Brief Table of Contents

Preface to the Instructor   xi

Preface to the Student   xix

Part One ▲ Building Foundation Skills

Chapter One: Self-Assessment
and Choosing Majors   1–1

Chapter Two: Emotional Intelligence:
The Essential Personal Qualities   2–1

Chapter Three: Managing Your Time   3–1

Part Two ▲ Basic Skills and Strategies

Chapter Four: Active Listening
and Note Taking   4–1

Chapter Five: Active Reading   5–1

Chapter Six: Memory Skills   6–1

Chapter Seven: Test Taking   7–1

Chapter Eight: Expressing
Yourself in Writing and Speech   8–1

Part Three ▲ Application

Chapter Nine: Critical Thinking
and Creative Problem Solving, with
Applications for Math and Science   9–1

Chapter Ten: Health and Stress   10–1

Chapter Eleven: Building Healthy
and Diverse Relationships   11–1

Chapter Twelve: Managing
Your Resources   12–1

Chapter Thirteen: Developing
Good Habits   13–1

Chapter Fourteen: Career
Development Portfolio:
Connecting School with Career   14–1

Photo Credits   P–1

Index   I–1

Table of Contents

Preface to the Instructor	xi
Preface to the Student	xix
Worksheet	
Worksheet P.1: Progress Assessment	xxxii

PART ONE ▲ Building Foundation Skills

Chapter One ▲ Self-Assessment and Choosing Majors — 1–1

What Is a "Peak Performer"?	1–2
The Benefits of Self-Assessment	1–3
Using Critical Thinking Skills	1–3
Peak Progress 1.1: Visualization: A Self-Management Tool	*1–4*
Skills for School and Job Success	1–5
Personal Performance Notebook 1.1: Peak Performance Self-Assessment Test	*1–7*
Discovering Your Learning Style	1–8
Are you a Reader, a Listener, or a Doer?	1–8
Visual Learners	1–8
Auditory Learners	1–8
Personal Performance Notebook 1.2: Learning Style Inventory	*1–9*
Kinesthetic Learners	1–11
Redefining Intelligence: Other Learning Styles	1–11
Using Inventories for Self-Assessment	1–12
Discovering Your Personality and Team Type	1–13
Connecting Learning Styles and Personality Types: The Four-Temperament Profile	1–14
Personal Performance Notebook 1.3: The Four-Temperament Profile	*1–16*
Analyzers	1–18
Supporters	1–18
Creators	1–19
Directors	1–20
Exploring Learning and Personality Tools	1–21
Integrating Styles	1–22
Integrating Both Sides of the Brain	1–23
The Adult Learning Cycle	1–23
Overcoming the Barriers to Self-Assessment	1–26
Self-Assessment and the Workplace	1–26
Choosing a Major	1–26
Career in Focus: Louis Parker: Setting Business Goals	*1–27*
Peak Progress 1.2: Applying the Adult Learning Cycle when Exploring Majors	*1–29*
Peak Performer Profile: Christy Haubegger	*1–31*
Case Study: Making a Commitment	*1–33*
Worksheets	
Worksheet 1.1: Applying the ABCDE Method of Self-Management	*1–34*
Worksheet 1.2: Assessing and Applying Learning Styles, Personality Types, and Temperaments	*1–35*
Worksheet 1.3: Checklist for Choosing a Major	*1–37*
Worksheet 1.4: Applying the Four-Temperament Profile	*1–39*
Career Development Portfolio: Autobiography	*1–40*

Chapter Two ▲ Emotional Intelligence: The Essential Personal Qualities — 2–1

Emotional Intelligence	2–2
Character First: Integrity, Civility, and Ethics	2–3
Personal Performance Notebook 2.1: Character and Ethics	*2–4*
Personal Performance Notebook 2.2: Skills and Personal Qualities	*2–5*
Creating and Following a Code of Ethics	2–5
Responsibility	2–6
Self-Management and Control	2–8
Peak Progress 2.1: Applying the Adult Learning Cycle to Self-Management and Control	*2–9*

Self-Esteem and Confidence 2–9

A Positive Attitude and Personal Motivation 2–10

*Peak Progress 2.2: Tips to Build
Self-Esteem and Confidence* 2–11

How Needs and Motives Influence
Attitudes and Motivation 2–12

*Personal Performance Notebook 2.3:
Needs, Motivation, and Commitment* 2–13

Motivational Strategies 2–13

*Personal Performance Notebook 2.4:
Self-Talk and Affirmations* 2–15

*Peak Progress 2.3: The Difference
Between High School and College* 2–16

Peak Performer Profile: Ben Carson, M.D. 2–17

The Motivation Cycle 2–18

The Benefits of a Higher Education 2–18

A Liberal Arts Education 2–19

The Connection Between School and Work 2–20

Peak Progress 2.4: Skills for School and Career 2–20

*Peak Progress 2.5: What Kind of
Student/Worker Are You?* 2–21

*Career in Focus: Jacqui Williams:
Positive Attitudes at Work* 2–22

*Peak Progress 2.6: The Most Common
Reason Students Do Not Graduate* 2–23

Overcoming the Barriers 2–23

Creating Positive Mind Shifts 2–24

Expanding Your Comfort Zone 2–24

Case Study: Getting Motivated 2–28

Worksheets

*Worksheet 2.1: Applying the ABCDE
Method of Self-Management* 2–29

*Worksheet 2.2: Rewarding Myself:
A Personal Reinforcement Contract* 2–30

Worksheet 2.3: Self-Esteem Inventory 2–31

Worksheet 2.4: Learning Styles 2–32

*Career Development Portfolio:
Assessment of Personal Qualities* 2–33

Chapter Three ▲ Managing Your Time 3–1

Self-Assessment 3–2

Where Does Your Time Go? 3–2

Committed Time 3–3

Maintenance Time 3–3

Discretionary Time 3–3

Where Should Your Time Go? 3–3

Setting Priorities 3–4

Personal Performance Notebook 3.1: Time Log 3–5

The First Weeks of College 3–5

*Personal Performance Notebook 3.2:
How Much Time Do You Spend?* 3–6

*Personal Performance Notebook 3.3:
Looking Ahead* 3–7

Time–Management Strategies 3–8

*Personal Performance Notebook 3.4:
Your Daily Energy Levels* 3–10

Time-Management and Learning Style 3–11

The Management Process 3–11

*Peak Progress 3.1: Applying the Adult
Learning Cycle to Taking Control of
Your Time and Life* 3–12

Planning 3–12

Organizing 3–13

Staffing 3–13

Delegating 3–13

Directing and Motivating 3–13

Evaluating 3–13

Managing College and Career Like a Pro 3–13

Assessment and Reflection 3–13

*Peak Progress 3.2: Investing Your Time
in High-Priority Items: The 80/20 Rule* 3–15

Overcoming Procrastination 3–15

*Personal Performance Notebook 3.5:
Delay or Procrastination?* 3–16

Controlling Interruptions 3–16

Strategies for Controlling Interruptions 3–17

*Personal Performance Notebook 3.6:
Interruptions!* 3–18

Juggling Family, School, and Job 3–19

The Returning Student 3–20

Balancing Your Life 3–21

*Personal Performance Notebook 3.7:
Your Life Area Goals* 3–22

*Career in Focus: Deborah Page: Focus
on Tasks, Not Time* 3–23

Peak Performer Profile: N. Scott Momaday 3–24

Case Study: Juggling Family and School 3–28

Worksheets

*Worksheet 3.1: Applying the ABCDE
Method of Self-Management* 3–29

Worksheet 3.2: To-Do List 3–30

Worksheet 3.3: Time Management 3–31

Worksheet 3.4: Time Wasters 3–32

Worksheet 3.5: Your Daily Energy Levels 3–34

*Career Development Portfolio:
Demonstrating Your Time-
Management Skills* 3–35

PART TWO ▲ Basic Skills and Strategies

Chapter Four ▲ Active Listening and Note Taking 4–1

Listening to the Message 4–2
    Active Listening Strategies 4–2
Note Taking 4–5
    Peak Progress 4.1: Applying the Adult Learning
        Cycle to Becoming an Active Listener 4–6
Recording the Message 4–6
    Personal Performance Notebook 4.1:
        Active Listening 4–7
    Formal Outline 4–8
    Creative Outline 4–9
        Mind Mapping 4–9
        Mind Map Template 4–10
    Cornell Method 4–10
    Combination Note-Taking System 4–11
    Personal Performance Notebook 4.2: Mind Map 4–12
Note-Taking Strategies 4–15
Assessment and Review 4–17
    Personal Performance Notebook 4.3:
        Reflection 4–19
    Peak Progress 4.2: Overcoming Barriers
        to Effective Note Taking 4–20
    Career in Focus: Danielle Sievert:
        Listening in the Workplace 4–21
    Peak Performer Profile: Anna Sui 4–22
    Case Study: Developing Active Listening Skills 4–25
    Worksheets
        Worksheet 4.1: Applying the ABCDE
            Method of Self-Management 4–26
        Worksheet 4.2: Sorting Information
            with a Mind Map 4–27
        Worksheet 4.3: Focus on Ideas 4–28
        Worksheet 4.4: Note-Taking Checklist 4–29
        Worksheet 4.5: Listening and
            Note Taking in the Workplace 4–30
        Worksheet 4.6: Life Assessment 4–31
        Worksheet 4.7: Ongoing Assessment
            and Action Plan 4–32
        Worksheet 4.8: Good Listening Habits 4–33
    Career Development Portfolio:
        Listening Self-Assessment 4–34

Chapter Five ▲ Active Reading 5–1

The Importance of Active Reading 5–2
Reading Systems 5–2
    The Five-Part Reading System 5–3
    Peak Progress 5.1 5–4
    The SQ3R Reading System 5–5
Preparation for Reading 5–5
    Personal Performance Notebook 5.1:
        Using the SQ3R System 5–6
Reading Strategies 5–9
    Reviewing 5–10
    Peak Progress 5.2: Symbols 5–11

    Peak Progress 5.3: Look It Up!
        Using the Dictionary 5–12
Barriers to Effective Reading 5–13
Managing Language Courses 5–13
Vocabulary Building 5–14
Technical Reading 5–15
Reading Forms 5–16
    Career in Focus: Brian Singer:
        Keeping Up-to-Date 5–17
    Peak Performer Profile: Oprah Winfrey 5–19
    Case Study: Effective Reading Habits 5–23
    Worksheets
        Worksheet 5.1: Applying the ABCDE
            Method of Self-Management 5–24
        Worksheet 5.2: Attitudes and Reading 5–25
        Worksheet 5.3: Different Types of Reading 5–26
        Worksheet 5.4: Summarize and Teach 5–27
        Worksheet 5.5: Creating a Reading Outline 5–29
        Worksheet 5.6: Analyzing Chapters 5–31
        Worksheet 5.7: Breaking Barriers to Reading 5–32
        Worksheet 5.8: Reading Matrix 5–33
    Career Development Portfolio:
        Demonstrating Competencies 5–34

Chapter Six ▲ Memory Skills 6–1

The Memory Process 6–2
    Peak Progress 6.1: Applying the Adult
        Learning Cycle to Increase Your Memory Skills 6–3
    Personal Performance Notebook 6.1:
        Being Observant 6–4
Memory Strategies 6–5
    Personal Performance Notebook 6.2:
        Mind Map—Organizing Information 6–6
    Personal Performance Notebook 6.3:
        Memory Assessment 6–8
    Personal Performance Notebook 6.4:
        Learning Styles and Memory 6–10
    Peak Progress 6.2: Mindfulness 6–11
    Peak Progress 6.3: Remembering Names 6–12
Review and Reflection 6–13
    Personal Performance Notebook 6.5:
        A Walk Down Memory Lane 6–14
    Peak Progress 6.4: More Memory Affirmations 6–17
Overcoming Barriers to Memory 6–17
    Career in Focus: Marla Bergstrom:
        Integrating Learning Styles 6–20
    Peak Performer Profile: Alberto Gonzales 6–21
    Case Study: Overcoming Memory Loss 6–23
    Worksheets
        Worksheet 6.1: Applying the ABCDE
            Method of Self-Management 6–24
        Worksheet 6.2: Connecting Learning
            Style with Memory 6–25

Worksheet 6.3: Memory   6–26
Worksheet 6.4: To-Do List   6–28
Worksheet 6.5: Memory Systems   6–29
Worksheet 6.6: Mental Picture   6–30
Career Development Portfolio: Applying
Memory Skills   6–32

Chapter Seven ▲ Test Taking   7–1

Preparing for a Test   7–2
Peak Progress 7.1: Test-Taking Factors   7–3
Personal Performance Notebook 7.1:
Test Taking   7–4
Test-Taking Strategies   7–5
Peak Progress 7.2: Special Strategies
for Math and Science Tests   7–6
After the Test   7–6
Taking Different Types of Tests   7–7
The Objective Test   7–7
True/False Test   7–7
Multiple-Choice Test   7–8
Matching Test   7–8
Fill-In-The-Blank Test   7–9
Open-Book Test   7–9
The Essay Test   7–9
Personal Performance Notebook 7.2:
Essay Test Preparation   7–10
Peak Progress 7.3: Sample Essay Test   7–11
Peak Progress 7.4: Important Words
in Essay Questions   7–13
Last-Minute Study Tips   7–13
Overcoming Test Anxiety   7–14
Personal Performance Notebook 7.3:
Test Anxiety   7–16
Peak Progress 7.5: Applying the Adult
Learning Cycle to Improve Your
Test-Taking Skills and Reduce
Test Anxiety   7–17
Preparing for a Performance Appraisal   7–17
Career in Focus: Carlos Fuentes:
Test in the Workplace   7–18
Personal Performance Notebook 7.4:
Performance Reviews   7–19
Peak Performer Profile: Kirk Perron   7–22
Case Study: Coping with Anxiety   7–24
Worksheets
Worksheet 7.1: Applying the ABCDE
Method of Self-Management   7–25
Worksheet 7.2: Exam Schedule   7–26
Worksheet 7.3: Preparing for Tests
and Exams   7–27
Worksheet 7.4: Performance Reviews   7–29
Worksheet 7.5: Matrix for Test Taking   7–30

Career Development Portfolio:
Assessing Your Skills and Competencies   7–31

Chapter Eight ▲ Expressing Yourself in Writing and Speech   8–1

The Importance of Writing and Speaking   8–2
Preparation for Writing   8–3
Peak Progress 8.1: How to Generate Topic Ideas   8–5
Organizing a Writing Plan   8–6
Personal Performance Notebook 8.1:
Preparing Research Papers   8–7
Writing Strategies   8–8
Editing   8–9
Peak Progress 8.2: Overcoming Writer's Block   8–10
Review and Assessment   8–12
Peak Progress 8.3: Writing Do's   8–13
Using the Library for Research   8–15
Peak Progress 8.4: Checklists for
Writing Papers and Giving Speeches   8–16
Taking Your Search Online   8–17
Public Speaking Strategies   8–17
Personal Performance Notebook 8.2:
Controlling Stage Fright and Writer's Block   8–19
Peak Progress 8.5: Applying the Adult
Learning Cycle to Improve Your
Public Speaking   8–21
Career in Focus: Lori Benson:
Communication Skills   8–23
Peak Performer Profile: Toni Morrison   8–25
Case Study: Learning Communication Skills   8–27
Worksheets
Worksheet 8.1: Applying the ABCDE
Method of Self-Assessment   8–28
Worksheet 8.2: Rehearsing   8–29
Worksheet 8.3: Essay Writing Tips   8–30
Worksheet 8.4: Planning Grid   8–32
Career Development Portfolio: Your
Writing and Speaking Skills   8–33

PART THREE ▲ Application

Chapter Nine ▲ Critical Thinking and Creating Problem Solving, with Applications for Math and Science   9–1

Preparing for Critical Thinking and
Problem Solving   9–2
Problem-Solving Steps   9–3
Personal Performance Notebook 9.1:
Using Critical Thinking to Solve Problems   9–4
Peak Progress 9.1: Problem-Solving Checklist   9–5

Common Errors in Judgment	9–6
Math and Science Applications	9–6
Problem-Solving Strategies for Math and Science	9–7
Overcoming Math and Science Anxiety	9–10
Personal Performance Notebook 9.2: The History of Your Anxiety	*9–11*
Creative Problem Solving	9–12
Peak Progress 9.2: Applying the Adult Learning Cycle to Overcoming Math and Science Anxiety	*9–13*
Personal Performance Notebook 9.3: Nine-Dot Exercise	*9–14*
Personal Performance Notebook 9.4: Brainstorming Notes	*9–15*
Personal Performance Notebook 9.5: Mind-Sets	*9–16*
Personal Performance Notebook 9.6: Decision-Making Application	*9–18*
Personal Performance Notebook 9.7: Solving Problems and Making Choices	*9–20*
Peak Progress 9.3: Creative Ideas Checklists	*9–22*
Career in Focus: Marina and Josef Koshetz: Creativity at Work	*9–23*
Peak Performer Profile: Scott Adams	*9–24*
Case Study: Conquering Fear of Failure	*9–27*
Worksheets	
Worksheet 9.1: Applying the ABCDE Method of Self-Management	*9–28*
Worksheet 9.2: Problem Solving	*9–29*
Worksheet 9.3: Preparing for Critical Thinking	*9–30*
Worksheet 9.4: You Can Solve the Problem: Sue's Decision	*9–31*
Worksheet 9.5: You Can Solve the Problem: Casey's Dilemma	*9–33*
Worksheet 9.6: Matrix for Critical Thinking	*9–35*
Career Development Portfolio: Assessing and Demonstrating Your Critical Thinking Skills	*9–36*

Chapter Ten ▲ Health and Stress · 10–1

Your Body as a System	10–2
Awareness	10–2
Five Strategies for Good Health Management	10–2
Personal Performance Notebook 10.1: Becoming Attuned to Your Body	*10–3*
Peak Progress 10.1: Eating for Health and Energy	*10–4*
Personal Performance Notebook 10.2: Reviewing Your Health	*10–6*
Personal Performance Notebook 10.3: Getting Proper Rest	*10–7*
Personal Performance Notebook 10.4: Committing to Exercise	*10–9*
Effects of Caffeine	10–10
Alcohol Abuse	10–10
Critical Thinking About Alcohol	10–11
Facts About Cigarette Smoking	10–12
Facts About Illegal Drugs	10–12
Critical Thinking About Drugs	10–12
Dealing with Addictions	10–13
Codependency	10–14
Emotional Health	10–15
Depression	10–15
Signs and Symptoms of Depression	10–15
The Suicidal Person	10–16
Protecting Your Body	10–16
Avoid Sexually Transmitted Diseases (STDs)	10–17
Birth Control	10–18
Preventing Rape	10–18
Date Rape	10–19
Facts About Rape	10–20
Managing Stress	10–20
Career in Focus: Tony Ferraro: Preventing Stress and Fatigue at Work	*10–21*
Peak Progress 10.2: Stress Leads to Burnout	*10–22*
Stress-Reduction Strategies	10–22
Peak Progress 10.3: Applying the Adult Learning Cycle to Create a Healthier Lifestyle	*10–25*
Peak Performer Profile: Lance Armstrong	*10–26*
Case Study: Increasing Your Energy Level	*10–29*
Worksheets	
Worksheet 10.1: Applying the ABCDE Method of Self-Management	*10–30*
Worksheet 10.2: Stress Performance Test	*10–31*
Worksheet 10.3: Better Health	*10–33*
Career Development Portfolio: Inventory of Interests	*10–34*

Chapter Eleven ▲ Building Healthy and Diverse Relationships · 11–1

The Importance of Communication	11–2
Strategies for Building Rapport	11–2
Understanding Diversity	11–2
Communication Strategies	11–5
Peak Progress 11.1: Applying the Adult Learning Cycle to Become a Better Communicator	*11–6*
Peak Progress 11.2: Thinking About Diversity	*11–7*
Personal Performance Notebook 11.1: Appreciating Diversity	*11–8*

Personal Performance Notebook 11.2:
    Stereotypical Thinking   *11–9*
Cultural and Gender Diversity at Work   11–10
Sexual Harassment at School and at Work   11–10
    Peak Progress 11.3: Team Effectiveness   *11–11*
Assertive Communication   11–12
Communicating with Instructors
    and Advisors   11–12
    Personal Performance Notebook 11.3:
        Assertive Communication Role-Playing   *11–13*
Accepting Criticism and Overcoming Conflict   11–14
    Personal Performance Notebook 11.4:
        Observing Conflict   *11–16*
    Personal Performance Notebook 11.5:
        Conflict Resolution   *11–17*
Overcoming the Barriers to Communication   11–17
    Personal Performance Notebook 11.6:
        Patterns in Relationships   *11–18*
Overcoming Shyness   11–19
Building Good Relationships   11–19
    Getting Along with Roommates and Family   11–21
    Personal Performance Notebook 11.7:
        Healthy Relationships   *11–22*
    Career in Focus: Kathy Brown:
        Team Building at Work   *11–26*
    Peak Performer Profile: Ellen Ochoa   *11–27*
    Case Study: Successful Team Work   *11–29*
    Worksheets
        Worksheet 11.1: Applying the ABCDE
            Method of Self-Management   *11–30*
        Worksheet 11.2: Study-Team Relationships   *11–31*
        Worksheet 11.3: Appreciating Diversity   *11–32*
        Worksheet 11.4: Are You Assertive,
            Aggressive, or Passive?   *11–33*
    Career Development Portfolio: Assessing Your
        Relationship Skills   *11–34*

Chapter Twelve ▲ Managing Your Resources   12–1

The Importance of Building Community   12–2
Exploring Campus Resources   12–2
    Personal Performance Notebook 12.1:
        Building Community   *12–3*
    People Resources   12–4
    Paper and Materials Resources   12–4
    Personal Performance Notebook 12.2:
        Making Time for Commitments   *12–5*
    Program Resources   12–6
    Personal Performance Notebook 12.3:
        Important Contacts   *12–7*
    Peak Progress 12.1: Campus Facilities   *12–8*
    Financial Resources   12–9

Commuter Students   12–10
Students with Disabilities   12–10
The Returning Student   12–11
Transfer Students   12–12
Students on Probation   12–12
Community Resources   12–13
    People Resources   12–13
    Financial Resources   12–14
    Paper and Material Resources   12–14
    Program Resources   12–15
You Are a Great Resource   12–15
Handling Money Wisely   12–15
    Getting Financial Help if You're in Trouble   12–16
    Personal Performance Notebook 12.4:
        Money In/Money Out   *12–17*
    Peak Progress 12.2: Applying the Adult
        Learning Cycle to Managing
        Financial Resources   *12–18*
    Other Tips to Save Money   12–18
    Building a Savings Account   12–20
    Career in Focus: Donna Washington:
        Benefits of Community Resources   *12–21*
    Peak Performer Profile: Condoleezza Rice   *12–22*
    Case Study: Building Community   *12–25*
    Worksheets
        Worksheet 12.1: Applying the ABCDE
            Method of Self-Management   *12–26*
        Worksheet 12.2: Resources   *12–27*
        Worksheet 12.3: Budgeting Each Term   *12–28*
        Worksheet 12.4: Money Management   *12–29*
        Worksheet 12.5: Building Community   *12–30*
        Worksheet 12.6: Assessing Your
            Community Involvement   *12–31*
        Worksheet 12.7: Networking   *12–33*
    Career Development Portfolio: Your
        Community Service   *12–34*

Chapter Thirteen ▲ Developing Good Habits   13–1

The 10 Habits of Peak Performers   13–2
Making a Commitment to Change Your Habits   13–7
    Peak Progress 13.1: Applying the Adult
        Learning Cycle to Develop Positive Habits   *13–8*
Strategies for Creating Positive Change   13–9
    Personal Performance Notebook 13.1:
        Make a Commitment to Learn and
        Apply Positive Habits   *13–10*
Peak Performance Success Formula   13–12
    Personal Performance Notebook 13.2:
        Commitment Contract   *13–13*

Practice the ABCDE Method of
  Self-Management 13–14
  Peak Performance Notebook 13.3:
    Assessment Is Lifelong 13–15
Resistors and Rears 13–16
  Peak Progress 13.2: Seven Positive Attitudes
    of Peak Performers 13–17
  Career in Focus: Rick Torres: Good Habits
    in the Workplace 13–19
  Peak Performer Profile: Mia Hamm 13–20
  Case Study: Spreading Good Habits 13–23
  Worksheets
    Worksheet 13.1: Applying the ABCDE
      Method of Self-Management 13–24
    Worksheet 13.2: Overcoming Resistance
      to Change 13–25
    Worksheet 13.3: Developing Positive Habits 13–26
    Worksheet 13.4: Building Positive Attitudes 13–27
    Worksheet 13.5: Changing Habits 13–28
  Career Development Portfolio:
    Planning Your Career 13–29

**Chapter Fourteen ▲ Career
Development Portfolio:
Connecting School with Career** 14–1

The Importance of a Career Development
  Portfolio 14–2
When Should You Start Your Portfolio? 14–3
How to Organize and Assemble Your Portfolio . 14–3
Elements of Your Portfolio 14–5
  Cover Letter 14–5
  Cover Page 14–5
  Title Page 14–7
  Contents Page(s) 14–7
  Introduction 14–7
  List of Significant Life Experiences 14–8
  Analysis of Accomplishments 14–8
  Inventory of Skills and Competencies 14–8
  Documentation 14–9
  Work Philosophy and Goals 14–9
  Personal Performance Notebook 14.1:
    Transferable Skills 14–10
  Personal Performance Notebook 14.2:
    Inventory of Personal Qualities 14–11

  Personal Performance Notebook 14.3:
    Inventory of Interests, Aptitudes, and Values 14–13
  Résumé 14–13
  Personal Performance Notebook 14.4:
    Assessing Your Goals 14–14
      Putting Your Résumé On–Line 14–16
  Cover Letters 14–16
Interview Planning 14–18
  Samples of Work 14–19
  Summary of Transcripts 14–19
  Credentials, Certificates, Workshops 14–19
  Bibliography 14–19
  Appendix 14–20
Overcoming the Barriers to Portfolio
  Development 14–20
Choosing Your Career 14–21
  Peak Progress 14.1: Tips for Exploring
    Your Career 14–22
Workplace Trends 14–22
  Peak Progress 14.2: Applying the Adult
    Learning Cycle to Connect School
    with Job Success 14–23
  Career in Focus: Steven Price:
    Career Planning is Lifelong 14–24
Business Ethics 14–25
  Personal Performance Notebook 14.5: Values 14–25
  Peak Performer Profile: David Filo
    and Jerry Yang 14–26
  Case Study: Exploring Careers 14–29
  Worksheets
    Worksheet 14.1: Applying the ABCDE
      Method of Self-Management 14–30
    Worksheet 14.2: Career Planning Grid 14–31
    Worksheet 14.3: Preparing Your Resume ... 14–32
    Worksheet 14.4: Interviewing the Employed 14–33
  Career Development Portfolio:
    Exploring Careers 14–34

Index I–1

Preface

TO THE INSTRUCTOR

Why I Wrote This Book

I have spent more than 25 years working with students as a college professor, an advisor, and a dean and more than 15 years as a management consultant. I began my research into personal productivity and human relations early in my teaching career and began compiling data from years of teaching classes in organizational behavior and giving hundreds of workshops to managers and executives. I have always been interested in transitions, which led me to teaching classes to help students successfully make the transition from high school to college and from college to the world of work.

It is apparent that there is a strong connection between the world of college and the world of work, yet college is often viewed as separate and distinct from the real world. This text, more than any other, presents the relationship of college with the larger systems of work and life. It focuses on responsibility and the consequences of one's decisions and actions. It goes further and shows how decisions and actions can affect others and the larger world.

I contend that it is the nature of people to love learning and to strive for peak performance. As educators, we have the unique opportunity to provide our students with the knowledge and skills they will use in their journey to becoming a peak performer. This book provides the strategies, personal qualities, and habits that will help students put knowledge into action.

As I have developed this edition, I have kept a number of definite goals at the forefront. Essentially, to be successful, students need to

◆ **Learn how they learn best—and incorporate new ways to learn.** Throughout this text, students are given the opportunity to explore learning styles and to develop personal strategies that work for them. Features throughout the text reinforce the core principles and give students the opportunity to practice their critical thinking skills.

◆ **Maximize their available resources and seek out new opportunities.** Oftentimes, students overlook what is already available to them. Thus, throughout the text we provide strategies for making the most of surrounding resources and tips for seeking out new resources and opportunities.

◆ **Relate what they are exploring and learning now to future success on the job.** Students are more motivated when they can make the connection between school and job success. Throughout this text, we provide numerous examples and features that directly tie the knowledge, skills, and habits learned in class today to what they will experience in their career.

◆ **Be challenged to strive to become the best individuals they can be.** Our hope is that not only do our students become successes in the business world but also that they are productive contributors to their communities. Throughout this text, we focus on the key personal qualities, habits, and strategies that will help students become peak performers in all facets of life.

Additionally, it is critical that we

◆ **Provide you, the instructor, with the most useful and practical teaching tools possible.** The goals of your course may vary and you may be dealing with a variety of students—from incoming freshmen straight out of high school, to returning students coming from the workforce, to transferring students coming from other schools. Thus, we have developed a number of teaching tools to suit your situation and your ultimate goals.

New to the Fifth Edition

The fifth edition of *Peak Performance: Success in College and Beyond* has been thoroughly updated and refined based on the many helpful comments and suggestions of adopters and reviewers of the previous edition. Revised with our main objectives in mind, following are a number of features and concepts that are new to this edition:

- **New student preface.** A new preface has been designed that not only walks the student through the numerous beneficial features that reinforce the text's goals but also includes "As You Get Started in Your New School: What You Need to Know and Should Not Be Afraid to Ask." This new section helps students explore the reasons they are attending college, a checklist of the tasks to accomplish the first week of school, and the critical questions that they should get answers to in their situation and school (derived from the top questions asked of advisors). It also includes information on topics such as graduation requirements, registering, adding and dropping classes, incomplete grades, taking a leave of absence, and transferring. Also included are the top 50 strategies for success in college.

- **The Adult Learning Cycle.** Introduced in Chapter 1 and carried throughout each chapter, the Adult Learning Cycle is a five-step process that demonstrates that learning comes from repetition, practice, and recall. This process offers a critical fifth stage not included in other learning theories: (1) relate, (2) observe, (3) think, (4) do, and (5) teach. Each chapter provides the reader an opportunity to apply the chapter material to the Adult Learning Cycle within a Peak Progress box.

- **The ABCDE Method of Self-Management.** New to this edition and introduced in Chapter 1, the ABCDE Method of Self-Management will help

students manage thoughts, feelings, and behaviors, so that they create positive results and achieve goals. This five-step process (A = Actual event; B = Beliefs; C = Circumstances; D = Dispute; E = Energized) uses visualization to show the connection among thoughts, feelings, and actions and empowers the reader to dispel negative thoughts and replace them with realistic and positive thoughts and behaviors.

- **Visualization exercise.** As the new discussion in Peak Progress 1.1: "Visualization: A Self-Management Tool" in Chapter 1 indicates, visualization is a powerful tool for envisioning success and critically thinking through difficult situations. Each chapter begins with a Visualization box that includes new scenarios that students can relate to. The student is then given the opportunity to reflect on personal experiences in the follow-up journal entry. A Revisualization exercise at the end of the chapter then helps the student practice the ABCDE Method of Self-Management to work through difficult situations and determine positive solutions. A chapter worksheet is provided to record the journal entry and follow-up scenario.

- **Chapter 1: "Self-Assessment and Choosing Majors."** Included is a new discussion defining the characteristics of a peak performer. The discussion of learning styles and personality types has been refined, including a new section on other intelligences. A new discussion of the research of David Kolb is presented, along with introduction of the Adult Learning Cycle.

- **Chapter 2 retitled "Emotional Intelligence: The Essential Personal Qualities."** This chapter has been completely reorganized to focus on character first, stressing that good character, integrity, and ethics are the hallmarks of truly successful leaders in both business and the community.

- **Chapter 9 retitled "Critical Thinking and Creative Problem Solving, with Applications for Math and Science."** This chapter has been reorganized and expanded to address achieving personal success in math and science courses. New strategies and examples have been included that allow the student to practice problem-solving techniques when solving equations and word problems.

◆ **Chapter 10: "Health and Stress."** The material has been updated to include the latest statistics in regard to alcohol and other drug use, as well as a new discussion on addictive behaviors, including gambling and sexual addictions, and resources for help.

◆ **Chapter 12 retitled "Managing Your Resources."** This chapter includes a new section devoted to commuter students, including tips on how to become more active at school and to make the most of commuting time. Under "Handling Money Wisely," there is a new section on saving for the future, including the benefits of a 401(K) or an IRA.

◆ **Chapter 13: "Developing Good Habits."** Reorganized to focus on the top 10 habits of a peak performer, this chapter shows how to translate and support essential personal qualities with everyday habits.

◆ **Taking Charge end-of-chapter summary.** Every chapter now concludes with a summary of the main points presented in the chapter. Written as "I" statements, they reinforce that the chapter presents a number of potential strategies to implement and master.

Successful Features

A number of pedagogical features throughout this text reinforce learning, critical thinking, and the main goals of the text. Every feature has been fine-tuned to support the chapter material more succinctly.

◆ **Secretary's Commission on Achieving Necessary Skills (SCANS).** Found on pages xvii–xviii and introduced in Chapter 1, this is the list of the competencies employees need to be able to demonstrate on the job. Included in this handy chart are the corresponding chapters in this text. The many exercises, strategies, case studies, and guidelines throughout the text correlate with several SCANS requirements,

as well as systems thinking, diversity, and critical thinking.

◆ **Chapter Objectives.** Clear and concise objectives at the beginning of each chapter identify the chapter's key concepts.

◆ **Visualization.** Each chapter begins with a revised Visualization box that includes new scenarios that students can relate to. The student is then given the opportunity to reflect on personal experiences in the follow-up journal entry.

◆ **Success Principle.** Each chapter begins with a success principle that succinctly communicates the important lesson to be learned from the chapter. The success principles in total provide a unique and powerful guide to striving for success in school, career, and life.

◆ **Words to Succeed.** Found throughout the text, these quotes provide insight, motivation, and food for thought and are tied to the chapter's content.

◆ **Peak Tip.** Sprinkled through the text's margins are quick tips for applying the text's content.

◆ **Personal Performance Notebook.** The Personal Performance Notebook exercises that appear in every chapter give opportunities to practice critical thinking and decision-making skills. Spaces are provided for recording answers and thoughts directly within the activity.

◆ **Peak Progress.** The Peak Progress boxed feature demonstrates the themes and concepts of each chapter and includes helpful suggestions to accelerate and assess progress.

◆ **Tech for Success.** Appearing in every chapter, this feature has been updated to offer tips for making the most out of technology applications for both school and job.

◆ **Career in Focus.** This feature provides real-world career profiles that illustrate examples of the relationship between the study skills necessary for college success and the skills needed for career success. Work situations that directly call on chapter skills are highlighted to show the relationship between school and career skills.

- **Peak Performer Profile.** Each chapter presents a noted person in the area of business, education, the arts, or public service. These peak performers have overcome obstacles and challenges to become successful.

- **Taking Charge end-of-chapter summary.** Every chapter now concludes with a summary of the main points presented in the chapter.

- **Performance Strategies.** Included in every chapter is a recap of the top 10 strategies for success in applying the chapter's concepts.

- **Review Questions.** Each chapter includes five basic questions to help the student review the chapter's main concepts.

- **Revisualization.** As a follow-up to the initial visualization exercise, this end-of-chapter feature allows the student to practice the ABCDE Method of Self-Management. A chapter worksheet is provided to record the journal entry and follow-up scenario.

- **Case Study.** Each chapter includes a case study activity that presents college students dealing with real-life situations that reflect the chapter's concepts. Additional case study opportunities are provided on the text's web site.

- **Worksheet activities.** Retitled Worksheets, each chapter concludes with numerous activities that are perforated and thumb-tabbed for ease of use. New Worksheets have been added to offer more critical thinking opportunities. Many of the useful forms are also available on the book's web site, www.mhhe.com/ferrett5e, so they can be customized.

- **Career Development Portfolio worksheet.** Found at the end of every chapter, the Career Development Portfolio gives the student the opportunity to track and showcase skills, competencies, accomplishments, and work. Chapter 14, "Career Development Portfolio: Connecting School with Career," shows the student how to develop a personal Career Development Portfolio and the various elements of the interview process.

Ancillaries

We have designed an extensive and convenient ancillary package that focuses on course goals, allows you to maximize your time with students, and helps students understand, retain, and apply the main principles.

Annotated Instructor's Edition (AIE) (0-07-298696-4). The AIE contains the full text of the student edition of the text, along with instructional strategies that reinforce and enhance the core concepts. Notes and tips in the margin provide topics for discussion, teaching tips for hands-on and group activities, and references to materials provided in the Instructor's Resource Manual and the Online Learning Center web site.

Instructor's Resource Manual, Test Bank, and Student Retention Kit (0-07-298705-7). Included in this extensive resource are chapter goals and outlines, teaching tips, additional activities, essay exercises, and transparency masters. Also provided is an extensive section on course planning, with sample syllabi. The extensive test bank includes matching, multiple choice, true/false, and short answer questions. The test bank is also available in an electronic format in the Instructor's Resource CD-ROM. The kit also includes unique resource guides that give instructors and administrators the tools to retain students and maximize the success of the course, using topics and principles that last a lifetime. Specialized sections include:

- Facilitator's Guide
- Tools for Time Management
- Establishing Peer Support Groups
- Developing a Career Portfolio
- Involving the Faculty Strategy
- Capitalizing on Your School's Graduates

Instructor's Resource CD-ROM (0-07-298701-4). All the core supplements are conveniently provided on this CD. Included are the computerized test bank, the Instructor's Resource Manual, and PowerPoint presentations.

New! Implementing a Student Success Course CD-ROM (0-07-310690-9). This innovative CD assists you in developing and sustaining your Student Success course. The features include a "how to" guide for designing and proposing a new course, with easy-to-use templates for determining budget needs and resources. Examples of model programs are provided from two-year, four-year, and career schools. The CD explores course goals, such as orientation and retention, and provides research data to support your proposal. Also included are materials to help sustain your course, such as faculty development programs and on-line resources.

Online Learning Center web site (www.mhhe.com/ ferrett5e). The book's web site includes features for both instructors and students—downloadable ancillaries, web links, student quizzing, additional information on topics of interest, and much, much more. Access to the web site is provided free to students when they purchase a new copy of this text.

PageOut, WebCT, Blackboard, and more. The Online Learning Center content of *Peak Performance* is supported by WebCT, eCollege.com, and Blackboard. Additionally, our PageOut service, free to qualified adopters, is available to get you and your course up and running on-line in a matter of hours! To find out more, contact your McGraw-Hill representative or visit www.pageout.net.

Customized text options. *Peak Performance* can be customized to suit your needs. The text can be abbreviated for shorter courses or can be expanded to include semester schedules, campus maps, additional essays, activities, or exercises, along with other materials specific to your curriculum or situation. Contact your McGraw-Hill representative for more information or

Canada: 1-905-430-5034

United States: 1-800-446-8979

E-mail: FYE@mcgraw-hill.com

More Resources for Teaching and Learning

New! LASSI: Learning and Study Strategies Inventory. The LASSI is a 10-scale, 80-item assessment of students' awareness about and use of learning and study strategies related to skill, will, and self-regulation components of strategic learning. The focus is on both the covert and overt thoughts, behaviors, attitudes, and beliefs that relate to successful learning and that can be altered through educational interventions. Research has repeatedly demonstrated that these factors contribute significantly to success in college and that they can be learned or enhanced through educational interventions, such as learning and study skills courses.

The LASSI provides standardized scores and national norms for 10 different scales. The LASSI is both diagnostic and prescriptive. It provides students with a diagnosis of their strengths and weaknesses, compared with other college students in the areas covered by the 10 scales, and it is prescriptive in that it provides feedback about areas where students may be weak and need to improve their knowledge, attitudes, beliefs, and skills.

The LASSI student assessment is available in print and packaged with *Peak Performance* (Package ISBN: 0-07-360450-X). An Instructor's Guide is also available; please contact your local McGraw-Hill sales representative for details.

Student Planner. Updated annually, this convenient organizational tool is available as a stand-alone or with the student text. The planner provides daily tips for success, time-management techniques, a daily calendar, and contact information. Contact your McGraw-Hill sales representative for the latest order information.

Study Smart: Study Skills for Students 2.0 (Online at www.mhhe.com/studymart2 or on CD-ROM 0-07-245515-2. Developed by Andrea Bonner and Mieke Schipper of Sir Sanford Fleming College, this innovative study skills tutorial teaches students essential note-taking methods, test-taking strategies, and time-management secrets. Study Smart can be ordered free when packaged with new copies of *Peak Performance.*

Random House Webster's College Dictionary (0-07-366069-8). Updated for the twenty-first century, this dictionary is available for a nominal cost when packaged with the text.

Acknowledgments

We would like to thank the many instructors whose insightful comments and suggestions provided us with inspiration and ideas that were incorporated into this new edition:

Janet Cutshall	Sussex County Community College
Mark Garth	Roxbury Community College
Laurie Grimes	Lorain County Community College
Henry Johnson	Florida Metropolitan University
Sharon Meredith	Des Moines Area Community College
Sherry Rhoden	Grand Rapids Community College
Magali Rubio	Miami-Dade College
Jane Santos	Katharine Gibbs School
T.C. Stuwe	Salt Lake Community College
Amy Tratt	Baker College
Patricia Twaddle	Moberly Area Community College
Bonnie Vorwerk	Central Florida Community College
Alan Walczak	Davenport University

We would especially like to thank the instructors who provided follow-up feedback and helped shape some of the new concepts and features presented in this edition:

Sharon Occhipinti	Florida Metropolitan University
T.C. Stuwe	Salt Lake Community College
John Whitman	Community College of Rhode Island

We would also like to send a special thank-you to the following instructors and their students for providing us guidance as we designed this new edition:

Mark Garth, Roxbury Community College, and his students: Isabel Compres, Heru Setepenra Heq-m-Ta, Joyce Marshall, and Keisha Mateo

Magali Rubio, Miami-Dade College, and her students: Catalina Castaneda, Patria Paulino, Yenlee Quinones, Leslie Rose, and Christopher Zuniga

Also, we would like to gratefully acknowledge the contributions of the McGraw-Hill editorial staff—specifically, Vicki Malinee, for her considerable effort, suggestions, ideas, and insights.

Dedication

To the memory of my father, Albert Lawrence Ferrett, for setting the highest standards.
To my mother, Velma Mary Hollenbeck Ferrett, for her seamless expression of love.
To my husband, Sam, and my daughters, Jennifer Katherine and Sarah Angela, for making it all worthwhile.

—Sharon K. Ferrett

SCANS: Secretary's Commission on Achieving Necessary Skills

Competency Chart

Competencies and Foundations	Peak Performance Chapters That Address SCANS Competencies
Resources: identifies, organizes, plans, and allocates resources	
• Managing time	Chapter 3
• Managing money	Chapter 12
• Managing space	Chapters 3, 13
• Managing people	Chapter 11
• Managing materials	Chapters 3, 4, 5, 8
• Managing facilities	Chapters 4, 8, 10, 12
Information: acquires and uses information	
• Acquiring information	Chapters 4, 5
• Evaluating information	Chapters 6, 7
• Organizing and maintaining information	Chapters 6, 7, 8, 9
• Using computer to process	Chapter 9
Systems: understands complex interrelationships	
• Understanding systems	All chapters, with a strong emphasis in Ch. 10
• Designing systems	Chapters 4, 5
• Monitoring systems	Chapters 3, 4, 5, 10
• Correcting systems	Chapters 3, 4, 5, 10
Interpersonal skills: works with others	
• Positive attitudes	Chapter 2
• Self-control	Chapter 2
• Goal setting	Chapter 2
• Teamwork	Chapters 2, 13
• Responsibility	Chapter 11
• Stress management	Chapter 10
Technology: works with a variety of technologies	
• Selecting technology	Chapters 8, 14
• Applying technology	Chapters 8, 14
• Maintaining technology	Chapters 8, 14
• Solving problems	Chapter 9
• Staying current in technology	Chapters 13, 14

continued on next page

Competencies and Foundations	Peak Performance Chapters That Address SCANS Competencies
Personal Qualities	
Responsibility, character, integrity, positive habits, self-management, self-esteem, sociability	Chapters 2, 14
Basic Skills	
• Reading—locates, understands, and interprets written information in prose and in documents such as manuals, graphs, and schedules	Chapter 5
• Writing—communicates thoughts, ideas, information, and messages in writing and creates documents, such as letters, directions, manuals, reports, graphs, and flow charts	Chapter 8
• Arithmetic/mathematics—performs basic computations and approaches practical problems by choosing appropriately from a variety of mathematical techniques	Chapter 9
• Listening—receives, attends to, interprets, and responds to verbal messages and other cues	Chapter 4
Thinking Skills	
• Creative thinking—generates new ideas	Ch. 9, Personal Performance Notebooks
• Decision making—specifies goals and constraints, generates alternatives, considers risks, and evaluates and chooses best alternative	Ch. 9, Case Study, Personal Performance Notebooks
• Listening—receives, attends to, interprets, and responds to verbal messages and other cues	Chapters 4, 11
• Seeing things in the mind's eye—organizes and processes symbols, pictures, graphs, objects, and other information	All chapters, with a strong emphasis in Ch. 2
• Knowing how to learn—uses efficient learning techniques to acquire and apply new knowledge and skills	Chapter 1
• Reasoning—discovers a rule or principle underlying the relationship between two or more objects and applies it when solving a problem	Chapter 9

Preface
TO THE STUDENT

Getting the Most Out of This Book

Congratulations! You are about to start or restart an amazing journey of opportunity, growth, and adventure. You may be at this point in your life for a number of reasons: You may be furthering your education right after high school, you may be focusing on a specific career or trade and want to acquire the appropriate skills or certification; or you may be returning to school after years in the workforce, needing additional skills or just looking for a change.

Whatever your reasons, this is an opportunity for you to learn new things, meet new people, acquire new skills, and better equip yourself both professionally and personally for the years ahead. This book is designed to get you started on that journey by helping you (1) learn how you learn best—and incorporate new ways to learn; (2) maximize available resources and seek out new opportunities; (3) relate what you are exploring now to future success on the job; and (4) strive to become the best person you can be.

Learn How You Learn Best—and Incorporate New Ways to Learn

We Learn
Ten percent of what we read
Twenty percent of what we hear
Thirty percent of what we see
Fifty percent of what we see and hear
Seventy percent of what we discuss with others
Eighty percent of what we do and experience
Ninety-five percent of what we teach others

In this text, you will find a number of features and discussion topics that will help you become a better learner:

- **Exploration of learning styles and personality types.** As you will discover in Chapter 1, each person has a preferred learning style and dominant personality type(s). However, the truly successful learner not only maximizes current preferences but also incorporates other styles and applications, thus becoming a more well-rounded learner. As you complete the exercises in this chapter, you will discover how you learn best and what strategies you can incorporate to maximize your learning efforts and environment.

- **The Adult Learning Cycle.** New to this edition, the Adult Learning Cycle is introduced in Chapter 1 and carried throughout each chapter. This is a five-step process that demonstrates that learning comes from repetition, practice, and recall: (1) relate; (2) observe; (3) think; (4) do; and (5) teach. You can apply this method to any new skill or information you want to learn and master. In each chapter, you will find a Peak Progress box that helps you see how the Adult Learning Cycle applies the chapter's content. This exercise will help you increase your awareness of how you learn best and how to explore and practice other learning styles. It will also help you overcome obstacles to learning in many different settings by giving hands-on, practical examples.

- **Critical thinking and creative problem solving.** Introduced in Chapter 1, critical thinking is more than just an educational buzzword—it is an important skill you will use and practice in every situation in life. Chapter 9 further explores how to solve problems creatively, including new and extended examples and applications to use in relation to math and science concepts. You will learn to overcome any anxieties you may have in these course areas by focusing on problem-solving techniques.

- **Personal Performance Notebook.** The Personal Performance Notebook exercises that appear in every chapter give you opportunities to practice your critical thinking and decision-making skills. You are asked to observe, evaluate, and apply chapter concepts to your life. Spaces are provided for you to record your answers and thoughts directly within the activity.

- **Chapter Objectives.** Clear and concise objectives at the beginning of each chapter aid you in identifying and mastering each chapter's key concepts.

- **Peak Progress.** In every chapter, the Peak Progress boxes demonstrate the themes and concepts of the chapter and includes helpful suggestions to accelerate and assess your progress.

- **Taking Charge end-of-chapter summary.** Every chapter now concludes with a summary of the main points presented in the chapter. Written as "I" statements, they reinforce that the chapter presents a number of potential strategies for you to implement and master.

- **Review Questions.** Each chapter includes five basic questions to help you review the chapter's main concepts.

- **Worksheet activities.** Each chapter concludes with numerous activities, now entitled Worksheets and perforated and thumb-tabbed for ease of use, that help you apply what you have learned to other classes and situations. New Worksheets have been added to offer more critical thinking opportunities. Many of the useful forms are also available on the book's web site, www.mhhe.com/ferrett5e, so you can customize and make multiple copies.

Maximize Available Resources and Seek Out New Opportunities

Oftentimes, we overlook the obvious resources and opportunities available to us. Some areas of the text that will guide you in how to maximize your resources as well as seeking out new ones include

- **Time is money, and vice versa.** In Chapter 3, you will explore time management, prioritizing, and where your time is spent—and where it should be spent. Also included is a discussion of the management process to show how mastering time management now will help you become a better manager of people and tasks in your career. Chapter 12 then explores external resources and tips on handling money and financial opportunities. Also included are strategies for commuter students, students with disabilities, and returning and transfer students.

- **Web site for this text.** The book's web site, www.mhhe.com\ferrett5e, offers a number of activities and resources for mastering and applying each chapter's content and for further study and exploration. Access to the web site is provided free with a new copy of this text. The password can be found at the beginning of this text.

- **Tech for Success.** The Tech for Success boxed feature appears in every chapter and has been updated to offer tips for making the most out of technology applications for both school and job.

- **Peak Tip.** Sprinkled through the text's margins are quick tips for applying the text's content in your everyday routine.

Relate What You Are Exploring Now to Future Success on the Job

Chances arc, one of your main reasons for attending college is to better your career opportunities. Throughout this text, you will find numerous features and examples that directly relate your experiences in college to your future success on the job. Just a few examples include

◆ **Secretary's Commission on Achieving Necessary Skills (SCANS).** Found on pages xix–xx and introduced in Chapter 1, this is a list of the ideal competencies you will need to be able to demonstrate on the job and the corresponding chapters in this text. The many exercises, strategies, case studies, and guidelines throughout the text correlate with several SCANS requirements, as well as systems thinking, diversity, and critical thinking.

◆ **Creating a Career Development Portfolio.** Chapter 14 walks you through the importance of developing a personal Career Development Portfolio. It is critical for you to create an ongoing account of your experiences, skills, and achievements. Additionally, you will learn to develop an effective resume and cover letter and to prepare for a successful interview.

◆ **Career Development Portfolio worksheet.** Found at the end of every chapter, the Career Development Portfolio presents the best of your skills, competencies, accomplishments, and work. When completed, the portfolio will contain sections on self-analysis, an inventory of skills and competencies, goals, educational and career plans, an inventory of interests, cover letters, resumes, and samples of work. You can use the portfolio to create and update your resume, to help you prepare for an interview, and to advance your career. The portfolio will give you the opportunity to assess your strengths, set goals, and possess an organized system of important documents. It will also help you explore possible majors and careers.

◆ **Career in Focus.** This feature provides real-world career profiles that illustrate examples of the relationship between the study skills necessary for college success and the skills you will need for career success. Work situations that directly call on chapter skills are highlighted, so that you can see the interrelationships.

◆ **Case Study.** Each chapter includes a case study activity that presents college students dealing with real-life situations that reflect the chapter's concepts. This feature stresses that the same issues that you deal with in school also exist in the workplace; the same skills and strategies that you use in the classroom can be adapted to your job. Additional case study opportunities are provided on the text's web site.

Strive to Become the Best Person You Can Be

In this text, you are introduced to the concept of a "peak performer" (Chapter 1) and are provided strategies for maximizing your success in school, career, and life. Our hope is that you are empowered to "walk the walk" and put these strategies and perspectives into practice, starting today. To be successful, you must not only adapt to college and the larger community but also acquire the necessary skills, personal qualities, habits, and motivation to face the challenges of tomorrow's workplace and the tremendous opportunities provided by a world that is increasingly rich in its demographic and cultural diversity.

This preface includes a number of features that provide you with handy guides for future success (such as the "Best Strategies for Success in School"). Additional features in the text include

◆ **The essential personal qualities.** Chapter 2 explores emotional intelligence and focuses on character first, stressing that good character, integrity, and ethics are the hallmarks of truly successful leaders in both business and the community.

◆ **Good habits.** Chapter 13 follows up on how to translate and support essential personal qualities with everyday habits. Included are the top 10 habits of a peak performer.

◆ **The ABCDE Method of Self Management.** New to this edition and introduced in Chapter 1, the ABCDE Method of Self Management will help you manage your thoughts, feelings, and behavior, so that you create the results you want and achieve your goals. This five step process (A = Actual event; B = Beliefs; C = Circumstances; D = Dispute; E = Energized) helps you see the connection among your thoughts, feelings, and actions and empowers you to dispel negative thoughts and replace them with realistic and positive thoughts and behaviors.

◆ **Visualization exercise.** As discussed in Chapter 1, visualization is a powerful tool you can use to imagine your success and think critically through difficult situations. A scenario is presented at the beginning of every chapter, including a journal exercise that asks you to think about your own experiences. A Revisualization exercise at the end of the chapter helps you use the ABCDE Method of Self-Management to work through difficult situations and determine positive solutions. A chapter Worksheet is provided to record your journal entry and follow-up scenario.

◆ **Success Principle.** Each chapter begins with a success principle that succinctly communicates the important lesson to be learned from the chapter. The success principles in total provide a unique and powerful guide to striving for success in school, career, and life.

◆ **Peak Performer Profile.** Each chapter presents a noted person in the area of business, education, the arts, or public service. These peak performers have overcome obstacles and challenges to become successful. You will see that having a positive attitude and perseverance is important for success.

◆ **Words to Succeed.** Found throughout the text, these quotes provide you with insights, motivation, and food for thought and are tied to the chapter's content.

◆ **Performance Strategies.** Included in every chapter is a recap of the top 10 strategies for success in applying the chapter's concepts.

The Text at a Glance

Here are many of the features we just explored and where they can be found throughout the text:

At the Beginning of the Chapter

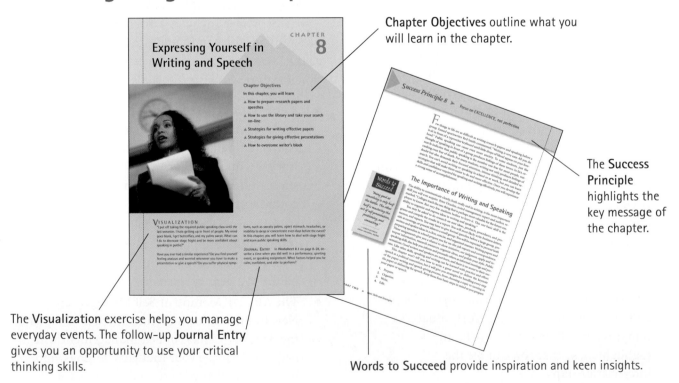

Chapter Objectives outline what you will learn in the chapter.

The **Success Principle** highlights the key message of the chapter.

The **Visualization** exercise helps you manage everyday events. The follow-up **Journal Entry** gives you an opportunity to use your critical thinking skills.

Words to Succeed provide inspiration and keen insights.

Throughout the Chapter

The **Peak Progress** feature provides important strategies, lists, and further discussion of a key topic.

The **Personal Performance Notebook** provides opportunity for self-assessment and critical thinking.

The **Peak Performer Profile** highlights a public figure who has achieved success by overcoming the odds and being a peak performer.

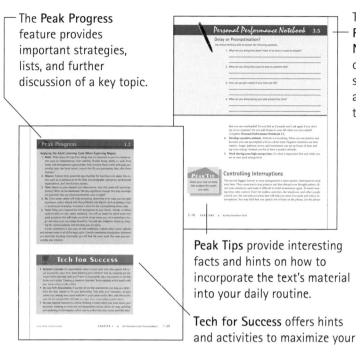

Peak Tips provide interesting facts and hints on how to incorporate the text's material into your daily routine.

Tech for Success offers hints and activities to maximize your use of technology.

The **Career in Focus** feature shows that the strategies you are learning now are essential to your on-the-job success.

At the End of the Chapter

Start preparing for your career now by completing the **Career Development Portfolio** worksheet.

Written as "I" statements, the **Taking Charge** box is a unique summary of the chapter, reinforcing that the key strategies can be mastered.

The **Revisualization** exercise provides examples and opportunities for applying the ABCDE method of Self-Management.

The chapter's ten most important **Performance Strategies** are listed, as well as five **Review Questions** to test understanding and application of the content.

The **Case Study** demonstrates the relationship between school and career success.

The numerous **Worksheets** provide activities for self-assessment, critical thinking, time management, and career planning.

As You Get Started in Your New School: What You Need to Know and Should Not Be Afraid to Ask

Now that you have your book in hand, you are ready to get started. Or are you really ready? What else should you be aware of at this point? You may have already attended a basic orientation session, offered by most schools, which reviews campus and community resources and school requirements. Going through orientation, meeting with your advisor, and reviewing your catalog will help you get oriented. Additionally, the quick review provided here in this text is designed to outline the essentials that you will want to know, so that you not only survive but also make your first year a success. **Peak Progress P-1** provides a handy checklist for the essential tasks you need to consider and accomplish the first week of school. Add to this list any tasks that are unique to your situation or school.

Why Are You Here?

College success begins with determining your goals and mapping out a plan. A good place to start is to have you reflect on why you are in college and what is expected of you. You will be more motivated if you clarify your interests and values concerning college. You will read in Chapter 2 the reasons students don't graduate from college, including poor study skills and habits, lack of preparation, motivation, and effort. College is a commitment of many precious resources you can't afford to waste—time, money, and mental energies. Consider the following statements and your reasons for being in college and share this in your study group or with students whom you meet the first few weeks of class:

◆ I value education and want to be a well-educated person.

◆ I want to get a good job that leads to a well-paying career.

◆ I want to learn new ideas and skills and grow as a person.

◆ I want to get away from home and be independent.

Peak Progress P-1

Tasks to Accomplish the First Week of School

- Attend orientation and meet with an advisor. Ask questions and determine available resources. (See **Peak Progress P-2** for questions to ask.)
- Register and pay fees on time.
- Set up an e-mail account.
- Check deadlines and procedures. *Never* just quit going to class.
- Buy books and keep receipts. Establish a record-keeping system.
- Find out the location of classrooms, parking, and campus resources.
- Go to all classes on time and sit in the front row.
- Know expectations and requirements. Get a syllabus for each class. E-mail instructors for clarification.
- Create an organized study area. Post instructors' names, office locations, and hours, as well as important deadlines.
- Form study teams and exchange e-mails and phone numbers. Get to know instructors and other students.
- Explore resources, such as the library, learning skills center, health center, and advising center.

- I want to make new friends.
- I want to have new experiences and stretch myself.
- I want to fulfill my goal of being a college-educated person.

Jot down what you want from college and why you're motivated to get it.

List four values that are most important to you and how college will help you achieve them.

1. _____
2. _____
3. _____
4. _____

What Should You Be Asking?

You don't want to learn the hard way that you need one more class to graduate, only to find it's offered only once a year (and you just missed it). Make your time with your advisor productive by getting answers to important questions that will help you map out your coursework. **Peak Progress P-2** provides a handy checklist of common questions to get you started.

What Do You Need to Do to Graduate?

You will be more motivated and confident if you understand graduation requirements. If you are a transfer student, requirements vary among schools. Don't rely on the advice of friends. Go to orientation and meet with your advisor early and often. Check out the catalog and make certain you know what is required to graduate. Fill in the following:

Graduation Requirements

- Number of units required:
- General education requirements:
- Curriculum requirements:
- Residency at the school:
- Departmental major requirements:
- Cumulative GPA required:
- Other requirements, such as special writing tests and classes:

How to Register for Classes

Meet with your advisor, carefully select classes, and review general education and major requirements. Add electives that help keep you active and interested, such as an exercise or a weight-training class. Make certain that you understand why you are taking each class and double-check with your advisor that it is meeting certain requirements.

Know the Grading System

Learn the minimum grade point average that you need to maintain good standing. If your GPA falls below 2.0, you may be placed on academic probation. The GPA is calculated according to the number of credit hours each course represents and your grade in the course. In the traditional system, A = 4 points, B = 3 points, C = 2 points, D = 1 point and F = 0 points (your school may have a different system, so ask to be sure). To calculate your GPA, first determine your total number of points. Following is an example:

Course	Grade Achieved	Number of Credit Hours	Points
Political science	C	2	$2 \times 2 = 4$
Psychology	B	3	$3 \times 3 = 9$
English	A	3	$4 \times 3 = 12$
Personal finance	A	1	$4 \times 1 = 4$
TOTAL		9	29

Then, to arrive at your GPA, you must divide your total points by your total number of credit hours:

GPA = Total points divided by total number of credit hours

Thus, in this example,

GPA = 29 divided by 9 = 3.22

Monitor your progress and meet with your instructors often, but especially at midterm and before final exams. Ask what you can do to improve your grade.

Adding or Dropping Classes

Make certain that you know the deadlines for dropping and adding classes. This is generally done in the first few weeks of classes. A withdrawal after the deadline could result in a failing grade. Also make certain before you drop the class that

◆ You will not fall below the required units for financial aid.

◆ You will not fall below the required units for playing sports.

◆ If required, the class is offered again before you plan to graduate.

Peak Progress   P-2

The Most Common Questions Students Ask Advisors

1. What classes do I need to take for general education?
2. Can a course satisfy both a general education and a major requirement?
3. Can I take general elective (GE) courses for Credit/No Credit if I also want to count them for my major?
4. How can I remove an *F* grade from my record?
5. What is the deadline for dropping courses?
6. Can I drop a course after the deadline?
7. What is an "educational leave"?
8. What is the difference between a withdrawal and a drop?
9. Do I need to take any placement tests?
10. Are there other graduation requirements, such as a writing exam?
11. Where do I find out about financial aid?
12. Is there a particular order in which I should take certain courses?
13. Are there courses in which I must earn a *C−* or better?
14. How do I change my major?
15. Which of my transfer courses will count?
16. What is the minimum residency requirement for a bachelor's degree?
17. Is there a GPA requirement for the major?
18. Is there a tutoring program available?
19. If I go on exchange, how do I make sure that courses I take at another university will apply toward my degree here?
20. What is a major contract and when should I get one?
21. When do I need to apply for graduation?
22. How do I apply for graduation?
23. What is a degree check?
24. What is the policy for incomplete grades?
25. Can I take major courses at another school and transfer them here?
26. As a nonresident, how can I establish residency in this state?
27. How do I petition to substitute a class?
28. Once I complete my major, are there other graduation requirements?
29. What is academic probation?
30. Is there any employment assistance available?
31. Is there a mentor program available in my major department?
32. Are there any internships or community service opportunities related to my major?

- You don't need the class or units to meet graduation requirements.
- You are meeting important deadlines.
- You talk with the instructor first.
- You talk with your advisor.

If you choose to withdraw from all your classes, take an academic leave. Don't just walk away from your classes. Remember, it is your responsibility to drop or withdraw from a class. The instructor will not drop you, nor will you be dropped automatically if you stop going to class at any time during the semester. You must complete required forms.

An Incomplete Grade

If you miss class due to illness or an emergency, you may be able to take an incomplete if you can't finish a project or miss a test. Check out this option with your instructor before you drop a class. Make certain you have a written agreement to finish the work at a specific time and that you stay in touch with the instructor through e-mail and phone.

Withdrawing or Taking a Leave of Absence

Some students withdraw because they don't have the money, they can't take time off from work, they lack child care, or they are having difficulty in classes. Before you drop out of college, talk with your advisor and see if you can get the support and motivation to succeed. If you want to take a leave to travel, want to explore other schools, are ill, or just need to take a break, make certain that you take a leave of absence for a semester, year, or longer. Taking a leave means that you do not have to reapply for admissions, and generally you fall under the same category as when you entered school.

Transferring

Before you transfer to another school, make certain you understand the requirements, which courses are transferable, and if there is a residency requirement. If you plan to transfer from a two-year school to a four-year school, your advisor will help you clarify the requirements.

Expectations of Instructors

Most instructors will hand out a syllabus that will outline expectations for the class. Make certain you understand and clarify expectations and have a good understanding of the course requirements. **Worksheet P-1** on page xxxii is a convenient guide to complete when checking your progress with your instructor.

The Best Strategies for Success in School

In this text, we will focus on a number of strategies that will help you determine and achieve your goals. **Peak Progress P-3** provides a comprehensive list of the proven strategies you will find woven throughout this text. Apply these to your efforts in school now and through your course of study. You will find that, not only are they key to your progress in school, but they will also help you develop skills, behaviors, and habits that are directly related to success on the job and in life in general.

The Best Strategies for Success in School

1. **Attend every class.** Going to every class engages you with the subject, the instructor, and other students. Think of the tuition you are paying and what it costs to cut a class.

2. **Be an active participant.** Show that you are engaged and interested by being on time, sitting in front, participating, asking questions, and being alert.

3. **Go to class prepared.** Preview all reading assignments. Highlight key ideas and main concepts and put question marks next to anything you don't understand.

4. **Write a summary.** After you preview the chapter, close the book and write a short summary. Go back and fill in with more details. Do this after each reading.

5. **Know your instructors.** Choose the best instructors, call them by their preferred names and titles, e-mail them, and visit them during office hours. Arrive early for class and get to know them better.

6. **Know expectations.** Read the syllabus for each course and clarify the expectations and requirements, such as tests, papers, extra credit, and attendance.

7. **Join a study team.** You will learn more studying with others than reading alone. Make up tests, give summaries, and teach others.

8. **Organize your study space.** Create a quiet space, with a place for school documents, books, catalogs, a dictionary, a computer, notes, pens, and a calendar. Eliminate distractions by closing the door and focus on the task at hand.

9. **Map out your day, week, and semester.** Write down all assignments, upcoming tests, meetings, daily goals, and priorities on your calendar. Review your calendar and goals each day. Do not socialize until your top priorities are completed.

10. **Get help early.** Know and use all available campus resources. Go to the learning center, counseling center, and health center; get a tutor; and talk with your advisor and instructors about concerns. Get help at the first sign of trouble.

11. **Give school your best effort.** Commit yourself to being extra disciplined the first three weeks—buy your textbooks early; take them to class; get to class early; keep up on your reading; start your projects, papers, and speeches early; and make school a top priority.

12. **Use note cards.** Jot down formulas and key words. Carry them with you and review them during waiting time and right before class.

13. **Review often.** Review and fill in notes immediately after class and again within twenty-four hours. Active reading, note taking, and reviewing are the steps that improve recall.

14. **Study everywhere.** Review your note cards before class, while you wait for class to begin, while waiting in line, before bed, and so on. Studying for short periods of time is more effective than cramming late at night.

15. **Summarize out loud.** Summarize chapters and class notes out loud to your study team. This is an excellent way to learn.

16. **Organize material.** You cannot remember information if it isn't organized. Logical notes help you understand and remember. Use a mind map for outlining key facts and supporting material.

17. **Dig out information.** Focus on main ideas, key words, and overall understanding. Make questions out of chapter headings, review chapter questions, and always read summaries.

18. **Look for associations.** Improve memory by connecting patterns and by linking concepts and relationships. Define, describe, compare, classify, and contrast concepts.

19. **Ask questions.** What is the obvious? What needs to be determined? How can you illustrate the concept? What information is the same and what is different? How does the lecture relate to the textbook?

20. **Pretest yourself.** This will serve as practice and reduces anxiety. This is most effective in your study team.

21. **Study when you are most alert.** Know your energy level and learning preference. Maximize reviewing during daytime hours.

22. **Turn in all assignments on time.** Give yourself an extra few days to review papers and practice speeches.

23. **Make learning physical.** Read difficult textbooks out loud and standing up. Draw pictures, write on a chalkboard, and use visuals. Tape lectures and go on field trips. Integrate learning styles.

24. **Review first drafts with your instructor.** Ask for suggestions and follow them to the letter.

25. **Pay attention to neatness.** Focus on details and turn in all assignments on time. Use your study team to read and exchange term papers. Proofread several times.

26. **Practice!** Nothing beats effort. Practice speeches until you are comfortable and confident and visualize yourself being successful.

27. **Recite and explain.** Pretend that you are the instructor and recite main concepts. What questions would you put on a test? Give a summary to others in your study group. Make up sample test questions in your group.

28. **Take responsibility.** Don't make excuses about missing class or assignments or about earning failing grades. Be honest and take responsibility for your choices and mistakes and learn from them.

29. **Ask for feedback.** When you receive a grade, be reflective and ask questions: "What have I learned from this?" How did I prepare for this?" "How could I improve this grade?" "Did I put in enough effort?" Based on what you learn, what new goals will you set for yourself?

30. **Negotiate for a better grade before grades are sent in.** Find out how you are doing at midterm and ask what you can do to raise your grade. Offer to do extra projects or retake tests.

31. **Always do extra credit.** Raise your grade by doing more than is required or *expected*. Immerse yourself in the subject and find meaning and understanding.

32. **Take responsibility for your education.** You can do well in a class even if your instructor is boring or insensitive. Ask yourself what you can do to make the class more effective (study team, tutoring, active participation). Be flexible and adapt to your instructor's teaching style.

33. **Develop positive qualities.** Think about the personal qualities that you need most to overcome obstacles and work on developing them each day.

34. **Stay healthy.** You cannot do well in school or in life if you are ill. Invest time in exercising, eating healthy, and getting enough sleep and avoid alcohol, cigarettes, and drugs—all involve memory loss.

35. **Dispute negative thinking.** Replace it with positive, realistic, helpful self-talk and focus on your successes. Don't be a perfectionist. Reward yourself when you make small steps toward achieving goals.

36. **Manage your life.** Hang up your keys in the same place, file important material, and establish routines that make your life less stressful.

37. **Break down projects.** Overcome procrastination by breaking overwhelming projects into manageable chunks. Choose a topic, do a rough draft, write a summary, preview a chapter, do a mind map, and organize the tools you need (notes, books, outline).

38. **Make school your top priority.** Working too many hours can cut into study time. Learn to balance school, your social life, and work, so you're effective.

39. **Meet with your advisor to review goals and progress.** Ask questions about requirements, and don't drop and add classes without checking on the consequences. Develop a good relationship with your advisor and your instructors.

40. **Be persistent.** Whenever you get discouraged, just keep following positive habits and strategies and you will succeed. Success comes in small, consistent steps. Be patient and keep plugging away.

41. **Spend less than you make.** Don't go into debt for new clothes, a car, CDs, gifts, travel, or other things you can do without. Education is the best investment in future happiness and job success that you can make. Learn to save.

42. **Use critical thinking and think about the consequences of your decisions.** Don't be impulsive about money, sex, smoking, or drugs. Don't start a family until you are emotionally and financially secure. Practice impulse control by imagining how you would feel after making certain choices.

43. **Don't get addicted.** Addictions are a tragic waste of time. Ask yourself if you've ever known anyone whose life was better for being addicted. Do you know anyone whose life has been destroyed by alcohol and other drugs? This one decision will affect your life forever.

44. **Know who you are and what you want.** Visit the career center and talk with a career counselor about your interests, values, goals, strengths, personality, learning style, and career possibilities. Respect your style and set up conditions that create results.

45. **Use creative problem solving.** Think about what went right and what went wrong this semester. What could you have done that would have helped you be more successful? What are new goals you want to set for next semester? What are some creative ways to overcome obstacles? How can you solve problems instead of letting them persist?

46. **Contribute.** Look for opportunities to contribute your time and talents. What could you do outside of class that would complement your education and serve others?

47. **Take advantage of your texts' resources.** Many textbooks have accompanying web sites, CDs, and study materials designed to help you succeed in class. Visit this book's web site at www.mhhe.com/ferrett5e.

48. **Respect yourself and others.** Be supportive, tolerant, and respectful of people who are different from you. Look for ways to learn about other cultures and different views; expand your friendships. *Respect yourself.* Surround yourself with people who are positive and successful, who value learning, and who are supportive and respectful of you and your goals.

49. **Focus on gratitude.** Look at the abundance in your life—your health, family, friends, and opportunities. You have so much going for you to help you succeed.

50. **Just do it.** Newton's first law of motion says that things in motion tend to stay in motion, so get started and keep working on your goals!

PROGRESS ASSESSMENT

Course: _____

Instructor: _____

Office: _____ Office Hours: _____

Phone: _____ E-mail: _____

1. How am I doing in this class?

   _____

   _____

   _____

2. What grades have you recorded for me thus far?

   _____

   _____

   _____

3. Are there any adjustments that I should make?

   _____

   _____

   _____

4. Am I missing any assignments?

   _____

   _____

   _____

5. Do you have any suggestions as to how I can improve my performance or excel in your class?

   _____

   _____

   _____

Self-Assessment and Choosing Majors

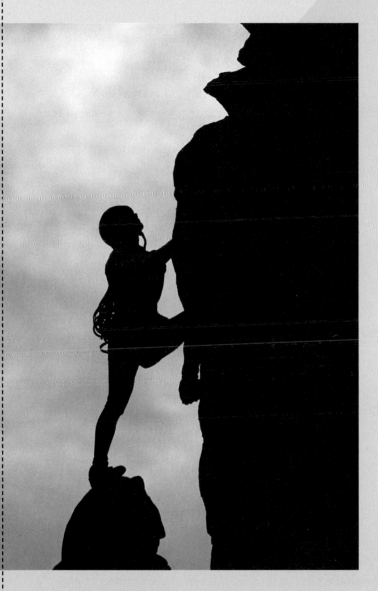

Chapter Objectives

In this chapter, you will learn

▲ The characteristics of a peak performer

▲ To use critical thinking skills in self-assessment

▲ Visualization techniques to help you focus on positive outcomes

▲ The skills and competencies for school and job success

▲ About learning styles and personality types and how to integrate them

▲ The Adult Learning Cycle and how to apply it

▲ About choosing your major

VISUALIZATION

"It's the first day of class and I'm already overwhelmed. What have I gotten myself into?"

Are you already feeling like this? Are you afraid you will never achieve your goals, or do you even know what your goals are? Instead of focusing on negative feelings, channel your energies into positive results and envision yourself being successful. In this chapter, you will learn "visualization" and will practice it throughout the text. This is a valuable

self-management tool that will help you focus on positive outcomes and achieve your goals.

JOURNAL ENTRY In **Worksheet 1.1** on page 1–34, write down two major goals that you'd like to accomplish in five years. List the obstacles that may keep you from achieving them. In this chapter, you will apply visualization to help you overcome those obstacles.

Use
- TM 1.1 Success Principle 1.
- TM 1.2 Attributes of a Peak Performer.
- TM 1.3 Benefits of Being a Peak Performer.
- TM 1.4 Benefits of Self-Assessment.

LEARNING IS A LIFELONG JOURNEY. People who are successful—"peak performers"—are on this journey. They are lifelong learners. We are constantly faced with many types of changes—economic, technological, societal, etc. To meet these challenges, you will need to continually learn new skills in school, on your job, and throughout your life. You will meet these challenges through your study and learning strategies, in your methods of performing work-related tasks, and even in the way you view your personal life and lifestyle.

Lately, you may have been asking yourself, "Who am I?" "What course of study should I take?" "What kind of job do I want?" "Where should I go to school?" "What should I do with my life?" When thinking about making a change, the first step is self-assessment. Self-assessment requires seeing yourself objectively.

Throughout this book, as you journey on the road to becoming a peak performer, you will discover methods that will help you with the task of self-assessment and change. In this chapter, you begin by assessing your learning and personality styles. The chapter's assessment exercises will help you look at your life as a dynamic motion picture rather than as a brief snapshot. These exercises will be the foundation for your Career Development Portfolio. This portfolio will furnish you with a lifelong assessment tool for learning where you are and where you want to go and for providing a place for documenting the results. This portfolio of skills and competencies will become your guide for remaining marketable and flexible throughout your career.

What Is a "Peak Performer"?

Peak performers come from all lifestyles, ages, cultures, and genders. They can be famous, such as the people profiled in this book. However, anyone can become a peak performer by setting goals and developing appropriate attitudes and behaviors to achieve the results they want. Peak performers are those who become masters at creating excellence by focusing on results. They know how to change their negative thoughts into positive and realistic affirmations. They focus on their long-term goals and know how to break down goals into daily action steps. They are not perfect or successful overnight. They learn to face the fear of making mistakes and working through them. They use the whole of their intelligence and abilities.

Every day thousands of individuals quietly overcome incredible setbacks, climb over huge obstacles, and reach within themselves to find inner strength. Many are neither rich nor famous, nor have they reached the top of their careers. They are successful because they know that they possess the personal power to produce results in their lives and find passion in what they contribute to life. They are masters, not victims, of life's situations. They control the quality of their lives. In short, they are their own best friend.

Peak performers:

◆ Take risks and move beyond secure comfort zones
◆ Creatively think and solve problems
◆ Make sound judgments and effective decisions
◆ Know their learning styles and how to maximize their learning
◆ Involve themselves in supportive relationships
◆ Continually acquire new skills and perfect their competence
◆ Remain confident and resilient
◆ Are motivated to overcome barriers
◆ Take small steps that lead to long-term goals

Use
TM 1.5 Critical Thinking
Guidelines.

The Benefits of Self-Assessment

The first step in becoming a peak performer is self-assessment. Out of self-assessment comes recognition of the need to learn new tasks and subjects, relate more effectively with others, set goals, manage time and stress, and create a balanced and productive life. Self-assessment requires facing the truth and seeing yourself objectively. For example, it is not easy to admit that you procrastinate or lack certain skills. Even when talking about your strengths, you may feel embarrassed. However, honest self-assessment is the foundation for making positive changes in your life. Self-assessment can help you

◆ Understand how you learn best
◆ Work with your strengths and natural preferences
◆ Learn to balance and integrate your preferred learning style with other styles
◆ Learn to use critical thinking and reasoning
◆ Make sound and creative decisions about school and work
◆ Learn to change ineffective patterns of thinking and behaving
◆ Create a positive and motivated state of mind
◆ Work more effectively with diverse people
◆ Learn how to handle stress and conflict
◆ Achieve better grades

and, most importantly,

◆ Work smarter, not harder; you will develop strategies that help you maximize your energies and resources

Words to Succeed

"It is to measure oneself against Truth, and not the other way around. The first product of self-knowledge is humility."

—FLANNERY O'CONNOR, *writer*

Using Critical Thinking Skills

Self-assessment involves using your critical thinking skills. What exactly is critical thinking? Critical thinking is a logical, rational, and systematic thought process used

Teaching Tip
Explain the importance of
being honest about strengths
and weaknesses. Ask
students if it is difficult to be
honest when they self-assess.

Teaching Tip
Emphasize the importance of
using the ABCDE Method of
Self-Management to visualize
success and create positive
results.

to think through a problem or situation. Since critical thinking determines the quality of the decisions that you make in all areas of your life, it is an important theme throughout this book. To help you fine-tune your critical thinking skills, make a habit of assessing your thinking skills regularly.

Also, complete the exercises and activities throughout this book. You will enhance your critical thinking skills by practicing visualization and self-management, which is discussed further in **Peak Progress 1.1,** as well as by completing the many **Personal Performance Notebook** exercises. Use the following guidelines in your journey to becoming a more critical thinker:

◆　Suspend judgment until you have gathered facts and reflected on them.

◆　Look for evidence that supports or contradicts your initial assumptions, opinions, and beliefs.

◆　Adjust your opinions as new information and facts are known.

◆　Ask questions, look for proof, and examine the problem closely.

◆　Reject incorrect or irrelevant information.

◆　Consider the source of the information.

Peak Progress   1.1

Visualization: A Self-Management Tool

Visualization is a powerful tool to help you focus on positive action and outcomes. You are not a victim or passive spectator; you are responsible for your thoughts and behaviors. When you observe and dispute negative thoughts and replace them with positive, appropriate, and realistic thoughts and behaviors, you are practicing your critical thinking and creativity skills. You are taking charge of your life, focusing on what you can change, and working toward your goals.

You may have noticed that your mood affects how your day will go. By using visualization, disputing negative thoughts, and using affirmations, you become aware of patterns and thoughts that may be keeping you from achieving your goals. Visualization uses the power of positive thinking, but it also shows you how to dispute and replace negative thoughts with accurate and realistic statements. You are really managing yourself, becoming action-oriented, and feeling energized, confident, and motivated. Optimism and hope create positive results. Focusing on positive results minimizes the energy negativity wastes.

You can practice visualization any time and anywhere throughout the day. For example, between classes, find a quiet place and close your eyes. Take several deep breaths and see yourself calm, centered, and focused on your goals. This is especially effective when your mind starts to chatter and you feel overwhelmed, discouraged, or stressed. Visualize yourself graduating, working steadily, and accomplishing your goals.

continued

Peak Progress 1.1

Visualization: A Self–Management Tool *(concluded)*

You can come to this place within your mind and find peace and calm at anytime. You may also find it effective to write down your thoughts in a journal or this text.

Visualization is as easy as ABC (and D and E). These five simple steps help you manage your thoughts, feelings, and behavior, so that you create the results you want and achieve your goals.

A = Actual event—state the situation, goal, or objective

B = Beliefs—describe your thoughts about the situation

C = Consequences—express the feelings that were created by your thoughts

D = Dispute—challenge any negative thoughts by countering with accurate and positive statements

E = Energized—visualize yourself focused, motivated, and positive

For example, when you read the Visualization box on the first page of this chapter, you may have felt the same—overwhelmed. You are in a new situation with many new expectations—of you and by you. Let's apply the ABCDE visualization method to focus your energies on developing a positive outcome. For example, you might say:

A = Actual event: "It is only the first week and I already have an overload of information from this class."

B = Beliefs: "Maybe this was a bad idea. What if I fail? What if I can't keep it all straight—learning styles, personalities, temperaments? These other people are probably a lot smarter than me."

C = Consequences: "I'm feeling overwhelmed and depressed. I'm panicking and totally stressed out."

D = Dispute: "Going to college is a big change, but I have handled new and stressful situations before. I know how to overcome feeling overwhelmed by breaking big jobs into small tasks. Everyone tells me I'm hardworking, and I know I'm talented and smart in many different ways. I know that going to college is a very good idea, and I want to graduate."

E = Energized: "I'm excited about discovering my learning and personality styles and how I can use them to my advantage. There are so many resources available to me—my instructor, my classmates, the book's web site, etc. I will get to know at least one person in each of my classes, and I will take a few minutes to explore at least one resource at school that can provide support. I see myself confident and energized and achieving my goals."

Hands-On Application
In small groups, have students come up with an actual event and apply the ABCDE method. Stress that they can learn to dispute irrational, negative thoughts and replace them with positive thoughts.

Skills for School and Job Success

Have you ever asked yourself, "What does it take to be successful in a job?" Many of the skills and competencies that characterize a successful student can also apply to the successful employee. Becoming aware of the connection between school success and job success helps you see how the skills learned in the classroom will eventually apply to the skills needed in the workplace.

Teaching Tip
Explain to students that
SCANS will be used as a
guide to help them connect
what they learn in class to the
world outside.

Class Discussion
1. Applying SCANS.
   Learning how to learn.
   How does this competency
   create college and job
   success?
2. Ask students if they would
   want their surgeon to be
   operating on them if he or
   she had not passed a test
   indicating technical
   competencies.

Over the years, employers have told educators what skills they want employees to have. In 1990, Elizabeth Dole, who was then the Secretary of Labor, created SCANS (Secretary's Commission on Achieving Necessary Skills). The commission members included business and industry leaders, human resource personnel, and other top advisors in labor and education. The Peak Performance Competency Wheel in **Figure 1.1** illustrates the skills and competencies recommended by SCANS for job success. These skills and competencies are necessary not only for job success but also for school success. You can apply and practice them now by completing the Peak Performance Self-Assessment Test in **Personal Performance Notebook 1.1** on page 1–7. Be honest and use critical thinking skills as you complete the test.

Notice that Statement 23 on the assessment test deals with commitment and effort. Commitment to your goals is vital if you are to succeed. Results happen with commitment and effort. One of the reasons people may not succeed in school or in their careers is a lack of willingness to make the necessary effort. If success does not come quickly, they give up without examining the real reasons for not succeeding.

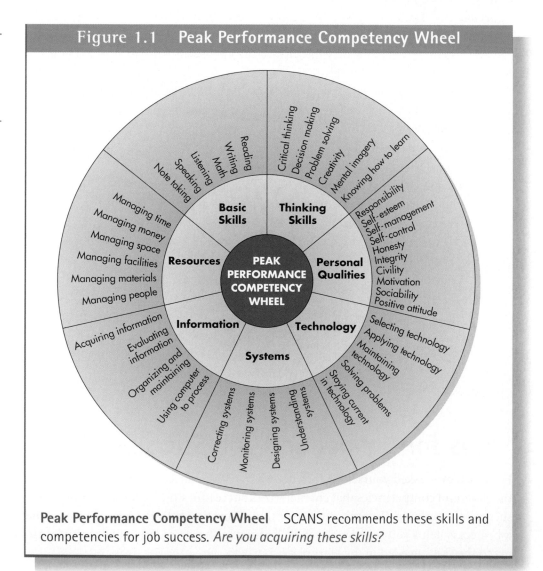

Figure 1.1   Peak Performance Competency Wheel

Peak Performance Competency Wheel   SCANS recommends these skills and competencies for job success. *Are you acquiring these skills?*

Peak Performance Self-Assessment Test

Assess each skill. Rate yourself on a scale of 1 to 5 by placing a checkmark. Then review your answers to discover your strongest skills and weakest skills.

Area	Good 5	4	OK 3	2	Poor 1
1. Reading	___	___	___	___	___
2. Writing	___	___	___	___	___
3. Speaking	___	___	___	___	___
4. Mathematics	___	___	___	___	___
5. Listening and note taking	___	___	___	___	___
6. Critical thinking and reasoning	___	___	___	___	___
7. Creative problem solving	___	___	___	___	___
8. Positive visualization	___	___	___	___	___
9. Knowing how you learn	___	___	___	___	___
10. Honesty and integrity	___	___	___	___	___
11. Positive attitude and motivation	___	___	___	___	___
12. Responsibility	___	___	___	___	___
13. Flexibility/ability to adapt to change	___	___	___	___	___
14. Self-management and emotional control	___	___	___	___	___
15. Self-esteem and confidence	___	___	___	___	___
16. Time management	___	___	___	___	___
17. Money management	___	___	___	___	___
18. Management and leadership of people	___	___	___	___	___
19. Interpersonal and communication skills	___	___	___	___	___
20. Ability to work well with culturally diverse groups	___	___	___	___	___
21. Organization and evaluation of information	___	___	___	___	___
22. Understanding technology	___	___	___	___	___
23. Commitment and effort	___	___	___	___	___

Teaching Tip
Encourage students to be honest with themselves as they fill out the test.

Use
TM 1.9 Peak Performance Self-Assessment Test.

Key Teaching Concept
Effort and commitment are often more important than ability or talent.

Key Teaching Concept

The most important concept in this chapter is to learn how to learn.

Teaching Tip

Bring in a laptop computer to demonstrate learning styles. Ask students how they would learn to use the computer. Would they read the manual? Would they take a class? Would they turn it on and experiment?

Class Discussion

Ask students: How would a visual learner approach learning the computer? How would an auditory learner approach learning the computer? How would a kinesthetic learner approach learning the computer?

Discovering Your Learning Style

As a lifelong learner, you need to know *how* to learn to maximize your learning potential. Everyone processes information differently. Knowing your preferred learning style can increase your effectiveness in school or at work and can enhance your self-esteem. Knowing how you learn best can help you reduce frustration, focus on your strengths, and integrate various styles.

ARE YOU A READER, A LISTENER, OR A DOER?

One way to explore how you learn best is to ask yourself if you are a reader, a listener, or a doer. Do you get more information from reading and seeing, talking and listening, or doing? Of course, you do all these things, but your learning strength or style may be in one of these areas.

A person who learns better by reading possesses a visual learning style. Someone who learns better by listening is considered an auditory learner. A kinesthetic learner learns by touch. The **Personal Performance Notebook 1.2** on page 1–9 has a Learning Style Inventory that will help you discover your learning style.

VISUAL LEARNERS

Visual learners prefer to see information and read material. They learn more effectively with pictures, graphs, illustrations, diagrams, timelines, photos, pie charts, and visual design. They like to contemplate concepts, reflect, and summarize information in writing. They might use arrows, pictures, and bullets to highlight points. Visual learners are often holistic in that they see pictures in their mind that create feelings and emotion. Visual learners tend to

- Remember what they see better than what they hear
- Prefer to have written directions they can read
- Learn better when someone shows them rather than tells them
- Like to read, highlight, and write summaries
- Keep a list of things to do when planning the week
- Tend to be quiet in class and watch facial expressions
- Like to read for pleasure and to learn
- May want to be an interior designer, a drafter, a proofreader, a writer, or an artist

AUDITORY LEARNERS

Auditory learners prefer to rely on their hearing sense. They like tapes and music, and they prefer to listen to information, such as lectures. They like to work in study teams and enjoy class discussions. They like to talk, recite, and summarize information aloud. Auditory learners may create rhymes out of words and play music that helps them concentrate. When they take study breaks, they listen to music or chat with a friend. Auditory learners tend to

- Remember what they hear better than what they see
- Prefer to listen to instructions

Learning Style Inventory

Name _____ Date _____

Determine your learning preference. Complete each sentence by checking a, b, or c. No completion is correct or better than another.

1. I learn best when I

   _____ a. see information.

   _____ b. hear information.

   _____ c. have hands-on experience.

2. I like

   _____ a. pictures and illustrations.

   _____ b. listening to tapes and stories.

   _____ c. working with people and going on field trips.

3. For pleasure and relaxation, I love to

   _____ a. read.

   _____ b. listen to music and tapes.

   _____ c. garden or play sports.

4. I tend to be

   _____ a. contemplative.

   _____ b. talkative.

   _____ c. a doer.

5. To remember a ZIP code, I like to

   _____ a. write it down several times.

   _____ b. say it out loud several times.

   _____ c. doodle and draw it on any available paper.

6. In a classroom, I learn best when

   _____ a. I have a good textbook, visual aids, and written information.

   _____ b. the instructor is interesting and clear.

   _____ c. I am involved in doing activities.

7. When I study for a test, I

   _____ a. read my notes and write a summary.

   _____ b. review my notes aloud and talk to others.

   _____ c. like to study in a group and use models and charts.

8. I have

   _____ a. strong fashion sense and pay attention to visual details.

   _____ b. fun telling stories and jokes.

   _____ c. a great time building things and being active.

Teaching Tip

Explain that there is no one way to learn or one instrument that can indicate a precise learning style. The purpose of the Learning Style Inventory is to provide a guide.

Learning Style Inventory—continued

9. I plan the upcoming week by

_____ **a.** making a list and keeping a detailed calendar.

_____ **b.** talking it through with someone.

_____ **c.** creating a computer calendar or using a project board.

10. When preparing for a math test, I like to

_____ **a.** write formulas on note cards or use pictures.

_____ **b.** memorize formulas or talk aloud.

_____ **c.** use marbles, LEGO® blocks, or three-dimensional models.

11. I often

_____ **a.** remember faces but not names.

_____ **b.** remember names but not faces.

_____ **c.** remember events but not names or faces.

12. I remember best

_____ **a.** when I read instructions and use visual images to remember.

_____ **b.** when I listen to instructions and use rhyming words to remember.

_____ **c.** with hands-on activities and trial and error.

13. When I give directions, I might say,

_____ **a.** "Turn right at the yellow house and left when you see the large oak tree. Do you see what I mean?"

_____ **b.** "Turn right. Go three blocks. Turn left onto Buttermilk Lane. OK? Got that? Do you hear what I'm saying?"

_____ **c.** "Follow me," after giving directions by using gestures.

14. When driving in a new city, I prefer to

_____ **a.** get a map and find my own way.

_____ **b.** stop and get directions from someone.

_____ **c.** drive around and figure it out by myself.

Score: Count the number of check marks for all your choices.

Total a choices _____ (visual learning style)

Total b choices _____ (auditory learning style)

Total c choices _____ (kinesthetic learning style)

The highest total indicates your dominant learning style.

- Like to listen to music and talk on the telephone
- Plan the week by talking it through with someone
- Use rhyming words to remember
- Learn best when they hear an assignment as well as see it
- May enjoy being a disc jockey, trial lawyer, counselor, or musician

KINESTHETIC LEARNERS

Kinesthetic learners are usually well coordinated, like to touch things, and learn best by doing. They like to collect samples, write out information, spend time outdoors, and relate to the material they are learning. They like to connect abstract material to something concrete. Kinesthetic learners tend to

- Create an experience
- Use hands-on activities and computer games
- Build things and put things together
- Use models and physical activity
- Draw, doodle, use games and puzzles, and play computer games
- Take field trips and collect samples
- Relate abstract information to something concrete
- May enjoy being a chef, a surgeon, a medical technician, a nurse, an automobile mechanic, an electrician, an engineer, a forest ranger, a police officer, or a dancer

Know how you learn.
Everyone has his or her own way of learning. *What type of learning style do you think best suits this person?*

Use
TM 1.10 Learning Styles.

Teaching Tip
Have students discuss how they can develop and integrate different learning styles. For example, they may enhance their visual sense by reading and looking at pictures. They can enhance their auditory skills by listening to tapes. They can enhance their kinesthetic sense by getting more involved in hands-on activities.

REDEFINING INTELLIGENCE: OTHER LEARNING STYLES

Because each of us has our own unique set of abilities, perceptions, and needs, learning styles vary widely. Besides visual, auditory, and kinesthetic learning styles, there are other, more specific styles, and some people may have more than one learning style.

Plus, in the last decade, intelligence has been redefined. We used to think of intelligence as measured by an IQ test. Research by Thomas Armstrong, author of *7 Kinds of Smart: Identifying and Developing Your Many Intelligences,* and Howard Gardner, who wrote *Frames of Mind: The Theory of Multiple Intelligences,* illustrated that we all possess many different intelligences. For example, there are people who are

1. **Word smart.** They have verbal/linguistic intelligence and like to read, talk, and write about information. They have the ability to argue, persuade, entertain, and teach with words. Many become journalists, writers, and lawyers.
2. **Picture smart.** They have spatial intelligence and like to draw, sketch, and visualize information. They have the ability to perceive in three-dimensional

Class Discussion
Explain that Carl Jung's contribution was to describe how people process information differently. Most students have heard of people being either extroverts or introverts. They may also be aware that some people are primarily thinkers and others process information through their feelings. Review other categories and ask students if some of the descriptive words fit their personalities.

space and re-create various aspects of the visual world. Many become architects, photographers, artists, and engineers.

3. **Logic smart.** They have logical/mathematical intelligence and like numbers, puzzles, and logic. They have the ability to reason, solve problems, create hypotheses, think in terms of cause and effect, and explore patterns and relationships. Many become scientists, accountants, and computer programmers.

4. **Musical smart.** They have rhythm and melody intelligence. They have the ability to appreciate, perceive, and produce rhythms and to keep time to music. Many become composers, singers, and instrumentalists.

5. **Body smart.** They have physical and kinesthetic intelligence. They have the ability to understand and control their bodies; they have tactile sensitivity, like movement, and handle objects skillfully. Many become dancers, physical education teachers or coaches, and carpenters and enjoy outdoor activities and sports.

6. **Outdoor smart.** They have environmental intelligence. They are good at measuring, charting, and observing plants and animals. They like to keep journals, to collect and classify, and to participate in outdoor activities. Many become park and forest rangers, surveyors, gardeners, landscape architects, outdoor guides, wildlife experts, and environmentalists.

7. **Self smart.** They have intrapersonal and inner intelligence. They have the ability to be contemplative, self-disciplined, and introspective. They like to work alone and pursue their own interests. Many become writers, counselors, theologians, or self-employed businesspeople.

8. **People smart.** They have interpersonal intelligence. They like to talk and work with people, join groups, and solve problems as part of a team. They have the ability to work with and understand people, as well as to perceive and be responsive to the moods, intentions, and desires of other people. Many become mediators, negotiators, social directors, social workers, motivational speakers, or teachers.

USING INVENTORIES FOR SELF-ASSESSMENT

You just completed the Learning Style Inventory, which helped you determine if you are primarily a visual, an auditory, or a kinesthetic learner. Just as there is no one or best way to learn, there is no one instrument, assessment, or inventory that can categorize how you learn best. There are many theories about learning styles, and none of them should be regarded as air-tight explanations. Any learning style assessment or theory is, at best, a guide.

The assessment instruments discussed in this text have been adapted from various sources and involve 25 years of research. They are simple, yet they provide valuable clues and strategies for determining how you learn, process information, and relate to others. They also provide you with clues for possible college majors and careers that fit your personality and style.

The purpose of these inventories is to provide a guide, not to categorize you into a specific box, and to show you how to integrate all learning styles. You are encouraged

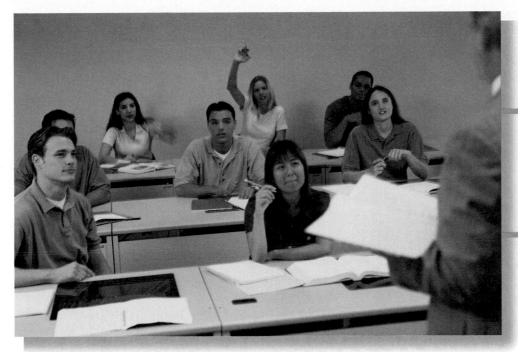

Learning Styles.
There is no one best way to learn. *How do you think you can develop and integrate different learning styles?*

to review many different instruments through your career or learning centers. The goals are to develop positive strategies based on your natural talents and abilities and to expand your effectiveness by integrating all learning styles.

Discovering Your Personality and Team Type

The concepts of personality and temperaments are not new. Early writings of ancient Greece, India, the Middle East, and China addressed various temperaments. Hippocrates, the ancient Greek founder of modern medicine, classified people according to personality types.

In 1921, psychologist Carl Jung proposed in his book *Psychological Types* that people are fundamentally different but also fundamentally alike. He identified three main attitudes/psychological functions, each with two types of personalities:

1. First, he classified *how people relate to the external or internal world.* **Extroverts** are energized by people, tending to be outgoing and social. **Introverts** are energized by time alone, preferring the world of ideas and thoughts.

2. Next, he determined *how people prefer to perceive information.* **Sensors** learn best from their senses and like to organize information systematically. **Intuitives** rely on hunches, intuition, and nonverbal perceptions.

3. Then, he characterized *how people prefer to make decisions.* **Thinkers** depend on rational logic and analysis. They tend to be unemotional and use a systematic evaluation of data and facts for problem solving. **Feelers** are sensitive to the concerns and feelings of others, value harmony, and dislike creating conflict.

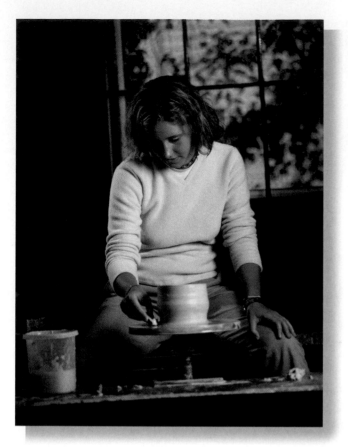

Understanding personality types.

Psychologists have developed a variety of categories to identify how people function best. *What personality type or types might apply to the person in this photograph?*

Jung suggested that differences and similarities among people could be understood by combining these types. Although people are not exclusively one way or the other, he maintained that they have basic preferences or tendencies.

Jung's work inspired Katherine Briggs and her daughter, Isabel Briggs Myers, to design a personality test, the Myers-Briggs Type Indicator (MBTI), which has become the most widely used typological instrument. They added a fourth function (judgment/perception), which they felt was implied in Jung's writings. This function focuses on *how people live*. **Judgers** prefer orderly, planned, structured learning and working environments. They like control and closure. **Perceivers** prefer flexibility and spontaneity and like to allow life to unfold. Thus, with the four attitudes/functions (extroverts vs. introverts, sensors vs. intuitives, thinkers vs. feelers, and judgers vs. perceivers), the MBTI provides 16 possible personality combinations. Although we may use all 8 preferences, 1 in each pair tends to be more developed.

David Keirsy and Marilyn Bates then combined the 16 Myers-Briggs types into four temperaments. Review **Figure 1.2** on page 1–15, which is an adaptation of Keirsy and Bates' work, listing the characteristics and likes of *extroverts, introverts, sensors, intuitives, thinkers, feelers, judgers,* and *perceivers.* What four types make up your personality combination?

Connecting Learning Styles and Personality Types: The Four-Temperament Profile

You now are aware of your preferred learning styles and have a sense of your personality type. How are these connected? How can you use this information to improve your learning skills and participate in productive group or team situations?

The Four-Temperament Profile demonstrates how learning styles and personality types are interrelated. Essentially, there are four main categories: analyzer, supporter, creator, and director. **Personal Performance Notebook 1.3** on page 1–16 includes a number of questions that will help you determine your dominant temperament.

The following descriptions elaborate on the four temperaments in Personal Performance Notebook 1.3. Which was your dominant temperament: analyzer, creator, supporter, or director? Did the answer surprise you? Please keep in mind that inventories only provide clues. People change over time and react differently in different situations. However, use this knowledge to discover your strengths and to become a well-rounded and balanced learner. Peak performers know not only their dominant style but also the way to integrate other styles when appropriate.

Figure 1.2   Characteristics of Personality Types

Extroverts (E) vs. Introverts (I)		Sensors (S) vs. Intuitives(iN)	
Gregarious	Quiet	Practical	Speculative
Active, talkative	Reflective	Experience	Use hunches
Speak, then think	Think, then speak	See details	See the big picture
Outgoing, social	Fewer, closer friends	Sequential, work steadily	Work in burst of energy
Energized by people	Energized by self	Feet on the ground	Head in the clouds
Like to speak	Like to read	Concrete	Abstract
Like variety and action	Like quiet for concentration	Realistic	See possibilities
Interested in results	Interested in ideas	Sensible and hardworking	Imaginative and inspired
Do not mind interruptions	Dislike interruptions	Good and precise work	Dislike precise work

Thinkers (T) vs. Feelers (F)		Judgers (J) vs. Perceivers (P)	
Analytical	Harmonious	Decisive	Tentative
Objective	Subjective	Closure	Open-minded
Impersonal	Personal	Plan ahead	Flexible
Factual	Sympathy	Urgency	Open time frame
Want fairness	Wants recognition	Organized	Spontaneous
Detached	Involved	Deliberate	Go with the flow
Rule	Circumstances	Set goals	Let life unfold
Things, not people	People, not things	Meet deadlines	Procrastinate
Lineal	Whole	Just the facts	Interested and curious

Characteristics of Personality Types   This chart reflects information gathered by David Keirsy and Marilyn Bates. Their work was influenced by psychologists Carl Jung and Myers and Briggs. *How can understanding your own personality and temperament help you succeed in school and life?*

Hands-On Application

In small groups, discuss possible problems and opportunities for each situation:

1. One roommate is an extrovert, and the other is an introvert.
2. The instructor is very logical, facts only, thinker type and the student processes information through feelings.
3. A boss has a sensing preference; the employee has an intuitive preference.
4. One co-worker has a judging preference, and the other co-worker has a perceiving preference.

The Four-Temperament Profile

The following statements indicate your preference in working with others, making decisions, and learning new information. Read each statement, with its four possible choices. Mark 4 next to the choice MOST like you, 3 next to the choice ALMOST like you, 2 next to the choice SOMEWHAT like you, and 1 next to the choice LEAST like you.

Teaching Tip
Indicate to students that there is no "best" style. Each style has effective and ineffective traits.

1. I learn best when I

   _____ **a.** rely on logical thinking and facts.

   _____ **b.** am personally involved.

   _____ **c.** can look for new patterns through trial and error.

   _____ **d.** use hands-on activities and practical applications.

2. When I'm at my best, I'm described as

   _____ **a.** dependable, accurate, logical, and objective.

   _____ **b.** understanding, loyal, cooperative, and harmonious.

   _____ **c.** imaginative, flexible, open-minded, and creative.

   _____ **d.** confident, assertive, practical, and results-oriented.

3. I respond best to instructors and bosses who

   _____ **a.** are factual and to the point.

   _____ **b.** show appreciation and are friendly.

   _____ **c.** encourage creativity and flexibility.

   _____ **d.** expect me to be involved, be active, and get results.

4. When working in a group, I tend to value

   _____ **a.** objectivity and correctness.

   _____ **b.** consensus and harmony.

   _____ **c.** originality and risk taking.

   _____ **d.** efficiency and results.

5. I am most comfortable with people who are

   _____ **a.** informed, serious, and accurate.

   _____ **b.** supportive, appreciative, and friendly.

   _____ **c.** creative, unique, and idealistic.

   _____ **d.** productive, realistic, and dependable.

6. Generally, I am

   _____ **a.** methodical, efficient, trustworthy, and accurate.

   _____ **b.** cooperative, genuine, gentle, and modest.

   _____ **c.** high-spirited, spontaneous, easily bored, and dramatic.

   _____ **d.** straightforward, conservative, responsible, and decisive.

The Four-Temperament Profile—continued

7. When making a decision, I'm generally concerned with

_____ **a.** collecting information and facts to determine the right solution.

_____ **b.** finding the solution that pleases others and myself.

_____ **c.** brainstorming creative solutions that feel right.

_____ **d.** quickly choosing the most practical and realistic solution.

8. You could describe me in one word as

_____ **a.** analytical.

_____ **b.** caring.

_____ **c.** innovative.

_____ **d.** productive.

9. I excel at

_____ **a.** reaching accurate and logical conclusions.

_____ **b.** being cooperative and respecting people's feelings.

_____ **c.** finding hidden connections and creative outcomes.

_____ **d.** making realistic, practical, and timely decisions.

10. When learning at school or on the job, I enjoy

_____ **a.** gathering facts and technical information and being objective.

_____ **b.** making personal connections, being supportive, and working in groups.

_____ **c.** exploring new possibilities, tackling creative tasks, and being flexible.

_____ **d.** producing results, solving problems, and making decisions.

Score: To determine your style, mark the choices you made in each column below. Then add the column totals. Highest number in

- a column, you are an analyzer.
- b column, you are supporter.
- c column, you are a creator.
- d column, you are a director.

	Choice a	Choice b	Choice c	Choice d
1.	_____	_____	_____	_____
2.	_____	_____	_____	_____
3.	_____	_____	_____	_____
4.	_____	_____	_____	_____
5.	_____	_____	_____	_____
6.	_____	_____	_____	_____
7.	_____	_____	_____	_____
8.	_____	_____	_____	_____
9.	_____	_____	_____	_____
10.	_____	_____	_____	_____
Total	_____	_____	_____	_____
	Analyzer	**Supporter**	**Creator**	**Director**

Class Discussion
Review the traits of the analyzer style. Ask students how many of them fit the style. What strategies help them learn best? Do they know people who fit this profile? How can they relate best to this style?

Hands-On Application
Role Playing:
1. In small groups, have one student play the instructor with an analyzer-style profile. Have three or four team members play students in the analyzer's class. One observer should take notes. Discuss findings in small groups.
2. List suggestions for dealing effectively with an instructor with a dominant analyzer style. Discuss in large groups with the class.

Teaching Tip
Discuss possible majors and careers for the analyzer style.

Teaching Tip
Discuss possible majors and careers for the supporter style.

Class Discussion
Review the traits of the supporter style. Ask students:
1. Do you fit into this style?
2. What strategies would help you learn best?
3. Do you know people who fit this profile?
4. How could you best relate to this style?

Figure 1.3   Profile of an Analyzer

Effective Traits	Ineffective Traits	Possible Majors	Possible Careers	How to Relate to Analyzers
Objective	Too cautious	Accounting	Computer programmer	Be factual
Logical	Abrupt	Bookkeeping	Accountant	Be logical
Thorough	Unemotional	Mathematics	Bookkeeper	Be formal and thorough
Precise	Aloof	Computer science	Drafter	
Detail-oriented	Indecisive	Drafting	Electrician	Be organized, detached, and calm
Disciplined	Unimaginative	Electronics	Engineer	
		Auto mechanics	Auto mechanic	Be accurate and use critical thinking
			Technician	
			Librarian	State facts briefly and concisely

Profile of an Analyzer   Analyzers want things done right. Their favorite question is "What?" *Do you recognize any analyzer traits in yourself?*

ANALYZERS

Analyzers tend to be logical, thoughtful, loyal, exact, dedicated, steady, and organized. They like following direction and work at a steady pace. The key word for analyzers is *thinking*. (See **Figure 1.3.**)

Strengths: Creating concepts and models and thinking things through

Goal: Intellectual recognition. Analyzers are knowledge seekers.

Classroom style: Analyzers relate to instructors who are organized, know their facts, and present information logically and precisely. They dislike the ambiguity of subjects that do not have right or wrong answers. They tend to be left-brained and seem more concerned with facts, abstract ideas, and concepts than with people.

Learning style: Analyzers often perceive information abstractly and process it reflectively. They learn best by observing and thinking through ideas. They like models, lectures, textbooks, and solitary work. They like to work with things and analyze how things work. They evaluate and come to a precise conclusion.

SUPPORTERS

People who are supporters tend to be cooperative, honest, sensitive, warm, and understanding. They relate well to others. They value harmony and are informal, approachable, and tactful. In business, they place emphasis on people and are concerned

Figure 1.4   Profile of a Supporter

Effective Traits	Ineffective Traits	Possible Majors	Possible Careers	How to Relate to Supporters
Understanding	Overly compliant	Counseling or therapy	Elementary teacher	Be friendly
Gentle	Passive	Social work	Physical therapist	Be positive
Loyal	Slow to act	Family and consumer science	Social worker	Be sincere and build trust
Cooperative	Naive	Nursing	Therapist	Listen actively
Diplomatic	Unprofessional	Medical assisting	Counselor	Focus on people
Appreciative	Can be overly sensitive	Physical therapy	Nurse	Focus on personal values
		Education	Medical assistant	Create a comfortable, relaxed climate
				Create an experience they can relate to

Profile of a Supporter   Supporters want things done harmoniously and want to be personally involved. Their favorite question is "Why?" *Do you recognize any supporter traits in yourself?*

Hands-On Application

Role playing:

1. In small groups, have one student play the instructor with a supporter-style profile. Have three or four team members play students in the supporter's class. One observer should take notes. Discuss in small groups.

2. List suggestions for dealing effectively with an instructor with a dominant supporter style. Discuss with the class.

with the feelings and values of those around them. The key word for supporters is *feeling*. (See **Figure 1.4.**)

Strengths: Clarifying values, creating harmony, and being a loyal team player

Goal: To create harmony, meaning, and cooperation. They are identity seekers.

Classroom style: Supporters tend to learn best when they like an instructor and feel accepted and respected. They are easily hurt by criticism. They like to integrate course concepts with their own experiences. They relate to instructors who are warm and sociable, tell interesting stories, use visuals, and are approachable. They learn best by listening, sharing ideas and feelings, and working in teams.

Learning style: Supporters perceive information through inner intuitions and process it reflectively. They are intuitive and like to deal with their feelings. They prefer learning information that has personal meaning, and they are patient and likeable. They are insightful and take the intuitive approach to problem solving. They are imaginative thinkers and need to be personally involved.

CREATORS

Creators are innovative, flexible, spontaneous, creative, and idealistic people. Creators are risk takers and love drama, style, and imaginative design. They like fresh

Teaching Tip
Discuss possible majors
and careers for the
creator style.

Class Discussion
Review the traits of the
creator style. Ask
students:
1. Do you fit into this
   style?
2. What strategies
   would help you learn
   best?
3. Do you know people
   who fit this profile?
4. How can you relate
   best to this style?

Hands-On Application
Role playing:
1. In small groups, have
   one student play an
   instructor with a
   creator-style profile.
   Have three or four team
   members play students in
   the creator's class. One
   observer should take
   notes. Discuss in small
   groups.
2. List suggestions for
   dealing effectively with
   an instructor with a
   dominant creator style.
   Discuss with the class.

Figure 1.5　Profile of a Creator

Effective Traits	Ineffective Traits	Possible Majors	Possible Careers	How to Relate to Creators
Imaginative	Unrealistic	Art	Writer	Be enthusiastic
Creative	Unreliable	English	Politician	Be involved
Visionary	Inconsistent	Music	Travel agent	Be flexible
Idealistic	Hasty	Design	Hotel manager	
Enthusiastic	Impulsive	Hospitality	Cartoonist	Be accepting of change
Innovative	Impatient	Travel	Musician	
	Fragmented	Theater	Composer	Focus on creative ideas
		Communications	Artist	
			Journalist	Talk about dreams and possibilities
			Craftsperson	
			Florist	
			Costume designer	
			Salesperson	
			Scientist	

Profile of a Creator　Creators want things done with a sense of drama and style. Their favorite question is "What if?" *Do you recognize any creator traits in yourself?*

ideas and are passionate about their work. The key word for creators is *experience*. (See **Figure 1.5.**)

Strengths: Creating visions that inspire people

Goal: To make things happen by turning ideas into action. They are experience seekers.

Classroom style: Creators learn best in innovative and active classrooms. They relate to instructors who have a passion for their work; are challenging, imaginative, and flexible; present interesting ideas; and make the topic exciting.

Learning style: Creators learn by doing and being involved in active experiments. They perceive information concretely and process it actively. They like games, role-playing, stories, plays, illustrations, drawings, music, and visual stimuli. They ask questions and enjoy acting on ideas. They are usually good public speakers. They are future-oriented and good at seeing whole systems.

DIRECTORS

Directors are dependable, self-directed, conscientious, efficient, decisive, and results-oriented people. They like to be the leader of groups and respond to other people's ideas when they are logical and reasonable. Their strength is in the practical application of ideas. Because of this ability, they can excel in a variety of careers, such as law enforcement, banking, and legal professions. The key word for directors is *results*. (See **Figure 1.6.**)

Figure 1.6   Profile of a Director

Effective Traits	Ineffective Traits	Possible Majors	Possible Careers	How to Relate to Directors
Confident	Aggressive	Business	Lawyer	Set deadlines
Assertive	Pushy	Law enforcement	Police officer	Be responsible for your actions
Active	Insistent	Construction	Detective	Focus on results
Decisive	Overpowering	Woodworking	Consultant	Focus on achievements
Forceful	Dominating	Carpentry	Banker	Do not try to take control
Effective leader		Business management	Park ranger	Do not make excuses
Results oriented		Wildlife conservation	Forest ranger	Have a direction
		Forestry	Administrator for outdoor recreation	Make known time or other changes in schedule

Profile of a Director Directors want to produce results in a practical manner. Their favorite question is "How?" *Do you recognize any director traits in yourself?*

Teaching Tip
Discuss possible majors and careers for the director style.

Class Discussion
Review the traits of the director style. Ask students:
5. Do you fit into this style?
6. What strategies would help you learn best?
7. Do you know people who fit this profile?
8. How can you relate best to this style?

Strengths: Integrating theory with practical solutions

Goal: To find practical solutions to problems. They are security seekers.

Classroom style: Directors relate to instructors who are organized, clear, to the point, punctual, and results-oriented. They prefer field trips and hands-on activities.

Learning style: Directors learn by hands-on, direct experience. They learn best by practical application. They like classes that are relevant. They work hard to get things done.

Exploring Learning and Personality Tools

There are numerous learning inventories and personality tests. You may want to contact your learning skills center or advising or career center for more information. For example, the following two inventories are widely used.

The **Learning and Study Strategies Inventory (LASSI)** is designed to gather information about learning and studying attitudes and practices. It is a self-assessment tool that looks at attitude, interest, motivation, self-discipline, willingness to work hard, time management, anxiety, concentration, test strategies, and other study skills. The Peak Performance Notebook 1.1 Self-Assessment Test covers many of the same areas and will help you assess your study skills and attitude.

The **Enneagram** is an ancient personality tool that has been growing in popularity. In many ways, it combines the personality inventories we have discussed and can be related to the Myers-Briggs inventory and the Four-Temperament Profile. The

Hands-On Application
Role playing:
3. In small groups, have one student play an instructor with a director-style profile. Have three or four team members play students in the director's class. One observer should take notes. Discuss in small groups.
4. List suggestions for dealing effectively with an instructor with a dominant director style. Discuss with the class.

Key Teaching Concept
Integrate all styles to
enhance learning.

Use
TM 1.11 Peak
Performance Learning
Pyramid.

Hands-On Application
Have students explore
how they can develop
and integrate different
learning styles.

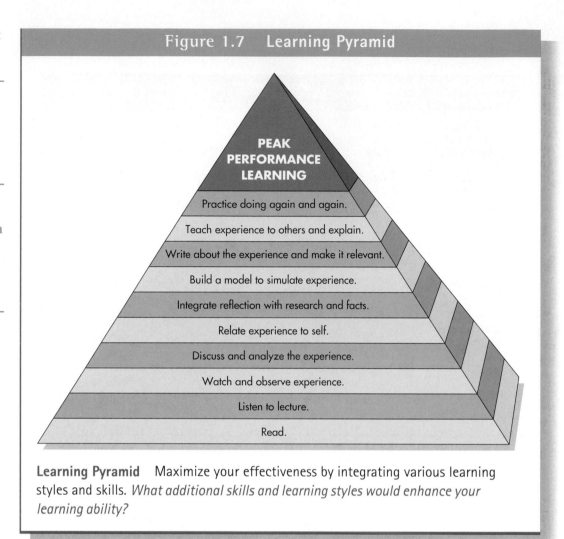

Figure 1.7   Learning Pyramid

PEAK PERFORMANCE LEARNING

Practice doing again and again.

Teach experience to others and explain.

Write about the experience and make it relevant.

Build a model to simulate experience.

Integrate reflection with research and facts.

Relate experience to self.

Discuss and analyze the experience.

Watch and observe experience.

Listen to lecture.

Read.

Learning Pyramid   Maximize your effectiveness by integrating various learning styles and skills. *What additional skills and learning styles would enhance your learning ability?*

Enneagram presents nine basic types of people with specific characteristics. The goals of the Enneagram are self-knowledge and growth. The heart of the system is the various ways the types relate to each other. Therefore, the Enneagram is currently in vogue in business circles as a way to understand and resolve workplace conflict. For more information, read

◆ *The Enneagram Made Easy,* by Renee Baron and Elizabeth Wagele
◆ *Understanding the Enneagram: The Practical Guide to Personality Types,* by Don R. Riso and Russ Hudson

Integrating Styles

Psychologist Henry James believed that people use less than 5 percent of their potential. Think of what you could accomplish if you could learn to work in alignment with your natural preferences and integrate various learning styles and techniques. The Learning Pyramid in **Figure 1.7** illustrates how you can maximize your effectiveness by integrating learning styles.

INTEGRATING BOTH SIDES OF THE BRAIN

Do you use both sides of your brain? "I use my whole brain!" you might answer—and you do. However, in the 1960s, Dr. Roger Sperry discovered that the left and right sides of the brain specialize in different modes of thinking and perception. Some researchers have suggested that the dominant brain hemisphere may play a significant role in how people learn.

Studies show that the brain has two systems by which it classifies information. One is linguistic (left brain), and the other is visual (right brain). These two half-brains do not work like separate departments but in an interconnected way. However, people who are left-brain dominant use a logical, rational, and detailed approach, whereas people who are right-brain dominant use an intuitive and insightful approach to solving problems and processing new information. When you integrate both sides of the brain while incorporating all the learning styles, you enhance learning, memory, and recall, and you achieve a synergistic effect. **Figure 1.8** on page 1–24 integrates the four temperaments and learning style types.

Hands-On Application
Ask students to write in their journals about how they approach a writing project. Based on their learning style, what can they do to support their efforts?

Teaching Tip
Have students discuss and apply the Adult Learning Cycle to various situations, i.e. riding a bike, learning to use the computer.

The Adult Learning Cycle

You can become a more effective learner, problem solver, and decision maker when you understand how you learn best and when you integrate all learning and personality styles. David Kolb, a professor at Case Western Reserve University, identified four stages of learning:

1. Concrete experience: learn by feeling and personal experience
2. Reflective observation: learn by observing and reflecting
3. Abstract conceptualization: learn by thinking and gathering information
4. Active experimentation: learn by doing and hands-on activities

Kolb's theory about learning styles is similar to Carl Jung's four functions (feeling, intuition, thinking, and sensation). The crux of it is that you learn by practice, repetition, and recognition. Thus, do it, and then do it again, and then again.

The following Adult Learning Cycle is an adaptation of both Kolb's and Jung's theories. It includes a fifth stage and illustrates how they are complementary to one another.

1. **RELATE. Why do I want to learn this?** What personal meaning and interest does this have for me? I learn by feeling, personal experience, and talking with others.
2. **OBSERVE. How does this work?** I learn by watching, listening, and experiencing.
3. **THINK. What does this mean**? I learn by thinking, gathering information, and reflecting.
4. **DO. What can I do with this?** I learn by doing, finding practical applications, and defining procedures.
5. **TEACH. How can I relay this information to others?** I learn by demonstrating and explaining, as well as by acknowledging and rewarding positive outcomes.

Figure 1.8 Integrated Brain Power

ANALYZER — **INTEGRATED BRAIN POWER** — **SUPPORTER**

ANALYZER	SUPPORTER
Logical	Gentle
Analytical	Caring
Literal	Sensitive
Factual	Harmonious
Precise	Peacemaker
Accurate	Emotional
Orderly	Loyal instead of sociable
Objective	Cooperative
Systematic	Understanding
Technical	Adaptable
Likes models	Seeks meaning

Learns by thinking and gathering new information
iNT Temperament

Learns by finding meaning and interests
iNF Temperament

Less Assertive

Left-Brain Studying
- Neat, organized study area
- Daily schedules
- Work on one project at a time
- Study alone
- Study consistently
- Plan studying

Right-Brain Studying
- Cluttered desk
- Flexible study times
- Jump from project to project
- Study with others
- Study in bursts of energy
- Cram last minute

Abstract Conceptual — *Concrete Experimental*

DIRECTOR — **CREATOR**

DIRECTOR	CREATOR
Confident	Innovative
Practical	Imaginative
Realistic	Free-spirited
Disciplined	Visionary
Problem solver	Impulsive
Controlled	Open-minded
Dependable	Creative
Results oriented	Curious
Pragmatic	Energetic
Traditional	Spontaneous
Wants results	Wants to create

More Assertive

Learns by practical application and doing
SJ Temperament

Learns by observing, reflecting, and experiencing
SP Temperament

Integrated Brain Power Integrating both sides of the brain boosts learning, memory, and recall. *Do you think you are left- or right-brain dominant?*

Depending on your learning style, the information to be learned, and the situation, you may find yourself starting the Adult Learning Cycle at different stages. **The key to learning is practice and repetition.** As you repeat the stages, meaning and recall are strengthened. To make learning long-lasting, you need to find ways to make learning meaningful and physical. For example, let's say you are taking a computer class.

1. **RELATE personal meaning, interests, and relevance.** Why do you want to use the computer? What are the benefits to you, your coursework, and your career? How does this relate to what you already know, such as typing skills? In what programs or skills would you like to become proficient? Think about the opportunities and talk with other people about practical uses of a computer. Study and learn in a group.

2. **OBSERVE your instructor and watch other people using the computer.** Listen and ask questions. Talk, read, and write about your experiences. What is new and different? Jot down instructions, draw, sketch, and add color to your notes. Find music to illustrate ideas or use background music as you learn. Experience doing a task as your instructor or a friend helps you.

3. **THINK about problems critically and in sequence.** Build on information and qualify it. What works and doesn't work? Test new ways of doing things. Ask people when you get stuck. Find new ways to solve problems. Relate what you know to new information. Review instructions when you are stumped.

4. **DO it and learn by trial and error.** Jump in and try new tasks. Learning to use a computer is a great example of hands-on learning. Find new applications.

5. **TEACH it to others.** Demonstrate to someone else what you have learned. Answer questions and ask for feedback.

Now, return to Stage 1 and reaffirm the benefits of learning this valuable new skill.

Here's another example. Susan owns a bed and breakfast inn that has a combination lock on the front door. Her guests need to learn how to use the lock.

1. **Relate:** "I don't want to get locked out!" Guests have a personal interest in learning the combination, since that will be how they get in and out of the inn. It is important and relevant information.

2. **Observe:** "Here's how it works." Susan shows them how to use the combination lock and talks to them as she demonstrates. They watch and gather information. Often, they repeat what she has said.

3. **Think:** "Did I get it?" They integrate information and Susan offers an overview: "Don't forget to turn the knob all the way to the right."

4. **Do:** "Now I'll try it." They practice learning by doing it, and Susan offers instruction as they are doing it. "Press the 5 button four times and turn all the way to the right."

5. **Teach:** "Let me show you." Often, they teach it to their spouse or practice it again while they say the combination out loud.

You can adapt the Adult Learning Cycle to best fit your preference, but you will be most effective if you integrate all learning styles and make learning physical and meaningful.

Class Discussion
In small groups, have
students:
• Review their barriers to
  self-assessment.
• Look for common barriers
  and list strategies to
  overcome these barriers.
• Discuss tips for choosing a
  major or career path.

Words to
Succeed

*"Let him that would
move the world first
move himself."*

—SENECA, *philosopher*

PEAK TIP

Peak performers learn to
bounce back. R.H. Macy
failed 7 times before his
New York store caught
on. Babe Ruth hit 714
home runs but struck out
1,330 times!

In each chapter, we will explore practical examples of the Adult Learning Cycle. For example, in Chapter 11, the Adult Learning Cycle will be applied to effective communication and how you can enhance your communication skills.

Overcoming the Barriers to Self-Assessment

The biggest barriers to self-assessment may be lazy and faulty thinking. A lack of critical thinking may keep you from making a commitment to reality. Look honestly at all areas of your life. Use critical thinking to assess your performance and creative problem solving and plan new ways to overcome discouragement and setbacks. For example, you may have discovered in your assessment exercises that you tend to be late for class or work. Create ways to help you become punctual, such as setting your clock ten minutes early and getting organized the night before. Positive habits help you overcome counterproductive behavior. Do not get discouraged. Acknowledge and work on your shortcomings and focus on your successes. Realize that everyone gets off course sometimes, so don't dwell on mistakes. Focus on your strengths and positive habits to get back on track.

SELF-ASSESSMENT AND THE WORKPLACE

Self-assessment is important for job success. Self-assessment and feedback are tools for self-discovery and positive change. Keep a portfolio of your awards, letters of appreciation, training program certificates, and projects you have completed. Assess your expectations with the results achieved and set goals for improvement. Keep your performance evaluations and comments, as well as a record of informal evaluations. Try to integrate all types of learning styles to enhance your own natural learning preferences.

Choosing a Major

For many students, deciding on a major is a daunting task. It is fine to stay undecided the first year or so of college. At some point, however, you will need to make a decision and work to make it successful. Not only can perpetual indecisiveness cause a lack of motivation and create a self-defeating cycle, but it can also waste your time and money—two very precious commodities.

You can explore all the options by taking advantage of any general education classes offered at your school. General education is a great way to experience various disciplines and get to know different instructors and students. It is also a great way to learn about the various majors as you gain a good education.

One of the main goals of exploring learning styles and personality types is to expand self-awareness. Discovering your interests, how you learn, how you process

Louis Parker

ACCOUNTANT AND FINANCIAL PLANNER

Related Majors: Accounting, Business Administration, Economics, Finance

Setting Business Goals

Louis Parker is a certified public accountant (CPA) and financial planner. In 1984, he started his own business, Parker, Inc., by offering accounting services. Louis prepares taxes, financial reports, and payroll, and he does bookkeeping for individuals and small businesses. He employs three full-time and one part-time assistant but needs five full-time workers to help during peak tax season (January–April).

To get feedback on his services, Louis occasionally does a survey of his clients. The survey shows whether his clients are getting the services they want at prices they believe are reasonable. Louis uses the results of the survey to set goals and plan for the future.

Another of Louis' goals is to continually increase business, as Louis believes that, without marketing and growth, his business will decline. Louis has used telemarketing services to help him set up appointments with prospective clients.

A few years ago, Louis decided to add financial planning because his clients were continually asking for his advice in financial areas. Financial planners help clients attain financial goals, such as retirement or a college education for their children. Louis was able to get certified in financial planning. Because he is affiliated with a financial services organization, he sometimes helps clients invest in the stock market, mainly in mutual funds. Currently, financial planning is only 10 percent of his business, but Louis' goal is to eventually increase that amount to 30 percent.

CRITICAL THINKING

How might a survey of his clients help Louis assess his personal strengths and weaknesses? What strategies should he put in place to follow up on client feedback? How can he incorporate the feedback into his long-term goals?

information, how you react under stress, and how you relate to others can be useful in choosing a college major and career. *Typing is not typecasting!* Personality typing isn't a science; it's just a guide. The more you integrate different styles, the more you will discover your interests, values, and strengths.

The following are guidelines to help you choose your major:

- **Assess yourself.** It is important not to rush when deciding a major. Take time to evaluate your goals, interests, skills, and competencies. Determine your personality and learning styles, which will help you narrow in on career areas. Visit the career center at your school. It will offer additional personality and interest assessment inventories, workshops, and course and career/life planning.

- **Talk with others.** Take the time to learn about the different fields of study, certain industries, and types of careers. Talk with your advisor, instructors, professionals, family, friends, and career counselors about various majors and options.

- **Explore options.** Be proactive about learning about the majors and what they offer. Go to a majors fair and career day. Visit academic departments and inquire about majors that interest you.

- **Establish a major selection time line.** Set milestone dates that will help you make the best decision, in your own time.

- **Gain experience.** Hands-on experience enables you to learn more about yourself and gives you an inside look at what certain careers entail. Some great ways to explore and discover your strengths, interests, and skills include
  - Internships
  - Co-ops
  - Volunteer work

Peak Progress

Applying the Adult Learning Cycle When Exploring Majors

1. **Relate.** Write down the top three things that are important to you in a future career, such as independence, high visibility, flexible hours, ability to work from home, and management opportunities. Now compare those wishes with your personality type. Are there certain careers that fit your personality that offer these features?

2. **Observe.** Explore three potential opportunities for learning more about this career, such as acquaintances in the field, knowledgeable instructors, professional organizations, and introductory courses.

3. **Think.** Based on your research and observations, does this career still sound appealing? What are the drawbacks? Are they significant enough that they outweigh the positives? Did any related professions come to light?

4. **Do.** If the career choice still looks promising, determine three ways you can gain experience and/or related skills the profession will require, such as joining a club or securing an internship. Construct a time line for accomplishing those tasks.

5. **Teach.** Relay your impressions and reservations to your family, friends, or fellow students who are also career searching. You will no doubt be asked some very good questions that will make you think about where you are in selecting a major and what your next steps should be. You will also enlighten others by relaying the various avenues and resources you are using.

If your conclusion is that you are still undecided, explore other career options and attempt some or all of the steps again. Consider practicing visualization whenever you need help focusing. Eventually, you will find the career path that suits your personality and interests.

TECH FOR SUCCESS

- **Semester Calendar** It's unavoidable—most of your tests and class papers will occur around the same time. Start planning your semester now by mapping out the major events and daily tasks you'll need to accomplish. Use a day planner or on-line forms, such as the "Creating a Semester Calendar" form available at this book's web site: www.mhhe.com/ferrett5e.

- **On-Line Self-Assessments** A number of on-line assessments can help you determine the best careers to fit your personality. Talk with your instructor, as your school may already have some available in your career center. Also, visit this book's web site for assessments and links to major sites: www.mhhe.com/ferrett5e.

- **On-Line Journal** Sometimes, critical thinking is easier when you write down your responses. Keeping an electronic self-assessment journal allows for easy updating and gathering of information, which can be pulled into your career portfolio later.

Teaching Tip
Stress the importance of using the computer every day to build skills. Encourage students to e-mail instructors, advisors, and friends. Have them keep a self-assessment journal on the computer.

Hands-On Application
Have students answer these questions:

1. What did you learn from the chapter that has been most helpful?
2. What is the most important thing you've learned so far in college?
3. What is the most important thing you've learned so far outside the classroom?

TAKING CHARGE

In summary, in this chapter, I learned to

- *Strive to become a peak performer.* Peak performers come from all walks of life, maximize their abilities and resources, and focus on positive results.

- *Self-assess.* Assessing and objectively seeing myself will help me recognize my need to learn new skills, relate more effectively with others, set goals, manage time and stress, and create a balanced and productive life.

- *Use my critical thinking skills.* Critical thinking is a logical, rational, and systematic thought process I use to think through a problem or situation to make sound choices and good decisions.

- *Get focused.* Visualization is a critical thinking and self-management tool that uses a five-step method (actual event, beliefs, consequences, dispute, energized) to help me focus on positive results and achieve my goals.

- *Make connections between skills for school and job success.* SCANS (Secretary's Commission on Achieving Necessary Skills) outlines skills and competencies that are critical to success in school as well as the job market.

- *Determine my learning style.* By knowing my preferred learning style, such as visual, auditory, or kinesthetic, I know how I learn best and how to incorporate features of other learning styles in order to maximize my learning opportunities.

- *Explore various personality types.* Although personality typing has been around for centuries, Jung identified extroverts vs. introverts, sensors vs. intuitives, and thinkers vs. feelers. Briggs and Briggs-Myers added judgers and perceivers and developed the Myers-Briggs Type Indicator. Further work by Keirsy and Bates focuses on four main temperaments: analyzer, supporter, creator, and director.

- *Integrate learning styles and personality types.* Once I understand my learning style(s) and personality type(s), I can incorporate features of other styles to maximize my learning. Although I may tend to be either left-brain dominant (linguistic) or right-brain dominant (visual), the goal is to use all my brain power to learn new skills and information.

- *Apply the adult learning cycle.* This five-step process (relate, observe, think, do, and teach) demonstrates that learning comes from repetition, practice, and recall.

- *Choose a major.* As I decide on a major, I will take advantage of general education courses; assess my goals and learning styles; consult with advisors, professionals, and friends; and set a time line for acquiring information and new skills.

Peak Performer Profile

Christy Haubegger

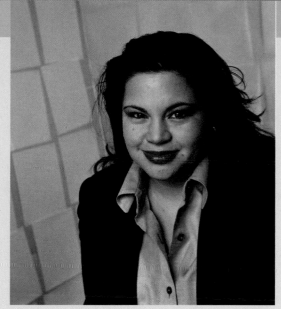

At first glance, the glossy magazine looks like many others on the newsstands The front cover offers a snapshot of the current issue: a profile of a famous celebrity, beauty and fashion tips, and a self-help article to improve the inner being. The big, bold letters across the top, however, spell the difference. This is *Latina,* the first bilingual magazine targeted for Hispanic-American women and the inspiration of founder Christy Haubegger.

Born in Houston, Texas, in 1968, Haubegger has described herself as a "chubby Mexican-American baby adopted by parents who were tall, thin, and blond." As a teenager during the mega-media '80s, she was especially sensitive to the lack of Hispanic role models in women's magazines. It was a void waiting to be filled. At the age of 20, Haubegger received a bachelor's degree in philosophy from the University of Texas. At 23, she went on to earn her law degree from Stanford, where she joined the editorial staff of the *Law Review,* rising to the position of senior editor. "My experience as senior editor gave me a start in the worlds of journalism and publishing."

Haubegger also took a course in marketing. In this class, she had to write a business plan for a favorite enterprise. *Latina* magazine was born. As one of the best-known publications for Hispanic-American women, *Latina* covers issues such as health, politics, family, and finance, as well as beauty and entertainment. *Latina* provides Hispanic women a voice and reminds them that they, too, are part of the American Dream.

Hispanic Americans are expected to be America's largest ethnic group by the year 2010. With numbers like that, Haubegger envisions the magazine as only "the first brick in a media empire."

PERFORMANCE THINKING If you were assessing the characteristics that make Christy Haubegger a successful publisher, which would you say were the most important?

Performance Strategies

Following are the top 10 strategies for self-assessment and exploring majors:

◆ Strive to become a peak performer in all aspects of your life.

◆ Use critical thinking and honesty in self-assessment.

◆ Make the connection between school and job success.

◆ Focus on commitment and effort.

◆ Practice visualization and self-management to create the results you want.

◆ Discover your learning and personality styles.

◆ Apply the adult learning cycle to maximize your learning.

◆ Integrate all learning styles.

◆ Connect personality styles with possible majors and careers.

◆ Focus on strengths and successes.

Review Questions

1. What is a peak performer?

2. Explain the differences among the three types of learners.

3. Why is it important to know your learning style and personality type?

4. How does critical thinking help you overcome barriers to self-assessment?

5. List three strategies you can use to explore possible majors.

REVISUALIZATION

Look back at the Visualization box on page 1–1 of this chapter and review your two goals and the obstacles you listed in **Worksheet 1.1** or your journal. Now, revisit **Worksheet 1.1** and apply the ABCDE method of self-management (actual event, beliefs, consequences, dispute, and energized). Focus on today's priorities and use the resources around you to succeed. See yourself feeling confident that you can stay on track and achieve your goals.

To get you started, let's consider one example of focusing on choosing a major:

A = Actual event: "I thought I wanted to major in graphic arts, but now I'm not sure that is the best choice for me."

B = Beliefs: "If I don't make a decision soon about my major, I may waste time in classes that delay my goal of graduating on time."

C = Consequences: "I'm nervous I may make a decision that I will regret later. I want to have a career that I find challenging and fulfilling. What if I don't ask all the right questions right now?"

D = Dispute: "College is an ideal time for exploring new ideas and interests, and most students change their majors two or three times without serious repercussions. The largest major at many colleges is undeclared students. For now, I will focus on courses that interest me and explore related areas. I'm here at college not only to learn information and new skills but also to learn about opportunities for the future."

E = Energized: "I know graduating on time in an interesting career field is definitely attainable. I am taking active steps to explore potential majors and careers. Today I will make my first visit to the career center. They may have leads on a related part-time job that can give me valuable experience."

Teaching Tip
Stress that it is important for students to practice the ABCDE Method of Self-Management so it becomes a positive habit.

MAKING A COMMITMENT

In the Classroom

Eric Silver is a freshman in college. He doesn't know what major to choose and isn't even sure if he wants to continue going to college. His parents are urging him to pursue his college career, but Eric wants to go to work instead. In high school, he never settled on a favorite subject, though he did briefly consider becoming a private investigator after reading a detective novel. His peers seem more committed to college and have better study habits. Eric prefers a hands-on approach to learning, and he finds it difficult to concentrate while studying or listening to a lecture. However, he enjoys the outdoors and is creative. Once he gets involved in a project he finds interesting, he is very committed.

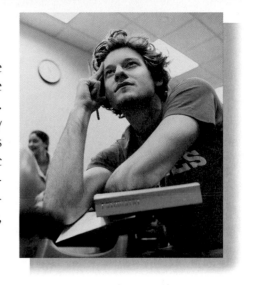

1. What strategies from this chapter would be most useful to help Eric understand himself better and gain a sense of commitment?

   _____

   _____

   _____

2. What would you suggest to Eric to help him find direction?

   _____

   _____

   _____

In the Workplace

Eric has taken a job as a law enforcement officer. He feels more comfortable in this job than he did in school, since he knows he performs best when actively learning. He enjoys teamwork and the exchange of ideas with his coworkers. Eric also realizes that, in order to advance in his work, he needs to continue his education. He is concerned about balancing his work, school, and family life. He does admit that he did not excel in subjects he was less interested in. Eric never learned effective study habits but realizes that he must be disciplined when returning to college.

3. What suggestions would you give Eric to help him do better in school?

   _____

   _____

   _____

4. Under what category of learning style does Eric fall and what are the ineffective traits of this style that he needs to work on most?

   _____

   _____

   _____

REVIEW AND APPLICATIONS   CHAPTER 1

APPLYING THE ABCDE METHOD OF SELF-MANAGEMENT

In the Visualization box on page 1–1, you were asked to consider two major goals that you would like to achieve in the next five years. List those two goals:

1. _____
   _____

2. _____
   _____

List some of the potential obstacles to achieving those goals:

_____

_____

_____

_____

Now, apply the ABCDE method to one or both of those goals and visualize yourself successfully tackling those obstacles.

A = Actual event:

B = Beliefs:

C = Consequences:

D = Dispute:

E = Energized:

- Do those goals seem more achievable now?

- Were the obstacles not really as big as they first seemed?

- Did this exercise help you determine certain steps you need to take, skills you need to learn, or behaviors you need to change?

ASSESSING AND APPLYING LEARNING STYLES, PERSONALITY TYPES, AND TEMPERAMENTS

Learning Styles

I am a(n) (circle one):

Visual learner

Auditory learner

Kinesthetic learner

The following learning habits make me most like this learning style:

What features of the two other learning styles should I incorporate to make me a well-rounded learner?

Personality Types

I am a(n) (circle one for each):

Extrovert or Introvert

Sensor or Intuitive

Thinker or Feeler

The following characteristics make me most like these personality types:

How can I incorporate positive features of the opposite personality types?

Temperaments

I am a(n) (circle one):

Analyzer

Supporter

Creator

Director

The following characteristics make me most like this temperament:

What positive behaviors/traits can I incorporate from the other three temperaments?

Creating the Ideal Team

In school and at work, you will often be a member of a project team. In most cases, you do not have the opportunity to select your team members but, instead, need to learn how to maximize each other's strengths.

Let's pretend, however, that you have the opportunity to select a four-person team to tackle an assignment. Now that you know your preferences, indicate the characteristics of three potential teammates who would be complementary. Indicate why you think each person would be an asset to the team.

Person #1

Learning style:

Personality type:

Temperament:

What this person will add to the team:

Person #2

Learning style:

Personality type:

Temperament:

What this person will add to the team:

Person #3

Learning style:

Personality type:

Temperament:

What this person will add to the team:

And ME

What I add to the team:

CHAPTER 1 ▶ REVIEW AND APPLICATIONS

CHECKLIST FOR CHOOSING A MAJOR

Earlier in this chapter, we used the Adult Learning Cycle to explore majors and career opportunities. Follow this handy guide as you put this into practice.

Relate

- What are the most important criteria for my future career, such as independence, high visibility, flexible hours, ability to work from home, and management opportunities?

- What is my personality type and/or temperament?

- Are there certain careers that fit my personality that offer these features?

- What skills do I already have that would be useful or necessary?

Observe

- Whom do I know who is currently working in this field whom I could interview or talk to?

- Which instructors at my school would be the most knowledgeable about the field? Who are the most approachable and are available to advise me?

- What are the major professional organizations in this field? Have I explored their web sites for additional information? Can I join these organizations as a student? Would it be worth the investment?

- Which courses should I be enrolled in right now or next semester that will further introduce me to this area?

- I've visited the career center at my school and have talked with my advisor and/or a career counselor.

Think

- What are the positives I am hearing?

- What are the drawbacks I am hearing?

- What education and skills will be necessary for me to pursue this major and career?

- Are there related professions that seem appealing?

Do

- I've constructed a time line for gaining experience in this area that includes tasks such as

  - Securing an internship; to be secured by:

  - Joining a student club; to be involved by:

  - Participating in related volunteer activities; to be accomplished by:

  - Getting a related part-time job; to be hired by:

  - Other:

Teach

- I have relayed my impressions to my family and/or friends. Some of the questions/responses they have given are

- I have talked with fellow students about their major and career search. Some tips I have learned from them are

- The most important resources I have found that I would recommend to others are

As of now, the major/career I would like to continue exploring is _____ .

APPLYING THE FOUR-TEMPERAMENT PROFILE

You've explored your temperament and discovered your preferred learning style and personality type. Apply this knowledge by associating with people who have various styles and find ways to relate to and work more effectively with different people.

For example, let's say that you are assigned to a five-person team that will present a serious public health issue to your personal health class. You are a supporter type, and you find yourself having a conflict with Joe, a director type. You are in your first meeting, and Joe is ready to choose a topic for the group project, even though one team member is absent.

Apply the ABCDE visualization method to focus your energies on building rapport and understanding:

A = Actual event: "Joe wants to choose a topic for the group project, even though one person isn't here to voice her opinion."

B = Beliefs: "I think that we are not taking the time to be sensitive to the needs of all the team members. Everyone should be present before we make a decision. Joe is trying to take control of the group and is just impatient."

C = Consequences: "I'm worried that the absent group member will not like the decision or may even be hurt that she wasn't involved. I resent being rushed and I'm afraid that conflict will result. Maybe this person will even quit the group."

D = Dispute: "What is the worst thing that could happen if we choose a topic today? We can always refocus later if we find this topic doesn't fit our goals. Chances are the absent member would agree with the topic in question, anyhow. Joe is probably not impatient—he just wants to make a decision and get us moving."

E = Energized: "I'm glad our group is made up of different strengths and personalities. I'm psyched that our team members have complementary strengths and can respect and work well with each other. I know that Joe will keep us moving forward and that he will be sensitive to my concerns that we listen to each other and respect each other's feelings."

Are you experiencing a similar situation or conflict in your school, work, or personal life? If so, use the ABCDE method to visualize a positive solution:

A = Actual event:

B = Beliefs:

C = Consequences:

D = Dispute:

E = Energized:

CHAPTER 1 ▲ REVIEW AND APPLICATIONS

AUTOBIOGRAPHY

The purpose of this exercise is to look back and assess how you learned skills and competencies. Write down the turning points, major events, and significant experiences of your life. This autobiography, or chronological record, will note events that helped you make decisions, set goals, or discover something about yourself. Record both negative and positive experiences and what you learned from them. Add this page to your Career Development Portfolio—for example,

For Example:

Year/Event	Learned Experience
1997 Moved to Michigan.	Learned to make new friends and be flexible.
1998 First job babysitting.	Learned responsibility and critical thinking.
1999 Grandmother became ill.	Helped with care. Learned dependability, compassion.

Year/Event	Learned Experience

Emotional Intelligence: The Essential Personal Qualities

Chapter Objectives

In this chapter, you will learn

▲ About emotional intelligence and the key personal qualities

▲ To focus on character first, including integrity, civility, and ethics

▲ Responsibility, self-management, and control

▲ How to develop self-esteem and confidence

▲ The importance of a positive attitude and motivation

▲ The benefits of higher education

▲ How to overcome the barriers to staying positive and motivated

VISUALIZATION

"On my commute to class, a car cut me off. I was furious and yelled at the driver. I was fuming and distracted during classes, and later I blew up at a coworker. This just ruined my entire day. How can I handle my angry feelings in a more constructive way?"

Have you ever had a similar experience? Are you easily offended by what others do or say? Have you said things in anger that have caused a rift in a relationship? In this chap-

ter, you will learn how to control your emotions and create a positive and resourceful state of mind.

JOURNAL ENTRY   In **Worksheet 2.1** on page 2–29, describe a time when you were angry and lost control of your emotions. How did you feel? How did others react to your outburst? What would you do differently? Visualize yourself calm and in control and realize that you have a choice in how you interpret events.

Key Teaching Concept
Emotional intelligence is key for peak performance.

Use
TM 2.1 Success Principle 2.

Teaching Tip
Emphasize the importance of using the ABCDE Method of Self-Management to visualize success and create positive results.

There is a tendency to define intelligence as a score on an IQ test or SAT or as school grades. Educators have tried to predict who will succeed in college and have found that high school grades, achievement test scores, and ability are only part of the picture. Emotional intelligence, or maturity, has more effect on school and job success than traditional scholastic measures. In fact, research has indicated that optimism and effort are major predictors of college success. A landmark study by the American College Test (ACT) indicated that the primary reasons for first-year students' dropping out of college were not academic but, rather, were emotional difficulties, such as feelings of inadequacy, depression, loneliness, and a lack of motivation or purpose.

Employers also list a positive attitude, motivation, honesty, the ability to get along with others, civility, and the willingness to learn as more important to job success than a college degree or specific skills. Earlier in this text, you learned that SCANS identifies many personal qualities as important competencies for success in the workplace. These qualities and competencies are also essential for building and maintaining strong, healthy relationships through life. Essential personal qualities should be viewed as a foundation on which to build skills, experience, and knowledge.

Thus, success in your personal life, school, and career is more dependent on a positive attitude, motivation, responsibility, self-control, and effort than on inborn abilities or a high IQ. In this chapter, you will learn the importance of emotional intelligence and why character is so important for school and job success. You will also develop personal strategies for maintaining a positive attitude and becoming self-motivated. You may realize that you are smarter than you think. You are smarter than your test scores or grades. You can maximize your success by developing emotional maturity. Peak performers use the *whole* of their intelligence—and so can you.

Emotional Intelligence

Emotional intelligence has become a popular topic as we learn more about the importance of personal qualities, communication, the management of feelings, and social competence. Researchers have demonstrated that people who have developed a set of traits that adds to their maturity level will increase their sense of well-being, assist their ability to get along with others, and enhance their school, job, and life success. Best-selling author and psychologist Daniel Goleman says that the business world rates emotional intelligence over job skill or expertise in its managers. The ability to regulate emotions is vital for school and job success. Emotional maturity contributes to competent behavior, problem-solving ability, socially appropriate behavior, and good communication. Being unaware or the inability to control emotions can result in restlessness, short attention span, negativism, impulsiveness, and distractibility. Clearly, having emotional intelligence distinguishes peak performers from mediocre ones. Becoming more emotionally mature involves three stages:

1. *Self-awareness*—tuning into yourself
2. *Empathy*—tuning into others
3. *Change*—tuning into results

In Chapter 1, you explored many strategies to help you increase your self-awareness and tune into yourself. You had an opportunity to assess many skills and personal qualities in the Peak Performance Self-Assessment Test on page 1–7. By learning personality types, you also began to "tune in" to others as well. The central theme throughout the remainder of this book is that you can use this information to begin changing your thoughts, images, and behaviors to produce the results you want in every aspect of your life. Enhancing your emotional intelligence and focusing on positive personal qualities are key to achieving those successful results.

Class Discussion
Ask students how these competencies create college and job success. Applying SCANS:
Attitude
Motivation
Personal Qualities

Class Discussion
Ask students how they feel when someone is dishonest with them.

Character First: Integrity, Civility, and Ethics

Integrity comes from the Latin word *integre,* meaning "wholeness." When we focus on character, integrity, and civility, we become a whole person—an emotionally mature person.

Good character is the most essential personal quality for true success in school, work, and life. Recent surveys of business leaders indicate that dishonesty and lying are the number one reason for on-the-job difficulties. If a company believes that an employee lacks integrity, all of that person's positive qualities—from skill and experience to productivity and intelligence—are meaningless. Employers usually list honesty or good character as an essential personal quality, followed by the ability to relate to and get along with others. In short, they want people who have integrity and civility. Also, a number of books have been written by successful top executives who claim that good character, honesty, and a strong value system are what make you an effective leader. All the corporate scandals seen in the news lately are testimonials that business leaders with poor ethics and values will eventually meet their demise.

Integrity helps us understand what is right and gives us the courage to do it, even when it is difficult. Civility is a set of tools for interacting with others with respect, kindness, and good manners, or etiquette. Empathy—sympathy and compassion for others—is essential for integrity and civility. Ethics, then, deals with more precise and often written standards of conduct and morals in a particular society.

Dr. Stephen L. Carter, Yale professor and best-selling author of *Integrity* and his follow-up book, *Civility,* suggests that following The Golden Rule (treating others as we want to be treated) is a simple way to weave integrity and civility into our everyday lives. If you put character first in your life, you will have a strong foundation in which to add other key elements of emotional maturity, such as motivation, a positive attitude, responsibility, confidence, and self-control.

Every day, you run into situations that test your character. **Personal Performance Notebook 2.1** on page 2–4 includes a number of questions and situations to get you

Character and Ethics

Integrity and honesty are essential qualities. It is important for you to assess and develop them as you would any skill. Use critical thinking to answer these questions.

1. What is the most difficult ethical dilemma you have faced in your life?

   _____

2. Do you have a code of ethics that helps guide you when making decisions? Explain.

   _____

3. When did you learn about honesty?

   _____

4. Who have you known that is a role model for displaying integrity and honesty?

   _____

5. Do you have a code of ethics at your college? Look it up in your school's catalog or ask the dean of students for a copy.

   _____

6. Does your company have a code of ethics?

   _____

7. If you were the chief executive officer (CEO) or owner of a small company, what would you want to include in your code of ethics?

   _____

8. How would you make certain that employees understood and honored your company's code of ethics?

   _____

Hands-On Application
Have students think of a difficult ethical decision that they have had to make. Have them assess how they learned about honesty.

thinking critically about how you respond when tested. In this exercise, include the personal qualities that make you smarter than you think, such as positive attitude, motivation, dependability, and honesty—for example, "I was raised on a farm in Michigan. What personal quality makes me smarter than my IQ or test scores?" If you answered hard work, you're right. That one personal quality—putting in extra effort—has helped many people be more successful in life.

Personal qualities, especially honesty, are important when you think of hiring someone to work for a business that you own. Let's say that a candidate sends in an outstanding resume. She has a college degree, experience, and a great personality, and she is positive and motivated, but you find out that she stole from her last employer. No matter how bright or talented someone is, you may realize you cannot have

Personal Performance Notebook 2.2

Skills and Personal Qualities

1. Jot down the skills, personal qualities, and habits you are learning and demonstrating in each of your classes.

Skills	Personal Qualities	Habits
_____	_____	_____
_____	_____	_____
_____	_____	_____

2. Pretend that you own your own business. List the skills and personal qualities you would want in the employees you hire.

Type of business: _____

Employees' Skills	Employees' Personal Qualities
_____	_____
_____	_____
_____	_____

Hands-On Application
Stress that this is an important exercise. Have students pretend that they own their own business. What qualities do they want most in their employees?

Teaching Tip
Emphasize character. Ask students if they included character, honesty, and integrity on their list of important qualities that they want in a worker.

---

a dishonest person working for you. Complete **Personal Performance Notebook 2.2** to see what qualities you would look for in a potential employee and which of those qualities you possess.

CREATING AND FOLLOWING A CODE OF ETHICS

There is no universal code of ethics. However, individuals take actions that are generally viewed as either good (ethical) or as wrong (unethical). You will be faced with situations in your personal, school, and business lives that will force you to make decisions that will be viewed as either ethical or unethical. Sometimes it is not easy. Everyone is faced at one time or another with situations that demand tough decisions. The following examples illustrate those situations:

Peggy Lyons has a midterm test to take. This test will determine 50 percent of her final grade. She has been very busy at home and has not attended class or her study group for the past week. She knows she probably won't do well on the test, but she needs a good grade. She knows the instructor is fair and has been asking about her. Someone Peggy met in the cafeteria tells her she can buy a copy of the test. She's tempted. What do you think she will do? What would you do?

> ### Words to Succeed
>
> "No man becomes suddenly different from his habit and cherished thought."
>
> —JOSHUA L. CHAMBERLAIN
> Civil War general

Class Discussion
1. What are the similarities of various codes of ethics?
2. Ask students what questions they use to keep themselves honest.

Class Discussion
How do the following competencies create college and job success: Write them on the board. Applying SCANS:
Responsibility
Self-management
Motivation
Self-control
Integrity
Character

While in college, Rey Armas has been working part-time at an electronics store. Rey's supervisor, Joe, has worked in the store for 10 years. Joe is about 50 and has a family. This is his only means of support. Rey has discovered that Joe is stealing some of the electronics components to sell on the side. Rey likes Joe. What should Rey do? What would you do?

Tora Veda is walking home from the bus stop one evening when she witnesses a mugging. She realizes she knows the mugger and the victim but is terrified by the incident and runs for home. She debates whether or not she should call the police and report the crime. What should she do? What would you do?

Peggy, Rey, and Tora are all faced with tough decisions. Their final decisions will be viewed by others as either ethical or unethical. They will have to call on their own personal code of ethics. When defining their code and their subsequent actions, they may find the following questions helpful. You, too, may find them helpful when developing a code of ethics.

◆ How would I feel if this situation were on the front page of a newspaper?
◆ Would I feel good telling my mother or child about this situation?
◆ Would I feel comfortable telling the truth about this situation?
◆ What could be the negative consequences of this decision or action?
◆ What could be the future repercussions?
◆ Is this decision or action illegal or morally wrong?
◆ Am I causing unnecessary harm to someone because of this decision?
◆ Am I treating others as I would want to be treated?

Responsibility

Now let's look at other personal qualities that SCANS and business leaders say are essential for success. Peak performers take responsibility for their thoughts, state of mind, and behavior. They don't blame others for their problems but, rather, use their energy to solve them. They are persistent and patient. They know they must exert a consistent amount of high effort to achieve their goals. They keep their word and agreements. When they say they are going to do something, they keep their commitment. People can depend on them.

Examples of being responsible include showing up prepared and on time for work, meetings, study teams, and so on; paying bills and repaying loans on time; and cleaning up personal messes at home and elsewhere. Responsible people own up to their mistakes and do what they can to correct them.

Other personal qualities related to responsibility include displaying a high level of perseverance, punctuality, concentration, attention to details, and follow-through and setting high standards. What you do or don't do in one area of your life affects other areas of your life and other people as well.

Peak performers realize they are responsible for their attitudes and actions, and they know they have the power to change them. A negative attitude is sometimes the

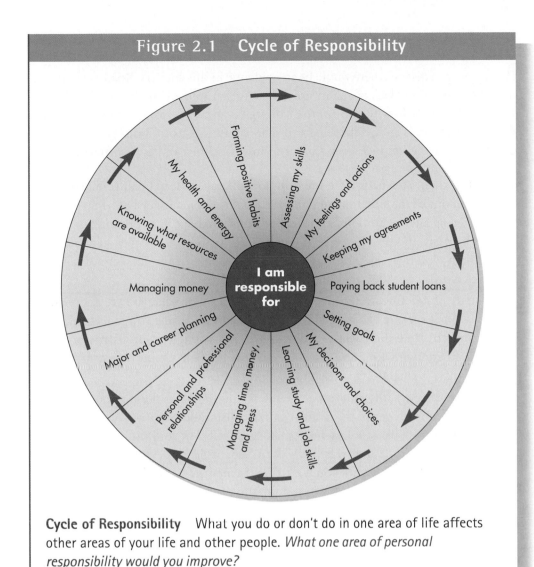

Figure 2.1   Cycle of Responsibility

Center: **I am responsible for**

Wheel segments:
- Forming positive habits
- Assessing my skills
- My feelings and actions
- Keeping my agreements
- Paying back student loans
- Setting goals
- My decisions and choices
- Learning study and job skills
- Managing time, money, and stress
- Personal and professional relationships
- Major and career planning
- Managing money
- Knowing what resources are available
- My health and energy

Cycle of Responsibility   What you do or don't do in one area of life affects other areas of your life and other people. *What one area of personal responsibility would you improve?*

Use
TM 2.4 Cycle of Responsibility.

Hands-On Application
Have students write down all the examples they have seen or that they have read about people who do not take responsibility and blame others. Discuss and list the best examples on the board.

Teaching Tip
Emphasize that students are part of a system and their actions affect others.

Class Discussion
1. How does not repaying student loans affect the college and other students? Ask for other examples of how students' actions affect others.
2. How do these competencies create college and job success?

result of not coping effectively with change, conflict, and frustration. Emotional, physical, and social changes are part of the growing process at any age. Learning to adjust to frustration and discouragement can take many forms. Some people may withdraw or become critical, cynical, shy, sarcastic, or unmotivated and listless. Blame, excuses, justification, and criticism of others are devices for those who cannot accept personal responsibility for their behavior and state of mind. Acknowledge your feelings and attitudes. Decide if they support your goals; if they do not, choose a state of mind and actions that support you.

Being responsible creates a sense of integrity and a feeling of self-worth. For example, if you owe money to a friend, family member, or bank, take the responsibility to repay the loan. If you have a student loan, repay it on schedule or make new arrangements with the lender. Not repaying can result in years of guilt and embarrassment, as well as a poor credit rating. It is important to your sense of self-worth to know you are a person who keeps agreements and assumes responsibility. The model in **Figure 2.1** illustrates how responsibility has a cyclical effect.

Self-Management and Control

Hands-On Application

Ask students to think of a time when they said or did something that they wished they could take back. Have them write what happened. If they could replay the scene, ask what they would do differently.

Class Discussion

Discuss tips for self-control, such as counting to ten. Ask students if that would help. Ask for examples of tips that students use to gain their own self-control and manage anger.

Hands-On Application

Role playing: Have one student do something that is annoying to his or her roommate or family member. Samples are tapping a pen, eating food noisily, leaving dirty clothes on the floor. Have the partner use the "I" statement to diffuse anger and resolve the problem without blaming. Discuss in small groups.

If anger were a disease, there would be an epidemic in this country. Road rage, spousal and child abuse, and lack of civility are just a few examples of anger. Emotionally mature people know how to control their thoughts and behaviors and how to resolve conflict. Conflict is an inevitable part of school and work, but it can be resolved in a positive way. Following are seven tips for trying to redirect and transform your anger:

1. **Calm down.** Step back from the situation and take a deep breath. Take the drama out of the situation and observe what is happening, what behavior is triggering angry emotions, and what options you have in responding in appropriate and positive ways. If you lash out without thinking and attack verbally, you may cause serious harm to your relationship. You cannot take back words once they are spoken. Resist the urge to overreact.

2. **Clarify and define.** Determine exactly with whom or what you are angry and why. What specific behavior in the other person is causing you to feel angry or frustrated? Determine whose problem it is. For example, your instructor may have an annoying tone and style of lecturing. If a behavior annoys only you, perhaps it is something you alone need to address.

3. **Listen with empathy and respect.** Understand the other person's point of view. Take the tension out of the conflict by really listening. See if you can restate the other person's position. Listen to yourself as well. Ask yourself how you feel. Are you tired, hot, hungry, frustrated, rushed, or ill? If so, you may not want to deal with your anger until you feel better. Sometimes, getting a good night's sleep or having a good meal will put the situation into perspective, and your anger will dissolve.

4. **Use "I" statements.** Take ownership of your feelings. Using "I" statements—direct messages you deliver in a calm tone with supportive body language—can diffuse anger. You are not blaming another person but, rather, expressing how a situation affects you. For example, you can say, "Carlos, when I hear you clicking your pen and tapping it on the desk, I'm distracted from studying." This is usually received better than saying, "Carlos, you're so rude and inconsiderate. You must know that you're annoying me when you tap your pen."

5. **Focus on one problem.** Don't pounce on every annoying behavior you can think of to dump on the person. Let's continue with the example in Tip 4: "And in addition to clicking your pen, Carlos, I don't like how you leave your dishes in the sink, drop your towels in the bathroom, and make that annoying little sound when you eat." Work to resolve only one behavior or conflict at a time.

6. **Focus on win-win solutions.** How can you both win? Restate the problem and jot down as many different creative solutions as possible that you can both agree on.

7. **Reward positive behavior.** As you use praise and reinforce positive behaviors, you will find that the person will exert less resistance. You can now be more direct about the specific behaviors and ask for a commitment: "Julie, if you could be here right at 8:00, we could get through this study session in two hours. Can we agree on this?" Focus on behavior, not personality or name calling, which just angers you and antagonizes the other person. Don't let anger

Class Discussion
How do these competencies
create college and job
success?
Applying SCANS:
Self-esteem
Sociability

Peak Progress   2.1

Applying the Adult Learning Cycle to Self-Management and Control

The Adult Learning Cycle can help you increase your emotional intelligence. For example, you may have felt the same angry and frustrated feelings mentioned in the Visualization box on the first page of this chapter. It could be because someone cut you off or you've lost your keys, you may have three papers due, or you are so overwhelmed with school, work, and family that your motivation dropped and you developed a negative attitude.

1. **RELATE. Why do I want to learn this?** What personal meaning and interest does controlling my anger have for me? Has it been a challenge for me? Has it hurt important relationships in my personal life or at school or work? How will controlling my anger help me in those situations?

2. **OBSERVE. How does this work?** I can learn a lot about anger management by watching, listening, and engaging in trial and error. Whom do I consider to be an emotionally mature person? Whom do I respect because of his or her patience, understanding, and ability to deal with stressful events? When I observe the problems that people around me have in their lives, how do they exhibit their emotional maturity in general and anger specifically?

3. **THINK. What does this mean?** Test new ways of behaving and break old patterns. Explore creative ways to solve problems rather than getting angry. Gather and assess information about anger management and reflect on what works and doesn't work.

4. **DO. What can I do with this?** Learn by doing and finding practical applications for anger management. Practice the seven steps outlined on page 2-00. Apply the ABCDE visualization techniques to specific situations to determine positive outcomes.

5. **TEACH. Whom can I share this with?** Talk with others and share experiences. Demonstrate to and teach others the methods you've learned. Model by example.

Now return to Stage 1 and realize your accomplishment in taking steps to controlling your anger better.

---

and conflict create more stress in your life and take a physical and emotional toll. You can learn to step back automatically from explosive situations and control them, rather than let your emotions control you. **Peak Progress 2.1** explores how you can use the Adult Learning Cycle to manage your emotions.

Self-Esteem and Confidence

Self-esteem is how you feel about yourself. Peak performers have developed confidence and believe in themselves. They assess themselves honestly and focus on their

Hands-On Applications

1. Role playing: Have one student play a confident person with high self-esteem. Have another student play a person with low self-esteem. Discuss appearance, posture, attitude, tone of voice, stance, walk, eye contact, etc.

2. Have students write down all the barriers that keep them from being motivated and positive. Jot down strategies for overcoming these barriers.

Use

• TM 2.2 A Positive Attitude.

Words to Succeed

"Nothing great was ever achieved without enthusiasm."

—RALPH WALDO EMERSON
poet

Key Teaching Concept
Change your attitude and you change your life.

strengths. They constantly learn new skills and competencies that build their confidence. They accept responsibility for their attitudes and behavior. They know that blame and anger only diminish confidence. They focus their energies on becoming a person of integrity and character.

People with a positive self-esteem have the confidence that allow them to be more open to new experiences and accepting of different people. They tend to be more optimistic. They are more willing to share their feelings and ideas with others and are willing to tolerate differences in others. Because they have a sense of self-worth, they do not find it necessary to put down or discriminate against others.

In contrast, people with low self-esteem may tend to mistrust others and reject people who are different. They lack self-confidence and may fail to meet their goals. Some may be more concerned with their rights than with their responsibility to act with respect and integrity.

Confidence can develop from

◆ Having honesty and integrity

◆ Gaining competence and skills

◆ Accepting and respecting yourself and your work

◆ Being responsible for your choices

◆ Seeing the big picture

◆ Setting high but attainable goals and expectations

If you want to change your outer world and experiences for the better, you must begin by looking at your thoughts, feelings, and beliefs about yourself. Assess your self-esteem at the end of the chapter in **Worksheet 2.3** and follow the tips in **Peak Progress 2.2.**

A Positive Attitude and Personal Motivation

There is an old story about three men working on a project in a large city in France. A curious tourist asked them, "What are you three working on?" The first man said, "I'm hauling rocks." The second man said, "I'm laying a wall." The third man said with pride, "I'm building a cathedral." The third man had a sense of vision of the whole system. When college and work seem as tedious as hauling rocks, focus on the big picture.

A positive attitude is essential for achieving success in school, in your career, and in life. Your attitude influences the outcome of a task more than any other factor. Motivation is the inner drive that moves you to action. Even when you are discouraged or face setbacks, motivation can help you bounce back and keep on track. You may have skills, experience, intelligence, and talent, but you will accomplish little if you are not motivated to direct your energies toward specific goals.

A positive attitude results in enthusiasm, vitality, optimism, and a zest for living. When you have a positive attitude, you are more likely to be on time, aware, and alert

Needs, Motivation, and Commitment

1. What needs motivate you at this time?

_____

_____

2. What do you think will motivate you in 20 years?

_____

_____

3. Complete this sentence in your own words: "For me to be more motivated, I need . . . "

_____

_____

4. Describe a time in your life when you were committed to something, such as a goal, a project, an event, or a relationship, that was important to you.

_____

_____

5. Regarding your answer to question 4, what were the main factors that kept you motivated?

_____

_____

Class Discussion

In small groups, tell students:

1. List the most common answers and put four or five of the best samples on the board.
2. Discuss the different factors that motivate people based on the four or five examples on the board.

Teaching Tip

After students have completed Personal Performance Notebook 2.3 ask students to reflect on a time of depression or when they were not motivated. How did they overcome depression and setbacks?

Use

TM 2.6 For Me to Be More Motivated, I Am Waiting for. . . .

As your lower-level needs are satisfied and cease to motivate, you begin to direct your attention to the higher-level needs for motivation. For example, once you feel confident, you will find that you have more energy and focus for defining and pursuing your dreams and goals. You will want to discover and develop your full potential. You will not only love learning new ideas but also value emotional maturity, character, and integrity. You will be well on the path to self-actualization. Complete the **Personal Performance Notebook 2.3** to assess what motivates you.

MOTIVATIONAL STRATEGIES

Keeping yourself motivated isn't always easy with all the pressures you may be feeling from school, work, family, and so on. However, there are some key motivational strategies you can put into action:

1. **Act as if you are motivated.** Attitude can influence behavior, and behavior can influence attitude. The way you act every day can affect your self-esteem, and

Words to Succeed

"What makes life dreary is the want of motive."

—GEORGE ELIOT
nineteenth-century English novelist

Hands-On Application
Ask students which of the
motivating factors are
internal (negative thoughts)
and which are external (such
as the weather). Ask them
what they can do to change
internal factors. What can
they do to change external
factors?

Hands-On Application
Role playing: Have students
pretend they are auditioning
for a part in a play that calls
for a very motivated,
positive, and enthusiastic
person. They should take
turns in their small groups.
One person should act as the
director and recorder and list
important traits.

Class Discussion
Ask students what they are
postponing in life. What do
they think will make them
happy? Write on the board
what many students are
waiting for to be more
motivated, for example,
graduation or a better job.

Key Teaching Concept
What you say to yourself
when you first wake up sets
the stage for the day.

Hands-On Application
Ask how many of your
students plan to graduate
from college. Have students
visualize how they will look,
feel, and act when they walk
across the stage at the
graduation ceremony.
Ask them who will be there
watching them. Have
students write out this image
and visualize it every week
or so.

your self-esteem can affect the things you do. You can attempt to change your behavior anytime. You don't need to wait until your attitude changes or until you feel motivated to begin the positive behaviors. Act as if you are already motivated.

For example, pretend you are performing in a movie. Your character is a positive, motivated student. How would you enter the room? Would you be smiling? What would your breathing, posture, and muscle tension be like? What kinds of gestures and facial expressions would you use to create this character? What kinds of friends would this person enjoy being with? Try acting out the part when you wake up in the morning and throughout the day. If you develop positive study and work habits and do them consistently, even when you don't feel like it, you'll be successful, and this will create a positive state of mind. You are what you do consistently. Positive habits create success.

2. **Use affirmations.** Any discussion of motivation must include your self-talk, what you say to yourself throughout the day. Once you start paying attention to your self-talk, you may be amazed at how much of it is negative. Throughout the day, countless thoughts, images, and phrases go through your brain almost unnoticed, but they have a tremendous influence on your mood and attitude. Your mind is most receptive just before sleep and when first waking up. The first step, then, is to replace negative self-talk with affirmations. For example, don't say, "I won't waste my time today." That just reminds you that you have a habit of wasting time. Instead, affirm, "I am setting goals and priorities and achieving the results I want. I have plenty of energy to accomplish all that I choose to do, and I feel good when I'm organized and centered." Complete the **Personal Performance Notebook 2.4** to determine if your self-talk needs to become more positive.

3. **Use visualization.** As we explored in Chapter 1, visualization is seeing things in your mind's eye by organizing and processing information through pictures and symbols. You imagine yourself behaving in certain ways, so that behavior will become real. For example, businessman Calvin Payne knows the power of visualization. He bought his college graduation cap and gown and kept them in his room. He visualized himself crossing the stage in his gown to accept his diploma. This visual goal helped him when he suffered setbacks, frustration, and disappointments. He graduated with honors and now incorporates visualization techniques in his career.

Most right-brain-dominant people are visual and use imagery a great deal. They can see scenes in detail when they read or daydream. In fact, their imagery is like a movie of themselves, with scenes of how they will react in certain situations, or a replay of what has occurred in the past. These images are rich in detail, expansive, and ongoing. Left-brain-dominant people tend to use imagery less, but using imagery is a technique that can be learned, developed, and practiced.

Visualization will help you see problems through formulas; read a recipe and see and taste the finished food; read blueprints and visualize the building; and see scenes and characters through narratives. You can also use mental imagery to create a positive, calm, and motivated state of mind.

4. **Use goals as motivational tools.** Just as an athlete visualizes crossing the finish line, you, too, can visualize your final goal. Often, peak performers write out their goals. Try keeping yours in your wallet, taping them on your bathroom

Self-Talk and Affirmations

Listen to your self-talk for a few days. Jot down the negative thoughts you say to yourself. For example, when you first wake up, do you say, "I don't want to go to class today"?

Do your thoughts and self-talk focus on lack of time, lack of money, or other problems? Observe when you are positive. How does this change your state of mind and your physical sense of well-being? List examples of your negative self-talk and positive affirmations:

Negative Self-Talk	Positive Affirmations
1. _____	1. _____
2. _____	2. _____
3. _____	3. _____

Hands-On Application

Have students:

1. Keep a log of their negative thoughts, self-talk, and images for a few days.
2. Rewrite their negative thoughts, self-talk, and images into positive statements and images.
3. Discuss in small groups.

---

mirror, or putting them on yellow sticky notes around your computer screen. Without a specific goal, it's not easy to find the motivation, effort, and focus required to go to classes and complete assignments. Make certain your goals are realistic. Excellence doesn't mean attaining perfection or working compulsively toward impossible or unrealistic goals. If you try to be a perfectionist, you set yourself up for frustration, which can lead to decreased motivation, lowered productivity, increased stress, and failure.

5. **Understand expectations.** You will be more motivated to succeed if you understand what is expected of you in each class. Most instructors hand out a syllabus on the first day. Review it carefully and keep a copy in your class notebook. Review the syllabus with a study partner and clarify expectations with your instructor. Meet with your academic advisor to review general college and graduation requirements. College is different from high school, and, the more you understand expectations, the more focused you'll be to reach your goals. (See **Peak Progress 2.3** on page 2–16.)

6. **Study in teams.** Success in the business world relies on team skills—the sharing of skills, knowledge, confidence, and decision-making abilities. The term *synergy* means that the whole is greater than the sum of the parts. It means seeing and using the whole system, not just isolated parts. You can increase your school and job success by learning, studying, and working in teams. You can also

   a. Teach each other material and outline main points

   b. Read and edit each other's reports

   c. Develop sample quizzes and test each other

   d. Learn to get along with and value different people

7. **Stay physically and mentally healthy.** It is difficult to motivate yourself if you don't feel well physically or emotionally. If you are ill, you miss classes, fall behind in studying, or both. Falling behind can cause you to worry and feel stressed. Talk out your problems, eat well, get plenty of exercise and rest, and create a balance of work and play.

Class Discussion

Ask students how important they think it is to interact with their instructors.

Teaching Tip

You may want to share examples of students who missed deadlines, signed up for classes that were not required, or prepared for a different type of test.

Hands-On Application

Explain the importance of forming study groups in each class. With a study group or study partner, students should review the syllabus and expectations of the class. They should list questions that they still have. Next, they should go to the instructor in each of their classes and review questions and expectations. Clarify the type of tests, projects, papers, and speeches that they should expect.

Teaching Tip

Emphasize the connection between feeling good physically and being motivated. Ask students if they have ever felt depressed at night, but after a good night's rest and a good breakfast, they felt better.

Teaching Tip
Reframing is choosing to see a situation or person in the best possible light.

Hands-On Application
Role playing: Have students think of a situation that they don't like. Have them list the negative aspects, then reframe and look for all the positive factors in the situation. Have study partners play their positive attitude and help them focus on the positive. Every student should take turns describing a situation and role-playing the positive attitude.

Class Discussion
Ask students what they do to reward themselves when they achieve a goal or complete a task. Stress the importance of focusing on what they have accomplished and not what they have yet to do.

The Differences Between High School and College

In college, you will be expected to

- Have more responsibilities and budget your time and money
- Express your opinions logically, not just give facts
- Motivate yourself
- Have more freedom and independence
- Have larger classes that meet for longer periods but less often
- Be responsible for knowing procedures and graduation requirements
- Write and read more than you have before
- Think critically and logically
- Receive less feedback, and be tested less often but more comprehensively
- Have several textbooks and supplemental readings
- Have more work and be required to turn in higher-quality work
- Interact with people of different values, cultures, interests, and religions
- Learn to be tolerant and respectful of diversity
- Be exposed to new ideas and critique these ideas in a thoughtful way
- Get involved in the community, school clubs, volunteer work, and internships related to your major

8. **Learn to reframe.** You don't have control over many situations or the actions of others, but you do have total control of your responses. Reframing is choosing to see a situation in the best possible light. For example, Joan Bosch works at a fast-food hamburger place. She has reframed this work situation to focus on essential job skills. She is learning to be positive, dependable, hardworking, service-oriented, flexible, and tolerant.

9. **Reward yourself.** The simplest tasks can become discouraging without rewards for progress and for completion. Set up a system of appropriate rewards and consequences. Decide what your reward will be when you finish a project. For an easier task, the reward might be small, such as a snack, a hot shower, or a phone call to a friend. For a larger project, the reward might be listening to a new CD, going out to dinner, or throwing a small party. What are some rewards that would motivate you? The following are some additional examples of rewards:

Listen to music	Cook your favorite meal	Play sports
Read a novel	Go to a museum	Go to a movie
Go to a sporting event	Take a walk	Visit friends
Take photos	Work in a garden	Watch television

10. **Make learning relevant.** You will be more motivated if you make the connection between college and the world of work. Essentially, make sure you understand the benefits of gaining knowledge and learning new skills in your coursework and the ways they will relate to your performance on the job. You may be attending college just because you love to learn and meet new

Peak Performer Profile

Ben Carson, M.D.

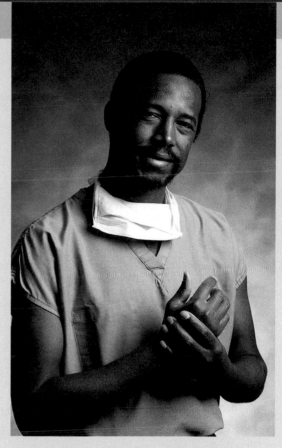

Ben Carson's life is a testament to having a positive attitude, motivation, and integrity. Despite major obstacles, he has become a world-renowned neurosurgeon and author who has touched many lives.

Overcoming the disadvantages of growing up in an economically depressed neighborhood in Detroit, Carson has lived by the words "no excuses." As a child, when difficult situations would confront him or his brother, his mother would ask, "Do you have a brain? Then you can think your way out of it." Carson did just that.

During the 1950s, Carson's mother worked multiple domestic jobs to keep the family afloat. Though life at home was challenging, days at school were even more so. Carson recalls, "There was an unspoken decree that the black kids were dumb." His mother knew better. When the two brothers brought home failing grades, she turned off the TV and required the boys to read two books a week and write reports. Eventually, Carson rose to the top of his class and went on to graduate from Yale University and the University of Michigan School of Medicine.

However, one biographer wrote that, during Carson's youth, his temper made him seem "most qualified for putting someone else in the hospital." It was only after a life-threatening confrontation that Carson realized his choices were "jail, reform school—or the grave."

Today, Carson is the director of pediatric neurosurgery at Johns Hopkins Hospital. Even working under primitive conditions in South Africa in 1997, Carson succeeded against the odds when he separated 11-month-old conjoined twins who were joined at the head. The man who was tagged "dummy" now saves the lives of children whom others label as hopeless.

PERFORMANCE THINKING   Explain how attitude, motivation, and integrity played a part in Ben Carson's success.

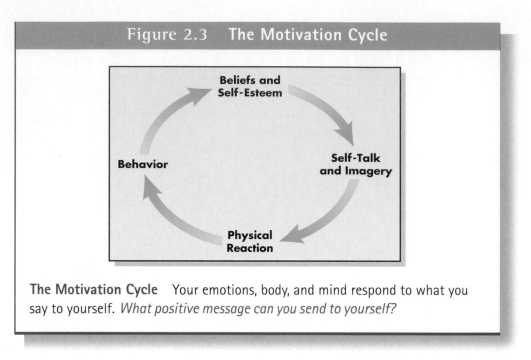

Figure 2.3   The Motivation Cycle

The Motivation Cycle   Your emotions, body, and mind respond to what you say to yourself. *What positive message can you send to yourself?*

Hands-On Application
Have students list all the reasons they're in school. Ask: What are the benefits? Discuss in small groups.

people. However, it's more likely you are enrolled to acquire or enhance your knowledge and skills, which will increase your marketability in the workforce.

THE MOTIVATION CYCLE

The motivation cycle in **Figure 2.3** amplifies what you learned in Chapter 1 about the power of visualization. It illustrates how your self-esteem influences what you say to yourself, which in turn influences your physical reactions—breathing, muscular tension, and posture. These physical reactions influence your behavior—both your verbal and your nonverbal responses.

Isn't it amazing how the emotions, body, and mind are interrelated? You cannot change one part without changing the whole system. Try to remember how important affirmations and visualization are for creating a resourceful state of mind.

The Benefits of a Higher Education

As mentioned earlier, you will be more motivated to put in long hours of studying when you feel the goal is worth it. Higher education is an excellent investment. No one can take your education away from you, and it pays large dividends. College graduates earn an average of well over $800,000 more in a lifetime than do high school graduates. (See **Figure 2.4.**) Although graduating from college or a career school won't guarantee you a great job, it pays off with more career opportunities, better salaries, more benefits, more job promotions, increased workplace flexibility, better workplace conditions, and greater job satisfaction. Many career centers at colleges make a commitment to help their students find employment.

Society and the workplace benefit when people improve their literacy. Various reports from the U.S. Department of Labor indicate that people who attend at least two years of college tend to

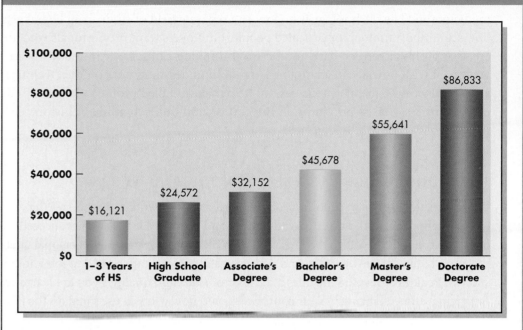

Figure 2.4 Annual Earnings and Education

SOURCE: Census 2000, U.S. Census Bureau, U.S. Department of Commerce.

Annual Earnings and Education Statistically, the level of your education is directly related to your income. These figures are average earnings for the U.S. population in 1999. Incomes vary within each category. *What other advantages, besides a good job and income, do you think education offers?*

◆ Make better decisions
◆ Be willing to learn new skills
◆ Have more hobbies and leisure activities
◆ Have a longer life expectancy
◆ Be healthier
◆ Be more involved in the community
◆ Have more discipline and perseverance
◆ Have more self-confidence
◆ Learn to adapt to change

A LIBERAL ARTS EDUCATION

Higher education has its roots in the liberal arts. Many years ago, being an educated person meant having a liberal arts education. *Liberal* comes from the Latin root word *liber*, which means "to free." A broad education is designed to free people to think and understand themselves and the world around them. The liberal arts include such areas as the arts, the humanities, the social sciences, mathematics, and the natural sciences. Classes in philosophy, history, language, art, and geography focus on how people think, behave, and express themselves in our culture and in the world.

The liberal arts integrate many disciplines and provide a foundation for professional programs, such as criminal justice, electronics, computer systems, business, medicine, and law. Technology is no longer a separate field of study from liberal arts but is an important tool for educated people. Employers want professionals who are creative problem solvers, have good critical thinking skills, can communicate and work well with others, can adapt to change, and understand our complex technical and social world. Liberal arts classes can help make a skilled professional a truly educated professional by providing an integration and understanding of history, culture, ourselves, and our world.

THE CONNECTION BETWEEN SCHOOL AND WORK

The connection between school and job success is a major theme in this book. What you learn in school correlates directly with finding and keeping a job, as well as succeeding in a chosen career. As you go through school, think about how the skills, personal qualities, and habits you are learning and demonstrating in class are related to job and life success. **Peak Progress 2.4** includes a number of skills and qualities you are learning, practicing, and enhancing in your coursework, and how you will use them on the job.

Peak Progress   2.4

Skills for School and Career
Keep the following skills in mind as you see the connection between school and job success.

Skills	School Application	Career Application
Basic skills	Foundation for schoolwork	Foundation for work tasks
Motivation	Motivated to attend classes	Motivated to excel at work
Thinking skills	Solve case studies, equations	Solve work problems
Creativity	Creative experiments	Creative work solutions
Control of time	Homework first	Work priorities in order
Control of money	Personal budget	Departmental budgets
Writing	Writing papers	Writing reports, memos
Speeches	Classroom speeches	Presentations
Test taking	Tests in classes	Performance reviews
Information	Selecting class information	Selecting work information
Learning	Learning for classes	Learning job skills
Systems	Learning college system	Learning organization
Resources	Using college resources	Using work resources
Technology	Using computers for papers	Using computers for work

As you develop your time- and stress-management skills, which we will explore in more detail later in this text, you will see improvement in your habits in school and on the job. Time management may help you show up for class on time and be prepared every day, thus leading to better grades. Punctuality in school will carry over to punctuality for work. Stress management may help you get along better with your roommates, instructors, or coworkers. Learning how to succeed in the school or college system can serve as a model for working effectively in organizational systems. Do you think you are maximizing your strengths, skills, and personal qualities? See **Peak Progress 2.5** to determine what kind of student/worker you are and to determine what you need to do to improve your performance.

Peak Progress   2.5

What Kind of a Student/Worker Are You?

A peak performer or an *A* student
- Is alert, actively involved, and eager to learn
- Consistently does more than required
- Consistently shows initiative and enthusiasm
- Is positive and engaged
- Can solve problems and make sound decisions
- Is dependable, prompt, neat, accurate, and thorough

A good worker or a *B* student
- Frequently does more than is required
- Is usually attentive, positive, and enthusiastic
- Completes most work accurately, neatly, and thoroughly
- Often uses critical thinking to solve problems and make decisions

An average worker or a *C* student
- Completes the tasks that are required
- Shows a willingness to follow instructions and learn
- Is generally involved, dependable, enthusiastic, and positive
- Provides work that is mostly thorough, accurate, and prompt

A problem worker or a *D* student
- Usually does the minimum of what is required
- Has regular attendance, is often late, or is distracted
- Lacks a positive attitude or the ability to work well with others
- Often misunderstands assignments and deadlines
- Lacks thoroughness

An unacceptable worker or an *F* student
- Does not do the work that is required
- Is inattentive, bored, negative, and uninvolved
- Is undependable and turns in work that is incorrect and incomplete

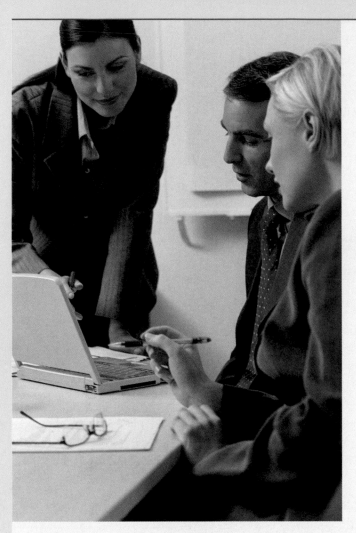

Jacqui Williams

SALES REPRESENTATIVE

Related Majors: Business, Marketing, Public Relations

Positive Attitudes at Work

As a sales representative for a large medical company, Jacqui Williams sells equipment, such as X-ray and electrocardiograph (EKG) machines, to hospitals nationwide. Her job requires travel to prospective clients, where she meets with buyers to show her products and demonstrate their installation and use. Because Jacqui cannot take the large machines with her, she relies on printed materials and a laptop computer, from which she can point out the new aspects of the machines she sells. The sales process usually takes several months and requires more than one trip to the prospective client.

Jacqui works on commission, being paid only when she makes a sale. Because she travels frequently, Jacqui must be able to work independently without a lot of supervision. For this reason, being personally motivated is a strong requirement for her position. Jacqui has found that the best way to remain motivated is to believe in the products she sells. Jacqui keeps up on the latest in her field by reading technical information and keeping track of the competition. She sets sales goals and then rewards herself with a short vacation.

Because personal relations with buyers are so important, Jacqui is careful about her appearance. While traveling, she keeps a positive mindset through affirmations, and she gets up early to eat a healthy breakfast and exercise in the hotel gym. She uses integrity by presenting accurate information and giving her best advice, even if it means not making a sale. Her clients would describe Jacqui as positive and helpful, someone whom they look forward to seeing and whose advice they trust.

CRITICAL THINKING

In what way does having integrity, good character, and a code of ethics enhance a sales representative's business?

Peak Progress   2.6

The Most Common Reasons Students Do Not Graduate

Between 30 and 50 percent of all college freshmen never graduate. The top 10 reasons are

1. Poor study skills and habits
2. Lack of time-management skills
3. Lack of preparation for the demands and requirements of college
4. Inability to handle the freedom at college
5. Too much partying
6. Lack of motivation or purpose
7. Failure to attend class regularly
8. Failure to ask for help early
9. Lack of effort and time spent in studying
10. Failure to take responsibility for education (such as getting to know instructors, knowing expectations, setting goals, understanding deadlines, making up tests, redoing papers)

Teaching Tip
Emphasize the importance of resiliency. Ask for examples of people who bounced back after setbacks. Ask students to keep a file of these stories.

Overcoming the Barriers

Discouragement is the number one barrier to motivation. Even peak performers sometimes feel discouraged and need help climbing out of life's valleys. Creating and maintaining a positive state of mind does not happen by reading a book, attending a lecture, or using a few strategies for a day or two. It takes time and effort. Everyone gets off course now and then, but the key is to realize that setbacks are part of life. Don't allow setbacks to make you feel as if you have failed and can no longer reach your goal. Find a formula that works for you to create a positive and resourceful mind.

Don't postpone developing your personal qualities. **Peak Progress 2.6** shows that a lack of personal qualities has a direct effect on the main reasons students don't graduate. If you think, "I'll be more motivated as soon as I graduate and get a real job," you may never develop the necessary qualities and skills to achieve that. Starting today, you should:

◆ Focus on being motivated and positive.

◆ Focus on your successes and accomplishments.

◆ Surround yourself with positive, supportive, and encouraging friends.

◆ Tell yourself, "This is a setback, not a failure."

◆ Make certain you are physically renewed. Get more rest, exercise more, and do something every day that you love.

◆ Replace negative and limiting thoughts and self-talk with affirmations and positive visualization.

◆ Collect short stories about people who were discouraged, received negative messages, and bounced back.

Words to Succeed

"The path was worn and slippery. My foot slipped from under me, knocking the other out of the way. But I recovered and said to myself, 'It's a slip and not a fall.'"

—ABRAHAM LINCOLN
U.S. president

PEAK TIP

Set goals and expectations and adjust them when necessary.

Class Discussion

Ask students how a support group can encourage them to expand and grow.

Hands-On Application

Have students write about their comfort zone. Ask them how they have expanded it. What were the risks?

CREATING POSITIVE MIND SHIFTS

Having both a positive attitude and high self-esteem is important, but neither will help you reach your goals if your beliefs or perceptions are misguided. Sometimes, a mind shift is necessary to see new possibilities and adjust perceptions. Your beliefs are your mind maps, and they influence how you see life. It is important to use critical thinking to assess your beliefs to see if they are accurate and support your goals. Let's say that you are driving a car to New York. If your map is wrong, positive attitude and self-esteem won't get you to New York.

Expectations may also influence how you see yourself and others. You may let your beliefs, assumptions, or expectations get in the way of seeing a person or situation clearly. Sometimes, the closer you are to a situation, the more difficult it is to see it clearly.

EXPANDING YOUR COMFORT ZONE

Your beliefs and expectations about yourself can either limit or expand your success. Other people's expectations of you may cause you to redefine who you think you are and what you think you are capable of achieving. You may start to believe what you tell yourself or hear from others again and again, which may be limiting your thinking.

For example, Steve Delmay comes from a long line of lumber mill workers. Although they have lived for generations in a college town, his family has never had anything to do with the college. Steve was expected to go to work at the mill right after high school. He never thought about other options. However, during his senior year in high school, he attended Career Day. He met instructors and students from the local college who were friendly, supportive, and encouraging. His world opened up, and he saw opportunities he had never considered before. Steve experienced a major mind shift. Although he had to overcome a lack of support at home, he is now a successful college student with a bright future.

Creative problem solving can expand your mind and comfort zone and shift your thinking, so that you can see new possibilities and broader and more exciting horizons. College is an ideal time to develop your natural creativity and explore new ways of thinking. Try the following steps:

1. **Create a support system.** Without support and role models, you may question whether you can be successful. First-generation college students, women in technical programs, or men in nursing programs may feel uncomfortable and question whether they belong. Cultural minorities, veterans, or physically challenged or returning students may feel that they don't belong. Some students may be told that they are not college material. You can find encouragement with a support system of positive and accepting people. Get involved and join a variety of clubs. Make friends with diverse groups of students, instructors, and community leaders.

2. **Reprogram your mind.** Affirmations and visualization can create a self-fulfilling prophecy. If you think of yourself as a success and are willing to put in the effort, you will be successful. Focus on your successes and accomplishments

and overcome limitations. For example, if you need to take a remedial math class, take it and don't label yourself as "dumb" or "math impaired." Instead, focus on how improved your math skills will be.

3. **Use critical thinking.** Question limiting labels and beliefs. Where did they come from and are they accurate? Be mentally active and positive.

4. **Use creative thinking.** Ask yourself, "What if?" Explore creative ways of achieving your goals. Find out how you learn best and adopt positive habits.

5. **Take responsibility.** You are responsible for your thoughts, beliefs, and actions. You can question, think, and explore. You can achieve almost anything you dream.

6. **Learn new skills.** Focus on your strengths, but be willing to learn new skills and competencies continually. Feeling competent is empowering.

7. **Use the whole of your intelligence.** You definitely are smarter than you think. Use all your experiences and personal qualities to achieve your goals. Develop responsibility, self-control, dependability, sociability, character, manners, and all the other qualities necessary for school, job, and life success.

TECH FOR SUCCESS

- **Ethics Information on the Web** Search for articles on ethics, business etiquette, and codes of ethics. Check out different businesses, the military, government agencies, and colleges to find out if each has a code of ethics. Print some samples and bring them to class. What do all the codes of ethics have in common?
- **On-line Discussion Groups** When you are interested in a topic or goal, it's very motivating to interact with others who have the same interests. Join a discussion group or listserv and share your knowledge, wisdom, and setbacks with others. You will learn their stories and strategies in return.

TAKING CHARGE

In summary, in this chapter, I learned to

- *Use the whole of my intelligence.* Developing emotional maturity and strong personal qualities is just as, if not more, important to my future success as learning new skills and information. Essential personal qualities include character, responsibility, self-management and self-control, self-esteem, confidence, attitude, and motivation.
- *Focus on character first.* Strong leaders are those who have an equally strong set of values. Having personal integrity gives me the courage to do the right thing, even when it is difficult. I display civility and empathy by interacting with family,

continued

friends, and colleagues with respect, kindness, good manners, sympathy, and compassion. It's important for me to have a personal code of ethics that I follow in all facets of my life.

- *Take responsibility for my thoughts, actions, and behaviors.* I don't blame others for my setbacks, and I focus my energy on positive solutions. Others can depend on me to keep my commitments.

- *Manage and control my emotions, anger, and negative thoughts.* Conflict is an inevitable part of life, but it can be resolved in a positive way. Seven steps I can follow to redirect my negative thoughts and anger are (1) calm down; (2) clarify and define; (3) listen with empathy and respect; (4) use "I" statements; (5) focus on one problem; (6) focus on win-win solutions; and (7) reward positive behavior.

- *Develop self-esteem and confidence.* Through self-assessment, I understand my strengths and will continue to learn new skills and competencies that will build my confidence.

- *Maintain a positive attitude and keep myself motivated.* A positive attitude is essential for achieving success, and it influences the outcome of a task more than any other factor. Motivation is the inner drive that moves me to action. Needs and motives influence attitude and motivation. Maslow's hierarchy of needs shows that I can fulfill my higher needs for self-esteem and self-actualization only when I have fulfilled my more basic needs first. The motivation cycle further demonstrates how affirmations, visualization, and self-talk affect my physical responses and behavior.

- *Realize the benefits of higher education.* My pursuit of a higher education should pay off with more career opportunities, a higher salary, more benefits, more job promotions, increased workplace flexibility, better workplace conditions, and greater job satisfaction. Higher education has its roots in the liberal arts. Liberal arts classes can help make me a truly educated professional by providing an integration and understanding of history, culture, ourselves, and our world.

- *Overcome the barriers to staying positive and motivated.* Discouragement is the number one barrier to motivation. Setbacks will occur, but I will focus on my successes and accomplishments, surround myself with supportive and encouraging people, keep physically renewed, and replace negative self-talk with positive affirmations and visualization.

- *Create positive mind shifts and expand my comfort zone.* My beliefs and perceptions must be realistic. If they aren't, I must refocus my expectations in order to achieve my goals. I should not allow my beliefs to limit my potential, and I will use critical thinking techniques to expand my mind and comfort zone.

Performance Strategies

Following are the top 10 strategies for developing emotional intelligence and personal qualities:

◆ Focus on the positive.

◆ Use affirmations and visualization.

◆ Reward yourself for making progress and strive for excellence, not perfection.

◆ Use goals as motivational tools.

◆ Develop and practice positive personal qualities.

◆ Cultivate character and integrity.

◆ Take responsibility.

◆ Expand your comfort zone.

◆ Be physically active and stay healthy.

◆ Focus on effort, not ability.

Review Questions

1. What is motivation?

2. List at least five motivational strategies.

3. Explain how affirmations and visualization affect the motivation cycle.

4. How can focusing on career success help you become a more successful student?

5. What personal qualities are essential to success in school and work?

REVISUALIZATION

Revisit the Visualization box on the first page of this chapter. Have you ever been a victim of road rage? If you commute, do you waste mental energy with negative thoughts about your fellow commuters? Revisit the situation you described in **Worksheet 2.1.** Now, apply the ABCDE method and visualize how you can diminish those negative thoughts and control your anger.

Let's consider the road rage example:

A = Actual event: "I was cut off in traffic."

B = Beliefs: "That driver shouldn't be allowed on the road. After yelling at him, I snapped at my roommate."

C = Consequences: "I was angry, frustrated, and in a bad mood all day."

D = Dispute: The other driver made a mistake, but that doesn't mean he's a bad driver all the time. Maybe he was late for work or rushing to pick up someone. It's better to take a deep breath, be thankful there wasn't an accident, and let it go."

E = Energized: "I feel good that I can control my emotions and not allow one event to ruin my day. This incident reminds me that driving takes focus and attention."

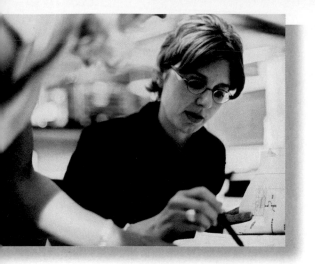

GETTING MOTIVATED

In the Classroom

Carol Rubino is a drafting major at a community college. In order to pay her expenses, she needs to work several hours a week. She is very organized and responsible with her school and work obligations. Most of her peers would describe Carol as motivated because she attends every class, is punctual, and works hard in both school and work. Throughout high school, Carol participated in extracurricular activities but never really enjoyed herself. She likes college but questions the connection between school and real life. As a result, Carol sometimes feels as if she is just wasting time and postponing life until graduation.

1. What strategies in this chapter can help Carol find a strong sense of purpose and motivation?

_____

_____

_____

2. What would you recommend to Carol for creating a more resourceful and positive attitude?

_____

_____

_____

In the Workplace

Carol is now a draftsperson for a small industrial equipment company. She has been with the company for 10 years. Carol is a valuable employee because she is competent and well liked. Carol has a supportive family, is healthy, and travels frequently. Although she enjoys her job, Carol feels bored with the mundane routine of her work. She wants to feel more motivated and excited on the job, as well as in her personal life.

3. What strategies in this chapter can help Carol become more enthusiastic about work or find new interest in her personal life?

_____

_____

_____

4. What would you suggest to Carol to help her get motivated?

_____

_____

_____

APPLYING THE ABCDE METHOD OF SELF-MANAGEMENT

In the Visualization box on page 2-00, you were asked to describe a time when you were angry and lost control of your emotions. Describe that event below, and indicate how others reacted and what you might have done differently.

_____

_____

_____

_____

_____

Now apply the ABCDE method to the situation and visualize a situation under control:

A = Actual event:

B = Beliefs:

C = Consequences:

D = Dispute:

E = Energized:

While completing this exercise, did you discover that you spend more time than you thought on negative thoughts?

CHAPTER 2 ▲ REVIEW AND APPLICATIONS

REWARDING MYSELF: A PERSONAL REINFORCEMENT CONTRACT

Use this example as a guide; then fill in the following contract for one or all of the courses you are taking this term.

Name _Sara Jones_

Course _General Accounting_   Date _September 2005_

If I _study for six hours each week in this class and attend all lectures and labs_

Then I will _reword myself with a long bike ride and picnic lunch every Saturday._

I agree to _learn new skills, choose positive thoughts and attitudes, and try out new behaviors._

I most want to accomplish _an "A" in this course to quality for advanced accounting courses._

The barriers to overcome are _my poor math skills._

The resources I can use are _my study group and the Tutoring Center._

I will reward myself for meeting my goals by _going out to dinner with some friends._

The consequences for not achieving the results I want will be _to find a new major._

Reinforcement Contract

Name _____

Course _____ Date _____

If I _____

Then I will _____

I agree to _____

I most want to accomplish _____

The barriers to overcome are _____

The resources I can use are _____

I will reward myself for meeting my goals by _____

The consequences for not achieving the results I want will be _____

CHAPTER 2 ▼ REVIEW AND APPLICATIONS

SELF-ESTEEM INVENTORY

Do this simple inventory to assess your self-esteem. Circle the number of points that reflects your true feelings.

     4 = all the time

     3 = most of the time

     2 = some of the time

     1 = none of the time

	4	3	2	1
1. I like myself and I am a worthwhile person.	4	3	2	1
2. I have many positive qualities.	4	3	2	1
3. Other people generally like me and I have a sense of belonging.	4	3	2	1
4. I feel confident and know I can handle most situations.	4	3	2	1
5. I am competent and good at many things.	4	3	2	1
6. I have emotional control and I am respectful of others.	4	3	2	1
7. I am a person of integrity and character.	4	3	2	1
8. I respect the kind of person I am.	4	3	2	1
9. I am capable and willing to learn new skills.	4	3	2	1
10. Although I want to improve and grow, I am happy with myself.	4	3	2	1
11. I take responsibility for my thoughts, beliefs, and behavior.	4	3	2	1
12. I am empathetic and interested in others and the world around me.	4	3	2	1

Total points   ____   ____   ____   ____

Add up your points. A high score indicates high self-esteem. If you have a high sense of self-esteem, you see your-self in a positive light. If your self-esteem is low, you may have less confidence to deal with problems in college or on the job.

CHAPTER 2 ▲ REVIEW AND APPLICATIONS

LEARNING STYLES

You will feel more motivated and positive when you align your efforts with your learning and personality styles. Review your preference and style and think of the factors that help motivate you.

For example, *auditory learners* may find that they are more motivated when they listen to a tape of their favorite inspirational music and say affirmations. *Visual learners* may find that they are motivated when they surround themselves with pictures and practice visualizing themselves as motivated and positive. *Kinesthetic learners* may be more motivated when they work on activities, dance, hike, jog, and work with others.

Analyzers may be more motivated when they think, reflect, and organize information into sequential steps. *Supporters* may be more motivated when they work in a group and make information meaningful. *Creators* may be more motivated when they observe, make active experiments, and build models. *Directors* may be more motivated when they clearly define procedures and make practical applications.

List the ways you can motivate yourself that are compatible with your learning style and personality type:

1. _____

   _____

   _____

2. _____

   _____

   _____

3. _____

   _____

   _____

4. _____

   _____

   _____

5. _____

   _____

   _____

6. _____

   _____

   _____

ASSESSMENT OF PERSONAL QUALITIES

Category	Assessment	Yes	No
Emotional intelligence	Do I value and practice essential personal qualities?		
Character	Do I value and practice being a person of character and integrity?		
Civility	Do I treat others with respect and courtesy?		
Ethics	Do I have a code of ethics?		
Responsibility	Do I take responsibility for my thoughts and behavior?		
Self-control	Do I have self-control and know how to manage anger?		
Self-esteem	Do I have a realistic and positive sense of myself?		
Positive attitude	Do I strive to be positive and upbeat?		
Motivation	Do I create the inner drive and determination to achieve my goals?		
Self-actualization	Am I committed to growing and realizing my full potential?		
Visualization	Do I use visualization as a powerful tool for change and growth?		
Affirmation	Do I dispute and replace negative self-talk with affirmations?		
Critical thinking	Do I use critical thinking to challenge my beliefs and see new possibilities?		

Managing Your Time

Chapter Objectives

In this chapter, you will learn

▲ How to set goals and priorities

▲ How to create a time-management system

▲ How to assess your energy level and time wasters

▲ How to work in alignment with your learning style

▲ How to overcome procrastination

▲ How to handle interruptions

VISUALIZATION

"It's 7:30 A.M., I'm late for class, and I can't find my keys. I'm frustrated and overwhelmed by too little time and too much to do. I feel as if I have no control over my life. How can I manage my time and get organized?"

Have you ever had a similar experience? Do you find yourself spending hours looking for things? Do you get angry at yourself and others because you feel frustrated and unorganized? In this chapter, you will learn how to take control of your time and your life and focus on priorities. Visualize

yourself going through the day organized and centered. You have a clear vision of your goals and priorities and work steadily until tasks are finished. Feel the sense of accomplishment and completion. Visualize yourself in charge of your time and your life.

JOURNAL ENTRY   In **Worksheet 3.1** on page 3-29, describe a time or situation when you felt overwhelmed by too much to do and too little time. What were the consequences?

Key Teaching Concept
Time is money, invest it wisely.

Use
TM 3.1 Success Principle 3.

Teaching Tip
Emphasize the importance of using the ABCDE Method of Self-Management to visualize success and create positive results.

Key Teaching Concept
Assessment is key in making change.

Teaching Tip
Explain to students that managing their time is similar to managing other areas of their lives. For example, sports requires taking a benchmark of current abilities before new goals are set. All change starts with assessment.

This chapter looks at time management with a positive attitude. Instead of controlling, suppressing, or constricting your freedom, time management enables you to achieve the things you really want and frees up time to enjoy life. Peak performers use a systematic approach that allows them to

◆ Organize projects and achieve results

◆ Accomplish goals and priorities

◆ Be effective, not just efficient

◆ Avoid crises

◆ Feel calm and productive

◆ Work smarter, not harder

◆ Feel a sense of accomplishment

◆ Have more free time to enjoy life

Everyone has the same amount of time—24 hours in each day. You can't save or steal time. When it's gone, it's gone. However, you can learn to invest it wisely. This chapter will help you learn how to get control of your life by managing your time wisely and by choosing to spend it on your main goals. It will also help you think about the contributions you want to make during your lifetime and the legacy you want to leave behind after you are gone. You will discover that there is always time to do the things you really want to do. Too many people waste time doing things that can be done in a few moments or doing things that should not be done at all and then ignoring their main goals.

As you go through this chapter, think about what you want to achieve and how you can use your time skillfully to perform at your peak level. This chapter will help you become effective, not just efficient. Being efficient is about doing things faster. Being effective is about doing the right things in the right way. As a wise time manager, you can avoid overwhelming feelings of losing control of tasks and falling behind in school, at work, or in your personal life.

Self-Assessment

Time management is much more than focusing on minutes, hours, and days. Your attitude, energy level, and ability to concentrate have a great impact as well. Try to evaluate clearly situations that may have spun out of control because of lack of planning or procrastination. Recall how these events may have affected other people. You are part of the whole system. When you are late for class, miss a study-group meeting, or don't do your share of a team project, it affects others.

Let's look at two important questions concerning your present use of time. The answers will help you develop a plan that will fine-tune your organizational and time-management skills—ultimately leading you to become an efficient peak performer.

1. Where does your time go? (Where are you spending your time and energy?)
2. Where should your time go?

Where Does Your Time Go?

You can divide time into three areas: committed time, maintenance time, and discretionary time.

COMMITTED TIME

Committed time is devoted to school, labs, studying, work, commuting, and other activities involving your immediate and long-term goals.

MAINTENANCE TIME

Maintenance time is the time you spend maintaining yourself. Activities such as eating, sleeping, bathing, exercising, and maintaining your home—cooking, cleaning/laundry, shopping, bill paying—use up your maintenance time.

DISCRETIONARY TIME

The time that is yours to use as you please is discretionary time. Separate your commitments and maintenance from your discretionary time and put all your activities into certain categories. For example, grooming may include showering, styling your hair, cleaning your contact lenses, and getting dressed. Don't spend too much time trying to determine in which category an activity fits. You want to use your discretionary time for the things you value most in life. These important items may include building relationships with family and friends; service to the community; intellectual development; and activities that give you a lot of joy and relaxation and that contribute to your physical, mental, and spiritual well-being. These are important goals that tie in with your long-term goals of being healthy, feeling centered and peaceful, and having loving relationships. Make certain your discretionary activities are conscious choices and that you make them top priorities.

Remember that this section asked you where your time goes and if you are using most of the day for commitments. A good place to determine your answer is with an assessment of how your time and energy are spent. Look at **Figure 3.1** on page 3–4 and then complete **Personal Performance Notebook 3.1** on page 3–5. The point of this exercise is to determine the best way to use your time to achieve important goals.

Where Should Your Time Go?

Peak performers know that the first rule of time management is to set goals to determine what they want to accomplish. Sometimes, it's hard to know how to spend time because there are so many things to spend it on. Conflicting demands on your time can be overwhelming and stressful. However, goals help clarify what you want and can give you energy, direction, and focus. Goal setting usually isn't quick or

Teaching Tip
Explain to students that time management is more than minutes or hours. Everyone has the same amount of time, but some people use it more effectively. Ask students what other factors are involved.

Words to Succeed

"Decide what you want, decide what you are willing to exchange for it, establish your priorities and go to work."

H. L. HUNT
financier

Teaching Tip
To illustrate the importance of setting goals, ask students if they would drive cross-country without a map or an idea of where they wanted to go.

Hands-On Application
In teams, have students discuss possible solutions to common time wasters. List the best strategies on the board. (see p. 3–32)

Teaching Tip
Share what you do each day to create time for yourself to do something enjoyable. Ask students what they do every day just for themselves.

Figure 3.1 Sample Time Log

Teaching Tip
Explain to students that it is often helpful to break their time into areas of commitments.

Use
TM 3.2 Weekly Schedule.

Hands-On Application
Have students keep a log of their activities and time. Have them discuss their logs in small groups.

Use
TM 3.3 Sample Time log.

Time	Activity	Notes	My Energy Level (High or Low)
6:00 – 7:00	shower, dress	maintenance	low
7:00 – 8:00	drive kids to school	committed	low
8:00 – 9:00	make to-do list	committed	high
9:00 – 10:00	coffee and calls	disc./committed	high
10:00 – 11:00	write proposal	committed	high
11:00 – 12:00	meeting	committed	low
12:00 – 1:00	lunch	maintenance	high
1:00 – 2:00			
2:00 – 3:00			
3:00 – 4:00			
4:00 – 5:00			
5:00 – 6:00			
6:00 – 7:00			
7:00 – 8:00			
8:00 – 9:00			
9:00 – 10:00			
10:00 – 11:00			

Sample Time Log Knowing how you spend your time is the first step toward managing it. *Are your discretionary activities conscious choices?*

easy. You need to take time to focus inward and think about your deepest values and desires.

Complete **Personal Performance Notebook 3.2** on page 3–6. It will help you create major targets in your life or long-term goals. From these goals, you can write midterm goals (two to five years), short-term goals (one year), and then immediate goals.

Setting Priorities

There is always time for what is most important. You want to make certain that your days are not just a treadmill of activities, crises, and endless tasks but that you focus on what is important as well as what is urgent. Review your goals and jot down your

Personal Performance Notebook 3.1

Time Log

Fill in this time log to chart and plan your activities throughout the day. Under "Notes," identify activities as maintenance, committed, or discretionary.

Time	Activity	Notes	My Energy Level (High or Low)
6:00–7:00			
7:00–8:00			
8:00–9:00			
9:00–10:00			
10:00–11:00			
11:00–12:00			
12:00–1:00			
1:00–2:00			
2:00–3:00			
3:00–4:00			
4:00–5:00			
5:00–6:00			
6:00–7:00			
7:00–8:00			
8:00–9:00			
9:00–10:00			
10:00–11:00			

Use
TM 3.4 First Weeks of College

Class Discussion
Ask students:
1. Do you have a weekly schedule you keep with you?
2. List the type of information this schedule should include.

Hands-On Application
Have students review their schedules and establish priorities to rearrange their weekly schedules. Review in small groups.

Class Discussion
Discuss students' time logs. Were they surprised at the amount of time spent in certain areas or on certain activities?

Use
TM 3.5 Assessing Your Time Log.

top priorities. If you are in the first month of classes, make certain you are completing items that are a top priority.

THE FIRST WEEKS OF COLLEGE

1. Register and pay fees on time.
2. Buy books and supplies and obtain an ID card.
3. Make an appointment with your advisor to review requirements.

How Much Time Do You Spend?

Fill in the following chart to determine how much time you spend on certain activities. Use the information you compiled in **Personal Performance Notebook 3.1.** Typical activities are listed. You may, of course, change or add activities to the list. Remember, the total number of hours should be 24.

Activity	Time Spent	Activity	Time Spent
Attending class		Eating	
Working		Sleeping	
Commuting		Cooking	
Studying		Shopping	
Attending meetings		Running errands	
Grooming		Socializing	
Exercising		Doing hobbies	
Doing household chores		Talking on the telephone	
Waiting in line		Watching television	
Other		**Total time**	

Teaching Tip

1. Illustrate how attending to details now can save students time later. Ask for examples of things they can do. Sample answers include: Add a class early; see an advisor before adding classes; pay fees on time.

2. Emphasize planning. Remind students that writing down their instructor's phone number, e-mail address, and fax number can save time later. Ask students why. Sample answer is: A student may be stuck out of town and can fax in a paper.

4. Check deadlines for adding and dropping courses. Never just stop attending class.

5. Keep a syllabus in your notebook and review expectations often.

6. Make a project board with deadlines. Start projects immediately.

7. Keep up with reading and assignments. Preview chapters before class.

8. Make an appointment with each of your instructors.

9. Get help immediately. Don't wait until you're in trouble.

10. Form a study team or get a study partner for each class.

11. Go to all your classes on time and sit in the front if possible.

12. Get organized. Keep a file for receipts, grades, and important papers.

13. Keep a daily to-do list.

Setting priorities helps you focus on immediate goals. These essential, small steps lead you to your big goals. Thus, it's important to have a realistic picture of what your goals are and to observe and reflect constantly on how your daily activities are leading to larger goals. Complete **Personal Performance Notebook 3.3** to map out your goals. Then, in Chapter 14, return to these goals when you are completing your Career Development Portfolio.

Looking Ahead

Complete this activity and save it in your Career Development Portfolio. Use additional paper if necessary or save it on the computer.

A. Mission Statement

1. Think of what you value most in life; then list those things:*

   _____

2. What is your life's purpose?

   _____

3. What legacy do you want to leave?

   _____

B. Long-Term Goals

Brainstorm all the goals that you want to accomplish during your lifetime. You should include goals for all areas of your life, such as education, career, travel, financial security, relationships, spiritual life, community, and personal growth. This list will be long, and you will want to add to it and revise it every year if goals change. Following are a few incomplete statements that might help you as you brainstorm:

1. My dreams include _____ .
2. I most want to accomplish _____ .
3. The places I most want to visit are _____ .
4. One thing I've always wanted to do is _____ .

C. Midterm Goals

Brainstorm the goals you want to accomplish in the next five years. Following are some examples:

1. I will complete my degree.
2. I will graduate with honors.
3. I will buy a new sports car.
4. I will take a trip to Europe.

D. Short-Term Goals

List goals that you want to accomplish in the next year. Consider your answers to these questions:

1. What is the major goal for which I am striving this year?
2. How does this goal relate to my life's mission or purpose?
3. Is this goal in conflict with any other goal?
4. What hurdles must I overcome to reach my goal?
5. What resources, help, and support will I need to overcome these hurdles?
6. What specific actions are necessary to complete my goal?
7. What will be my reward for achieving this goal?

E. Semester Goals

List goals you want to accomplish this semester—for example,

1. I will preview chapters for 10 minutes before each lecture.
2. I will go to all of my classes on time.
3. I will jog for 30 minutes each day.

Class Discussion

Ask students how time management is related to values. Ask if they spend time every day on what they value or consider important in life.

Hands-On Application

Have students keep a journal entry of the following questions and update it often:
- What do I want to be?
- What do I want to do?
- What do I want to have?
- What do I want to become?
- What do I want to leave behind as my legacy?

Use the following 10 strategies to improve your time-management skills and to help you achieve your goals in a balanced and effective way.

1. **Write a daily to-do list.** Use a daily planner to schedule classes, work, priorities, and due dates. Devote a section to your goals and objectives; devote another section to writing a to-do list. Include shopping, paying bills, making photocopies, cleaning, attending a meeting, seeing an instructor, returning books to the library, and so on. Put the number "1" next to the item with the highest priority. Assign numbers to the rest of the items, with the highest number going to the least important item.

   Some people like to write a to-do list for the next day, taking some time at the end of a day to review briefly what they want to focus on for the next day. Others like to write their list in the morning at breakfast or when they first get to school or work.

   Once you have written your list, get going! Begin your day with the first item on your list. Don't do the least important items until the most important ones are done. Check off each item as you complete it. When you see all the items checked off, you'll be inspired. It's OK if you don't get to everything on your list. If there are tasks left over, add them to your next to-do list. Do first things first. Ask yourself, "What is the best use of my time right now?" The "To-Do List" (**Worksheet 3.2**) at the end of this chapter may be helpful.

2. **Make a project board.** Refer to **Figure 3.2.** During the first week of class, mark down deadlines for each assignment, paper, project, and test you must complete for that semester. Set daily and weekly goals for meeting these deadlines. Put your class schedule in your planner and make a copy for your study space. Include your classes, labs, work hours, and sports or club commitments. Once you have recorded your committed time, add in study time and other daily activities, such as exercising and commuting. Make certain you build in time for family. If you have children, plan special events that you can all look forward to. Bear in mind that the schedule should be flexible; you will want to allow for free time and unexpected events. Follow this schedule for two weeks and see how accurate it is. For each major project, use a project board. Working your way backward from the due date will indicate the daily and weekly goals necessary for completing the project. Make certain you allow extra time for proofreading and possible computer problems.

3. **Do the tough tasks first.** Your energy level will be high, and you will feel a sense of accomplishment as you tackle your tough tasks first. Start out with your most difficult subjects, while you're fresh and alert. For instance, if you are avoiding your statistics homework because it is difficult, get up early and do it before your classes begin. Start projects when they're assigned. Work first and then play. Using a weekly activity schedule might prove helpful.

4. **Break projects down into smaller tasks.** Begin by seeing the whole project or each chapter as part of a larger system. Then break it into manageable chunks. You may get discouraged if you face a large task, whether it's writing a major term paper or reading several chapters. Getting started is half the battle. Spend

Figure 3.2   Sample Project Board

Project: Term Paper for Business Class 110

Today's Date: January 23, 2005   Due Date: April 23, 2005

Key Activities	Date Completed
Paper finished and turned in	April 23
Type final draft and proof.	April 15
Proof second draft; revise.	April 10
Do additional research and spell-check.	April 5
First draft	March 27
Detailed outline	March 15
Detailed library research	March 10
Library research	March 5
General outline	February 22
Initial library research	February 8
Mind map outline	February 4
Finalize topic.	January 28
Explore topics.	January 23

Sample Project Board   Making a project board is one good time-management strategy. *What is the advantage of working your way backward from the due date of a major project?*

Use
TM 3.7 Project Board.

Hands-On Application
Have students take a paper, speech, or project that is assigned and create a schedule on the project board. Discuss in small groups.

Teaching Tip
Emphasize the importance of scheduling several days or a week to review a draft. The best tip for students is to remind them to see their instructor after they have written a draft and clarify expectations and ask for suggestions.

Class Discussion
Emphasize **consolidation**. Ask students how they might consolidate tasks. Sample answers include: Socialize while jogging with a friend or have lunch with a friend.

just 15 minutes before you go to bed outlining your chapter for the next day or mind mapping the main ideas for your term paper. If your paper is due on a certain date, plan all the steps necessary prior to that date. Write a summary after each section and at the end of each chapter. You will find inspiration in completing smaller tasks, and you will feel more in control.

5. **Consolidate similar tasks.** If you group similar tasks, you can maximize your efforts. For example, if you need to make several calls, make them all at a specific time and reduce interruptions. Set aside a block of time to shop, pay bills, go to the post office, and run errands. Write a list of questions for your advisor, instructor, or study team. Make certain you know expectations, so you don't have to repeat tasks. Save your energy and use your resources by planning and combining similar activities, such as taking a walk with a friend, thus combining exercise with socializing.

6. **Study at your high-energy time.** Know your body rhythms and study your hardest subjects during your high-energy time. Review the time log to determine the time of day when you have the most energy. See **Personal Performance Notebook 3.4** on page 3–10. Guard against interruptions and don't do mindless tasks or socialize during your peak energy period. For example, if your peak time is in the morning, don't waste time by answering

Your Daily Energy Levels

Take a more detailed look at your daily energy levels, so you can become more aware of your patterns. Keep track of them every day for a week or more and answer the following questions.

Key Teaching Concept
It's not how long you work; it's the energy level and focus you bring to a task.

Hands-On Application
Have students record their energy levels to determine their high-energy time.

Class Discussion
Review students' energy logs. Ask them if they complete priority items during their high-energy times. Do they study during the day?

Energy Level	7:00 A.M.	Noon	10:00 P.M.
100 percent			
80 percent			
50 percent			
25 percent			

1. What tasks do you want to focus on during your high-energy time?

_____

2. What can you do to increase your energy at your low-energy time?

_____

Key Teaching Concept
Use small chunks of time to review note cards and study.

Teaching Tip
Emphasize organization. Encourage students to write down important phone numbers and keep a copy of them posted in their study area.

Class Discussion
Ask students what they can do the night before to make their mornings less stressful.

Use
TM 3.8 Daily Energy Levels.

mail, socializing, cleaning, checking out books at the library, or doing other routine work. Use your high-energy time to do serious studying and work that requires thinking, writing, and completing projects. Use your low-energy time to do mindless physical work, chores, or easy reading or previewing of chapters.

7. **Study everywhere and anywhere.** Of course, it is important to have a regular study space, but be prepared to study everywhere and anywhere. Carry note cards with you to review formulas, dates, definitions, facts, and important data. Bring class notes or a book with you and study while waiting. Be prepared for the idle time that is part of every day. Review during the 5 or 10 minutes of waiting between classes, for the bus, in line at the grocery store, or for appointments. Tape important material and lectures, and play these tapes while commuting, exercising, dressing, walking, or waiting for class to begin. Avoid crowded times in the library and computer labs. Even if you plan well, you will occasionally get stuck in lines, but you can make the most of this time.

8. **Study in short segments throughout the day.** Studying in short segments is much more effective than studying in marathon sessions. Your brain is much more receptive to recall when you review in short sessions at various times.

9. **Get organized.** Manage your time by consistently creating good habits. Lay out your clothes and pack your lunch the night before, put your keys on the same hook, put your backpack by the door, put your mail and assignments in the

same space, and keep records of bills, grades, and so on in your file. Think of the time that you waste looking for items. Getting organized saves time and reduces stress.

10. **Be flexible, patient, and persistent.** Don't try to make too many changes at once and don't get discouraged if a strategy doesn't work for you. You are striving for excellence, not perfection. Change certain aspects until a strategy fits your style. Be flexible. If it works, do it. If not, try something new. Just make sure you've given yourself at least 30 days to develop new habits. It often feels strange and uncomfortable to do any new task or vary your schedule of daily events. For example, you might discover that you have a habit of getting a donut and coffee every morning and spending an hour or so socializing with friends before your morning classes. You might try changing this habit by doing it only once a week.

TIME-MANAGEMENT AND LEARNING STYLE

Many time-management strategies are designed for people with left-brain dominance. Left-brain-dominant people tend to be convergent thinkers because they are good at looking at several unrelated items and bringing order to them. Right-brain-dominant people are usually divergent thinkers because they branch out from one idea to many. They are good at brainstorming because one idea leads to another. They are able to focus on the whole picture. However, they can also learn to break the global view of the whole project into steps; break each of these steps into activities; and schedule and organize activities around the big goal. It is very important for right-brain-dominant people to focus their efforts on one or two top-priority items instead of being scattered and distracted by busywork. Imagine putting on blinders when you focus on one step until it is completed.

A creative way to brainstorm, plan, and put your vision into action is to use a mind map (see Chapter 4, pages 4–10 to 4–12) and integrate learning styles. Use visual cues and yellow sticky notes. When you think of an activity that will help you meet your goal, write it down. Visualize yourself completing the project. Use auditory cues by dictating ideas and planning your project on tape. Talk about the great feeling you will have when you complete this project. Make your project physical by adapting a hands-on approach and working with others to complete your project. Ask yourself, "Is there a way to simplify this task?" Planning is important, even if you are a creative person. **Peak Progress 3.1** explores the process of learning to take control of your time.

The Management Process

The management process is a key business concept. Well-run organizations use the management process to ensure efficiency. Effective managers use planning, organizing, staffing, delegating, directing and motivating, and evaluating to meet the organization's goals. You can apply the same principles to your education and job.

Class Discussion
How does this competency create college and job success? Applying SCANS:
Managing time.

Teaching Tip
1. Learning Style Application. Stress the importance of working in alignment with one's learning style. Ask students what strategies might work for creative, right-brain people. Use a mind map to illustrate one technique that works.
2. Illustrate the importance of planning by asking if students would fly with a pilot who did not plan a flight schedule.

Words to Succeed

"Nothing is so fatiguing as the eternal hanging of an uncompleted task."

—WILLIAM JAMES
psychologist

Class Discussion
1. Emphasize critical thinking. Have students discuss the time that can be spent on doing something that someone else could do, on procrastination, or on trying to be a perfectionist. (see p. 3–32)
2. Discuss these sample situations:
 • A roommate who is responsible for getting a roommate up for classes.
 • A coworker who whines and complains all day.
 • A friend who wants to talk when you have research to do.
 • A study team member who procrastinates on a large portion of the project.
3. Discuss with students possible solutions to these situations.
4. Have students write down all their time wasters and discuss in small groups.

Peak Progress 3.1

Applying the Adult Learning Cycle to Taking Control of Your Time and Life

When you read the Visualization box on the first page of this chapter, you may have recognized the same feelings of frustration. It could be because you've lost your keys, you may have three papers due, or you are overwhelmed with school, work, and family and don't feel as if you are doing justice to any one area of your life. Applying the learning cycle will help you establish goals and create a plan to meet them.

1. **RELATE. Why do I want to learn this?** Planning my time better and getting organized are essential for me to juggle the demands of school, work, and life. What are the areas where I need the most work?

2. **OBSERVE. How does this work?** I can learn a lot about time management by observing people who are on time, get their work done, work calmly and steadily, and seem to accomplish a lot in a short time. I'll also observe people who are unorganized, often late, miss classes, and waste a lot of time blaming, complaining, and being overly involved in other people's lives. Do their problems relate to time management and self-management? How do I manage my time?

3. **THINK. What does this mean?** What strategies are working for me? What are some new strategies I can try out? I will explore creative ways to solve problems rather than feeling overwhelmed.

4. **DO. What can I do with this?** Practice the ABCDE method for making changes and creating positive habits. Each day, I'll work on one area. For example, I'll choose one place to hang my keys and consistently put them there. If I find them in my purse or on the table, I'll put them on the hook until it becomes a habit.

5. **TEACH. Whom can I share this with?** I'll share my tips and experiences with others and find out their strategies in return. I should continue to reward myself, at least mentally, for making positive changes.

Now, return to Stage 1 and think about how it feels to learn this valuable new skill of managing your time and priorities.

PLANNING

Specify your goals and visualize the results you want to achieve. Break these large goals into semester goals and weekly and daily priorities. Keep these posted by your study area. Detail the steps you must take to meet your goals. Be prepared for frustrating barriers and setbacks and deal with them calmly. Planning involves knowing how the system works and finding the resources and information you need. For example, attending college includes seeing your advisor, attending orientation, registering, waiting in lines to pay fees, finding classrooms and parking spaces, getting a library card, obtaining an ID card, and so on. This is part of the process. Don't be tempted to take shortcuts or let the little irritations discourage or distract you from your goals.

ORGANIZING

Organize your office, study area, and activities in order to achieve your goals. Post charts of major projects, due dates, and class schedules. A project board is very important for keeping you on track. Use a detailed calendar and create action steps for your goals. Don't forget to follow through on details.

STAFFING

Use the resources available to help you succeed. Your study-team members, coworkers, advisors, instructors, and tutors are part of your success team. Know how to reach at least two students in each of your classes. You can take notes for each other in an emergency, share information, ask questions, and study together. Your instructors are key staff in your school career. If you have a choice, pick the best instructors and build supportive relationships with them. Know their names and expectations, take an active part in class discussions, and get to know them as people. Become familiar with support services for students.

DELEGATING

Every executive knows the importance of delegating tasks to subordinates and coworkers. You can also learn to delegate by assigning certain housekeeping tasks to roommates or family members and by dividing the workload equally for your study team. If you have children, make certain everyone does his or her share. Delegate whatever you can and build independence, skills, and competencies in others.

DIRECTING AND MOTIVATING

Use positive reinforcement to motivate yourself. Keep a list of all the ways you can reward yourself. Take frequent short breaks for walks or exercise. Keep a list of your goals on your desk. Reward yourself and others. Treat yourself to a night out once a week for pizza and a movie. When you are with family or friends, enjoy them totally. Reward yourself after each project and study task. For example, take a few minutes to enjoy time with your children, spouse, or a friend after you complete a study goal.

EVALUATING

Monitor your attitude, behavior, and expectations, as well as the results you are creating. Detach yourself and, in a nonjudgmental way, measure your results. Be honest and don't allow excuses or blame to distract you from finding solutions to achieve the results you want. Use creative thinking to overcome barriers.

Managing College and Career Like a Pro

The same qualities that get you hired and promoted can also help you in school. Your instructor will be just as impressed as your boss with good communication skills, thorough preparation, good manners, and adherence to commitments. Approach your education as if it were a major career move, because it is! Try the following eight strategies to plan your education like a professional.

1. **Plan your course of study.** First, sit down with your school catalog and scan it to review majors, fields of study, resources available, and school requirements. After you have done some planning on your own and have made a tentative schedule, make an appointment to talk with your advisor, dean, or department head. Make certain that you have taken the necessary requirements, such as math and English placement tests, and the background courses for certain classes.

2. **Research the best instructors in the subject.** By talking with several students who have had the course, other instructors, your advisor, and staff members, you'll get a good idea of who the best instructors are.

3. **Register on time.** You will have a much better chance of getting the classes you need if you register on time.

4. **Be persistent.** If a class you want is closed, go to the first class meeting. Students often drop out and space becomes available. Some instructors will let students in if they show they are committed and interested.

5. **Go to summer school.** You may want to attend summer school for difficult courses or popular courses that are usually full, or to get a few units out of the way, so you can get through the program sooner or take a lighter load during the year.

6. **Audit classes.** If a course is difficult, consider auditing it. You can gain a good background and become familiar with the tests, assignments, and requirements. Then, you will have a much better chance of getting a good grade when you take it for credit.

7. **Get organized.** Planning your education requires time and organization. Keep an academic file for planning each term. Keep a record of tests, reports, projects, grades, transcripts, and so on. If you need to negotiate a grade, you will have the background information. Invest in equipment such as a computer. Videotape your speeches; use a calendar, note cards, and an erasable pen; and market yourself as you would in your career. Write out your short- and long-term goals. Set daily priorities. Plan your work, and work your plan.

8. **Evaluate your performance regularly.** Just as career professionals monitor their performance, you, too, can use feedback from tests and papers to gauge how you are doing in school. You don't need to wait for formal evaluations. See your instructor throughout the term and ask for feedback, suggestions, and ideas for improvement.

Assessment and Reflection

Having a purpose and clearly defined goals gives wings to your dreams. Self-assess often. Your awareness of where your time goes becomes a continual habit of assessing, planning, and choosing tasks in the order of their importance, and this leads to

Peak Progress 3.2

Investing Your Time in High-Priority Items: The 80/20 Rule

According to the 80/20 rule of time management, people tend to spend 80 percent of their time on activities that produce only 20 percent of the results they want.

Taking a look at your time wasters may reveal that you are spending too much time on low-priority activities and shortchanging your top priorities. Wasting time on low-priority activities is unproductive and a major reason for not accomplishing major tasks. Other ways to look at it include

1. Eighty percent of your time is spent on 20 percent of your activities.
2. Eighty percent of the clothes you wear come from 20 percent of your favorite wardrobe.
3. Eighty percent of the interruptions come from 20 percent of the people.
4. Eighty percent of the profits come from 20 percent of the sales.
5. Eighty percent of your phone calls come from 20 percent of the people you know.
6. Twenty percent more effort can result in an 80 percent better paper or speech.

Sometimes, to increase results by 20 percent, you must exert 80 percent more activity. Other times, increasing your effort by just 20 percent results in a dramatic 80 percent improvement. For instance, you may spend just 20 percent more effort polishing a speech, and it produces an 80 percent improvement. Can you think of other examples?

success. Ask yourself the following questions: Do I have a sense of purpose and direction? Are my goals clearly defined? Are any in conflict with each other? Are they flexible enough to be modified as needed? Do I forget to write priorities and phone numbers in my planner? Do I daydream too much and have a problem with concentration? Do I invest time in high priority tasks? Do I attend to small details that pay off in a big way? See **Peak Progress 3.2** to see if the 80/20 rule applies to you.

Overcoming Procrastination

Procrastination is a barrier to time management. Some people prefer to do the things they like to do, rather than doing what should be done. To avoid procrastination, try the following five techniques.

1. **Set daily priorities.** Begin by becoming clear on your goals and the results you want to achieve.
2. **Break the project into small tasks.** A large project can seem overwhelming. Do something each day that brings you closer to your goal.
3. **Assess the payoffs for procrastination.** Do you feel important when you are late for class, meetings, or work? Do you get sympathy when you tell friends

Delay or Procrastination?

Use critical thinking skills to answer the following questions.

1. What are you doing that doesn't have to be done or could be delayed?

   _____

   _____

2. What are you doing that could be done by someone else?

   _____

   _____

3. How can you get control of your time and life?

   _____

   _____

4. What are you doing during your peak productivity time?

   _____

   _____

that you are overloaded? Do you feel as if people won't ask again if you don't say yes to requests? Do you add drama to your life when you are rushed? Complete **Personal Performance Notebook 3.5.**

4. **Develop a positive attitude.** Attitude is everything. When you are positive and focused, you can accomplish a lot in a short time. Negative emotions are time wasters. Anger, jealousy, worry, and resentment can eat up hours of time and sap your energy. Instead, resolve to have a positive attitude.

5. **Work during your high-energy time.** Do what is important first and while you are at your peak energy level.

PEAK TIP

Invest your time on items that produce the results you want.

Controlling Interruptions

The second biggest barrier to time management is interruption. Interruptions steal your time. They cause you to stop projects, and they disrupt your thought pattern, divert your attention, and make it difficult to build momentum again. To avoid wasting time, take control. Don't let endless activities, the telephone, and other people control you. Set everyday priorities that will help you meet your goals and reduce interruptions. You may find that you spend a lot of time on the phone. Use the phone for convenience, to save time, or as a reward for accomplishing a task, but don't allow it to become an interruption. For instance, if your friend calls, set a timer for 10 minutes or postpone the call until later in the day, after you have previewed an assigned chapter or outlined a speech. Set the answering machine if you are studying, or tell the caller that you will call back in an hour. When you return a call, chat for 5 or 10 minutes instead of 45 minutes. Combine socializing with exercising or eating lunch or dinner. If you watch a favorite program, turn the set off right after that show. The essence of time management is taking charge of your life and not allowing interruptions to control you. Complete **Peak Performance Notebook 3.6** to determine the sources of your interruptions and time wasters.

Teaching Tip
Bring in a "Do Not Disturb" sign to illustrate one tip for creating quiet time. Ask students for other suggestions.

STRATEGIES FOR CONTROLLING INTERRUPTIONS

Peak performers know how to live and work with other people and manage interruptions. Try these six tips to help you reduce interruptions:

1. **Create an organized place to study.** A supportive, organized study space can help you reduce interruptions and keep you focused. Have all your study tools—a dictionary, pencils, pens, books, papers, files, notes, a calendar, a semester schedule, and study-team and instructor names and phone numbers—in one place, so you won't waste time looking for the items you need. Keep only one project on your desk at one time and file everything else away or put it on a shelf. You can increase your learning by studying in the same space and by conditioning your brain for serious studying and attention. If you have children, include a study area for them, close to yours, where they can work quietly with puzzles, crayons, or paint. This will allow study time together and create a lifelong study pattern for them.

2. **Create a good time to study.** You will find that, when you are focused, you can study anywhere, any time. However, to increase your effectiveness, do your serious studying when your energy level is at its peak. Guard against interruptions and use this time for serious studying.

3. **Create quiet time.** Discuss study needs and expectations with your roommates or family and ask for an agreement. You might establish certain study hours or agree on a signal to let each other know when you need quiet time, such as closing your door or hanging a quiet sign. Make certain that you balance study time with breaks to eat and socialize with your roommates or family.

4. **Study in the library.** If it is difficult to study at home or in the dorm, study in the library. Many students go to the library for quiet time. Once you enter, your brain can turn to a serious study mode. Sitting in a quiet place and facing the wall can reduce interruptions and distractions. You will find that you can accomplish far more in less time, and then you can enjoy your friends and family.

5. **Do first things first.** You will feel more in control if you have a list of priorities you work through every day. Having a clear purpose of what you want and need to do makes it easier to say no to distractions. Make certain that these important goals include your health. Taking time to exercise, eat right, and relax will not only save time but will also help increase your energy and focus.

PEAK TIP

To avoid wasting time surfing the Internet or playing video games, have a specific task to complete when using your computer.

Interruptions!

1. List all the interruptions you experience and their origins. Try to keep a log of interruptions for a few days. Be aware of internally caused interruptions, such as procrastination, daydreaming, worry, negative thoughts, anger, and lack of concentration.

Interruptions	Frequency	Possible Solutions
Visitors		
Friends		
Family		
Telephone		
Daydreaming		
Lack of purpose		
Other		

2. Make a list of your most common time wasters. Some common time wasters are

- Socializing
- Doing what you like to do first
- Watching television
- Procrastinating
- Not setting goals and priorities
- Not keeping a calendar
- Not writing down deadlines

- Losing things and not organizing
- Failing to plan
- Having a negative attitude
- Complaining and whining
- Being overly involved with other people's problems

My common time wasters are

_____

_____

_____

_____

_____

_____

_____

_____

6. **Just say no.** Tell your roommate or family when you have an important test or project due. If someone wants to talk or socialize when you need to study, say no. Set aside time each day to spend with your family or roommates, such as dinner, a walk, or a movie. They will understand your priorities when you include them in your plans. The key is balance and communication.

Class Discussion
Have students practice saying no. Give a few examples of how difficult it is for you to say no to invitations to join committees, requests for help, community demands, etc. Ask students why many of us have difficulty saying no even when we don't want to do something.

Juggling Family, School, and Job

Anyone who lives with children knows how much time and energy they require. Having a family involves endless physical demands, including cleaning, cooking, chauffeuring to activities, helping with homework, and nonstop picking up. Children get sick, need attention, and just want you there sometimes for them. Focus on the big picture as you look at these 10 ways to juggle your many roles:

1. **Be flexible.** There are only certain kinds of studying that you can realistically expect to do around children and other kinds of studying that are hopeless to even attempt. If you expect to be interrupted a lot, use this to your advantage. Carry flash cards to use as you cook dinner or while supervising children's homework or playtime. Quiz yourself, preview chapters, skim summaries, review definitions, do a set number of problems, brainstorm ideas for a paper, outline a speech, review equations, sketch a drawing, or explain a chapter out loud. Save the work that requires deeper concentration for time alone.

2. **Communicate expectations.** Children as young as three or four years old can understand that you need quiet time. Make certain that they have lots of quiet activities to keep them busy when you are working. Small children can color, play with clay, or do puzzles when you are working on other projects. After quiet time, you can take a walk, read, or cook dinner together. Clear communication and expectations can save you time at home, school, and work.

3. **Increase your energy.** Find ways to revitalize yourself. Put time into keeping yourself healthy. Exercise, dance, get enough sleep and rest, and eat healthy foods.

4. **Find good day care.** This is essential for school and job success. Line up at least two backup sources of day care. Explore public and private day-care centers, preschools, family day-care homes, parent cooperatives, baby-sitting pools, other family members, and nannies. Explore renting a room in the basement or attic of your house to a child-care provider. Part of the rent can be paid with child care and light housecleaning. Trade off times with other parents.

5. **Create positive time.** Don't buy your children toys to replace spending time with them. They don't need expensive toys or elaborate outings. You can enjoy each other as you study, garden, shop, do household chores, eat, take walks, read, play games, or watch a favorite television show. The activity is secondary to your uninterrupted presence. Spend time at bedtime sharing your day,

Hands-On Application
Role playing: Have one student in every group play a student who works part-time and attends school full-time. Have another student play a boss who wants to increase the agreed upon 15 hours of work to 30+ hours. Discuss assertive responses that would focus on the original agreement but also allow for a good working relationship.

Hands-On Application
Have nontraditional students discuss how they juggle job, family, school, and other demands. Include at least one nontraditional or working student in each group. Have students explore strategies for creating balance.

talking about dreams, reading a story, and expressing your love and appreciation to them. Make this a positive time and avoid quarrels or harsh words. They will remember and cherish this warm and special time forever, and so will you.

6. **Model successful behavior.** Returning to school is an act that sends an important message. You are saying that learning, growing, and being able to juggle family, a job, and school are possible, worthwhile, and rewarding. It is important for children to see their parents setting personal and professional goals while knowing that the family is the center of their lives. You are providing a model by demonstrating the importance of education, setting goals and achieving them, and creating balance.

7. **Delegate and develop.** Clarify expectations with your children, so that everyone contributes to the family. Even young children can learn to be team members and important contributors to making the family unit work. Preschool children can help put away toys, fold napkins, set the table, and feel part of the team. Preteens can be responsible for cooking a simple meal one night a week and for doing their own laundry. When your children go to college, they will know how to cook, clean, do laundry, get up on time in the morning, and take responsibility for their lives. An important goal of being a good parent is to raise independent, capable, competent, responsible adults.

8. **Create a support system.** A support system is essential for survival. Check out resources on campus through the reentry center. Set up study teams for all your classes. Make friends with other people who have children.

9. **Get organized.** The night before, take your shower; lay out your clothes; pack lunch; organize homework in your backpack; and check for keys, books, any signed notes, and supplies. Good organization means good time management and reduces your stress level.

10. **Balance your life.** Make certain that you take time each day to do at least one thing you like to do. Take time to relax, exercise, meditate, walk, and read for pleasure. Remind yourself that you are blessed with a full and rewarding life.

THE RETURNING STUDENT

The college classroom and workplace are changing. According to the National Center for Education Statistics, more than 40 percent of college students are over 25 years old. Reentry students are the fastest growing group of college students. Since many reentry students have families and jobs, child care, flexible schedules, relevant classes, and financial aid are all important issues. Many colleges allow people over 60 to take courses for a nominal fee. Older students bring a wealth of experience, practical application, and different viewpoints to the classroom.

The early baby boomers are now past 50, and this large group is changing the nature of the workplace. Many adults change jobs or careers, start working after raising a family, or do volunteer work. Older adults also bring a wealth of experience and a different perspective to the workplace. Many of these older workers are returning to school, especially to learn computer skills.

The following are a few tips for reentry students. Think about how these tips can be applied to the workplace.

1. **Observe, read, and notice procedures, deadlines, resources, and policies.** Read the catalog and schedule of classes.

2. **Explore campus resources.** If your school has a reentry center, go there and sign up for tutoring services, check out campus care, and explore the career center.

3. **Explore community and family resources.** Create a support system of people who can help. Have backup child care and transportation.

4. **Develop an organized record-keeping system.** Keep all your grades, transcripts, and other paperwork in one place.

5. **Join study groups.** This really works. You will be more effective when you learn to use the talents and skills of others.

6. **Integrate all learning styles.** Create experiences, write, reflect, observe, listen, read, summarize, teach, demonstrate, and do.

7. **Find a mentor.** Build relationships with your advisors and instructors (or bosses and coworkers).

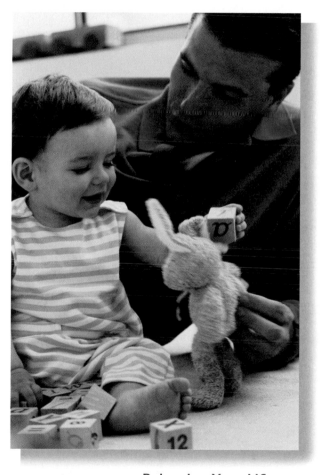

Balancing Your Life
Balancing your personal and family lives with your work sometimes requires making trade-offs to have a more fulfilling life. *What can you do to create a more balanced life?*

BALANCING YOUR LIFE

Take time to reflect on all areas of your life and the time you are presently investing in them. Decide if you are investing too much or too little time in each area. Also, look at the roles you play in each area of your life. In the family area, you may play the role of wife, mother, daughter, and so on. In the work area, you may be a manager, a part-time worker, or an assistant.

Your Life Area Goals

Several life areas are listed on this chart. Write one goal you have for each major area. Explain how you can commit a certain amount of time to meeting that goal and still maintain overall balance.

Use
TM 3.9 Life Areas.

Hands-On Application
Have students write goals for each area of their lives. Ask: What are the major barriers to reaching these goals? Discuss balancing their lives. Ask students to list strategies for overcoming each barrier. Discuss in small groups.

Hands-On Application
Tell students:
1. Review your semester goals.
2. List lifetime goals as well as immediate goals. Sample answers include health, family, career, monetary.
3. Explore ways of creating positive habits out of important lifetime goals. Sample answer is: "I will jog with a friend for exercise at least three times a week."
4. List other priorities and goals for the first weeks of college. Add to the list.

Life Areas	Goals
1. Career (job, earning a living)	_____
2. Education	_____
3. Spirituality (your inner being, peace of mind)	_____
4. Relationships (your family, friends, associates)	_____
5. Health (weight, exercise, food, stress, personal care)	_____
6. Recreation (hobbies, sports, interests)	_____
7. Finance	_____
8. Home	_____
9. Community involvement and service	_____
10. Personal growth and renewal	_____
11. Other	_____

Accompanying each role in your life are certain goals. Some goals demand greater time than others. It is OK to make a trade-off for a specific goal, but realize that you may neglect a vital area of your life. For instance, you may have a big term paper due, so you trade off a family outing to accomplish this goal. Complete **Personal Performance Notebook 3.7** to determine how you can achieve balance.

CAREER IN FOCUS

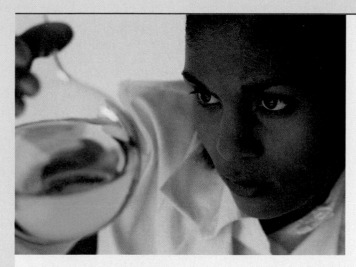

Deborah Page

FOOD SCIENTIST

Related Majors: Agricultural Science, Chemistry, Microbiology, Nutrition

Focus on Tasks, Not Time

Deborah Page is a food scientist for a large company in the food-processing industry. Her job is to develop new food products and ways to preserve or store foods. To do this, she engages in research and conducts tests and experiments, keeping in mind consumer demand for safety and convenience. Occasionally, she analyzes foods to determine levels of sugar, protein, vitamins, or fat.

Because her job is task-oriented, Deborah has a great deal of freedom in structuring her day. Her company allows flexible scheduling, so Deborah arrives at work at 9:30 A.M., after her children have left for school. Deborah is able to work until 6:30 P.M., because her children are involved in after-school activities and because her husband can pick them up by 5 P.M.

Deborah finds that she does her best work in late mornings and early afternoons. She plans research and testing during those times. She schedules most calls during the first hour at work, and she uses the latter part of her day to organize tasks for the next day. Good prior planning helps her manage her time well and focus on her tasks at hand.

Deborah's job includes a fair amount of reading, and she sometimes takes work home with her for the evening. That way, she can often leave work early to take her children to an appointment or to attend one of their sports activities. Giving attention to her family and personal interests helps Deborah create a balanced life.

CRITICAL THINKING

Why is it important for Deborah to organize her time wisely? What are some of the prioritization strategies she uses daily to manage her time? What are some strategies to help her balance her personal and career commitments with a healthy, fulfilling lifestyle? Explore ways for Deborah to find time for herself for personal renewal.

N. Scott Momaday

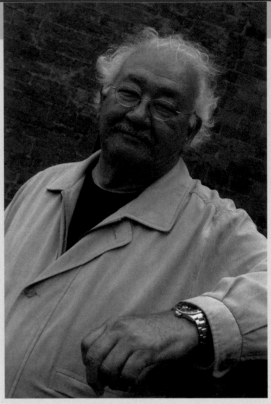

N. Scott Momaday has claimed many titles—dean of Native American authors, Pulitzer Prize winner, scholar, and Kiowa Indian.

Though born during the Great Depression, in Oklahoma, Momaday grew up in a world rich with tradition. His childhood was spent on the reservations and pueblos of the Apache, Navaho, Pueblo, and Jemez Indians, where his parents taught school. The vast southwestern landscape that Momaday calls the "Indian world" was his playground. It was also his teacher and a colorful source of material for his future career. Horses, cowboy stories, and even comic books fed his imagination. As a boy, what did Momaday want to be when he grew up? A cowboy. "Comes with the territory," he explains.

Fortunately, Momaday followed in the footsteps of his mother and father, after pursuing his education at the University of New Mexico and then Stanford, where he received his doctorate. His mother, a descendent of American pioneers with Cherokee roots, was a writer and teacher. His Kiowa father was an artist and accomplished storyteller in the Kiowa oral tradition. One reviewer described Momaday's style as using the language of his mother to tell "his story in the manner of his father's people." He later developed his innate talent as a painter and printmaker. He settled in Arizona, where he is currently a professor at the University of Arizona.

Through his novels, plays, poems, essays, folktales, artwork, and teaching, Momaday has kept the culture and beliefs of an old world alive and relevant. In his Pulitzer Prize–winning novel, *House Made of Dawn*, the central character, like Momaday, faces the conflicts of straddling both the Indian and the white worlds. Momaday, however, has always known who he is: "I am an Indian and I believe I'm fortunate to have the heritage I have."

PERFORMANCE THINKING   In what ways do you think good time management has enabled Momaday to accomplish his goals?

TAKING CHARGE

In summary, in this chapter, I learned to

- *Assess where my time goes.* Knowing where I am already spending my time is essential for time management. I assess how much time I (1) commit to school, work, and other activities; (2) spend maintaining myself and home; and (3) devote to discretionary time.

- *Determine where my time should go.* I set goals to determine what I want to accomplish. I look at my values and priorities and use them to write a mission statement. I evaluate my dreams as I write my long-term goals. I break down my tasks and goals by short-term (this week, this semester) and long-term (in a year, in five years). I use a daily to-do list to keep me focused on top priorities. I know what I'd like to accomplish, what I should accomplish, and what is urgent and *must be accomplished.*

- *Assess my energy level.* "Doers" are organized and know how to pace themselves. They know when their energy level is high and work on top-priority goals when they are alert and focused. Having a sense of my body rhythms and high-energy time gives me confidence that I can accomplish more in less time.

- *Break down projects.* I look at a large project and then break it into manageable chunks. I make a project board, with deadlines for each assignment, and break down the assignment into realistic steps that I can do each day. I consolidate similar tasks to maximize my efforts.

- *Study everywhere and anywhere.* I make the most of waiting time, commuting time, and time between classes. I know it is more effective to study in short segments throughout the day than to study late at night in a marathon session.

- *Get organized.* I will develop a habit of putting everything in its place and getting organized. I found that spending a few extra minutes spent organizing my space and schedule pay off later.

continued

- *Integrate learning styles.* Visualizing myself completing a project, talking to others about the project, working in groups, working alone, and using hands-on approaches whenever possible help me integrate learning styles. I look at the whole project and break it into steps, focusing on top-priority items and setting deadlines. I observe, plan, think, and do and then evaluate and do again until the project is completed. I model successful behavior and teach others.

- *Be patient and flexible.* I reward myself for making progress and don't expect perfection. I'm flexible when appropriate and know that there is time to do whatever is most important.

- *Apply the principles of the management process.* I invest my time in planning based on my goals, organizing my space and schedule, developing study teams and a support system, delegating tasks when possible, rewarding myself, and monitoring results.

- *Overcome procrastination and interruptions.* By setting daily priorities, breaking large projects into manageable tasks, being positive, creating an organized place to study, and being disciplined, I can accomplish what needs to be done. I've learned to just say no when necessary, and I reward myself when I complete projects and withhold rewards until I do first things first.

- *Take responsibility for my time.* I don't rely on others to be my alarm clock or blame others for not completing my work. I maintain a positive attitude and keep myself motivated. I manage and control my emotions, anger, and negative thoughts. Conflict and negative emotions can eat up a lot of time and energy. When I'm positive and focused, I can accomplish a lot in a short amount of time.

- *Balance my life.* I invest time in exercise and take time to rest and relax. I cannot be effective if I'm not rested and renewed. I take time to enjoy life.

Performance Strategies

Following are the top 10 strategies for time management:

- ◆ Set goals and priorities.
- ◆ Study at the right time and in the right space.
- ◆ Study everywhere and anywhere.
- ◆ Break down projects and consolidate similar tasks.
- ◆ Make a schedule.
- ◆ Say no to interruptions.
- ◆ Get organized.
- ◆ Be flexible.
- ◆ Create balance.
- ◆ Just do it!

Review Questions

1. How does time management help you achieve your goals?
2. Name at least five time-management strategies.
3. How can you apply the management process to meeting your personal goals?
4. What can you do to avoid procrastination?
5. Why is it important to control interruptions?

REVISUALIZATION

Revisit the Visualization box on the first page of this chapter and your journal entry on **Worksheet 3.1**. Now, apply the ABCDE method to approach that situation armed with new strategies you have learned in this chapter.

Let's take the example of the student running late for class:

A = Actual event: "I lost my keys."

B = Beliefs: "I'm so disorganized. What's wrong with me that I always lose things? Maybe I've taken on too much, between school and work."

C = Consequences: "I'm frustrated and angry with myself."

D = Dispute: "I've simply misplaced my keys. It doesn't mean I can't handle my obligations. It just means I need to come up with a strategy to avoid this happening again."

E = Energized: "I feel good that I didn't allow my negative thinking to ruin my day. I can apply simply tips for helping myself get more organized and save time. I will consciously choose to hang up my keys each night on the hook by the back door. Before I go to bed, I'll make certain my keys are hung up, my backpack is packed with my books and to-do list, and my lunch is ready to go."

Do you feel more equipped to manage your frustrated thoughts, so you can focus on goals and priorities that offer you direction and accomplishment? Practice deep breathing with your eyes closed for just one minute. See yourself calm, centered, and at peace. See yourself effortlessly completing all tasks and achieving your goals.

JUGGLING FAMILY AND SCHOOL

In the Classroom

Laura Chen is a returning part-time student. She also works full-time and takes care of her family. Her husband is verbally supportive of her goal to become a dental hygienist but is not very helpful with taking care of the children or with housework. Their children are 12 and 14 and have always depended on Laura to help them with their homework and drive them to their activities. Laura prides herself on being efficient at home, as well as being a loving mother and wife.

1. What can Laura do to get more control over her life?

   _____

   _____

2. What strategies in the chapter would be most helpful to Laura?

   _____

   _____

In the Workplace

Laura is now a dental hygienist. She has always had a busy schedule, but she expected to have more free time after she graduated. Instead, she finds herself being even busier than before. Her children are active in school, and she feels it is important for her to be involved in their activities and schoolwork. Laura is also a member of two community organizations, volunteers at the local hospital, and is active in her church. Lately, she has been late for meetings and has been rushing through her day. Because she knows her health is important, Laura has resumed her regular exercise program. Since graduation, she has had difficulty finding time for herself.

3. What strategies can help Laura gain control over her time and her life?

   _____

   _____

4. What areas of her life does she need to prioritize?

   _____

   _____

APPLYING THE ABCDE METHOD OF SELF-MANAGEMENT

In the Visualization box on page 3–1, you were asked to describe a situation when you were overwhelmed by too much to do and too little time. Describe that event below. What were the consequences?

_____

_____

_____

_____

Now, apply the ABCDE method and visualize a more organized situation:

A = Actual event:

B = Beliefs:

C = Consequences:

D = Dispute:

E = Energized:

While completing this exercise, did you determine ways you can become more organized and efficient?

TO-DO LIST

Use this form to organize your tasks, goals, and objectives for each day. It's OK if you don't get to everything on your list, but work on your top-priority items first.

Urgent	Priorities	To See or Call		

Continuing Attention	Awaiting Developments		
	What	Who	When

TIME MANAGEMENT

Complete the following statements with a Yes or No response.

	Yes	No
1. I do the easiest and most enjoyable task first.	_____	_____
2. I do my top-priority task at the time of day when my energy is the highest and I know I will perform best.	_____	_____
3. I use my time wisely by doing high-return activities—previewing chapters, proofreading papers.	_____	_____
4. Even though I find interruptions distracting, I put up with them.	_____	_____
5. I save trivial and mindless tasks for the time of day when my energy is low.	_____	_____
6. I don't worry too much about making lists. I don't like planning and prefer to be spontaneous and respond as events occur.	_____	_____
7. My work space is organized, and I have only one project on my desk at a time.	_____	_____
8. I set goals and review them each semester and each year.	_____	_____
9. My work space is open and I like to have people wander in and out.	_____	_____
10. My study team socializes first and then we work.	_____	_____
11. I have a lot of wasted waiting time, but you can't study in small blocks of time.	_____	_____
12. I block out a certain amount of time each week for my top-priority and hardest classes.	_____	_____

Scoring

1. Add the number of Yes responses to questions 2, 3, 5, 7, 8, 12.   _____ _____
2. Add the number of No responses to questions 1, 4, 6, 9, 10, 11.   _____ _____
3. Add the two scores together.   _____ _____

The higher the score, the more likely you are to be organized.

CHAPTER 3 ◀ REVIEW AND APPLICATIONS

TIME WASTERS

Getting control of your time and life involves identifying time wasters and determining your peak energy level. It also involves identifying goals, setting priorities, and creating an action plan. Determining what task should be done first and overcoming procrastination are major factors in creating success. All these steps and issues involve critical thinking skills. Use critical thinking to complete the following questions.

1. What are the major activities and tasks that take up much of your time?

_____

_____

2. What activities cause you to waste time?

_____

_____

3. What activities can you eliminate or reduce?

_____

_____

4. When is your high-energy time?

_____

_____

5. When do you study?

_____

_____

6. Look at your committed time. Does this block of time reflect your values and goals?

_____

_____

7. How can you increase your discretionary time?

_____

_____

8. Do you complete top-priority tasks first?

_____

_____

—continued

9. Look at the common reasons and excuses that some students use for not being organized and focused. Add to this list and use creative problem solving to list strategies for overcoming these barriers.

Reasons	Strategies
I ran out of time.	
I overslept.	
I'm easily distracted.	
People interrupt me.	
Instructors put too much pressure on me.	
I feel overwhelmed and panic at deadlines.	
I forgot about an assignment.	
Other	

YOUR DAILY ENERGY LEVELS

Take a detailed look at your daily energy levels, so you can become aware of your patterns. Keep track for a week or more. What tasks do you want to focus on during your high-energy time? Write these tasks on the chart.

Energy Level	7:00 A.M.	Noon	10:00 P.M.
100 percent			
80 percent			
50 percent			
25 percent			

DEMONSTRATING YOUR TIME-MANAGEMENT SKILLS

List all the factors involved in time management. Indicate how you would demonstrate them to employers. Add this page to your Career Development Portfolio.

Areas	Your Demonstration
Dependability	Haven't missed a day of work in my job
Reliability	
Effectiveness	
Efficiency	
Responsibility	
Positive attitude	
Persistence	
Ability to plan and set goals and priorities	
Visionary	
Ability to follow through	
High energy	
Ability to handle stress	
Ability to focus	
Respect for others' time	
Ability to overcome procrastination	
Reputation as a doer and self-starter	

Active Listening and Note Taking

Chapter Objectives

In this chapter, you will learn

▲ Active listening strategies

▲ How to take notes in alignment with your learning style

▲ The various note-taking systems

▲ Effective note-taking strategies

VISUALIZATION

"I am having a problem staying focused and alert in my afternoon class. The instructor speaks in a monotone and I have a hard time following his lecture. What can I do to listen more effectively and take better notes?"

Have you ever had a similar experience? Do you find yourself daydreaming during class? Do you ever leave a class and feel frustrated because you've not been focused and your notes are unreadable? In this chapter, you will learn how to be an active listener and to take clear and organized notes.

JOURNAL ENTRY In **Worksheet 4.1** on page 4–26, describe a time when you had difficulty in making sense out of a lecture and staying alert. Are there certain classes in which it is more challenging for you to be an active listener?

Key Teaching Concept
You must want to listen.

Use
TM 4.1 Success Principle 4.

Teaching Tip
Emphasize the importance of using the ABCDE Method of Self-Management to visualize success and create positive results.

Words to Succeed

"I only wish I could find an institute that teaches people how to listen. After all, a good manager needs to listen as much as he needs to talk. . . . Real communication goes in both directions."

—LEE IACOCCA
former chairman of Chrysler Corporation

Class Discussion
How do these competencies create college and job success? Applying SCANS:
Listening
Designing a note-taking system
Thinking skills
Evaluating skills

Attending lectures or meetings, listening, taking notes, and gathering information are a daily part of school and work. However, few people give much thought to the process of selecting, organizing, and recording information. Active listening and note taking are not just tools for school. They are essential job skills. Throughout your career, you will be processing and recording information. The volume of new information is expanding in this computer age, and the career professional who can listen, organize, and summarize information will be valuable. This chapter addresses the fine points of active listening and note taking.

Listening to the Message

Before you can be an effective note taker, you must become an effective listener. Most people think of themselves as good listeners. However, listening should not be confused with ordinary hearing. Active listening is a decision to be fully attentive and to understand the intent of the speaker. It is a consuming activity that requires physical and mental attention, energy, concentration, and discipline. Not only is listening fundamental to taking good classroom notes, but it also is directly related to how well you do in college and in your career. As a student, you will be expected to listen actively to other student presentations and small-group and class discussions. Active listening is also important for job success. Career professionals attend meetings, follow directions, work with customers, take notes from professional journals and lectures, and give and receive feedback.

ACTIVE LISTENING STRATEGIES

You can apply the following 10 active listening strategies for building effective relationships at school, at work, and in life.

1. **Desire to listen.** The first place to start is with your intention. You must want to be a better listener and realize that listening is an active rather than a passive process. Is your intention to learn and understand the other person? Or is your intention to prove how smart you are and how wrong the other person is? The best listening strategies in the world won't help if you are unwilling to listen.

2. **Be open and willing to learn.** Be aware of the resistance you have to learning new information. Many students resist change, new ideas, or different beliefs. This resistance gets in the way of actively listening and learning. Be open to different points of view, different styles of lecturing, and new ideas. Students sometimes have problems listening to lectures because they have already

made up their minds, or they want to prove the instructor wrong and mentally challenge everything that is said. It is easy to misinterpret the meaning of a message if you are defensive, judgmental, bored, or emotionally upset.

3. **Postpone judgment.** Don't judge your instructor or his or her message based on clothes, reputation, voice, or teaching style. Go to class with an open and curious mind and focus on the message, the course content, and your performance.

4. **Be mindful.** Being mentally and physically alert is vital for active listening. It's true that everyone's mind wanders during a long lecture, but being mentally preoccupied is a major barrier to effective listening. It's up to you to focus your attention, concentrate on the subject, and bring your mind back to the present. Make a determined effort to stay focused and in the present.

5. **Use empathy and respect.** Focus on understanding the message and viewpoint of the speaker. Look for common views and ways in which you are alike. Listen with empathy, respect, and the intention to understand.

6. **Observe.** A large part of listening and note taking is observing. Observe your instructor and watch for obvious verbal and nonverbal clues about what information is important. If your instructor uses repetition, becomes more animated, or writes information on the board, it is probably important. Overhead transparencies or handouts may also include important diagrams, lists, drawings, facts, or definitions. Watch for examples and connect similar ideas. Observe words and phrases that signal important information or transition, such as "One important factor is…" Review the list of signal words and phrases that appears in **Figure 4.1** on pages 4–4 and 4–5.

7. **Predict and ask questions.** Keep yourself alert by predicting and asking yourself questions. Is this story supporting the main topic? What are the main points? How does this example clarify the readings? What test questions could be asked about these main points? Pretend that you are in a private conversation and ask your instructor to elaborate, give examples, or explain certain points. Make certain that you are paying attention in class and that you have previewed the chapter and done your homework.

8. **Look as if you are listening.** Active listening requires high energy. Sit up, keep your spine straight, and uncross your legs, and you will have more energy. Maintain eye contact and lean slightly forward. Participate in discussions or ask questions.

9. **Reduce distractions.** Avoid sitting next to a friend or someone who likes to talk or is distracting. Sit near the front. Bring a sweater if it is cold in the classroom or sit by an open window if it is warm. Carry a bottle of water with you to drink when your energy starts to lag.

10. **Be quiet.** The fundamental rule of listening is to be quiet while the speaker is talking. Don't interrupt or talk to classmates. As a listener, your role is to understand and comprehend. The speaker's role is to make the message clear and comprehensible. Don't confuse the two roles. When you are listening, listen attentively until the speaker is finished.

Class Discussion
Ask students if they have ever judged an instructor based on clothes or reputation, and later were surprised at how much the instructor had to offer. Ask students for ways to keep an open mind.

Teaching Tip
Illustrate the importance of being in the present. Ask students if their minds have wandered since class started. Ask them what they do to refocus attention.

Words to Succeed

"Listening to learn isn't about giving advice—at least not until asked—but about trying to understand exactly what someone means."

—ELIZABETH DEBOLD
businesswoman

Teaching Tip
Stress that much of listening is observing. Being observant means looking for verbal and nonverbal clues. Which words indicate importance, or contrast, and what behavior may indicate what is on the test?

Teaching Tip
Explain that one way of staying alert is to predict and ask questions. Have students pretend that they are in a private conversation with their instructor. How would they sit? What would their eye contact and facial expressions be?

Figure 4.1 Signal Words and Phrases

To Show Addition or Another Fact		To Show Contrast or Change an Idea	
again	in addition	although	in contrast
also	in fact	anyhow	nevertheless
and	last	anyway	notwithstanding
and then	likewise	at the same time	on the contrary
another	moreover	but	on the other
besides	next	despite this	hand
but also	nor	even though	otherwise
equally	plus the fact that	for all that	still
important	second	however	yet
finally	then too	in any event	
first	third		
further	too		

To Show Summary		To Show Amount	
as has been	in essence	few	over
noted	in other words	greater	several
as I have said	in short	less than	smaller
finally	in summary	many	some
in brief	on the whole	more than	under
in closing	to conclude	most	
in conclusion	to sum up		

To Show Comparison		To Show Purpose	
in like manner	likewise	all things	to this end
in the same way	similarly	considered	with this in mind
		for this purpose	with this object

Signal Words and Phrases Listening for certain words and phrases that signal or highlight ideas can increase your understanding of information. *Which words or phrases do your instructors use most often?*

Peak Progress 4.1 explores how you can become a more active listener by applying the Adult Learning Cycle. Then, **Personal Performance Notebook 4.1** asks you to think critically about your listening skills and how you can improve them.

Figure 4.1   Signal Words and Phrases—continued

To Show Place		To Show Time	
above	here	after a few days	immediately
across	nearby	afterward	in the meantime
adjacent to	on the opposite	at last	later
below	side	at length	not long after
beneath	opposite to	before	soon
beside	over	between	then
between	there	finally	while
beyond	under		
farther			

To Show a Specific Case		To Show Result	
a few of these	let us consider	accordingly	so
are	the case of	as a result	then
especially	the following	because	therefore
for example	you can see	consequently	thereupon
for instance	this in	for this reason	thus
in particular		hence	

To Strengthen a Point	
basically	undeniably
essentially	without a doubt
indeed	without any
truly	question

Note Taking

Note taking is an individualized process comprised of a series of complex activities. It is not a passive act of simply writing down words. It is a way to order and arrange thoughts and material to help you remember information. Effective note-taking strategies include highlighting main ideas, organizing key points, comparing and contrasting relationships, and looking for patterns. You will accomplish this by observing, listening, reviewing, organizing, and recording. No two people take notes in the

Words to
Succeed

"He listens well, who takes notes."

—DANTE
author

Hands-On Application
Role playing: Have a student play a bored listener while another student is trying to tell the listener something very important. Ask the speaker how it felt to be ignored. Now have a student play an attentive listener. What body language is important?

Hands-On Application
Ask assertive, talkative, or extroverted students to practice being quiet and listening for one full day. Ask introverted, quiet students to practice being more outgoing for one full day by giving their opinions and approaching someone they don't know and introducing themselves.

Peak Progress 4.1

Applying the Adult Learning Cycle to Becoming an Active Listener

Becoming an active listener and learning to take good notes take time and effort.

1. **RELATE. Why do I want to learn this?** How will being an active listener help me in school, work, and life? How would I rate my listening skills now? What areas do I need to improve?

2. **OBSERVE. How does this work?** I can learn a lot about active listening by watching others. I'll observe people who are good listeners and who take good notes. I'll also observe people who are not good listeners. Do their poor listening skills cause other problems for them?

3. **THINK. What does this mean?** I will gather information about listening and note taking and determine the better strategies for me to apply. What works and what doesn't seem to work? I'll explore creative ways to listen and take notes.

4. **DO. What can I do with this?** I will make a commitment to be a more active listener. I'll find opportunities to try my new listening skills. Each day, I'll focus on one area and work on it. For example, I'll choose one class in which I'm having trouble listening and experiment with new strategies.

5. **TEACH. Whom can I share this with?** I'll talk with others and share my tips and experiences. I'll demonstrate and teach the methods I've learned to others.

Now, return to Stage 1 and think about how it feels to learn this valuable new skill of active listening.

PEAK TIP

Think of note taking as sorting and organizing information while you listen and read.

same way, because each person's beliefs about the subject and instructor, biases and assumptions, mental state of mind, and listening skills are all factors that affect the note-taking process.

Recording the Message

Now that you are prepared and have sharpened your listening and observation skills, let's look at the structure and format of your notes. To help you organize and record information, you will want to use a system that enhances your learning and is compatible with your personality style. There are several note-taking systems that will help you organize information while you listen and read. Find one that supports your learning and personality styles.

If you are primarily an auditory learner, listen attentively and consider taping certain lectures (be sure to ask the instructor before you tape). Recite your book notes into a tape recorder and play the tape several times.

If you are an analytical type, you may be more comfortable with a linear and sequential or formal method of note taking.

Active Listening

Use critical thinking to answer the following questions.

1. Do you come to class prepared and with a positive and receptive state of mind? Write down one tip that you would be willing to try to improve your listening.

   _____

   _____

   _____

2. Jot down the name of a person whom you consider to be a good listener. Consider your feelings toward this person. It is usually difficult not to like someone whom you consider to be a good listener. Active listening shows respect and caring and is one of the best gifts one person can give to another.

   _____

   _____

   _____

3. Write a list of daily situations in which active listening is required. Some situations could include talking to your child about his or her day at school, listening to your spouse's or roommate's views on politics, and meeting with a community group to plan a fundraising event. What listening strategies would increase your attention and responsiveness in the situations you've listed?

   _____

   _____

   _____

If you are primarily a visual learner, supplement your lecture notes with drawings, illustrations, and pictures. Take special note of material on the board, overhead transparencies, and handouts. Read your notes right after class to reinforce your learning and compare your notes with the material in the textbook.

If you are a creative type, you can look for information that is different and does not match. You may like using a creative outline or mind map, because it presents the big picture visually and allows a creative flair.

If you are supportive, you can process information that is personally relevant and connect similar patterns. You may want to use the Cornell note-taking system in

Use
TM 4.3 Traditional or
Formal Outline.

Figure 4.2   Sample Formal Outline

Topic: Note taking   Jana Rosa
                                                           April 9, 2005

Effective Strategies for Taking Notes

   A. The traditional outline for note taking
      1. Advantages
         a. Occupies your attention totally
         b. Organizes ideas as well as records them
      2. Disadvantages
         a. Too structured for right-brain person
         b. Time consuming

   B. The mapping system for note taking
      1. Advantages
         a. Presents a creative and visual model
         b. Can start anywhere on the page
      2. Disadvantages
         a. Too busy for a left-brain person
         b. Too unorganized for a left-brain person

Sample Formal Outline   A formal outline provides an orderly, sequential way to organize information. *What is one advantage of using a formal outline?*

which you can jot stories in the margin or create a mind map to connect ideas and patterns. The Cornell method is discussed later in this chapter.

If you are a kinesthetic learner, you may also have a director style personality and like active learning. You can make learning more physical by writing and rephrasing material; working with your study team or study partner; collecting examples, stories, and diagrams; using note cards; and standing when taking notes from your textbook. You may find the Mind Map Template to be practical for use in many classes (discussed later in this chapter), or you may want to use a combination of systems that produces the results you want. The following sections discuss a few common outline systems.

FORMAL OUTLINE

A formal outline shows headings, main points, and supporting examples, and requires consistency. For example, if you have an A.1, you should have a B.1. Likewise, if you have an A.2, you should have a B.2. Left-brain-dominant people tend to like neat, orderly notes and are often comfortable with a sequential format. However, formal outlines may also be time-consuming. See **Figure 4.2** for a sample formal outline.

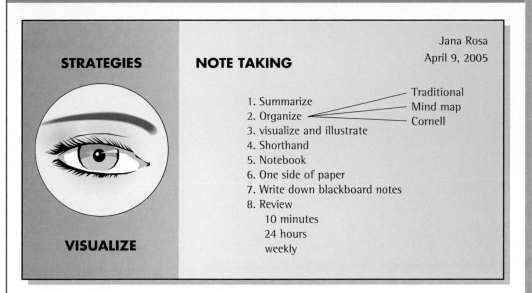

Figure 4.3   Sample Creative Outline

Sample Creative Outline   Students who are right-brain dominant may prefer an outline that allows for illustrations. *What other items might you include on the left side of the outline?*

CREATIVE OUTLINE

If you tend to be right-brain dominant, you may feel more comfortable with a creative outline. You can simply divide the paper and use the left side for key words, illustrations, questions, graphs, definitions, stories, dates, or formulas. Use the right side to list topics. See **Figure 4.3** for an example of a creative outline.

MIND MAPPING

You can also use mind mapping, which is another type of creative outline. See the sample mind map in **Figure 4.4** on page 4–10. A mind map is a visual, holistic form of note taking. The advantage is that you can see connections and the big picture. You can also see connections to the main idea. Mapping starts from the main idea placed in the center of a page and branches out with subtopics through associations and patterns. Two styles of mind maps are illustrated in this chapter, in **Figure 4.4,** and **Figure 4.5** on page 4–11. You may find that mapping helps you increase your comprehension, creativity, and recall. You can draw a map for each chapter and put them on your bulletin board, or you may want to use a combination of maps and traditional outlines.

A left-brain-dominant student may be uncomfortable mapping because the outline is not sequential; it is difficult to follow the instructor's train of thought; there is little space for corrections or additions; and the notes must be shortened to key words and only one page. One option is to use a mind map to illustrate the whole chapter and use the traditional outline for daily notes.

Figure 4.4 Sample Mind Map

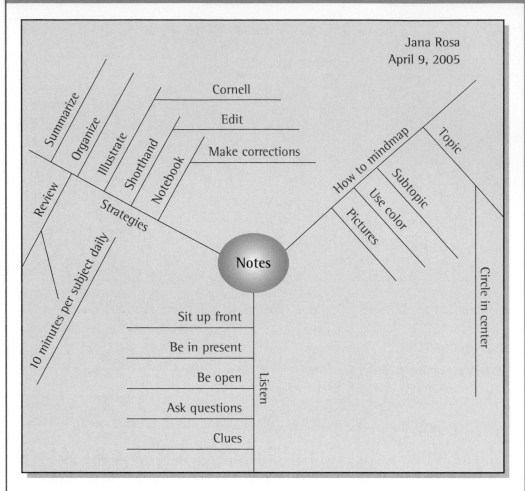

Sample Mind Map   This is one type of mind map. Mind maps use branches to reveal concept connections and patterns. *What is another advantage of using a mind map?*

MIND MAP TEMPLATE

In certain classes, you will study several different topics that have the same patterns. For example, you may study different cultures, and the categories or patterns are the same for each culture. You can adapt the template in **Figure 4.5** to many subjects. Personal Performance Notebook 4.2 provides a blank template to get you started.

CORNELL METHOD

The Cornell method, or T note-taking system, has been used for more than 45 years and is effective for integrating text and lecture notes. See **Figure 4.6** on page 4–13 for an example of the Cornell method of note taking.

Figure 4.5 Mind Map Template

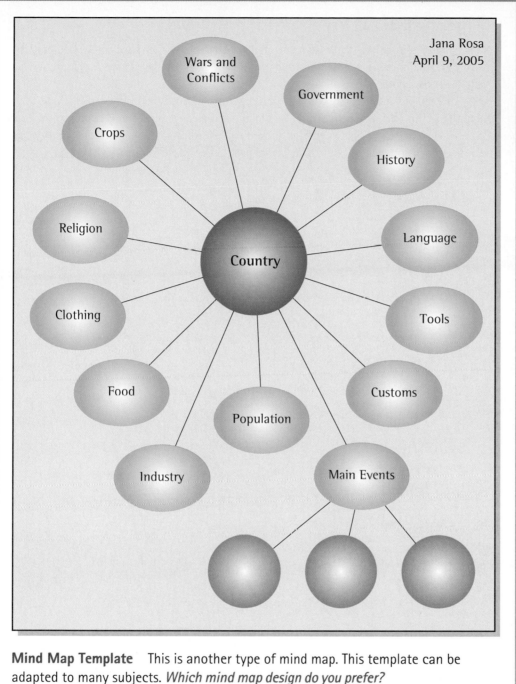

Jana Rosa
April 9, 2005

Mind Map Template This is another type of mind map. This template can be adapted to many subjects. *Which mind map design do you prefer?*

COMBINATION NOTE-TAKING SYSTEM

Figure 4.7 on page 4–14 shows the combination note-taking system, using a formal outline, mind mapping, and the Cornell method.

Mind Map

Make a mind map of a chapter from one of your textbooks in the space below. Compare it with the mind maps drawn by other students in your class. Use the sample in **Figure 4.5** on page 4–11 as a guide.

For example, let's say you will map out Chapter 3 in this text. In the middle circle, you might put "Time Management Strategies." In one of the surrounding circles, you might enter "Study everywhere and anywhere." In offshoot circles from that, you might put "Carry note cards," "Listen to taped lectures," and "Avoid peak times in the library."

Use
TM 4.6 Mind Map Template.

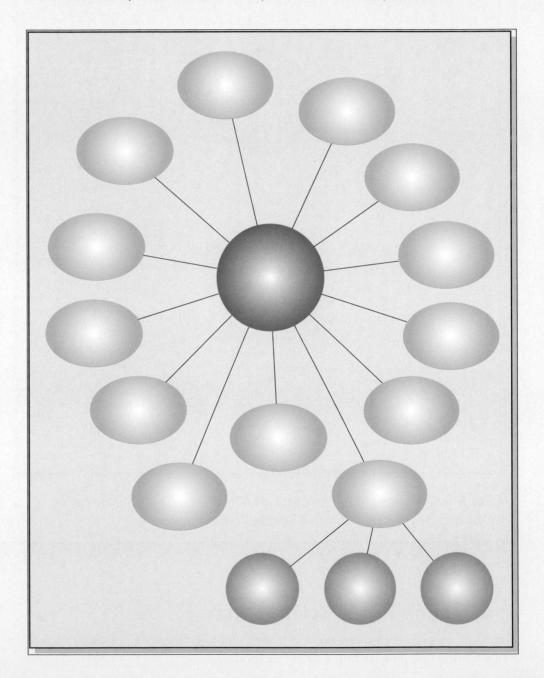

Figure 4.6   The Cornell Method

	Seminar	Jana Rosa
	Peak Performance 101	Oct. 2, 2005
	Topic: Note taking	Tuesday

What is the purpose of note taking?	I. Purpose of Note Taking
	   A. To accurately record information
	   B. To become actual part of listening
	   C. To enhance learning

Different Systems of Note Taking	II. A. Formal outline
	   B. Cornell method
	   C. Mind map

Summary: Use the note-taking system
that is right for you or create a combination.
Remember to date and review.

The Cornell Method   Also called the T note-taking system, this diagram integrates text and lecture notes and also includes a summary section. *Which personality type might prefer the Cornell method?*

Figure 4.7   Combination Note-Taking System

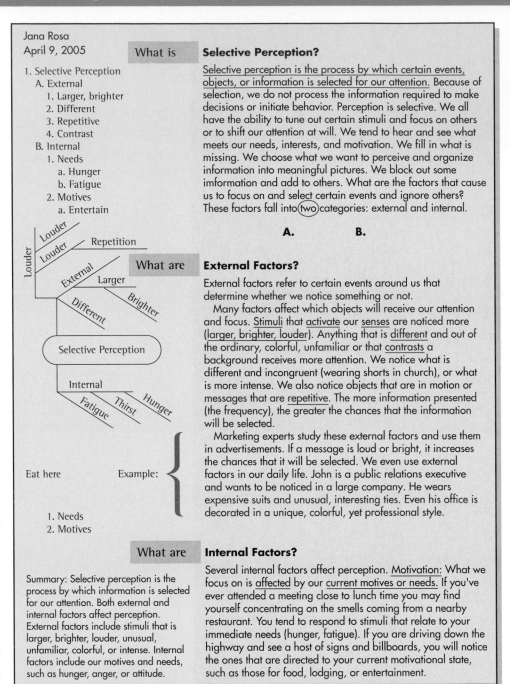

Jana Rosa
April 9, 2005

1. Selective Perception
   A. External
      1. Larger, brighter
      2. Different
      3. Repetitive
      4. Contrast
   B. Internal
      1. Needs
         a. Hunger
         b. Fatigue
      2. Motives
         a. Entertain

What is   Selective Perception?

Selective perception is the process by which certain events, objects, or information is selected for our attention. Because of selection, we do not process the information required to make decisions or initiate behavior. Perception is selective. We all have the ability to tune out certain stimuli and focus on others or to shift our attention at will. We tend to hear and see what meets our needs, interests, and motivation. We fill in what is missing. We choose what we want to perceive and organize information into meaningful pictures. We block out some imformation and add to others. What are the factors that cause us to focus on and select certain events and ignore others? These factors fall into two categories: external and internal.

A.   B.

What are   External Factors?

External factors refer to certain events around us that determine whether we notice something or not.

Many factors affect which objects will receive our attention and focus. Stimuli that activate our senses are noticed more (larger, brighter, louder). Anything that is different and out of the ordinary, colorful, unfamiliar or that contrasts a background receives more attention. We notice what is different and incongruent (wearing shorts in church), or what is more intense. We also notice objects that are in motion or messages that are repetitive. The more information presented (the frequency), the greater the chances that the information will be selected.

Marketing experts study these external factors and use them in advertisements. If a message is loud or bright, it increases the chances that it will be selected. We even use external factors in our daily life. John is a public relations executive and wants to be noticed in a large company. He wears expensive suits and unusual, interesting ties. Even his office is decorated in a unique, colorful, yet professional style.

What are   Internal Factors?

Several internal factors affect perception. Motivation: What we focus on is affected by our current motives or needs. If you've ever attended a meeting close to lunch time you may find yourself concentrating on the smells coming from a nearby restaurant. You tend to respond to stimuli that relate to your immediate needs (hunger, fatigue). If you are driving down the highway and see a host of signs and billboards, you will notice the ones that are directed to your current motivational state, such as those for food, lodging, or entertainment.

Summary: Selective perception is the process by which information is selected for our attention. Both external and internal factors affect perception. External factors include stimuli that is larger, brighter, louder, unusual, unfamiliar, colorful, or intense. Internal factors include our motives and needs, such as hunger, anger, or attitude.

Combination Note-Taking System   You can use several different note-taking systems on the left, reflecting the main text on the right. *Which note-taking system do you prefer?*

Note-Taking Strategies

The following strategies will help you make the most of the note-taking system you use.

1. **Be prepared.** Can you imagine going to an important class without doing your homework; being unprepared to participate; or lacking pen, paper, and necessary material? Preview or skim textbook chapters for main ideas, general theme, and key concepts. Previewing is a simple strategy that enhances your note taking and learning. In a sense, you are priming your brain to process information efficiently and effectively. You will also want to review previous notes and connect what you have learned to new ideas. Use index cards to jot down key words, formulas, definitions, and other important information.

2. **Go to every class.** The most obvious and important part of being prepared is to attend all your classes. You cannot take effective notes if you are not there. Having someone else take notes for you is not the same as being in class. Make a commitment that you will go to every class unless you are ill. Check bus schedules in case your car breaks down. Have several backup plans if you have children. Don't schedule other appointments when you have classes. In other words, be prepared and make a commitment to treat your education as a top priority.

3. **Be on time.** Walking in late for class indicates an attitude that class is not important and disrupts the instructor and other students. Set your watch five minutes ahead and arrive early enough to preview your notes and get settled. Punctuality also helps you prepare emotionally and mentally.

4. **Sit up front.** You will be more physically alert, and you will see and hear better, if you sit in the front of the class. You are also more likely to ask questions and engage the instructor in eye contact when you sit in front. You will be less likely to talk with other students, pass notes, doodle, finish your homework, or daydream when you sit in front.

5. **Use all your senses.** Many people view note taking not only as a passive activity but also as an auditory activity. Actually, you will find note taking more effective if you integrate learning styles and use all your senses.

   If you are primarily an auditory learner, listen attentively and capitalize on this style of processing information. You might want to tape lectures. Explain your notes to your study group, so you can hear the material again.

   If you are primarily a visual learner, develop mental pictures and use your right-brain creativity. Draw and illustrate concepts. Practice visualizing images while the speaker is talking and form mental pictures of the topic. Visualize the whole of the subject and associate the image with key words. You might try using colored pencils, cartoons, or any illustrations that make the material come alive. Supplement your lecture notes with drawings, and take special note of material on the board, overhead transparencies, and handouts.

   Make note taking more kinesthetic by writing and rephrasing material, drawing diagrams, discussing your notes with your study team, outlining your

Words to Succeed

"Eighty-five percent of success in life is just showing up."

—WOODY ALLEN
entertainer

PEAK TIP

Sit in the front of the class, observe, and actively listen to your instructor by asking questions, looking for patterns, and summarizing main points.

Hands-On Application
Have students bring in samples of their notes, exchange them, and ask for feedback. Review effective note taking.

Teaching Tip
Stress that lectures in college
are often a major part of
classroom learning. Review
the list of how college is
different from high school.

Class Discussion
Have students discuss some
of the problems they face
with lectures. Ask students
how they can be more
prepared for large lectures,
instructors who talk too fast,
distractions, etc. Jot down
major problems of note
taking on the board.

Class Discussion
Ask students how they can
make note taking more
active. For example, suggest
that they jot down questions
in the left margin while the
instructor is speaking.

notes on the board, and standing when you take notes from your textbook at home. Draw models and charts, collect samples, and write descriptive notes. Take notes on field trips.

Use left-brain organizational skills. Use large, bold headlines for the main ideas and large print for key words, important points, facts, places, and other supporting data. Write your name, topic, and date on each sheet of paper. You may want to purchase a binder for each class to organize notes, syllabi, handouts, tests, and summaries.

6. **Make note taking active and physical.** For your mind to be alert, your body also must be alert. Physical activity gets your blood flowing throughout your body, including your brain, which is why physical activity enhances academic performance for all learning styles. Observe your body, how you hold your pen, and how your back feels against the chair. Slouching produces fatigue and signals the brain that this activity is not important. Sit straight. When you are at home taking notes and you feel your energy dip, take a walk, stretch, do deep knee bends or head rolls, or jog in place for a few minutes. Exercise also helps relax the body, focuses the mind, and reduces stress.

7. **Link information.** Connect ideas and link similar information. Look for patterns and information that is different. Compare and contrast; find similarities and differences. Develop associations between what you are hearing for the first time and what you already know. When you link new knowledge to what you already know, you create lasting impressions. Ask yourself how this information relates to other classes or to your job.

8. **Use creative shorthand and focus on key words.** A common mistake students make is attempting to write down everything the instructor says. Notes are like blueprints, because they represent a larger subject and highlight main details. The essential element in taking effective notes is to jot down only main points and key words. Let's suppose that you are learning about groups and group dynamics. Your instructor may declare, "The essential ingredient for groupthink to occur is strong group cohesiveness." *Group cohesiveness* is a key term that will link to the concept of groupthink. Ask yourself, "How does all this new information relate to what I already know?" In the example of groupthink, you might list fraternities and sororities, political groups, sporting teams, and clubs as having strong group cohesiveness.

Focus on key words that link concepts, associate words, and emphasize main ideas. Illustrations, filler statements, stories, introductions, and transitions are important for depth, interest, and understanding, but you don't have to write down every word. Devise your own system for note taking that includes abbreviations and symbols. See **Figure 4.8** for examples.

9. **Leave space for revisions and additions.** Leave wide margins and plenty of space to make corrections, add notes, clarify, and summarize. Don't crowd your words, or the notes will be difficult to understand. Keep all handouts you receive in class. Use a question mark if you do not understand something, so you can ask about it later.

Figure 4.8 Note-Taking Shortcuts

Key Teaching Concept
Summarize information in your own words. This is a key strategy.

Symbol	Meaning	Abbreviation	Meaning
>	greater than; increase	i.e.	that is
<	less than; decrease	etc.	and so forth
?	question	lb.	pound
w/	with	assoc.	association
w/o	without	info	information
V or *	important ideas	ex.	example
+	positive		
—	negative		
X	times		
~	lost		
P	leads to (e.g., motivation p success)		
^	bridge of concepts		
#	number		

Note-Taking Shortcuts   This chart lists some common symbols and abbreviations you can incorporate into your own note-taking system. *What is the essential element in taking effective notes?*

Assessment and Review

After you've taken your notes, reinforce your memory and understanding of the material by assessing and reviewing your notes. Use these four strategies for assessment and review:

1. **Summarize in your own words.** When you finish taking text and lecture notes, summarize in your own words. You might want to write summaries on index cards. Summarizing can be done quickly and can cover only main concepts. This one small action will greatly increase your comprehension and learning. It is even more effective when you read your summary out loud to others; teaching is a good way to learn.

2. **Edit and revise your notes.** Set aside a few minutes as soon as possible after the lecture to edit, revise, fill in, or copy your notes. Ask yourself what questions might be on a test. Underline what the instructor has indicated is important. Fill in blanks with new material. Clean up, expand, and rewrite sections that are messy or incomplete.

Teaching Tip
Stress the importance of
reviewing notes within
24 hours.

Class Discussion
Ask students how computers
can help them take better
notes.

TECH FOR SUCCESS

- **PDA** Keep your notes literally on hand by using a personal digital assistant (PDAs). PDAs are available in a variety of price ranges and with endless features. You will be motivated to take notes throughout the day to help you organize priorities and remember good ideas.
- **Your Instructor's Visual Presentation** Many instructors lecture in conjunction with visual aids, such as a PowerPoint presentation. Ask your instructor if the lecture outline is available as a handout, on a course web site, or in the bookstore. This is a handy tool for note taking that helps you better follow the discussion and organize your notes.

If you are unclear on a point, leave a space and put a question mark in the margin. You can ask for verification from other students in class or your instructor.

3. **Review your notes.** Even if you have only 10 minutes, review your notes for the main ideas and write down any question you have. Experts say that, unless students review soon after the lecture, much of the new information will be lost within the first half-hour after the class. Research indicates that your memory is at its most receptive within 24 hours after hearing new information. You might try going to your next class early and spending 5 minutes reviewing your class notes from the previous class. Or you can review while the instructor passes out handouts, adjusts the overhead projector, or organizes. Reviewing right before you go to sleep is also a great strategy to help you remember. Your mind is receptive to new information at that time. Reviewing increases your memory and helps you perform better on exams.

4. **Monitor and evaluate.** Periodically assess your note-taking system. Try different systems and strategies until you find one that works best. Feedback from study-group members, your instructor, and tests will help you assess how well your system is working.

Complete **Personal Performance Notebook 4.3** to reflect on your listening and note-taking skills. **Peak Progress 4.2** on page 4–20 provides tips on overcoming obstacles to improve your skills.

Personal Performance Notebook 4.3

Reflection

Use critical thinking to answer the following questions.

1. Do you preview chapters, take textbook notes, and write summaries?

   _____

   _____

   _____

   _____

2. Are you prepared mentally to listen and learn?

   _____

   _____

   _____

   _____

3. Can you see the whole picture from your notes and gain a general understanding of the material? Explain how.

   _____

   _____

   _____

   _____

4. Describe how you can make your least interesting class more interesting and productive.

   _____

   _____

   _____

   _____

5. Give some examples of how being an active note taker can create a positive learning experience.

   _____

   _____

   _____

   _____

Hands-On Application
Have students write down their least favorite class and the barriers they are experiencing. Have group members brainstorm ideas for overcoming barriers. Discuss ABCDE Method on p. 4–26.

Peak Progress   4.2

Overcoming Barriers to Effective Note Taking

The first step in overcoming the barriers to effective note taking is to recognize its importance. Some students view note taking as a passive academic skill that they will never use once they graduate from college. As a result, their notes are often disorganized, incomplete, illegible, and of little help in preparing for tests.

Effective note taking changes the information that you hear into information that is distinctly yours. You have discarded the unessential, highlighted the essential, and organized information to give it meaning and focus. This process is an important job skill. Follow these simple steps until discipline and focus become a habit:

1. **Find meaning and interest** in the subject. Understand why taking better notes will help you in the long run. Determine specific reasons and situations in school, at work, or at home where taking good notes will be essential.

2. **Observe** your intention and willingness to listen and learn. Observe what is on the board, in handouts, and in overhead transparencies. Sit in the front to avoid distractions and to help you focus and observe the instructor. Observe how effective students take notes and compare.

3. **Listen** for understanding and for the main points and key words. Take notes during class discussions and lectures. If you are unsure of the main points, ask your instructor.

4. **Organize** the important information. Choose a system that helps you organize and record main points and key words. If a formal outline doesn't work for your learning style, try another method of note taking.

5. **Think** about the information and gather more if necessary. Reflect on what you know and what you don't know.

6. **Record** the date and topic, and leave room in the margins for revising.

7. **Review, revise, and practice** your notes as soon as possible. Review notes with your study team, so you can fill in information that you missed and summarize main points. Teaching what you've learned to someone else will also help you remember and understand the material better.

8. **Evaluate** your system of taking notes. Experiment with several methods. Ask your instructor and other students for feedback.

9. **Teach** others your system. Demonstrate what works for you.

10. **Reward** yourself when you make progress. Congratulate yourself for learning and enhancing your skills.

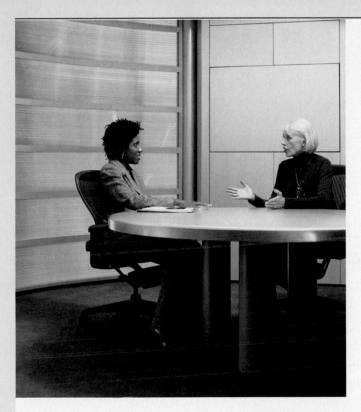

Danielle Sievert

PSYCHOLOGIST

Related Majors: Psychology, Counseling

Listening in the Workplace

Danielle Sievert provides mental health care as an industrial-organizational psychologist for a Fortune 500 company. When most people think of psychologists, they think of clinicians in counseling centers or hospitals, but many large companies hire psychologists to tend to the needs of staff on all levels. Most industrial-organizational psychologists hold master's degrees in psychology. Psychology is the study of human behavior and the mind and its applications to mental health. Danielle and other industrial-organizational psychologists use psychology to improve quality of life and productivity in the workplace.

Danielle conducts applicant screenings to select employees who will work well within the company. She provides input on marketing research. She also helps solve human relations problems that occur in various departments. Danielle occasionally conducts individual sessions with employees who face problems within or outside of the office. Danielle works a nine-to-five schedule and is occasionally asked to work overtime. She is often interrupted to solve pressing problems.

Active listening is an important part of Danielle's job. Managers and other employees will ask for her help, she says, only when they sense that she is empathetic and desires to be of help. To hone her listening skills, Danielle asks questions to make sure she understands exactly what the person is saying. She also takes notes, either during or after a session. By using such skills, Danielle is able to fulfill her role as a psychologist in the workplace.

CRITICAL THINKING

What kinds of problems might occur at the workplace that could be addressed by a firm's psychologist?

Peak Performer Profile

Anna Sui

"What should I wear?" This is a question that many people ask almost daily. For international fashion designer Anna Sui (pronounced *Swee*), the answer is simple? "Dress to have fun and feel great." Her showroom above noisy 8th Avenue in New York City illustrates her attitude with a Victorian-inspired mix of purple walls, ornate clothing racks, glass lamps, and red floors.

To the second of three children and only daughter born to Chinese immigrants, the Detroit suburbs of the early 1960s were a long way from the fashion mecca of New York City. However, even then Sui seemed to be visualizing success. Whether designing tissue-paper dresses for her neighbor's toy soldiers or making her own clothes with coordinating fabric for shoes, Sui had flair.

After graduating from high school, Sui headed for the Big Apple. She eventually opened her own business after two years of studying at the Parson's School of Design and years of working in the trenches at various sportswear companies. When Sui premiered her first runway show in 1991, the *New York Times* applauded the event as "producing a pastiche of hip and haute style." Sui's imaginative mix of styles was a hit.

To create such acclaimed designs, Sui takes note of the world around her. She continues to collect her "genius files"—clippings from pages of fashion magazines—to serve as inspiration. She listens to her clients, to music, to the street, and to her own instincts. Sui is quick to say that, although her moderately priced clothes are popular with celebrities, they are also worn by her mother. It's not about age and money, she explains, but about the "spirit of the clothing." By listening actively and staying attuned to the world around her, Sui continues to influence trends and enchant with her designs.

PERFORMANCE THINKING   For the career of your choice, how would active listening and note taking contribute to your success?

In summary, in this chapter, I learned to

- *Actively listen to the message.* Developing an interest in listening and making it meaningful to me are the first steps to being an active listener. I must want to listen and am open to new information, new ideas, and different beliefs. My intent is to understand others and to focus on the message.

- *Go to every class.* I know that it is very important to make a commitment to go to every class and form a relationship with my instructor and other students. I'm on time and sit up in front, where I'm alert and aware. I sit up straight, maintain eye contact, and act as if I'm listening and involved with the speaker. I reduce distractions and focus on listening, not talking. I'm in the present and concentrate on the subject.

- *Observe my instructor and watch for verbal and nonverbal clues.* I watch for examples, words, and phrases that signal important information or transitions. I take note of handouts and transparencies. I use critical thinking to postpone judgment. I focus on the message, not presentation. I look beyond clothes, voice, teaching style, and reputation and focus on what the other person is saying. Using critical thinking helps me look for supporting information and facts and ask questions.

- *Prepare prior to class.* I preview chapters before class, so I have a general idea of the chapter, and make notes of questions to ask or concepts that I want the instructor to give examples of or elaborate. I do homework and use index cards to jot down and memorize key words, formulas, and definitions.

- *Focus on key words.* I don't try to write down all information but, rather, look for key words and essential information. I use an outline that works for me. I look for patterns, link information, and connect ideas in a way that makes sense and organizes the information. I leave space for corrections and additions and use marks such as "?" for questions.

- *Integrate learning styles.* I not only use my preferred learning style but also integrate all styles. I make note taking active and physical. I draw pictures and make illustrations, use outlines, supplement my notes with handouts, take field trips, create models, and summarize out loud.

- *Get organized.* I know that information that is not organized is not remembered. I write the date and topic on each sheet and organize notes in a folder or binder. I use a system of note taking that works best for me and that records main points and organizes information. The mind map uses my creative side and helps me see connections and the big picture. A formal outline uses my left-brain, sequential side.

- *Summarize in my own words when I am finished taking notes in class or from the text.* This one action greatly improves my comprehension and learning. I review this summary with my book and study team and fill in essential information. I make notes on questions to ask my instructor or study group.

- *Review, monitor, and evaluate.* I review my notes for main ideas as soon as possible after class, but within 24 hours. This increases my memory and helps me make sense out of my notes. I edit and add to my notes. I evaluate my note-taking skills and look for ways to improve.

Performance Strategies

Following are the top 10 strategies for active listening:

- ◆ Find meaning and purpose in being an active listener.
- ◆ Postpone judgment and be open to new ideas.
- ◆ Seek to understand and show respect to the speaker.
- ◆ Reduce distractions and be alert and focused.
- ◆ Maintain eye contact and look interested and alert.
- ◆ Observe the speaker and watch for clues.
- ◆ Observe body language and look for meaning beyond words.
- ◆ Look for examples and main points.
- ◆ Ask questions to clarify.
- ◆ Paraphrase in your own words.

Following are the top 10 strategies for effective note taking:

- ◆ Listen actively.
- ◆ Predict and ask questions.
- ◆ Look for information that is similar to what you already know.
- ◆ Look for information that is different from what you already know.
- ◆ Listen for signal words and phrases.
- ◆ Organize information.
- ◆ Develop an outline that creates links between information.
- ◆ Make note taking active and physical.
- ◆ Summarize in your own words and review often.
- ◆ Edit and revise while information is still fresh.

Review Questions

1. What is active listening?
2. Why are active listening and note-taking skills important to learning?
3. Name five types of outline systems.
4. Why is "Go to every class" an important note-taking strategy?
5. What should you do with your notes after attending class?

REVISUALIZATION

Review the Visualization box on the first page of this chapter and your journal entry in **Worksheet 4.1.** Think of one of those challenging classes you described and apply the ABCDE method to help you focus on becoming a more active listener—for example,

A = Actual event: "I was hopelessly lost during my 2:00 class. I couldn't follow the lecture and my notes are a mess."

B = Beliefs: "Maybe I should drop this class and find an instructor who's more dynamic."

C = Consequences: "I'm frustrated with myself that I can't get more out of this class. I can't fail this class, as I need a good grade to graduate."

D = Dispute: "But I'm passing all the quizzes and I like my study group. I know with a little more effort I can become better focused during lectures."

E = Energized: "I'm confident that I can apply simple strategies to become a more active listener. Even though this instructor has a different teaching style than my learning style, I can adjust and be flexible. I see this as a good learning experience all around."

DEVELOPING ACTIVE LISTENING SKILLS

In the Classroom

Roxanne Jackson is a fashion design student who works part-time at a retail clothing store. She has two roommates, who are also students. Roxanne is a very social person. She is outgoing, enjoys being around people, and loves to talk and tell stories. However, Roxanne is a poor listener. In class, she is often too busy talking with the person next to her to pay attention to the class assignments. She always starts off as a popular study-group member, but it soon becomes clear that her assignments are always late and incorrect. Roxanne's roommates have finally confronted her. There is tension between them, because the roommates feel that Roxanne is not pulling her weight on household chores. Another major problem is that Roxanne does not seem to take accurate phone messages. She never seems to write down the correct information.

1. What strategies in this chapter can help Roxanne be a more effective listener?

   _____

   _____

2. What would you suggest she do to improve her relationship with others and help her become better at taking down information?

   _____

   _____

In the Workplace

Roxanne is now a buyer for a large department store. She enjoys working with people. She is very talented and a responsible employee when she is actively aware and tuned in to others. People respond to her favorably and enjoy being around her. The problem with Roxanne is that she is often too busy or preoccupied to listen actively or take correct notes. She often forgets directions, misunderstands conversations, and interrupts others in her haste and enthusiasm.

3. What would you suggest to help Roxanne become a better listener?

   _____

   _____

4. What strategies in this chapter would help her become more aware, more sensitive to others, and able to record information more effectively?

   _____

   _____

APPLYING THE ABCDE METHOD OF SELF-MANAGEMENT

In the Visualization box on page 4-0, you were asked to describe a time when you had a difficulty in making sense out of a lecture and staying alert. Are there certain classes in which it is more challenging for you to be an active listener?

_____

_____

_____

Now, apply the ABCDE method to the situation and visualize yourself a more active listener:

A = Actual event:

B = Beliefs:

C = Consequences:

D = Dispute:

E = Energized:

Practice deep breathing, with your eyes closed, for just one minute. See yourself calm, centered, and alert. See yourself enjoying your lectures, staying alert, and taking good notes.

SORTING INFORMATION WITH A MIND MAP

Use the following example as a guide for developing a mind map of key points. In the blank space, create your own mind map for one of your class lectures.

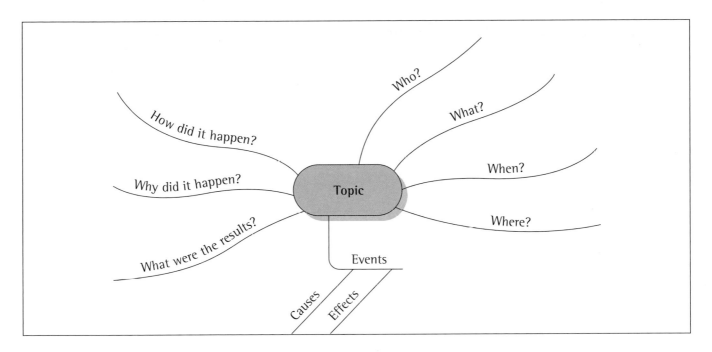

Lecture   Class

FOCUS ON IDEAS

Fill in this guide to create a list of the important ideas presented in a class lecture. You can use this list to create an outline on a separate sheet of paper.

Class _____ **Instructor** _____ **Date** _____

Lecture topic _____

Chapters covered _____

Main ideas _____

Supporting ideas _____

Examples _____

Vocabulary terms _____

Key words _____

Important concepts and theories _____

Applications _____

How this information is similar to known information _____

How this information is different from known information _____

Overall theme _____

Summary of lecture _____

NOTE-TAKING CHECKLIST

Use this checklist to inventory your note-taking skills for each class.

	Observe				Organize				Link				Review			
	Maintain a positive attitude.	Be alert and attentive.	Integrate learning styles.	Focus on main points and key words.	Outline material.	Illustrate.	Separate essential from nonessential.	Categorize and compare.	Link familiar with new.	Link similarities and differences.	Link key words and points.	Link questions and summary.	Review information.	Edit and modify.	Summarize.	Recall and evaluate.
Course 1																
Course 2																
Course 3																
Course 4																
Course 5																
Course 6																
Course 7																
Course 8																

LISTENING AND NOTE TAKING IN THE WORKPLACE

Write how you will demonstrate the listed listening and note-taking skills for future employers.

1. Finding meaning and interest in new information and projects _____

_____

2. Showing interest and being prepared _____

_____

3. Actively listening _____

_____

4. Observing and asking questions _____

_____

5. Acquiring information _____

_____

6. Thinking through issues _____

_____

7. Organizing information and taking good notes _____

_____

8. Staying alert and in the present _____

_____

9. Being willing to test new strategies and learn new methods _____

_____

10. Practicing active listening and note taking again and again _____

_____

11. Teaching effective methods to others _____

_____

LIFE ASSESSMENT

It may help you plan your life today by imagining yourself many years from now. Think about the personal qualities, character traits, friends, type of family, goals, and values that may be most important to you in later years. The kind of person you hope to be at 85 or 90 years old will not just happen; you must think about the future. By doing so, you will begin to define more clearly the values and goals you have today. It can also help you determine your current priorities and make decisions that will have an impact on your future.

Interview grandparents, elderly relatives, friends, or neighbors. Actively listen as you ask them questions about the challenges they have lived through. Take notes about key events. Ask such questions as the following:

- What values do you consider to be most important?
- If you had your life to live again, what would you do differently?
- What advice do you have for young people today?
- What legacy do you want to leave for the next generation?

Now, think about the legacy *you* want to leave behind. What do you want to be remembered for? What characteristics and qualities do you want your children and grandchildren to remember about you? Reflect on them and jot them down. Try to include what you think will be most important to you when you are 85 years old. Consider values, interests, attitudes, abilities, accomplishments, and talents as you assess and review. With this future image of yourself in mind, write your legacy in the following space.

_____

_____

_____

_____

_____

_____

_____

_____

_____

_____

_____

_____

_____

_____

_____

CHAPTER 4 ▲ REVIEW AND APPLICATIONS

ONGOING ASSESSMENT AND ACTION PLAN

One of the most important skills is to learn what you are good at doing. Focus on your strengths and remove barriers that limit you. An easy way to do this is to keep an ongoing assessment and action plan. Review your action plan at the end of the semester and compare expectations with results. Continue this practice in your career. You will soon learn what you do effectively. You will also see patterns of choices and thus identify barriers and limitations. This information will help you improve. Jot down your key activities, tasks, skills, and decisions and what you expect to happen.

Key Activity	Expectation	Results	Correction
Example: Presentation in class	Example: Earn an A grade	Example: Earned a B grade	Example: Must overcome my nervousness Practice

GOOD LISTENING HABITS

A. Can you identify good listening habits in a social, small-group, or conference setting? Read the following situations. Answer Yes or No in the blank after each question.

1. Jake keeps his eyes as much as possible on each person in his study group as he or she speaks. Is Jake practicing good listening habits? _____

2. Kara does not like the way her math instructor dresses, so she never listens very carefully to the lectures. Is Kara practicing good listening habits? _____

3. Donald knows his lab partner, Joe, is shy. He avoids eye contact with Joe whenever Joe speaks. Is this a good listening habit? _____

4. Lucy always tries to decide in advance whether it is worthwhile to listen to the speaker. Is she practicing good listening habits? _____

5. Keisha's boss called her department into a meeting concerning work hours. She paid attention to both his words and his nonverbal cues—gestures, posture, and facial expression. Did she practice good listening habits? _____

B. What would you do in the following situations? Check Yes or No in the spaces provided.

	Yes	No
1. I continue to listen even if a great deal of effort is needed to understand what the speaker is saying.	_____	_____
2. I wait until the speaker has finished before asking for an explanation about an important concept I did not fully understand.	_____	_____
3. I try to identify the major points of a class lecture and decide if each point has been supported.	_____	_____
4. I try not to do another activity—such as watching television—while trying to listen to what someone is saying.	_____	_____
5. I try to prepare my response while the speaker is still speaking.	_____	_____

CHAPTER 4 ▲ **REVIEW AND APPLICATIONS**

LISTENING SELF-ASSESSMENT

This simple assessment tool will give you an idea of your active listening skills. Read each statement. Then check Yes or No as to whether these statements relate to you.

	Yes	No
1. My intention is to be an active and effective listener.	_____	_____
2. I concentrate on meaning, not on every word.	_____	_____
3. I focus on the speaker and use eye contact.	_____	_____
4. I am aware of emotions and nonverbal behavior.	_____	_____
5. I withhold judgment until I hear the entire message.	_____	_____
6. I am open to new information and ideas.	_____	_____
7. I seek to understand the speaker's point of view.	_____	_____
8. I do not interrupt, argue, or plan my response; I listen.	_____	_____
9. I am mentally and physically alert and attentive.	_____	_____
10. I paraphrase to clarify my understanding.	_____	_____
11. When I'm in class, I sit in the front, so I can hear and see better.	_____	_____
12. I mentally ask questions and summarize main ideas.	_____	_____
13. I increase the value of my listening by previewing the textbook before class.	_____	_____
14. I adapt to the instructor's speaking and teaching style.	_____	_____

Total Yes responses:

Count your Yes responses. If you marked Yes to 10 or more questions, you are well on your way to becoming an active and effective listener. If you did not, you have some work to do to improve those skills. Review this chapter again. Add this page to your Career Development Portfolio.

Active Reading

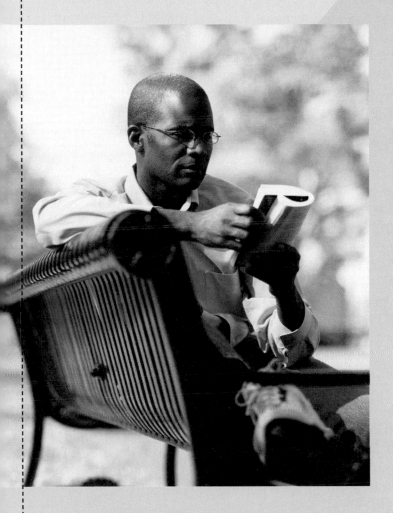

Chapter Objectives

In this chapter, you will learn

▲ The benefits of active reading

▲ The Five-Part Reading System

▲ The SQ3R Reading System

▲ Active reading strategies

▲ Strategies for managing language courses

▲ How to build a better vocabulary

▲ Tips for reading technical material and completing forms

VISUALIZATION

"I usually love to read, but lately I feel like I'm on information overload. Sometimes, I read several pages and realize that I haven't understood a word I've read. What can I do to read more effectively and actually remember what I've read?"

Do you ever close a book and feel frustrated because you don't remember what you've just read? In this chapter, you will learn how to become an active reader and how to maximize your reading. You will visualize yourself reading

quickly, comprehending, and recalling information. You will see yourself discovering new information, building on facts and concepts, developing skills to retain and recall, and feeling the joy of reading.

JOURNAL ENTRY In **Worksheet 5.1** on page 5–24, describe a time when you enjoyed being read to. Why was the experience pleasurable? What types of books did you enjoy most? Did you have a favorite book or story?

Key Teaching Concept
Reading is an active skill that requires focus and concentration.

Use
TM 5.1 Success Principle 5

Teaching Tip
Emphasize the importance of using the ABCDE Method of Self-Management to visualize success and create positive results.

Teaching Tip
Ask students to bring a textbook(s) from a different class(es). Stack seven or eight of them to illustrate how students see the "mountain of reading" facing them.

Class Discussion
How do these competencies create college and job success? Applying SCANS:
Basic Skills
Reading
Create a reading system

Words to Succeed

"To read a writer is for me not merely to get an idea of what he says, but to go off with him, and travel in his company."

—ANDREW GIDE
author

Some students express dismay at the mountain of reading they have to complete each week. Let's approach reading as a climber approaches a towering mountain. Experienced climbers are alert and aware of the terrain and weather. They are certain of their purpose, goals, and objectives and confident of their skills. They know the importance of concentration, and they maintain a relaxed, calm, and centered focus but never allow themselves to get too comfortable or inattentive.

The same sense of adventure and purpose, concentration, and attentiveness is necessary if you are going to make reading more enjoyable and increase your comprehension. The amount of reading required in school is enormous and demanding, and it is easy to get discouraged and put off reading until it piles up. In this chapter, you will learn to create a reading system that helps you keep up with your reading assignments and increase your comprehension.

The Importance of Active Reading

When you were a child at home, you may have been told, "This is quiet time; go read a book," or "Curl up with a book and just relax." In school, your instructor may have said, "Read Chapters 1 through 5 for tomorrow's test," or "You didn't do well on the test because you didn't read the directions carefully." On the job, someone may have said to you, "I need your reactions to this report. Have them ready to discuss by this afternoon."

Whether you are reading material for enjoyment, for a test, or for a research project on the job, to be an effective reader you must become actively involved with what you are reading. Previewing, taking notes, outlining main points, digging out ideas, jotting down key words, finding definitions, asking and answering questions, underlining important points, looking for patterns and themes, summarizing in your own words, and reviewing for recall can all greatly improve your comprehension. This is active reading because you, the reader, are purposeful, attentive, and physically active.

Reading Systems

Many factors affect your reading comprehension. Your skill level, vocabulary, ability to concentrate, and state of mind, as well as the type of distractions, all affect your comprehension and ability to recall what you have read. Over the years, you may have developed a reading system that works best for you. Once such system is known as the Five-Part Reading System.

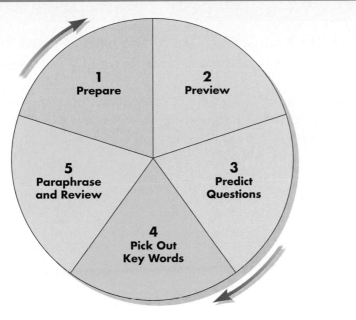

Figure 5.1   The Five-Part Reading System

1 Prepare

2 Preview

3 Predict Questions

4 Pick Out Key Words

5 Paraphrase and Review

The Five-Part Reading System   This system can be useful for increasing your reading comprehension and recall. *In what ways is this system similar to your own reading system?*

Use
TM 5.2 The Five-Part Reading System.

THE FIVE-PART READING SYSTEM

The Five-Part Reading System (see **Figure 5.1**) is similar to the Adult Learning Cycle that is explored throughout this text (see **Peak Progress 5.1**).

1. **Prepare.** Prepare yourself mentally for reading by creating a positive, interested attitude. Look for ways to make the subject matter meaningful. Focus your attention on what you are about to read. Clarify your purpose and how you will use the information. Think about what you already know about the subject before you begin reading. Prepare yourself physically by being rested, and read during high-energy times. Eliminate distractions by choosing a study area that encourages concentration. Make a conscious choice to become a better reader.

2. **Preview.** A quick survey of the chapter you are about to read will give you a general overview. Pay attention to the title, chapter headings, illustrations, and key and boldface words. Look for main ideas, connections between concepts, terms, formulas, and general understanding. By gaining a general understanding of the assignment, you will be better prepared to actively read the material and to understand the classroom lecture. Reinforce your reading by being an active listener in class. Observe the instructor and listen to key chapter points. Observe your study-group members explain and summarize the chapter.

Class Discussion
Ask students how the Five-Part Reading System helps keep them alert and mindful.

Teaching Tip
Emphasize the importance
of going through the Adult
Learning Cycle to create
interest and skill.

Teaching Tip
Stress to students the
importance of summarizing
information in their own
words. This is the best tip for
creating real understanding.

Peak Progress 5.1

Applying the Adult Learning Cycle to Becoming a Better Reader

Becoming an active reader and learning to like reading takes time, effort, and practice.

1. **RELATE. Why do I want to learn this?** Being an effective reader can help me get ahead in school, work, and life. Through reading, I continually learn new things and explore new ideas. I can also escape through fiction, thus relieving the stress of the day. What do I want to improve overall about my reading?

2. **OBSERVE. How does this work?** I can learn a lot about active reading by watching, listening, and trying new things. I'll observe people who are avid readers and who remember information. Do I know someone who isn't a good or committed reader? I will try new techniques and strategies for active reading and mark my improvement.

3. **THINK. What does this mean?** Which techniques work and which ones don't work for me? Can I find creative ways to make reading more enjoyable and effective?

4. **DO. What can I do with this?** I will make a commitment to be a more active reader. I'll find practical applications for practicing my new reading skills. Each day, I'll work on one area. For example, I'll choose one class in which I'm having trouble reading and experiment with new strategies.

5. **TEACH. Whom can I share this with?** I'll talk with others and share my tips and experiences. I'll demonstrate and relay the methods I've learned to others. I'll read more for pleasure and read to others when possible.

Remember, the more you go through the cycle, the more interest and meaning reading will have for you.

3. **Predict questions.** Next, change every heading into a question and think about connections. Predict test questions and search for answers as you read. Ask what, who, when, where, why, and how. The more questions you ask, the better prepared you will be to find answers. Experiment and make reading physical whenever possible. For example, you might try reading while standing up or reading out loud.

4. **Pick out key words.** Outline, underline, and highlight key words, main ideas, definitions, facts, and important concepts. Look for main ideas, supporting points, connections, and answers to the questions you have raised. This is the time to develop an outline, either a traditional outline or a mind map, to help you organize the information. Integrate what you are reading into classroom lectures, notes, field trips, study-group discussions, models, and graphs.

5. **Paraphrase.** Rewrite in your own words, summarize, and review. Write a short summary and then recite it out loud or share it in your study group. Practice

reciting this summary right after class and again within 24 hours of previewing the chapter. Review several times until you understand the material and can explain it to someone else. Recite out loud and in your own words and teach someone else. This helps you integrate learning styles and remember the main points at the end of each major section. Review in your study teams and take turns listening to each other's summary. Remember that the best way to learn is to teach. Carry your note cards, so you can review questions and answers and can summarize often.

Class Discussion
Ask students how they can prepare their minds for reading. What is the connection between attitude and reading?

THE SQ3R READING SYSTEM

The method of reading called the SQ3R Reading System has helped many students improve their reading comprehension since it was first developed by Professor Francis Robinson in 1941. It suggests that the reader apply these five steps to be an effective reader.

1. **S—Survey** the material before reading it. Quickly peruse the contents, scan the main heads, look at illustrations and captions, and become familiar with the special features in each chapter.
2. **Q**—Find the main points and ask **questions.**
3. **R—Read** the material.
4. **R—Recite** the main ideas and key points in your words.
5. **R—Review** the material carefully.

See **Personal Performance Notebook 5.1** on page 5–6 for further explanation and application.

Preparation for Reading

Before you begin a reading assignment, prepare yourself mentally through affirmations. Avoid telling yourself that the book is too hard or too boring. Instead, try saying to yourself, "This book looks interesting," or "The information in this book will be helpful."

If you approach reading with a lack of interest or importance, you will read only what is required. Your ability to retain will be influenced negatively. Retention is the process by which you store information. If you think something is important, you will retain it. *Remember:* Critical reading requires skill accompanied by a positive attitude.

Being in the present means being mindful and keenly aware. Whether you are playing a sport, performing a dance, giving a speech, acting in a play, talking with a friend, or focusing on a difficult book, being in the present is the key to concentration. Keep your reading goals in mind and concentrate on understanding main points as you prepare to read. If your mind does wander, take a quick break, drink a glass of water, or stretch. Become aware of your posture, your thoughts, and your

PEAKTIP

To succeed in business, learn to be a critical reader. You will be able to keep up with journals, professional readings, memos, reports, surveys, and a stack of daily mail.

Using the SQ3R System

Look at the following table for a review of the SQ3R System. Then, do the activity that follows.

Letter	Meaning	Reading Activity
S	Survey	Survey the assigned reading material. Pay attention to the title, boldface terms, the introduction, and the summary.
Q	Question	Find the major heads. Try to make questions out of these heads.
3R	1. Read	Read the material section by section or part by part.
	2. Recite	After reading a section or part, try to summarize aloud what you have read. Make sure your summary answers the question you formed for the section's or part's head.
	3. Review	After reading the entire assigned reading material, review your question heads. Make sure you can recall your original questions and answers. If you cannot, then go back and reread that section or part.

Use the SQ3R system for the following reading selection; then complete the questions that follow.

Job Searching

Point of Departure

Before you begin to look for a job, it is important to decide what you want to do, what you like to do, and what skills and abilities you have to offer.

Self-knowledge is an understanding of your skills, strengths, capabilities, feelings, character, and motivations. It means you have done some serious reflection about what is important to you and what values you want to live your life by. It is very hard to make a career decision unless you really know yourself.

Know Yourself

The more you know about yourself—your skills, values, and attitudes and the type of work you like best—the easier it will be to market your skills. Your entire job search will be faster and smoother if you
- Identify your most marketable skills.
- Assess your strengths.
- Review your interests.
- Identify creative ways you solve problems.

Using the SQ3R System—continued

S—Survey

1. What is the title of the selection?

   _____

2. What is the reading selection about?

   _____

3. What are the major topics?

   _____

4. List the boldface terms.

   _____

Q—Question

5. Write a question for the first heading.

   _____

6. Write a question for the second heading.

   _____

3 Rs

R—Read

Read the selection section by section.

R—Recite

Briefly summarize to yourself what you read. Then, share your summary with a study team member.

R—Review

7. Can you recall the questions you had for each head?   Yes _____   No _____

8. Can you answer those questions?   Yes _____   No _____

Write your answers for each section head question on the following lines.

9. Heading 1

   _____

10. Heading 2

    _____

Preview Your Reading
You get the big picture by quickly scanning through a book, and you enhance your learning. *Besides identifying key concepts, what else should you look for when previewing?*

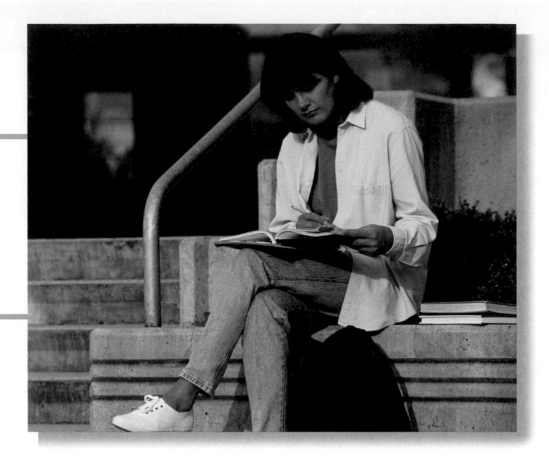

surroundings, and then gently bring your thoughts back to the task at hand. Do this consistently.

Since active reading requires an alert mind, it is important to get enough sleep. Read when you are most rested and alert. Prepare yourself physically by sitting up in your chair and taking deep breaths frequently. Read at your study area, which you have organized and supplied with the necessary study material. Your mind will begin to associate this spot with being alert and producing results.

Determine whether you are reading for pleasure, previewing information, enhancing classroom lectures, looking for background information, understanding ideas, finding facts, memorizing formulas and data, or analyzing and comprehending a difficult or complex subject. In this way, you clarify your purpose for reading. Determine what you want to get from an assignment, plan the amount of material you intend to read, and set a goal for the time it will take. Ask yourself, "Why am I reading this?" You will be more motivated when there is a set goal and time for completion.

Previewing is a major step in making the most of your reading. Just as an athlete warms up before a jog, previewing warms up your brain for incoming information. Therefore, the goal in previewing is to read quickly for an overall understanding of main concepts and ideas. You want to get the big picture, not memorize facts or details. Identify the main idea of each section to get a feel for the chapter. Look at how it is organized; its level of difficulty; and the illustrations, diagrams, pictures, summaries, and graphs. Look for familiar concepts and connections.

Reading Strategies

To improve your reading, here are some active reading strategies you may wish to use as you read:

1. **Outline the main points.** Organizing information in an outline creates order and understanding. Use a traditional outline or mind map to outline the main points quickly. The purpose of a brief outline is to add meaning and structure to material, as well as to simplify and organize complex information. The physical process of writing and organizing material creates a foundation for committing it to memory. Use section titles and paragraph headlines to provide a guide. Identify the main ideas.

2. **Predict questions.** Dig out key points and questions. Jot down questions as you read either in the margin or in your reading notes. Asking questions gets you interested and involved, keeps you focused, organizes information, and helps you prepare for tests. As you preview the chapter, make questions out of chapter headings, section titles, and definitions. If there are sample questions at the end of the chapter, review them and tie them in with your other questions. Ask yourself, "What are some possible test questions?" List them on note cards and review them as you walk to classes or while eating or waiting in lines. Exchange questions with your study team or partner.

3. **Read actively.** Stay focused and alert by reading quickly and making it an active experience. Reading phrases instead of individual words and concentrating on main points will help you stay focused. Read difficult material aloud or stand when you read. Pretend you are explaining concepts to others or giving a lecture on the chapter. Several readings may be required to comprehend. Pay close attention to headings, main topics, key ideas, first and last sentences in paragraphs, summaries, and questions.

4. **Take frequent breaks.** Try to schedule a short stretching break about every 40 minutes. A person's brain retains information best in short study segments. Don't struggle with unclear material now. Go back to the difficult areas later when you are refreshed and when the creative process is not blocked.

5. **Make connections.** Try to link new information with what you already know. Ask yourself the following questions. They may help you make associations and jog your memory.
   - What conclusions can you make as you survey the material?
   - How can you apply this new material to other material, concepts, and examples?
   - What information does and does not match?
   - What has been your experience with reading similar subjects or with reading in general?
   - What do you know about the topic that may influence how you approach the reading?

6. **Talk with the author.** Pretend you are talking with the author and jot down points with which you agree or disagree. When your brain has been exposed

Teaching Tip
Stress that students will read with more comprehension if they develop a system that makes reading more active. Illustrate this concept by comparing reading to driving a car. If a driver becomes too relaxed, sleepy, bored, or distracted, accidents are much more likely to happen. Safe driving requires an active, alert, and mindful focus. Ask students what they do to keep themselves alert while driving.

Class Discussion
Ask how reading can be more active. Sample answers include: reading aloud, pretending to lecture in class, talking in front of a mirror.

Teaching Tip
Stress the importance of taking frequent breaks. Ask students if they have had the experience of reading for an hour and not remembering a word. Taking a short break every 30 or 40 minutes will help the mind stay alert.

Teaching Tip
Encourage students to develop a relationship with the author. Pretend they know the author and enjoy a conversation while reading material.

Words to Succeed

"To read without reflecting is like eating without digesting."

—EDMUND BURKE
British statesman and orator

to a subject before, it is far more receptive to taking in more information, so jot down in the margins everything you can think of that you already know about this topic, even if it is just a word or an image.

7. **Read in alignment with your learning style.** For example, if you are a visual learner, you can draw pictures, charts, and diagrams and highlight illustrations as you read. Develop mental pictures in your head. If you are primarily an auditory learner, read out loud or into a tape recorder and then listen to the tapes. If you are a kinesthetic learner, collect samples and recite and summarize your material with your study team. Integrate different learning styles. Write your vocabulary, formulas, and key words on note cards. Visualize key words and main ideas, and read them to yourself. Read while standing up.

8. **Identify key words.** Focus on your purpose of finding key words and main ideas by using these techniques:
   - Write in the margins.
   - Draw illustrations.
   - Underline.
   - Sketch.
   - Take notes on cards.
   - Underline or highlight important material.

   Many students use highlighters to emphasize main points and mark sections that are important to review later. Use a graphic device, such as wavy lines (~ ~), to indicate difficult material that needs to be reviewed later. Refer to **Peak Progress 5.2** on page 5–11 for sample symbols you might find helpful. Don't underline until you have previewed information. Underline just the key points and words, and think about the ideas expressed. Use a colored highlighter for marking only important material. Also, see **Peak Progress 5.3,** which shows you how to navigate around a dictionary.

Reviewing

PeakTip

Summarize your material after a lecture. Then, explain it to your study partner. Teaching something to someone else reinforces your learning.

1. **Summarize in writing.** After you finish reading, close your book. Write down everything you can recall about the chapter and the main topics. In just four or five minutes, brainstorm main ideas and key points and summarize the material in your own words. Writing is an active process that increases comprehension and recall. Write quickly and test yourself by asking questions like these:
   - What is the major theme?
   - What are the main points?
   - What are the connections to other concepts?
   - What can I summarize in one paragraph?

2. **Recite aloud.** Summarizing aloud can increase learning. Read aloud when you are previewing main points and outlining important material, as well as when you want to memorize it. Practice giving summaries in front of a mirror. Some students use an empty classroom and pretend they are lecturing. Summarize or explain the material to a study partner. Recite the

Class Discussion
Ask students:
1. Do you review often?
2. Do you take book notes or use note cards to record key words?
3. Could you find five or ten minutes twice a day to review?

Symbols

Set up a chart of the notations you plan to use in each of your courses this term. A sample chart is provided. Be methodical about using the symbols by adapting them to your needs.

You may need to use different symbols in each course, although some can be shared.

Symbol	Exploration
>	greater than
<	less than
Q	question
w/	with
w/o	without
V or *	important ideas
+	positive
–	negative
×	times
~	Lost
→	leads to (motivation → success)

Symbols	Math	English	Basic Finance
	= equals	→ leads to	$ American dollars

main ideas to your study team. You can take turns summarizing, and the benefits are enormous.

3. **Review.** You have previewed your material for an overall view, summarized main concepts, and recited aloud. Now, it is important to review for understanding main ideas and to commit the information to long-term memory. You can increase your comprehension by reviewing the material within 24 hours of your first reading session. You may want to review your outline, note cards, key words, and main points. Review headings, main topics, key ideas, first and last sentences in paragraphs, and summaries. Carry your note cards with you and review them when you have a few minutes before class. Your note cards are the most effective tool for reviewing information.

4. **Review often.** Reviewing often and in short sessions kicks the material into long-term memory. Review weekly and conduct a thorough review a week or so before a test. Keep a list of questions to ask your instructor and a list of possible test questions. Review right before you go to bed, when your mind is relaxed and is more receptive to information. As you review, use all your senses. Visualize what something looks like. Look at graphs, charts, and pictures, and actively use your imagination. Hear yourself repeat words. Read and summarize difficult material out loud. Draw illustrations. Imagine what something feels like or what it smells like.

Look It Up! Using the Dictionary

Here is a quick guide for using the dictionary.

Guide words: Boldface words at the top of the page indicate the first and last entries on the page.

Syllabication: This shows how the word is divided into syllables.

Pronunciation: The key at the bottom of right-hand page shows pronunciation.

Capital letters: The dictionary indicates if a word should be capitalized.

Part of speech: The dictionary uses nine abbreviations for the parts of speech:

n.—noun	adv.—adverb	v.t.—transitive verb
adj.—adjective	cong.—conjunction	pron.—pronoun
v.i.—intransitive verb	prep.—preposition	interj.—interjection

Etymology; This is the origin of the word, which is especially helpful if the word has a Latin or Greek root from which many other words are derived. Knowing the word's history can help you remember the word or look for similar words.

Restrictive labels: Three types of labels are used most often in a dictionary. Subject labels tell you that a word has a special meaning when used in certain fields (mus. for music; med. for medicine, etc.). Usage labels indicate how a word is used (slang, dial. for dialect, etc.). Geographic labels tell you the region of the country where the word is used most often.

Homographs: The dictionary indicates when a single spelling of a word has different meanings.

Variants: These are multiple correct spellings of a single word (ax or axe).

Illustrations: These are drawings or pictures used to help illustrate a word.

Definition: Dictionaries list the definition chronologically (oldest meaning first).

Source: By permission. From *Merriam-Webster's Collegiate® Dictionary*, 10th edition. © 2000 by Merriam-Webster, Incorporated.

Barriers to Effective Reading

The greatest barrier to effective reading is attitude. Many people are not willing to invest the time in becoming a better reader. If the material is difficult, is boring, or requires concentration, they may not continue to read or complete the reading assignment. Many students were raised in the era of videos and computer games. There is so much instant entertainment available that it is easy to watch a movie or television program or listen to the news instead of reading a newspaper or news magazine. Reading takes time, effort, concentration, and practice. Some students and career professionals say that they have too much required reading and have little time for pleasure reading. However, it is important to read for pleasure, even if you have only a few minutes a day. Carry a book with you. You might keep one in the car and another by your bed. The more you read, the more your reading skills will improve. As you become a better reader, you will find you enjoy reading more and more. You will also find that, as your attitude improves, so will your reading ability and your vocabulary.

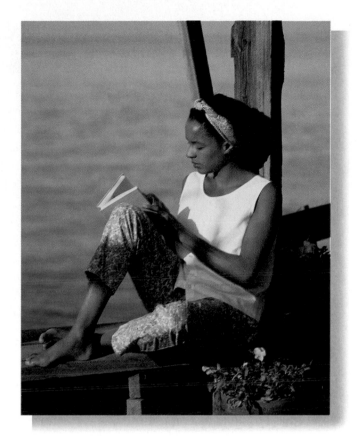

Finding Time to Read
Investing time in reading pays off. Your reading skills improve when you read more. *How can you make time to read for pleasure?*

Managing Language Courses

Building vocabulary is also important if you are taking an English as a second language course or learning a foreign language. Following are 10 reading and study tips for students who are studying different languages.

1. **Do practice exercises.** As with math and science, doing practice exercises is critical in learning another language.

2. **Keep up with your reading.** You must build on previous lessons and skills. Therefore, it is important to keep up your readings; preview chapters, so you have a basic understanding of any new words; and then complete your practice sessions several times.

3. **Carry note cards with you.** Drill yourself on the parts of speech and verb conjugation through all the tenses and practice vocabulary building.

4. **Recite out loud.** Recite new words to yourself out loud. This is especially important in a language course. Tape yourself and play it back.

5. **Form study teams.** Meet with a study team and speak only the language you are studying. Recite out loud to each other, explain verb conjugation, and use words in various contexts. Recitation is an excellent strategy when studying languages.

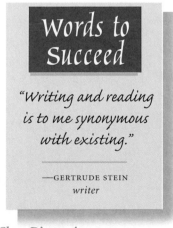

Words to Succeed

"Writing and reading is to me synonymous with existing."

—GERTRUDE STEIN
writer

Class Discussion
Have students:
1. List the barriers they experience in reading.
2. Come up with a way to overcome each major barrier to reading.
3. Name their best reading strategies.

TECH FOR SUCCESS

- **Books On-Line** Many of your textbooks can now be purchased on-line and downloaded to your computer. Most of these books are formatted to be read on-line, rather than printed out. Does this sound appealing, or would you rather read from a printed copy of the text? List some of the advantages and disadvantages of both options.
- **All the News That's Fit to Click** What's your source for the latest news? Most major newspapers are available on-line and often archive previous articles. Take a poll of your classmates to see who still opts for newsprint, who prefers the local and cable networks, and who relies on the Web. Discuss the pros and cons. Do your classmates' preferences match their learning styles? Which sources do the more avid readers prefer?

6. **Listen to tapes.** Play practice tapes while commuting, jogging, exercising, and so on.

7. **Visualize.** During an exam, visualize yourself listening to a tape, seeing the diagrams you have drawn, and hearing yourself reciting the material.

8. **Model and tutor.** Invite a student whose primary language is the one you are studying out for coffee. Speak only his or her native language. Offer to teach the person your language in exchange for private tutoring. You can meet foreign students in classes where English as a second language is taught, usually in local schools and communities.

9. **Focus on key words.** Study the meanings, tenses, and pronunciation of key words. You can also keep these exercises on note cards. Carry them with you to review.

10. **Have fun.** Do research on the country of the language you're studying. Make the language come alive for you. Invite your study group over for an authentic meal, complete with music and costumes. Invite foreign students and your instructor.

The same principles and strategies you use for reading English can be applied to reading and learning a foreign language. Your efforts will be worthwhile especially when you are able to speak, read, and understand another language as you communicate in the real world. Remember, as you become a better reader, you will enjoy the new language more and more.

Words to Succeed

"If you wish to know the mind of a man, listen to his words."

—CHINESE PROVERB

Vocabulary Building

You will need a fundamental vocabulary to master any subject. Developing a good vocabulary is important for reading comprehension and success in college. To succeed in a career, you must know and understand the meaning of words that you encounter in conversations, reports, meetings, and professional reading. People often judge the intelligence of another person by the ability to communicate through words. Words are the tools of thinking and communicating. Try the following methods for building your vocabulary:

- **Realize the power and value of words.** An effective speaker who has a command of language can influence others.
- **Observe your words and habits.** You may be unaware that you fill your conversations with annoying words, such as *you know, OK, like,* and *yeah.*
- **Be creative and articulate.** Use precise, interesting, expressive words.
- **Associate with articulate people.** Surround yourself with people who have effective and extensive vocabularies.
- **Be aware and alert.** Listen for new words. Observe how they are used and how often you hear them and see them in print.
- **Look up words you don't know.** Keep a dictionary at your desk or study area.
- **Study the word.** How can you use it in conversation?
- **Write new words.** Write new words in your journal or on note cards.
- **Practice mentally.** Say new words again and again in your mind as you read and think of appropriate settings where you could use the words.
- **Practice in conversation.** Use new words until you are comfortable using them.
- **Read.** The best way to improve your vocabulary is to read more.
- **Review great speeches.** Look at how Abraham Lincoln, Benjamin Franklin, Winston Churchill, and Thomas Jefferson chose precise words. Read letters written during the Revolutionary and Civil Wars. You may find that the common person at that time was more articulate and expressive than many people today.
- **Invest in a vocabulary book.**
- **Look for contextual clues.** Try to figure out a word by the context in which it is used.
- **Learn common word parts.** Knowing root words, prefixes, and suffixes makes it easier to understand the meaning of many new words. Also, learn to recognize syllables. When you divide words into syllables, you learn them faster, and doing so helps with pronunciation, spelling, and memory recall.

Root	Meaning	Example
auto	self	autograph, autobiography
sub	under	submarine, submerge
circum	around	circumference, circumspect
manu	hand	manuscript, manual, manufacture

Technical Reading

Some of the subjects you are taking now or will take, as your course of study progresses, will involve technical information. Science, math, computer science, accounting, and statistics courses tend to present their data in specialized formats. You may find yourself interpreting graphs, charts, diagrams, or tables. You may be reading technical material, such as the directions for a chemistry experiment, a flowchart for a computer program, the steps for administering medication, or the statistical analysis of a financial statement.

Such material can be complicated and difficult. This is why many readers—student readers, in particular—tend to skip over it or become discouraged. However, there are some reading strategies you can implement when you encounter technical material in your studies or on the job:

- Do not skip over any graphics.
- Read the
  1. Graphic title
  2. Accompanying captions
  3. Column titles
  4. Labels or symbols and their interpretations
  5. Data (percentages, totals, figures, etc.)
- Identify the type of graphic you are looking at. Are you looking at a table, chart, or graph?
- Identify the purpose of the graphic. Is it demonstrating to the reader similarities or differences; increases or decreases; comparisons or changes; and so on?
- See a connection between the topic of the graphic and the chapter or section topic in which it appears.
- Explain in your own words the information depicted on the graphic.
- Share your interpretation of the graphic with your study-group members. Did they feel your interpretation was clear and on target?

Reading Forms

Whether you are entering school, applying for a job, filling out medical papers, or requesting a bank loan, you will probably have to fill out some type of form. Although forms differ in many ways, there are many elements of information that are requested on all forms. You can expect to provide your name, address, social security number, and phone numbers.

Reading the form carefully and accurately can save time and prevent complications (see **Figure 5.2**)—for example,

- Directions may ask you to print your name in black or blue ink. Make sure you do not use a pencil or write your name in cursive handwriting.
- A job application may ask that you answer all questions in your own handwriting. Make sure you do not type the application.

In both cases, the forms would most likely be returned to you because you did not read the directions carefully. For instance, if you type the job application, and it is returned to you for failing to follow the directions, you may miss the deadline for

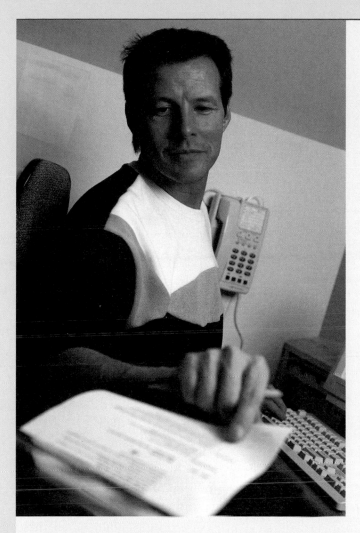

Brian Singer

INFORMATION TECHNOLOGY SPECIALIST

Related Majors: Computer Science, Mathematics, Information Systems

Keeping Up-to-Date

Brian Singer is an information technology specialist, or computer programmer. His job is to write instructions that computers follow to perform their functions. His programs instruct computers what to do, from updating financial records to simulating air flight as training for pilots.

When writing a program, Brian must first break the task into various instructional steps that a computer can follow. Then, each step must be coded into a programming language, such as COBOL. When finished, Brian tests the program to confirm it works accurately. Usually, he needs to make some adjustments, called debugging, before the program runs smoothly. The program must be maintained over time, updated, or modified as the need arises. Because critical problems can be intricate and time-consuming and must be fixed quickly, Brian usually finds himself working long hours, including evenings and weekends. Although his office surroundings are comfortable, Brian must be careful to avoid physical problems, such as eyestrain or back discomfort.

To stay current in his field, Brian reads about 500 pages of technical materials each week. Brian also took a class on reading technical information to improve his reading skills. Because he concentrates best when he is around people, Brian likes to read and study in a coffeehouse. When he has difficulty understanding what he reads, he gets on the Internet and asks for help from an on-line discussion group. To help him remember and better understand what he has read during the week, Brian tries to implement the new information in his work.

CRITICAL THINKING

What skills might help an information technology specialist when reading technical information?

Teaching Tip
Distribute a school
application form for
students to practice
filling out.

Figure 5.2   Filling Out Forms

APPLICATION FOR EMPLOYMENT
SUPERIOR MARKETS

DIRECTIONS: Please use a pen and print.
Answer all sections completely and accurately.

NAME			SOCIAL SECURITY NUMBER
LAST	FIRST	MIDDLE	
Cortez	Mark	A.	032-32-3712

HOME ADDRESS				
NUMBER	STREET	CITY	STATE	ZIP
134	North Avenue	Indianapolis	IN	46268

TELEPHONE	ALTERNATE #
(317) 555-2492	

Filling Out Forms   You can even apply good reading skills when filling out forms and applications. *What could happen if you were to use handwriting and a pencil to fill out this form?*

submitting it and lose the job opportunity. Some of this carelessness in reading forms can be avoided by using the following reading tips:

◆ Scan the entire form before you begin to fill it out.

◆ If you are unsure of any questions and what information is actually needed, ask or call the appropriate office or person for clarification.

◆ When filling out the form, read the small print directions carefully. Often, these directions appear in parentheses below a fill-in blank.

◆ Fill in all questions that pertain to you. Pay attention when you read the directions that tell you what sections of the form or application you should fill out and what sections are to be completed by someone else.

◆ Make sure you write clearly—particularly numbers.

◆ When reporting somewhere to fill out forms, take with you any pertinent information that may be needed. Call ahead and ask what you are expected to have with you (for example, Social Security card; proof of citizenship; dates of employment or schooling; names, addresses, and phone numbers of references, former employees, or teachers).

◆ Reread your responses before submitting your form or application.

Peak Performer Profile

Oprah Winfrey

Accomplished actress, film producer, and magazine publisher, Oprah Winfrey is best known as the popular host and producer of an Emmy-award-winning talk show that aims to inspire.

Winfrey's career began when she entered Tennessee State University and soon began working in radio and television broadcasting in Nashville, Tennessee. Later, she moved to Baltimore, Maryland, where she hosted a TV talk show, which became a hit. After eight years, a Chicago TV station recruited Winfrey to host a morning show. The success of that show led her to launch the celebrated *Oprah Winfrey Show*.

A straightforward and winning approach has characterized Winfrey throughout her career. At 17, she was a contestant in a Nashville pageant for "Miss Fire Prevention." She was asked what she would do if she had a million dollars. Her response was "I would be a spending fool." She won the pageant. Over three decades later, she still displays the same bravado that propelled her from rural Mississippi to *Time* magazine's list of the 100 most influential people of the twentieth century.

However, Winfrey's success doesn't rest simply on accolades but, rather, on her connection with her audience. She shares the ups and downs of her own life and the ways in which she has overcome adversity. As an abused child and runaway teenager, Winfrey found refuge with her father, a man who expected the best from her and encouraged one of her lifelong passions—reading. Her love of books inspired her to establish a book club, which opened up the world of reading to millions of people in her audience. Winfrey credits books with saving her life and making her the person she is today. She says her goal is to help make the same kind of difference in other people's lives.

PERFORMANCE THINKING   Choose a favorite book you have read and explain why you like it. Do you set time aside for reading for pleasure? Have you considered joining a book club and meeting people with similar interests? How can you inspire others to become avid readers?

TAKING CHARGE

In summary, in this chapter, I learned to

- *Be an active reader.* I stay focused and alert by reading quickly and making it an active experience. I concentrate on main points and general understanding. I read difficult material out loud or standing up. I write in the margins, draw illustrations, underline, sketch, take notes, and dig out key points and words. I pretend that I'm giving a lecture on the chapter and that I'm talking with the author and jotting down questions.

- *Apply the Five-Part Reading System.* Very similar to the Adult Learning Cycle, this system is useful for increasing my comprehension and recall. The steps include (1) prepare; (2) preview; (3) predict questions; (4) pick out key words; and (5) paraphrase and review.

- *Apply the SQ3R Reading System.* A five-step process, this method can improve my reading comprehension: S = Survey; Q = Questions; R = Read; R = Recite; R = Review.

- *Prepare for reading.* I prepare myself by creating meaning, purpose, and interest in the material. I make certain that I'm attentive and alert and look for ways to make reading physically active. I replace negative self-talk with affirmations and visualize myself reading with confidence and pleasure.

- *Preview the material and predict questions.* Scanning chapters gives me a quick overview of main concepts and ideas. I look for information that I already know and link it to information that is new. I look for key words, main ideas, definitions, facts, and important concepts. I make questions out of chapter headings and definitions. I go back over the chapter to find answers and jot them down in the margin or on note cards and compare my answers with those of my study team.

- *Outline main points and make connections.* Organizing information in an outline creates order, meaning, and understanding and makes it easier to recall the material. It helps simplify difficult information and make connections. I link new information with what I already know and look for connections to what I don't know. I look for similarities and differences. I look for examples and read end-of-chapter summaries.

- *Integrate learning styles.* I draw pictures, charts, and diagrams and use different-color pens to highlight. I read difficult material out loud and read sum-

continued

maries to my study group. I tape sections I want to memorize and play them back. I visualize key words and main ideas. I integrate learning styles and make reading active.

- *Summarize.* Summarizing in writing and out loud is a powerful reading and memory strategy. I close the book at various times, write summaries, and then check my brief summaries with the book. I summarize in writing after I finish a quick read of the chapter and then fill in with details. I summarize out loud to myself and my study group.

- *Review.* I increase my comprehension by reviewing my outline, note cards, key words, main points, and summaries. I review within 24 hours of reading and after lectures. Teaching what I know and presenting my summaries to my study team is a great way to prepare for tests and to make recall easier.

- *Practice.* The more I read, the better reader I become. Reading becomes a pleasurable activity, and my vocabulary and knowledge base increases.

- *Manage language courses.* Many of the same vocabulary building strategies work for second-language courses, such as focusing on key words, reciting out loud, carrying note cards, listening to tapes, keeping up with the reading assignments, and using practice exercises. I also take advantage of study teams, find a model or tutor, explore fun and creative ways to learn more about the language and culture, and visualize myself successfully understanding the material.

- *Build a strong vocabulary.* A good vocabulary is critical to my success in school and my career. I can improve my vocabulary by learning and incorporating new words into my writing and conversation, using resources such as a dictionary or vocabulary book, and observing my speech habits.

- *Tackle technical reading and forms.* Thorough and precise reading is critical when reading technical information, graphs, and forms. Tips for technical information include identifying the purpose of the material or graph, looking for connections, and explaining in my own words. Tips for forms include scanning before I begin, reading the small print, knowing what pertains to me, and asking questions when I'm unsure.

Performance Strategies · · · · · · · · · · · · ·

Following are the top 10 strategies for active reading:

◆ Find interest in the material.

◆ Outline main points and identify key words.

◆ Gather information and predict questions.

◆ Stay focused by reading quickly.

◆ Take breaks and make reading physical.

◆ Reduce distractions and stay alert.

◆ Make connections and link information.

◆ Create a relationship with the author.

◆ Summarize in writing in your own words.

◆ Teach by summarizing out loud and explaining it to others.

Review Questions

1. Name and describe each part of the Five-Part Reading System.

2. How does outlining the main points help you improve your reading?

3. What is the greatest barrier to effective reading?

4. Name five strategies for managing language courses.

5. Why should you try to build your vocabulary?

REVISUALIZATION

Revisit the Visualization box on the first page of this chapter and your journal entry in **Worksheet 5.1.** You relayed an early, positive experience with reading. Now, think about your current feelings about reading. Do you enjoy reading? If so, what are the benefits for you? Visualize either a recent positive or recent negative reading situation. A positive situation might be joining a book club. A negative situation might be having three major reading assignments due at once. Revisit **Worksheet 5.1** and apply the ABCDE method to visualize how the situation can enhance your reading skills—for example,

A = Actual event: "I am distracted and tired as I try to read today's assignment. I can't seem to comprehend what this chapter is about."

B = Beliefs: "My mind wanders too much when I read. I always wait until the last minute to prepare for class, and now I can't stay focused long enough to finish the required reading."

C = Consequence: "I'm nervous that I won't be prepared enough for class. What if I get called on to answer a question?"

D = Dispute: "Procrastination is a habit I can break if I just put forth the effort. Even if I don't finish all the required reading today, I can apply effective strategies to the material I am able to tackle."

E = Energized: "I'm energized because I know that it is worth the effort to become a better reader. It will help me in all areas of life. Reading is a skill I can learn and practice. It makes sense to invest the time in learning reading strategies and becoming a more effective reader. Like any skill, with practice comes interest, meaning, and confidence."

EFFECTIVE READING HABITS

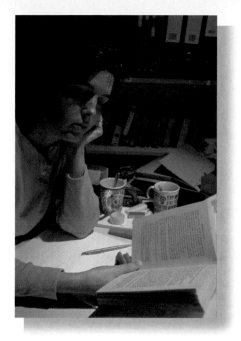

In The Classroom

Chris McDaniel has problems keeping up with her reading. She is overwhelmed by the amount of reading and the difficulty of her textbooks. She has never been much of a reader but enjoys watching television. She sometimes reads in bed or in a comfortable chair but often falls asleep. She realizes that this is not the most productive way to study, but it has become a habit. Chris has noticed that, after reading for an hour or so, she can recall almost nothing. This has caused her frustration and self-doubt about her ability to succeed in college.

1. What habits should Chris change to help her improve her reading skills?

   _____

   _____

   _____

2. Suggest one or two specific strategies Chris could implement to become a better reader.

   _____

   _____

In The Workplace

Chris is now a stockbroker. She never thought that she would work in this business, but a part-time summer job led her to a career in finance, and she really likes the challenge. She is surprised, however, at the vast amount of reading involved in her job: reports, letters, magazines, and articles. She also reads several books on money management each month.

3. What strategies in this chapter would help Chris manage and organize her reading materials?

   _____

   _____

4. What are some specific reading strategies that apply to both school and work?

   _____

   _____

CHAPTER 5 ▲ REVIEW AND APPLICATIONS

APPLYING THE ABCDE METHOD OF SELF-MANAGEMENT

In the Visualization box on page 5–1, you were asked to describe a time when you enjoyed being read to. Why was the experience pleasurable? What types of books did you enjoy most? Did you have a favorite book or story?

_____

_____

_____

_____

Now, think about your current experiences with reading. Do you enjoy reading? If so, what are the benefits to you? Visualize either a recent positive or a recent negative reading situation. Apply the ABCDE steps to visualize how the situation can enhance your reading skills.

A = Actual event:

B = Beliefs:

C = Consequences:

D = Dispute:

E = Energized:

When you are in a positive state of mind, do you see yourself reading quickly and comprehending and recalling information effortlessly? Enjoy becoming an active reader.

ATTITUDES AND READING

Read the following questions and write your answers on the lines provided.

1. What is your attitude toward reading?

_____

_____

2. What kind of books do you most like to read?

_____

_____

3. Do you read for pleasure?

_____

_____

4. Do you read the daily newspaper?   Yes _____   No _____

   If yes, what sections do you read? Place a check mark.

   _____ Comics   _____ Horoscope   _____ Weather

   _____ Sports   _____ Classified ads   _____ World news

   _____ Business   _____ Entertainment   _____ Other

5. Do you read magazines?   Yes _____   No _____

   If yes, which magazines?

   _____

   _____

6. Do you want to read faster?

   _____

   _____

7. Do you want to remember what you have read?

   _____

   _____

8. What techniques can you learn to read faster and remember more?

   _____

   _____

DIFFERENT TYPES OF READING

Find a sample of each of the following sources of reading material:

- Newspaper
- Chapter from a textbook
- Instructions for an appliance, insurance policy, or rental contract

Read each sample. Then, answer the following questions.

1. How does the reading process differ for each type of reading?

_____

_____

_____

_____

_____

_____

_____

_____

_____

_____

2. Does knowing your purpose for reading affect how you read? Why?

_____

_____

_____

_____

_____

_____

_____

_____

_____

CHAPTER 5 ▶ REVIEW AND APPLICATIONS

SUMMARIZE AND TEACH

1. Read the following paragraph on predicting questions. Underline, write in the margins, and write a summary of the paragraph. Compare your work with a study partner's work. There are many ways to highlight, so don't be concerned if yours is different. Comparing may give you ideas on creative note taking.

Predicting Questions

Dig out key points and questions. Jot down questions either in the margin or in your reading notes as you read. Asking questions gets you interested and involved, keeps you focused, organizes information, and helps you prepare for tests. As you preview the chapter, make questions out of chapter headings, sections, titles, and definitions. If there are sample questions at the end of the chapter, review them and tie them in with your own questions. What are possible test questions? List them on note cards and review them. Exchange questions with your study team or partner.

Summary

_____

_____

_____

_____

_____

_____

_____

_____

_____

_____

_____

_____

_____

_____

_____

_____

_____

continued

CHAPTER 5 ◀ REVIEW AND APPLICATIONS

2. Work with a study partner in one of your classes. Read a chapter and write a summary. Compare your summary with your study partner's summary. Now, summarize and teach the main concepts to your partner. Each of you can clarify and ask questions.

Summary

_____

_____

_____

_____

_____

_____

_____

_____

_____

_____

_____

_____

_____

_____

_____

_____

_____

_____

_____

_____

_____

_____

_____

_____

CREATING A READING OUTLINE

Outlining what you read can be a helpful study technique. Develop the habit of outlining. Use the following form as a guide. You may also develop your own form. Outline pages 5-2 through 5-9 of Chapter 5 on the lines below.

Course _____ Chapter _____ Date _____

I. _____

   A. _____

      1. _____

      2. _____

      3. _____

      4. _____

   B. _____

      1. _____

      2. _____

      3. _____

      4. _____

II. _____

   A. _____

      1. _____

      2. _____

      3. _____

      4. _____

   B. _____

      1. _____

      2. _____

continued

III. _____

   A. _____

      1. _____

      2. _____

      3. _____

      4. _____

   B. _____

      1. _____

      2. _____

      3. _____

      4. _____

IV. _____

   A. _____

      1. _____

      2. _____

      3. _____

      4. _____

   B. _____

      1. _____

      2. _____

      3. _____

      4. _____

ANALYZING CHAPTERS

As you start to read the next chapter in this book, fill in this page to prepare for reading. You may need to add additional headings. List each heading and then phrase it as a question. Then, summarize as you complete your reading. Use a separate sheet of paper if needed.

Course _____ Textbook _____

Chapter _____

Heading 1 _____

Question _____

Heading 2 _____

Question _____

Heading 3 _____

Question _____

Heading 4 _____

Question _____

Summary of Section

_____

_____

_____

_____

_____

Summary of Chapter

_____

_____

_____

_____

_____

_____

BREAKING BARRIERS TO READING

Following is a list of the common reasons that some students use for not reading effectively. Read this list; then add to it on the lines provided. Use creative problem solving to list strategies for overcoming these barriers.

Reasons for Not Reading	Strategies for Overcoming Reading Barriers
1. My textbooks are boring.	
2. I can't concentrate.	
3. I'm easily distracted.	
4. I fall asleep when I read.	
5. I never study the right material.	
6. There is too much information, and I don't know what is important.	
7. I read for hours, but I don't understand what I have read.	
8. I don't like to read.	

READING MATRIX

Use this matrix for the textbook assigned in each of your classes. As you read an assignment, place a check mark in each box when you complete each part of the Five-Part Reading System.

	Prepare				Preview				Predict Questions				Pick Out Key Words				Paraphrase			
	Create positive attitude.	Create an interested attitude.	Clarify your purpose.	Prepare yourself physically.	Preview contents.	Preview titles and chapter headings.	Preview for overall understanding.	Preview summary.	Predict topics.	Predict questions.	Predict answers.	Ask Who? What? Where? When? Why? How?	Pick out key words.	Pick out main ideas.	Underline important points.	Develop an outline.	Paraphrase.	Recite out loud.	Write a summary.	Review at interval times.
Class																				
Class																				
Class																				
Class																				

DEMONSTRATING COMPETENCIES

Follow these steps and fill in the chart to identify and demonstrate your competencies. Then, add this page to your Career Development Portfolio.

1. **Looking back:** Review your worksheets from other chapters to find activities from which you learned to read and concentrate.

2. **Taking stock:** Identify your strengths in reading and what you want to improve.

3. **Looking forward:** Indicate how you would demonstrate reading and comprehension skills to an employer.

4. **Documentation:** Include documentation of your reading skills.

5. **Inventory:** Make a list of the books you've read recently and include any classics. Use a separate sheet of paper.

6. Fill in the chart; explain how you demonstrate these competencies:

Competencies	Your Demonstration
Active reading	
Critical reading	
Willingness to learn new words	
Improvement in technical vocabulary	
Articulation	
Expressiveness	
Ability to use dictionary	
Positive attitude toward reading	
Technical reading	
Form reading	

Memory Skills

Chapter Objectives

In this chapter, you will learn

▲ How to prepare yourself mentally and physically for remembering

▲ How to use your senses and learning styles to enhance memory

▲ Memory strategies

▲ How to use mnemonic devices

▲ How to recall names

Visualization

"I have been meeting so many new people. I wish I could remember their names, but I just don't have a good memory. What can I do to increase my memory skills and actually remember names, facts, and information more easily?"

Do you ever find yourself feeling embarrassed because you cannot remember the names of new people you've met? Do you ever get frustrated because you don't remember material for a test? In this chapter, you will learn how to increase your memory skills.

Journal Entry In **Worksheet 6.1** on page 6–24, describe a situation when you needed to learn many new names or numerous facts for a test. How did you fare? What factors helped you remember?

Use
- TM 6.1 Success Principle 6.
- TM 6.2 The Memory Process.

Teaching Tip
Emphasize the importance of using the ABCDE Method of Self-Management to visualize success and create positive results.

Y ou may have heard someone say, "I just don't have a good memory." Do you have a good memory? Do you think some people are simply born with better memories? You will discover in this chapter that memory is a process. As a complex process, memory is not an isolated activity that takes place in one part of the brain; it involves many factors that you can control. How well you remember depends on factors, such as your attitude, interest, intent, awareness, mental alertness, observation skills, senses, distractions, memory devices, and willingness to practice. Most people with good memories say that the skill is mastered by learning the strategies for storing and recalling information. This chapter will summarize and highlight specific strategies that help you remember information.

The Memory Process

The memory process involves five main steps:

1. Intention—you are interested and excited about learning
2. Observation—you are alert and attentive and observe information
3. Organization—you experiment and organize information to make sense of it
4. Retention—you practice and repeat until you know the information
5. Recall—you recall, teach, and share information with others

As you can see, this process is quite similar to the Adult Learning Cycle, which is explored throughout this text. Read **Peak Progress 6.1** to see how you can use it to improve your memory skills.

1. **Intention.** The first step in using memory effectively is to prepare yourself mentally. As with learning any skill, your intention, attitude, and motivation are fundamental to success. Intention means that you are interested and willing to learn. You intend to remember by finding personal meaning and interest. You must want to remember. Have you ever said, "I wish I could remember names," "I'm just not good at remembering facts for tests," or "I can't remember formulas for math"? Instead, say, "I really want to remember JoAnne's name."

   If you make excuses or program your mind with negative self-talk, your mind refuses to learn new information. If you think a subject is boring or unimportant, you will have difficulty remembering it. Too often, students study just enough to get by on a quiz and forget the information immediately thereafter. It is much better to learn a subject so that it becomes interesting and part of your long-term memory. Uncover the facts, interesting points, related materials, details, and fascinating aspects of the subject. Ask your instructor for interesting stories to enhance a point. Read a novel on the subject or look for another textbook in the library that explains the subject from a different view.

Words to Succeed

"Remember people and learn their names."

—YUKI TOGO
former president of Toyota

Class Discussion
How do these competencies create college and job success? Applying SCANS:
Basic skills
Mental visualization
Acquiring and evaluating information
Organizing and maintaining information

Class Discussion
Ask students:
1. What is the connection between memory and attitude?
2. Does the material or the instructor affect the difficulty in remembering information?

Teaching Tip
Emphasize the importance
of using the Adult Learning
Cycle to increase interest
and skill.

Peak Progress 6.1

Applying the Adult Learning Cycle to Increase Your Memory Skills

1. **RELATE. Why do I want to learn this?** I must become more proficient at remembering names, facts, and information. This is critical not only for success in school but also in the workplace and social situations. What strategies do I already use to remember and retain information?

2. **OBSERVE. How does this work?** Whom do I know who is good at remembering names and information? What tips can I pick up from him or her? Whom do I know who seems to struggle with remembering important information? I'll try using new techniques and strategies and observe how I'm improving.

3. **THINK. What does this mean?** What strategies seem to work the best for me? What strategies are ineffective? Have I eliminated negative and defeating self-talk? I continue to look for connections and associations. I use humor, songs, rhymes, and other mnemonic techniques.

4. **DO. What can I do with this?** I will practice memory skills in many different situations and make a conscious commitment to improving my skills. I'll make games out of my practice and have fun. I'll find practical applications and use my new skills in everyday life. Each day, I'll work on one area. For example, I'll choose one class in which I'm having trouble recalling information and experiment with new strategies. Or, for one person or group of people with whom I having trouble remembering names, I'll focus on improving.

5. **TEACH. Whom can I share this with?** I'll talk with others and share my tips and experiences. I'll ask if they have any strategies they find useful that I might also try.

Continue to at least mentally congratulate yourself when you have made improvements. The more you go through the cycle, the more interest and meaning recall will have for you, and the better your memory skills will become.

Take full responsibility for your attitude and intention. Realize that you are in control of your memory. Develop an interest in whatever you are studying or in any task or project with which you are working. Make a conscious, active decision to remember, and state your intention with positive affirmations.

2. **Observation.** Observe and be attentive to details. How many times have you physically been in one place but mentally and emotionally were thousands of miles away? Mindfulness is the state in which you are totally in the moment and part of the process around you. Learning occurs when your mind is relaxed, focused, receptive, and alert. Relax, close your eyes, breathe deeply, create a quiet atmosphere, and let your mind be calm and open. Focus your attention by concentrating on one thing at a time. **Personal Performance Notebook 6.1** on page 6–4 helps you practice your observation skills.

3. **Organization.** Organization brings material together and makes sense out of it. Nothing is harder to remember than unconnected facts, dates, or theories. Use critical thinking to create an outline that works for you. Ask questions about how information is interconnected. You cannot retain or recall information unless you

Being Observant

How observant are you? Try the following experiments to determine if you are really observing the world around you.

Key Teaching Concept
Observation and awareness are keys to improving memory skills.

Hands-On Application
Ask the students to close their eyes. Walk to the back of the room and ask them to describe what you are wearing. (Wear something different, for example, an unusual tie, necklace, or glasses.) Then ask them to describe what the person sitting next to them is wearing. This exercise illustrates that most of us are not observant. Have students discuss ways to increase their observation skills in their groups.

Experiment 1

1. Look around the room.
2. Close your eyes.
3. Mentally picture what is in the room.
4. Open your eyes.
   a. Did you remember everything?   Yes _____   No _____
   b. If no, what didn't you remember?

   _____

   _____

   _____

Experiment 2

1. Look at a painting, photo, or poster for one minute.
2. Without looking back, write down the details you remember.
3. Then, compare your list of details with the painting, photo, or poster.
   a. What details did you remember? Colors? Faces? Clothing?

   _____

   _____

   _____

   b. What details didn't you remember?

   _____

   _____

   _____

   c. Did you remember the obvious things or did you remember subtle details?

   _____

   _____

   _____

   d. Why do you think those were the details you remembered?

   _____

   _____

   _____

understand it. Understanding means that you see connections and relationships in the information you are studying. Tips for organizing information include

- Use index cards for recording information you want to memorize. Write brief summaries and indicate the main points of each chapter on the backs of note cards.
- Carry these cards with you and review them during waiting time, before going to sleep at night, or any other time you have a few minutes to spare.
- Organize the cards according to category, color, size, order, weight, and other areas.
- Map each chapter. (See **Personal Performance Notebook 6.2** on page 6–6 for a sample of a mind map.)

4. **Retention.** Repetition and practice help you retain information. Do it, and do it again. Integrate what you have learned, find new applications, and connect this information to other information you already know. Continue to ask questions and look for more examples.

5. **Recall.** Share this information with others. Teach it, write about it, talk about it, and demonstrate that you know it. This will help you become more interested in the information, create more meaning for you, and build your confidence. Repeating this cycle will build your memory skills.

Memory Strategies

Following are a number of strategies that will help you improve your memory skills.

1. **Prepare yourself physically.** People often think of learning as a passive activity that happens quietly in the brain. Physical activity increases academic performance by getting the blood flowing and activating the senses. Your mental and physical states are interrelated. Trying to memorize information when you are tired is a waste of time. Get enough rest, so that you are alert. Study when you are alert and can concentrate. Sit up straight, take frequent breaks, and exercise to build energy and stamina. Practice reciting information while doing physical activity, such as showering, walking, or jogging.

2. **Reduce information overload and avoid distractions.** Reduce mental distractions by eliminating unnecessary information. You don't have to memorize certain types of information, such as deadlines, telephone messages, and assignment due dates. You just have to know where to find this information. Write deadlines and important information in your organizer or student planner or on a calendar. Write messages in a phone log, not on slips of paper that can get lost. You can refer to any of this written information again if you need it.

   Avoid becoming someone else's memory support. If someone asks you to call him or her with the notes from class, ask the person to call you instead. If a study team member asks you to remind him or her about a study meeting, suggest using a student planner to record important dates. You have enough to remember without taking responsibility for someone else's memory. If something is bothering you, write it down and tell yourself that, as soon as

Key Teaching Concept
Simplify your life. Don't be someone else's memory support.

Class Discussion
Ask students what suggestions they have for staying alert, mindful, and fully in the present.

Hands-On Application
Present these role-playing situations:
1. A roommate who oversleeps and wants to be awakened in time for class.
2. A coworker who wants to be reminded about deadlines.
3. A boss who wants to be reminded about buying bread on the way home.

Have a student play the responsible roommate, worker, or boss. Discuss options for these situations.

Words to Succeed

"I hear, I know. I see, I remember. I do, I understand."

—CONFUCIUS
philosopher

Hands-On Application
Have students list all the memory strategies they have already learned in previous chapters.

Class Discussion
Discuss the importance of reciting information. Ask students if they have been in a play. Did they find reciting information helpful in remembering?

Mind Map—Organizing Information

A mind map will help you organize information to be memorized. Not only will the map organize the information, but the physical act of writing will also help you commit the material to memory. Use the map figure that follows as a guide, and on the space provided create a mind map of this chapter.

Key Teaching Concept
If you want to remember information, you must organize it to understand it.

- Write the main topic in the middle and draw a circle or a box around it.
- Surround the main topic with subtopics.
- Draw lines from the subtopics to the main topic.
- Under the subtopics, jot down supporting points, ideas, and illustrations.
- Be creative.
- Use different-colored ink and write main topics in block letters.
- Draw pictures for supporting points.

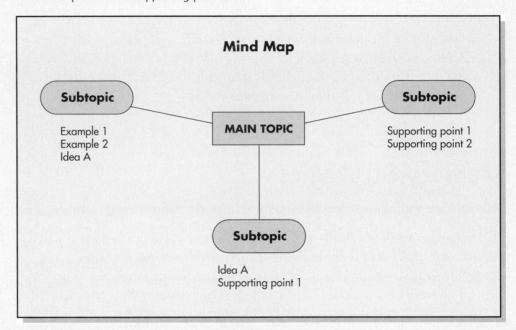

Mind Map

Create your own mind map.

your study time is over, you will address it. In this way, you can reduce distractions and focus completely on absorbing important information.

Distractions can keep you from paying attention and, consequently, from remembering what you're trying to learn. One way to avoid distractions is to study in a place designed for serious intent and where you will not be distracted. Libraries and designated study rooms are good places to use for quiet study.

3. **Use all your senses.** Memory is sensory, so using all your senses (sight, hearing, touch, smell, and taste) will give your brain a better chance of retaining information. Assume that you are taking a medical terminology or vocabulary-building course. You may want to look at pictures and visualize in your mind images with the new terms or words. Actively listen in class, tape all lectures (ask for the instructors' permission), and play them back later. Recite definitions and information aloud. Rewrite key words and definitions on note cards. Draw pictures and illustrations of these words whenever possible. Use the computer to write definitions or descriptions. Discuss the new terms with your study team. Try to use the new words in your own conversations. Listen for the new words and notice when and how others use them in conversation. Keep a log of new words, definitions, and uses of the word. Complete **Personal Performance Notebook 6.3** on page 6–8 to see how your senses relate to your childhood memories.

4. **Make learning visual.** Consider a student who is preparing for a test in a computer class. She is primarily a visual learner and feels most comfortable reading the manual, reading her textbook, and reviewing her notes. Visual learners recall information best when they see it. They like watching a video and looking at illustrations and pictures.

5. **Make learning auditory.** Another student in the computer class is an auditory learner. He remembers best when he hears instructions and responds more to spoken words. Auditory learners need to hear the message by listening to tapes and CDs and by talking aloud when they study.

6. **Make learning physical.** A third student in the computer class likes hands-on experience. He writes out commands and directions and gets actively involved. Whether you like to learn by reading or listening, you will retain information better if you use all your senses and make learning physical. Read aloud, read while standing, jot down notes, lecture in front of the classroom to yourself or your study team, go on field trips, draw diagrams and models, and join a study group. Complete **Personal Performance Notebook 6.4** on page 6–10 to determine how to integrate your learning style and use all your senses.

7. **Write down information.** Writing is physical and enhances learning. When you write down information, you are reinforcing learning by using your eyes,

Key Teaching Concept
Bring your planner to class. Illustrate the importance of writing important information in a convenient place. Encourage students to keep a calendar with deadlines or a project board with due dates; to write phone numbers in address books; and to keep copies of the e-mail addresses and fax numbers of instructors, advisors, and other key personnel in their study areas and in their planners. (see p. 6–28)

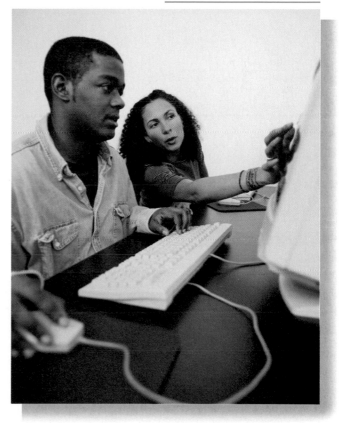

Learning Memory
Focusing on your preferred learning style strengthens your memory skills. *How does your learning style affect the way in which you learn memory?*

Memory Assessment

A. Sometimes, your perceptions differ from reality, particularly when you are assessing your skills and personal qualities. Assess your memory and your intention. Then check Yes or No as it pertains to you.

1. Do you remember names?   Yes _____   No _____
2. Do you remember important information for tests?   Yes _____   No _____
3. Did you use your senses more as a child?   Yes _____   No _____

B. Read each statement that follows and write your comments on the lines provided.
   1. Write a few lines about your earliest memory.

   _____

   _____

   _____

   _____

   _____

   _____

   2. Does it help your memory to look at family photos or hear about your childhood?

   _____

   _____

   _____

   _____

   _____

   _____

   3. What smells do you remember most from home?

   _____

   _____

   _____

   _____

   _____

   _____

hand, fingers, and arm. Writing uses different parts of the brain than do speaking and listening.

- Writing down a telephone number helps you remember it.
- Taking notes in class prompts you to be logical and concise and fills in memory gaps.
- Underlining important information and then copying it onto note cards reinforces information.
- Writing a summary after reading a chapter also reinforces information.
- Summarizing in your own words helps transfer information to long-term memory.

8. **Study in short sessions.** The brain retains information better in short study sessions. After about an hour, the brain needs a break to process information effectively. Break large goals into specific objectives and study in short sessions. For example, if you are taking a marketing course, preview a chapter in your textbook for 20 minutes and mind map the chapter on sales for 20 minutes. Then, take a 10-minute break. Tips for this type of studying include

- Take regular, scheduled breaks.
- Treat yourself to a small snack.
- Return to complete your goal.

Even when you are working on something complex, such as completing a term paper or a major project, you are more effective when you take frequent breaks. Try **Peak Progress 6.2** on page 6–11 to practice refocusing on the task at hand.

9. **Integrate your left brain and your right brain.** Think of both sides of your brain as members of a team that can cooperate, appreciate, and support each other. Recall the discussion about right- and left-brain dominance in Chapter 1. (See **Figure 1.9** on page 00.) By using both sides of your brain, you can enhance your memory. For example, you may have a term paper assignment that constitutes 50 percent of your final grade. You want to turn in a well-researched, accurately written, neatly typed paper. The left side of your brain insists that it be error-free. Your preferred style of learning leans toward the right side, so your reaction to this assignment might be frustration, fear, and resistance.

By using a word processor, you can support both sides of the brain. You satisfy the structured side, which wants a flawless paper, while allowing your creative side to correct mistakes easily by using the spell-check.

10. **Go from the general to the specific.** Many people learn best by looking at the big picture and then learning the details. Try to outline from the general (main topic) to the specific (subtopics). Previewing a chapter gives you an overview and makes the topic more meaningful. Your brain is more receptive to specific details when it has a general idea of the main topic.

11. **Associate and connect.** By associating and linking new material with old material, you make it meaningful. Suppose you are learning about explorer Christopher Columbus' three ships. Think of three friends whose names start with the same first letters as the ships' names: Pinta, Santa Maria, and Nina (e.g., Paul, Sandy, and Nancy). Associate these names with the three ships, and you should be able to recall the ships' names.

Class Discussion
Ask students:
1. What can a visual learner do to enhance his or her memory?
2. What can an auditory learner do to enhance his or her memory?
3. What can a kinesthetic learner do to make his or her memory active and physical?

PEAKTIP

Devote at least two hours of studying outside of class for each hour you spend in class.

Learning Styles and Memory

Answer the following questions on the lines provided.

1. How can you use your preferred learning style to enhance your memory?

_____

_____

_____

_____

_____

_____

_____

_____

_____

_____

2. What can you do to integrate both sides of the brain and to use all your senses to help yourself recall information?

_____

_____

_____

_____

_____

_____

_____

_____

_____

_____

Figure 6.1   Stages of Memory

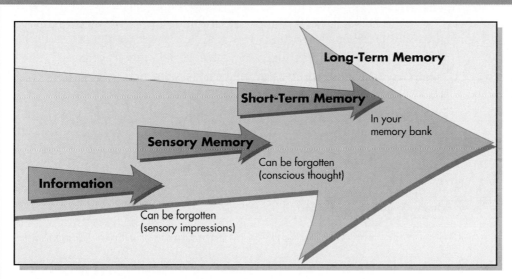

Stages of Memory   When we perceive information with our five senses, important information is processed into short-term memory and eventually into long-term memory. By using memory strategies and techniques, you can improve your long-term memory. *What kinds of memory techniques will work best for you?*

12. **Recite.** When you say information aloud, you use your throat, voice, and lips and you hear yourself recite. You may find this recitation technique helpful when you are dealing with difficult reading materials. Reading aloud and hearing the material will reinforce it for you and help move information from your short-term memory to your long-term memory. (See **Figure 6.1.**)

Class Discussion
Ask students how they remember names.

Hands-On Application
Role playing: Have one student make up a name and introduce him- or herself to the group. Have group members go through each memory technique. Discuss the results. Ask students to try these techniques next time they are introduced to a new person.

Teaching Tip
Ask students if they feel important when people remember their names. Remembering names is a key school and job skill.

Peak Progress   6.3

Remembering Names

Here are some techniques that may help you remember someone's name.

1. Imagine the name. See the name clearly in your mind: Tom Plum.
2. Be observant. Pay attention to his features and mannerisms.
3. Use exaggeration. Caricaturing the features is a fun and effective way to remember names. Single out and amplify one outstanding feature. For example, if Tom has red hair, exaggerate it to bright red and see the hair much fuller and longer than it is.
4. Visualize the red hair and the name Tom. See this vision clearly.
5. Repeat Tom's name to yourself several times as you are talking to him.
6. Recite Tom's name aloud during your conversation. Introduce Tom to others.
7. Use association. Associate the name with something you know ("Tom is the name of my cat") or make up a story using the person's name.
8. As soon as you can, jot down the name. Use a key word, or write or draw a description.
9. Use rhyming to help you recall: "Tom is not glum, nor is he dumb."
10. Use your preferred learning style. It may help if you see the name (visual), hear it pronounced (auditory), or practice saying it and writing it several times and connecting the name with something familiar (kinesthetic).
11. Ask people their names. Do this if you forget or say your name first. "Hi, I'm Sam and I met you last week." If they don't offer their names, ask.
12. Relax. Being nervous can make you forget. For example, suppose you are with a good friend and you meet Tom. You may be so anxious to make a good impression that Tom's name is lost for a moment. Learn to relax by being totally in the moment instead of worrying about forgetting, how you look, what others may think, or your nervousness.

Reciting may be helpful when preparing to give a speech. Try to practice in the actual place where you will be speaking. Visualize the audience; practice demonstrating your visual aids; write on the board; use gestures and pauses. Tape your speech and play it back. To remember names, recite the person's name when you meet and say it several times to yourself and out loud. **Peak Progress 6.3** provides a number of additional tips for remembering names.

13. **Use mnemonic devices.** Mnemonic (nee-mon-nik) devices are memory tricks that help you remember information. However, there are problems with memory tricks. It can take time to develop a memory trick, and it can be hard to remember the trick if you make it too complicated. Also, memory tricks don't help in understanding the information or develop skills in critical thinking. They are best used for sheer rote memorization. Some mnemonic devices include

- *Rhythm and rhymes.* In elementary school, you might have learned the rhyme "In 1492 Columbus sailed the ocean blue." It helped you remember the date of Columbus' voyage. Rhythms can also be helpful. Many people have learned to spell the word *Mississippi* by accenting all the *i*s and making the word rhythmic.

- *Acronyms.* Acronyms are words formed from the first letters of a series of other words, such as *HOMES* for the Great Lakes (Huron, Ontario, Michigan, Erie, and Superior) and *EPCOT* (Experimental Prototype Community of Tomorrow).

- *Grouping.* Grouping long lists of information or numbers can break up the task and make it easier for you. Most people can remember up to seven numbers in a row, which is why phone numbers are that long.

- *Association.* If your ATM identification number is 9072, you might remember it by creating associations with dates. Maybe 1990 is the year you graduated from high school, and 1972 is the year you were born.

- *The method-of-place technique.* As far back as 500 B.C., the Greeks were using a method of imagery called *loci*—the method-of-place technique. This method is still effective today because it uses imagery and association to aid memory.

   Memorize a setting in detail and then place the item or information you want to remember at certain places on your memory map. Some people like to use a familiar street, their home, or their car as a map on which to place their information. The concept is the same. You memorize certain places on your street, in your home, or in your car. You memorize a specific order or path in which you visit each place. Once you have this map memorized, you can position various items to remember at different points. **Personal Performance Notebook 6.5** on page 6–14 provides an opportunity to practice this technique.

14. **Practice, practice, practice.** Repetition creates long-term memory and recall. Think positively, incorporate affirmations, and reward yourself when you see improvement. See **Peak Progress 6.4** on page 6–17 about memory affirmations.

These strategies are very effective in strengthening your memory skills. Certain strategies might work better for you than others, depending on your personality and learning styles. Everyone has his or her personal strengths and abilities. You can master the use of memory strategies with effort, patience, and practice. As you build your memory skills, you will also enhance your study habits and become more disciplined and aware of your surroundings.

Teaching Tip
Stress the importance of practice for improving memory.

Review and Reflection

The sooner and the more often you review information, the easier it is to recall. Ideally, your first review should be within the first hour after hearing a lecture or reading an assignment. Carry note cards with you and review them again during the first

A Walk Down Memory Lane

Creating a memory map is a visual way to enhance and practice your memory skills. It uses the method-of-place technique. The key to this method is to set the items clearly in your memory and visualize them.

Think of your memory map as a garden rich in detail and full of flowers representing thoughts, images, and ideas. You always enter the garden through a white garden gate. You are actively involved, attentive to all the details, and in control of your memory. You can see each distinct point in the garden: the garden gate, the birdbath, the gazebo, the fountain, a garden bench, and a flowerbed. The key is to set the items clearly in your memory and visualize them. Draw a picture of your garden in detail in the space provided.

A Walk Down Memory Lane—continued

Using your drawing of the garden, let's say that you want to memorize four stories that emphasize four key points for a speech you are giving in your Speech 101 class.

The first story in your speech is about a monk, so you draw a monk and place him at the garden gate. You want to tell a joke about a robin, so you place the robin in the birdbath. Your third point involves people of a bygone era, and you have chosen a Victorian woman as the image to represent this key point, so you place her in the gazebo. Your fourth point involves the younger generation, so you choose a little girl and place her playing in the fountain. Follow the steps to the method-of-place technique:

1. Imagine your beautiful memory garden.

2. Imagine each distinctive detail of the location: the garden gate, birdbath, gazebo, fountain, flowerbed, and flowers arranged by colors.

3. Create a vivid image for each item you want to remember and place it at a specific location.

4. Associate each of the images representing the items with points in the garden and see the images at each location.

5. As you mentally stroll down the garden lane, create pictures in your mind of each of your items through association.

If you have additional points you want to remember, place one at the garden bench and one at the flowerbed. If you have more than six items to remember, illustrate a rainbow over your flowerbed. Flowers in various colors of the rainbow can represent each item you wish to remember. It is easier to remember information grouped together and associated by categories.

Be creative and flexible with the method-of-place technique. If a garden doesn't work for you, use a car, a bike, or your home. Just make certain that your illustration is clear and you always start in the same place. Draw it in detail and color it.

Use a Checklist in Your Memory Garden
A checklist provides a way to review and check off each item you want to remember. You can combine it with the method-of-place technique.

Memory Checklist

1. Garden gate	Monk	**4.** Fountain	Little girl
2. Birdbath	Bird	**5.** Garden bench	
3. Gazebo	Victorian woman	**6.** Flowerbed	

Check off each memory point and the item you want to remember.

Go to page 6-00 to see a drawn interpretation of a memory garden.

A Walk Down Memory Lane—continued

Memory Garden

SOURCE: *The Memory Book* by Harry Lorayne, & Jerry Lucas. Stein & Day, 1996.

Peak Progress 6.4

More Memory Affirmations

Improving your memory skills takes concentration, effort, and practice. It helps you establish stronger study habits. Integrate the following affirmations into your daily routine. These will help you as you create effective study habits and enhance your memory skills.

- I use memory techniques to help me study and recall information.
- My memory gets better every day.
- I relax, focus, and complete my project, and then I will socialize.
- I take short breaks throughout my study time.
- I have a positive attitude about the information I am studying.
- I summarize material in my own words.
- I am organized and review the information often.
- I look forward to accomplishing my goals in study teams.
- I can see myself successfully remembering whatever I want.

Class Discussion

Ask students:

1. What are their earliest memories?
2. Does it help to review scrapbooks, talk to relatives, and visit with old friends?
3. What smells do they remember most from home?
4. What are the biggest barriers to an efficient memory?
5. What are the best strategies for overcoming barriers to an efficient memory?

day. Studies show that, within 48 hours, you forget 85 percent of what you have learned. If you review right after you hear it and again within 24 hours, however, your recall soars to 90 percent. Discuss, write, summarize, and recite in your own words what you have just read or heard.

Practice information that you want to remember. For example, when you first start driver training, you learn the various steps involved in driving. At first, they may seem overwhelming. You may have to stop and think through each step. After you have driven a car for a while, however, you don't even think about all the steps required to start it and back out of the driveway. You check your mirror automatically before changing lanes, and driving safely has become a habit. The information is in your long-term memory. The more often you use information, the easier it is to recall. You could not become a good musician without hours of practice. Playing sports, speaking in public, flying an airplane, and learning to drive all require skills that need to be repeated and practiced many times.

Overcoming Barriers to Memory

The number one barrier to memory is mental laziness. People often say, "If only I could remember names" or "I wish I had a better memory." Avoid using words such as *try, wish,* or *hope.* You can overcome the barrier of mental laziness by creating a positive attitude, intending to remember, using all your senses, and using memory techniques.

Practice becoming more observant and aware. For example, let's say that you want to learn the students' names in all your classes. Look at each student as the instructor takes roll, copy down each name, and say each name mentally as you look

PEAK TIP

It takes effort and a positive attitude to enhance your learning and memory skills.

TECH FOR SUCCESS

- **Stored Memory.** Your computer is one big memory tool, storing thousands of hours of your work and contact information. For example, if you use the "Favorites" feature in your web browser to catalog web sites, consider how long it would take for you to reconstruct this information if it were suddenly wiped out. Do you have back-up plans if your hard drive were inaccessible, or if you lost your PDA or cell phone containing countless stored numbers? Use these many tools and features to help you organize and save time, but don't forget to write down and keep hard copies of very important documents and contact information.

around the classroom. As you go about your day, practice becoming aware of your surroundings, people, and new information.

To make sure your memory skills stay sharp, review and assess your answers to the following questions periodically. Can you answer yes to them?

1. Do I want to remember?
2. Do I have a positive attitude about the information?
3. Have I eliminated distractions?
4. Have I organized and grouped material?
5. Have I reviewed the information often?
6. Have I reviewed right after the lecture?
7. Have I reviewed class notes within 24 hours?
8. Have I set up weekly reviews?
9. Have I used repetition?
10. Have I summarized material in my own words?
11. Have I compared, contrasted, and associated new material with what I know?
12. Have I used memory techniques to help associate key words?

In summary, in this chapter, I learned to

- *Apply the five-step memory process.* Similar to the Adult Learning Cycle, the memory process consists of five steps: intention, observation, organization, retention, and recall.

- *Intend to remember.* People who have better memories *want* to remember and make it a priority. It's important for me to increase my memory skills, and I take responsibility for my attitude and intention. I create personal interest and meaning in what I want to remember.

- *Be observant and alert.* I observe and am attentive to details. I am relaxed, focused, and receptive to new information. I reduce distractions, concentrate, and stay focused and mindful of the present. I look at the big picture, and then I look at details. Memory is increased when I pay attention.

- *Organize information.* Organization makes sense out of information. I look for patterns and connections. I look for what I already know and jot down questions for areas that I don't know. I group similarities and look for what is different.

- *Retain information.* I write summaries in my own words and say them out loud. I jot down main points, key words, and important information on note cards and review them often. I study in short sessions and review often.

- *Recall.* I recall everything I know about the subject. I increase my recall by writing down information, reciting out loud, and teaching others. Practicing and reviewing information often are key to increasing recall. I reward myself for concentration, discipline, and effort.

- *Use my senses.* I draw pictures and illustrations, use color, tape lectures, play music, write out summaries, jot down questions, collect samples, give summaries to my study group, recite out loud, and go on field trips.

- *Integrate learning styles.* I incorporate various learning styles by making learning visual, auditory, and physical.

- *Take frequent breaks.* I study in 40- to 60-minute sessions, since I know that the brain retains information best in short study periods. I take breaks to keep up my motivation.

- *Go from the general to the specific.* I first look at the big picture for gaining general, overall understanding and meaning. I then focus on the detail and specific supporting information.

- *Use mnemonic devices.* I use rhythm and rhymes, acronyms, grouping, association, and method-of-place techniques to help me memorize and recall information.

- *Find connections and recite.* I link new information with familiar material, and I summarize what I have learned, either out loud or in writing.

Marla Bergstrom

JOURNALIST

Related Majors: Journalism, English, Social Studies

Integrating Learning Styles

As a journalist, Marla Bergstrom's job is to find newsworthy local issues, collect accurate information from both sides of the story, and write an article that treats the subject fairly. As a general assignment reporter for a large newspaper, she covers stories from politics to crime, education, business, and consumer affairs.

Marla works closely with her editor when selecting a topic for an article. She often investigates leads for a story, only to realize later that she does not have enough information to make a strong story. She organizes the information she gathers, not knowing how or if it will fit into the article. Marla usually works on more than one story at a time, as some stories take weeks of research. Her hours are irregular. In one week, Marla might attend an early morning political breakfast and attend a school board meeting the same evening.

Each week, Marla interviews a wide variety of people, including the mayor, police chief, school supervisor, and other community leaders. She always says hello to people using their names. She prides herself on being able to remember names after only one meeting. When conducting an interview, the first thing Marla does is write down the name of the person, asking for the correct spelling. By doing this, she not only checks spelling but also sees a person's name in print. Because Marla is a visual learner, this helps her remember the name. On the way home from an interview, Marla orally reviews the names of the people she met. After an interview, Marla types her notes and memorizes pertinent information, such as the names of people, businesses, and locations. Marla knows that having good memory skills is essential for being a capable journalist.

CRITICAL THINKING
Which learning styles help Marla remember pertinent information?

Peak Performer Profile

Alberto Gonzales

His rise to the top appears meteoric. In less than a decade, Alberto Gonzales advanced from partner at a Houston law firm to general counsel to the governor of Texas, the 100th Texas secretary of state, a justice on the Texas Supreme Court, the first Hispanic-American counsel to the White House, and most recently the appointed Attorney General. However, Gonzales reached this influential position through hard work, dedication, and perseverance.

Born in San Antonio, Texas, Gonzales was raised in Houston by his parents who had been migrant farm workers. For most of Gonzales' childhood, the family's two-bedroom house, home to eight children, had neither a telephone nor hot running water. These circumstances, however, did not diminish Gonzales' drive. Though lacking material wealth, his mother and father taught him the "value of self-responsibility."

In 1975, after graduating from high school, Gonzales joined the U.S. Air Force. Originally aiming at a career as a pilot, he opted out of the military after two years, changed his career goals, and chose to study law.

Within the next five years, he had earned a bachelor's degree in political science from Rice University and then a law degree from Harvard Law School.

In 2001, Gonzales was appointed White House counsel. As top legal advisor, Alberto Gonzales commanded a powerful position in the administration. Not only did he advise the presidential office on all legal matters, but also selected and evaluated judicial nominees, including those for the U.S. Supreme Court.

PERFORMANCE THINKING Relatively new to the nation's capital, Gonzales has had to remember a myriad of legal details. What three memory strategies would you recommend?

Performance Strategies •••••••••••••

Following are the top 10 strategies for improving memory:

- ◆ Intend to remember and prepare yourself mentally.
- ◆ Be observant, be alert, and pay attention.
- ◆ Organize information to make it meaningful.
- ◆ Integrate learning styles.
- ◆ Write down information.
- ◆ Study in short sessions.
- ◆ Use mnemonic devices.
- ◆ Go from general to specific.
- ◆ Summarize.
- ◆ Practice, use repetition, and relax.

Review Questions ••••••••••••••••

1. What are the five main steps of the memory process?
2. Why is intending to remember so important to enhancing memory?
3. Why does writing down information help you remember it?
4. What are mnemonic devices and what do they help you remember?
5. What is the purpose of reviewing information sooner and more often?

REVISUALIZATION ••

Review the Visualization box at the beginning of this chapter and your journal entry in **Worksheet 6.1.** Continuing with this exercise, describe a situation in which you forgot some important information or someone's name that you really wanted to remember. Work through the ABCDE method and incorporate the new strategies you have learned in this chapter—for example,

A = Actual event: "I just ran into my instructor and he called me by name. I could not for the life of me remember his name until after he walked away."

B = Beliefs: "I am one of many students, but somehow he remembers my name. Why can't I remember his? Will I freeze the same on tests when I need to remember much more difficult material?

C = Consequences: "I hope he didn't catch on. I need to do well in this class, and he is one of the key instructors in my major. I'm so embarrassed."

D = Dispute: "This makes me realize that I need to become more organized and focused on what is important. I know having a good memory is not an innate talent or ability and that I can improve mine by trying some new strategies. For example, the next time I see Mr. Baker, I'll remember my favorite food (donuts), and I'll make a point to start the conversation by saying his name."

E = Energized: "I'm energized because I know that applying even just a few little tricks will help me improve my retention. I know this is a powerful skill that will help me in school, at work, and in social situations."

OVERCOMING MEMORY LOSS

In the Classroom

Erin McAdams is outgoing, bright, and popular, but she also has a reputation for being forgetful. She forgets appointments, projects, and due dates. She is continually losing her keys and important papers. She is often late and forgets meetings and even social events. She always tells herself, "I'm just not good at remembering names" and "I really am going to try harder to get more organized and remember my commitments." She blames her bad memory for doing poorly on tests and wishes that people would just understand that she's doing the best she can. She insists that she's tried but just can't change.

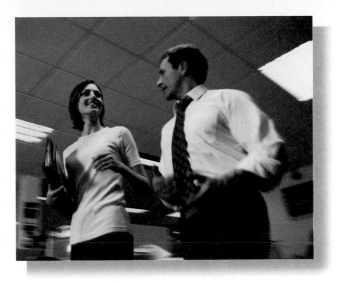

1. What would you suggest to help Erin improve her memory skills?

_____

_____

2. What strategies in this chapter would be most helpful?

_____

_____

In The Workplace

Erin is now in hotel management. She loves the excitement, the diversity of the people she meets, as well as the daily challenges. She has recently been assigned to plan and coordinate special events, which include parties, meetings, and social affairs. This new job requires remembering many names, dates, and endless details.

3. How can Erin learn to develop her memory skills?

_____

_____

4. Suggest a program for her that would increase her memory skills.

_____

_____

APPLYING THE ABCDE METHOD OF SELF-MANAGEMENT

In the Visualization box on page 6–1, you were asked to describe a situation when you needed to learn many new names or numerous facts for a test. How did you fare? What factors helped you remember?

_____

_____

_____

_____

Now, describe a situation in which you forgot some important information or someone's name that you really wanted to remember. Work through the ABCDE method and incorporate the new strategies you have learned in this chapter.

A = Actual event:

B = Beliefs:

C = Consequences:

D = Dispute:

E = Energized:

Relax, take a deep breath, and visualize yourself recalling facts, key words, dates, and information easily.

CONNECTING LEARNING STYLE WITH MEMORY

For each course you are taking, consider your best learning style. Write the name of the course in the Course column. Then, put a check mark in the column of the learning style that best accommodates the course.

Course	Visual	Auditory	Kinesthetic

CHAPTER 6 ▲ REVIEW AND APPLICATIONS

MEMORY

A. Quickly read these lists once. Read one word at a time and in order.

1	2
the	Disney World
work	light
of	time
and	and
to	of
the	house
and	the
of	packages
light	good
of	praise
care	and
the	coffee
chair	the
and	of

B. Write as many words from the lists as you can remember on the lines that follow. Then, check your list against the lists in Part A.

_____   _____

_____   _____

_____   _____

_____   _____

_____   _____

_____   _____

_____   _____

_____   _____

_____   _____

_____   _____

—continued

CHAPTER 6 ▶ REVIEW AND APPLICATIONS

1. How many words did you remember from the beginning of the list?

_____

_____

2. How many words did you remember from the middle of the list?

_____

_____

3. How many words did you remember from the end of the list?

_____

_____

4. Did you remember the term *Disney World?*   Yes _____   No _____

_____

_____

Most people who complete this exercise remember the first few words, the last few words, the unusual term *Disney World,* and the words that were listed more than once (*of, the,* and *and*). Did you find this to be true about yourself?   Yes _____   No _____

C. Remembering names

   1. Do you have problems remembering names?   Yes _____   No _____

   2. What do you think you are still resisting?

   _____

   _____

   3. What are the benefits of remembering names now and in a career?

   _____

   _____

D. What memory techniques will you commit to learning and using?

_____

_____

_____

CHAPTER 6 ▲ REVIEW AND APPLICATIONS

NAME: _____   DATE: _____

TO-DO LIST

Use this to-do list to place and organize your appointments, project due dates, and other information that is important for you to remember.

URGENT

PRIORITIES

TO SEE OR CALL	AWAITING DEVELOPMENTS		
	What	Who	When
Name _____ Telephone # _____ Reason for call _____			
Name _____ Telephone # _____ Reason for call _____			
Name _____ Telephone # _____ Reason for call _____			

CHAPTER 6 ▼ REVIEW AND APPLICATIONS

MEMORY SYSTEMS

Use this grid when preparing for a test. Place a check mark next to each task as it is completed.

	Observe				Organize				Associate				Summarize			
	Pay attention to details.	Listen and observe.	Avoid distractions.	Stay alert.	Organize with an outline.	Use index cards.	Organize whole to part.	Organize part to whole.	Associate, compare, and contrast.	Link information.	Connect material.	Use imagery.	Summarize.	Recite out loud.	Use repetition.	Review.
Test 1																
Test 2																
Test 3																
Test 4																
Test 5																
Test 6																
Test 7																
Test 8																

CHAPTER 6 ▲ REVIEW AND APPLICATIONS

MENTAL PICTURE

Use a clock or a study partner to time you as look at the following pictures for a duration of two minutes. As you look at these pictures, create a mental picture. After the two minutes have passed, make up a story using all of these elements.

1. Write your creative story on the following lines.

_____

_____

_____

_____

_____

_____

—continued

2. What memory strategies did you use to recall the information?

_____

_____

_____

_____

_____

_____

_____

_____

_____

_____

_____

_____

3. What connections were you able to make among the photos?

_____

_____

_____

_____

_____

_____

_____

_____

_____

_____

_____

_____

_____

_____

APPLYING MEMORY SKILLS

Assess your memory skills by answering the following questions. Add this page to your Career Development Portfolio.

1. **Looking back:** Review an autobiography you may have written for this or another course. Indicate the ways you applied your memory skills.

   _____

   _____

2. **Taking stock:** What are your memory strengths and what do you want to improve?

   _____

   _____

3. **Looking forward:** How would you demonstrate memory skills for employers?

   _____

   _____

4. **Documentation:** Include examples, such as poems you have memorized, literary quotes, and techniques for remembering names.

   _____

   _____

5. **Assessment and demonstration:** Critical thinking skills for memory include

   - Preparing yourself mentally and physically
   - Creating a willingness to remember
   - Determining what information is important and organizing it
   - Linking new material with known information (creating associations)
   - Integrating various learning styles
   - Asking questions
   - Reviewing and practicing
   - Evaluating your progress

   Assess your memory skills. Review your life to discover how you learned these various skills. How do you use your memory skills in class? How would you use memory skills at work?

   _____

   _____

   _____

   _____

Test Taking

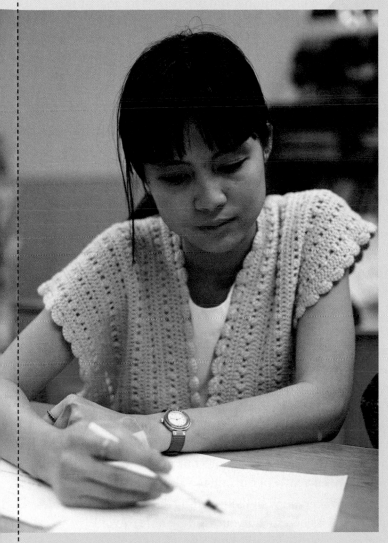

Chapter Objectives

In this chapter, you will learn

▲ How to prepare for tests

▲ Strategies for taking tests

▲ How to take different types of tests

▲ Special tips for math and science tests

▲ How to overcome test anxiety

Visualization

"I studied very hard for my last test, but my mind went blank when I tried to answer the questions. What can I do to decrease my anxiety and be more confident about taking tests?"

Have you ever had a similar experience? Do you find yourself feeling anxious and worried when you take tests? Do you suffer physical symptoms, such as sweaty palms, upset stomach, headaches, or inability to sleep or concentrate? In this

chapter, you will learn how to decrease your anxiety and learn test-taking strategies.

Journal Entry   In **Worksheet 7.1** on page 7–25, describe a time when you did well in a performance, sporting event, or test. What factors helped you be calm, be confident, and remember information?

Key Teaching Concept
Reviewing is the best way to prepare for tests.

Use
TM 7.1 Success Principle 7.

Teaching Tip
Emphasize the importance of using the ABCDE Method of Self-Management to channel test anxiety into positive action. (p. 7–25)

Class Discussion
How do these competencies create college and job success? Applying SCANS:
Memory skills
Processing and storing information

Use
TM 7.5 Chapter Application Worksheet 7.2 Preparing for Tests and Exams.

All successful athletes and performers know how important it is to monitor and measure their techniques and vary their training programs to improve results. Taking tests is part of school; performance reviews are part of a job; and tryouts and performing are part of the life of an athlete, a dancer, or an actor. In fact, there are few jobs in life that don't require you to assess skills, attitude, and behavior. The goal of this chapter is to explore specific test-taking strategies.

Preparing for a Test

The following tips will help you as you prepare for taking a test.

1. **Prepare early.** The best way to do well on tests is to begin by preparing on the first day of class. Prepare by attending all classes, arriving on time, and staying until the end of class. Set up a review schedule on the first day. Observe your instructors during class to see what they consider important and what points and key words they stress. As you listen to lectures or read your textbook, ask yourself what questions might be on the examination. Prepare yourself both mentally and physically by reviewing the test-taking factors in **Peak Progress 7.1.**

2. **Know expectations.** The first day of class is important because most instructors outline the course and clarify the syllabus and expectations concerning grading, test dates, and the types of tests. During class or office hours, ask your instructors about test formats. Ask for sample questions, a study guide, or additional material that may be helpful for studying. You are in a partnership with your instructors, and it is important in any relationship to understand expectations. A large part of fear and anxiety comes from the unknown. The more you know about what is expected concerning evaluations and exams, the more at ease you will be. **Personal Performance Notebook 7.1** on page 7–4 gives you a handy guide for approaching your instructors about upcoming tests and how you are currently performing in class.

3. **Keep up.** Manage your time and keep up with daily reading, homework, and assignments. Consolidate your class notes with your reading notes. Avoid waiting until the night before to prepare for an exam.

4. **Ask questions.** Ask questions in class. As you read take notes and review chapter material. Chapter summaries, key concepts, reviews, and end-of-chapter questions and exercises all provide examples of possible test questions. Save all quizzes, course materials, exercise sheets, and lab work. Ask if old tests or sample tests are available at the library.

5. **Review early.** Start the review process by previewing chapters before classes. Take a few minutes to review your class notes immediately after class. When

Peak Progress 7.1

Test-Taking Factors

The factors involved in taking tests and performing well on them are

1. Preparing yourself both mentally and physically
2. Determining what information is important
3. Processing information
4. Linking new material with known information
5. Creating associations
6. Creating a willingness to remember
7. Staying focused
8. Reasoning logically
9. Overcoming fear
10. Evaluating

information is fresh, you can fill in missing pieces, make connections, and raise questions to ask later. Set up a schedule, so that you have time to review daily notes from all your classes each day. Review time can be short; 5 or 10 minutes for every class is often sufficient. Daily review should also include scanning reading notes and items that need memorization. This kind of review should continue until the final exam.

6. **Review weekly.** Spend about an hour or so for each subject to investigate and review not only the week's assignments but also what has been included thus far in the course. These review sessions can include class notes, reading notes, chapter questions, note cards, mind maps, flash cards, a checklist of items to study, and summaries written in your own words. One of the best ways to test yourself is to close your book after reading and write a summary; then, go back and fill in missing material.

7. **Final review.** A week or so before a test, commit yourself to a major review. This review should include class and book notes, note cards, and summaries. You can practice test questions, compare concepts, integrate major points, and review and recite with your study team. Long-term memory depends on organizing the information. Fragmented information is difficult to remember or recall. Understanding the main ideas and connecting and relating information transfer the material into long-term memory.

8. **Rehearse.** One of the best tips for doing well on tests is to pretest yourself by predicting questions and creating and taking sample tests.

9. **Summarize.** Pretend the instructor said that you could bring one note card to the test. Choose the most important concepts, formulas, key words, and points and condense them onto one note card. This exercise highlights important material. You will do better on a test even if you cannot use the note card during the test.

Test Taking

This exercise involves a lot of risks, and you may be tempted to avoid it—but do it! Students almost always find it to be helpful. To help you prepare for tests, do the following activities and write your findings on the lines provided.

Use
TM 7.2 What to Do Before Midterms.

Class Discussion
Ask students to list what they should do before midterms.

Hands-On Application
Tell students that they can simulate the test-taking experience by having each study team member write five to ten questions. Create sample tests and take them. Discuss possible answers. Report the results in class.

Class Discussion
Ask students if they know what the campus policy is on cheating.

Hands-On Application
Have students keep a log of how they are changing the way they prepare for tests. Have them discuss with their groups the best strategies and list the best habits.

1. Go to each of your instructors and ask how you are doing in each class.
2. Discuss your expectations and the style of test questions you can expect on their tests.
3. Ask the instructors and make note of what you can do to earn a good grade.

Course _____

_____

_____

Course _____

_____

_____

Course _____

_____

_____

Course _____

_____

_____

Course _____

_____

_____

Use
TM 7.4 Chapter Application Worksheet 7.1 Exam Schedule.

10. **Use your study team.** You may be tempted to skip studying one night, but you can avoid temptation if you know other people are waiting for you and depending on your contribution. Have each member of the study team provide 5 to 10 questions. Share these questions and discuss possible answers. Word the questions in different formats—multiple-choice, true/false, matching, and essay. Then, simulate the test-taking experience by taking, giving, and correcting each other's timed sample tests.

Test–Taking Strategies

The following strategies will help you as you take a test.

1. **Arrive early.** You don't want to be frantic and late for a test. Arrive a few minutes early. Deep breathing and affirmations along with visualization may help you relax and complete the test successfully. While waiting for other students to arrive, the instructor will sometimes answer questions or explain material to those students who are in class ahead of schedule. Use anxiety-reducing strategies to stay focused and positive. Look over your note cards calmly. Avoid negative conversations that may make you feel anxious—for example, if someone mentions the length of time he or she has studied.

2. **Organize yourself.** As soon as you start the test, write words, facts, formulas, dates, principles, or statistics in pencil on the back of your paper or in the margins. If you wait until you are reading each question, you may forget important material while under pressure.

3. **Write clearly.** Your instructor must read many exams in the process of grading tests. If your writing is difficult to read, your grade may be affected because what you write is either indecipherable or messy.

4. **Focus and get to the point.** When you are answering questions that require a short response, avoid using extra words or filler sentences. Remember that these types of answers shouldn't become long essays. Most instructors will appreciate concise, accurate responses that don't require a lot of reading time.

5. **Read and listen to all instructions.** Scan the entire test briefly. Preview the questions to see which you can answer quickly and which will take more time. Some questions may help you answer others. Dates, key words, or related facts may stimulate your memory for another question.

6. **Pace yourself.** Keep moving through the test according to your plan. Make your time count. Look at points for each question and determine the importance that should be given to each section. For example, you will want to spend more time on an essay worth 25 points than on a multiple-choice worth 5. Don't panic if you don't know an answer right away. Leave it and answer all the questions you do know. Build on success and don't block your thinking. Rephrase questions you find difficult. It may help you change the wording of a sentence. Use memory strategies if you are blocked: Draw a picture or a diagram, use a different equation, or make a mind map and write the topic and subtopics. Use association to remember items that are related. You can refer back to Chapter 6 for memory skills.

7. **Review.** Once you have finished, reread the test and check for mistakes or spelling errors. Stay the entire time, answer extra-credit questions, and fill in details, if time permits. See **Peak Progress 7.2** on page 7–6 for specific strategies for math and science texts.

Teaching Tip
Remind students to breathe deeply, stay focused, and use all the time available.

Teaching Tip
1. Remind students how important assessment is to improving test-taking skills.
2. Tell students to watch for words such as *sometimes, usually, generally,* and *frequently.* They can be indicators of a true statement.
3. Tell students to eliminate the choices they know are incorrect.

Use
TM 7.3 Test-Taking Factors.

Use
TM 7.7 Chapter Application Worksheet 7.4 Matrix for Test Taking.

Class Discussion
Ask students how they
reward themselves.

Teaching Tip
Remind students that all the
study strategies so far will
help them with math and
science tests. Review special
strategies and ask for more
suggestions.

Peak Progress   7.2

Special Strategies for Math and Science Tests

During your years of study, you will probably take math and science courses. Following are some strategies for preparing to take a math or science test.

1. **Use note cards.** Write formulas, definitions, rules, and theories on note cards and review them often. Write out examples for each theorem.

2. **Write notes.** As soon as you are given the test, jot down theorems and formulas in the margins.

3. **Survey the test.** Determine the number of questions and the worth and difficulty of each question.

4. **Answer easy to hard.** Do the easy questions first. Spend more time on questions that are worth the most points.

5. **Answer general to specific.** First, read to understand the big picture. Ask, "Why is this subject in the book? How does it connect with other topics?"

6. **Write the problem in longhand.** For example, for $A = 1/2bh$, "*For a triangle, the area is one-half the base times the height.*"

7. **Think.** Use critical thinking and creative problem solving. Let your mind ponder possibilities.

8. **Make an estimate.** A calculated guess will give you an approximate answer. This helps you when you double-check the answer.

9. **Illustrate the problem.** Draw a picture, diagram, or chart that will help you understand the problem—for example: "The length of a field is 6 feet more than twice its width. If the perimeter of the field is 228 feet, find the dimensions of the field."

After the Test

1. **Reward yourself.** Reward yourself with a treat, such as a hot bath, a walk, an evening with friends, or a special dinner. Always reward yourself with a good night's sleep.

2. **Analyze and assess.** When you receive the graded test, analyze and assess it. Be a detached, curious, receptive observer and view the results as feedback. Feedback is essential for improvement. If you don't receive a grade you're pleased with, ask yourself the following questions:

   • Did I prepare enough?
   • What should I have studied more?
   • Did I anticipate the style, format, and questions?
   • What didn't I expect?
   • What did I do right?
   • How was my recall?
   • Did I test myself with the right questions?

Special Strategies for Math and Science Tests *(continued)*

Let l = the length of the field.

Let w = the width of the field.

Then $l = 6 + 2w$

So $6w + 6 = 228$

$6w + 12 = 228$

$6w = 216$

$w = 36$

So $l = 6 + 2w = 6 + 2(36) = 78$

Translating: The width of the field is 36 ft. and its length is 78 ft.

Checking: The perimeter is $2w + 2l = 2(36) + 2(78) = 72 + 156 = 228$.

10. **Ask yourself questions.** Ask, "What is being asked? What do I already know? What are the givens? What do I need to find out? How does this connect and relate with other concepts? What is the point of the question?"

11. **Show your work.** If you get stuck, try to retrace your steps.

12. **Do a similar problem.** If you get stuck, try something similar. Which formula worked? How does this formula relate to others?

13. **Be logical.** Break the problem down step by step. Look for proof of your answer.

14. **Check your work.** Does your answer make sense?

15. **Review.** Review your test as soon as you get it back. Where did you make your mistakes? What will you do differently next time?

Class Discussion
Ask students what other strategies have helped them in math and science or language classes.

Hands-On Application
Have each group bring to class strategies that have helped them work through science and math problems. Each group should have a minimum of one math and one science example. Have the group leader present the problems to the class.

- Did I handle test anxiety well?
- Would it have helped if I had studied with others?

If you honestly don't know why you received the grade you did, see the instructor. Approach the meeting with a positive attitude, not a defensive one. Remember, a test is information and feedback on how you are doing, not an evaluation of you as a person. You cannot change unless you can understand your mistakes. Learn from your mistakes and move forward. Assess what you did wrong and what you will do right the next time.

Taking Different Types of Tests

The following tips will help you as you take different types of tests.

THE OBJECTIVE TEST

TRUE/FALSE TEST

1. **Listen and read carefully.** Read the entire question carefully before you answer it. For the question to he true, the *entire* question must be true. If any part of the statement is false, the entire statement is false.

2. **Pay attention to details.** Read dates, names, and places carefully. Sometimes the dates are changed around (1494 instead of 1449) or the wording is changed slightly. Any changes such as these can change the meaning.

3. **Watch for qualifiers.** Watch for such words as *always, all, never,* and *every.* The question is often false because there are almost always exceptions. If you can think of one exception, then the statement is false. Ask yourself, "Does this statement overstate or understate what I know to be true?"

4. **Watch for faulty cause and effect.** Two true statements may be connected by a word that implies cause and effect, and this word may make the statement false—for example, "Temperature is measured on the centigrade scale because water freezes at zero degrees centigrade."

5. **Always answer every question.** Unless there is a penalty for wrong answers, answer every question. You have a 50 percent chance of being right.

6. **Trust your instincts.** Often, your first impression is correct. Don't change an answer unless you are certain it is wrong. Don't spend time pondering until you have finished the entire test and have time to spare.

MULTIPLE-CHOICE TEST

1. **Read the question carefully.** Are you being asked for the correct answer or the best choice? Is there more than one answer? Preview the test to see if an answer may be included in a statement or question.

2. **Rephrase the question.** Sometimes, it helps to rephrase the question in your own words. You may also want to answer the question yourself before looking at the possible answers.

3. **Eliminate choices.** Narrow your choices by reading through all of them an eliminating those that you know are incorrect.

4. **Go from easy to difficult.** Go through the test and complete those questions for which you know the answers. This will give you a feeling of confidence. Don't use all your time on a few questions.

5. **Watch for combinations.** Read the question carefully and don't just choose what appears to be the one correct answer. Some questions offer a combination of choices, such as "All of the above" or "None of the above."

6. **Look at sentence structure.** Make sure the grammatical structure of the question matches that of your choice.

MATCHING TEST

1. **Read carefully.** Read both lists quickly and watch for clues.

2. **Eliminate.** As you match the items you know, cross them out unless the directions mention that an item can be used more than once. Elimination is the key in a matching test.

3. **Look at sentence structure.** Often, verbs are matched to verbs. Read the entire sentence. Does it make sense?

FILL-IN-THE-BLANK TEST

1. **Watch for clues.** If the word before the blank is *an,* the word in the blank generally begins with a vowel. If the word before the blank is *a,* the word in the blank generally begins with a consonant.

2. **Count the number of blanks.** The number of blanks often indicates the number of words in an answer.

3. **Watch for the length of the blank.** A longer blank may indicate a longer answer.

4. **Answer the questions you know first.** As with all tests, answer the questions you know first and then go back to those that are more difficult. Rephrase and look for key words.

5. **Answer all questions.** Try never to leave a question unanswered.

OPEN-BOOK TEST

The key to an open-book test is to prepare. Students often think that open-book tests will be easy, so they don't study. Generally, these tests go beyond basic recall and require critical thinking and analysis. Put markers in your book to indicate important areas. Write formulas, definitions, key words, sample questions, and main points on note cards. Bring along your detailed study sheet. The key is to be able to find information quickly. Use your own words to summarize. Don't copy from your textbook.

THE ESSAY TEST

Being prepared is essential when taking an essay test. Make certain that you understand concepts and relationships, not just specific facts. (See **Peak Progress 7.2** on page 7–6 for a sample essay test.) in addition, use the following strategies to help you take an essay test.

1. **Organize.** Organizing your notes and reading material will help you outline important topics.

2. **Outline.** An outline will provide a framework to help you remember dates, main points, names, places, and supporting material. Use **Personal Performance Notebook 7.2** on page 7–10 to practice outlining key words and topics. See **Peak Progress 7.3** on page 7–11 for a completed example.

3. **Budget your writing time.** Look over the whole test, noticing which questions are easiest. Allot a certain amount of time for each essay question and include time for review when you're finished.

4. **Read the question carefully.** Make certain you understand what is being asked in the question. Respond to key words such as *explain, classify, define,* and *compare.* Rephrase the question into a main thesis. Always answer what is being asked directly. Don't skirt around an issue. If you are being asked to compare and contrast, do not describe, or you will not answer the question

Key Teaching Concept
An essay should be a minipaper. Write a thesis statement, introduction, body and conclusion.

Key Teaching Concept
Know what is being asked.

Essay Test Preparation

Pretend you are taking an essay test on a personal topic—your life history. Your instructor has written the following essay question on the board:

Write a brief essay on your progress through life so far, covering the highs and lows, major triumphs, and challenges.

Before you begin writing, remind yourself of the topics you want to cover in this essay. What key words, phrases, events, and dates would you jot down in the margin of your essay paper? List your thoughts on the lines provided.

Teaching Tip

1. Encourage students to organize the material for an essay test. They should know what is being asked.
2. Remind students to use all the available time. Don't leave an essay question blank.

Hands-On Application

Have students keep a list of important words for essay questions. They should discuss these words in their groups and add them to the list. For example, discuss means to talk about a subject from several points of view.

Peak Progress

Hands-On Application
Have students bring to class samples of essay tests or essay questions that they have taken and review the key words.

Sample Essay Test

Steve Hackett

Intro to Economics Quiz

January 12, 2003

Question

Describe the general circumstances under which economists argue that government intervention in a market economy enhances efficiency.

Thesis statement

Well-functioning competitive markets are efficient resource allocators, but they can fail in certain circumstances. Government intervention can generate its own inefficiencies, so economists promote the forms of government intervention that enhance efficiency under conditions of market failure.

Outline

I. Well-functioning competitive markets are efficient.
   A. Incentive for firms to minimize costs and waste
   B. Price approximates costs of production.
   C. Effort, quality, and successful innovation are rewarded.
   D. Shortages and surpluses are eliminated by price adjustment.
II. Markets fail to allocate scarce resources efficiently under some circumstances.
   A. Externalities affect other people.
      1. Negative externalities, such as pollution
      2. Positive externalities and collectively consumed goods
   B. Lack of adequate information
   C. Firms with market power
III. Government intervention can create its own inefficiencies.
   A. Rigid, bureaucratic rules can stifle innovative solutions and dilute incentives.
   B. Politically powerful groups can subvert the process.
IV. Efficient intervention policy balances market and government inefficiencies.

—continued on page 7–12

correctly. **Peak Progress 7.4** lists a number of key words used in essay questions.

5. **Organize the material.** Organize your main points in an outline, so that you won't leave out important information.

6. **Write concisely and correctly.** Get directly to the point and use short, clear sentences. Remember that your instructor may be grading a pile of other students' tests, so get to the point and avoid using filler sentences.

7. **Write neatly.** Appearance and legibility are important. Use an erasable pen. Use wide margins and don't crowd your words. Write on one side of the paper only. Leave space between answers, so you can add to an answer if time permits.

Sample Essay Answer *continued*

Well-functioning competitive markets allocate resources efficiently in the context of scarcity. They do so in several different ways. First, in market systems, firms are profit maximizers and thus have an incentive to minimize their private costs of production. In contrast, those who manage government agencies lack the profit motive and thus the financial incentive to minimize costs. Second, under competitive market conditions, the market price is bid down by rival firms to reflect their unit production costs. Thus, for the last unit sold, the value (price) to the consumer is equal to the cost to produce that unit, meaning that neither too much nor too little is produced. Third, firms and individuals have an incentive to work hard to produce new products and services preferred by consumers because, if successful, these innovators will gain an advantage over their rivals in the marketplace. Fourth, competitive markets react to surpluses with lower prices and to shortages with higher prices, which work to resolve these imbalances.

Markets can fail to allocate scarce resources efficiently in several different situations. First, profit-maximizing firms have an incentive to emit negative externalities (uncompensated harms generated by market activity that fall on others), such as pollution, when doing so lowers their production costs and is not prevented by law. Individual firms also have an incentive not to provide positive externalities (unpaid-for benefits) that benefit the group, such as police patrol, fire protection, public parks, and roads. A second source of market failure is incomplete information regarding product safety, quality, and workplace safety. A third type of market failure occurs when competition is subverted by a small number of firms that can manipulate prices, such as monopolies and cartels.

Government intervention can take various forms, including regulatory constraints, information provision, and direct government provision of goods and services. Government intervention may also be subject to inefficiencies. Examples include rigid regulations that stifle the incentive for innovation, onerous compliance costs imposed on firms, political subversion of the regulatory process by powerful interest groups, and lack of cost-minimizing incentives on the part of government agencies. Thus, efficient government intervention can be said to occur when markets fail in a substantial way and when the particular intervention policy generates inefficiencies that do not exceed those associated with the market failure.

8. **Focus on main points.** Your opening sentence should state your thesis, followed by supporting information.

9. **Answer completely.** Make certain that the question is answered completely, with supporting documentation. Cover the main points thoroughly and logically.

Important Words in Essay Questions

The following words are used frequently in essay questions. Read them and become comfortable with their meanings.

Compare	Look for characteristics that are similar.
Contrast	Look for differences between objects, events, or problems.
Define	Give concise, clear meanings and definitions.
Describe	Relate in a story form or sequence.
Discuss	Give a complete discussion, including pros and cons, and give reasons as you examine the problem.
Evaluate	Carefully appraise the problem, citing authorities.
Explain	Clarify, analyze, and give examples of the problem.
Illustrate	Draw a picture or diagram to explain or clarify the problem.
Interpret	Comment on a problem or translate, giving examples and your opinion or judgment about a problem or situation.
Justify	Convince or give reasons for conclusions or decisions.
List	Enumerate or write a list of points, one by one.
Outline	Organize main points and subordinate supporting points in a logical arrangement.
Prove	Give factual evidence and logical reasons that something is true.

Key Teaching Concept
Cramming is not effective.

Hands-On Application
Pretend that you can have a note card with you at your test. Write the most important information on it and commit it to memory.

Class Discussion
Ask students what they can do to use their commuting or waiting time to study.

10. **Use all the available time.** Don't hurry. Pace yourself and always use all the available time for review, revisions, reflection, additions, and corrections. Proofread carefully. Answer all questions unless otherwise directed.

Last-Minute Study Tips

Cramming is not effective if you haven't studied or attended classes. You might ask yourself, however, "What is the best use of my time the night before the test?" or "What can I do right now in just a few minutes to prepare for a test?"

◆ *Focus on a few points.* Decide what is important. Focus on a few of the most important points or formulas instead of trying to cram everything into a short study time. Preview the chapter quickly.

◆ *Intend to be positive.* Don't panic or waste precious time being negative. State your intention of being receptive and open, gaining an overview of the material, and learning a few supporting points.

◆ *Use critical thinking.* What are the key words and points? Think logically.

- *Get a tutor or study partner.* Focus on main points and summarize. Do practice problems and tests. Several hours of intense study with a tutor can be far more effective than several late nights studying by yourself.
- *Focus on key words.* Write on note cards formulas, key words, dates, definitions, and important points.
- *Review your note cards.* In just a few minutes, you can review important points. Keep it simple, review quickly, and review often. Use flash cards or mind maps and review again in short segments. Carry your note cards with you.
- *Affirm your memory.* The mind is capable of learning and memorizing material in just a short time if you focus, concentrate, and apply it. Look for connections.

Words to Succeed

"Courage is not the absence of fear, but rather the judgment that something else is more important than fear."

—AMBROSE REDMOON
historian

PEAK TIP

Get sample tests and makeup questions and rehearse taking tests with a study partner. Recite, summarize, and practice to reduce test anxiety.

Class Discussion
What are the symptoms of test anxiety? Ask students what they experience mentally and physically. Is this anxiety similar to stage fright?

Teaching Tip
Stress the importance of practicing test taking. Indicate that practice can reduce anxiety.

Overcoming Test Anxiety

Many people see tests and performance assessments as huge mountains where one slip can cause them to tumble down the slope. Test anxiety is the number one barrier to doing well on tests. Even the thought of taking a test causes some people to feel anxious and sends others into a state of panic. Symptoms of test anxiety include nervousness, upset stomach, sweaty palms, and forgetfulness. Test anxiety is a learned response to stress. Since exams, tests, quizzes, tryouts, presentations, interviews, and performance reviews are all evaluations and part of life, it is worth the time to learn to overcome test anxiety.

The attitude you bring to a test has a lot to do with your performance. Approach tests with a positive attitude. Replace negative self-talk with affirmations, such as "I am well prepared and will do well on this test." Tests provide a chance to learn to face fear and transform it into positive energy. Tests are opportunities to show what you have mastered in a course. Tests do not measure how much you know, nor do they indicate your intelligence, creativity, self-esteem, personal qualities, character, or ability to contribute to society. Don't exaggerate the importance of tests. Keep them in their proper perspective. Even if the worst happens and you do poorly, you can meet with the instructor to discuss options. You can do additional work, take the test again, or take the class again if necessary. Following are 10 more suggestions that might help:

1. **Be prepared.** You will be prepared if you have attended every class; previewed chapters; reviewed your notes; and written, summarized, and studied the material in small amounts of time each day.
2. **Practice taking a sample text.** Athletes, actors, musicians, and dancers practice and rehearse for hours. When performers are on stage, their anxiety is channeled into focused energy. Practice taking sample tests

Hands-On Application
Have students:
1. Keep note cards of important information and use them as flash cards for two weeks. Then discuss the results in their groups.
2. Choose one positive habit that they would like to adopt to help them take tests.
3. Role-play possible barriers to successful test taking with a partner and have them respond with creative solutions.

Hands-On Application
Have students create a checklist or routine that they can follow to help reduce anxiety. Discuss the checklists in their small groups. Example list items are:
· Breathe deeply.
· Relax muscles.
· Focus.
· Be prepared.
· Write main facts on note cards.

with your study team, and you should be more confident during the actual test.

3. **Don't cram.** You should review the night before the test, not learn new information. Write the most important information, formulas, and key words on one note card. Don't try to cram several weeks or months of studying into one night. Last-minute, frantic cramming only creates a hectic climate and increases anxiety.

4. **Stay calm.** Make your test day peaceful by laying out your clothes, books, supplies, and keys the night before. Review your note cards just before you go to sleep, repeat a few affirmations, and then get a good night's rest. Set an alarm, so you'll be awake in plenty of time. Before you jump out of bed, relax and visualize your day unfolding in a positive way. Eat a light, balanced breakfast that includes protein, such as cheese or yogurt. Keep a piece of fruit or nuts and bottled water in your backpack for energy.

5. **Get to class early.** Use the few minutes before the test to take a few deep breaths. Review your note cards.

6. **Listen carefully to instructions.** Read all the instructions on the test.

7. **Jot down notes.** On the back of your test or in the margins write formulas, dates, or important information that you want to remember. Having this information may help you feel more confident.

8. **Preview the whole test.** Do the easiest problems first to build your confidence. Don't feel rushed. If you don't know the answer to a problem, don't panic. Move on and return to it later.

Test Anxiety

Use your critical thinking skills to answer the following questions.

1. Describe your test anxiety. Describe your emotions and thoughts associated with taking all types of tests.

_____

_____

_____

_____

Teaching Tip

Stress the importance of the portfolio assessment. Discuss the key factors involved in test taking and overcoming anxiety.

2 a. Do you have different feelings about nonacademic tests, such as a driving test or a vision test, compared with academic tests, such as quizzes and exams?

_____

_____

_____

_____

b. What do you think is the source of these differences?

_____

_____

_____

_____

3 a. What are your memories about your best and worst test-taking experiences?

_____

_____

_____

_____

b. What factors contributed to your ease or discomfort during these tests?

_____

_____

_____

_____

Applying the Adult Learning Cycle to Improve Your Test-Taking Skills and Reduce Test Anxiety

1. **RELATE. Why do I want to learn this?** I need to reduce my test anxiety and I want to do better on tests. Knowing how to control my anxiety will help me not only when taking tests but also in other performance situations. Do I already apply specific test-taking strategies or habits? What are some of my bad habits, such as last-minute cramming, that I should work to change?

2. **OBSERVE. How does this work?** Who does well on tests, and does that person seem confident when taking tests? What strategies can I learn from that person? Who seems to be just the opposite—does poorly on tests or seems to be full of anxiety? Can I determine what that person is doing wrong? I can learn from those mistakes. I'll try using new techniques and strategies for test taking and observe how I'm improving.

3. **THINK. What does this mean?** What strategies are working for me? Have I broken any bad habits, and am I more confident going into tests? Has my performance improved?

4. **DO. What can I do with this?** I will map out a plan before each major test, determining what I need to accomplish in order to be prepared and confident going in. I won't wait until the last minute to prepare. Each day, I can practice reducing my anxiety in many different stressful situations.

5. **TEACH. Whom can I share this with?** I'll talk with others and share what's working for me. Talking through my effective strategies reinforces their purpose.

   Now, return to Stage 1 and think about how it feels to learn this valuable new skill. Remember to congratulate and reward yourself when you achieve positive results.

Teaching Tip
Emphasize the importance of using the Adult Learning Cycle to increase interest and skills.

Teaching Tip
Have students compare taking college tests with taking a driver's test or having a performance review.

Use
TM 7.6 Chapter Application Worksheet 7.3 Performance Reviews.

9. **Get involved.** Focus on the subject. Get involved with answering the questions and be fully in the present.

10. **Get help.** If you are experiencing severe anxiety that prevents you from taking tests or performing well, seek help from a counselor at your school.

Reflect and use critical thinking to describe your test anxiety experiences in **Personal Performance Notebook 7.3** on page 7–16. **Peak Progress 7.5** explores how you can apply the Adult Learning Cycle to improve your test-taking skills and reduce anxiety.

Preparing for a Performance Appraisal

If you are employed, at some time you will more than likely receive a performance appraisal. A performance appraisal can be a valuable tool to let you know how your employer perceives the quality of your work, your work ethic, and your future

Words to Succeed

"Courage is not simply one of the virtues, but the form of every virtue at the testing point."

—C.S. LEWIS
writer

Carlos Fuentes

PHYSICAL THERAPIST

Related Majors: Physical Therapy, Biology

Tests in the Workplace

Carlos Fuentes is a physical therapist. A physical therapist works closely with physicians to help patients restore function and improve mobility after an injury or illness. Their work often relieves pain and prevents or limits physical disabilities.

When working with new patients, Carlos first asks questions and examines the patients' medical records, then performs tests to measure such items as strength, range of motion, balance and coordination, muscle performance, and motor function. After assessing the patients' abilities and needs, Carlos implements a treatment plan that may include exercise, traction, massage, electrical stimulation, and hot packs or cold compresses. As treatment continues, Carlos documents the patient's progress and modifies the treatment plan.

Carlos is self-motivated and an independent worker. He has a strong interest in physiology and sports, and he enjoys working with people. He likes a job that keeps him active and on his feet. Carlos spends much of his day helping patients become mobile. He often demonstrates an exercise for his patients while instructing them how to do it correctly. His job sometimes requires him to move heavy equipment or lift patients. Because Carlos is pursuing a master's degree in physical therapy, he works only three days a week:

Although he is not required to take tests as part of his job, Carlos does undergo an annual performance appraisal with his supervisor. After eight years of service, Carlos is familiar with the types of questions his supervisor might ask and keeps those in mind as he does his job throughout the year.

CRITICAL THINKING

How might understanding test-taking skills help Carlos work more effectively with his patients? How would test-taking skills help him prepare more effectively for performance reviews?

Personal Performance Notebook 7.4

Performance Reviews

Answer the following questions about your first performance review.

1. Describe your first performance review. Explain how you felt.

_____

_____

_____

_____

_____

2. How did you prepare for your first performance review?

_____

_____

_____

_____

3. Were you motivated by the feedback you heard? Did you become defensive after hearing criticism?

_____

_____

_____

_____

_____

4. What would you do differently?

_____

_____

_____

_____

_____

Tech for Success

- **Your Resources** Many of your textbooks have accompanying web sites that provide study materials, such as on-line study guides, animated flash cards, and possible essay questions. Often, this material is free when you purchase a new text. Take advantage of these resources to test your understanding of the information prior to taking the real test.
- **On-line Tutors** A number of companies and groups provide on-line tutors and live tutorial services. Your school or public library may also offer access to this kind of service. Often, these are paid services and you may find the assistance beneficial. However, you may be able to get limited assistance for free through a professional organization or related site. Ask your librarian for advice and explain how much assistance you think you need and in what content areas.

PEAKTIP

Performance reviews are an effective way to keep track of all your career achievements, goals, and support letters.

opportunities. It also gives you the opportunity to ask similar questions of your manager or reviewer. However, performance appraisals can be stressful and cause a great deal of unnecessary anxiety. The following questions will help you focus on getting the most out of your performance appraisal. Also, complete **Personal Performance Notebook 7.4** on page 7–19 to review your first performance appraisal experience.

- Write your job description, including the duties you perform.
- How do you view your job and the working climate?
- List goals and objectives and the results achieved.
- What areas do you see as opportunities for improvement?
- What are your strengths and how can you maximize them?
- What are your general concerns?
- What are your advancement possibilities?
- What additional training would be helpful for you?
- What new skills could assist in your advancement?
- How can you increase your problem-solving skills?
- How can you make more creative and sound decisions?
- What can you do to prepare yourself for stressful projects and deadlines?
- Give examples of how you have contributed to the company's profits.
- What relationships could you develop to help you achieve results?
- What project would be rewarding and challenging this year?
- What resources do you need to complete this project?

In summary, in this chapter, I learned to

- *Prepare for test taking.* The time before a test is critical. I must prepare early for tests, starting from the first day of class. I keep up with the daily reading and ask questions in class and while I read. I review early and often, previewing the chapter before class and reviewing the materials again after class. I save and review all tests, exercises, and notes and review them weekly. I rehearse by taking a pretest, and I predict questions by reviewing the text's chapter objectives and summaries. I summarize the chapter in my own words, either in writing or out loud, double-checking that I've covered key points. I recite my summary to my study team and listen to theirs. We compare notes and test each other.

- *Take a test effectively.* Arriving early helps me be calm and focused on doing well on the test. I get organized by reviewing key concepts and facts. I focus on neatness and getting to the point with short, clear responses. I read all the instructions, scanning the entire test briefly and writing formulas and notes in the margins. I pace myself by answering the easiest questions first, and I rephrase questions that I find difficult and look for associations to remember items. At the end, I review to make certain I've answered what was asked and check for mistakes or spelling errors. I stay the entire time that is available.

- *Follow up a test.* I should reward myself for successfully completing the test. Then I will analyze and assess how I did on the test. Did I prepare enough? Did I anticipate questions? What can I do differently for the next test? I'll use creative problem solving to explore ways to do better on future tests.

- *Be successful on different kinds of tests.* Objective tests include true/false, multiple-choice, matching, fill-in-the-blank, and open-book. I must read the question carefully, watch for clues, and look at sentence structure. Essay tests focus on my understanding of concepts and relationships. I outline my response, organize and focus on the main points, and take my time to deliver a thorough, neat, well-thought-out answer.

- *Incorporate last-minute study tips.* I know it's not smart to wait until the last minute, but a few important things I can do include focusing on a few key points and key words, reviewing note cards, looking for connections to memorize, and not wasting time panicking—I must stay focused!

- *Overcome test anxiety.* A positive attitude is key to alleviating anxiety before and during a test. I should prepare as much as possible and avoid last-minute cramming, practice taking a sample test, get to class early and stay calm, listen carefully to instructions, and preview the whole test and jot down notes.

- *Prepare for a performance appraisal.* I will make the most of my performance appraisal by critically thinking about my job description and duties, as well as my goals, objectives, and results. I will focus on opportunities to advance my knowledge and skills, and I will avoid the anxiety that comes with the appraisal process.

Peak Performer Profile

Kirk Perron

Jamba—it sounds like a dance, but it's actually an African word that means "celebration." Put it together with fruit juice and special ingredients, such as ginkgo and ginseng, and you have an industry leader in blended-to-order smoothies. Jamba Juice founder Kirk Perron thinks of these portable drinks as nutritious meals, a healthy alternative to fast food.

Perron's taste for business began at age five, when he was juicing lemons for his own lemonade stand. Twenty-one years later, he found himself back in business at the helm of a quickly growing company. In one five-year period, Jamba Juice was showing an increase of 2,500 percent in shops and 3,000 percent in revenues.

A serious cyclist and fitness buff, Perron first hit on the juice business idea when, after vigorous workouts, he would reward himself with a smoothie. Realizing that others might enjoy the same "sensory experience," he took a bold step. Using his experience as a former grocery store clerk with business courses from the local community college under his belt, Perron opened his first store in San Luis Obispo, California, called Juice Club. Other stores followed and evolved into what is now Jamba Juice. Today, millions of health-conscious patrons are lining up in more than 300 stores nationwide.

Perron's advertising philosophy is based on good word of mouth and use of the best ingredients. No detail is too small, including biodegradable cups and straws that are tested for the "suckability factor." The real test, however, is in the tasting. Recently, one smoothie fan actually took a "straw poll" to compare the country's best smoothies. The verdict? Jamba Juice scored at the top, with "clear fruit flavors" and a "lovely consistency," passing the test as a four-straw winner.

PERFORMANCE THINKING Jamba Juice has expanded its menu to include soups, breads, and snacks. If you had to judge these newer items, what criteria would be important to you to test these items?

Performance Strategies

Following are the top 10 strategies for successful test taking:

◆ Prepare early.
◆ Clarify expectations.
◆ Observe and question.
◆ Review.
◆ Rehearse by pretesting yourself.
◆ Use your study team.
◆ Organize yourself.
◆ Move through the test quickly.
◆ Reread, recheck, rethink, and reward.
◆ Analyze, assess, and reprogram.

Review Questions

1. What are the 10 steps for preparing for a test?
2. Why is it important to pace yourself while taking a test?
3. What should you do after you take a test?
4. What is the key to being successful when taking an open-book test?
5. Describe three special strategies for taking math and science tests.

REVISUALIZATION

Revisit the Visualization box on the first page of this chapter and your journal entry on **Worksheet 7.1.** You described a time when you did well in a performance, sporting event, or test and explored the factors that helped you be calm, confident, and focused. Now, consider a situation in which your mind went blank or you suffered anxiety. Continuing in **Worksheet 7.1,** apply the ABCDE method to visualize a result in which you are again calm, confident, and focused—for example,

A = Actual event: "I just took a biology test and was so nervous that my mind went blank. It's as if I studied all the wrong information."

B = Beliefs: "I'm not good in stressful situations. I should avoid taking difficult classes."

C = Consequence: "I'm disappointed in myself. If I can't get over my anxiety taking tests, how will I ever survive a job interview?"

D = Dispute: "I have been successful in other stressful situations, such as sports, which required me to focus on my performance. My poor performance on this test was a wake-up call that I need to attempt some positive strategies to become better prepared and improve my confidence."

E = Energized: "I know that I can learn to control my anxiety and improve my test-taking skills. Since performance reviews are part of life, this skill is worth effort and time."

COPING WITH ANXIETY

In the Classroom

Sharon Oshinowa is a bright and hardworking student. She studies long hours, attends all her classes, and participates in class discussions. Sharon is very creative and especially enjoys her computer graphics course. When it comes to taking tests, however, she panics. She stays up late cramming, tells herself that she might fail, and gets headaches and stomach pains. Her mind goes blank when she takes the test, and she has trouble organizing her thoughts. Sharon could get much better grades and enjoy school more if she could reduce her stress and apply some test-taking strategies.

1. What techniques from this chapter would be most useful to Sharon?

_____

_____

_____

_____

2. What one habit could she adopt that would empower her to be more successful?

_____

_____

_____

In the Workplace

Sharon now works as a graphic designer for a large company. She likes having control over her work and is an excellent employee. She is dedicated, competent, and willing to learn new skills. There is a great deal of pressure in her job to meet deadlines, learn new techniques, and compete with other firms. She handles most of these responsibilities well unless she is being evaluated. Despite her proficiency, Sharon panics before her performance reviews. She feels pressure to perform perfectly and does not take criticism or even advice well.

3. What strategies in this chapter would be most helpful to Sharon?

_____

_____

_____

4. What would you suggest she do to control her performance anxiety?

_____

_____

_____

CHAPTER 7   ▶ REVIEW AND APPLICATIONS

APPLYING THE ABCDE METHOD OF SELF-MANAGEMENT

In the Visualization box on page 7–1, you were asked to describe a time when you did well in a performance, sporting event, or test. Write about that and indicate the factors that helped you be calm, confident, and focused.

_____

_____

_____

_____

Now, consider a situation in which your mind went blank or you suffered anxiety. Apply the ABCDE method to visualize a result in which you are again calm, confident, and focused.

A = Actual event:

B = Beliefs:

C = Consequences:

D = Dispute:

E = Energized:

Practice deep breathing with your eyes closed for just one minute. See yourself calm and centered and relaxed as you take a test or give a performance. See yourself recalling information easily. You feel confident about yourself because you have learned to control your anxiety. You are well prepared and you know how to take tests.

CHAPTER 7 ▲ REVIEW AND APPLICATIONS

EXAM SCHEDULE

Fill in the following chart to remind you of your exams as they occur throughout the semester or term.

Course	Date	Time	Room	Type of Exam
Student Success 101	November 7	2:15 P.M.	1012A	Essay

CHAPTER 7 ▶ REVIEW AND APPLICATIONS

PREPARING FOR TESTS AND EXAMS

Before you take a quiz, a test, or an exam, fill in this form to help you plan your study strategy. Certain items will be more applicable, depending on the type of test.

Course _____

Date of test _____   Test number (if any) _____

- Pretest(s)   Date given _____   Results _____
  Date given _____   Results _____
  Date given _____   Results _____

- Present grade in course _____

- Met with instructor   Yes _____   No _____   Date(s) of meeting(s) _____

- Study team members   Date(s) of meeting(s) _____

  Name _____   Phone number _____

  Name _____   Phone number _____

  Name _____   Phone number _____

  Name _____   Phone number _____

- Expected test format (Circle. There can be more than one test format.)

  Objective   Essay   True/false   Multiple-choice

  Other _____

- Importance (circle one)

  Quiz   Midterm   Final exam   Other

- Chapters covered in the test _____

  Date for chapter review _____

- Chapter notes (use additional paper)

  _____

  _____

  _____

- Date for review of chapter notes _____

- Note cards   Yes _____   No _____   Date note cards reviewed _____

- List of key words

  Word _____   Meaning _____

  Word _____   Meaning _____

  Word _____   Meaning _____

  Word _____   Meaning _____

CHAPTER 7 ▲ REVIEW AND APPLICATIONS

- Possible essay questions:

1. Question _____

   Thesis statement _____

Outline

   I. _____

       A. _____

       B. _____

       C. _____

       D. _____

   II. _____

       A. _____

       B. _____

       C. _____

       D. _____

   - Main points

     _____

     _____

   - Examples

     _____

     _____

2. Question _____

   Thesis statement _____

Outline

   I. _____

       A. _____

       B. _____

       C. _____

       D. _____

   II. _____

       A. _____

       B. _____

       C. _____

       D. _____

   - Main points

     _____

     _____

   - Examples

     _____

     _____

PERFORMANCE REVIEWS

The following are qualities and competencies that are included in many performance reviews.

Acceptance of diversity*	Safety practices
Effectiveness in working with others	Personal growth and development
Quality of work	Workplace security
Quantity of work	Technology
Positive attitude	Willingness to learn

*Diversity: Getting along with people from diverse backgrounds and cultures

1. Using this page and a separate sheet of paper, indicate how you would demonstrate each of the listed qualities and competencies to an employer.

_____

_____

_____

_____

_____

_____

_____

_____

2. Give examples of your willingness to accept assessment and feedback from an employer. Include sample performance reviews in your portfolio.

_____

_____

_____

_____

_____

_____

_____

_____

MATRIX FOR TEST TAKING

Use this checklist of strategies to support your test-taking skills for each class.

	Prepare				**Rehearse**				**Organize**				**Assess**			
	Go to every class; ask questions.	Keep up with homework.	Develop and predict questions.	Review often; join study team.	Clarify expectations.	Rehearse by summarizing.	Rehearse by predicting questions.	Take sample test.	Organize notes and materials.	Read and listen to all instructions.	Preview test and place yourself.	Organize thoughts; jot down words, formulas.	Reread, recheck, rethink.	Analyze and assess results.	Reward yourself.	Modify and adjust.
Test 1																
Test 2																
Test 3																
Test 4																

ASSESSING YOUR SKILLS AND COMPETENCIES

The following are typical qualities and competencies that are included in many performance reviews.

- Communication skills:
    Writing
    Speaking
  Reading
- Integrity
- Willingness to learn

- Decision-making skills
- Delegation
- Planning
- Organizational skills
- Positive attitude
- Ability to accept change

On the following lines, describe how you currently demonstrate each of the listed skills and competencies to an employer. Consider how you can improve. Add this page to your Career Development Portfolio.

1. How do you demonstrate the listed skills?

_____

_____

_____

_____

_____

_____

_____

_____

_____

_____

2. How can you improve?

_____

_____

_____

_____

_____

_____

_____

_____

_____

Expressing Yourself in Writing and Speech

Chapter Objectives

In this chapter, you will learn

▲ How to prepare research papers and speeches

▲ How to use the library and take your search on-line

▲ Strategies for writing effective papers

▲ Strategies for giving effective presentations

▲ How to overcome writer's block

VISUALIZATION

"I put off taking the required public speaking class until the last semester. I hate getting up in front of people. My mind goes blank, I get butterflies, and my palms sweat. What can I do to decrease stage fright and be more confident about speaking in public?"

Have you ever had a similar experience? Do you find yourself feeling anxious and worried whenever you have to make a presentation or give a speech? Do you suffer physical symp-

toms, such as sweaty palms, upset stomach, headaches, or inability to sleep or concentrate even days before the event? In this chapter, you will learn how to deal with stage fright and learn public speaking skills.

JOURNAL ENTRY　In **Worksheet 8.1** on page 8–28, describe a time when you did well in a performance, sporting event, or speaking assignment. What factors helped you be calm, confident, and able to perform?

Key Teaching Concept
You can overcome the fear of writing and speaking.

Use
TM 8.1 Success Principle 8.

Teaching Tip
Emphasize the importance of using the ABCDE Method of Self-Management to overcome anxiety. (p. 8–28)

Class Discussion
Discuss the importance of overcoming the barrier of perfection. Too many people avoid writing and speaking because they fear making a mistake.

Words to Succeed

"Being good at something is only half the battle. The other half is mastering the art of self-presentation, positioning, and connecting."

—ADELE SCHEELE
career counselor, author

Key Teaching Concept
Writing and speaking are the most important skills for college and job success.

Use
TM 8.2 The Four Basic Steps.

Few things in life are as difficult as writing research papers and speaking before a group. Famed sportswriter Red Smith commented, "Writing is very easy. All you do is sit in front of a typewriter keyboard until little drops of blood appear on your forehead." Public speaking can cause even more anxiety. To some students, just the thought of speaking in front of a group produces feelings of sheer terror. In fact, research indicates that public speaking is the number one fear for most people, outranking even fear of death. For many students, writing not only produces feelings of doubt but also demands their focused attention, intense thinking, and detailed research. You can't avoid writing or speaking in school or at work, but you can learn strategies that will make them easier to do and more effective. Once you develop the skills and confidence required for speaking and writing effectively, you will experience a strong sense of accomplishment.

The Importance of Writing and Speaking

The ability to communicate clearly, both orally and in writing, is the most important skill you will ever acquire. Peter Drucker, noted management expert and author, remarked, "Colleges teach the one thing that is perhaps most valuable for the future employee to know. But very few students bother to learn it. This one basic skill is the ability to organize and express ideas in writing and speaking."

You may be asked to do research on new ideas, products, procedures, and programs and compile the results in a report. You will most likely write business letters, memos, and reports. You may have to give formal speeches before a large group, preside at meetings, or present ideas to a small group. You will be expected to present both written and spoken ideas in a clear, concise, and organized manner. Writing papers and preparing speeches in school prepare you for on-the-job reports and correspondence. These assignments give you a chance to show initiative, use judgment, apply and interpret information, research resources, organize ideas, and polish your style. Public speaking skills also help you inform and persuade others at informal meetings and presentations. Good writers and speakers are not born, and there is no secret to their success. Like other skills, speaking and writing can be learned with practice and effort.

This chapter won't tell you how to write a great novel or deliver the keynote speech at a political convention, but it will give you strategies for handling every step of the paper-writing and speech-giving process, from choosing a topic to turning in the paper or delivering the speech. Keep these four basic steps in mind as you prepare your paper or speech:

1. Prepare.
2. Organize.
3. Write.
4. Edit.

Teaching Tip
Review the
importance of setting
a schedule and
looking at the big
picture. Urge
students to complete
the first draft early
and see the instructor
for suggestions and
help.

Figure 8.1　Sample Schedule

Term Paper for Criminal Justice 101, Due April 3

Final Check. Make copy.	April 2
Edit, revise, and polish.	March 29 (Put away for one or two days)
Complete bibliography.	March 28
Revise.	March 26
Edit, review, revise.	March 24 (Confer with instructor)
Final draft completed.	March 22 (Proof and review with a good writer)
Complete second draft.	March 20
Add, delete, and rearrange information.	March 17
First draft completed.	March 15 (Share with writing group)
Write conclusion.	March 12
Continue research and flesh out main ideas.	February 16
Write introduction.	February 10
Organize and outline.	February 3
Gather information and compile bibliography and notes.	January 29
Narrow topic and write thesis statement.	January 23
Do preliminary reading.	January 20
Choose a topic.	January 16
Brainstorm ideas.	January 15
Clarify expectations and determine purpose.	January 14

Sample Schedule　This schedule for preparing a term paper starts where it's finished. *Why does this schedule begin at the due date of the term paper?*

Preparation for Writing

1. **Set a schedule.** Estimate how long each step will take and leave plenty of time for proofing. Work backward from the due date and allow yourself ample time for each step. See **Figure 8.1** on page for an example.

2. **Choose a general topic.** Choose a topic that meets your instructor's requirements, one that is narrow enough to handle in the time available and one in which you have an interest. If you have any questions concerning

expectations, talk with your instructor and clarify length, format and style, purpose, and method of citation. Determine if your purpose is to entertain, inform, explain, persuade, gain or maintain goodwill, gain respect and trust, or gather information. Consider the age, education level, and size of your audience and their knowledge of the topic. Use the tips in **Peak Progress 8.1** on page 8–5 to help you come up with a topic.

3. **Do preliminary reading.** Begin to gather general information by reviewing reference materials, such as articles or an encyclopedia. Your initial research is intended to give you an overview of the subject and key issues. Ask questions to help you begin structuring your topic and compiling a working bibliography. Make certain you check the list of related references at the end of reference books and reference book articles. You may want to develop a list of questions that can lead to new directions and additional research:

   • What do I already know about the topic? What do I want to know?
   • What questions do I want to explore? What interests me most?
   • What is the point I want to research?

   Write these questions on note cards and include them later with your research cards.

4. **Narrow your topic.** After you have finished your preliminary reading, you can focus on a specific topic. For example, instead of "Health Problems in America," narrow the subject to "Cigarette Smoking Among Teenage Girls" or "Should Cigarette Advertising Be Banned?"

5. **Write a thesis statement.** Writing a thesis statement will help you clarify what you plan to cover in your paper. The thesis is the main point, or central idea, of a paper. In one sentence, your thesis should describe your topic and what you want to convey about it. A good thesis statement is unified and clear—for example, "Smoking among teenage girls is on the rise."

6. **Prepare a bibliography.** Go through the on-line catalog in the library. Most libraries have electronic access and, as with the card catalog, you can browse by subject or author. You can also use the Internet to discover what is available on your topic and start putting together a preliminary bibliography. Skim the references to see if they contain useful information. List all materials available on your topic. Put them in alphabetical order and number them. Write down each author's full name (last name first), the exact title (underline newspapers, magazines, and book titles and put article titles in quotations marks), the place of publication, the name of the publisher, and the date of publication and write the call number in the upper left-hand corner.

7. **Take notes.** Jot down quotations and ideas that clarify your research topic. Put this information on note cards. At the top of each card, write the topic; below that, write a summary in your own words, a brief statement, or a direct quotation. If you are quoting, use quotation marks and be sure to write the words exactly as they appear and the source. If there is an error in the text, in brackets write the term *sic,* which means "thus in the original." If you omit words, indicate missing words with ellipsis points

How to Generate Topic Ideas

- *Brainstorm.* Brainstorming is generating as many ideas as possible without evaluating their merit. The brainstorming process often works well in small groups. Your goal is to get a list of as many topics as you can in the specific time you have set aside. No one should evaluate the ideas. Within 10 minutes, you can often generate a sizable list of potential topics.

- *Go to the library.* Look in the *Reader's Guide to Periodical Literature* for possible ideas. Look through newspapers, magazines, and new books.

- *Brainstorm on-line.* The Internet is a valuable source of ideas.

- *Keep a journal.* Keeping a journal is a great way to generate ideas for a paper or speech and is a good way to practice your writing skills. Write down ideas, feelings, opinions, summaries of books and articles, and reactions to other speeches or papers.

- *Keep a file.* Collect articles, poems, and a list of topics you find interesting. Listen to good speeches and collect stories or ideas from current newspapers that you could research and write about from a different perspective.

- *Develop observation skills.* Be aware of life around you. Think of possible topics as you read, watch television and movies, and talk with friends. What topics are in the news? What are people talking about?

- *Complete a sentence.* This technique can help generate potential topics. Write open-ended sentences and brainstorm completions—for example,

  The world would be better if _____

  Too many people _____

  In the future _____

  A major problem today is _____

  A most wondrous event in life is _____

  The best thing about _____

  What I enjoy most is _____

  I learned that _____

  It always makes me laugh when _____

  The components of a perfect day are _____

  If I had unlimited funds, I would buy _____

  I get through a tough day by _____

Teaching Tip
Avoid discussion of grammar, punctuation, and spelling. Focus on the importance of communication and generating ideas. Grammar can be covered during final drafts.

Hands-On Application
1. Have students bring in a petition, application, or other form that they may use in college. Have them examine these forms for purpose. They should discuss writing tips that are important for clarity.
2. Have students brainstorm ideas for a paper or speech for each class member. Tell students that completing sentences is a good way to brainstorm ideas. Have them come up with more sentences. Discuss in groups.

Use
TM 8.4 How to Generate Ideas.

(three dots with a space between each dot, or period). Also write down each reference source on a separate card. You will need exact information for your final bibliography and footnotes and for researching material. Put a rubber band around your cards and keep them in a small folder. Sorting these cards into subject divisions will help you prepare your outline. See **Figure 8.2** for a sample bibliography card.

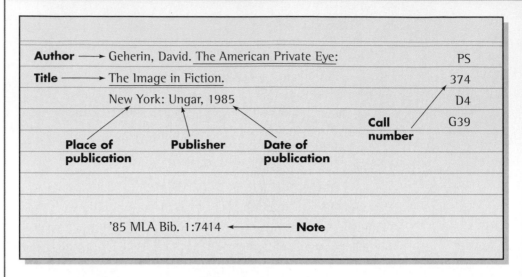

Figure 8.2   Bibliography Card

Author ──→ Geherin, David. The American Private Eye: PS

Title ──→ The Image in Fiction.   374

New York: Ungar, 1985   D4

Call   G39
number

Place of   **Publisher**   **Date of**
publication   **publication**

'85 MLA Bib. 1:7414 ←──── **Note**

Source: *MLA Handbook for Writers of Research Papers,* 4th edition, by Joseph Garibaldi. New York: The Modern Language Association of America, 1995.

Bibliography Card   As you research, write down reference information for each source on a card. *What is the advantage of creating these cards?*

Organizing a Writing Plan

1. **Organize and outline information.** Organize your note cards into a logical order using either a traditional or a mind map outline. This outline should contain main points and subtopics. An outline is a road map that illustrates your entire project. If you use a computer, check applicable software packages that offer an outline feature. Or you can use this traditional outline format:

   Sample Outline
     I. Smoking among teenage girls is increasing.
         A. Smoking has increased by 24 percent.
             1. Supporting information
             2. Supporting information
         B. Girls are smoking at younger ages.
    II. Advertising targets young girls directly.
         A. Example of advertising
             1. Supporting information
             2. Supporting information
         B. Effects of advertising
   Use **Personal Performance Notebook 8.1** to help you organize your paper.

2. **Continue your research.** Look for specific information and data that support your main points and thesis. Research the books and articles you noted on your bibliography cards. Organize and separate the information.

Personal Performance Notebook 8.1

Preparing Research Papers

When you start thinking about assigned research papers, use this form to prepare and organize your paper.

Topic _____ Due date _____

Thesis _____

_____

_____

Introduction _____

_____

_____

Interest and importance _____

_____

_____

Introduce thesis in concise statement. _____

_____

_____

Review your paper and check for these elements:

Main Body

_____ Background of topic

_____ Thesis emphasized

_____ Terminology, facts, data

_____ Key words

_____ Main points and arguments

_____ Supporting points

Conclusion

_____ Restate thesis.

_____ Summarize key points.

_____ Present a clear and strong conclusion.

3. **Revise your outline.** Revise your outline as you continue to research. You may also want to refine your writing strategy by focusing on how best to accomplish your purpose. What is your major topic? What subtopics do you want to include? What examples, definitions, quotations, statistics, stories, or personal comments would be most interesting and supportive? Continue to look for specific information to support your thesis.

Writing Strategies

1. **Write your first draft.** Now is the time to organize all your note cards according to sections and headings and write in your own words according to your revised outline. Write freely and don't worry about spelling, grammar, or format. The key is to begin writing and keep the momentum going. Both papers and speeches should have three sections: an introduction, a main body, and a conclusion.

2. **Write the introduction.** The introduction should be a strong opening that clearly states your purpose, captures the attention of your audience, defines terms, and sets the stage for the main points. "More than 450,000 people will die this year from the effects of cigarette smoking" is a stronger introduction than "This paper will present the dangers of smoking."

3. **Write the main body.** The main body is the heart of your paper or speech. Each main point should be presented logically and stand out as a unit. Explain main points in your own words and use direct quotes when you want to state the original source. See **Figure 8.3** for a visual representation of

Key Teaching Concepts

1. The introduction and the conclusion are the most important elements in a speech or paper. They capture the audience and move them to action.

2. Explain the importance of the conclusion. Ask students if they want the audience to do something.

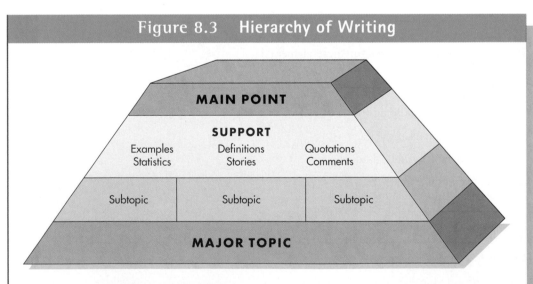

Figure 8.3   Hierarchy of Writing

MAIN POINT

SUPPORT

| Examples Statistics | Definitions Stories | Quotations Comments |

| Subtopic | Subtopic | Subtopic |

MAJOR TOPIC

Hierarchy of Writing   Remember these key elements for making a main point from your main topic. *Why are "support" elements so important?*

how to develop your major topic in order to make your main point. Refer often to your outline and your thesis statement. Your research note cards will help you find the support elements you need. If you find gaps, do more research.

4. **Write the conclusion.** Your final paragraph should tie together important points, our reader or listener should have an understanding of the topic and be aware that you have achieved your purpose. You might try using a story, a quotation, or a call to action. You may want to refer again to the introduction, reemphasize main points, or rephrase an important position. Keep your conclusion brief, interesting, and powerful. **Peak Progress 8.2** provides some helpful hints on overcoming writer's block.

Editing

1. **Revise.**

   - Revise your first draft for attention to overall meaning and effect. Revise again for punctuation, grammar, and style.
   - Read your paper out loud to get an overall sense of meaning and the flow of your words. Vary sentence lengths and arrangements to add interest and variety. For example, don't start each sentence with the subject or overuse the same words or phrases.
   - Rework paragraphs for clarity and appropriate transitions. Does each paragraph contain one idea in a topic sentence? Is the idea well supported? Transitions should be smooth and unobtrusive. In a speech, they should be defined clearly, so that listeners stay focused.
   - Recheck your outline. Have you followed your outline logically? Have you included supporting information in the correct places? Break up the narrative with lists if you are presenting series of data. As you revise, stay focused on your purpose rather than on the ideas that support your conclusion. Make sure your points are clearly and concisely presented with supporting stories, quotes, and explanations.
   - The paper should be concise and clear. Information should contribute, not just fill in space. Revision also involves deleting and/or moving information from one section to another. If you are using a computer or word processor, you can cut and paste with your word processing program. Save often and make a copy on a disk.
   - Review sentence structure, punctuation, grammar, and unity of thought. Check carefully for typographical and spelling errors, grammatical mistakes, and poor transitions.

2. **Revise again.** Often, the difference between an *A* paper and a *B* paper, or speech, is that extra polish. If you can set it aside for a day or two before

> ## Words to Succeed
>
> *"Every discourse, like a living creature, should be so put together that it has a body of its own and lacks neither head nor feet, a middle nor extremities, all composed in such a way that they suit both each other and the whole."*
>
> —PLATO
> *Greek philosopher*

Hands-On Application
In groups, have students list the symptoms, physical and mental, of writer's block. Ask students: How have you overcome these symptoms? Brainstorm ideas.

Teaching Tip
Hold up a blank sheet of paper to illustrate what can happen to the mind when faced with a writing project. Tell students that mind mapping, outlining ideas, or free writing can get ideas flowing.

Peak Progress   8.2

Overcoming Writer's Block

- **Read.** Reading will give you ideas and improve your writing. Read novels, classic literature, biographies, and newspapers. Read other students' papers and exchange papers with your study team.

- **Write e-mail and letters.** Write e-mail and letters every day. Nothing improves your writing like daily practice.

- **Keep a journal.** Again, there is no better way to become a writer than to practice writing.

- **Write in a conversational tone.** Don't use technical, artificial, or stilted language. Use everyday, common words as if you were talking to someone. Try using a tape recorder to hear how your words sound.

- **Write in short blocks of time.** Like any other large task, you'll become discouraged if you try to write a large paper in one sitting. Write a little every day—anywhere you happen to be. Write for five minutes before bed, in the morning, or between classes.

- **Review your purpose.** Have a clear understanding of your purpose. Make a list of key points you want to make. In one or two words or phrases, write what you want to accomplish. What do you want to say?

- **Go to a restaurant.** Go out for a cup of coffee or tea and give yourself an hour of uninterrupted time to outline or mind map your paper or speech. If you are a visual learner, you may find that a mind map breaks your writing block. Start with your central purpose and topic. Outline main points, subtopics, and so on and fill in with additional ideas. A map allows your ideas to flow freely and allows you to see the connections between topics. You can then use this visual map as you type your paper. Don't feel that you must start with the introduction and work in a linear fashion.

- **Find a conference room or classroom.** You may need space to be alone, spread out papers, and work without interruptions.

- **Free write.** After you have completed your map outline, write for 30 or 40 minutes. Don't worry about spelling, organization, or grammar; just keep writing. Timed free writing is a powerful writing tool to break a writing block. Free writing is especially useful if you start early, allow the first draft to sit for a few days, and then revise.

- **Take a break or vary your routine.** If you get frustrated, take a short break or change the pace and work on your conclusion instead of starting with the introduction. Write your conclusion in one sentence to check for clarity. Then you can go back and write your paper.

- **Set a deadline.** Write a schedule and stick to it. Complete each task, even if it isn't what you would like it to be. You can revise and change later.

Figure 8.4   Writing Citations

MLA Style

For Footnotes

1. Lee, Ann. *Office Reference Manual.* New York: Irwin, 1993.

For Bibliography or Works Cited

- **Book: one author**
  Allen, James D. *Coming of Age.* New York: Macmillan, 1992.
- **Book: two authors**
  Arkin, Terry C., and Nancy A. Kelly. *Smoking Too Soon.* New York: Basic Books, 1991.
- **Government publication**
  U.S. Congressional Quarterly Service. A Review of Smoking.
  Washington, D.C., 1989: 28.
- **Nonprint Source**
  Morgan, David E. *Reference Software for Smoking Studies.* DOS Version. CD-ROM.
  New York: Macmillan, 1995.
- **Journal**
  "Risking the Future Adolescent." *National Research Council Journal.*
  Washington, D.C.: National Academy Press, 1990.
- **Editorial**
  "Some Better Ways to Curb Teen Smoking." Editorial. Los Angeles Times
  14 August 1995: sec. 1-2.
- **Encyclopedia or other reference work**
  Walton, Tom E. "Smoking." *World Book Encyclopedia.* 2001 ed.

Writing Citations   The Modern Language Association's (MLA) style of citation is used for humanities subjects, such as English and languages. *To what subject area does the APA style apply?*

you give it a final revision, you can approach what you have written with a fresh view. Go through your entire paper or speech. Is your central theme clear and concise? Read your paper out loud. Recite your speech to a friend or tape it. Does it flow? Could it use more stories or quotes to add flair? Is it too wordy or confusing? Can you make it more concise? Does it have an interesting introduction and conclusion? Share your paper with a friend or member of your study team. Ask one of them to proofread your work. Other people can sometimes see errors that you can't, and they can provide a fresh viewpoint.

3. **Use a computer to compile footnotes and bibliography.** There are many ways to write citations. The Modern Language Association (MLA) of America format is often the preferred method for English and classical languages (see **Figure 8.4**). The American Psychological Association (APA)

format is commonly used for social science topics. Computer programs are available to format according to MLA and APA. Make sure you have written the references according to your instructor's preference. Footnotes can he placed at the bottom of a page or listed at the end of the paper, where they are referred to as endnotes. The bibliography is a list of books and articles, and it is found at the end of a paper after the endnotes. In MLA format, this list is called "Works Cited."

4. **Confer with your instructor.** Make an appointment with your instructor to review your paper. Some students make an appointment when they have completed their outline or first draft. Other students like to wait until they have proofed their second draft. Most instructors will review your paper with you and give you suggestions. Discuss what to add and what to revise and the preferred method of citation.

5. **Prepare your final draft.** Following your instructor's guidelines and suggestions, prepare your final draft. Leave a margin of 1 inch on all sides, except for the first page, which should have a 3-inch margin at the top of the paper. Double-space your entire paper, except for the footnotes and the bibliography, which are often single-spaced. Make corrections, revise, run a spell-check, and print out a clean, corrected copy on good-quality paper. It's always a good idea to proofread this hard copy, because it's easy to miss errors on a computer screen. See **Peak Progress 8.3** for writing tips.

6. **Number your pages.** Number all pages except the first page, or the cover page. You can number the pages in the upper right-hand corner 1/2 inch from the top of the page. Number your endnotes and bibliography as part of the text.

7. **Add a title page.** To create a title page, center the title one-third of the page from the top. Two-thirds from the top, center your name, instructor's name, course title, and date. See **Figure 8.5** for a sample of a title page.

Review and Assessment

1. **Final review.** Do a final check of your paper by reading through all of it one more time. You want your paper to be error-free. **Peak Progress 8.4** on page 8–16 provides a handy checklist to use as you finalize your paper.

2. **Make a copy.** Copy your final paper or speech in case your instructor loses the original. You should also keep copies of your major research papers in your Career Development Portfolio to show documentation of writing, speaking, and research skills.

3. **Present your paper or speech on time.** Deliver your paper on time and be prepared to give your speech when it's due. Delaying the date just adds to the anxiety and may result in a lower grade.

4. **Assess and evaluate.** Review your graded paper or speech when it is returned to you. Ask your instructor for improvement tips.

Class Discussion

Ask students:

1. How important is it to meet with instructors to review drafts and clarify expectations? How many have done this? Did it help?

2. How important is it to deliver work on time? Should you keep a hard copy? How important is it to make a backup disk?

Key Teaching Concept

Indicate to students that the key to revising involves having time for proofreading, meeting with the instructor, modifying, and asking friends to review.

Teaching Tip
Ask how many students participate in sports or in a play or musical activity. Stress that learning how to write and speak also takes hours of practice.

Writing Do's

Be concise.
Eliminate unnecessary words. Write in plain language and avoid wordiness.

Be concrete.
Emphasize verbs for active, powerful writing. Use vivid action words rather than vague, general terms. The sentence "Jill wrote the paper" is in the active voice and is easy to understand; "The paper was written by Jill" is in the passive voice and sounds weak. Favor familiar words over the unfamiliar. Include stories and quotes for interest and support. Avoid vague adjectives and adverbs, such as *nice, good, greatly,* and *badly.*

Be clear.
Keep in mind the purpose of your writing. Make certain that your message is complete and includes all the information the audience needs to understand your intent. Never assume that the audience has any prior information. Use simple words and avoid stuffy, technical terms; clichés; slang; and jargon. If you must be technical, include simple definitions for your audience.

Be correct.
Choose precise words and grammatically correct sentences. Make sure your supporting details are factual and that you interpret them correctly.

Be coherent.
Your message should flow smoothly. Transitions between topics should be clear and logical.

Be complete.
Make certain you have included all necessary information. Will your listeners or readers understand your message? Reread your speech or paper from their point of view. What questions might the audience have? If there are any unanswered questions, answer them.

Be considerate
Use a respectful tone. Don't talk down to your audience or use pompous language. Always write with courtesy, tact, and consideration.

Class Discussion
Ask students if they have ever read something or listened to a speech that made them feel the author or speaker was condescending or offensive. Discuss the importance of being respectful of your audience.

Writing Do's

Be interesting.
Use variety. Vary the length of sentences for interest and a sense of rhythm. Include stories, examples, and interesting facts.

Be neat.
Neatness counts. Papers should always be typed. If you find an error in the final draft, it's OK to use white-out fluid or pen to make a correction. A word processor or computer, of course, can help you make the correction quickly and print out a flawless page.

Edit and proofread several times.
Make certain you use correct grammar and check spelling and punctuation carefully. It is easy to miss errors with only one proofing, so proof at least twice and don't rely completely on your computer's spell-check feature.

Avoid biased language.
Make substitutions for biased words. Language is so powerful that it is important to avoid using words that are biased in terms of sex, disabilities, or ethnic groups—for example,

Instead of . . .	You can substitute . . .
mankind	humanity, people, humankind
manmade	manufactured, handcrafted
policeman	police officer
fireman	firefighter
housewife	homemaker
crippled	disabled, a person with disabilities
Indian (American)	Native American
Negro	African American
Oriental	Asian American
Chicano	Hispanic

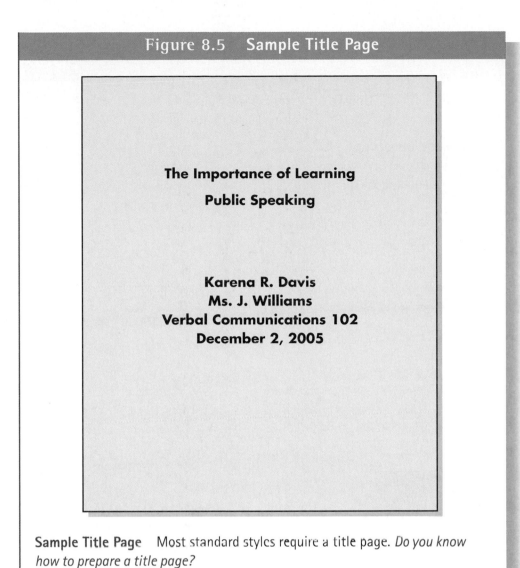

Figure 8.5   Sample Title Page

> The Importance of Learning
>
> Public Speaking
>
>
> Karena R. Davis
> Ms. J. Williams
> Verbal Communications 102
> December 2, 2005

Sample Title Page   Most standard styles require a title page. *Do you know how to prepare a title page?*

Hands-On Application

1. Arrange a class tour of a library. Stress to students the importance of feeling comfortable at the library and on the Internet.
2. Encourage students to use the Internet for research and the computer to write papers and speeches.
3. Have students work in pairs and create their own Web site or review the school's Web site.
4. Encourage students to e-mail each of their instructors.

Using the Library for Research

The library contains a wealth of information. Besides books, libraries have newspapers, magazines, encyclopedias, dictionaries, indexes, audiovisual equipment, telephone directories, maps, catalogs, research aids, computer software, and computers. Librarians are trained to find information about every subject. They can often order special materials from other libraries or direct you to other sources. Asking for their guidance at the beginning of your search can save you hours of time and frustration. When planning your research strategy, remember the three basic types of sources found in most libraries: books, periodicals, and reference materials.

◆ *Books.* Books make up a large part of every library. Books are designed to treat a subject in depth and offer a broad scope. In your research project,

Words to Succeed

"*What's another word for Thesaurus?*"

—STEPHEN WRIGHT
comedian

Checklists for Writing Papers and Giving Speeches

Review these checklists before submitting a paper or giving a speech.

Papers and Speeches

_____ Appropriate and focused topic	_____ Good examples
_____ Attention-getting introduction	_____ Good visuals
_____ Thesis statement clear	_____ Sources credited
_____ Word choice appropriate	_____ Smooth transitions
_____ Plenty of factual support	_____ Effective summary/conclusions

Papers

_____ Spelling and grammar checked	_____ Neat appearance/format
_____ Proofread at least twice	_____ Deadline met
_____ Pages numbered	_____ Copies made

Speeches

_____ Eye contact	_____ Relaxed body language
_____ Appropriate voice level and tone	_____ Appropriate attire
_____ No slang or distracting words	_____ Access to watch or clock

A Good Source

Libraries provide the most research options, with books, periodicals, reference materials, on-line access, and trained librarians. *What's the best source for recent data?*

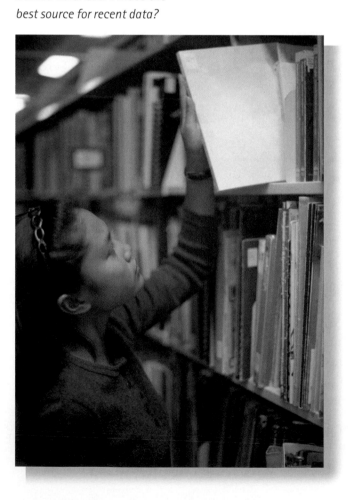

use books for historical context; thorough, detailed discussions of a subject; or varied perspectives on a topic.

◆ *Periodicals.* A periodical is anything published regularly, such as daily or weekly newspapers, weekly or monthly news magazines, professional and scholarly journals, and trade and industry magazines. Articles in periodicals provide current printed information. For your research, use periodicals when you need recent data.

◆ *Reference materials.* Reference materials may be in print or on the computer. Examples of reference materials include encyclopedias, dictionaries, chronologies, abstracts, indexes, and compilations of statistics. In your research strategy, use reference materials when you want to obtain or verify specific facts.

The *Reader's Guide to Periodical Literature* is a helpful source for locating articles. Other standard reference materials that may give you a general understanding of specific topics and help you develop questions include the *Encyclopedia Americana,* the *Encyclopaedia Britannica,* the *New York Times* index, and the *Wall Street Journal* index.

Check these sources for historical speeches:

◆ *Speech Index*
◆ *Index to American Women Speakers,* 1828–1978
◆ *Representative American Speeches,* 1937+
◆ *Facts on File,* 1941+
◆ *Vital Speeches of the Day,* 1941+
◆ *Historic Documents of* [Year]
◆ *Public Papers of the Presidents of the United States*

Taking Your Search On-Line

The Internet is the world's largest information network. It is often referred to as the information superhighway, because it is a vast network of computers connecting people and resources worldwide. The Internet was developed in the 1960s because the U.S. Department of Defense was interested in creating a network through which leaders could communicate after a nuclear attack. The RAND Corporation, a military think tank, worked on a system that evolved into the Internet.

The Internet is an exciting medium to help you access the latest information. You can access data on-line and access resources such as dictionaries, encyclopedias, and library catalogs; news publications and electronic journals; and databases from universities and government agencies. You can learn about companies by visiting their web sites. Anyone with a computer and a modem can use the Internet.

◆ The World Wide Web is a collection of mechanisms used to locate, display, and access information available on the Internet. A web site or page is multimedia and can use colored pictures, video, sound, images, and text. You can use browser software, such as Netscape or Explorer, and click on highlighted words, called hyperlinks, to investigate additional information. The World Wide Web is a popular way to advertise businesses, departments, and products.

◆ Telnet is an Internet tool that allows you to access another computer without having a special account. For example, some Telnet sites, such as libraries, allow you to log on from a home computer.

◆ File Transfer Protocol (FTP) is a tool to transfer files between two Internet sites. You can send (upload) or retrieve (download) a file from a remote site to your own. Thus, thousands of files are available to any Internet user.

Public Speaking Strategies

Many of the strategies for choosing a topic and organizing a speech are similar to those for writing papers. Following are a few additional strategies specifically for public speaking:

Teaching Tip
1. Remind students that all speaking is public speaking. Review the speaking they have been doing in this class.
2. Encourage students to be in the present and have a conversation with their audience.

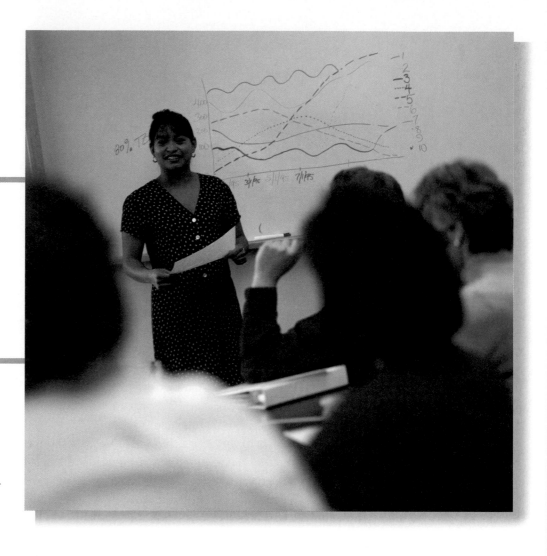

Eye Contact

When you look at the audience as you speak, you create a rapport that makes everyone more comfortable. *What other strategies could help you become a good speaker?*

Class Discussion
Ask students if visuals are important to a speech. Ask for examples of visuals they have seen that work well.

Class Discussion
Ask students if they have ever listened to themselves on tape. Ask them if they were amazed at how they sounded. Then ask why they think some people may be reluctant to videotape themselves.

Hands-On Application
Role playing: Have students videotape themselves interviewing someone for four or five minutes. Exchange places. Review and discuss with their groups. Have them list the improvements they can make.

◆ *Be prepared.* Practice giving your speech several times.

◆ *Look at the audience.* Establish eye contact and speak to the audience members. Smile, develop rapport, and notice when your audience agrees with you or looks puzzled or confused.

◆ *Develop visuals.* When it is appropriate, use overheads, slides, handouts, and demonstrations. They can focus audience attention, add drama, reduce your stress, and reinforce your speech. Make sure that the type on your visuals is large enough to read, the projector works, and you have practiced working with the visual aids.

◆ *Prepare your prompters.* Don't memorize the speech but be well acquainted with your topic, so that you are comfortable talking about it. Prepare simple notes to prompt yourself. Write key phrases in large letters. Write key phrases, stories, and quotes on note cards.

◆ *Practice.* Rehearsal is everything! Practice the speech aloud several times in front of a mirror, an empty classroom, or friends. Practice speaking slowly and calmly but louder than usual. Vary the pitch and speed for emphasis. Practice will also help you overcome stage fright. Complete **Personal Performance Notebook 8.2** to determine how you handle stage fright and writer's block.

Controlling Stage Fright and Writer's Block

A. Use your critical thinking skills to answer the following questions. Be prepared to discuss your answers in your study teams.

   1. Describe your typical physical reaction to giving a speech.

   _____

   2. What has helped you control stage fright?

   _____

   3. Describe the processes of writing that are easiest for you and those that are the hardest.

   _____

B. Read the following common reasons and excuses that some students use for not writing effective speeches. Add to this list. Use creative problem solving to list strategies for overcoming these barriers.

Reasons/Excuses

   1. I have panic attacks before I write or give speeches.

   Strategy: _____

   _____

   2. I can't decide on a topic.

   Strategy: _____

   _____

   3. I don't know how to research.

   Strategy: _____

   _____

   4. I procrastinate until the last minute.

   Strategy: _____

   _____

   5. I don't know what my instructor wants.

   Strategy: _____

   _____

   6. My mind goes blank when I start to write or give a speech.

   Strategy: _____

   _____

Hands-On Application

Have students prepare a one- or two-minute talk about stage fright and present it in small groups. Have students take turns speaking and giving positive suggestions.

Teaching Tip
Discuss the importance
of rehearsing (review
worksheet p. 8–29).

Hands-On Application
1. Have students keep a
journal of words they
hear speakers use for
fillers.
2. Ask students to listen
to themselves and be
aware of the words
they use as fillers.
3. Have students explore
strategies for
eliminating annoying
and unnecessary
words.
4. Have each student
ask a partner to be
honest and tell the
student when he or
she is using fillers.

Figure 8.6   Speech Evaluation Form

Name _____   **Topic** _____

Introduction
__ Gained attention and
interest
__ Introduced topic
__ Topic related to
audience
__ Established credibility
__ Previewed body of speech

Body
__ Main points clear
__ Organizational pattern
evident
__ Established need
__ Presented clear plan
__ Demonstrated practicality
__ Language clear
__ Gave evidence to
support main points
__ Sources and citations clear
__ Reasoning sound
__ Used emotional appeals
__ Connectives effective

Delivery
__ Spoke without rushing and
at an appropriate rate
__ Maintained eye contact
__ Maintained volume and
projection
__ Avoided distracting
mannerisms
__ Used gestures effectively
__ Articulated clearly
__ Used vocal variety and
dynamics
__ Presented visual aids
effectively
__ Departed appropriately
__ Other: _____

Conclusion
__ Prepared audience for
ending
__ Reinforced central idea
__ Called audience to
agreement/action
__ Used a vivid ending

Suggestions
_____
_____
_____
_____
_____
_____
_____
_____
_____
_____
_____

General Notes
_____
_____
_____
_____
_____
_____
_____
_____
_____

Key: Superior (1), Effective (2), Average (3), Weak (4)

Speech Evaluation Form   Feedback on your speaking skills can help you improve.
How would you assess your last speech in a class?

◆ *Be in the present.* Take a deep breath before beginning your speech. Look at
your audience and smile. Keep your purpose in mind and stay focused on
the message and the audience. Remember to pause at important points for
emphasis and to connect with your audience.

◆ *Avoid unnecessary words.* Use clear, concise words. Don't use pauses as fillers,
irritating nonwords, or overused slang, such as *uh, ur, you know, stuff like
that, sort of,* and *like.* Use brief pauses for emphasis; then take a deep breath
and continue.

◆ *Review your performance.* Ask your instructor and fellow students for
feedback. Be open to learning and strive to improve. Review the sample
speech evaluation form shown in **Figure 8.6.**

See **Peak Progress 8.5** on page 8–21 to explore how you can apply the Adult
Learning Cycle to become more proficient at public speaking.

Teaching Tip
Emphasize the importance
of using the Adult Learning
Cycle to increase interest and
improve skills.

Peak Progress 8.5

Applying the Adult Learning Cycle to Improve Your Public Speaking

Increasing your public speaking skills takes time, effort, and practice.

1. **RELATE. Why do I want to learn this?** I've always admired people who are confident speaking in front of others, and I want to feel that confident, poised, and in control. Becoming an effective public speaker will be a valuable skill for both school and career. What areas do I need to work on? What are my physical systems of anxiety?

2. **OBSERVE. How does this work?** I can learn by observing people who are effective and confident at giving speeches. What makes them successful? Do I understand the message? I'll also analyze ineffective speeches. Did stage fright play a role? Did the speaker seem uncomfortable and nervous? I'll try using new techniques and strategies for dealing with fear and stage fright and observe how I'm improving.

3. **THINK. What does this mean?** What strategies are working for me? Am I more confident and relaxed? Am I reducing anxiety and negative self-talk?

4. **DO. What can I do with this?** I will practice my public speaking skills whenever possible. I'll find practical applications to use my new skills in everyday life. Each day, I'll work on one area. For example, I'll choose less stressful situations, such as my study group or a club meeting, and offer to give a presentation on an interesting topic. I will ask for feedback.

5. **TEACH. Who can I share this with?** I'll talk with others and share my tips and experiences and listen to theirs in return. I'll volunteer to help other students in my study group.

Now, return to Stage 1 and think about how it feels to learn this valuable new skill. Remember, the more you practice speaking in front of others, the more relaxed and confident you will become.

TECH FOR SUCCESS

- **Visual Aids** As many of your instructors facilitate their lectures with handouts, overhead transparencies, and PowerPoint presentations, you, too, will want to consider enhancing your presentations with visual aids. Many employers do not provide training for such programs, but knowing how to incorporate them into business meetings and presentations is often expected. Thus, learning at least the basics of PowerPoint or a similar program now will be a valuable skill you can use in both school and on the job.

- **Spell-Check, Spell-Check, Spell-Check** As e-mail has replaced the traditional memo, it's much easier to send out correspondence quickly to a group of people at one time. However, it's not uncommon to receive important e-mails that are riddled with typos and grammatical mistakes. Get in the habit of always using the spell-check function prior to sending all e-mails or documents. The few seconds it takes to check your outgoing correspondence can save you from unnecessary embarrassment (and follow-up e-mails) later on.

In summary, in this chapter, I learned to

- *Become a more effective writer and speaker.* Being a good communicator is essential in all facets of life. It is the most important skill I will ever acquire. Although public speaking can be stressful, I can learn to reduce my anxiety and become more successful if I prepare, organize, write, and edit my presentation carefully.

- *Prepare effectively.* When writing a paper or presentation, I need to first set a schedule for accomplishment. I carefully and thoughtfully choose my topic and do the preliminary reading and information gathering. I can then narrow my topic and write a thesis statement that helps me clarify what I plan to cover. I prepare a bibliography of references and original sources, and I take notes that support my topic.

- *Organize my writing plan.* I must organize my thoughts and research into a coherent outline. I continue to look for specific data that supports my main points. I revise my outline as necessary as I consider the subtopics that support my main theme. I include examples, definitions, quotations, and statistics that are interesting and supportive.

- *Write a draft of my paper or presentation.* Now that I have done the preliminary research and outline, I prepare a draft, writing freely and with momentum. My draft includes (1) an introduction, (2) the main body, and (3) a conclusion. The introduction clearly states the purpose or theme, captures attention, and defines terms. The main body includes the subtopics that support the main theme, as well as visual aids. The conclusion ties the important points together and supports the overall theme of the presentation.

- *Revise and edit my paper or presentation.* Now that I have prepared a draft, I must revise it often. I check to make sure that the overall theme and supporting points are clear and revise my outline when necessary. I correct spelling and grammatical mistakes and review my transitions and sentence structure. It helps to read it out loud to make sure the writing is varied and interesting. I will make sure I have accurately prepared the bibliography, and I will ask my instructor to review my paper. I will then finalize my paper, number the pages, and add a title page.

- *Review and assess my paper or presentation.* After a final check of my paper, I make additional copies and include one in my Career Development Portfolio. I deliver it on time, go over my graded results, and ask my instructor for tips for improvement.

- *Use the library and Internet for research.* The library provides a wealth of resources, including books, periodicals, and reference materials. Originally conceptualized by a military think tank, the Internet has become the world's largest information network, providing access to a myriad of resources, databases, and content.

- *Incorporate new strategies for effective public speaking.* When I speak in public, it's important for me to be prepared, establish eye contact with my audience, develop visual aids, and prepare simple notes or cues to prompt myself. I avoid unnecessary words and fillers, and I connect with my audience. Rehearsing is key to a successful presentation, and I review my performance by asking others for feedback.

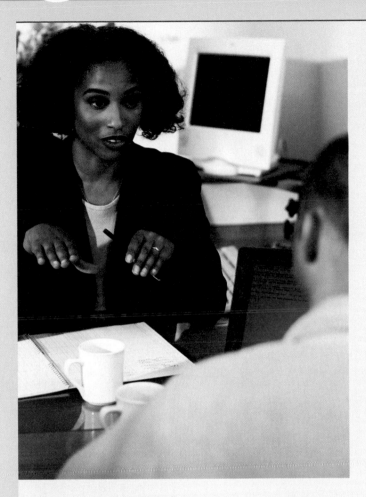

Lori Benson

HUMAN RESOURCES DIRECT

Related Majors: Human Resources, Personnel Administration, Labor Relations

Communication Skills

Lori Benson is the human resources director for a small advertising firm. Lori is her company's only human resources employee. Besides recruiting and interviewing potential employees, Lori also develops personnel programs and policies. She serves as her company's employee benefits manager by handling health insurance and pension plans. Lori also provides training in orientation sessions for new employees and instructs classes that help supervisors improve their interpersonal skills.

Possessing excellent communication skills is essential for Lori's job. To recruit potential employees, Lori sends letters to colleges to attract recent graduates. She also places want ads in newspapers and magazines. In addition, Lori often sends memos to the employees at her company regarding parking or a change in health insurance coverage. This kind of writing must be clear, accurate, and brief. Lori first writes a draft and then sets it aside for a few days before doing revisions. She usually asks the CEO to review the ads and letters sent to the media. See **Figure 8.7** on page 8–24 for an example of a memo that Lori wrote regarding the company parking garage.

Lori does research to find out what programs and policies other companies are offering. She uses public speaking strategies when preparing for training and other classes. First, she makes notes and then writes prompts to help her remember what she wants to say. Lori practices her lecture several times and reviews her notes before each class. She keeps her notes in a file for the next time she gives a class on the same subject.

CRITICAL THINKING

How does Lori incorporate the communication skills she learned in college into the workplace?

Figure 8.7 Sample Memo

Media Plus Agency

MEMO

October 7, 2005

To: All Employees

From: Lori Benson
         Human Resources

Subject: New Card Key for Parking Garage

Please be advised that on November 1, 2005, Golden Parking Services will convert the entry gate activators to magnetic card keys. The new entry system is designed to facilitate ease of entry and quicker response. (No more waiting in line to go to work!)

If you have not recived your new card key by OCTOBER 21st, please inform the Human Resources office.

Thank you for your patience as we implement this improved system.

cc: Edward Haskell
    Jenny Lopez

Deadline is highlighted

October 21st

Please respond!

Graphics

All capitals to highlight importance

Clear message

Sample Memo The format for a memo is different from the format for a letter. *What specific differences do you notice between memo and letter styles?*

Peak Performer Profile

Toni Morrison

Her books have been described as having "the luster of poetry" illuminating American reality. However, one reader once commented to acclaimed novelist Toni Morrison that her books were difficult to read. Morrison responded, "They're difficult to write." The process, Morrison sums up, "is not [always] a question of inspiration. It's a question of very hard, very sustained work."

An ethnically rich background helped provide Morrison's inspiration. The second of four children, she was born Chloe Anthony Wofford in a small Ohio steel town in 1931 during the Great Depression. The family's financial struggle was offset by a home strengthened by multiple generations and traditional ties. Storytelling was an important part of the family scene and black tradition.

In the late 1940s, Morrison headed to the East Coast. After earning a bachelor's degree in English from Howard University and a master's degree from Cornell University, she was still years away from literary recognition. While working as an editor at Random House in New York City, she began her writing career

in earnest, and in 1970 her first novel, *The Bluest Eye*, was published.

Since then, Morrison has produced a body of work described as standing "among the 20th century's richest depictions of Black life and the legacy of slavery." Her dedication was rewarded in 1987, when Morrison's fifth novel, *Beloved*, won the Pulitzer Prize. Based on a true incident that took place in 1851, this novel has been read by millions. Then, in 1993, Morrison was awarded the Nobel Prize in Literature. She is the first black woman and only the eighth woman to receive this supreme honor.

Through Morrison's writing skills and self-expression, she has provided insight into American cultural heritage and the human condition.

PERFORMANCE THINKING The novel *Beloved* is dedicated to "Sixty Million and more." What is Morrison trying to express?

Performance Strategies ••••••••••••••

Following are the top 10 strategies for giving speeches and writing papers:

◆ Determine your purpose and set a schedule.

◆ Choose and narrow your topic.

◆ Read and research. Prepare a bibliography.

◆ Organize information into an outline and on note cards.

◆ Write a draft.

◆ Refine your purpose and rewrite the draft.

◆ Edit and proof.

◆ Use your study team to practice and review.

◆ Revise, polish and practice.

◆ Practice. Practice. Practice.

Review Questions ••••••••••••••••••

1. What is the one basic skill taught in college that Peter Drucker feels is the most valuable for the future employee to know?

2. How should you establish a schedule to research and write a paper?

3. Explain how to use the Internet for research.

4. Describe four strategies you can use to overcome writer's block.

5. What are five public speaking strategies?

REVISUALIZATION •••

Review the Visualization box at the beginning of this chapter and your journal entry in **Worksheet 8.1.** Now, think of a situation in which your mind went blank or you suffered stage fright. How would increasing your presentation or public speaking skills have helped you? How would visualization have helped you? Continuing in **Worksheet 8.1,** apply the ABCDE method to that situation and visualize yourself calm and focused—for example,

A = Actual event: "I just gave a speech in my personal health class and was so nervous that, at the beginning, my mind went blank, my hands shook, and I stumbled over my words."

B = Beliefs: "Nothing is more frightening for me than getting up before a group. I'm sure everyone in class was laughing at me. I'm just not good at public speaking and never will be."

C = Consequence: "I'm embarrassed about my presentation."

D = Dispute: "I know I'm not alone. Many people rank public speaking as a major fear. Several students have told me that they suffer from stage fright, too. As I'm more critical of myself than others, I'm sure it went better than I thought. Even so, it was a good learning experience to help me realize I need to be better prepared and relaxed when I present."

E = Energized: "I know that public speaking is a skill that can be learned with practice. It's definitely worth the effort, since it's a skill I can use in both school and career. If I visualize myself remaining calm and confident and avoid negative self-talk, I know I will improve."

LEARNING COMMUNICATION SKILLS

In the Classroom

Josh Miller is a finance student at a business college. He likes numbers and feels comfortable with order, structure, and right-or-wrong answers. As part of the graduation requirements, all students must take classes in speech and writing. Josh becomes nervous about writing reports or giving speeches and doesn't see the connection between the required class and his finance studies. One of Josh's biggest stumbling blocks is thinking of topics. He experiences writer's block and generally delays any project until the last possible minute.

1. What strategies in this chapter would help Josh think of topics and meet his deadlines?

   _____

   _____

2. What would you suggest to help him see the value of speaking and writing well?

   _____

   _____

In the Workplace

Josh has recently been promoted to regional manager for an investment firm. He feels very secure with the finance part of his job but feels pressure with the new promotion requirements. He will need to present bimonthly speeches to top management, run daily meetings, and write dozens of letters, memos, and reports. He must also give motivational seminars at least twice a year to his department heads. Josh would like to improve his writing skills and make his presentations clear, concise, and motivational.

3. What suggestions would you give Josh to help make his presentations more professional and interesting?

   _____

   _____

4. What strategies could he use to improve his writing?

   _____

   _____

APPLYING THE ABCDE METHOD OF SELF-MANAGEMENT

In the Visualization box on page 8–1, you were asked to describe a time when you did well in a performance, sporting event, or speaking assignment. What factors helped you be calm, confident, and able to perform?

_____

_____

_____

_____

Now, describe a situation in which your mind went blank or you suffered stage fright. How would increasing your presentation or public speaking skills have helped you? Apply the ABCDE method to visualize a result in which you are again calm, confident, and focused.

A = Actual event:

B = Beliefs:

C = Consequences:

D = Dispute:

E = Energized:

Practice deep breathing with your eyes closed for just one minute. See yourself calm, centered, and relaxed as you give a performance or make a speech. See yourself presenting your ideas in a clear, concise, and confident manner. You feel confident about yourself because you have learned to control stage fright, you're well prepared, and you know how to give speeches.

REHEARSING

Today, your boss asked you to give an important presentation to the management staff about a program you have been developing for budgeting. You want to start preparing for the presentation and give yourself enough time to create a unique way to present your new ideas and information. You want to enhance your own delivery style and improve your performance, so that management will understand your budget program fully.

The following are some ideas about presentations. Read this list and then add your own ideas on the lines provided.

1. Begin gathering materials and taking notes.
2. Practice visualizing yourself speaking successfully.
3. Prepare a rough draft of your presentation.
4. List the main points you want to make.
5. Prepare your handouts and overheads or visuals.
6. Recite material out loud.
7. Listen to how your presentation sounds.
8. Practice while you are jogging.
9. Give the presentation to a friend.
10. Go to the room where the presentation will be given.
11. Write a summary of the material on the board.
12. Integrate different learning styles as you explain material to your audience.
13. Time yourself.
14. Get a sense of the room, where you should stand, how you would arrange the chairs, and so on. Now, sit and review.
15. Eat a light meal, take a walk, or do a few jumping jacks before your presentation. Eat a nutritious and light breakfast.
16. Wear a professional outfit and follow good grooming habits.
17. Walk to the front of the class with confidence.
18. _____
    _____
19. _____
    _____
20. _____
    _____

ESSAY WRITING TIPS

An essay needs more than the right topic, thorough research, and a finely tuned thesis statement. It also requires *good writing.* Good writing involves using these elements:

- Good grammar
- Complete sentences
- Accurate punctuation
- Active verbs instead of passive verbs whenever possible
- Appropriate vocabulary

Several areas of grammar can present problems for writers. Check yourself.

Subject-Verb Agreement

Sentences should always have subjects and verbs agree. This means that, when the subject in a sentence is singular (such as *John, girl,* or *car*), the verb also is singular (such as *walks, sings,* or *is*). However, if the subject in a sentence is plural (such as *John and Mary, girls,* or *cars*), then the verb also is plural (such as *walk, sing,* or *are*).

Subject-Verb Examples

John walks to school.

The girl sings very well.

The car is old.

John and Mary walk to school.

The girls sing together.

The cars are old.

Write the correct verb that agrees with the subject on each line:

1. Parents often _____ their children nicknames. (give, gives)
2. A baby might _____ the nickname Red because of his hair color. (get, gets)
3. Most people _____ their nicknames. (enjoy, enjoys)
4. Nicknames _____ people. (interest, interests)
5. The seats _____ very uncomfortable in the stadium. (is, are)

Proper Use of Pronouns

In most cases, the pronouns *I* and *we* should be used as subjects. The pronouns *me* and *us* should be used as objects.

Subject Examples

Joe and I went to the concert.

We also went to the concert.

Object Examples

The usher stood between the stage and me. The music sounded wonderful to us.

Write the correct verb that agrees with the subject on each line:

6. The boss gave raises to _____. (us, we)
7. _____ couldn't wait to begin. (We, Us)
8. _____ watched the sunset. (We, Us)
9. Marge and _____ enjoyed the party. (I, me)
10. The next day, she told _____ about the party. (I, me)

—continued

Indefinite Pronoun and Verb Agreement

Do you know indefinite pronouns? Indefinite pronouns can be either singular or plural, depending on the meaning of the sentence. But they must always agree with the verb in the sentence. Use singular verbs with singular indefinite pronouns. Use plural verbs with plural indefinite pronouns. Following are lists to help you. You can refer to them when you are writing. Use them to fill in the exercise.

Indefinite Pronouns

Singular		Plural	Singular or Plural
one	nobody	few	most
no one	anybody	both	none
each	anyone	others	
someone	anything	many	
something	everybody		
everyone	either		
	neither		

Write the correct verb on each line:

11. Every night something _____ over our trash can. (knock, knocks)

12. Everybody _____ the game tic-tac-toe. (play, plays)

13. Most _____ their lunch to school. (bring, brings)

14. Others _____ their lunch. (buy, buys)

15. Neither of the books _____ finished. (are, is)

Commas

A comma has many uses. Here are just a few of those uses:

- To set off the part of an address:
  I am going to Buffalo, New York.

- To set off parts of a date:
  I will be leaving on Monday, August 8, 2005.

- To set off introductory words or phrases:
  Wake her up, Vicki!
  No, I don't want to go.

- To set off a series of words:
  Bring a pen, pencil, and paper to class.
  Joe, Margo, Liz, and Pete are going to class.

  Add commas where they are needed in each sentence:

16. Put those boxes in the attic Sam.

17. On August 10 2005 I will deliver my report.

18. I invited Jill Mary Tom and Sue to the party.

19. I live in Williamsburg Virginia.

20. His sales call is at ZZZ Company 34 Putnam Street Olean New York.

CHAPTER 8 ▲ REVIEW AND APPLICATIONS

NAME: DATE:

PLANNING GRID

Fill in this grid as you prepare your written assignments and speeches.

	Preparation					Writing					Rewriting						Final Review			
	Topic: general, narrow topic.	Focus: thesis statement.	Identify audience and gather information.	Compile bibliography and notes.	Organize and outline.	Introduction.	Flesh out main idea.	Conclusion.	Write first draft.	Review.	Add, delete, rearrange information.	Write second draft.	Proof.	Confer with instructor.	Revise/share with writing group.	Revise again/compile bibliography.	Final check: grammar, spelling.	Make copy and meet deadline.	Evaluate results.
Paper #1																			
Speech #1																				

YOUR WRITING AND SPEAKING SKILLS

Looking Back

1. Recall any activities and events through which you learned to write and speak. Jot down examples of classes, presentations, essays, journals, and papers.

   _____

   _____

2. What are your strengths in writing and speaking?

   _____

   _____

3. What would you like to improve?

   _____

   _____

4. What are your feelings about writing and speaking?

   _____

   _____

Looking Forward

5. How can you demonstrate to employers that you have effective writing and speaking skills?

   _____

   _____

6. Include in your portfolio samples of speeches you have given. List the titles on the following lines.

   _____

   _____

7. Include in your portfolio samples of your writing. List the titles.

   _____

   _____

8. Include in your portfolio samples of your research. List the titles.

   _____

   _____

Add this page to your Career Development Portfolio.

Critical Thinking and Creative Problem Solving, with Applications for Math and Science

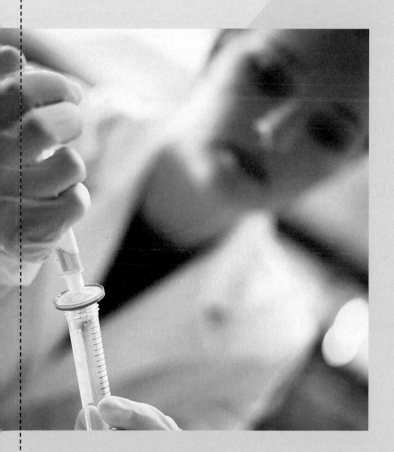

Chapter Objectives

In this chapter, you will learn

▲ To prepare your mind for problem solving

▲ The importance of critical thinking

▲ Common fallacies and errors in judgment

▲ How to use problem solving for mathematics and science

▲ How to overcome math anxiety

▲ The importance of creativity in problem solving

VISUALIZATION

"I've never been a wiz at math. Even balancing my checkbook is a challenge. I love to debate and tackle problems, but for some reason I just can't get my mind around numbers and formulas."

Do you ever find yourself feeling anxious or worried whenever you have to take a mathematics or science class? Do you understand the practical connections math and science have to critical thinking and problem solving? In this chapter, you will learn to put your critical thinking and creative problem-solving skills into action and to use strategies to

help you feel more comfortable with math and science applications. You will visualize yourself approaching math and science with curiosity and a willingness to learn.

JOURNAL ENTRY   In Worksheet 9.1 on page 9–28, describe a personal situation in which understanding basic math or science skills was necessary, such as paying your taxes, applying for a loan, or following up on a medical condition. Did you feel prepared and understand the results? What did you learn in the process?

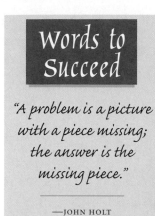

"A problem is a picture with a piece missing; the answer is the missing piece."

—JOHN HOLT
educator and author

Use
TM 9.1 Success Principle 9.

Class Discussion
How do these competencies
create school and job
success? Applying SCANS:
Thinking skills
Decision making
Problem solving
Reasoning

Teaching Tip
Emphasize the importance of
using the ABCDE Method of
Self-Management to reduce
anxiety and create positive
habits.

All problem solving—whether personal or academic—involves decision making. You have to make decisions to solve a problem; conversely, some problems occur because of the decision you have made. For example, in your private life you may decide to smoke cigarettes; later, you face a subsequent problem of nicotine addiction. In your school life, you may decide not to study mathematics and science because you consider them too difficult. Because of this decision, certain majors and careers will be closed to you. You can see that many events in your life do not just happen; they are the result of your choices and decisions. In this chapter, you will learn to use critical thinking and creativity to help you make effective decisions and solve problems. Mathematics and science will be discussed, as these are key areas where you can develop and improve your critical thinking and problem-solving skills. You will also learn to overcome math anxiety and develop a positive attitude.

Preparing for Critical Thinking and Problem Solving

The following strategies are based on a logical and scientific approach to problem solving:

1. **Have a positive attitude.** Your attitude has a lot to do with how you approach and solve a problem or make a decision. Positive thinking requires a mind shift. You may have had a negative attitude toward math or science, perceiving the material too difficult or not relevant. Much of math anxiety, like stage fright and other fears, is compounded by this negative thinking and self-talk. You can apply the ABCDE method of self-management you have learned in this text and dispel myths and irrational thinking. Approach math and science with a positive "can do" and inquisitive attitude. Perceive problems as puzzles to solve, rather than homework or difficult courses to avoid. Instead of looking for the "right answer," focus on problem-solving strategies.

2. **Use critical thinking.** Critical thinking is a multidimensional process that involves decoding, analyzing, processing, reasoning, and evaluating information. It is also an attitude: a willingness and passion to explore, probe, question, and search for answers and solutions. (See **Figure 9.1.**) Critical thinking is fundamental to all problem solving. Use your critical thinking skills to complete **Personal Performance Notebook 9.1** on page 9–4.

3. **Persistence pays off.** Coming to a solution requires sustained effort. A problem may not always be solved with your first effort. Sometimes a second or third try will see the results you need or want. Analytical thinking requires time, persistence, and patience.

Figure 9.1 Critical Thinking Qualities

Attributes of a Critical Thinker

- Willingness to ask pertinent questions and assess statements and arguments
- Ability to suspend judgment and tolerate ambiguity
- Ability to admit a lack of information or understanding
- Curiosity and interest in seeking new solutions
- Ability to clearly define a set of criteria for analyzing ideas
- Willingness to examine beliefs, assumptions, and opinions against facts

Critical Thinking Qualities Being able to think critically is important for understanding and solving problems. *Do you apply any of the attributes of a critical thinker when you are faced with solving a problem?*

Hands-On Application
Have students: Write a paragraph about an issue on which they hold strong opinions, using Figure 9.1.

Hands-On Application
Bring in different newspapers. In groups, ask students to find examples of irrational thinking. Cut out the best examples and use them to illustrate common errors in judgment.

Teaching Tip
Ask students how defining the problem relates to solving problems successfully in their other classes, in their jobs, and in their personal lives.

Problem-Solving Steps

Problem solving involves four basic steps:

1. **Define and restate the problem.** What are you trying to find? What is known and unknown? What is the situation or context of the problem? Can you separate the problem into various parts? Organize the problem. Restate the problem in your own words—for example, "We want to know a temperature in degrees Celsius instead of degrees Fahrenheit."

2. **Choose an appropriate strategy.** Ask yourself what formula or calculation would be helpful—for example, "Since we have a formula that relates Celsius and Fahrenheit temperatures, I'll replace F in the formula with the value given for degrees Fahrenheit."

3. **Solve the problem.** Find needed and assumed information. Use all the data, conditions, and known factors in the problem. For example, the formula you're given is $F = 1.8C + 32$. Substituting -22 for F in the equation leads to the following solutions:

    $-22 = 1.8C + 32$

    $-22 - 32 = 1.8C$

    $-54 = 1.8C$

    $-54 / 1.8 = C$

    $-30 = C$

    The answer is $-30C$.

Words to Succeed

"The value of a problem is not so much coming up with the answer as in the ideas and attempted ideas it forces on the would-be solver."

—I.N. HERSTEIN
mathematician

Using Critical Thinking to Solve Problems

Stating a problem clearly, exploring alternatives, reasoning logically, choosing the best alternative, creating an action plan, and evaluating your plan are all critical thinking skills involved in making decisions and solving problems.

Look at the common reasons or excuses that some students use for not solving problems creatively or making sound decisions. Use creative problem solving to list strategies for overcoming these barriers.

1. I'm not a creative person.
   Strategy:

   _____

   _____

2. Facts can be misleading. I like to follow my emotions.
   Strategy:

   _____

   _____

3. I avoid conflict.
   Strategy:

   _____

   _____

4. I postpone making decisions.
   Strategy:

   _____

   _____

5. I worry that I'll make the wrong decision.
   Strategy:

   _____

   _____

Peak Progress 9.1

Use
- TM 9.2 Mathematics and Science Checklist.
- TM 9.3 Problem-Solving Plan for Science.

Problem-Solving Checklist

When you enroll in any course, including a math or science course, consider these questions:

- Have you approached the class with a positive attitude?
- Have you built confidence by getting involved in problems?
- Have you clearly defined the problems?
- What do you want to know and what are you being asked to find out?
- Have you separated essential information from the unessential?
- Have you separated the known from the unknown?
- Have you asked a series of questions: How? When? Where? What? If?
- Have you devised a plan for solving the problem?
- Have you gone from the general to the specific?
- Have you explored formulas, theories, and so on?
- Have you made an estimate?
- Have you illustrated or organized the problem?
- Have you made a table or a diagram, drawn a picture, or summarized data?
- Have you written the problem?
- Have you discovered a pattern to the problem?
- Have you alternated intense concentration with frequent breaks?
- Have you tried working backward, completing similar problems, and solving small parts?
- Have you determined if you made careless errors or do not understand the concepts?
- Do you think, apply, reflect, and practice?
- Have you asked for help early?
- Have you been willing to put in the time required to solve problems?
- Have you analyzed the problem? Was your guess close? Did your plan work? How else can you approach the problem?
- Have you rewarded yourself for facing your fears, overcoming anxiety, and learning valuable skills that will increase your success in school, your job, and in life?

4. **Study in groups.** Learning does not take place in isolation but, rather, in a supportive environment where anxiety is reduced and each person feels safe to use trial and error methods. Creativity, interaction, and multiple solutions are proposed when you study in groups. You will build confidence as you learn to think out loud, brainstorm creative solutions, and solve problems. See **Peak Progress 9.1** for a comprehensive checklist of questions to use as you problem solve.

Common Errors in Judgment

Here are some common errors in judgment that interfere with effective critical thinking:

- *Stereotypes* are judgments and overgeneralizations held by a person or a group about members of another group—for example, "All instructors are absent-minded intellectuals." Learn to see individual differences between people and situations.

- *Snap judgments* are decisions made before all necessary information or facts are gathered. Too often, people attempt to solve a problem before it is even determined exactly what the problem is.

- *Unwarranted assumptions* are beliefs and ideas that are taken for granted. For example, your business instructor allows papers to be turned in late, so you assume that your real estate instructor will allow the same.

- *Projection* is the tendency to attribute to others some of our own traits in an attempt to justify our own faulty judgments or actions. For example, Jack might perceive that others are behaving in a certain way in order to justify his behavior: "I cheat because everyone else is cheating."

- *The halo effect* is the tendency to label a person good at many things based on one or two qualities. For example, Serena sits in the front row, attends every class, and gets good grades on papers. Based on this observation, you decide that she is smart, organized, and nice and is a great student in all her classes. First impressions are important in the halo effect and are difficult to change.

- *Sweeping generalizations* are based on one experience and generalized to a whole group. For example, if research has been conducted using college students as subjects, you cannot generalize the results to the overall work population.

Class Discussion

1. Discuss with students how they can use problem-solving skills in their lives while focusing on the benefits of learning math and science.

2. Discuss with students their earliest memories of math and science.

Teaching Tip

Focus on the benefits of learning math and science. Ask students how they can use problem-solving skills in their lives.

Math and Science Applications

Critical thinking and creative problem solving are essential strategies for success in mastering mathematics, science, and computer science courses. A critical and creative approach is not only important in all academic classes but also vital for job and life success. For example, using logic and the analytical process can help you write papers, prepare for tests, compare historical events, and learn different theories in philosophy. By studying mathematics and science, you will learn such everyday skills as understanding interest rates on credit cards, calculating your tuition, managing your personal finances, computing your GPA, and understanding how our bodies and the world around us works. Basic arithmetic can help you figure out a tip at a restaurant, algebra can help you compute the interest on a loan, basic probability can help you determine the chance that a given event will occur, and statistics can help you with the collection, analysis, and interpretation of data. Critical thinking and creative problem solving will help you make day-to-day decisions about relationships, drugs, alcohol, which courses to take, how to find a job, where to live, how to generate creative ideas for speeches and papers, and how to resolve conflicts. Making sound decisions and solving problems are important skills for school, career, and life.

PROBLEM-SOLVING STRATEGIES FOR MATH AND SCIENCE

To be successful in math and science, you need to know a variety of problem-solving strategies. Most of these strategies are designed to get you physically involved. The following strategies integrate all learning styles and make learning physical and personal. Included are sample problems to help you practice these strategies.

1. **Make a model or diagram.** Physical models, objects, diagrams, and drawings can help organize information and can help you visualize problem situations. Use objects, cut up a model, measure lengths, and create concrete situations—for example,

   Problem: What is the length of a pendulum that makes one complete swing in one second?

   Strategy: Make a model. With a 50 cm string and some small weights, make a pendulum that is tied to a pencil taped to a desk. To determine the length of the pendulum, measure the distance from the pencil to the center of the weight.

   Solution: Since it is difficult to measure the time period accurately, time 10 swings and use the average. The correct answer is approximately 25 cm.

   Evaluation: If the length is fixed, the amount of weight does not affect the time period. The amount of deflection does affect the period when large deflections are used, but it is not a factor for small amounts of 5 cm or less. The length of the pendulum always affects the time period.

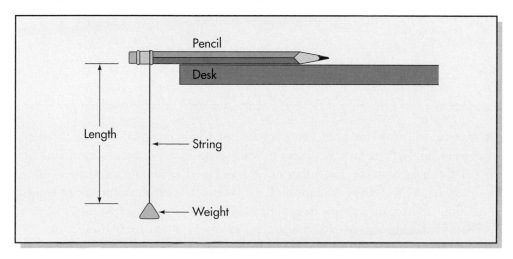

2. **Draw, illustrate, and make tables, charts, or lists.** This is a way to organize data presented in a problem, and it helps you look for patterns. For example, a fruit

Words to Succeed

"The Universe is a grand book which cannot be read until one first learns to comprehend the language and become familiar with the characters in which it is composed. It is written in the language of mathematics."

—GALILEO
discoverer

punch dispenser mixes 4 ml of orange juice with 6 ml of pineapple juice. How many milliliters of orange juice does it mix with 240 ml of pineapple juice?

			Answer
ml Orange Juice	4	16	**160**
ml Pineapple Juice	6	24	**240**

3. **Look for patterns and connections.** A pattern is a regular, systematic repetition that helps you predict what will come next. Field trips and laboratory work can help you find patterns and categorize information, and so can creating tables. For example, an empty commuter train is picking up passengers at the following rate: One passenger got on at the first stop, three got on at the second stop, five got on at the third stop. How many passengers got on the train at the sixth stop?

						Answer
Stops	1	2	3	4	5	**6**
Number of passengers	1	3	5	7	9	**11**

4. **Act out the problem.** Sometimes it is helpful to physically act out the problem. For example, there are five people in your study group and each person initiates a handshake with every member one time. How many total handshakes will there be? There will be 20 handshakes total, because each person shakes hands 4 times (since you cannot shake your own hand). Thus, 5 people times 4 handshakes equals 20 total handshakes. You multiply the total number of people times one number fewer for the handshakes.

5. **Simplify.** Sometimes the best way to simplify a problem is first to solve easier cases of the same problem. For example, consider the study group handshakes

and simplify by solving it for two people instead of five. Two people shake hands a total of two times. Using the formula determined above, you see that the equation is $2 \times 1 = 2$. Fill in the rest of the table below:

Number of People	Each Person Initiates Handshake X Times	Total Number Handshakes
2	1	2
3	2	
4		
5	4	20
6		

Along the same lines, when working on homework, studying in your group, or taking a test, always do the easiest problems first. When you feel confident about your ability to solve one kind of problem, you gain enthusiasm to tackle more difficult questions or problems. Also, an easier problem may be similar to a more difficult problem.

6. **Translate words into equations.** Highlight visual and verbal learning by showing connections between words and numbers. Write an equation that models the problem. For example, Sarah has a total of $82.00, consisting of an equal number of pennies, nickels, dimes, and quarters. How many coins does she have in all? You know how much all of Sarah's coins are worth and you know how much each coin is worth. (In the following equation, p = pennies, n = nickels, d = dimes, and q = quarters).

$p + 5n + 10d + 25q = 8,200$

We know that she has an equal number of each coin; thus, $p = n = d = q$. Therefore, we can substitute p for all the other variables:

$1p + 5p + 10p + 25p = 41p = 8,200$, so $p = 200$

Sarah has 200 pennies, 200 nickels, 200 dimes, and 200 quarters. Therefore, she has 800 coins.

7. **Estimate, make a reasonable guess, check the guess, and revise.** Using the example in number 6, if you were told that Sarah had a large number of coins that added up to $82.00, you could at least say that the total would be no more than 8,200 (the number of coins if they were all pennies) and no less than 328 (the number of coins if they were all quarters).

8. **Work backwards and eliminate.** For example, what is the largest two-digit number that is divisible by 3 whose digits differ by 2? First, working backwards from 99, list numbers that are divisible by 3:

99, 96, 93, 90, 87, 84, 81, 78, 75, 72, 69, 66, 63, 60, . . .

Now, cross out all numbers whose digits do not differ by 2. The largest number remaining is 75.

9. **Summarize in a group.** Working in a group is the best way to integrate all learning styles, keep motivation and interest active, and generate lots of ideas and support. Summarize the problem in your own words and talk through the problem out loud. Explain the problem to your group and why you arrived at the answer. Talking out loud, summarizing chapters, and listening to others clarifies thinking and is a great way to learn.

10. **Take a quiet break.** If you still can't find a solution to the problem as a group, take a break. Sometimes it helps to find a quiet spot and reflect. Sometimes working on another problem or relaxing for a few minutes while listening to music helps you return to the problem refreshed.

OVERCOMING MATH AND SCIENCE ANXIETY

Many people suffer from some math and science anxiety, just as almost everyone gets a little nervous when speaking before a large group. The first step in learning any subject is to use critical thinking and creative problem solving to manage and overcome stage fright or anxiety. (See **Personal Performance Notebook 9.2** to evaluate your comfort level.)

PEAK TIP

If you have a case of anxiety overtaking a required math class, try enrolling in a summer refresher course. You'll be prepared and confident when you take the required course later.

◆ **Be aware.** Observe how your body responds to anxiety and keep a journal of your thoughts and reactions. Don't suppress or deny your anxiety, but acknowledge it and choose to let it go. Become aware of how you relax. Try deep breathing and relaxation techniques to help you become calm and centered.

◆ **Take control.** Anxiety is a learned emotional response. You were not born with it. Since it is learned, it can be unlearned. Take responsibility and don't allow unreasonable fears to control your life.

◆ **Be realistic.** Don't take a math or science class if you don't have the proper background. It is better to spend the summer or an additional semester to gain the necessary skills, so that you don't feel overwhelmed and discouraged.

◆ **Keep up and review often.** If you prepare early and often, you will be less anxious. The night before your test should be used for reviewing, not learning, new material.

◆ **Get involved.** Focus your attention away from your fears and concentrate on the task at hand. You can overcome your math anxiety by jotting down ideas and formulas, drawing pictures, and writing out the problem. You keep your energy high when you stay active and involved. Reduce interruptions and concentrate fully for 45 minutes. Discipline your mind to concentrate for short periods. Time yourself on problems to increase speed and make the most of short study sessions.

The History of Your Anxiety

If you've experienced anxiety with math or science, it may be helpful to retrace the history of your anxiety. Write your responses to the following questions and exercises:

1. Try to recall your earliest experiences with math and science. Were those experiences positive or negative? Explain what made them negative or positive.

_____

_____

_____

_____

2. a. Did you struggle with math or science?

_____

_____

   b. Did you get help?

_____

   c. Recall these memories as vividly as possible and write them down.

_____

_____

_____

_____

3. a. Summarize your feelings about math.

_____

_____

_____

   b. List all the reasons you want to succeed at math.

_____

_____

_____

◆ **Have a positive attitude.** As mentioned earlier, having a positive attitude is key to learning any subject. Do you get sidetracked by negative self-talk that questions your abilities or the reason for learning math skills? Choose to focus on the positive feelings you have when you are confident and in control. Replace negative and defeating self-talk with positive "I can" affirmations.

◆ **Ask for help.** Don't wait until you are in trouble or frustrated. Ask for help from day one. Get a tutor, see the instructor, and join a study group. If you continue to have anxiety or feel lost, go to the counseling center.

◆ **Dispute the myths.** Many times, fears are caused by myths, such as "Men are better at math and science than women" or "Creative people are not good at math and science." There is no basis for the belief that gender has anything to do with math ability, nor is it unfeminine to be good at math and science. Success in math and science requires creative thinking. As mathematician Augustus De Morgan said, "The moving power of mathematics is not reasoning, but imagination." Use critical thinking to overcome myths. See **Peak Progress 9.2** to apply the Adult Learning Cycle to overcoming anxiety.

Creative Problem Solving

Creativity is thinking of something different and using new approaches to solve problems. Many inventions have involved a break from traditional thinking and resulted in an "ah-ha!" experience. For example, Albert Einstein used many unusual approaches that revolutionized scientific thought.

Use creativity at each step to explore alternatives, look for relationships among different items, and develop imaginative ideas and solutions. Use critical thinking skills to raise questions, separate facts from opinions, develop reasonable solutions, and make logical decisions. Try the following strategies to unlock your mind's natural creativity:

1. **Use games, puzzles, and humor.** Turn problems into puzzles to be solved. Rethinking an assignment as a puzzle, a challenge, or a game instead of a difficult problem allows an open frame of mind and encourages your creative side to operate. Creative people often get fresh ideas when they are having fun and are involved in an unrelated activity. When your defenses are down, your brain is relaxed and your subconscious is alive; creative thoughts can flow.

2. **Challenge the rules.** Habit often restricts you from trying new approaches to problem solving. Often, there is more than one solution. List many alternatives, choices, and solutions and imagine the likely consequences of each. Empty your mind of the "right" way of looking at a problem and strive to see situations in a fresh, new way. How many times have you told yourself that you must follow certain rules and perform tasks a certain way? If you want to be creative, try new approaches, look at things in a new order, break the pattern, and challenge the rules. Practice a different approach by completing the Nine-Dot Exercise in **Personal Performance Notebook 9.3** on page 9–14.

3. **Brainstorm.** Brainstorming is a common creativity strategy that frees the imagination. With this strategy, a group thinks of as many ideas as possible.

Applying the Adult Learning Cycle to Overcoming Math and Science Anxiety

1. **RELATE. Why do I want to learn this?** I want to be confident in math and science. Avoiding math and science closes doors and limits opportunities. More than 75 percent of all careers use math and science, and these are often higher-status and better-paying jobs. This is essential knowledge I'll use in all facets of life.

2. **OBSERVE. How does this work?** I can learn a lot about applying critical thinking and creative problem solving to mathematics and science by watching, listening, and trying new things. I'll observe people who are good at math and science. What do they do? I'll also observe people who experience anxiety and don't do well and learn from their mistakes. I'll try using new critical thinking techniques for dealing with fear and observe how I'm improving.

3. **THINK. What does this mean?** I'll apply critical thinking to mathematics and science. What works and doesn't work? I'll think about and test new ways of reducing anxiety and break old patterns and negative self-talk that are self-defeating. I'll look for connections and associations with other types of anxiety and apply what I learn.

4. **DO. What can I do with this?** I will practice reducing my anxiety. I'll find practical applications for connecting critical thinking and creative problem solving to math and science. Each day, I'll work on one area. For example, I'll maintain a positive attitude as I approach math and science classes.

5. **TEACH. Whom can I share this with?** I'll form and work with a study group and share my tips and experiences. I'll demonstrate and teach the methods I've learned to others. I'll reward myself when I do well.

Remember, attitude is everything. If you keep an open mind, apply strategies you have learned in this chapter, and practice your critical thinking skills, you will become more confident in your problem-solving abilities.

Teaching Tip
Emphasize the importance of using the Adult Learning Cycle to increase interest and improve skills.

Teaching Tip
Emphasize creativity and practice:
1. Ask students if they have "slept on" a problem and thus solved it in a new way.
2. Ask students to be patient when solving a math problem or using critical thinking to solve a work problem.

Tech for Success

- **Working on Weak Areas** There are excellent on-line programs that help you determine the mathematical areas where you need the most work. ALEKS (www.highedmath.aleks.com) is a tutorial program that identifies your less proficient areas, then focuses on improvement through practice and targeted problems.

- **Math at Your Fingertips** In your studies, you will come across many standard calculations and formulas, most of which can be found on-line and downloaded. Although this should not replace working through the formulas yourself to make sure you understand their applications, it does make incorporating math into your everyday life much easier.

Nine-Dot Exercise

Connect the following nine dots by drawing only four (or fewer) straight lines without lifting the pencil from the paper. Do not retrace any lines. You can see the solution on this book's web site: www.ferrett5e.

Teaching Tip

Ask students how asking the question What if? Can encourage creativity.

Hands-On Application

Ask students for other mind games that can help them to be more creative.

Hands-On Application

Have students:

1. Write down three topics or ideas for a research paper.
2. Brainstorm these topics or ideas in small groups. How many ideas did they generate in just three to five minutes?

Teaching Tip

Cite examples of brainstorming in the business world. For example, Pringles Potato Chips was developed at a retreat where executives were asked to role-play a potato chip. Ask students to find other creative examples of brainstorming and ideas in the business world.

Hands-On Application

Have students:

1. Record any creative ideas in their journals for one week.
2. Discuss these creative ideas in small groups.

Brainstorming encourages the mind to explore new approaches without judging the merit of these ideas. In fact, even silly and irrelevant ideas can lead to truly inventive ideas. While brainstorming ideas for a speech, one study group started making jokes about the topic, and new ideas came from all directions. Humor can generate ideas, put you in a creative state of mind, and make work fun. Top executives, scientists, doctors, and artists know that they can extend the boundaries of their knowledge by allowing themselves to extend their limits. They ask, "What if?" Complete the brainstorming exercise in **Personal Performance Notebook 9.4.**

4. **Work to change mind-sets.** It is difficult to see another frame of reference once your mind is set. The exercise in **Personal Performance Notebook 9.5** on page 9–16 is an "ah-ha" exercise. It is exciting to watch people really see the other picture. There is enormous power in shifting your perception and gaining new ways of seeing things, events, and people. Perceptual exercises of this kind clearly demonstrate that we see what we focus on. You are conditioned to see certain things, depending on your beliefs and attitudes. Rather than seeing facts, you may see your interpretation of reality. Perceptual distortion can influence how you solve problems and make decisions. To solve problems effectively, you need to see objects and events objectively, not through perceptual filters.

Brainstorming Notes

Creating an idea is not always enough to solve a problem; it also involves convincing others that your idea is the best solution. Read the following brainstorming notes. Then, on the lines that follow, write your own brainstorming notes about how Basil can sell his ideas to his staff.

Basil's Pizza			Sept. 29, 2005

Brainstorming Notes

Problem: Should I hire temporary employees or increase overtime of my regular employees to meet new production schedule?

Ideas	Evaluation	Plus + or Minus −	Solution
hire temp. employees	may lack training	−	1. hire temps
	additional benefits	−	
work regular employees			
overtime	may result in fatigue	−	
	extra $ for employee	+	
	higher morale	+	
	possible advancement	+	
	cross training	+	
	save on overhead		
	and benefits	+	
turn down contract	not possible		
reduce hours store is open	not feasible		
reduce product line	not acceptable		
			2. work overtime explore further

Teaching Tip
Stress how important brainstorming is for creativity.

Class Discussion
Have students list all the barriers to creativity. Next have them list the strategies for overcoming these barriers. If time permits, have them explore the strategies for overcoming the barriers to critical thinking.

_____

_____

_____

_____

_____

_____

Mind-Sets

Look at the following figure. Do you see an attractive young woman or an old woman with a hooked nose?

I see a(n) _____ .

If you saw the young woman first, it is very hard to see the old woman. If you saw the old woman first, it is just as hard to see the young woman.

Teaching Tip

Using the image of the young/old woman, illustrate the power of perception. Once a person forms a perception, it is difficult to create a mind shift. Sometimes a person has to close his or her eyes and look again, or look at the pictures from a distance.

Examine police reports from eyewitnesses. Research indicates that what people see as "fact" is often filtered through beliefs and biases.

Hands-On Application

Have students:

1. Change part of their daily routines. Also ask them to suspend judgment in various situations.
2. Keep a daily journal of the change, including feelings and reactions—both personal and from others.
3. Discuss in their groups the most common experiences.

PEAK TIP

Try not to let your previous experiences influence your expectations on how to solve a new problem.

5. **Change your routine.** Try a different route to work or school. Order new dishes. Read different kinds of books. Become totally involved in a project. Stay in bed and read all day. Spend time with people who are different from you. In other words, occasionally break away from your daily routine and take time every day to relax, daydream, putter, and renew your energy. Look at unexpected events as an opportunity to retreat from constant activity and hurried thoughts. Perhaps this is a good time to brainstorm ideas for a speech assignment or outline an assigned paper. Creative ideas need an incubation period in which to develop.

6. **Allow failure.** Remember that, if you don't fail occasionally, you are not risking anything. Mistakes are stepping-stones to growth and creativity. Fear of failure undermines the creative process by forcing us to play it safe. Eliminate the fear and shame of failure experienced in earlier years and learn to admit mistakes. Looking at your mistakes as stepping-stones and opportunities for growth will

allow this shift. Ask yourself, "What did I learn from this mistake? How can I handle the same type of situation the next time? How can I prepare for a situation like this the next time?"

Creative people aren't afraid to look foolish at times, to generate unusual ideas, and to be nonconformists. They tend not to take themselves too seriously. Being creative has a lot to do with risk taking and courage. It takes courage to explore new ways of thinking and to risk looking different, foolish, impractical, and even wrong.

7. **Expect to be creative.** Everyone can be creative. To be a creative person, try to see yourself as a creative person. Use affirmations that reinforce your innate creativity:

   - I am a creative and resourceful person.
   - I have many imaginative and unusual ideas.
   - Creative ideas flow to me many times a day.
   - I live creatively in the present.
   - I act on many of these ideas.
   - When in the action stage, I act responsibly, use critical thinking, check details carefully, and take calculated risks.

8. **Support, acknowledge, and reward creativity.** If you honor new ideas, they will grow. Get excited about new ideas and approaches, and acknowledge and reward yourself and others for creative ideas. Give yourself many opportunities to get involved with projects that encourage you to explore and be creative. Monitor your daily life as well. How often do you put your creative ideas into action? Is there anything you want to change but keep putting it off? What new hobby or skill have you wanted to try? If you find yourself getting lazy, set a firm deadline to complete a specific project. If you find yourself running frantically, then take an hour or so to review your life's goals and to set new priorities. If you are feeling shy and inhibited, clear some time to socialize and risk meeting new people. Reward your creativity and risk taking by acknowledging them.

9. **Use both sides of the brain.** You use the logical, analytical side of your brain for certain activities and your imaginative and multidimensional side for others. When you develop and integrate both the left and the right sides of your brain, you become more imaginative, creative, and productive. Learn to be attentive to details and to trust your intuition.

10. **Keep a journal.** Keep a journal of creative ideas, dreams, and thoughts, and make a commitment to complete journal entries daily. Collect stories of creative people. Write in your journal about the risks you take and your imaginative and different ideas.

11. **Evaluate.** Go through each step and examine your work. Look at what you know and don't know and examine your hypotheses. Can you prove that each step is correct? Examine the solution carefully. Can you obtain the solution differently? Investigate the connections of the problem. What formulas did you use? Can you use the same method for other problems? Practice your decision-making skills by working through the case scenarios in **Personal Performance Notebook 9.6** and **9.7** on the following pages.

Words to Succeed

"I hear and I forget. I see and I remember. I do and I understand."

—CHINESE PROVERB

Class Discussion

Ask students:
1. What do they think of when they hear the term creative people? Do they think of artists, inventors, and writers?
2. How many consider themselves as being creative? Students may not think of themselves as being creative.

Class Discussion

Ask students what they can do to increase and enhance their creativity.

Decision-Making Application

Use critical thinking and creative problem-solving skills as you consider the following case scenario:

I am currently attending a career school and will soon earn my associate's degree in computer-aided design. Once I obtain my degree, should I continue my education or look for a full-time job? My long-term goal is to be an architect. My wife and I have been married for three years and we want to start a family soon.

- **Define the problem:** "Should I continue my education or get a job?"
- **Gather information and ask questions:** "What are the advantages and disadvantages? Whom should I talk with, such as my advisor, instructors at my current school and potential schools, family members, and career professionals?"
- **List pros and cons for each choice:** "What are the factors I should consider, such as cost, opportunities, and time?"

Consider the following pros and cons for each decision and list additional reasons that you think should be considered:

Decision: *Continue education at a local state university.*

Pros	Cons
I'll get a better job with a four-year degree.	I'll have to take out more student loans.
I'm enjoying school and the learning process.	I want to put my skills into practice on the job.
I'll meet new, diverse friends and contacts.	A lot of my time at home will be devoted to studying.

Decision: *Get a job.*

Pros	Cons
I can make more money than I am now and start paying off debts.	The opportunities would be better with a four-year degree.
We can start a family.	It will take longer to become an architect.
I get to put my skills to work.	Once I start working full-time, it may be hard to go back to school.

—continued

Decision–Making Application—continued

- **Choose what you believe is the best solution:** "I have decided to get a job."
- **Review and assess:** "My choice is reasonable and makes sense for me now in my situation. I won't have to work such long hours and juggle both school and work. I can pay back loans and save money. We can start our family. I can review my long-term goal and determine an alternate way to achieve it."

Would you arrive at the same decision? What would be your decision and your main reasons?

_____

_____

Now, set up a problem or decision that you are facing and follow the same steps.

- **Problem:**

    _____

    _____

- **Where can I get help or information?**

    _____

    _____

Possible solutions and pros and cons:

Solution #1: _____

Pros	Cons
1.	
2.	
3.	

Solution #2: _____

Pros	Cons
1.	
2.	
3.	

Solution chosen and why:

_____

_____

Solving Problems and Making Choices

Every day you solve problems. You make choices. Some problems are easy to solve: *What's for dinner?* Some problems are harder: *Can I afford to buy a car?* Some problems change a life forever: *Should I get married?*

You will face problems and choices. You might make good or poor choices. You don't know how a choice will turn out. However, you can follow some steps to help you review your options. They may help you see chances, show you risks, and point out other choices.

Step 1 Know what the problem really is. Is it a daily problem? Is it a once-in-a-lifetime problem?

Step 2 List the things you know about the problem. List the things you don't know. Ask questions. Seek help and advice.

Step 3. Explore alternate choices.

Step 4. Think about the pros and cons for the other choices. Rank them from best to worst choice.

Step 5. Pick the choice you feel good about.

Step 6. After choosing, study what happens. Are you happy about the choice? Would you make it again?

Read the following story and apply the steps in the following exercise.

Class Discussion
Ask students why they think unplanned pregnancy is still a problem when there is so much information available on birth control.

Teaching Tip
Encourage students to use critical thinking when they consider having sex. Tell them to imagine how their lives would change with a baby. Remind them that this is at least an 18-year investment, and most parents say it is a responsibility for life.

José's Choice

José is 50 years old. He has a wife and three kids. He has worked as a bookkeeper for 20 years for the same company. The company is relocating. Only a few people will move with the company. Many workers will be losing their jobs.

José's boss says he can keep his job, but he has to move. If he doesn't, he won't have a job. The family has always lived in this town. José's daughter is a senior in high school and wants to go to the local college next year. His twin boys will be in junior high and are looking forward to playing next year for the ninth-grade football team. José's wife works part-time in a bakery. She has many friends and all of her family live nearby.

The family talked about the move. His wife is afraid. His daughter doesn't want to move. The twins will miss their friends. The family has to decide about the move. What is their problem? What are the choices? Can you help them?

—continued

Solving Problems and Making Choices—continued

Step 1   The problem is _____

_____

_____

Is it a daily problem? _____

_____

_____

Is it a once-in-a-lifetime problem? _____

_____

_____

Step 2   You know _____

_____

_____

You don't know _____

_____

_____

Step 3   The other choices are _____

_____

_____

Step 4   Rank the choices. _____

_____

_____

Step 5   Pick a choice the family might feel good about. _____

_____

_____

Step 6   What might happen? _____

_____

_____

Class Discussion
Ask students how they can
use this creative ideas
checklist for other classes,
jobs, and life situations.

Peak Progress   9.3

Creative Ideas Checklist

Use this checklist of questions to challenge your usual thought patterns. When exploring alternative approaches to problem solving, you can put each category on a separate card. Here are some examples you might find helpful:

- What other idea does this situation suggest?
- How can I modify?
- What can I subtract? Can I take it apart?
- What can I streamline?
- What can I rearrange?
- Can I translate?
- Can I combine or blend?
- What are other uses if modified?
- What can I model?
- Can I use another approach?
- Can I interchange components?
- Are there any opposites?
- What are the positives and negatives?
- Have I used a mind map?
- Have I used a drawing?
- Have I acted it out?
- Can I draw a picture or visualize it?
- Should I sleep on it?
- List some of your own suggestions for creative problem solving:

_____

_____

_____

_____

12. **Practice and be persistent.** Problem solving requires discipline and focused effort. It takes time, practice, and patience to learn any new skill. Stay with the problem and concentrate.

Peak Progress 9.3 provides a handy checklist to help you think of new ways to find solutions.

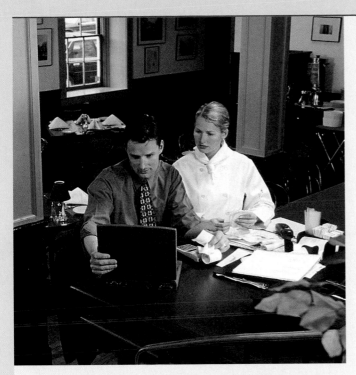

Marina and Josef Koshetz

RESTAURANT OWNERS

Related Majors: Restaurant and Food Service Management, Business

Creativity at Work

Marina and her husband, Josef Koshetz, have recently opened a small restaurant that serves foods from their homeland of Russia. Starting their restaurant was a great deal of work, requiring getting the correct permits, remodeling an existing building, purchasing equipment, and planning the menu. The couple works long hours, six days a week. Before opening the restaurant at 11 A.M., Marina makes bread while Josef mixes together the traditional dishes they will serve. Then, Marina remains in the kitchen to cook and prepare dishes while Josef waits tables and runs the cash register. At the end of the day, the couple washes the dishes and cleans the restaurant together. Although the restaurant is closed on Mondays, Marina and Josef use that day to plan the next week's specials and purchase food and other supplies.

Despite their hard work, the couple has made only enough money to cover costs. On a recent Monday afternoon, the two restaurateurs brainstormed ways to attract more customers. The restaurant is located in a quiet neighborhood on the edge of a district where many Russian immigrants live. So far, almost all of their customers have been Russian. Josef and Marina realized that they needed to do more to attract other residents to their restaurant. They decided to host an open house and invite everyone who lived within a mile radius of the restaurant. Then, they decided to add a couple of popular American dishes and began running ads in a local newspaper. Soon, their restaurant was attracting more customers, and the business began to show a profit.

CRITICAL THINKING
How did Josef and Marina use creativity and critical thinking to improve their business?

Peak Performer Profile

Scott Adams

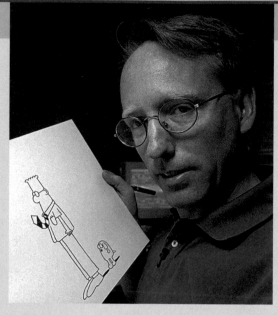

He's been described as a techie with the "social skills of a mousepad." He's not the sort of fellow you'd expect to attract media attention. However, pick up a newspaper, turn to the comics, and you'll find him. He's Dilbert. Cartoonist Scott Adams created this comic-strip character who daily lampoons corporate America and provides a humorous outlet for employees everywhere.

Though creative at a young age, Adams' artistic endeavors were discouraged early on. The Famous Artists School rejected him at age 11. Years later, he received the lowest grade in a college drawing class. Practicality replaced creativity. In 1979, Adams earned a B.A. in economics from Hartwick College in Oneaonta, New York, and, in 1986, an MBA from the University of California at Berkeley. For the next 15 years, Adams settled uncomfortably into a number of jobs that "defied description." Ironically, the frustrations of the workplace—power-driven coworkers, inept bosses, and cell-like cubicles—fueled his imagination. Adams began doodling, and Dilbert was born.

Encouraged by others, Adams submitted his work to United Media, a major cartoon syndicate. He was offered a contract in 1989, and "Dilbert" debuted in 50 national newspapers. Today, "Dilbert" appears in 2,000 newspapers in 56 countries and is the first syndicated cartoon to have its own web site, The Dilbert Zone, with 1.5 million hits daily.

With such mass exposure, coming up with new ideas for cartoons could be a challenge. However, Adams found the perfect source: He has made his e-mail address available. He gets about 300 messages a day from workers at home and abroad. His hope is that, through his creative invention, solutions will develop for the problems he satirizes.

PERFORMANCE THINKING   Of the 12 strategies on pages 9–12 to 9–22, which one do you think has been most helpful for Scott Adams and why?

TAKING CHARGE

In summary, in this chapter, I learned to

- *Appreciate the importance of critical thinking.* Critical thinking is fundamental for understanding and solving problems in coursework, in my job, and in all areas of my life. I have learned to examine beliefs, assumptions, and opinions against facts, to ask pertinent questions, and to analyze data. Critical thinking is especially important for mastering math and science.

- *Prepare for problem solving.* My attitude has a lot to do with how I approach problem solving, especially in math and science classes. I have developed a positive and inquisitive attitude and a willingness to explore, probe, question, and search for answers and solutions. I have created interest and meaning in studying math and science. I will replace negative self-talk with affirmations. I will use my critical thinking skills and be persistent in solving problems. I will participate in a supportive, group environment, such as a study group.

- *Avoid errors in judgment.* I will avoid using stereotypes, snap judgments, unwarranted assumptions, sweeping generalizations, and the halo effect. I will not project my habits onto others in order to justify my behavior or decisions.

- *Define the problem.* I observe, analyze, and define the problem clearly and state it in a sentence or two. I know what is being asked and have defined the main points. I write out the problem in words and go from the general to the specific.

- *Ask questions and gather information.* I think and reflect about what I know, what I need to know, and what I am trying to find out. What is my theory or hypothesis? How is this problem similar to or different from other problems I have solved? I look for patterns, connections, and relationships.

- *Choose a strategy.* How do I set up this problem? What model, formula, drawing, sketch, equation, chart, table, calculation, or particular strategy will help? I choose the most appropriate strategy and outline a step-by-step plan.

- *Solve the problem.* I use the strategy I've selected and work the problem. I show all my work, so I can review. I make an estimate of what I think the answer will be.

- *Review and check.* I look back and see if I answered the question asked. Did I solve the problem? Is my answer reasonable and does it make sense? If not, did I make careless errors or misunderstand the concepts? I will retrace my steps.

- *Use creative problem solving.* I will use creative problem solving to approach the problem from a different direction and explore new options. What problems are similar? Is there a pattern to the problem? I will brainstorm different strategies. I will act out the problem, move it around, picture it, take it apart, translate, and summarize in my own words. I will solve easier problems first and then tackle harder problems.

Performance Strategies

Following are the top 10 strategies for critical thinking and creative problem solving:

- ◆ Create a positive attitude.
- ◆ Use writing to draw sketches and critically solve problems.
- ◆ Use flash cards to practice formulas, equations, and terms.
- ◆ Think about and examine similar problems that you understand and try similar ways to solve this problem.
- ◆ Look for patterns.
- ◆ Make tables, diagrams, pictures, and charts.
- ◆ Go step by step and then work backwards.
- ◆ Translate equations into words and words into equations.
- ◆ Analyze problems and write out what you know and what you don't know.
- ◆ Integrate all learning styles and practice again and again.

Review Questions

1. How can you prepare your mind for problem solving?
2. What are the attributes of a critical thinker?
3. Name five strategies for problem solving in math and science.
4. Name five strategies for becoming more creative.
5. What are the steps to problem solving?

REVISUALIZATION

Review the Visualization box on the first page of this chapter and your journal entry in **Worksheet 9.1.** Now that you know more strategies for critical thinking and creative problem solving, consider a difficult situation you have encountered, such as a financial dilemma, a rigorous course, or a serious personal crisis. Apply the ABCDE method of self-management and use your critical thinking skills to work through the situation and arrive at a positive result—for example,

A = Actual event: "I have my first math test tomorrow and I'm so nervous that I'm having trouble concentrating. I always did well in math, but it's been so many years since my last course that I feel like I've had to learn it all over again."

B = Beliefs: "Returning to school after years of working isn't as easy as I thought it would be. I had hoped I could pick up where I left off."

C = Consequences: "I need a good grade in this course in order to stay in my program. I've worked so hard to get to this point; I can't let myself down now."

D = Dispute: "I know that lots of students struggle initially with math concepts. The more I review the material, the clearer it will be. I have more distractions to deal with today than I did years ago, but I've learned to focus, organize, and juggle all my responsibilities."

E = Energized: "I'm energized because I'm excited to be back in college, and I'm not going to let fear of one or two classes cause me to doubt my goals. I've learned to think critically and solve problems creatively in real life, and these skills will help me succeed in math and science."

CONQUERING FEAR OF FAILURE

In The Classroom

Gloria Ramone is a single mom who works part-time and lives and attends school in the inner city. She is eager to complete her education, begin her career, and have the opportunity to receive a higher salary. She is an electronics student who wants her classes to be practical and relevant. She is required to take a class in critical thinking, a class she is resisting because she sees no practical application to her job. Her attitude is affecting her attendance and participation.

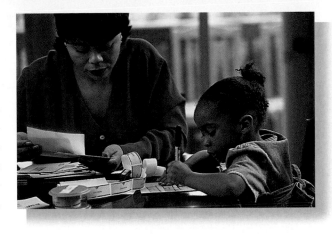

1. Can you offer ideas to help Gloria see the importance of critical thinking in decision making?

_____

_____

_____

2. Can you help her connect decisions in school with job decisions?

_____

_____

_____

In the Workplace

Gloria is now a manager in a small electronics business. She is also taking evening classes, working toward a business degree. She has received promotions quickly on her job, but she knows that she needs further management training. Gloria is very interested in the electronics field and loves to solve problems. On a daily basis, she is faced with issues to solve and has decisions to make. She has lots of practice predicting results and using critical thinking for problem solving. Gloria enjoys most of the business classes, but she doesn't want to take the classes in finance and statistics. Gloria has math anxiety and is dreading the upper-division math and statistics.

3. What strategies in this chapter can help Gloria overcome math anxiety?

_____

_____

_____

4. What are some affirmations Gloria could use to help her develop a positive attitude about math?

_____

_____

_____

CHAPTER 9 ▲ REVIEW AND APPLICATIONS

APPLYING THE ABCDE METHOD OF SELF-MANAGEMENT

In the Visualization box on page 9–1, you were asked to describe a personal situation in which understanding basic math or science skills was necessary, such as paying your taxes, applying for a loan, or following up on a medical condition. Did you feel prepared and understand the results? What did you learn in the process?

_____

_____

_____

_____

Now that you know more strategies for critical thinking and creative problem solving, apply the ABCDE method to a difficult situation you have encountered, such as a financial dilemma, a rigorous course, or a serious personal crisis. Use your critical thinking skills to work through the situation and arrive at a positive result.

A = Actual event:

B = Beliefs:

C = Consequences:

D = Dispute:

E = Energized:

Use positive visualization and practice deep breathing with your eyes closed for just one minute. See yourself calm, centered, and relaxed, learning formulas, practicing problem solving, and using critical thinking to work through problems. You feel confident about yourself because you have learned to control your anxiety and maintain a positive attitude.

CHAPTER 9 ▶ REVIEW AND APPLICATIONS

PROBLEM SOLVING

Write three problems you may be experiencing in the workplace or at school. Use critical thinking to find creative solutions to the problems.

Problems

1. _____

  _____

  _____

2. _____

  _____

  _____

3. _____

  _____

  _____

Possible Solutions

1. a. _____

  b. _____

  c. _____

2. a. _____

  b. _____

  c. _____

3. a. _____

  b. _____

  c. _____

PREPARING FOR CRITICAL THINKING

Brainstorm alternative approaches and solutions to the problems that arise in your day-to-day activities. By using critical thinking, you will be able to explore new ideas as you fill in this form.

Issues/Problems in Day-to-Day Activities

_____

_____

_____

_____

_____

Solution #1: _____

Pros	Cons	Potential Consequences	Costs	Timing

Solution #2: _____

Pros	Cons	Potential Consequences	Costs	Timing

Solution #3: _____

Pros	Cons	Potential Consequences	Costs	Timing

CHAPTER 9 ▸ REVIEW AND APPLICATIONS

YOU CAN SOLVE THE PROBLEM: SUE'S DECISION

Every day you solve problems. Some problems are easy to solve: *Should I do my shopping now or later?* Some problems are harder: *My car is in the shop. How will I get to work?* Some problems change your life forever: *Can I afford to go to school?*

Every day life brings problems and choices. The kinds of choices you make can make your life easier or harder. Often, you do not know which direction to take. But there are ways to help you be more certain. There are steps you can take. You can look at your choices before you make them. You can see some of the problems you may face. You may find you have other or better choices. Here are some steps to help you make choices:

Step 1   Know what the problem really is. Is it a daily problem? Is it a once-in-a-lifetime problem?

Step 2   List the things you know about the problem. List the things you don't know. Ask questions. Get help and advice.

Step 3   Explore alternate choices.

Step 4   Think about the pros and cons for the other choices. Put them in order from best to worst choice.

Step 5   Pick the choice you feel good about.

Step 6   Study what happens after you have made your choice. Are you happy about the choice? Would you make it again?

Read the following story and apply the steps in the following exercise.

Sue has been diagnosed with cancer. Her doctor has told her that it is in only one place in her body. The doctor wants to operate. He thinks that he will be able to remove all of it, but he still wants Sue to do something else. He wants her to undergo chemotherapy for four months, which will make her feel very sick. It will make her tired, but the medicine can help keep the cancer from coming back.

Sue is not sure what to do. She has two small children who are not in school. Sue's husband works days and cannot help care for the children during the day. Sue's family lives far away, and she cannot afford day care. She asks herself, "How will I be able to care for my children if I am sick?"

The doctor has told Sue that she must make her own choice. Will she take the medicine? Sue must decide. She will talk with her husband, and they will make a choice together.

What is Sue's problem? What are her choices? What would you decide? Apply the six steps to help Sue make a good choice by writing responses to the following questions and statements.

—continued

CHAPTER 9 ◤ REVIEW AND APPLICATIONS

Step 1   The problem is

_____

_____

_____

Step 2
a.   You know these things about the problem:

_____

_____

_____

b.   You don't know these things about the problem:

_____

_____

_____

Step 3   The other choices are

_____

_____

_____

Step 4   Rank the choices, best to worst.

_____

_____

_____

Step 5   Pick a choice the family might feel good about.

_____

_____

_____

Step 6   What might happen to Sue and her family?

_____

_____

_____

YOU CAN SOLVE THE PROBLEM: CASEY'S DILEMMA

You make choices and solve problems every day. Some choices are automatic and don't require much thought, such as stopping a car at a red light or stepping on the gas pedal when the light turns green. Other problems require you to make easy choices, such as which TV show to watch. Other problems are more difficult to solve—for example, what to say to your teenage son when he comes home past curfew smelling like beer.

In your life, you will face many problems and choices. You might make good or poor choices because you don't always know how a choice will turn out.

There are some steps you can follow to help you make a good choice and solve your problem. These steps can help you think of options and improve your problem-solving skills:

Step 1   Stop and think. Take a deep breath before you say or do something you will regret.

Step 2   Write a problem statement. Be sure to include who has the problem and state it clearly.

Step 3   Write a goal statement. Check to see that it has simple, realistic, and positive words.

Step 4   List all your choices, both the good and the bad choices.

Step 5   Remove choices that don't match your goal, will hurt others, or will cause more problems than they will solve.

Step 6   Make your best choice. Check Step 3 to be sure your choice matches your goal.

Read the following story and apply the steps in the following exercise.

Casey has been divorced for three years, and her children visit their father every other weekend. When he brought the children home this weekend, he told Casey that he is planning to remarry.

Now, her children will have a stepmother and Casey is worried how everyone will get along. She wants her children to continue to visit their dad and enjoy the visits.

Can you help Casey solve this problem? Follow the six steps to help Casey make a choice by writing responses to the following questions and statements.

—continued

CHAPTER 9 ◢ REVIEW AND APPLICATIONS

1. What is the first thing Casey should do?

_____

_____

_____

2. Write a problem statement.

_____

_____

_____

3. What is Casey's goal?

_____

_____

_____

4. List as many choices as you can for Casey.

_____

_____

_____

5. Which choices should Casey cross off her list?

_____

_____

_____

6. What is the best choice for Casey to make?

_____

_____

_____

7. Does your answer in #6 match her goal in Step 3?

_____

_____

_____

NAME: DATE:

MATRIX FOR CRITICAL THINKING

Use this checklist of strategies to sharpen your critical thinking skills in both the classroom and the workplace.

	Question				Anticipate				Analyze				Assess			
	Clearly state the problem.	Question your assumptions.	Question credentials.	Make a list of questions.	Anticipate outcomes and probabilities.	Predict consequences.	Look for cause and effect.	Anticipate trends and patterns.	Analyze facts.	Interpret data.	Make inferences and analyze.	Analyze flaws and inconsistencies.	Assess accuracy.	Assess facts and data.	Ensure that information is objective and reliable.	Adjust and modify.
Decision 1																
Decision 2																
Decision 3																
Decision 4																

CHAPTER 9 ▲ REVIEW AND APPLICATIONS

ASSESSING AND DEMONSTRATING YOUR CRITICAL THINKING SKILLS

1. **Looking back:** Review your worksheets to find activities through which you learned to make decisions and solve problems creatively. Jot down examples. Also, look for examples of how you learned to apply critical thinking skills to math and science.

   _____

   _____

   _____

   _____

   _____

2. **Taking stock:** What are your strengths in making decisions and in using critical thinking? Are you a creative person? What areas would you like to improve?

   _____

   _____

   _____

   _____

   _____

3. **Looking forward:** How would you demonstrate critical thinking and creative problem-solving skills to an employer?

   _____

   _____

   _____

   _____

   _____

4. **Documentation:** Include documentation of your critical thinking and creative problem-solving skills. Find an instructor or employer who will write a letter of recommendation. Add this letter to your portfolio.

   _____

   _____

   _____

   _____

   _____

   Add this page to your Career Development Portfolio.

Health and Stress

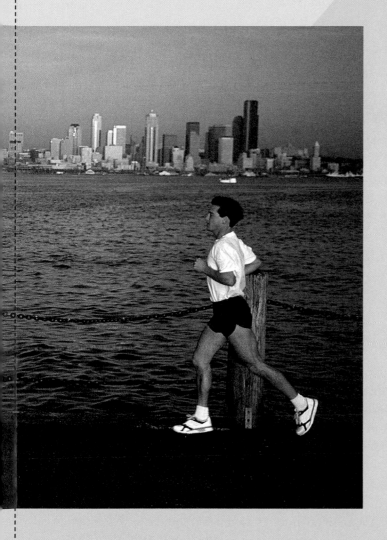

Chapter Objectives

In this chapter, you will learn

▲ The importance of health

▲ How to make healthy choices in your diet

▲ The importance of a regular exercise program

▲ How to make sound decisions about alcohol and other drugs

▲ How to recognize depression and suicidal tendencies

▲ How to protect yourself from disease, unplanned pregnancy, and rape

▲ How to control stress and reduce anxiety

VISUALIZATION

"I'm stressed out with so much homework and trying to juggle everything. I haven't been getting enough sleep, and I'm gaining weight from eating too much fast food and not exercising. What can I do to reduce my stress and be healthier?"

Do you find yourself feeling overwhelmed and stressed by too many demands? Do you lack energy from too little sleep or exercise or from excess calories? In this chapter, you will learn how to manage stress and create healthy habits to last a lifetime. You will see yourself healthy and in charge of your physical, mental, and emotional life.

JOURNAL ENTRY In Worksheet 10.1 on page 10–30, describe a time when you had lots of energy, felt healthy and rested, and was in control of your weight. What factors helped you be calm, confident, and healthy?

Words to Succeed

"Your health is bound to be affected if, day after day, you say the opposite of what you feel. Our nervous system is part of our physical body."

—BORIS PASTERNAK
Russian novelist

Words to Succeed

"Things which matter most must never be at the mercy of things which matter least."

—J.W. VON GOETHE
writer

Creating balance, increasing energy, and providing time for renewal are some of the keys to becoming a peak performer. The purpose of this chapter is to present principles and guidelines to help you develop the most effective methods of maintaining your health while dealing with daily demands.

Your Body as a System

Your body is a good example of a working system. If you take an aspirin for a headache, the tablet doesn't just isolate the pain in your head but travels through your bloodstream and affects other parts of your body. Many factors affect your health and energy and are interrelated, factors such as exercise, food, sleep, drugs, stress, and your state of mind.

You will encounter many demands that require an enormous amount of effort at various times. Papers, reports, deadlines, tests, performance reviews, conflicts, committees, commuting, family responsibilities, and presentations are all part of school, career, and life. These demands will also create a considerable amount of stress. Stress is not an external event but part of a larger system, and it affects every part of your body and mind.

Awareness

The first step in managing your health is awareness. Observe how your body feels, the thoughts going through your mind, and your level of stress. Be aware of negative habits. You may not even realize that you eat every time you watch television, drink several cans of soda while you study, or nibble while you fix dinner. Fast food may be part of a routine to save time, or you skip breakfast. Observe your daily habits and begin to replace unproductive ones with beneficial choices. Take a minute to observe your body's reactions by completing **Personal Performance Notebook 10.1.**

Have you experienced discomfort or a change in your body? If you can identify symptoms and early warning signs of an illness, you can take appropriate action that can lead to protection against diseases, such as cancer. (See **Figure 10.1.**)

Five Strategies for Good Health Management

1. **Eat healthy foods for high energy.** Eat a nutritional diet daily to control weight and blood pressure and to reduce depression, anxiety, headaches, fatigue, and insomnia. Many theories try to identify which foods are best to keep you

Personal Performance Notebook   10.1

Becoming Attuned to Your Body

Set aside a few minutes of quiet, private time. Stop what you are doing and close your eyes. Try to focus on your body. Observe its reactions to these few minutes of quiet. Notice your breathing. Write your observations on the lines provided.

1. How were you sitting? _____

2. What was your state of mind? _____

3. Were you feeling rested, energetic, or tired? _____ Yes _____ No

4. Did you observe pain anywhere in your body? Where? _____

5. Was there any feeling of tension? _____ Yes _____ No

6. Were you holding your shoulders up? _____ Yes _____ No

7. Were you clenching your jaw? _____ Yes _____ No

Try to stop and discern how you're feeling several times a day.

Hands-On Application
Ask students:
1. Are they aware of their bodies? (Have students keep a journal for a few days and record any discomfort.)
2. How do they feel? Where do they feel tension or stress?
_____

Figure 10.1   Observing Caution Signs

The American Cancer Society provides the following guidelines. See your doctor if you notice any of the following symptoms:

C   Change in bowel or bladder habits

A   A sore that does not heal

U   Unusual bleeding or discharge

T   Thickening or lump in the breast or elsewhere

I   Indigestion or difficulty in swallowing

O   Obvious changes in a wart or mole

N   Nagging cough or hoarseness

Source: The American Cancer Society, 2001.

Observing Caution Signs   Protect yourself by monitoring your health. *Can changes in your health always signal a serious condition?*

Teaching Tip
Illustrate how the body is an interrelated system. For example, researchers have found that flossing is not good just for teeth and gums; it can also prevent bacteria from causing damage to the heart and other areas of the body.
_____

healthy and whether you need vitamin and mineral supplements. Some nutritionists say that a good diet supplies all the vitamins and minerals you need. Others disagree.

The recommended daily allowances (RDAs) developed by the U.S. Senate Select Committee on Nutrition provide guidelines for determining if you

Class Discussion
1. Discuss what foods give students energy and keep them healthy. Ask them why they don't eat a healthier diet.
2. Ask students what they do to maintain their ideal weight. What are the excuses?

Use
TM 10.2 Food Pyramid.

Peak Progress 10.1

Eating for Health and Energy

Beneficial eating and exercise habits can pay off big dividends for success in life. Researchers have studied the effects of diet for years and have attempted to agree on the best diet for most people. In 1993, the Harvard School of Public Health sponsored a major conference on nutrition. Scientists and nutritionists from the United States and Europe met to look at the traditional Mediterranean diet, which may have prolonged life and prevented disease for centuries in Mediterranean countries. The experts released a model similar to that of the United States Department of Agriculture food guide pyramid. The Mediterranean model suggests more beans and legumes over animal-based proteins and advocates the use of olive oil in a daily diet.

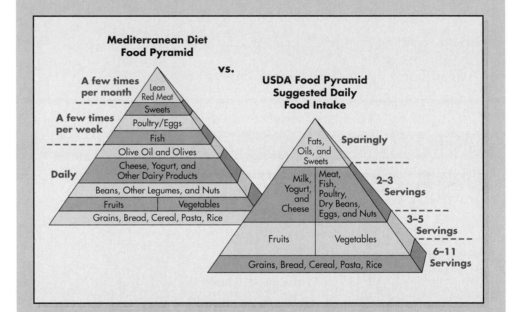

Source: U.S. Department of Agriculture, U.S. Department of Health and Human Services.

Note: The U.S.D.A. food pyramid is currently under review and may be replaced with new guidelines. This is the most current presentation as we go to press.

consume enough vitamins and minerals. The following general guidelines will help you make healthy choices in your diet.

- *Eat a variety of foods.* Include whole grains, lots of fruits and vegetables, milk, meats, poultry, fish, and breads and cereals in your diet. See **Peak Progress 10.1** above for suggested balanced diets illustrated by the food pyramids.
- *Cut down on salt and caffeine.* Caffeine is found in soft drinks, coffee, tea, and chocolate. Salt is often an ingredient in prepared foods.
- *Eat plenty of fresh fruits and vegetables.* Fruits and vegetables are excellent sources not only of disease-preventing fiber but also of vitamins.

- *Take a multivitamin supplement every day.* Many experts advise taking vitamin and mineral supplements for optimal health. Some recommend extra C, E, B complex, and A vitamins if you are under stress.
- *Increase whole-grain cereals and breads.* Whole grains contain fiber, vitamins, and minerals. They are also filling and will keep you from snacking.
- *Reduce the amount of animal fat in your diet.* Too much animal fat can increase the level of cholesterol in your blood, which can affect your cardiovascular system, causing your body to get less oxygen.
- *Broil or bake meats rather than fry them.* Use olive oil or other mono-unsaturated fat instead of butter.
- *Cut down on sugar.* Sugar has no nutritional value and promotes tooth decay. You don't have to eliminate treats, but keep in mind that they are filled with nonnutritional calories.
- *Use alcohol in moderation.* If you drink alcoholic beverages, do it in moderation. Too much alcohol increases the risk for certain cancers, cirrhosis of the liver, damage to the heart and brain, and strokes. Never drink and drive.

2. **Maintain your ideal weight.** You will have more energy and be generally healthier when you maintain your ideal weight. Weight maintenance is a major problem for many people, and millions of dollars are spent every year on fad diets, exercise equipment, and promises of a quick fix. There are many support groups for weight control that can be very helpful. If you do need to lose weight, don't try to do it too quickly with fad diets or fasting. Consult a physician to discuss the best method for you. Slow weight loss is more effective and helps you keep the weight off longer. Fasting can lead to major health problems. Building energy by nourishing and helping the body do its job effectively takes a long-term commitment to changing habits. Try taking a walk when you have the urge to snack.

   The following general guidelines will help you maintain your ideal weight.
- *Eat only when you're hungry.* Make sure you eat to sustain your body and not because you are depressed, lonely, bored, or worried.
- *Don't fast.* When a person fasts as a way to reduce daily caloric intake, the body's metabolic rate decreases, so the body burns calories more slowly than before. Then, at a certain point, the body has an urge to binge, which is nature's way of trying to survive famine.
- *Eat regularly.* Don't skip meals. If you are really rushed, carry a banana, an apple, raw vegetables, or nuts with you. Establish a three-meals-a-day pattern. You need to eat regularly and have a balanced diet to lose weight and keep it off.
- *Create healthy patterns.* Eat slowly and enjoy your food. Eat in one or two main places. For example, eat in the dining room or at the kitchen table. Resist the urge to eat on the run, sample food while you are cooking, munch in bed, or snack throughout the day.
- *Get help.* Do you have a problem with weight control or are you overly concerned with being thin? Do you have a problem with eating too little or with fasting (anorexia)? Do you eat and then throw up as a way to control your weight (bulimia)? Anorexia and bulimia are illnesses and need medical

Teaching Tip
Discuss the resources available, including:
Anorexia/Bulimia Ranch Treatment Center, (800) 445-1906
American Anorexia/ Bulimia Association, (212) 734-1114
National Cancer Institute, (800) 4-CANCER

Class Discussion
How have eating habits changed in the past 50 years? We know more about health, but are we healthier?

Reviewing Your Health

Read the following and write your comments on the lines provided.

1. Do you maintain your ideal weight? If not, what can you do to achieve your ideal weight?

_____

_____

_____

Class Discussion
What resources are available to help keep students healthy?

Hands-On Application
Have student teams find phone numbers for campus and community resources. Discuss in class.

2. Describe a few of your healthy eating habits.

_____

_____

_____

3. Describe a few of your unhealthy eating habits.

_____

_____

_____

4. Do you feel you have control over your eating? Explain.

_____

_____

_____

5. What can you do to make positive and lasting changes in your eating habits?

_____

_____

_____

treatment. You might feel isolated and powerless, but there are many resources that can offer help. Look in the yellow pages or discuss your problem with your doctor or counselor. Don't wait. There are many resources that can help you. Use critical thinking as you explore your eating patterns in **Personal Performance Notebook 10.2.**

Getting Proper Rest

Read the following and write your comments on the lines provided

1. Do you wake up in the morning feeling rested and eager to start the day?

_____

_____

_____

2. What prevents you from getting enough rest?

_____

_____

_____

3. What activities can renew your body and spirit besides sleep?

_____

_____

_____

Hands-On Application

Ask students:

1. To pair up with friends who are committed to healthy living and who will help them keep their goals.
2. To be honest about their commitments to exercise and health.
3. To list their barriers and excuses. Have their friends act as critics and come up with solutions.

---

3. **Renew energy through rest.** It is important for good health and energy to get enough rest. Although amounts vary from one person to the next, most people need between six and nine hours of sound sleep a night. The key is not to be concerned about the number of hours of sleep that you require but, rather, whether or not you feel rested, alert, and energized. Some people wake up rested after five hours of sleep; others need at least nine hours to feel energized and refreshed. If you wake up tired, try going to bed earlier for a night or two and then establish a consistent bedtime. Notice if you are using sleep to escape conflict, depression, or boredom. It is also important to find time to relax each day. Use critical thinking in **Personal Performance Notebook 10.3** to assess your commitment to getting rest.

4. **Exercise for energy.** Aerobic exercise raises the heart rate above its normal rate and keeps it there for 20 or more minutes. Regular aerobic exercise is essential for keeping your body at peak performance. Aerobic exercise strengthens every organ in the body (especially the heart), reduces stress, strengthens the immune system, increases muscle strength, reduces excess fat, stimulates the lymph system, and increases your endurance and

Teaching Tip
Stress the importance of getting enough rest.

Increasing Energy
Most people benefit from as little as 20 minutes of exercise three times a week. *What is your exercise goal?*

stamina. Exercise can also alter body chemistry by changing hormones, adjusting metabolism, and stimulating the brain to release more endorphins. Endorphins are natural chemicals in the body that affect your state of mind and increase feelings of well-being. How much exercise you need to stay in good physical health depends on your goals, your present fitness level, your overall health, and your physician's advice. For most healthy people, a regular program of 20 to 30 minutes of aerobic exercise is needed at least three times a week for optimum health. There are many ways to exercise aerobically. Walking, swimming, bicycling, dancing, and jogging are some popular ways. The key is to start slowly, build up gradually, and be consistent! If you experience pain during aerobic exercise, stop. Assess your commitment to exercise in **Personal Performance Notebook 10.4.**

5. **Healthy relationships provide energy.** Healthy relationships can be a wonderful source of increased energy. We all know the deep satisfaction of sharing a good talk or a wonderful evening with a friend, or the sense of pride and accomplishment when we've completed a team project. Indeed, other people can help us think through problems, develop self-confidence, conquer fears, develop courage, brainstorm ideas, overcome boredom and fatigue, and increase our joy and laughter. Some barriers to healthy relationships are
   - Getting so busy at school and work or with your goals that you ignore your friends and family
   - Being shy and finding it difficult to build friendships
   - Approaching friendship as a competitive sport

   It takes sensitivity and awareness to value others' needs. It also takes courage to overcome shyness. The key is to see the enormous value of friendships. Personal friends bring a deep sense of joy and fellowship to life. Life's sorrows

Committing to Exercise

Read the following and write your comments on the lines provided.

1. Describe your current commitment to exercising your body.

_____

_____

_____

2. What are your excuses for not exercising? What can you do to overcome these barriers?

_____

_____

_____

3. Now, set your exercise goal.

_____

_____

_____

TECH FOR SUCCESS

- **Health on the Web** There are more sites on the Internet devoted to the topic of health than to any other subject. However, how do you know which sites are providing accurate information? Start with government, professional organizations, and nonprofit sites. Many of these sites offer "questions to ask" or red flags to look for when consulting with physicians or purchasing products on the Internet.

- **Assess Yourself** You will find a vast array of free personal assessment tools on the Internet. You can explore everything from ideal body weight to your risk of developing a certain cancer. Use assessments to help you determine what patterns and behaviors you want to change. As with all information on the Internet, check the source or research behind the assessment tool.

- **Just What *Is* in That Burger?** Almost every fast-food chain provides the caloric breakdown of its most popular items on the company's web site. Before your next trip to your favorite restaurant, look up the calories and fat content of your usual order. Is it what you expected, or even higher? Does knowing this information make an impact on your selections?

Class Discussion
Ask students if alcohol abuse
is a problem on their
campus. Recent studies
indicate that college binge
drinking is a major problem
on many college campuses.
Over half of college students
drink to get drunk. Every
year deaths occur from
alcohol overdoses. Campus
police report that alcohol is
almost always involved in
rape and campus violence.
Ask students what they think
could be done to educate
students.

and setbacks are lessened when you have friends to support and help you through difficult times. You will find yourself energized by good friends.

Effects of Caffeine

A small amount of caffeine can enhance alertness and effectiveness and be a source of comfort. A cup or two of coffee in the morning can give you a burst of energy, create a sense of well-being, and does not pose a health problem for most people. Caffeine is not found just in coffee, however; it is also found in tea, many soft drinks, chocolate, and some medications, such as aspirin products. Thus, it is easy to consume too much caffeine and become anxious, nervous, jittery, irritable, and insomnia-prone. Too much caffeine may deplete your B vitamins, minerals, and other nutrients that your body needs to cope with stress. Caffeine can also be addictive: The more you take in, the more it takes to produce that desired burst of energy. If you find yourself experiencing caffeine-induced symptoms, reduce your intake but do so gradually. Headaches can result from rapid caffeine withdrawal. Try substituting decaffeinated coffee, tea, or soft drinks or herbal tea. Even decaffeinated coffee can contain traces of caffeine. Check labels to confirm that your substitutions are indeed caffeine-free.

Alcohol Abuse

Alcohol can be one of the biggest energy drains to your body. Because it is a drug, it can alter moods, become habit-forming, and cause changes in the body. Because alcohol is also a depressant, it actually depresses the central nervous system.

Coffeehouse Blues
The caffeine in coffee can be pleasurable in moderate amounts, but, because it is addictive, there's a downside to drinking too much. *What are some other ways to increase your energy besides ingesting caffeine?*

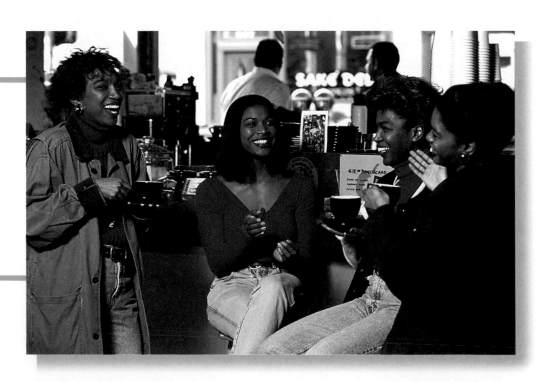

Alcoholism can begin as early as childhood and is often influenced by peer pressure. A major life lesson is to think for yourself and be responsible for your choices and behavior. Alcoholism is considered a chronic disease that can be progressive and even fatal. For most adults, a glass of wine or a beer at dinner will not be a problem, but it is important to realize that even a small amount of alcohol can cause slowed reactions and poor judgment.

CRITICAL THINKING ABOUT ALCOHOL

It is important to use critical thinking to make sound decisions about drinking. High school and college drinking have become major social and health problems. U.S. students consume over 430 million gallons of alcohol per year. There are more than 25 million alcoholics in the United States today, and most say they began drinking in high school and college.

Students often believe that there isn't a problem if they drink just beer, but it is possible to be an alcoholic by drinking only beer. A six-pack of beer contains the same amount of alcohol as six drinks of hard liquor—or one beer is equivalent to one shot of hard liquor. Take a close look at some of the facts about alcohol and alcoholism in **Figure 10.2.**

Although one in five college students report that they don't drink at all, the Core Institute, an organization that surveys college drinking practices, reports the following:

◆ Three hundred thousand of today's college students will eventually die of alcohol-related causes, such as drunk driving accidents, cirrhosis of the liver, various cancers, and heart disease.

Teaching Tip
Stress the importance of using critical thinking to respond to addiction. Denial and blame are common responses to addiction.

Class Discussion
1. Stress the costs of alcohol and smoking. The average student spends more on beer than on textbooks. Many students complain that they don't have money for college materials, textbooks, and even food, and yet they smoke and drink.
2. Ask students why they think so many students still smoke when the facts about the dangers of smoking are so well documented.
3. Are they using critical thinking in their choices?
4. Have students experienced this kind of faulty thinking?
5. What is a possible explanation?

Figure 10.2   The Costs of Alcohol

- 15,786 fatalities were caused by alcohol-related crashes in 1999. That means 1 alcohol-related fatality every 33 minutes.
- 300,000 of today's college students may die of alcohol-related causes, such as drunk-driving accidents, cirrhosis of the liver, cancer, and heart disease.
- 3 out of 10 Americans may be involved in an alcohol-related crash.
- 1.4 million people were arrested in the United States in 1999 for driving under the influence (DUI) or driving while intoxicated (DWI)—more than all other reported criminal offenses, except larceny and theft.
- According to the Department of Justice, each year 37 percent of rapes and sexual assaults involve alcohol use by the offender, as do 15 percent of all robberies, 27 percent of aggravated assaults, and 25 percent of simple assaults.

SOURCES: National Highway Traffic Safety Association; www.factsontap.org/collexp/stats.htm; U.S. Department of Justice, *Alcohol and Crime: An Analysis of National Data on the Prevalence of Alcohol Involvement in Crime.*

The Costs of Alcohol   Knowing the facts can help you make the right choices. *Would you allow yourself or a friend to drink and drive?*

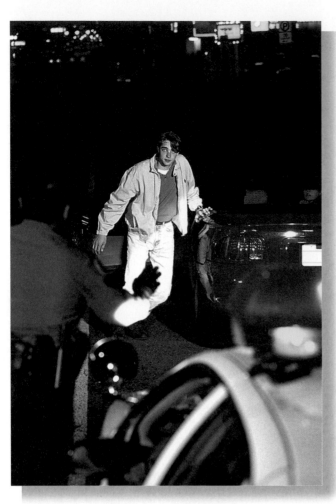

- One hundred fifty-nine thousand of today's first-year college students will drop out of school for alcohol- or other drug-related reasons.
- The average student spends $900 on alcohol each year, compared with $450 on textbooks.
- Almost one-third of college students admit to having missed at least one class because of their alcohol use.
- One night of heavy drinking can impair your ability to think abstractly for up to 30 days.

Facts About Cigarette Smoking

It is hard to believe that anyone would smoke after hearing and viewing the public awareness campaigns that present the risks of cigarette smoking. Perhaps the billions of dollars advertisers spend each year convince enough people that smoking makes you more attractive, sexier, cooler, and calmer. Those advertising claims are in stark contrast to the facts shown in **Figure 10.3.**

Walking the Line
The Highway Patrol will sometimes set up checkpoints for screening out drunk drivers on the road. *Do you think this is a wise practice in light of the statistics for alcohol-related fatalities?*

Facts About Illegal Drugs

Drug addiction also causes major social and health problems. Almost 80 percent of people in their mid-twenties have tried illegal drugs. Here are some pertinent facts concerning drug abuse:

- Certain patterns of behavior among marijuana users, especially adolescents, show loss of memory and intellectual reasoning.
- The cost of drug abuse to American society is almost $50 billion a year.
- According to the National Council on Alcoholism and Drug Dependence, marijuana releases five times more carbon dioxide and three times more tar into the lungs than tobacco does.
- Crack addiction can occur during less than two months of occasional use.
- Intravenous drug use causes 24 percent of AIDS cases in the United States.

CRITICAL THINKING ABOUT DRUGS

Drugs (both legal and illegal), including alcohol and tobacco, are everywhere. People want to feel good and forget their pain and troubles. Every drug-induced high, however, has a crashing low. Try to rely on your inner strength, not on external means, to

Figure 10.3   The Costs of Cigarette Smoking

- Cigarette smoking-related diseases cause about 430,700 deaths each year in the United States.
- Cigarette smoking is directly responsible for 87 percent of all lung cancer cases and causes most cases of emphysema and chronic bronchitis.
- The Environmental Protection Agency estimates that secondhand smoke causes about 3,000 lung-cancer deaths and 37,000 heartdisease deaths in nonsmokers each year.
- Nonsmokers married to smokers have a 30 percent greater risk for lung cancer than those married to nonsmokers.
- The effects of secondhand smoke, especially on children, include respiratory problems, colds, and other illnesses, such as cancer.
- Secondhand smoke contains over 4,000 chemicals: 200 are poisons and 63 cause cancer.
- Smoking costs the United States approximately $97.2 billion each year in health-care costs and lost productivity.

SOURCES: American Lung Association, http://www.lungusa.org/tobacco.

The Costs of Cigarette Smoking   Cigarette smoking causes major health problems for those who smoke, as well as for those exposed to it through secondhand smoke. *Why do you think many people still smoke in spite of the expense and health risks involved?*

Hands-On Application
Role-play: One person is addicted to a drug, gambling, an unhealthy relationship, or has an eating disorder, and has a list of barriers to overcome. The other person explores solutions. Reverse roles. Have students think of the best solutions and discuss in their groups.

Teaching Tip
Stress the importance of using critical thinking to respond to addiction. Denial and blame are common responses to addiction.

feel good about life. Be aware of the facts about alcohol and other drug abuse and the high cost of addiction.

You need energy and concentration if you are to be successful at school and in your job. Only you can take responsibility for your life and determine if harmful substances are costing you more than the pleasure you get from them. Ask yourself if you really need to complicate your life, if using drugs will actually make your life better.

Dealing With Addictions

Addictive behavior comes in many forms and is not relegated to substance abuse solely. Just as an alcoholic feels happy when drinking, the food addict feels comforted when eating, the sex addict gets a rush from new partners, the shoplifter feels a thrill with getting away with something, the addictive shopper feels excited during a shopping spree, the gambler feels in control when winning, and the workaholic feels a sense of importance while working late each night or on weekends. Addiction is an abnormal relationship with an object or event and is characterized by using a substance or behavior repeatedly. Beginning as a pleasurable act, it progresses until it becomes a compulsive behavior and causes significant problems.

PEAK TIP
Some people spend too much time in front of their computer screens and become isolated with little face-to-face contact. This can even become an addiction.

Teaching Tip
Don't preach. Stick to the facts, ask questions, and bring in speakers or recovering addicts.

Teaching Tip
Addiction is a good example of how a person's behavior affects many others.

Class Discussion
Ask students how an addict's behavior affects others. Give an example of how a codependent person keeps an addicted person from taking responsibility.

Teaching Tip
Here are other resources that students might find helpful:
Alcoholics Anonymous
    World Services, Inc.,
    (212) 870-3400
National Institute on Drug
    Abuse, (301) 443-1124
American Council on
    Alcoholism Hot Line,
    (800) 527-5344
National Clearinghouse
    for Alcohol and Drug
    Information,
    (800) 729-6686
ACA WSO, P.O. Box 3216,
    Torrance, CA 90510
    (310) 534-1815
Poison Control Center,
    (800) 222-1222

If you are trying to overcome an addiction, you may experience anxiety, irritability, or moodiness. Some people switch addictions to help them cope and to give them the illusion that they have solved the problem. For example, many former alcoholics become chain smokers. Some people take up gambling as a way to have fun and get a rush, but then it becomes a problem. Compulsive gambling can leave people deep in debt and devastate families and careers. A key question to ask is "Is this behavior causing ongoing disruption in my life or the lives of those close to me?" Warning signs include secrecy; a change in discipline, mood, or work habits; a loss of interest in hobbies or school; and altered eating and sleeping habits; you may become withdrawn, depressed, or aggressive. You must take the initiative to get help. Ask your school counselor or go to the health center.

Here are some additional steps to take to deal with an addiction:

◆ *Admit there is a problem.* The first step toward solving a problem is to face it. Denial is often a reaction for someone with an addiction. He or she may do well in school or hold down a job and, therefore, doesn't see a problem. If you think you have lost control or are involved with someone who has, admit it and take charge of your life.

◆ *Take responsibility for addiction and recovery.* You are responsible for and can control your life. Several support groups and treatment programs are available for a number of addictions. Search the Internet or your local phone book for resources in your area, or contact
   Alcoholism: Alcoholics Anonymous: www.alcoholics-anonymous.org
   Drug abuse: National Institute on Drug Abuse: www.drugabuse.gov
   Gambling: National Council on Problem Gambling: www.ncpgambling.org
   Sexual Behavior: The Society for the Advancement of Sexual Health: www.ncsac.org
   Smoking: The Centers for Disease Control and Prevention, Tobacco Information and Prevention Source (TIPS): www.cdc.gov/tobacco

CODEPENDENCY

Even if you are not directly involved with alcohol or other drugs, your life may be affected by someone who is involved. Families and friends can find themselves affected by the addicted person. A common term used when discussing people whose lives are affected by an addict is *codependency*. There are many definitions of *codependency*, and they include numerous self-defeating behaviors, such as low self-esteem; lack of strong, solid, and emotionally fulfilling relationships; lack of self-control; and over-controlling behavior. A codependent person may

◆ Avoid *facing the problem of addiction.* Denying, making excuses, justifying, rationalizing, blaming, controlling, and covering up are all games that a codependent person plays in an effort to cope with living with an addict.

◆ *Take responsibility for the addict's life.* This may include lying; taking over a job, an assignment, or a deadline; or somehow rescuing the addict.

◆ *Be obsessed with controlling the addict's behavior.* For example, the codependent may hide bottles; put on a happy face; hide feelings of anger; confuse love and pity; and sometimes feel that, if only he or she could help more, the addict would quit.

If you feel that you have problems in your life as a result of growing up in an alcoholic family or that you may be codependent, get help. Organizations such as ACA (Adult Children of Alcoholics) address the issues of people who grew up in alcoholic homes. There are many agencies and groups that can make a difference.

Emotional Health

Everyone has the blues occasionally. Sometimes stress and emotional problems interfere with your goals or ability to cope. A variety of emotional problems can affect college students and professionals from all walks of life.

DEPRESSION

It has been estimated that over 60 million people suffer from mild forms of depression each year. Mild depression is relatively short-term. Severe depression is deeper and may last months or years. Over 6 million Americans suffer serious depression that impairs their ability to function. Depression accounts for 75 percent of all psychiatric hospitalizations. It is an emotional state of sadness ranging from mild discouragement to feelings of utter hopelessness. Depression can occur as a response to the following situations:

◆ *Loss.* The death of a loved one, the loss of a job, or any other major change or disappointment in your life can trigger depression.

◆ *Health changes.* Physical changes, such as a serious disease or illness, childbirth, or menopause, can result in chemical changes that may cause depression.

◆ *Conflicts in relationships.* Unresolved conflicts in relationships can cause depression.

Depression can be triggered by many events. Some of these events are tied to certain stages in life. For example, adolescents are just beginning to realize who they are and are trying to cope with the responsibilities of freedom and adulthood. Setting unrealistic goals can also cause depression. If you are facing middle age, you may feel the loss of youth or unrealized career success, or you may miss children who are leaving home. For an elderly person, the loss of physical strength, illness, the death of friends, and growing dependency may prompt depression.

SIGNS AND SYMPTOMS OF DEPRESSION

Recognize some of the common symptoms associated with depression:

◆ Sleep disturbance (sleeping too much or too little or waking up)
◆ Increase in or loss of appetite
◆ Overuse of prescription drugs
◆ Use of nonprescription drugs
◆ Drinking too much
◆ Withdrawal from family and friends, leading to feelings of isolation
◆ Recurring feelings of anxiety
◆ Anger for no apparent reason

Key Teaching Concept
Loss and disappointment are part of life. Help is available to work through depression.

Class Discussion
Ask students if they think depression is a serious problem in college. What are a few of the triggers? How do they cope?

Hands-On Application
Have students write about a situation that has caused them to be depressed or stressed. Have them pass the written piece to the person on the right in their small group. This person should write solutions to the problem. Continue until all group members are included. Discuss in class.

PEAKTIP

Keep in mind that mild depression is an emotion created by realistic and reasonable reactions to loss.

Teaching Tip
Review the warning signs of depression, what to do, and what not to do.

Class Discussion
What are the signs of depression? Why don't people who are depressed seek help?

- Loss of interest in formerly pleasurable activities
- A feeling that simple activities are too much trouble
- A feeling that other people have much more than you have

When depression causes persistent sadness and continues for longer than a month, severe depression may be present.

THE SUICIDAL PERSON

Suicidal thoughts occur when a feeling of hopelessness sets in, and problems seem too much to bear. Suicidal people think that the pain will never go away. Suicidal people usually respond to help. Be concerned if you or others exhibit the following warning signs:

- Excessive alcohol or other drug use
- Significant changes in emotions (hyperactivity, withdrawal, mood swings)
- Significant changes in sleeping, eating, or studying patterns or weight gain or loss
- Feelings of hopeless or helpless
- Little time spent with or a lack of close, supportive friends
- Nonsupportive family ties
- Rare participation in group activities
- Recent loss or traumatic or stressful events
- Suicidal statements
- Close friend or family member having committed suicide
- Attempted suicide in the past
- Participation in dangerous activities
- A plan for committing suicide or for giving away things

You should be concerned if you know someone who exhibits several of these warning signs. If you do know someone who is suffering from depression and seems suicidal, take the following steps:

- Remain calm.
- Take the person seriously; don't ignore the situation.
- Encourage the person to talk.
- Listen without moralizing or judging. Acknowledge the person's feelings.
- Remind the person that counseling can help and is confidential.
- Remind the person that reaching out for help is a sign of strength, not weakness.
- Call a suicide hot line or a counselor at school and get the name of a counselor for the person to call, or make the call with him or her.
- Stay with the person to provide support when he or she makes the contact. If possible, walk or drive the person to the counselor.
- Seek support yourself. Helping someone who is suicidal is stressful and draining.

Protecting Your Body

Reliable information about sex can help you handle the many physical and emotional changes you will experience in life. It can also help you make better decisions about difficult choices. Although sex is a basic human drive and a natural part of

Figure 10.4 STDs: Symptoms, Treatments, and Risks

Class Discussion
Why is the incidence of sexually transmitted diseases increasing on college campuses?

Sexually Transmitted Diseases	What Are the Common Symptoms?	What Is the Treatment?	What Are the Risks?
Genital herpes Cold sores can spread genitally via oral sex.	Ulcers (sores) or blisters around the genitals.	There is no cure; antiviral medications can shorten and prevent outbreaks.	Highly contagious; become more susceptible to HIV infection.
Genital warts	The virus lives in the skin or mucous membranes and usually causes no symptoms; some people get visible genital warts.	There is no cure, although the infection usually goes away on its own. Cancer-related types are more likely to persist.	Higher risk of cervical cancer.
Chlamydia	Known as the "silent" disease, because most infected people have no symptoms. Others may experience discharge from genitals or burning sensation when urinating.	Antibiotics	Infertility
AIDS/HIV	No symptoms for years. Some carriers can be HIV+.	There is no known cure; medical treatments can slow the disease.	Weakening of the immune system; life-threatening infections.

SOURCE: Centers for Disease Control and Prevention, Division of Sexually Transmitted Diseases www.cdc.gov/nchstp/od/nchstp.html.

STDs: Symptoms, Treatments, and Risks Because STDs are a serious health risk, it is important to separate fact from myth when considering your options for protection. *In what ways can knowing the facts about STDs protect you?*

life, there are also dangers that include unplanned pregnancies, sexually transmitted diseases, and rape. Your level of sexual activity is a personal choice and can change with knowledge, understanding, and awareness. Just because you were sexually active at one time does not mean you cannot choose to be celibate now. No one should pressure you into sexual intercourse. If you decide to be sexually active, you need to make responsible choices and decisions and to be aware of the risks. Know the facts and protect your body.

AVOIDING SEXUALLY TRANSMITTED DISEASES (STDs)

Sexually transmitted diseases, or STDs, are spread through sexual contact (including genital, vaginal, anal, and oral contact) with an infected partner. A person may be infected yet appear healthy and symptom-free. See **Figure 10.4** on page 10-00 for a list of STDs and their symptoms, treatments, and risks. Despite public health efforts and classes in health and sexuality, STDs continue to infect significant numbers of young adults. Even if treated early, STDs are a major health risk and can have a devastating effect on your life. They can result in damage to the reproductive organs, infertility, or cancer.

AIDS (acquired immune deficiency syndrome) is a fatal STD. It weakens the immune system and leads to an inability to fight infection. AIDS is transmitted through sexual or other contact with the semen, blood, or vaginal secretions of someone with HIV (human immunodeficiency virus) or by sharing nonsterile intravenous needles with someone who is HIV-positive. Occasionally, it is contracted through a blood transfusion. AIDS is not exclusively a homosexual disease. In fact, in other countries worldwide, it is most commonly spread by heterosexual intercourse. AIDS cannot be transmitted by saliva or casual contact, such as by sharing utensils or shaking hands. Recently, drug therapies using a combination of drugs have been successful in controlling the progression of the disease. However, there is currently no cure for AIDS.

To avoid contracting an STD, follow these guidelines:

◆ Remember that, for any type of sex, prevention is the best rule.

◆ Ask a prospective partner about his or her health.

◆ No matter what the other person's health status is, explain that you always use safety precautions.

◆ Latex condoms and dental dams can help protect against most sexually transmitted diseases. However, abstinence is the only method totally effective in preventing the spread of STDs. It is vital to know the facts, the latest treatments, and the ways you can protect your body.

BIRTH CONTROL

If your relationship is intimate enough for sex, it should be open enough to discuss birth control, STDs, and pregnancy if birth control fails. Both men and women need to stop and ask, "How would an unwanted pregnancy change my life?"

Many contraceptives are available, but you must understand that none are 100 percent foolproof (except abstinence). Current contraceptives include birth control pills, condoms, diaphragms, sponges, spermicidal foams, cervical caps, IUDs, and long-term implants. Douching and withdrawal do not prevent pregnancy and should not be used for birth control. Discuss birth control methods with your partner and with a qualified health professional. Make an informed decision and choose what is best for you.

PREVENTING RAPE

Rape is a serious crime. To help prevent rape, you need to be proactive. Make certain you know your campus well. Ask the campus police or security what you can do to prevent a sexual assault or rape. If you are taking a night class, find the safest place to park your car. Find out if the school has a security escort policy for students taking a night class or using the library in the evening. (If such a service does not exist, request one, or perhaps you can organize one.) If there is no campus escort policy, arrange to walk to your car with a friend or group from your class. Another preventive measure is taking a course on self-defense. Consult a rape crisis counseling center or the campus police to learn if a course is available.

DATE RAPE

Date rape often goes unreported because the victim knows the attacker. The victim may blame him- or herself because he or she had too much to drink or wonders if he or she said or did something to give the attacker the wrong idea. Date rape is not your fault! Check with the counseling center, health center, or campus police for ways to protect yourself from date rape. Here are a few preventive measures:

Teaching Tip
Stress the importance of safety. You may want to bring in a guest speaker from the campus police.

1. **Use assertive language.** In a direct, forceful, and serious tone, let others know when their advances are not welcome.

2. **Trust your intuition.** Be attuned to body cues and trust your intuition. If it doesn't feel right, leave the situation and get help as soon as you can.

3. **Take your time.** Take time to know a person before you spend time alone with him or her. Meet someone you don't know very well in a public place, or double date with a couple you know well. If you are going to a party or to a movie, or for a walk at night, ask a friend to accompany you. Don't take chances because someone looks nice or knows someone that you know.

4. **Recognize that alcohol and other drugs can be dangerous.** Everyone is aware of how dangerous it is to drive while under the influence of alcohol or other drugs. Alcohol and other drugs are also dangerous while dating and are often factors in date rape. If you are intoxicated, you may not be able to protect yourself or be aware of the signals that would otherwise warn you of danger. In some cases, date rapists have added the drug Rohypnol (also called Roofie) to the victim's drink, causing the victim to become unconscious and experience temporary amnesia.

5. **Be aware of the danger signals of an unhealthy relationship.** Be concerned if you are dating someone who
   - Pressures you sexually
   - Refers to people as sex objects
   - Doesn't respect your wants
   - Is possessive
   - Is bossy or aggressive
   - Has a temper and acts rashly
   - Is emotionally or physically abusive

6. **Send clear messages.** Try to make certain that your body language, tone of voice, and choice of words match your feelings. If you do not want to get physically intimate, don't allow anyone to talk you into it. Be aware of your own limits and feelings and communicate them assertively to your date. Respect yourself. Don't do anything that you do not feel comfortable doing. Say no loudly and clearly. Scream for help if you need it. An effective tactic is to yell, "Fire!" to ensure other people's assistance.

7. **Get professional help.** Date rape is a traumatic experience and a violent crime. Report it immediately to a rape crisis center or call the local police. Make certain you get counseling to deal with the trauma. Remember, it is not your fault!

Class Discussion
Experts say that rape (especially date rape) is the most underreported crime. Ask the class why they think this is so. What can be done to protect students?

Hands-On Application
In small groups, have students discuss strategies and solutions for keeping themselves safe. Write down campus and community resources.

Teaching Tip
Discuss these resources:
Rape, Abuse, and Incest
    National Network,
    (800) 656-HOPE
National Domestic Hotline,
    (800) 799-SAFE

Teaching Tip
Have students add to this list of stress factors.

Teaching Tip
Indicate that going or returning to school (and juggling work and family) is a major transition. Major transitions can be stressful. Discuss campus resources. You may want to bring in a speaker.

FACTS ABOUT RAPE

1. **Rape is not just a woman's problem.** Besides the fact that both men and women can become victims of rape, many men have girlfriends, wives, or relatives who could also be targets. Both men and women can become aware and speak up against such stereotypical attitudes as women who are raped ask for it or that women are sex objects. No one asks to be raped because of his or her clothing or behavior. Forced sexual intercourse is degrading and humiliating—and it is rape. You can challenge demeaning and cruel jokes and attitudes by taking a mature, caring stand against violence whenever possible.

2. **Rape is a serious crime.** Rape is a violent crime and can result in the offender spending years in prison. It is an act of violence, aggression, and force.

3. **Your date has the right to say no.** Respect another person's right to say no under any conditions and at any time. Do not misinterpret the word *no*. Don't expect sex in exchange for dinner or just because you have had sex with this person before. People have a right to change their minds, and this right should be respected.

4. **Alcohol and other drugs can be dangerous.** Alcohol and other drugs reduce sexual inhibition and the ability to read body language and cues. Some people blame alcohol consumption for their actions that take advantage of someone else or for their own aggressive behavior. This is not an excuse for unacceptable or illegal behavior.

5. **Understand and state your intentions.** Be clear about your feelings and intentions and respect your date's feelings and intentions. If you believe you are getting mixed messages, talk about it and clear up any miscommunication. Listen to your intuition. If the situation doesn't feel right, leave.

6. **Take your time getting to know someone.** Rushing a relationship is a danger sign. Take your time and get to know someone as a person. Look for and create healthy and fulfilling relationships.

Managing Stress

Stress is a natural reaction of the body to any demand, pleasant or unpleasant. Stress is simply your body's reaction to external events (e.g., taking an exam or giving a speech) or internal events (e.g., fear, worry, or unresolved anger). Everything you experience stimulates your body to react and respond. Stress is normal and, in fact, necessary for a vital life. With too little positive stress, many people are bored and unproductive. The key is knowing how to channel stress. Look at the early warning signs in **Peak Progress 10.2** on page 10–22 to see if you are under too much stress.

Life is a series of changes, and these changes require adaptive responses. The death of a close family member or friend, a serious illness, exams, divorce, financial problems, and the loss of a job are all changes that require adjustment and cause some types of stress. It is important to emphasize, however, that your perception of and reaction to these inescapable life events determine how they affect you. Even positive events can be stressful. Events such as marriage, a promotion, the birth of a baby, a new romantic relationship, a new roommate, graduation, even vacations

Preventing Stress and Fatigue at Work

Tony Ferraro has been a member of the fire department in his city for 25 years. Three years ago, he was promoted to captain of his station. He and the other firefighters at his station respond to fire alarms, using various techniques to put out fires. They also respond to medical emergencies by providing emergency medical assistance until an ambulance arrives. When not out on calls, Tony and his crew maintain their equipment, participate in drills and advanced fire fighting classes, and keep physically fit.

Tony works two or three 24-hour shifts a week, during which time he lives and eats at the fire station. Because fire fighting involves considerable risks for injury or even death, it is a stressful and demanding job. Being alert, physically fit, energized, calm, and clear-headed are critical for making sound decisions. To stay healthy mentally and physically, Tony studies a form of karate that helps him not only stay in shape but remain calm and focused. In addition, he drinks no more than one to two cups of coffee a day and has given up smoking.

As captain of his fire station, Tony initiated better eating habits in the kitchen by posting a food pyramid and talking to the other firefighters about reducing fat and sugar in their diet. In addition, he observes the firefighters for signs of stress and makes suggestions when needed, such as taking time off or getting sufficient rest. The company's health insurance policy includes coverage for counseling. Once after a particularly stressful period, Tony invited a stress counselor to speak and offer services at the station.

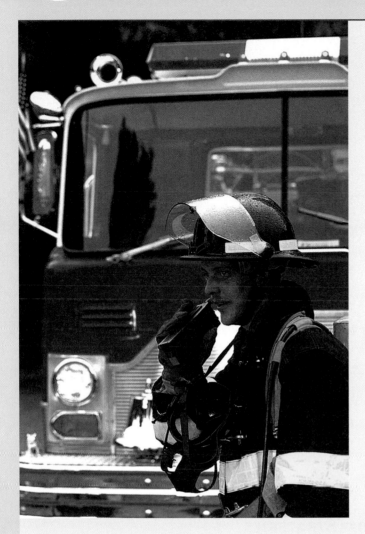

Tony Ferraro

FIREFIGHTER

Related Majors: Fire Science, Public Administration

CRITICAL THINKING

Why is it important for firefighters to work toward healthy goals in physical, emotional, and mental areas?

Hands-On Application
Even beneficial change is stressful. Have students write a list of some changes they can recall in the last year. Have them discuss solutions for dealing with change in their group.

Class Discussion
What are some beneficial habits that can help with addiction? Would stress-reduction strategies such as exercise, yoga, meditation, or hobbies help in replacing negative behaviors? Ask students what they do to create positive habits.

Peak Progress 10.2

Stress Leads to Burnout

Here are early warning signs that your body is pushing too hard and too long and may be on its way to burnout. If you have more than four of the following symptoms, you may want to consider getting help for dealing with stress overload.

- Frequent headaches, backaches, neck pain, stomachaches, or tensed muscles
- Insomnia or disturbed sleep patterns
- No sense of humor; nothing sounds like fun
- Fatigue, listlessness, or hopelessness, and low energy
- Increase in alcohol intake, smoking, or taking drugs
- Depression or moodiness
- Racing heart
- Appetite changes (eating too much or too little)
- Frequent colds, flu, or other illnesses
- Anxiousness, nervousness; difficulty concentrating
- Irritability, losing your temper, and overreacting
- Lack of motivation, energy, or zest for living
- A feeling that you have too much responsibility
- Lack of interest in relationships

and holidays may be disruptive and demanding for some people and, therefore, stressful. Public speaking may be exciting and fun for one person but may cause an anxiety attack in another. Stress is something you can manage in many cases. You can choose to respond to it in a calm, centered way and rechannel that energy in a positive way.

STRESS-REDUCTION STRATEGIES

Prolonged stress can wear you down and produce burnout. It can lead to physical problems, such as migraine headaches, ulcers, high blood pressure, or serious illnesses. Research has indicated that constant change over a long period of time can cause excessive levels of stress. Too many negative or positive changes stimulate the production of certain hormones and chemicals that affect the body. The solution is not to avoid stress but to acknowledge it directly and learn to manage and channel it. Try the following strategies:

1. **Become attuned to your body and emotions.** Many of us have been taught to deny emotions or physical symptoms and ignore stress. Become aware of your body and its reactions. Stress produces physical symptoms. Are you having physical symptoms of stress, such as frequent headaches? Are you finding it difficult to relax? Are you emotionally upset, depressed, or irritable?

   The transition to college forces you to become more self-reliant and self-sufficient. Give yourself permission to feel several different emotions, but also learn strategies to pull yourself out of a slump. (See **Figure 10.5.**) You might set a time limit: "I accept that I'm feeling overwhelmed or down today. I will allow

Figure 10.5   Student Stress Factors

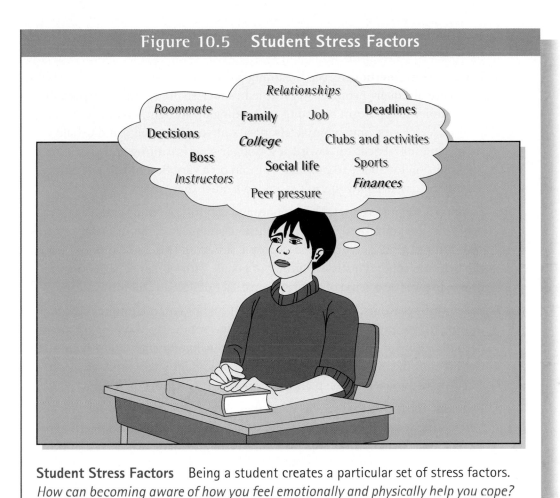

Student Stress Factors   Being a student creates a particular set of stress factors. *How can becoming aware of how you feel emotionally and physically help you cope?*

Key Teaching Concept
Exercise is a great way to reduce stress and create energy and stay healthy.

a few hours to feel these emotions; then, I will do what I know works to make me feel better." Remember that you have the power to change negative, hurtful thoughts and to create positive habits.

2. **Exercise regularly.** Experts say that exercise is one of the best ways to reduce stress, relax muscles, and promote a sense of well-being. Most people find that they have more energy when they exercise regularly. Sometimes the best way is to make exercise a daily habit and a top priority in your life.

3. **Rest and renew your body and mind.** Everyone needs to rest, not only through sleep but also through deep relaxation. Too little of either causes irritability, depression, inability to concentrate, and memory loss. Yoga is a great way to unwind, stretch and tone the muscles, and focus energy. Many people find that meditation is essential for relaxation and renewal. You don't have to practice a certain type of meditation; just create a time for yourself when your mind is free to rest and quiet itself. Other people find that a massage relieves physical and mental tension. Visualization is another powerful technique for relaxing your body.

4. **Develop hobbies and interests.** Hobbies can release stress. Sports, painting, quilting, reading, and collecting can add a sense of fun and meaning to your life. Many find satisfaction and focus by developing an interest in the

Words to Succeed

"Breathing exercises can calm your emotions, clarify your mind, and benefit your involuntary nervous system and metabolism."

—DR. ANDREW WEIL
author

Class Discussion
1. Discuss ways to build balance in one's life.
2. List the strategies for balance that would work for them.
3. Ask students if they think people take themselves too seriously.
4. Could the world use more people with the ability to see humor and to laugh?
5. Ask each student to bring in their favorite humorous cartoon or story.

environment, the elderly, politics, children, animals, or the homeless. Investigate volunteering opportunities in your area.

5. **Use breathing methods.** Deep breathing reduces stress and energizes the body. If you are like many people, you breathe in short, shallow breaths, especially when under stress. Begin by sitting or standing up straight, breathe through your nose, fill your lungs completely, push out your abdomen, and exhale slowly and fully. Focus on a word, a sound, or your breathing and give it your full attention for about 10 minutes. You can do a variation of this anytime during the day, even if you can't escape to a quiet spot.

6. **Develop a support system.** The support and comfort of family and friends can help you clear your mind, sort out confusion, and make better decisions. Express your feelings, fears, and problems to people you trust. Dozens of support groups can help you cope with stress. A group of people with similar experiences and goals can give you a sense of security, personal fulfillment, and motivation.

7. **Take mini-vacations.** Next time you are put on hold on the phone or kept waiting in line, pull out a novel and enjoy a few moments of reading. Practice deep breathing or head rolls, or visualize the tension flowing out of your body. Get up and stretch periodically while you're studying. These mini-vacations can keep you relaxed and expand your creativity.

8. **Rehearse the feared event.** When you mentally rehearse beforehand, you are inoculating yourself against a stressful event. Your fears become known and manageable. Visualization is an excellent technique for rehearsing an event.

9. **Exercise and stretch the mind.** Mental exercise can refresh and stimulate your entire life. Reading, doing crossword puzzles, and playing challenging board games renew the spirit and stretch the mind. Attend lectures, take workshops and seminars, and brainstorm creative ideas or current subjects with well-read friends. Think of all the ways that you can renew and expand your thinking. Make friends with creative people who inspire you and renew your perspective.

10. **Create balance in your life.** Peak performers recognize the importance of balance between work and play in their lives. They want quality and a balanced life. Assess your activities and determine if they are distractions or opportunities. Learn to say no to requests that do not enrich your life or the lives of others. Set a time limit on work, demands from other people, and study; reward yourself for tasks accomplished.

11. **Develop a sense of humor.** Nothing reduces stress like a hearty laugh or spontaneous fun. Discovering the child within helps us release our natural creativity. Laughing produces endorphins, natural chemicals that strengthen the immune system and produce a sense of well-being. Laughter also increases oxygen flow to the brain and causes other positive physiological changes.

12. **Plan; don't worry.** Leading a disorganized life is stressful. Write down what has to be done each day; don't rely on your memory. Take a few minutes the night before to lay out your clothes, pack your lunch, and jot down a list of the next day's priorities. Get up 20 minutes early, so you don't have to rush. Worrying is stressful and depletes your energy. You can have only one thought in your mind at a time, so don't allow self-defeating thoughts to enter. Set aside 20 minutes a day to plan, solve problems, and explore solutions. Get involved in the

Peak Progress 10.3

Applying the Adult Learning Cycle to Create a Healthier Lifestyle

1. **RELATE. Why do I want to learn this?** I know I must reduce my stress, control my eating habits, and exercise and maintain my ideal weight. What areas do I struggle with, and what would I like to improve? Having strong physical energy will boost my mental energy.

2. **OBSERVE. How does this work?** Who do I know that seems to "have it all together"? What behaviors do I want to emulate? What factors or benefits will motivate me to make positive changes about my health behaviors? I'll try developing new habits and using new techniques and strategies and observe how I'm improving.

3. **THINK. What does this mean?** What strategies are working, and where do I continue to struggle? What tools or information would keep me motivated?

4. **DO. What can I do with this?** I will make a commitment to improve my health by eating healthy and exercising. Each day, I'll work on one area. For example, I'll use my time-management skills and find ways to build exercise into my day. I'll practice reducing my stress in many different situations. I'll find practical application and use my new skills in everyday life.

5. **TEACH. Whom can I share this with?** I'll try to find a partner with similar interests and we'll keep each other motivated. I'll share my tips, experiences, and setbacks.

Living a healthy lifestyle is a life-long commitment. You will repeat the cycle many times in order to stay focused and successful.

---

solutions, not the problem. When your time is up, leave the problems until your next scheduled session.

13. **Be assertive.** Stand up for your rights, express your preferences, and acknowledge your feelings. Assertive communication helps you solve problems, rather than build resentment and anger, and increases confidence and control over your life.

14. **Keep a log.** A log can be helpful in gaining insight into the types of situations that are stressful for you and how you respond to them. Write journal entries in this book. Be honest with yourself and record daily events and your reactions. Writing in a journal also helps clarify concerns and decisions and can give you a fresh perspective.

15. **Get professional help.** It is normal to experience grief after a loss or a major transition, and you should allow yourself time to grieve, so that you can experience and release your emotional pain. However, if your sadness, depression, or anger continues despite your best efforts, or if you are suicidal, get professional help. Call a crisis hot line, health center, counseling center on campus or in the community, or mental health department for a list of agencies that can provide help. With a counselor's guidance, you can gain insight into your pattern of reacting to stress and modify your perception and behavior. (See **Peak Progress 10.3** on using the Adult Learning Cycle to create a more healthy balance.)

Teaching Tip
Urge students to use critical thinking:
- To review the symptoms of stress.
- To review the stress in their lives.

Teaching Tip
Emphasize the importance of using the Adult Learning Cycle to create interest and improve skills.

Class Discussion
In small groups, ask students to discuss the stresses in their lives and the strategies for overcoming them.

Peak Performer Profile

Lance Armstrong

Most of us bicycle for fun. For Lance Armstrong, the Olympic world-champion cyclist, it's a job he loves to do. Athletic from an early age, Armstrong grew up in the suburbs of Dallas, Texas, and was competing as a triathlete at age 16. By his senior year in high school in the late 1980s, the U.S. Olympic development team had spotted him as a world-class cyclist, and he was invited to train in Colorado. Many championships and titles followed.

However, in 1996, when Armstrong was only 25, he faced the most difficult trial of his life. Diagnosed with advanced testicular cancer that had spread to his lungs, lymph nodes, abdomen, and brain, he was given about a 50/50 chance of survival. Although shaken, Armstrong was determined to overcome the disease. He underwent surgery, changed his diet, and began months of aggressive chemotherapy. He also focused on the future: "I might have a bald head and not be as fast, but I'll be out there. I'm going to race again." He was pronounced cancer-free a year later.

July 30, 2001, was a landmark day for America's "golden boy of cycling." After pedaling more than 2,000 grueling miles, he crossed the finish line near the Champs Elysées in Paris as winner of the prestigious Tour de France for the third consecutive year. He was the first American to have won three years in a row.

Armstrong's web site notes that October 2, 2001, was the five-year anniversary of his cancer diagnosis and survival. Past this point, doctors begin using the word *cured*. As for the Tour 2002, this peak performer commented, "I'll be back. . . . And I won't be back to finish second." Armstrong did come back, and finished first.

PERFORMANCE THINKING   Lance Armstrong has said, "If I never had cancer, I never would have won the Tour de France." Armstrong views this disease in a positive way. Do you think his attitude affected his recovery? Why?

TAKING CHARGE

In summary, in this chapter, I learned to

- *Be aware and observe.* I envision my body and mind as a whole system and realize that everything is connected. I observe how my body feels, my thoughts, level of stress, negative habits, what I eat and drink, and changes or discomfort in the body.

- *Eat a variety of healthy foods in moderation.* I increase my consumption of fresh fruits and vegetables, eat whole grains, limit animal fat, cut down on sugar and caffeine, and take a multivitamin supplement every day. This helps me maintain my ideal weight, increases my self-esteem, and gives me energy.

- *Exercise regularly.* I participate in an aerobic activity for 30 minutes three times a week. I balance rest and relaxation with active sports, such as bicycling, dancing, or swimming. Being active not only helps me maintain my ideal weight but also gives me energy and increases my sense of well-being.

- *Develop healthy relationships.* Spending time with friends who are supportive and share my interests is a great source of satisfaction, and it helps increase my energy and enjoyment of life. Friendships bring a deep sense of joy and fellowship.

- *Reduce my caffeine consumption.* Too much caffeine can make me anxious, nervous, irritable, and insomnia-prone, and it can become addictive.

- *Use critical thinking to avoid drugs.* Since alcohol is a toxin, heavy drinking can cause brain damage, increase the risk for heart disease, depress the immune system, and cause liver failure. Alcohol and other drugs can cause a loss of memory and intellectual reasoning.

- *Get help for addictions.* I recognize the signs of addiction to food, gambling, and alcohol and other drugs and when to seek help. I know that there are resources on campus and in the community that can help me or someone I know who has a drinking or drug problem.

- *Observe my emotional health.* Although I know that life has its ups and downs, I am aware of times when I don't seem to bounce back after a disappointment or loss. Some of the warning signs of depression are changes in sleep patterns and appetite, the use of drugs, and feelings of anxiety, anger, isolation, and disinterest. Severe depression and suicidal tendencies occur when feelings are extreme.

- *Protect my body.* I protect myself from illness, sexually transmitted diseases, unwanted pregnancies, and rape. I am knowledgeable, aware, and proactive. I make certain that I visit the health center, use safety precautions, and learn self-defense techniques.

- *Reduce stress.* I have developed strategies for reducing stress, including exercising, doing deep breathing, disputing negative thoughts and beliefs, developing a sense of humor, rehearsing feared events, and creating balance in my life.

Performance Strategies

Following are the top 10 tips for achieving a healthy lifestyle:

◆ Be aware of your body, your emotions, and the reasons you eat. Is it because you're hungry or because you're bored, anxious, lonely, or stressed?

◆ Maintain your ideal weight.

◆ Focus on healthy eating, not dieting. (Fill up on vegetables, fruits, whole grains, and a balanced diet.)

◆ Exercise for energy and health.

◆ Get enough rest and renewing time.

◆ Develop supportive and healthy relationships.

◆ Create balance in your life.

◆ Avoid harmful substances, such as cigarettes and other drugs.

◆ Protect yourself from sexually transmitted diseases and pregnancy.

◆ Get help immediately for physical and mental distress.

Review Questions

1. What are five strategies for good health management?

2. What are some of the benefits of aerobic exercise?

3. Cite two statistics or facts involving alcohol.

4. How does smoking marijuana compare with smoking tobacco?

5. Why is it important to manage your stress?

REVISUALIZATION

Revisit the Visualization box on the first page of this chapter and your journal entry in **Worksheet 10.1.** Now, describe a situation in which you suffered from lack of sleep, were not eating healthy, or were stressed out. Apply the ABCDE method to work through the scenario and achieve a positive outcome—for example,

A = Actual event: "I was doing great, exercising three times a week at the gym. I lost a few pounds and suddenly had more energy. After the gym closed for two weeks for maintenance, I haven't been able to get motivated to get back to my routine. Each week, I say I'll start on Monday, but the Mondays come and go."

B = Beliefs: "I've lost my momentum and motivation."

C = Consequences: "I don't think I'll ever get back on track, and I'm afraid I'm going to gain those pounds right back."

D = Dispute: "I successfully incorporated exercise into my schedule once already, and I know I can do it again. I just have to make an appointment with myself and follow through. Once I'm back in the groove, I know I can stick with it."

E = Energized: "I'm motivated to get back on track with my exercise routine because I know it boosts my energy levels, benefits my overall health, and makes me feel more confident when I look in the mirror. This is a commitment to myself that I know I can and will keep."

INCREASING YOUR ENERGY LEVEL

In the Classroom

Danny Mendez is a business major in marketing, works part-time at a sporting goods store, is president of his fraternity, and is on the crew team. This demanding schedule is manageable because Danny's energy is high. However, around midterm he feels overwhelmed with stress. He needs to find ways to increase his energy level, maintain his good health, and manage his stress.

1. What strategies would you suggest to Danny that would help reduce his stress?

   _____

   _____

2. What can you suggest to Danny to increase his energy level?

   _____

   _____

In the Workplace

Danny is now a marketing manager for a large advertising agency. He often travels to meet with current and prospective clients. When Danny returns, he finds work piled on his desk—advertising campaign issues, personnel problems, and production delays. Danny's energy has always been high, but lately he eats too much fast food, has started smoking again, and rarely exercises anymore. He keeps saying that he'll get back on track when his stress is reduced.

3. What habits should Danny adopt to reduce his stress and fatigue?

   _____

   _____

4. What strategies in this chapter can help him increase his energy?

   _____

   _____

CHAPTER 10 ▲ REVIEW AND APPLICATIONS

APPLYING THE ABCDE METHOD OF SELF-MANAGEMENT

In the Visualization box on page 10–1, you were asked to describe a time when you had lots of energy, felt healthy and rested, and were in control of your weight. What factors helped you be calm, confident, and healthy?

_____

_____

_____

Describe a situation in which you suffered from lack of sleep, were not eating healthy, or were stressed out. Apply the ABCDE method to work through the scenario and achieve a positive outcome.

A = Actual event:

B = Beliefs:

C = Consequences:

D = Dispute:

E = Energized:

Use visualization to see yourself healthy and in charge of your physical, mental, and emotional life. You feel confident about yourself because you have learned to invest time in exercising, eating healthy, and being rested.

STRESS PERFORMANCE TEST

Read the following statements. Now, think back over the last few months. Have you experienced stress as described in the statements? If so, put a checkmark in the column that best indicates the amount of stress you have experienced.

	Severe (3)	Moderate (2)	Little (1)	None (0)
1. No time for goals	_____	_____	_____	_____
2. Lack of money	_____	_____	_____	_____
3. Uncomfortable living and study areas	_____	_____	_____	_____
4. Long working hours	_____	_____	_____	_____
5. Boring, uninteresting job	_____	_____	_____	_____
6. Conflict with roommate, family, etc.	_____	_____	_____	_____
7. Conflict with instructors	_____	_____	_____	_____
8. Too many responsibilities	_____	_____	_____	_____
9. Deadline pressures	_____	_____	_____	_____
10. Boring classes	_____	_____	_____	_____
11. Too many changes in life	_____	_____	_____	_____
12. Lack of motivation	_____	_____	_____	_____
13. Difficulty finding housing	_____	_____	_____	_____
14. Little emotional support from family	_____	_____	_____	_____

—continued

CHAPTER 10 ◢ REVIEW AND APPLICATIONS

	Severe (3)	Moderate (2)	Little (1)	None (0)
15. Poor grades	_____	_____	_____	_____
16. Parents/partners have set standards and expectations that are too high	_____	_____	_____	_____
17. Unclear on goals	_____	_____	_____	_____
18. Too many interruptions	_____	_____	_____	_____
19. Health problems	_____	_____	_____	_____
20. Dependency on alcohol, other drugs	_____	_____	_____	_____
21. Too much socializing	_____	_____	_____	_____
22. Lack of career/life goals	_____	_____	_____	_____
23. Speaking/test-taking anxiety	_____	_____	_____	_____
24. Lack of relationships, friends	_____	_____	_____	_____
25. Lack of self-esteem	_____	_____	_____	_____
Subtotals	_____	_____	_____	_____

Add your 1s, 2s, and 3s to give yourself a total score:

Totals   _____ + _____ + _____ = _____

Total Score

Scores:

24–36 Peak Performer (You have learned how to function effectively under stress.)

37–48 Persistent Coper (You cope and handle stress in most situations, but you have some difficulty coping and feel overwhelmed sometimes.)

49–60 Stress Walker (You have frequent feelings of being overwhelmed and exhausted, and they affect your performance.)

60+ Burnout Disaster (You need help coping; stress is taking its toll on your health and emotions and you are facing burnout.)

BETTER HEALTH

On the following lines, list four ways you can improve your health.

1. _____

_____

_____

_____

_____

2. _____

_____

_____

_____

_____

3. _____

_____

_____

_____

_____

4. _____

_____

_____

_____

_____

CHAPTER 10 ▲ REVIEW AND APPLICATIONS

INVENTORY OF INTERESTS

Developing outside interests can be a helpful way to reduce stress in your life. Interests are activities that you enjoy and pique your curiosity. Besides helping you reduce your stress level, they may help you determine your life's work and career path. For example, an interest in the outdoors may lead to a major in natural resources, which could lead to a career as a park ranger. A passion for working with cars may lead to a certificate in auto mechanics and thus to your own auto repair shop.

    Fill in the following inventory and add this page to your Career Development Portfolio.

1. My interests are

_____

_____

_____

_____

2. Answer the following questions:
    a. What magazines do I like to read?

    _____

    _____

    _____

    _____

    b. What kinds of books do I like to read?

    _____

    _____

    _____

    _____

    c. When I have free time, what do I like to do? (Check the areas that interest you.)

Reading	_____	Working with people	_____
Writing	_____	Working with computers	_____
Sports	_____	Building or remodeling	_____
Outdoor activities	_____	Creating artwork	_____
Traveling	_____	Public speaking	_____

Other activities:

_____

_____

_____

_____

Building Healthy and Diverse Relationships

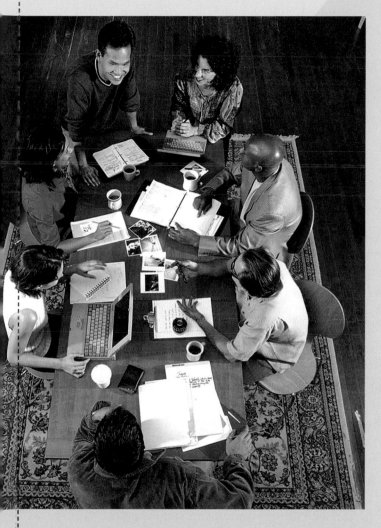

Chapter Objectives

In this chapter, you will learn

▲ Strategies for communicating and building rapport

▲ To understand and appreciate college and workplace diversity

▲ Assertive communication

▲ How to build rapport with instructors and advisors

▲ How to accept criticism

▲ How to overcome shyness

VISUALIZATION

"I never realized I would interact with so many new people at college. It's both exciting and frightening. I've been so focused on planning my coursework that I wasn't prepared to think beyond my own little world."

Attending college gives you the opportunity to interact with a wide variety of people with different backgrounds, opinions, and interests. This also forces you to become a better communicator and an effective participant in social and group settings. In this chapter, you will learn how to create

healthy relationships, work effectively in a team, become more assertive, and handle criticism. You will see yourself communicating with others in a clear, concise, confident, and direct manner.

JOURNAL ENTRY In Worksheet 11.1 on page 11–30, describe a difficult or confrontational situation in which you felt comfortable communicating your needs and ideas in an assertive, direct, and calm manner. What factors helped you be confident and respectful?

No one exists in a vacuum. You can learn to read more efficiently, write more fluid prose, take tests well, or memorize anything you want, but success will elude you if you don't have the ability to communicate and build rapport with different people. People spend nearly 70 percent of their waking hours communicating, listening, speaking, writing, and reading. Communication skills and the ability to build rapport and foster diverse relationships are key strengths for school and job success. SCANS lists interpersonal relationships, communication, an understanding of diversity, and team skills as important for job success.

This chapter will discuss ways to improve your ability to understand and relate to people. Developing these skills is one of the most important challenges you will face in your personal, school, and work lives.

The Importance of Communication

Communication is the giving and receiving of ideas, feelings, and information. Note the word *receiving*. Some people are good at speaking but are not effective listeners. Poor listening is one of the biggest barriers to effective communication. Miscommunication wastes billions of dollars in business and damages relationships.

Think of what you really want when you communicate with someone else. Do you want people to really listen to you, understand your feelings, and relate to your message? Building rapport is more than just giving and receiving information. It is the ability to find common ground with another person based on respect, empathy, and trust. Common ground is the intent to focus on similarities and core values that are diverse or cross-cultural.

Some people seem to have a knack for building rapport and making others feel comfortable and accepted. They are highly sensitive to nonverbal cues and the responses that they elicit from other people. They have developed empathy and make you feel valued. They are comfortable with themselves and comfortable communicating with people from different cultures and backgrounds. They can put themselves aside and focus on the other person with genuine interest and appreciation. You can learn this skill, too. People will want to be near you because you will make them feel good about themselves, give them a sense of importance, and create a climate in which they feel comfortable. People who are good at building rapport not only look for similarities in others but also appreciate and value differences.

Strategies for Building Rapport

Let's look at a few strategies for building rapport.

1. **Assess and clarify intention.** The first step in building rapport is to assess your intention. Your intention sets the tone and direction and often determines the results. If your goal is to build understanding, acceptance, and rapport, it will usually be reflected in your tone, body language, and style. If you are judgmental, however, this message will come through, regardless of your choice of words. For example, let's say that your arms are crossed and you frown, lean back in your chair, have indirect eye contact, sigh, and shake you head. You indicate that you are willing to listen, but your nonverbal body language is shouting, "I don't like you, and I don't want to listen." Choose to listen for understanding and to find common ground.

2. **Be an active listener.** Here are a few tips:
   - *Listen; don't talk.* Don't change the subject unless the speaker is finished. Be patient and don't interrupt others. Listen for feelings and the undertones and meanings of what people are really saying. You can accomplish this by being attuned to nonverbal cues—posture, tone of voice, eye contact, body movements, and facial expressions.
   - *Put the speaker at ease.* Listeners who want to build rapport put the talker at ease by creating a supportive and open climate. Being warm and friendly, showing interest, and smiling all help put others at ease.
   - *Withhold criticism.* Criticizing puts people on the defensive and blocks communication. Arguing almost never changes someone's mind, and it may widen the communication gap.
   - *Paraphrase.* Restating what the speaker has said shows that you are really interested in understanding, not just in getting your point across. Encourage others to talk and explain. Ask questions and seek to understand another person's point of view.
   - *Know when you cannot listen.* If you know you do not have time to pay close attention to the speaker, say so. For example, if you have a lot of studying to do and your roommate wants to talk about a date, you may want to say in a kind and respectful tone. "I'd like to know more about your date, but I have to read this chapter. Can we have a cup of tea in an hour and talk about it?" You also may want to delay talking and listening if you are angry, tired, or stressed. Just make certain you respond in a respectful tone of voice.

3. **Look attentive, alert, and interested.** Look at the speaker and appear interested. When your eyes wander, you appear uninterested or bored. You can create an attentive and supportive climate by communicating openness with facial expressions, relaxed and uncrossed arms, and a posture of leaning slightly toward the person. Try not to sit behind a desk but closer to the other person. Some experts say that 70 percent of what is communicated is done through nonverbal communication, or body language. If you intend to build rapport, your body language must be warm and open and convey interest and acceptance.

4. **Be respectful.** Many organizations are implementing employee-training programs that emphasize the importance of business etiquette—respect and consideration of the feelings and needs of others. Good manners and respect

Teaching Tip
Ask students to think of a problem in their personal lives. Did the problem involve communication?

Words to Succeed

"Minds are like parachutes. They only function when they are open."

—SIR JAMES DEWAR
chemist and physicist

Hands-On Application
Have one person play a roommate who is angry because of frequent overnight guests. Have students paraphrase what is said.

are the foundation of all healthy relationships. People need to feel they are getting the consideration and appreciation that they deserve, whether it is in the classroom, on the job, or at home. Therefore, if you want to build rapport with others, be respectful.

5. **Use warmth and humor.** You can also build rapport by knowing how to use humor. Avoid sarcasm and jokes at the expense of another person's feelings. Don't take yourself too seriously. Humor puts people at ease. A joke or easy laughter can dissipate tension. Humor, wit, and a sincere smile create warmth and understanding and can open the door to further effective communication.

6. **Relate to a person's team style.** There are many different types of people in this world, who learn, think, and relate differently. Knowing this can help you interact and work more effectively with diverse people and teams. For example, if your boss has an analyzer type of personality, you will want to make certain that your report is based on facts and that your presentation is clear, concise, and correct.

7. **Relate to a person's learning style.** You can build rapport with your instructors, coworkers, and supervisors by relating to their personality, learning, and teaching styles. For example, perhaps your instructor prefers the visual mode. She writes on the board, shows overheads and films, and uses phrases such as "Do you see what I'm saying?" For an instructor who prefers a visual mode, enhance your visual presentation. For example, turn in an especially attractive visual paper by taking note of neatness and spelling and using pictures, diagrams, and drawings whenever appropriate. Try to maintain eye contact while this instructor is lecturing and return visual clues, such as nods, smiles, and other reassurances.

Understanding Diversity

Colleges and workplaces are becoming more and more diverse. Diversity includes factors such as gender, race, age, ethnicity, physical ability, social and economic background, and religion. College is an excellent place to get to know, understand, and value other cultures.

More and more people travel to different countries for business or personal reasons, and they encounter varied cultures and customs. Coupled with television, newspapers, computers, the Internet, telephones, and fax machines, the opportunities to link nations and interact with many cultures are on the rise. Statistics provided by the Bureau of Labor projects that the workforce of the twenty-first century will include more women, minorities, and part-time workers. These diverse people will bring a different and broader worldview to schools, society, and organizations. As a result of this cultural explosion, many organizations offer diversity awareness training to help employees relate comfortably and appreciate diversity. These programs provide opportunities for employees to develop and strengthen critical thinking skills and reduce stereotypical thinking and prejudice.

As a contributing member of society and the work-force, it is essential that you use critical thinking to assess your assumptions, judgments, and views about people who are different from you. Building cultural sensitivity will be the foundation for building common ground with diverse groups. (See **Figure 11.1.**)

Communication Strategies

Here are some strategies you may wish to use when developing acceptable communication with diverse groups. (See **Peak Progress 11.1** on page 11–6 on how to apply the Adult Learning Cycle to make best use of your strategies.)

1. **Be aware of your feelings.** If you have a negative attitude or reaction to a group or person, examine

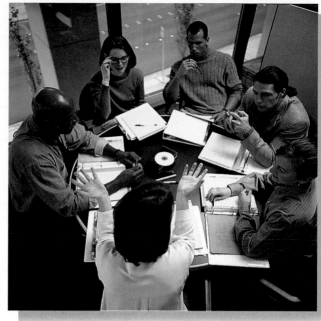

Working Together
The composition of the workforce will continue to change and diversify in the twenty-first century. To be effective and get along with coworkers, people will need to deal with any prejudices they've learned. *What can companies do to help employees understand and appreciate diversity?*

Use
TM 11.2 Cultural
Awareness Pyramid

Figure 11.1   Cultural Awareness Pyramid

PEAK AWARENESS

Acts on commitment
to eliminate oppression.
Seeks to include full participation of
diverse cultural groups in decision making.

CULTURALLY SENSITIVE AND RESPECTFUL

Respects people from diverse cultural and social backgrounds.
Seeks out contacts with people from diverse backgrounds.
Encourages people to value and respect their cultural identity.

CULTURALLY AWARE

Attempts to understand and increase awareness.
Is aware that experiences differ for people based on their culture.

CULTURALLY IN DENIAL

Believes there is no problem. Everyone should be the same.

Cultural Awareness Pyramid   This diagram summarizes four different levels of cultural awareness. *Why is the ability to be sensitive to diversity a valuable asset in the workplace?*

Class Discussion

Ask students:

1. What other groups create certain images? Sample answers: *farmer's daughter, lawyer, environmentalist.*

2. What stereotypes exist for different geographic areas? Sample answers: *California, the South, Alaska, Hawaii.*

3. A friend tells you, "I'm dating someone from California. He loves to surf, and his college major is outdoor recreation." What image would you draw from this description?

Hands-On Application

Have students write their negative reactions to people. Stress that everyone has stereotypes, fears, and prejudices. Tell students that the first step toward change is to admit that certain people annoy them. Ask if this annoyance is based on a stereotype or a personal characteristic.

Peak Progress 11.1

Applying the Adult Learning Cycle to Become a Better Communicator

1. **RELATE. Why do I want to learn this?** Being able to communicate effectively is the most important skill I can acquire, practice, and perfect. It's not only important in my personal relationships, but it's also essential to my success in school and career. By being more direct and assertive, I avoid negative feelings of resentment or thoughts that I'm being taken advantage of. I can succinctly express my views, wants, and impressions, as well as my innovative ideas and decisions. I want to feel confident that I can handle difficult situations and avoid overreaching and creating unnecessary conflict.

2. **OBSERVE. How does this work?** I've always admired people who are assertive and confident when expressing themselves and their views. What makes them successful? What are specific techniques or mannerisms they use when communicating with others? I'll also observe people who are passive or aggressive and learn from their mistakes. How do others react or respond? I'll try using new techniques and strategies for dealing with fear, resentment, and upset feelings.

3. **THINK. What does this mean?** What seems to work for me? Do I feel more confident and comfortable interacting with others? Do I believe I'm presenting my ideas so that others clearly understand my point of view? Am I more respectful of others' opinions and feelings? Have my personal and professional relationships improved? I'll continue to avoid negative self-talk and focus on a positive attitude and outlook.

4. **DO. What can I do with this?** I will practice being more assertive. I will make a commitment to be direct, kind, and respectful. Each day I'll work on one area. For example, when my roommate plays her music too loudly, I'll express my needs in an assertive and respectful manner.

5. **TEACH. Whom can I share this with?** I'll ask others if they have ever felt misunderstood and what they have changed to express themselves more effectively. I'll share my experiences and the strategies that have worked for me. I'll volunteer to help other students in my study group.

Now, return to Stage 1 and continue to monitor your progress and think of new ways to enhance your communication skills.

---

it and see where it is coming from. (See **Figure 11.2.**) Be aware of how you talk to yourself about other people. Be willing to admit your own prejudices. This is the first step toward change.

2. **See the value in diversity.** We are a rich nation because of different races and cultures. Knowledge and understanding can break through barriers. The value of education is the appreciation of different views and the tools for building understanding and tolerance. Learn to think instead of react. By sharing different viewpoints, you can learn new and interesting ways of seeing situations and approaching problems. Shift your thinking about diversity by reviewing **Peak Progress 11.2.** Are you accepting of others and appreciate our

Figure 11.2   Understanding the Meaning

Attitudes have three parts: what you think, feel, and do. These definitions make up parts of a prejudiced attitude:

Stereotype	Prejudice	Discrimination
A mental or emotional picture held in common by members of a group that represents an oversimplified belief, opinion, or judgment about members of another group	An unjustified negative feeling directed at a person or group based on preconceived opinions, judgments, and stereotypes	An unjustified negative behavior toward a person or group based on preconceived opinions, judgments, and stereotypes

Understanding the Meaning   Having a better understanding of prejudice can help reduce its effect. *Have you ever felt prejudice? How have you dealt with that feeling?*

Class Discussion
How does critical thinking relate to stereotypes, prejudice, and discrimination? Ask students how they can use critical thinking to assess their assumptions about people.

Peak Progress   11.2

Thinking About Diversity

If you could shrink the earth's population to a village of precisely 100 females and males—but maintain the existing demographic ratios—the group would look like this:

- 57 Asians
- 21 Europeans
- 14 Western Hemisphere dwellers (North and South Americans)
- 8 Africans
- 70 nonwhites
- 30 whites
- 70 non-Christians
- 30 Christians
- 70 unable to read
- 50 malnourished
- 80 living in substandard housing
- 1 university graduate
- Fifty percent of the wealth worldwide would be in the hands of 6 people—all citizens of the United States.

diversity? Complete **Personal Performance Notebook 11.1** on page 11–8 to determine your attitudes.

3. **Treat people as individuals.** It is important to look beyond preconceived notions and see people as individuals and not members of a particular group. Try to see people as unique and valued. Use critical thinking to assess how you

Appreciating Diversity

A. Read the following and write your comments on the lines provided.

1. What is your attitude toward people who are different from you in gender, race, sexual orientation, or culture?

   _____

2. Is your attitude one of acceptance or exclusion?

   _____

3. Would you speak up if someone's gender, cultural, racial, sexual, or ethnic background were discussed in a stereotypical manner?

   _____

4. Do you consider yourself to be a sensitive and respectful person?

   _____

5. How do you show a sensitive and respectful attitude?

   _____

B. Look at the reasons and excuses some students use for not meeting different people. Write strategies for overcoming these excuses.

1. **Reason:** It's not polite to notice differences.

   Strategy: _____

2. **Reason:** I'm afraid of rejection.

   Strategy: _____

3. **Reason:** People who are different want to stick with their own kind.

   Strategy: _____

4. **Reason:** I feel uncomfortable around people who are different from me.

   Strategy: _____

5. **Reason:** I might say something embarrassing.

   Strategy: _____

6. **Reason:** People who are different from me wouldn't want me in their group.

   Strategy: _____

Teaching Tip
Indicate that multiculturalism is a process of valuing and celebrating the contributions of people from different cultures.

Hands-On Application
Encourage students to participate in events where different groups celebrate their traditions. For example, they can attend a Cinco de Mayo celebration. Have them taste foods, listen to music, and learn a few new facts about different cultures and religions. Encourage students to get to know other people in their classes. Stress that their years in college are opportunities to expand their circle of friends.

Stereotypical Thinking

Do you know someone who views people in a stereotypical way? Can you describe some stereotypical reactions you may have observed or heard concerning people like those in the following list? Write your comments on the lines provided:

1. Welfare recipient _____

2. Asian female _____

3. Truck driver _____

4. Homemaker _____

5. Lawyer _____

6. Farmer _____

or others may view people in stereotypical ways in **Personal Performance Notebook 11.2.**

4. **Treat people with respect.** Treat people with respect and consideration. You can be respectful even if someone's behavior is unacceptable.

5. **Be aware of differences.** It is important to focus on similarities. We are very much alike in our humanness. Don't let differences dominate your interactions. However, don't act as if people were all alike and their experiences were the same. Be aware that values and experiences differ for people based on their culture, religion, and background.

6. **Listen.** Listen and don't talk. Be supportive and don't criticize. Paraphrase, ask questions, and be willing to learn.

7. **Get involved.** Take a cultural diversity course at college or in the community. Visit with people from other religions. Be willing to seek out people from different cultures. Go to lectures, read, and look for opportunities to become acquainted with other cultures.

8. **Take risks.** Don't avoid contact with other cultures because you may be afraid of making a mistake, saying the wrong thing, or inadvertently offending someone. Cultivate friendships with people from different cultures and races. Share your own culture's traditional foods and customs with others. Knowledge of other cultures can help you appreciate your own roots. When you take a risk, you become more aware of how other people relate to you, and you will become more comfortable dealing with diversity. The only way you can bridge the gaps between cultures is to risk getting involved.

9. **Apologize when you make a mistake.** Mistakes happen, even with the best intentions. Ask for clarification and apologize. However, be prepared at times for strong feelings or misunderstandings that may result from past experiences

Words to Succeed

"Civil rights were about respect. Gender equality was about respect. The environment is about respect. . . . Let's start when kids are young—teaching them the habits of being citizens of the world."

—PETER YARROW
musician

with racism or sexism. Don't take it personally if someone does not respond as positively as you had hoped. Sometimes bridging the gap requires that you make an extra effort to understand.

10. **Speak out.** It is not enough to be aware that values and experiences differ for people from different cultures; you must act on this knowledge. Stand up and speak out whenever you hear or see discrimination in school or at work. Encourage your school to welcome and celebrate diversity.

11. **Encourage representation.** Encourage active participation by members of diverse cultural and social groups in various clubs, student government, local government, college meetings and boards, community groups and boards, and any decision-making groups.

Cultural and Gender Diversity at Work

Attention to cultural and gender diversity is increasingly important because the workplace has become more diverse. Attitudes and behavior from top management set the tone for the whole company. Many top managers approach the issue by asking themselves, "How can I instruct others to tolerate differences in race, gender, religion, and sexual preference?" Perhaps a better question would be "How can I set an example, create a climate of respect, and encourage people to value differences?" Managers can create an atmosphere of respect and understanding.

There are many seminars and workshops that offer ideas on working successfully with people of different cultures and genders. Firm guidelines need to be established and clearly communicated about the consequences of discrimination.

Discrimination is illegal and can be grounds for court action. Organizations have a responsibility and an obligation to make certain that all employees know what behaviors are illegal and inappropriate and the consequences for such behavior. Top managers are responsible for establishing procedures and need to offer a safe atmosphere for complaints. In short, companies must provide education, create guidelines and procedures, and set a tone of serious concern and respect toward all differences in the workplace. Think about what you learned about personality and team styles in Chapter 1. Diversity can have many positive effects on team effectiveness. Consider your study or work teams as you complete **Peak Progress 11.3.**

Sexual Harassment at School and at Work

Sexual harassment is behavior that is unwelcome, unwanted, and degrading. It can be destructive to the school and work climate. It is also costly. Employee turnover, loss of productivity, expensive lawsuits, and a negative work environment are just some of the consequences of sexual harassment.

Class Discussion

Ask students:

1. What is meant by professional behavior?

2. List these qualities on the board and make certain the list includes considerate behavior.

3. Have they known people who look good on paper but lacked courtesy, composure, etiquette, or professionalism?

4. How important are humor and warmth in building rapport? Some employers have expressed concern about using humor because it might offend.

5. Is society becoming too politically correct?

6. What would they suggest to retain a fun environment while still showing sensitivity?

Teaching Tip
Bring to class your school's policy about sexual harassment. Ask students if they know the sexual harassment policy for their places of employment, if they work.

Team Effectiveness

Most organizations function with teams. Even the most educated and skillful people will falter if they can't work effectively and cooperatively with one another. When you need to review the effectiveness of a work team, a study team, or any other team, use the following list of skills and score each item from 1 to 10 (10 = most effective).

Team Function

- Commitment to tasks _____
- Oral communication skills _____
- Listening skills _____
- Writing skills _____
- Conflict resolution _____
- Decision-making skills _____
- Creative problem solving _____
- Openness to brainstorming and new ideas _____
- Team spirit and cohesiveness _____
- Encouragement of critical thinking _____
- Interest in quality decisions _____
- Professionalism _____
- Team integrity and concern for ethics _____
- Starting and ending meetings on time _____

When a score is totaled, the team can discuss answers to these questions:

1. How can this team be more effective?

_____

_____

_____

2. What can individual members do to strengthen the team?

_____

_____

_____

Organizations are responsible for establishing accepted guidelines. Most campuses and companies employ someone you can talk to if you have a complaint or concern. Organizations that have more than 25 employees are legally required to have written procedures concerning sexual harassment and should practice the following procedures.

◆ Define sexual harassment and the disciplinary actions that may result because of inappropriate behavior.

◆ Make certain that all employees are informed of the policy and are aware of the procedures for filing a complaint.

Hands-On Application
Role-playing assertiveness: Have students write a script with assertive language and role-play a current, real-life situation. The other group members should give passive and aggressive responses to the same situation. Each person should have an opportunity to play a situation of his or her own choosing.

Teaching Tip
Encourage students to visit their advisors several times a quarter or semester, to get to know them as people, and to work together as a team.

◆ Designate a person to handle confidential complaints and concerns.

◆ Ensure that common work practices are in compliance with the policy.

Assertive Communication

You may not always feel that you have the right to speak up for what you need, particularly in new situations where you see yourself as powerless and dependent. Assertive communication should help in these situations. Assertive communication is expressing yourself in a direct, above-board, and civil manner. Only you can take responsibility for clarifying expectations, expressing your needs, and making your own decisions. You might find yourself acting passively in some situations, aggressively in others, and assertively in still others. In most situations, however, strive to communicate in an assertive, direct, clear, and respectful manner.

◆ Passive people rarely express feelings, opinions, or desires. They have little self-confidence and low self-esteem, have difficulty accepting compliments, and often compare themselves unfavorably with others. Sometimes they feel that others take advantage of them, which creates resentment.

◆ Aggressive people are often sarcastic, critical, and controlling. They want to win at any cost and sometimes blame others for making them angry. They sometimes resort to insults and criticisms, which breaks down communication and harms relationships.

◆ Passive-aggressive people appear to be passive but act aggressively. For example, a passive-aggressive student will not respond in class when asked if there are any questions about an assignment but will then go to the dean to complain. A passive-aggressive roommate will leave nasty notes or complain to others rather than confront a roommate directly.

◆ Assertive people state their views and needs directly; use confident body language; and speak in a clear, strong voice. They take responsibility for their actions. Assertive people respect themselves and others. Practice developing assertive responses in **Personal Performance Notebook 11.3.**

Communicating with Instructors and Advisors

Develop professional relationships with your instructors and advisors just as you would with your supervisor at work. Try a few of these tips to increase rapport:

1. **Clarify expectations.** Make certain you understand the objectives and expectations of your instructors and advisors. Most instructors will give you extra help and feedback if you take the initiative. For instance, before a paper is due, hand in a draft and say, "I want to make sure I am covering the important

Assertive Communication Role-Playing

Read the following situations. Then, develop an assertive response for each one.

1. **Situation:** You receive a *B* on your test, and you think you deserve an *A*. What would you say to your instructor?

   Assertive response: _____

2. **Situation:** A friend asks you to read her term paper. She tells you it is the best paper that she has ever written. However, you find several glaring errors.

   Assertive response: _____

3. **Situation:** Your roommate asks to borrow your new car. You don't want to lend it.

   Assertive response: _____

4. **Situation:** An acquaintance makes sexual advances. You are not interested.

   Assertive response: _____

5. **Situation:** You go to a party and your date pressures you to drink.

   Assertive response: _____

6. **Situation:** Your roommate's friend has moved in and doesn't pay rent.

   Assertive response: _____

7. **Situation:** Your sister borrowed your favorite sweater and stained it.

   Assertive response: _____

8. **Situation:** A friend lights up a cigarette, and you are allergic to smoke.

   Assertive response: _____

9. **Situation:** You want your roommate or spouse to help you keep the apartment clean.

   Assertive response: _____

10. **Situation:** Your mother wants you to come home for the weekend, but you have to study for a major test.

    Assertive response: _____

Hands-On Application

Role-playing: Tell students that a student has been given a B on a paper and feels that she or he should have been given an A. Students can create any situation that they would like to role-play. Have students discuss the situations and scripts in their small groups.

Hands-On Application
Have students:
1. Make an appointment to meet with at least two of their instructors during office hours.
2. Find out what their instructor's interests are, if they are working on a new project, and what they like about teaching.

points in this paper. Am I on the right track? What reference sources would you like me to use? What can I add to make this an *A* paper?"

2. **Clarify concerns.** If you don't understand or you disagree with a grade you have received on a test or paper, ask for an appointment with the instructor. Approach the situation with a supportive attitude: "I like this course and want to do well in it. I don't know why I got a *C* on this paper, because I thought I had met the objectives. Could you show me exactly what points you think should be changed? Could I make these corrections for a higher grade?" Make certain you are respectful and appreciative of your instructor's time and help.

3. **Adapt to your instructor's teaching style.** Approach each class with a positive attitude and don't expect that all instructors will teach according to your learning style.

4. **Be open to learn.** Attend every class with an inquisitive and open mind. Some instructors may be less interested, but you owe it to yourself to be as supportive as possible. If you are a returning student, you may find that the instructor is younger than you are and may lack life experiences. Be open to learn and value the training, education, and knowledge that the instructor brings to class. The same rule applies in the workplace, too. Be supportive and open to learning, and consider yourself on the same team.

5. **Take responsibility for your own learning.** Don't expect your instructor to feed you information. Take an active role in each class. You are ultimately responsible for your own learning and your own career. You may be tempted to cut classes when you don't like your instructor, but you will miss valuable class discussions, question-and-answer sessions, explanations, reviews of concepts, expectations about tests, contact with students, and structure to help you stay focused. Furthermore, you miss the opportunity to see your instructor improve because your initial impression may be false. Students have reported that, once they gave the instructor a chance and worked hard, their attitudes changed. In fact, in some instances, this instructor became their favorite, and they excelled in the class.

6. **Take an interest in your instructors.** Visit them during office hours to discuss your work, goals, grades, and future coursework. When it is appropriate, ask about your instructor's academic background as a guide for yours. Ask about degrees, colleges attended, work experience, and what projects they are working on for professional growth. A large part of building rapport is showing genuine interest, appreciation, and respect.

7. **Ask for a letter of reference.** If you have built a rapport with your instructor or advisor, ask for a letter of recommendation soon after the class is over. Your instructor and advisor can help you in school and in your career.

Accepting Criticism and Overcoming Conflict

Being reminded that you aren't perfect is never easy or pleasant. However, try to listen with an open mind when your instructor, boss, coworker, roommate, or spouse or other students point out mistakes, mention concerns, or make suggestions. Learning to accept and grow from feedback is key to job success. Start with the attitude that the critic has good intentions and goodwill. Also, admit that you have shortcomings.

Conflict usually occurs when people have different needs, opinions, and expectations. One of the best ways to resolve conflict is by actively listening to the other person's concerns and criticism. Conflict can be positive if it brings problems to the surface and encourages new ideas and approaches. Use your observation and critical thinking skills to complete **Personal Performance Notebook 11.4** and **11.5** on pages 11–16 to 11–17 about conflict resolution.

Here are 10 more tips on how to receive criticism and overcome conflicts:

1. **Stay calm.** Don't lose your temper. Take time to compose a response. Ask him or her to calm down: "I can see that you are upset, and I really want to know what your concerns are. Please talk more slowly." It is important to listen to the message without overreacting or becoming defensive.

2. **Establish an open environment.** It helps if you can create an open dialogue that invites feedback. People need to feel safe when giving feedback or criticism. Let people know that you like them and that you will not get angry if they give you negative feedback or suggestions. For example, get to know your instructors and bosses. Don't wait for formalized feedback in the form of grades; ask the instructors how you are doing in class, on quizzes, on papers, and so on. Keep copies or records of your quizzes and papers and review them with your instructors. Just as a hiker needs a compass to check direction, check your own direction at times. Open communication keeps issues from reaching a boiling point.

3. **Be open to nonverbal cues.** Sometimes people have difficulty expressing criticism and may express nonverbal criticism. If the person is aloof, angry, or sad, you might ask if you did something to offend him or her. If he or she is sarcastic, perhaps there is underlying hostility. If appropriate, you can say something like "You have been very quiet today. Is there something that I did to offend you?"

4. **Listen.** Listening is key. Don't interrupt or start your defense. Really concentrate on the other person's perceptions, feelings, and expectations. Listen for understanding and stay calm and detached.

5. **Don't justify.** Practice saying, "Thank you. I appreciate your viewpoint and your courage in telling me what is bothering you." It's fine if you need to explain a situation, but don't make excuses for your behavior. If the criticism is true, change your behavior. If not, then continue without arguing or becoming sarcastic. Criticism is feedback about how another person views your behavior. It is not necessarily reality but an interpretation. Relax and put it in perspective. Someone is reacting to a certain behavior at a specific time, not to your whole personality or the way you really are at all times. You might try being more detached and observing your behavior with more awareness, or ask others if it is offensive.

6. **Ask for clarification.** If you are unclear, ask for specific details, the time of the incident, and clarification: "Can you give a specific incident or time

Teaching Tip
Stress that it is important to listen to body language and hidden messages.

Observing Conflict

Read the following questions and write your answers on the lines provided.

1. Observe how others handle conflict, compliments, and criticism. Do you notice any ineffective behaviors? If so, list them.

   _____

   _____

2. If you were a consultant in conflict resolution, what are some conflict resolution tips you would give?

   _____

   _____

3. What behaviors do you use under stress that you would like to change?

   _____

   _____

4. What do you intend to do the next time you are in a conflict with someone else?

   _____

   _____

Words to Succeed

"Maturity involves being honest and true to oneself . . . assuming responsibility for one's decisions, having healthy relationships with others and developing one's own true gifts."

—MARY PIPHER
psychologist

when you think that I was rude?" Keep comments in perspective, and ask for clarification. The key is to understand the issue at hand.

7. **Focus on the problem.** Don't use detours and attack the person—for example, "You think I'm messy. Look at your room. You're a real pig." Instead, focus on the problem: "If I do the dishes the same evening I cook, will that make you feel more comfortable?" Trust that you can both speak your minds in a calm and nondefensive manner without damaging your relationship.

8. **Ask for specific instructive feedback.** Remember, you have a right to ask for clarification. Make certain you understand—for example, "Professor Walker, you gave me a *B* on this paper. Could you explain what points you consider to be inadequate? How can I improve it?" Summarize the discussion.

9. **Focus on solutions.** Focus on the problem and possible solutions instead of the person. You might say, "I can see that this is a problem for you. What can I do to solve it? What procedures or options can we explore?"

10. **Apologize.** If you think the situation warrants it, apologize. If you feel that criticism is unfair, discuss it openly. You don't want to let resentments smolder and build.

Conflict Resolution

Describe a conflict that you have not yet resolved. Think of resolution techniques that would be helpful. Respond to the following statements.

1. Describe the problem.

_____

_____

2. Express your feelings.

_____

_____

3. State what you want.

_____

_____

4. Predict the consequences.

_____

_____

Overcoming the Barriers to Communication

The number one barrier to effective communication is the assumption that the other person knows what you mean. It is easy to think that what you say is what the other person hears. Communication is a complex system, with so many barriers to overcome that it is a wonder anyone ever really communicates. Other barriers include

◆ Faulty perception
◆ Poor listening skills
◆ Misunderstandings
◆ The need to be right
◆ Cultural, religious, social, and gender differences

Communication is the lifeblood of personal relationships and the foundation of effective team and work groups. Learning how to work effectively with your study team, advisors, instructors, roommates, coworkers, and supervisors will help you be

Class Discussion
Ask students: What are the barriers to effective communication? Have students list strategies for overcoming these barriers.

Patterns in Relationships

Look at the pattern of some of your relationships. Recall situations that occur again and again. For example, you may have the same problem communicating with instructors or advisors. You may have had conflicts with several roommates, coworkers, or supervisors. Once you see the pattern and consequences of your interactions, you can begin to think and act differently. When you take responsibility for changing your inner world of beliefs and thoughts, your outer world will also change. Write about what seems to be a recurring theme or pattern in your relationships.

_____

_____

_____

_____

_____

_____

_____

_____

_____

_____

_____

_____

_____

Hands-On Application
Have students jot down the names of people who are effective at handling conflicts, building rapport, and communicating. Observe what they say and do and jot down effective strategies.

successful at school, at work, and in personal relationships. Many professional and personal problems involve a failure in communication.

The first step to effective communication is the desire and willingness to understand and build rapport with others. Seek to clarify intentions and be an active listener. Show that you are interested in others and establish common bonds. Paraphrase conversations to assess mutual understanding. Develop healthy relationships based on integrity, respect, trust, and honesty. Look for patterns that seem to occur in your relationships as you complete **Personal Performance Notebook 11.6.**

Overcoming Shyness

Shyness is common. Behavioral experts say it affects thousand of people. Shyness is not a problem unless it interferes with your life. It is perfectly acceptable to enjoy your privacy, be quiet, be modest, prefer a few close friends to many, and even embarrass easily. However, if shyness prevents you from speaking up in class, getting to know your instructors and other students, giving presentations, or making new friends, it is keeping you from fulfilling your potential for success. In school and in the workplace, it is important to ask questions, clarify assignments, and ask for help. The inability to ask for help is one of the biggest drawbacks to being shy. In addition, shy people may not contribute to classroom discussions, ask questions, build rapport with instructors, or offer feedback. They can appear emotionally detached and withdrawn. You can overcome your shyness, built rapport, and be an effective conversationalist by following these strategies:

Teaching Tip
Have students keep a journal of their feelings, focusing on relationships with others. Ask students if they are shy and if it interferes with their lives.

1. **Use positive self-talk.** Reinforce your self-confidence and self-image by using positive talk. Instead of saying, "I'm shy. I can't change," tell yourself, "I am confident, people like me, and I like people. I find it easy and enjoyable to get to know new people. I am accepted, appreciated, and admired."

2. **Use direct and relaxed eye contact.** Many shy people look down or avoid making eye contact. Direct eye contact reinforces your confidence and shows interest and empathy. Look at your instructors and show interest in what they are presenting.

3. **Ask questions.** You don't have to talk a lot to be an effective conversationalist. In fact, you don't want to deliver monologues. Ask questions and give others a chance to talk and to change the subject. Asking open-ended questions shows interest and concern. For example, instead of asking Jennifer if she is in your English class, ask her how she is progressing with the assigned term paper. If you are asking questions of an instructor, be clear and to the point and focus on understanding the concept.

4. **Listen to other points of view.** You don't have to agree with other people's points of view, but you can listen and respond tactfully and thoughtfully. You have something to contribute, and exchanging different views is a great way to learn and grow.

5. **Use humor.** Most people like to laugh. Poking good-natured fun at yourself lightens the conversation, as does a funny joke or story. Just make certain to be sensitive; don't tell off-color or racial jokes or stories. Smiling at others will improve your own outlook.

Building Good Relationships

Problems in relationships can consume a great deal of your time and energy, and they may affect your self-esteem. Because feeling good about yourself is one key to all-around success, it is important to look at friendships and romantic relationships. Here are a few tips to help you build healthy relationships:

Class Discussion
Ask students:
1. Do they know anyone who feels resentful, is often angry, blames others, or has recurring problems that stem from a communication style?
2. How can they be supportive without enabling inappropriate or negative behavior?
3. Do they know anyone who is involved in an unhealthy relationship? What are the factors?

1. **Progress slowly.** A healthy relationship progresses slowly. Take the time to get to know the other person and how he or she feels and reacts to situations. Relationships that move too fast or have intense and instant sexuality as a basis often end quickly. Some people go from casual to intimate in one date. Solid relationships need time to grow and develop through the stages of companionship and friendship. Take the time to know people in many different situations. Develop good acquaintances and solid friendships. Perhaps from one of these friendships a romantic relationship will develop.

2. **Have realistic expectations.** Some people think that having a good romantic relationship will magically improve their lives, even if they make no effort to change their thinking or behavior. If you are a poor student, are unmotivated, are depressed, or lack confidence, you will still have these problems even if you have a great relationship. It is unrealistic to expect a relationship to solve life's problems or transform them; only you can solve your problems. Knowing this, you can put more energy into improving your life than you do in looking for someone else to change it.

3. **Be honest.** A healthy relationship is based on commitment to the truth. You certainly don't want to reveal to a casual acquaintance or a first date everything in your past. At the appropriate time, however, honesty about your feelings, basic values, and major life experiences is the foundation of a healthy relationship. For example, if you are an alcoholic or have been married before, the other person should know that as your relationship progresses.

4. **Be supportive.** A healthy relationship is supportive of the growth and well-being of each partner; an unhealthy relationship is not. No one owns another person, nor does anyone have a right to physically or emotionally harm another. An unhealthy relationship is possessive and controlling. A healthy relationship is mutually supportive.

5. **Have respect.** A healthy relationship is based on respect for the feelings and rights of the other person. An unhealthy relationship is self-centered and disrespectful.

6. **Have trust and be trustworthy.** A healthy relationship works in a relaxed, loving, and comfortable way. When an occasional problem comes up, there is an inherent trust that it will be faced and resolved. If a relationship is obsessive, controlling, and distrustful, it is unhealthy. When problems arise, the focus should be on solving them, not on assigning blame.

7. **Know that change can occur.** It is easy for healthy relationships to change. Emotionally healthy people know that not all relationships will develop into romantic and intimate commitments. Letting go and knowing how to end a relationship are as important as knowing how to form healthy relationships. It is acceptable and normal to say no to an acquaintance who asks you out or to decide that you don't want a romantic relationship or a friendship to continue after a few dates. No one should date, have sex, or stay in a relationship out of guilt, fear, or obligation. It is more difficult to terminate a relationship that has progressed too fast or one in which the expectations for

the relationship are perceived differently. Talk about your expectations and realize that your sense of personal worth does not depend on someone's wanting or not wanting to date you.

8. **Keep the lines of communication open.** Healthy relationships are based on open communication. Trouble occurs in relationships when you think you know how the other person feels or would react to a situation. For example, you may assume that a relationship is intimate, but the other person may regard it as a casual affair. Expectations for the relationship can be vastly different. Make certain that you make your expectations clear.

Communication in a healthy relationship is open enough to discuss even sensitive topics, such as birth control, sexually transmitted diseases, and unplanned pregnancy. Take a moment to reflect on your relationships in **Personal Performance Notebook 11.7** on page 11–22.

Class Discussion
Discuss the best ways to get along with roommates and family members.

Teaching Tip
Stress the importance of clarifying expectations.

GETTING ALONG WITH ROOMMATES AND FAMILY

The following 10 suggestions will help you create rapport and improve communication with your roommates or family members.

1. **Clarify expectations.** List the factors that you feel are important for a roommate on the housing application or in an ad. If you don't want a smoker or pets, be honest about it.

2. **Discuss expectations during the first meeting.** Define what neatness means to both of you. Discuss how both of you feel about overnight guests.

Family Ties
Balancing honesty with courtesy and respect will strengthen your relationships and improve communication. *Besides communication, what other area would you want to improve in your family relationships?*

Healthy Relationships

Read the following statements and questions and respond to them on the lines provided.

1. List the factors that you believe are essential for a healthy relationship.

_____

_____

_____

Hands-On Application
Write the expectations that are most important for getting along with roommates and family.

2. What do you believe contributes to unhealthy relationships?

_____

_____

_____

Teaching Tip
Ask students if their relationships support their goals.

3. Who are your friends?

_____

_____

Hands-On Application
Have students:
1. Write the names of important people in their lives.
2. Write at least one strategy for improving their relationships with these people.
3. Discuss strategies in their small groups.

4. Describe some of your other relationships, such as support groups and study teams.

_____

_____

_____

5. List the ways that your relationships support you and your goals.

_____

_____

_____

6. List the ways that unhealthy relationships may undermine you and your goals.

_____

_____

_____

7. Describe your relationships with your instructors.

_____

_____

_____

3. **Clarify concerns and agree to communicate with each other.** Don't mope or whine about a grievance or leave nasty notes. Communicate honestly and kindly.

4. **Treat your roommate and family members with respect.** Don't give orders or make demands. Communicate openly and calmly. Listen to each other's needs. Treat each other with courtesy and civility. Be especially respectful of your roommate's need to study or sleep. Don't interrupt or make noise.

5. **Don't borrow unless necessary.** A lot of problems result over borrowing money, clothes, jewelry, bikes, cars, and CDs. The best advice is not to borrow. If you must, however, ask permission first and make certain you return the item in good shape or replace it if you lose or damage it. Fill the tank of a borrowed car with gas, for instance. Immediately pay back all money borrowed.

6. **Take responsibility for your life.** It isn't your roommate's responsibility to loan you money or food, clean up after you, entertain or feed your friends, or pay your bills.

7. **Keep your agreements.** Your life will improve greatly if you practice keeping your word and agreements. Agree on chores and do your share. Make a list of chores. You should all feel that you are keeping up a fair share of the load. When you say you will do something, do it. When you agree on a time, be punctual. Try to be flexible, however, so that annoyances don't build.

8. **Accept your roommate's beliefs.** Don't try to reform or change a roommate's beliefs. Listen openly and, when necessary, agree that your viewpoints are different.

9. **Accept your roommate's privacy.** Don't enter each other's bedroom or private space without asking. Don't pry, read personal mail, or eavesdrop on conversations. Don't expect to share activities unless you are invited. Give each other space.

10. **Get to know each other.** Set aside time for occasional shared activities. Cook a meal, go for walks, or go to a movie. Appreciate your roommate and/or family members and try not to focus on little faults.

Key Teaching Concept
The best time to clarify communication is before a commitment is made.

Class Discussion
Ask students, "How important is it to keep your agreement?" Ask students for examples of people agreeing to certain expectations and later trying to change the agreement. Sample answers include: *paying the rent by a certain date, sharing half of the expenses, no overnight guests, cleaning up after themselves, signing up for a certain study time, and so on.*

Class Discussion
Ask students to list other strategies for building healthy relationships.

TECH FOR SUCCESS

- **Relationships and Computers** Computers can help you build better relationships:
  - Keep in touch with family through e-mail.
  - E-mail is a great way to send messages to friends and professional colleagues almost anywhere in the world.
  - Chatrooms allow you to talk with others who share your interests.
  - E-mail your instructors and academic advisor one or more times during the semester. Your e-mail could be just a few lines recapping a conversation, confirming a meeting, or clarifying expectations.

In summary, in this chapter, I learned to:

- *Value and improve communication.* Effective communication, including the ability to build rapport with diverse people, is fundamental for school, work, and life success. It involves both the giving and receiving of ideas, feelings, and information.

- *Build rapport with others.* To build rapport effectively, I must first clarify my intention and use corresponding body language. I must be an active listener, including putting the speaker at ease, containing my criticisms, restating the speaker's point, and declining respectfully if the timing is not good for communicating. I should appear attentive and interested, be respectful and considerate, and use humor when appropriate. I relate to different learning and personality styles, understanding that people process and learn information and see the world in different ways. I look for the best in others and appreciate the strengths of different styles. I focus on people's strengths, not weaknesses. I am flexible and can adapt to different personality types.

- *Appreciate diversity.* Our diversity can be expressed by our race, age, ethnicity, gender, learning and physical abilities, and social, economic, and religious backgrounds. I value different cultures and seek to understand and build rapport with diverse people. By sharing different backgrounds, experiences, values, interests, and viewpoints, I can learn new and interesting ways of seeing situations and solving problems. I look for ways to become acquainted with other cultures and opportunities to work with a variety of people.

- *Recognize sexual harassment.* Sexual harassment is behavior that is unwelcome, unwanted, degrading, and detrimental to school and work.

- *Be assertive.* I express myself in a direct, above-board, and respectful manner. I can express feelings and opinions in a calm, confident, and authentic way that does not offend others. I do not use sarcasm or criticism to express myself. I can say no to inappropriate behavior that is unwelcome and unwanted.

- *Communicate with instructors.* I meet with my instructors often to (1) clarify expectations, (2) get help with homework, (3) consult on drafts of papers or speeches, (4) discuss ways to prepare for tests, (5) get advice about project requirements, (6) discuss grades or assignments, and (7) find additional help for studying and assignments. I attend every class, adapt to my instructor's teaching style, and am positive and open to learn. I take an interest in my instruc-
continued

tor's research, writing, or area of expertise. Since I have built rapport with my instructor, I feel comfortable asking for a letter of reference.

- *Communicate with my advisor.* Spending time with my advisor can help me schedule classes, clarify requirements, procedures, and deadlines; explore travel and internship opportunities; and explore majors and careers. Since I have built a positive relationship with my advisor, I feel comfortable asking for a letter of reference.

- *Accept feedback and criticism.* I know that, to grow and learn, I must be open to feedback and occasional criticisms. I do not take offense when it is offered in the spirit of helpfulness. I listen, stay calm, and ask for clarification and suggestions. My intent is to improve and grow in all areas of my life. If I make mistakes, I apologize and try to make amends.

- *Clarify miscommunications.* I do not assume that I know what the other person thinks or says. I clear up misunderstandings by asking for clarification and paraphrase what I think I heard. I focus on listening and seek to understand rather than to be right. I want to be a better listener and improve my communication with others.

- *Overcome shyness.* It is fine to be quiet, but, when shyness interferes with making friends, speaking in front of groups, working with others, or getting to know my instructors, I must learn to be more confident and outgoing. I use visualization and affirmations to dispute negative self-talk. I realize that shyness is a problem for many people and focus on making others feel comfortable and welcomed. I use direct eye contact, am warm and friendly, ask questions, and listen. I relax, am able to laugh at myself, and use humor when it is appropriate.

- *Develop healthy relationships.* I value friendships and take time to get to know others. My relationships are built on a foundation of honesty, trust, respect, and open communication. I am supportive of my friend's goals and values and I expect them to respect and support mine. I talk about expectations with friends—both casual and romantic.

- *Communicate with roommates and family.* To improve communication, I clarify and discuss expectations concerning guests, smoking, neatness, noise, borrowing, food, bills, privacy, and other issues that could cause problems. We agree to talk and get to know each other but also to respect each other's beliefs, views, and space. I take responsibility for my life and do not expect my roommate or family members to be my memory system, alarm clock, driver, or maid.

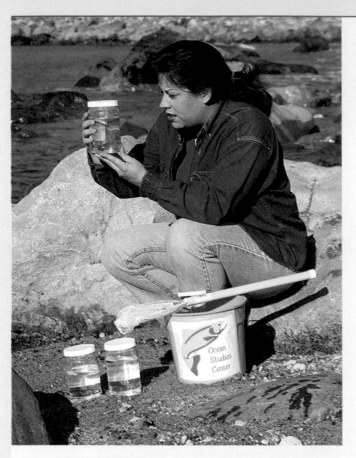

Kathy Brown

MARINE BIOLOGIST

Related Major: Biological Science

Team Building at Work

Kathy Brown is a marine biologist who manages teams doing research on saltwater organisms outside Monterey, California. Currently, she is head of a project to gain more knowledge on the navigation techniques of gray whales during migration.

Although Kathy is a top-rate biologist and researcher with a Ph.D., she can accomplish her project goals only by building teams of researchers who work together effectively. To do this, she carefully considers the personalities and leadership styles of each researcher while forming teams. Kathy provides pre-project training in communication skills, group decision making, diversity, and conflict resolution. She lets teams brainstorm ideas and come up with solutions for studying wild animals in a controlled experiment. To facilitate the teams, Kathy uses lots of humor. She also has teams rate their effectiveness in several key team functions, including creative problem solving and team spirit.

Finally, the teams are sent to sea to set up labs and conduct research from ocean vessels. Kathy travels from vessel to vessel to encourage teamwork, check research procedures, and help solve problems. She makes sure that each team knows how to reach her at all times, day and night.

Because teamwork is so important to the overall results, Kathy will not rehire anyone who cannot work as a part of a team. She knows that even the most educated and skillful researchers will fail if they are not able to work effectively and cooperatively with a variety of people.

CRITICAL THINKING

Why do you think team building is an important part of a science research project?

Peak Performer Profile

Ellen Ochoa

When astronaut Ellen Ochoa was growing up in La Mesa, California, in the 1960s and early 1970s, it was an era of space exploration firsts: the first walk in space, the first man on the moon, the first space station. Even so, it would have been difficult for her to imagine that one day she would be the first Hispanic woman in space, since women were excluded from becoming astronauts.

By the time Ochoa entered graduate school in the 1980s, however, the sky was the limit. Having studied physics at San Diego State University, she attended Stanford and earned her Ph.D. in electrical engineering. In 1985, she and 2,000 other potential astronauts applied for admission to the National Aeronautics and Space Administration (NASA) space program. Five years later, Ochoa, 18 men, and 5 other women made the cut. The training program at the Johnson Space Center in Houston, Texas, is a rigorous mix of brain and brawn. Ochoa tackled subjects such as geology, oceanography, meteorology, astronomy, aerodynamics, and medicine. In 1991, Ochoa officially became an astronaut and was designated a mission specialist. On her first mission in 1993, Ochoa carried a pin that read "Science Is Women's Work."

From 1993 to 1999, Ochoa logged in three space shuttle missions, or about 720 hours in space. Her first and second missions focused on studying the sun and its impact on the earth's atmosphere. Her third mission involved the first docking of the shuttle *Discovery* on the International Space Station.

In between shuttle flights, Ochoa enjoys talking to young people. Aware of her influence as a woman and a Hispanic, her message is that "education is what allows you to stand out"—and become a peak performer.

PERFORMANCE THINKING   In 1999, Ochoa and two other female astronauts posed for a picture of them raising a women's suffrage banner. What do you think they were trying to "say"?

Performance Strategies

Following are the top 10 tips for building healthy and diverse relationships:

◆ Determine your intention.

◆ Listen to understand.

◆ Show interest and empathy and ask questions.

◆ Use good eye contact, warmth, and humor.

◆ Build rapport and create common bonds.

◆ Communicate in an assertive, clear, calm, and direct yet kind manner.

◆ Make time to develop diverse, supportive, and healthy relationships.

◆ Take an interest in other people. Listen.

◆ Paraphrase to clarify.

◆ Ask yourself, "What is one thing that I could do to improve this relationship?"

Review Questions

1. What does it mean to be an active listener?

2. How do assertive people communicate?

3. Name five barriers to effective communication.

4. Can having a good romantic relationship dramatically improve your life or solve life's problems? Why or why not?

5. What are five strategies for creating rapport and improving communication with roommates?

Revisualization

In the Visualization box on the first page of this chapter, you were asked to describe a difficult situation in which you felt comfortable communicating your needs and ideas in an assertive, direct, and calm manner. Now, think of a confrontational situation in which you were passive or aggressive. How would being more assertive and understanding communication styles have helped you? How would using positive visualization have helped? How would the active listening strategies in Chapter 4 help improve your communication with others? In **Worksheet 11.1,** apply the ABCDE method to explore how you can achieve a positive outcome—for example,

A = Actual event: "Jack, a member of our study team, is not pulling his weight. He misses meetings or comes late, and he doesn't do his share of the work. Most of the time, I just ignore him or complain to the other members. I didn't know how to respond to Jack when he made more excuses for not attending class and not doing his small part in the group."

B = Beliefs: "It's just easier to go along with Jack rather than cause conflict. He may yell at me or quit the group. Besides, it's easier for me to just do his part of the presentation."

C = Consequences: "I'm upset and resentful that Jack is not doing his work. But I get nervous and anxious when I try to express my opinions or stand up for myself. I'm afraid I might lose control and overreact."

D = Dispute: "Based on past experience, Jack won't do his part unless others express their concerns. And it is unlikely that Jack will quit the group or become confrontational. I can express my concerns in a calm and nonthreatening manner. For example, I would say, 'Jack, I get upset that you are late and that you did not complete the library assignment that you committed to doing. I would appreciate it if you would complete it by tomorrow, so that the group can turn in the project on time. You can email it to us.' It is easier to stay calm when I don't let my frustration and resentment grow."

E = Energized: "My needs and ideas are as important as those of others, and I can express myself in clear and respectful terms. I know my boundaries, and I have tools for resolving conflict. I use direct eye contact, actively listen, and speak directly to Jack, rather than hoping that someone else in the group will respond or that the problem will go away."

SUCCESSFUL TEAM WORK

In The Classroom

Brian Chase is an electronics student and works part-time in an electronics firm. He likes working with his hands and enjoys his technical classes. However, he has one marketing class that he finds difficult. The instructor has formed permanent class teams with weekly case studies to present to the class and a final team project to complete. Brian dislikes relying on others for a final grade and gets frustrated trying to keep the team members focused on their tasks. Some people are late for meetings, others don't do their share of the work, and two team members have personality conflicts with each other.

1. What suggestions do you have for Brian to help him work more effectively with others?

   _____

   _____

2. What strategies in the chapter would increase Brian's listening and team-building skills?

   _____

   _____

In The Workplace

Brian is now a department manager of service technicians for a large security company that provides security equipment and alarm systems for banks, hotels, and industrial firms. His department must work closely with salespeople, systems design specialists, clerical staff, and maintenance personnel. Brian is having trouble convincing his technicians that they are part of the team. Sometimes they don't listen to the advice of the salespeople, clerical staff, or each other, which results in miscommunication and frustration.

3. What suggestions do you have for Brian that would help him build rapport within and among various departments?

   _____

   _____

4. What strategies in this chapter could help create a solid team?

   _____

   _____

CHAPTER 11 ▲ REVIEW AND APPLICATIONS

APPLYING THE ABCDE METHOD OF SELF-MANAGEMENT

In the Visualization box on page 11–1, you were asked to describe a difficult or confrontational situation in which you felt comfortable communicating your needs and ideas in an assertive, direct, and calm manner. What factors helped you be confident and respectful?

_____

_____

_____

    Now, think of a confrontational situation in which you were passive or aggressive. Apply the ABCDE method to explore how you can achieve a positive outcome.

A = Actual event:

B = Beliefs:

C = Consequences:

D = Dispute:

E = Energized:

    See yourself calm, centered, and relaxed as you state your needs, ideas, or rights. See yourself talking in a clear, concise, and confident manner. You feel confident about yourself because you have learned to communicate in an assertive and direct manner.

STUDY-TEAM RELATIONSHIPS

List some strategies for helping your study team be more organized and effective.

1. Before the meeting:

_____

_____

_____

_____

2. During the meeting:

_____

_____

_____

_____

3. After the meeting:

_____

_____

_____

_____

4. Think of effective ways to deal with the following list of challenges.

Challenges	Solutions
Latecomers or no-shows	_____
Passive members	_____
Negative attitudes	_____
Low energy	_____
Arguments	_____
Lack of preparation	_____
Socializing	_____
Members who dominate	_____

CHAPTER 11 ▲ REVIEW AND APPLICATIONS

APPRECIATING DIVERSITY

Assess your appreciation for diversity and check Yes or No for each of the following comments.

	YES	NO
1. I am committed to increasing my awareness and sensitivity to diversity.	_____	_____
2. I ask questions and don't assume that I know about different groups.	_____	_____
3. I use critical thinking to question my assumptions and examine my views.	_____	_____
4. I strive to be sensitive and respectful of differences in people.	_____	_____
5. I listen carefully and seek to understand people with different views and perspectives.	_____	_____
6. I realize that I have certain biases, but I work to overcome prejudices and stereotypes.	_____	_____
7. I do not use offensive language.	_____	_____
8. I readily apologize if I unintentionally offend someone. I do not argue or make excuses.	_____	_____
9. I celebrate differences and see diversity as positive.	_____	_____
10. I speak up if I hear others speaking with prejudice.	_____	_____
11. I try to read about other cultures and customs.	_____	_____
12. I do not tell offensive jokes.	_____	_____
13. I encourage active participation of members of diverse cultural and social groups in clubs, groups, and any decision-making group.	_____	_____

ARE YOU ASSERTIVE, AGGRESSIVE, OR PASSIVE?

Next to each statement, write the number that best describes how you usually feel when relating to other people.

3 = mostly true   2 = sometimes true   1 = rarely true

_____ 1. I often feel resentful because people use me.

_____ 2. If someone is rude, I have a right to be rude, too.

_____ 3. I am a confident and interesting person.

_____ 4. I am shy and don't like speaking in public.

_____ 5. I use sarcasm if I need to make my point with another person.

_____ 6. I can ask for a higher grade if I feel I deserve it.

_____ 7. People interrupt me often, but I prefer not to bring their attention to it.

_____ 8. I can talk louder than other people and can get them to back down.

_____ 9. I feel competent with my skills and accomplishments without bragging.

_____ 10. People take advantage of my good nature and willingness to help.

_____ 11. I go along with people so they will like me or to get what I want.

_____ 12. I ask for help when I need it and give honest compliments easily.

_____ 13. I can't say no when someone wants to borrow something.

_____ 14. I like to win arguments and control the conversation.

_____ 15. It is easy for me to express my true feelings directly.

_____ 16. I don't like to express anger, so I often keep it inside or make a joke.

_____ 17. People often get angry with me when I give them feedback.

_____ 18. I respect other people's rights and can stand up for myself.

_____ 19. I speak in a soft, quiet voice and don't look people in the eyes.

_____ 20. I speak in a loud voice, make my point forcefully, and can stare someone in the eye.

_____ 21. I speak clearly and concisely and use direct eye contact.

Scoring

Total your answers to questions 1, 4, 7, 10, 13, 16, 19 (passive): _____

Total your answers to questions 3, 6, 9, 12, 15, 18, 21 (assertive): _____

Total your answers to questions 2, 5, 8, 11, 14, 17, 20 (aggressive): _____

Your highest score indicates your prevalent pattern.

ASSESSING YOUR RELATIONSHIP SKILLS

Developing your skills in building diverse and healthy relationships is essential for success in school and throughout your career. Take stock of your relationship skills and look ahead as you do the following exercises. Add this page to your Career Development Portfolio.

1. **Looking back:** Review your worksheets to find situations in which you learned to build rapport, listen, overcome shyness, resolve conflict, work with diversity, and be assertive. List the situations on the lines provided.

   _____

   _____

   _____

   _____

   _____

2. **Taking stock:** Describe your people skills. What are your strengths in building relationships? What areas do you want to improve?

   _____

   _____

   _____

   _____

   _____

3. **Looking forward:** Indicate how you would demonstrate to an employer that you are able to work well with a variety of people.

   _____

   _____

   _____

   _____

   _____

4. **Documentation:** Include documentation and examples of team and relationship skills. Ask an advisor, a friend, a supervisor, or an instructor to write a letter of support for you in this area. Keep this letter in your portfolio.

   _____

   _____

   _____

   _____

   _____

Managing Your Resources

Chapter Objectives

In this chapter, you will learn

▲ To understand college systems and manage information

▲ The importance of building community

▲ How to explore resources at school

▲ How to research resources for nontraditional students

▲ How to explore resources in the community

▲ The importance of making a contribution

▲ Strategies for managing and saving money

VISUALIZATION

"Using a credit card is easy—in fact, much too easy. Before I knew it, I had rung up thousands of dollars, and I can barely handle the minimum monthly payments. I feel like I'll be in debt forever."

Are you struggling with your finances or finding it hard to make ends meet? Have you ever bought things that you didn't need or spent too much on a luxury item that you really couldn't afford? In this chapter, you will learn how to

find and maximize your school and local resources to help you get back on a debt-free track and contribute to the greater good of the community.

JOURNAL ENTRY   In Worksheet 12.1 on page 12–26, write about a time when you set a financial goal, such as buying a new car. How difficult was it to achieve? What sacrifices did you have to make?

In this chapter, we will look at ways for using the resources of your school and the greater community, as well as your own inner resources, to build your own community. A system is a unified structure of interrelated subsystems. A school—a large school district or a private school or college—is a system composed of interrelated parts that work together to graduate students. When you enter a college or job, you are entering a system. You become responsible for understanding how the system works. This understanding includes knowing the system's rules, regulations, deadlines, procedures, and requirements.

The Importance of Building Community

A sense of belonging is a basic and powerful human need. If you are a student living away from home, if you commute to school, if you live in a large urban area, or if you've moved often, you may not have experienced a sense of community or belonging. College is an ideal place to form relationships that will last a lifetime; to be accepted; to find activities, common interests, and issues; and to work together to achieve common goals.

The tools you have been learning for building rapport, listening, finding and managing resources, and forming relationships are all important for building a sense of community. Community is not just a physical place but also a spirit in which people are accepted despite their differences. You can create this sense of community and intimacy wherever you are. Use critical thinking and creativity as you explore ways to create a sense of belonging and community in **Personal Performance Notebook 12.1.**

Exploring Campus Resources

Resources are people, programs, paper and materials, facilities, time, and financial services that offer help and support for meeting goals and building community. Identify the resources most important to you, locate them on your campus, and include materials and phone numbers in a three-ring binder or your academic planner. Campus resources include

- *People resources:* faculty, advisors, administrators, friends, coworkers, classmates, and counselors
- *Paper and materials resources:* catalogs, directories, books, and brochures
- *Program resources:* areas of study, groups, clubs, and activities
- *Facility resources:* buildings and equipment

Building Community

Read the following statements and questions and write your comments in the lines provided. Be prepared to discuss your thoughts in class or with your study team.

1. When you hear the word *community*, what comes to mind?

_____
_____

2. Describe your experiences with community.

_____
_____

3. Did you grow up in a close-knit small town or rural community where you knew everyone?

_____
_____

4. Did you enjoy social events at churches or community centers? What community events did you attend?

_____
_____

5. Did you grow up in a city and didn't know your neighbors?

_____
_____

6. Can the same sense of community that many people experienced years ago in small communities be created in the new millennium, or have people become too isolated, busy, independent, or uncaring? Explain your answer.

_____
_____

7. What factors kept you out of certain groups in the past?

_____
_____

8. Would you like to have a stronger sense of community? If so, what are the barriers involved? Add strategies for dealing with the following reasons for not exploring or building a sense of community.

_____
_____

Class Discussion
Ask students:
1. What kind of community were they raised in?
2. What are the barriers to creating community?
3. What strategies foster a sense of community?

Hands-On Application
Have students write a paragraph or two about homesickness. Did they experience feelings of loneliness? How did the cope with these feelings? Have them discuss it in their small groups. If students did not go away to college, have them write about the changes in their lives after high school.

Class Discussion

1. What other people resources are important on campus?
2. What other paper and materials resources are important on campus?
3. What other program resources are important on campus?

◆ *Financial resources:* financial aid, credit agencies, and financial planning services

◆ *Time resources:* goals, priorities, activities, and scheduling (see **Personal Performance Notebook 12.2** to get a sense of how you juggle your commitments)

◆ *Inner resources:* personal skills, abilities, attitudes, qualities, motivation, and talents that enable you to cope, grow, contribute, and share; your greatest resource is yourself.

PEOPLE RESOURCES

The most important resources on campus are the people with whom you work, study, and relate. Faculty, administrators, advisors, study-team members, club members, sports-team members, guest speakers, and all the students with whom you connect and form relationships make up your campus community. These people will help you network for jobs and will provide information and support.

PAPER AND MATERIALS RESOURCES

Most schools have a vast amount of paper resources. Here are a few that will be most helpful:

◆ *School catalog.* The school catalog is a great place to start. The catalog will include procedures and guidelines, academic areas, basic graduation requirements, and information on most services offered at your school. Look under academic areas. What fields of study interest you the most or the least? Which areas are so unusual you didn't even know they existed?

◆ *School telephone directory.* The school telephone directory is an excellent source of information regarding staff, phone numbers, locations, activities, and services offered.

◆ *School newspaper.* This publication provides information about campus events and activities, jobs, roommates, rides, and so on. Working for newspapers and other campus publications is also a great way to develop writing and job skills and to meet new people.

◆ *Library.* When we think of libraries, most of us think of books. Indeed, the library is a rich source of books, magazines, newspapers, encyclopedias, dictionaries, pamphlets, directories, and more. Libraries also offer many services besides the written word. They may vary in size and services, but they all have information, ideas, facts, and a mountain of treasures just waiting to be explored. Besides books and periodicals, librarians and their staff are trained to find information about almost every subject. They can often order special materials from other libraries or direct you to other sources. Computer networks are now available in many libraries to retrieve information quickly. Many libraries have electronic access to books and periodicals.

Words to Succeed

"We must delight in each other, make others' conditions our own, rejoice together, mourn together, labor and suffer together, always having before our eyes our community as members of the same body."

—JOHN WINTHROP
governor of Massachusetts Bay Colony, 1630

PEAKTIP

Stay in touch with your community by reading the local newspaper on a regular basis to learn about new job opportunities, community activities, and volunteer services.

Making Time for Commitments

As you learned in Chapter 3, time is an important resource. Read the following questions and write your comments on the lines provided.

1. How involved are you in school events and activities?

   _____

   _____

   _____

Hands-On Application
In groups, list campus activities, clubs, and events. Have students discuss the events they have attended and describe the clubs to which they belong.

2. What school activities would you like to be more involved in?

   _____

   _____

   _____

3. What community activities would you like to be more involved in?

   _____

   _____

   _____

4. Is time a factor in being involved in school and community events and activities?

   _____

   _____

   _____

5. Explore ways that you could make time for one activity.

   _____

   _____

   _____

6. What have you learned about time management that has helped you manage this important resource?

   _____

   _____

   _____

◆ *Orientation guide.* Many colleges provide a student handbook or orientation guide. Explore campus resources by completing **Personal Performance Notebook 12.3.**

◆ *Other.* Add to this list.

_____

_____

_____

_____

_____

PROGRAM RESOURCES

Most schools have various programs, departments, and offices that provide services and help. Use these resources to build your sense of community.

◆ *Orientation programs.* Many schools offer an orientation program or preview weekend. If you had the opportunity to attend an orientation program, review your information packets and keep them in your binder. You may want to refer to planning guides and requirements before you register for classes for next term.

◆ *Advising center.* A central advising center is available at most colleges to provide general education advising and to answer questions concerning policies, procedures, graduation requirements, and deadlines. In addition, you are probably assigned an academic advisor for your major. Make certain that you keep your major contract, program changes, and graduation requirements in your binder or academic planner.

◆ *Admissions, records, and registration.* This office will have your transcripts, including information about grades, transfer credits, and the dropping or adding of classes. The registrar and staff can also assist you with graduation deadlines and requirements. Keep a copy of your transcripts, grades, grade changes, and other requirements in your binder or Career Development Portfolio.

◆ *Career development center.* This office provides career counseling and advising and often includes interview and resume workshops and materials. Keep a copy of inventories, materials, and possible majors and careers in either your binder or your Career Development Portfolio.

◆ *Job placement office.* Some schools offer a free placement service to help students find part- and full-time employment.

◆ *Exchange programs.* Your school may offer an exchange program, which is a great way to attend a different school without transferring. You stay enrolled at your own school but study for a term or a year at a designated school, either in this country or abroad.

◆ *Tutoring and special services.* Tutoring is offered through tutoring centers, academic departments, and special classes offered through student services.

Important Contacts

Write a list of people's names, facilities, and activities that you think you will need or use during most of your school term.

People

1. Person's Name: _____

   Phone Number: _____ Office Hours: _____

2. Person's Name: _____

   Phone Number: _____ Office Hours: _____

3. Person's Name: _____

   Phone Number: _____ Office Hours: _____

4. Person's Name: _____

   Phone Number: _____ Office Hours: _____

Facilities

1. Facility: _____ Phone Number: _____

   Purpose: _____

2. Facility: _____ Phone Number: _____

   Purpose: _____

3. Facility: _____ Phone Number: _____

   Purpose: _____

4. Facility: _____ Phone Number: _____

   Purpose: _____

Activities

1. Activity: _____

   Place: _____ Date/Time: _____

2. Activity: _____

   Place: _____ Date/Time: _____

3. Activity: _____

   Place: _____ Date/Time: _____

4. Activity: _____

   Place: _____ Date/Time: _____

Review the list of campus resources and find out where the offices are located. Choose two or three offices from this list and visit them. Discuss in a small group.

Hands-On Application

Have students list important resources, names, and phone numbers. Discuss these lists in groups to get more ideas.

Teaching Tip

You may want to bring to class representatives of different clubs to discuss the various campus activities or distribute a list of campus clubs.

Teaching Tip

Stress to students the importance of listing their instructors', advisors', and other key people's office locations, phone numbers, e-mail addresses, and fax numbers.

Campus Facilities

Many campus facilities provide equipment and services for students.

- *Student union or center.* This office often houses student organizations, clubs, the bookstore, student government, and student activities. It will also have information on various student vacations, special classes, religious organizations, retreats, sports, and political groups. Get involved with your school, meet new people, and contribute your talents.
- *Health Center.* There is usually an office or a center that offers free or low-cost medical treatment and information for students.
- *Alumni association.* This organization provides special discounts, travel arrangements, benefits, and information for graduates. These services are often available to all students.
- *Gymnasium and sports complex.* Some schools have athletic centers or field houses, weight rooms, swimming pools, and basketball and racquetball courts that are open to all students.
- *Security.* Many schools have security or police departments that provide information about safety, parking, and traffic rules. Some even provide safe escort for night-class students.
- *Child-care center.* Child care is often provided on campus, and sometimes there is a children's center sponsored by the early childhood education department.
- *Ride and carpooling boards.* There is often a bulletin board that lists information on rides, carpooling, and public transportation.
- *Off-campus housing.* Check for posted lists of available apartments, houses, people requesting roommates, and so on.

◆ *Counseling.* Many schools offer a free counseling service for students who are trying to cope with the enormous demands of school or who want to talk about personal problems. Most professionals are trained to deal with addiction, eating disorders, depression, excessive shyness, and relationship conflicts, or they can refer students to agencies for specific problems. Many counseling centers also offer classes in study skills, time and stress management, and other topics to help students succeed.

◆ *Clubs, campus events, and activities.* Whether you have moved to a new college or are attending a local school, join campus events. Approach these events with a positive attitude and a sense of adventure. Create a new sense of community by joining clubs and making new friends. Developing a support system of people who are facing the same problems and changes as you are can be very helpful. For example, returning students often find the reentry center to be a wonderful resource of support.

◆ *School facilities.* Take a walk or tour around your school or campus and make a note of the buildings and equipment available as you review **Peak Progress 12.1.**

FINANCIAL RESOURCES

Most schools provide many sources of jobs and financial aid. Be sure to explore them on your campus. Thousands of dollars of financial aid are available and go unclaimed each year. If you are having trouble paying for your education, check the financial aid office for loans, grants, scholarships, and information on programs available to students. Generally, scholarships and grants do not have to be paid back. However, student loans must be repaid. Make certain that you know the payback policy and treat your school loan with the same respect you would treat any loan. Unpaid loans hurt the lending agency or school and, of course, other students who need loans. Defaulting on student loans may also damage your credit, because this information appears on credit reports. Some sources of financial aid include the following loans and programs.

- *School scholarships and grants.* Scholarships and grants are awarded at most schools on the basis of academic achievement, athletics, music, art, or writing and usually do not have to be paid back. Check with the financial aid office for a complete list of scholarships and grants. Also, research scholarships offered by you and your parents' employers.
- *Pell grants.* This is the largest student aid program financed by the federal government; Pell grants do not have to be repaid. Check with your school's financial aid office for more information.
- *Loans.* Stafford and Perkins loans are low-interest loans to be repaid after you complete your education. Plus loans and supplemental loans for students (SLS) have variable interest rates; repayment of the principal and interest begins after the last loan payment. Check with the financial aid office for a complete list of loans.
- *The Internet.* Use the keyword "college scholarship" or "college loans" to search for available programs.
- *Work-study.* Student employment, or work-study, is an excellent way to earn money and gain valuable experience.
- *Other sources.* Loans, assistance programs, and aid programs may be available if you have special needs, such as visual impairments, hearing problems, speech difficulties, or a deceased parent.
- *Veterans programs.* Veterans can take advantage of money available through the Veterans Administration.
- *Programs for Native American students.* Native American students can find financial aid from the U.S. Bureau of Indian Affairs.
- *Programs for the unemployed.* Training programs, such as WIN (Work INcentive), are available for the unemployed. There are also scholarships, grants, fellowships, and loans available.

Check with your school's financial aid office for a complete listing of various financial resources, or visit the U.S. Department of Education web site at www.ed.gov. This web site provides general information about the major federal student aid programs, who is eligible and how to apply, tax credits for education expenses, and other federal, state, and private sources of information.

Commuter Students

Commuters make up the largest number of college students. Almost 80 percent of all college students are commuters. Here are some tips to help you succeed:

◆ **Get involved in school.** Students who get involved and join a club are more likely to graduate and have a positive college experience. Check out clubs and activities that are available.

◆ **Explore and take advantage of school resources.** Visit the student activities office and find out if there is a student newspaper or radio station and what support groups, special classes, tutorial and other activities, and support are offered. Check out the library, career center, computer center, and other available resources.

◆ **Get support from your family.** If you live at home, talk with your parents, spouse or partner, or children about your new responsibilities. Delegate duties and ask for help and support. Let them know when you have reports, papers, and projects due or need to study for a test.

◆ **Connect with others.** Build relationships with students, instructors, advisors, and staff. Find someone who cares about you. Build a connection with an instructor or advisor and join study groups.

◆ **Carry an emergency kit.** If you commute by car, carry a flashlight, water, snacks, medical supplies, a blanket, a pen and paper, jumper cables, a towel, a few dollars and change, extra clothes, and shoes. In the winter, pack extra gloves, a hat, boots, and even a down jacket or sleeping bag. People have been stranded for hours in snow storms. Talk with other commuters and add to your list.

◆ **Tape lectures.** With your instructor's permission, tape lectures or ask for tapes that would supplement your classes and make good use of your commuting time. However, never let a tape, music, or your thoughts distract you from your main job of driving safely.

◆ **Pack your lunch.** Also, pack granola bars or packets of nuts or raisins that you can keep in your backpack or car.

Students With Disabilities

Most schools realize the importance of providing services and resources for students with disabilities, such as learning disabilities, chronic illnesses, and physical limitations.

◆ *Check out resources.* The first step is to see what is available at your school, such as a center for students with disabilities or a learning skills center. Special services may be provided by student services or counseling. You can check out resources in the library or go online to the National Center for Learning Disabilities at www.ncld.org or call 1-888-575-7373. If you have a visual impairment, the library may have audiotapes or books in Braille. There are often classes in sign language for students with hearing impairments. There should be ramps in most buildings, and some schools offer a van to transport students to classes.

- *Recognize learning disabilities.* A learning disability is a neurological disorder that can affect reading, writing, speaking, math abilities, or social skills. If you think you have persistent problems in these areas, you can contact the learning center or student health center for a referral to a licensed professional. Most schools have tutors, student assistants, and special materials to help students with learning disabilities. Creating structure and routines, establishing deadlines, working in groups, and using the other strategies offered in this book can be especially helpful for students with learning disabilities.
- *Meet with instructors.* Talk with all of your instructors. You are not asking for special favors or treatment but, rather, for alternatives for meeting your goals. You may want to sit in the front row, tape the lectures, have an oral test, use a computer instead of writing assignments longhand, or need extra time taking a test.
- *Meet with your advisor.* Discuss your concerns with your academic advisor or an advisor from the learning center. It is critical that you get help early, focus on your strengths, get organized, and map out a plan for success.
- *Be realistic.* Outline what adjustments you may need to make to be successful. Design your educational plans with your disabilities in mind.
- *Be assertive.* Ask for what you need and want in polite, direct language. Treat yourself and others with respect.
- *Integrate all learning styles to reinforce learning.* Focus on your strengths and make learning physical and active. Study in groups, summarize in writing and out loud, set a timer to stay focused and disciplined, and reward yourself for completing tasks. Use the Adult Learning Cycle to reinforce interest and learning.
- *Focus on your goals.* Realize that, even though your mountain may be steeper, you have what it takes to adapt and succeed. Use the ABCDE Method of Self-Management to help you dispute negative thinking and apply visualization and positive affirmations.

Class Discussion
What resources are available for returning and older students? List phone numbers and discuss events.

The Returning Student

If you are a returning, or reentry, student, you have lots of company. Over one-third of all students are over age 25, and many are well over 40. These students are sometimes referred to as nontraditional students. Their numbers are growing every year as more and more people return to school to complete or further their education. Some returning students are veterans or single parents, some work full-time, and almost all have other commitments and responsibilities. Returning students often do better than younger students, because they have a sense of purpose, discipline, and years of experience to draw upon.

Two of their biggest concerns are finding time and dealing with interruptions. How can they manage school as well as the demands of families and jobs? Many find

Teaching Tip
Stress the importance of transfer students getting to know the new college or university system.

Hands-On Application
Have students compute their GPA or what they think it will be this term if they earn the grades they expect. (see page xxv in the Preface to the Student.)

Class Discussion
Ask students if they know what probation and disqualification mean on their campus. Ask students for the best tips to avoid probation.

that they must organize their time and use the available campus resources. More and more services are offered for the older, returning student, such as support groups, child care, tutoring, credit for work experiences, and special classes. There are many resources that are important for returning students:

- Adult reentry center
- Legal aid
- Continuing education
- Adult services
- Veterans Affairs
- Office for credit for prior experience
- Women's center
- Counseling center
- Job placement center
- Information/referral services
- Financial aid office
- On-campus child care

Transfer Students

Most colleges have an orientation or workshop for transfer students. The important point is to remember that every college is different. Don't assume you know policies and procedures because you have attended a different college.

You will also want to make certain that you have an advisor; you should know what upper division and general education courses are required, what credits were transferred from your previous school, and whether they were accepted as general education or as electives. Complete a major contract or plan of study, so that you have direction. If you transferred as a junior, you may have only two years of college to complete.

Students on Probation

Probation is a warning that you are doing substandard work. On many campuses, this means less than a 2.0 grade point average. If you continue to maintain a grade point average below 2.0 or if it falls to a certain level, you may be disqualified. Disqualification means that you are denied further school attendance until you are reinstated. Disqualified students may petition for reinstatement, usually through the Office of Admissions and Records.

Many resources are available to help you stay in school and avoid probation. Follow all the study strategies in this book. Check with the learning skills lab, advising center, counseling center, and academic support services. Most schools offer workshops on study skills.

Community Resources

Class Discussion
Ask students if they know the surrounding community. What activities have they joined to get involved and make a contribution?

As a college student, you have an opportunity to get to know a city and a chance to make a contribution to the campus and community. Even if you've always lived in the same city, you may not be aware of its rich resources and opportunities. When you get involved, you gain a sense of belonging and know that one person can make a difference. Many students have found enormous satisfaction in working with children, volunteering in nursing homes and hospitals, serving in a house of worship, or working with the homeless.

PEOPLE RESOURCES

Your community is made up of people who can provide you with great opportunities for growth, information, and services. Some people resources in the community include

- *Business professionals.* It is important to connect with business professionals in your field of study. They offer valuable information and advice, internships, scholarships, contacts, jobs, and career opportunities. You can make contacts by volunteering your services or joining professional organizations. Many professional groups have student memberships.

- *Government officials.* You will feel more involved in the community when you learn the names of your local political leaders. Go to a city council meeting, attend a county board of supervisors meetings, or meet the major. Sometimes city, county, and state governments have special programs, internships, and fellowships for students. Learn the names of your state senator and representative by searching on-line or calling the local political office or chamber of commerce.

- *Political parties.* Political activity is one way to meet people, become informed about local issues, and contribute your organizational talents. Political parties are always looking for volunteers.

- *Child care.* Child care is provided by both private and public agencies. Look in the yellow pages and call your city hall, houses of worship, or the local school district.

- *Health care.* Know the phone number of local hospitals and health clinics. They provide inexpensive vaccinations, birth control, gynecological exams, and general health care.

- *Houses of worship.* If you choose to seek a faith of your choice, houses of worship are also places to meet new friends. They hold social events, workshops, support groups, and conferences.

- *Crisis centers.* Hot lines are usually available 24 hours a day for such crises as suicidal feelings, physical and/or emotional abuse, rape, AIDS, and severe depression.

- *Helping organizations.* The American Cancer Society, American Heart Association, Red Cross, and Salvation Army provide information, services, and help. These organizations are always looking for volunteers.

- *Support groups.* Whatever your needs, there may be a support group to share concerns and to offer help. Among these are support groups for alcoholism, drug addiction, friends and family of addicts or alcoholics, physical and/or

Class Discussion
Ask students what their
favorite community
resources are and what they
would recommend to other
students.

emotional abuse, veterans, people making career changes, and cancer and
other terminal illnesses.

◆ *Counseling.* Counselors, psychiatrists, clergy, and therapists can help with
personal problems, such as depression, excessive shyness, or destructive
behavior, or are available just to talk about any problem you may be having.

FINANCIAL RESOURCES

Look in the yellow pages or call your chamber of commerce to obtain a list of resources that offer help with financial planning or saving money. Some community
financial resources include

◆ *Job placement services.* Job placement services provide career counseling, job
listings, and workshops for interviewing skills and resume writing.

◆ *Legal aid.* You may need free or low-cost legal aid services.

◆ *Community scholarships and grants.* Many community organizations (such as
the Rotary, Kiwanis, Lions, Elks, Soroptimist, and American Association of
University Women) offer scholarships and grants that do not have to be repaid.

◆ *Service learning.* Many schools encourage students to incorporate internships,
co-op programs, volunteering, or service learning into their education. The
emphasis is on students contributing their time and talents to improve the
quality of the community and to learn valuable job skills. Students often earn
college credits and obtain valuable experience while integrating what they learn
in classes into practical, on-the-job problem solving. Students also have an
opportunity to create their own learning experiences through directed study
and field experience. Some students tutor or work with the homeless, the
elderly, or people with disabilities. Many other students find that internships
and co-op programs are great ways to earn college credit and contribute their
talents. Businesses are looking for people who also take time to contribute to
the community. Many internships offer wages, and some lead to part-time or
full-time employment after graduation.

PAPER AND MATERIAL RESOURCES

Some printed material resources include

◆ *Community telephone directories.* Scanning the yellow pages is one of the best
ways to discover the services available in the area.

◆ *Local newspapers.* Read the local newspaper to learn about community events,
services, seminars, clubs, auctions, art showings, sporting events, concerts,
businesses, and entertainment. You'll also read about the local political and
community leaders and the current community issues.

◆ *Magazines and newsletters.* Almost every community has a few newsletters or
magazines describing the area, featuring local interest stories, and advertising
community resources.

◆ *Local libraries.* Check out the city and county libraries. As already discussed,
libraries are a tremendous resource. Besides printed material, they offer a
wealth of information, films, and classes.

PROGRAM RESOURCES

You may find a number of community programs available to you.

◆ *Chamber of commerce.* The local chamber of commerce has information about local attractions, special events, museums, bed and breakfast inns, hotels, motels, restaurants, libraries, clubs, and businesses. It also has information about economic development, the environment, political issues, clubs, and organizations.

◆ *Clubs and organizations.* Many clubs, such as the Rotary, Lions, Elks, Soroptimist, American Association of University Women, and Kiwanis, also offer scholarships for students. Clubs such as Toastmasters and the Sierra Club offer programs for people with specific interests. Big Brothers, Big Sisters, YWCA, YMCA, Girls Clubs, and Boys Clubs are always looking for volunteers and lecturers, and they offer many services free or at low cost.

◆ *Recreation centers.* Recreation centers, gyms, swimming pools, and local community education programs offer classes, programs, and recreation.

Teaching Tip
Stress that each student is his or her own best resource.

Teaching Tip
Invite an expert on financial planning to speak about the dangers of credit card debt.

Hands-On Application
Have each student prepare a budget. (see worksheet 12.3 on p. 12–28)

You Are a Great Resource

The most important resource you have is yourself. Call on your inner resources to make a difference in the world. School and community resources are also available for you to become involved and contribute your talents. Making a contribution is one of the best ways to connect to a school and community and to gain a real sense of satisfaction. What resources are you particularly interested in using? In what areas do you think you can make a contribution? Make time to get involved in at least one area of interest in school, the community, or the world.

Handling Money Wisely

Did you know that, according to the Consumer Credit Counseling Service (CCCS),

◆ The average student leaves college with a credit card debt of between $8,000 and $10,000 (this does *not* include student loans)? At a rate of 18 percent interest, it will take 25 years of minimum payments to pay off this loan and will ultimately cost $24,000.

◆ More young people filed for bankruptcy than graduated from college in 2001?

◆ The average college student spends more on beer than on textbooks?

◆ *Keep a budget.* The first step in planning is to write a budget. Calculate how much money you earn and how much money you spend. Write a long-term budget for a year or more, one for the school term, and a short-term monthly budget. You will then have a big picture of large expenses, such as tuition, and you will be able to modify and monitor your expenses each month. Keep receipts, bills, canceled checks, and credit card statements in a

Class Discussion

Ask students: How can they stay out of debt or at least keep their debt restricted to school-related expenses?

file or box in case you want to exchange your purchases and to help you revise for accuracy in your budget. Keep one file for taxes and file applicable receipts. Be realistic and monitor your budget each month. Refine it when necessary and then stick to it. **Personal Performance Notebook 12.4** provides a guide for planning a budget.

◆ *Beware of credit card debt.* You will want to establish a good credit rating. Credit cards are convenient and a way to establish a credit rating. However, be careful not to exceed your loan limit and make certain you have the money before you charge. Thousands of students find themselves in debt every year by using a credit card without backup funds. Many students don't even know the rate of interest that they are paying. Most cards charge at least 18 percent interest. Some people blame the financial industry for making it too easy to obtain credit cards. As an adult, however, you should make a point of being informed and take responsibility for your decisions and actions.

◆ *Save for the future.* Once you get out of college and have a good job, save 10 percent of your income in a savings account, your company's 401k plan, an Individual Retirement Account (IRA), or a similar investment. Some sacrifices now, such as buying a used car instead of a new one, will add up later. For example, $25,000 today earning 8 percent will equal $800,000 at retirement. If you were to save and invest just $1 every day—the price of a small soft drink at a fast-food restaurant—you would have $90,000 in the bank at your retirement. (See **Peak Progress 12.2** on page 12–18 for applications to the Adult Learning Cycle.)

GETTING FINANCIAL HELP IF YOU'RE IN TROUBLE

If you find that you are having financial problems and your credit rating might be damaged, get help. Don't borrow more money!

1. **First, admit to yourself that you have a problem.** Denial only makes the problem worse. There are some warning signs that you may be in financial trouble. If you experience two or more of these signs, you need to take action:
   • You make only the minimum monthly payments on credit cards.
   • You're having trouble making even the minimum monthly payments on your credit card bills.
   • The total balance on your credit cards increases every month.
   • You miss loan payments or often pay late.
   • You use savings to pay for necessities, such as food and utilities.
   • You receive second or third payment-due notices from creditors.
   • You borrow money to pay off old debts.
   • You exceed the credit limits on your credit cards.
   • You've been denied credit because of a bad credit bureau report.

2. **Get professional help.** Check the yellow pages or call the local chamber of commerce and ask if your community has a consumer credit agency that helps with credit counseling. Bring all your budget information, assets, bills, resources, loans, and any other requested items.

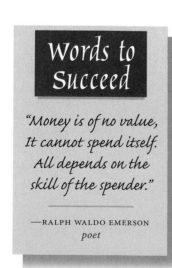

Words to Succeed

"Money is of no value, It cannot spend itself. All depends on the skill of the spender."

—RALPH WALDO EMERSON
poet

Money in/Money out

The following chart will help you get started on planning and organizing your budget. On a separate sheet of paper, make a copy of this chart and follow the instructions.

1. Monitor your spending for a month. To keep your budget simple, list money in and money out. Suggested categories are earnings, food, travel, and school items. At the end of the month, total your monthly income and your monthly expenses. Put them in the appropriate categories. Subtract your total expenses from your total income. The money left is your monthly surplus. If you have a deficit, you will need to explore ways of increasing revenue or decreasing expenses. Following is a sample budget.

Hands-On Application
Have small groups think of strategies for saving money. List the best strategies and discuss in class.

Date	Money In	Money Out
Monday, Jan. 2	$28.00 (typed paper)	
Tuesday, Jan. 3		$14.00 (dinner/movie) $12.00 (gas for car)
Wednesday, Jan. 4	$58.00 (snow removal)	

2. How can you increase your earnings?

_____

_____

_____

3. How can you decrease your spending?

_____

_____

_____

_____

4. List all the free or inexpensive entertainment available in your community. Discuss this list with your study team.

_____

_____

_____

_____

Teaching Tip
Emphasize the importance
of using the Adult Learning
Cycle to increase interest and
improve skills.

Class Discussion
Ask students:
1. How do they simplify their
   lives?
2. How do they save money?

Peak Progress   12.2

Applying the Adult Learning Cycle to Managing Financial Resources

1. **RELATE. Why do I want to learn this?** I know if I start a habit of wise spending and successful saving and investing now, it will pay off later. I want to stay debt-free and maintain a good credit rating.

2. **OBSERVE. How does this work?** Who do I know appears to be in good financial shape? What can I learn from resources such as investment web sites and money counselors? What are some on-line tools I can explore to determine what my goals should be?

3. **THINK. What does this mean?** Where can I further limit my expenses? I'll keep track of my progress and see what strategies work for me.

4. **DO. What can I do with this?** I will practice reducing my spending every chance I can. Each day, I'll work on one area. For example, instead of buying coffee and a bagel every day, I'll prepare my own at home and save about a few dollars every day. I'll also pack my lunch, rather than buying it on the run.

5. **TEACH. Whom can I share this with?** I'll ask others for tips and share my progress with a financial counselor.

Make a commitment to paying your obligations on time. Investing in a wise financial plan today will pay off with big dividends later.

Local branches of the Consumer Credit Counseling Service (CCCS) provide debt counseling for families and individuals, and it charges only a small fee when it supervises a debt-repayment plan. Other private and public organizations, such as universities, credit unions, the military, and state and federal housing authorities, also provide financial counseling services for a nominal fee or no charge at all.

3. **Spend less than you earn.** Write a budget and be absolutely firm about sticking to it. Once the habit of living within your means is part of your life, you will reap the rewards of confidence and control.

OTHER TIPS FOR SAVING MONEY

◆ *Shop wisely.* Refer to a list when you shop and don't buy on impulse. Don't shop as a means of entertainment. Avoid buying convenience items and snack foods. They all cost more and provide less nutrition. Pack your lunch, rather than buying snacks at school or work. You can save a considerable amount of money each week.

◆ *Pay cash.* Don't use a credit card. If you have one, use it only for emergencies or special items, such as airline tickets. Pay off the balance on a credit card immediately. Interest charges can be expensive. You will be tempted to buy more with credit, and it is difficult to monitor how much you spend. Follow this simple rule: If you don't have the money for an item, don't buy it. Keep

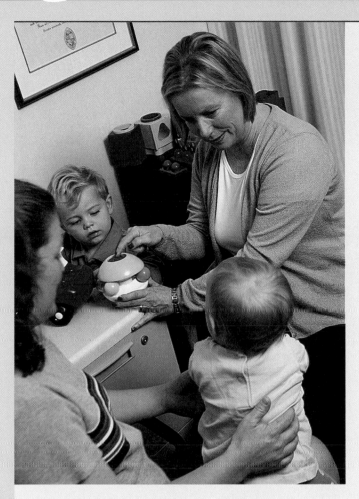

Donna Washington

SCHOOL SOCIAL WORKER

Related Majors: Social Work, Psychology, Sociology

Benefits of Community Resources

Donna Washington works as a social worker at an elementary school. School social workers help students, teachers, and parents cope with problems. Their work involves guidance and counseling regarding challenging issues in the classroom as well as in the home. They diagnose behavior problems and advise teachers on how to deal with difficult students. They work with families to improve attendance and help working parents find after-school child care. They also help recent immigrants and students with disabilities adjust to the classroom.

A long list of community resources helps Donna provide appropriate community referrals. She often uses the telephone to arrange services for children in need, such as counseling or testing. Other services on her list include legal aid societies, crisis hot lines, immigrant resource centers, and tutoring. Donnas has developed her list over a 20-year career span and remains in touch with key community leaders to keep her list up-to-date.

Donna chose to be a school social worker because of a strong desire to make a difference in the lives of children. She possesses all of the qualities that make her an excellent social worker: She is responsible, emotionally stable, warm and caring, and able to relate to a wide variety of clients, and she can work independently. Because of budget cuts, agencies in her district are understaffed, and Donna struggles with a huge caseload. Although she finds the work emotionally draining at times, Donna finds tremendous satisfaction when she sees the lives of her students improve due to her care.

CRITICAL THINKING

What qualities make a good social worker? Why?

Peak Performer Profile

Condoleezza Rice

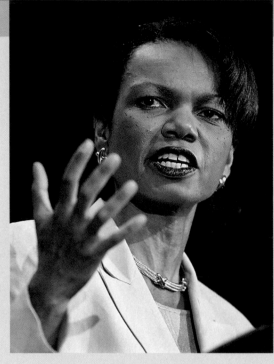

There's an anecdote that tells the story of a road trip Condoleezza Rice and her parents took many years ago from Birmingham, Alabama, to Washington, DC. When they finally reached the nation's capital, Rice stood in front of the White House for a traditional snapshot and reportedly said, "I'm standing in front of the White House now, but one day I'm going to be in it." In 2001, Rice became the first woman to serve as national security advisor. In 2004, she was nominated to the position of Secretary of State.

Rice grew up in Birmingham in the 1950s and 1960s, during some of the South's most turbulent years. She experienced racism firsthand, as well as the loss of a childhood friend in the infamous Birmingham church bombing of 1963. Beyond knowing that racism is a fact, she has said, "You need a strategy to deal with it." She has benefited from the teachings of her parents. Both Rice's mother and father were educators, who taught her the value of achievement through education, self-reliance, and discipline. They also taught her to be whatever she dreamed.

At age 15, Rice enrolled in the University of Denver, graduating *cum laude* in 1974 with a bachelor's degree in political science. She went on to earn a master's degree from Notre Dame and later returned to Denver for her Ph.D. in international studies. Later, while serving as a professor at Stanford University and the school's youngest provost, she distinguished herself as a Soviet expert.

As national security advisor, Rice helped shape the administration's foreign policy and advised the president on how to deal with the world's "hot spots." Rice has applied a firm hand when needed. As one colleague has described her, she displays "a kind of intellectual agility mixed with velvet-glove forcefulness."

PERFORMANCE THINKING When the World Trade Center and the Pentagon were attacked on September 11, 2001, Rice's position of national security advisor became even more vital. If she were to consider people who make contributions toward any community recovery effort, who would she name, and why?

In summary, in this chapter, I learned to

- *Explore and understand the campus system.* It is important to understand the rules, regulations, deadlines, policies, procedures, requirements, and resources for help at my school. I attend orientation sessions and find out how to register and pay fees. Exploring resources helps me create a sense of belonging and build a community of new friends, activities, and goals.

- *Determine campus resources.* I take advantage of all the resources that are available to help me succeed. I take time to go on a campus tour and go on-line to review the school's web site.

- *Seek out people resources.* I appreciate the faculty, advisors, administrators, study-team members, and all the students and relationships that make up the campus community. I explore and build relationships with all the people who provide information, help, and support. I meet with instructors and my advisor often to review and clarify my expectations and progress.

- *Research paper resources.* I spend time in the library exploring books, magazines, and newspapers, and reviewing this rich resource. I visit the bookstore and computer labs, read through the catalog, look at school material, and read the school newspaper.

- *Utilize program resources.* I explore various programs that offer help, support, and opportunities, such as the advising center, the career development center, counseling, the tutoring and learning center, exchange programs, the job placement office, clubs, campus events, and other activities. I explore resources available for my special needs, such as the adult reentry center and transferring student, legal aid, and veterans programs. As a commuting student, I check out carpooling boards and look for programs that can help me be more involved in campus activities.

- *Explore financial resources.* I explore scholarships and grants, loans, work-study, and special assistance programs. I also explore campus jobs, as well as student-assistant programs.

- *Visit campus facilities.* I explore various facilities on campus, such as the health center, the gymnasium, the sports complex, the swimming pool, the child-care center, the wood-working shop, the alumni center, ride boards, off-campus housing, and security, and I know where lost and found items are turned in.

- *Explore community resources.* I appreciate the opportunity that I have to explore the community and get involved. I look into internships and part-time jobs. I go to a city council meeting and become familiar with community leaders and projects. I read the local paper and am familiar with local topics and opportunities for service. I look in the yellow pages for resources and special support groups and agencies offering counseling and health services.

- *Participate in service learning.* I look for ways that I can combine learning with volunteer work. I volunteer for community projects and political parties, as well as in schools, nursing homes, hospitals, animal shelters, crisis centers, and areas of interest, such as historical buildings or environmental protection.

- *Manage my money.* I take full responsibility for my finances. I know how to make and stick to a budget, save money, and spend less than I earn. I limit my credit card use and seek help managing my money when necessary.

Performance Strategies

Following are the top 10 tips for managing your resources:

- Explore all available resources.
- Join clubs and activities and widen your circle of friends.
- Investigate one new campus resource each week.
- Explore one new community resource each week.
- Get involved and volunteer at school and in the community.
- Seek help at the first sign of academic, financial, health, or emotional trouble.
- Reduce spending and increase savings.
- Know where your money goes and where you want to invest it.
- Use a credit card for convenience only and don't go into debt for unnecessary items.
- Look for creative ways to save money.

Review Questions

1. What does *community* mean to you?
2. What type of campus programs would you seek to find a full- or part-time job while attending school?
3. Name two college financial resources cited in this chapter that you would like to investigate, and explain why.
4. What is your most important resource? Why?
5. How can staying healthy help you financially?

REVISUALIZATION

Revisit the Visualization box at the beginning of this chapter and your answer in **Worksheet 12.1.** Think of how gratified you felt to set a goal and achieve it. Now, think of a financial goal you may consider in the next few years and apply the ABCDE method to work through the obstacles and create a plan for achieving that goal as well—for example,

A = Actual event: "When I graduate, I will owe more than $20,000 in student loans."

B = Beliefs: "I don't see how I can pay that off quickly, and that debt will hang around for years. I'm excited about my chosen field, but it doesn't pay that well until I've been in the business for at least a few years."

C = Consequences: "This debt will keep me from getting loans for other things I really want, such as a new car or house."

D = Dispute: "If I put a plan in place and start saving now, I know I can get a head start on paying back the loan faster. I need to manage my money, rather than letting it manage me."

E = Energized: "I'm energized because I know that I can face up to my responsibilities, work hard, and pay back my loans quickly. I've made an appointment to get free money-management help. I'll develop a plan that lays out how I need to save, starting today. I'll investigate ways to help me earn additional income or provide experiences that will pay off."

BUILDING COMMUNITY

In The Classroom

Lorraine Peterson is a returning student at a two-year business school. She also works part-time selling cosmetics at a retail store and would like to advance to a managerial position. She was away from school for several years. During that time, she started a family and is now eager to become involved in school and its activities. On returning to school, she happily discovered other returning students. Several of them get together for coffee on a regular basis. Lorraine is especially interested in foreign students and international business. She also wants to learn more about available computer services, guest speakers, marketing associations, and scholarships.

1. What suggestions do you have for Lorraine about involvement in campus and community events?

   _____

   _____

2. How can she find out about scholarships and explore all the resources that would increase her success as a returning student?

   _____

   _____

In The Workplace

Lorraine has been a salesperson for several years with a large cosmetics firm. She recently was promoted to district manager for sales. Part of her job is to offer motivational seminars on the benefits of working for her firm. She wants to point out opportunities and resources available to employees, such as training programs, support groups, demonstrations, sales meetings, and conferences. The company also donates money for scholarships and sponsors community events. An elaborate incentive system offers awards and prizes for increased sales.

3. How can Lorraine publicize these resources to her sales staff?

   _____

   _____

4. What strategies in this chapter would help her communicate the importance of contributing time and talents to the community and the company?

   _____

   _____

NAME: DATE:

APPLYING THE ABCDE METHOD OF SELF-MANAGEMENT

In the Visualization box on page 12–1, you were asked to write about a time when you set a financial goal. How difficult was it to achieve? What sacrifices did you have to make?

_____

_____

_____

Now, think of a financial goal you may consider in the next few years and apply the ABCDE method to work through the obstacles and create a plan for achieving that goal as well.

A = Actual event:

B = Beliefs:

C = Consequences:

D = Dispute:

E = Energized:

Visualize yourself planning and saving money for investing in your goals. You feel confident about yourself, because you have learned to manage your money and your goals. See yourself feeling prosperous as you consider other aspects of wealth, such as being healthy, having supportive family and friends, having opportunities, and being surrounded by many campus and community resources.

RESOURCES

Research and list the various resources your community has to offer. Make a point to visit at least a few of them and place a check mark by those you have visited. You can copy this worksheet form to extend your list of resources.

Check

_____ Resource _____

Service Offered _____

_____

Contact Person _____

Phone Number _____

_____ Resource _____

Service Offered _____

_____

Contact Person _____

Phone Number _____

_____ Resource _____

Service Offered _____

_____

Contact Person _____

Phone Number _____

_____ Resource _____

Service Offered _____

_____

Contact Person _____

Phone Number _____

_____ Resource _____

Service Offered _____

_____

Contact Person _____

Phone Number _____

CHAPTER 12 ▲ REVIEW AND APPLICATIONS

BUDGETING EACH TERM

Creating a budget is the first step to financial success. As you plan for your expenses, take time and reflect on your spending habits. Spending within your budget will allow you to reach your financial goals. Complete the following list and review it every month to keep track of your expenses.

Budget for Each School Term

Tuition	$ _____
Books and supplies	$ _____
Housing	$ _____
Transportation	$ _____
Insurance	$ _____
Clothing	$ _____
Laundry	$ _____
Food	$ _____
Entertainment	$ _____
Utilities	$ _____
Phone	$ _____
Health care	$ _____
Household items	$ _____
Savings	$ _____
Miscellaneous	$ _____
Total	$ _____

Estimated Expenses for the Year

Tuition	$ _____
Books and supplies	$ _____
Housing	$ _____
Transportation	$ _____
Insurance	$ _____
Clothing	$ _____
Laundry	$ _____
Food	$ _____
Entertainment	$ _____
Utilities	$ _____
Phone	$ _____
Health care	$ _____
Household items	$ _____
Other	$ _____
Loans	$ _____
Total	$ _____

Estimated Resources   Month/Term

Parental contribution	$ _____
Summer savings	$ _____
Student savings	$ _____
Job	$ _____
Loans	$ _____
Other	$ _____
Total	$ _____

MONEY MANAGEMENT

1. List ways you can increase your income.

_____

_____

_____

_____

_____

_____

_____

_____

_____

_____

_____

_____

_____

2. List ways you can decrease your spending.

_____

_____

_____

_____

_____

_____

_____

_____

_____

_____

_____

_____

_____

_____

_____

CHAPTER 12 ▲ REVIEW AND APPLICATIONS

BUILDING COMMUNITY

Throughout the academic year, use this checklist to review your participation in the various school programs.

	People				Program				Facilities				Financial			
	Do you know your advisor?	Do you know your instructors?	Do you know key administrators?	Do you know your study team?	Have you attended orientation?	Do you know how to use computers?	Have you chosen a major?	Do you know about key programs?	Have you been to the student union?	Have you explored the library?	Have you used the computer facilities?	Have you explored key administrative offices?	Have you researched financial aid?	Work-study?	Student employment?	Loans, grants, internships?
First month																
Second month																
Third month																
Fourth month																
Fifth month																
Sixth month																
Seventh month																
Eighth month																

ASSESSING YOUR COMMUNITY INVOLVEMENT

The purpose of this worksheet is to look back and assess how involved you have been in community service. Write your responses to the following statements on the lines provided.

1. List ways you have integrated academic coursework with real-world, hands-on experiences.

   _____

   _____

   _____

2. List clubs and activities in which you were involved in high school.

   _____

   _____

   _____

3. List clubs and activities in which you are involved in college.

   _____

   _____

   _____

4. List internships you have completed.

   _____

   _____

   _____

5. List volunteer organizations in the community you have been involved with.

   _____

   _____

   _____

—continued

6. List professional clubs or organizations to which you belong.

_____

_____

7. List your role in the clubs and organizations you listed in Question 6.

_____

8. In what activities does your school club or organization involve itself?

_____

9. Choose two organizations from the following list. Use the Internet and other sources of information to find out about these organizations:

United Way

Volunteers of America

Lions Club

Salvation Army

AmVets

Other

Answer the following questions for one of the organizations you researched.

a. Who founded the organization?

_____

b. When was it founded? Where?

_____

c. Is it:

_____ local?

_____ national?

_____ international?

d. Where is its main headquarters?

_____

e. What is its purpose or mission statement?

_____

NETWORKING

Write information about your network of people on the following form. You can copy this worksheet form to extend your list of contacts.

Name _____

Company _____

Phone _____

Type of Work _____

Name _____

Company _____

Phone _____

Type of Work _____

Name _____

Company _____

Phone _____

Type of Work _____

Name _____

Company _____

Phone _____

Type of Work _____

YOUR COMMUNITY SERVICE

Exploring your personal resources and abilities is important for your career development. Answer the following questions and relate your community participation to your leadership skills. Add this page to your Career Development Portfolio.

1. Describe your ability to manage resources. What are your strengths in managing time, money, and information and in determining what resources are available to solve various problems?

_____

_____

_____

_____

_____

2. Indicate how you would demonstrate to an employer that you have made a contribution to the community.

_____

_____

_____

_____

_____

3. Indicate how you would demonstrate to an employer that you know how to explore and manage resources.

_____

_____

_____

_____

_____

4. Indicate how you would demonstrate to an employer that you have learned leadership skills.

_____

_____

_____

_____

_____

Developing Good Habits

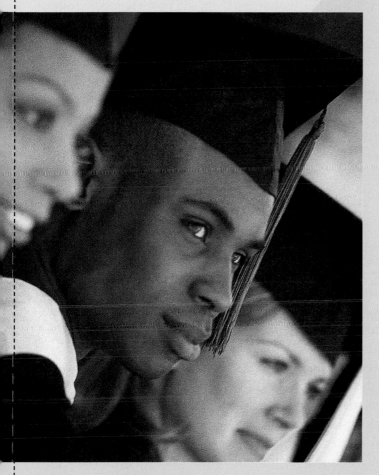

Chapter Objectives

In this chapter, you will learn

▲ The top 10 habits of peak performers

▲ The importance of positive habits

▲ The importance of commitment

▲ The best strategies for school and job success

▲ How to overcome resistors and fears

VISUALIZATION

"It's been a soul-searching journey to get to this point, but I now understand that I control my destiny. I make choices every day regarding what new things I will learn, how I will interact with others, and on what I will focus my energies. I will be successful because I have the power to become a peak performer in everything I do."

Are you ready for the exciting journey ahead of you? Do you know what your greatest assets are and the areas where you would like to improve? You and only you can determine what kind of person—student, employee, family member, and contributor to society—you will be. You have tremendous power to create your own success. Take a few minutes

each morning before you jump out of bed or as you shower to set the tone for the day. Visualize yourself being focused and positive and successfully completing your projects and goals. Imagine yourself overcoming fear and negative habits that are self-defeating. See yourself putting all the strategies that you've learned to work for you and creating positive, long-lasting habits.

JOURNAL ENTRY In Worksheet 13.1 on page 13–24, think of a time when you knew what to do but you kept repeating negative habits. How would positive visualization have helped you?

Words to Succeed

"We are what we repeatedly do. Excellence, then, is not an act, but a habit."

—ARISTOTLE
Greek philosopher

Use
TM 13.1 Success Principle 13.

Teaching Tip
Emphasize the importance of using the ABCDE Method of Self-Management to visualize success and create positive results.

Key Teaching Concept
You must want to change.

Y
ou can use many strategies and techniques for doing well in your school, career, and personal life. Many techniques are also available for managing your time, taking tests well, and developing healthy relationships. Reading about and discussing them is one thing, but actually making these techniques and strategies part of your everyday life is another. You will find that embracing them will prove rewarding and helpful as you begin developing and working on your goals. Knowing that you have the motivational skills to succeed in school and in your career can give you the confidence to take risks, grow, contribute, and overcome life's setbacks. You have what it takes to keep going, even when you feel frustrated and unproductive. This chapter will show you how to turn these strategies into lasting habits. It will also look at the importance of effort and commitment, without which there is no great achievement. Look at great athletes; the difference in their levels of physical skill is often not dramatic, but their sense of commitment is what separates the good from the truly great. Peak performers—in school, work, and life—achieve results by being committed.

The 10 Habits of Peak Performers

In Chapter 2, we discussed the importance of emotional maturity for school, job, and life success. You may have a high IQ, talent, skills, and experience, but, if you lack emotional maturity and such important qualities as responsibility, effort, commitment, a positive attitude, interpersonal skills, and especially character and integrity, you will have difficulty in school, in the workplace, and in your relationships. However, it is not enough to review essential traits and qualities of emotional maturity. You must be committed to making them long-lasting habits. The best way to learn anything is to practice, teach, and model. To create a habit, you must practice and teach deliberately and consistently. Commit yourself to making the following 10 essential qualities long-lasting habits. (See **Figure 13.1.**)

1. **Be honest.** A peak performer is a person of character. Character and integrity are the foundation of all other skills, competencies, personal qualities, and habits. If you are not trustworthy and honest, talent, intelligence, energy, and personality will not matter. This book has stressed using the whole of your intelligence for school, and job success. When you have a sense of wholeness, you are confident about thinking, speaking, living, and taking the right path. You know that you can trust yourself to do the right thing, keep your commitments, and play by the rules. Practice the habit of honesty every day by being truthful, fair, kind, compassionate, and respectful. Doing the right thing is a decision and a habit.

Figure 13.1   The 10 Habits of Peak Performers

THE TEN HABITS OF PEAK PERFORMERS

1. Be honest
2. Be positive
3. Be resilient
4. Be engaged
5. Be curious

6. Be responsible
7. Be supportive
8. Be a creative problem solver
9. Be disciplined
10. Be grateful

The 10 Habits of Peak Performers   Peak performers translate positive personal qualities into action. *Do you demonstrate these habits consistently?*

Key Teaching Concept
What you focus on expands.

Class Discussion
Ask students to think of something they really feared and worried about that never happened. Has fear ever caused them to sabotage themselves? What is a good way to deal with unrealistic fears?

Teaching Tip
Explain the concept of the self-fulfilling prophecy. Ask students if they expected the worst to happen and if their thoughts and behavior actually caused it to happen.

2. **Be positive.** Peak performers are positive, enthusiastic, and optimistic. They greet each day and every event as an opportunity. Focus on your strengths and be your own best friend by working for and supporting yourself. Focus on what is going right, on all the tasks you do well, and on your accomplishments. Relax and don't take yourself or others so seriously. Learn to laugh at yourself and the complexities of life. A negative attitude is often caused by fear. Fear blocks creativity, causes the imagination to run wild, and makes everyday frustrations look catastrophic. Fear can devastate your sense of self-confidence, make recall difficult, and harm your performance in school and at work. When you are faced with a new and fearful situation, such as a math exam, a public speaking class, or a new roommate, be positive and optimistic. It is easy to dwell on the worst that could happen, instead of looking at likely positive outcomes. As you've learned through practicing visualization and the ABCDE Method of Self-Management, you dispel negative thoughts and learn to see yourself and events realistically. You begin by telling the truth about who you are: your current skills, abilities, goals, barriers, and both positive and negative habits. Positive thinking is not wishful thinking but, rather, rational, hopeful thinking. Develop the habit of being positive and enthusiastic by looking for creative ways to create a motivated and resourceful state of mind. Look for the best in others and in every situation. You learn to be aware of the common barriers and setbacks that cause people to fail. Then, you set goals to focus your energy on the most appropriate path. Next, you create the specific thoughts and behaviors that will produce the results you want. You take positive action and empower yourself.

3. **Be resilient.** Adversity happens to everyone. Peak performers are resilient, flexible, and able to bounce back from disappointments, loss, and failure. Even when you are equipped with the best skills, self-understanding, and a positive and motivated attitude, life can hand you difficult situations. Even good students sometimes lose papers, forget assignments, miss deadlines, and do poorly on tests. Don't turn one mistake into a recipe for continued failure. You can't always change circumstances, but you always have a choice about how you come back and prepare to win again. Life is unpredictable and transitory, but persistence and endurance can get you back on your feet. The key is to make adversity and setbacks work for you. See everything as an opportunity to learn and grow. Refuse to accept that setbacks have the power to ruin your life. See failure as temporary instead of permanent and pervasive to all areas of your life. The way you interpret events is often more important than the events themselves. Consequently, the first step is to take control of how you interpret events, as well as your thoughts, reactions, and behaviors toward them. Again, the ABCDE Method of Self-Management is a useful tool to help you see events and people realistically. You will learn to reframe your setbacks as stepping-stones to your final goal and energize yourself to take positive action. Develop the habit of resiliency by using creativity and critical thinking to explore new options and achieve your goals.

4. **Be engaged.** Peak performers do not sit back and wait for life to happen. They are engaged, are active, and have a desire to contribute. Contributing means shifting a self-centered, "what's-in-it-for-me?" attitude to a "what can I do to be more involved and useful?" attitude. One way to sabotage your classes or career is to expect your instructors or supervisor to make your life interesting. All careers are boring or monotonous at times, and some classes are less than spellbinding. Develop the habit of using your imagination and creativity to make any situation challenging and fun. This habit of being engaged can help you take initiative in class and at work by being an active participant. It is going to each class prepared, asking questions, and being engaged with the subject matter, the instructor, and other students. Develop the habit of being engaged in the moment and looking for connections among your classes, the world of work, and the larger community. Look for school and community activities that will give you hands-on experiences, leadership opportunities, and a chance to contribute. This broader, long-range view requires a habit of not only setting daily goals and priorities but also reflecting on your life's mission. A full life is more than just a college degree, financial success, possessions, prestige, and career advancement. It is connecting and working with others and thinking about the legacy that you want to leave. Your short-term goals will make more sense when they are in alignment with your life mission and a desire to make the world a better place. Think about the kind of person you want to be when you're 80 or 90 years old, and start being that person today. Live with the end results in mind.

5. **Be curious.** Peak performers are curious, flexible, open, and willing to learn new skills, personal qualities, and positive attitudes. They are aware of popular culture, interested in life around them, open to feedback, and able to adapt to new situations. Skills and knowledge will help you be successful, but true learning is lifelong and depends on the willingness to continually learn, explore new ideas, and manage change. Some students feel that learning new information is not important for success. They cling to their own traditions and beliefs and argue with everything the instructor says. Successful students are curious, keep an open mind, and are willing to learn as well as unlearn and revise their maps of the world. Talented professionals can also find themselves at a dead end if they refuse to learn new skills and be flexible. Regardless of occupation, age, and education level, all of us must be involved in the exciting and sometimes frightening business of change. Shifts in the economy can result in layoffs for many competent, highly educated, and skilled workers. Corporate buyouts, downsizing, and mergers may also cause job turnovers, layoffs, and forced retirement. The competition for good jobs is fierce. Therefore, it is imperative that you continuously learn new skills, be aware of new trends, practice positive habits, obtain job training, and be flexible with your goals. If plan A doesn't work out, have plan B ready to go. Develop the habit of curiosity by having a sense of wonderment about life and asking questions. Take time to reflect on your dreams. If you could create your perfect job, what would you do? What could you do today to move closer to a fulfilling job? Update your resume often and be prepared to transfer basic job and career skills, such as problem solving, effective communication, listening, and the ability to maintain healthy relationships throughout your career.

6. **Be responsible.** Peak performers are emotionally mature people who take responsibility for their thoughts, feelings, words, behaviors, and habits. Assuming responsibility and following through with commitments are essential for success in all areas of your life. You may not always feel like keeping your commitments to yourself, your instructors, friends, coworkers, or supervisors, but meeting obligations is the mark of a mature, responsible person. You will get ahead in school, at work, and in life when you are known as a reliable, conscientious person who keeps agreements. A responsible person does not feel entitled but, rather, honors personal obligations. For example, a major obligation for many students is the repayment of student loans after completing a course of study. Deciding to pursue higher education is a partnership with your school. Keep your commitment by paying back loans. Develop the habit of responsibility by doing what you say you're going to do, showing up, being pro-active, and keeping your agreements.

7. **Be supportive.** Peak performers are supportive and work well with others. Look at instructors, advisors, classmates, coworkers, friends, family, and supervisors as part of your team. They deserve your support, tolerance, and willingness to work cooperatively. The world is made up of people from different cultures, religions, backgrounds, views, and lifestyles. School provides an excellent opportunity to develop the habit of understanding,

Key Teaching Concept
Don't blame others for your choices. Take responsibility.

Class Discussion
Is teamwork an important job skill? List all the ways you can enhance learning by working in a group.

cooperating, and supporting people from different backgrounds. Go beyond being tolerant of different cultures, religions, and views, and celebrate and support diversity. Pettiness is a major barrier to school and job success. Being supportive means being respectful and kind and listening with understanding. Listen to what you say and how you say it. If your tone is brusque, others won't cooperate. Don't interrupt or criticize. People need to be heard and respected. Listen for understanding instead of trying to persuade and influence. Through patience, self-control, and critical thinking, you will learn to listen, see the other person's point of view, and work to solve problems with a win/win approach. Ask yourself, "How can I see this differently?" "How can we both get what we want?" and "What can I do to make this relationship better?" Practice looking for the best in others and focus on strengths instead of shortcomings. Don't gossip or belittle others' accomplishments. Learn to be less defensive. If you must make suggestions, give positive feedback first and be gentle with suggestions. Focus on the problem, not the person. Working effectively with others is fundamental for school, job, and life success. You will find that most instructors, advisors, and supervisors will go the extra mile to help you if they know who you are, if you show interest and a willingness to learn, and are supportive of their efforts. Develop the habit of being supportive by building healthy relationships based on trust and respect.

8. **Be a creative problem solver.** Peak performers use critical thinking and creative problem solving. You can expand your sense of adventure and originality in problem solving and learn to think critically and creatively. You can challenge your beliefs and try new approaches. Creative problem solvers have a clear vision of where they want to go and they set realistic goals. Critical thinking helps you clarify values, set goals and priorities, and create steps to meet them. Critical thinking also helps you distinguish between an inconvenience and a real problem. Some people spend a great deal of time and energy getting angry at minor annoyances or events that they cannot change. They complain about the weather, become angry when their plane is late, become annoyed because other people don't meet their expectations, and are upset because they have to wait in line. For example, the plane being late is an inconvenience; the plane crashing is a real problem. A serious car accident is a problem; a fender bender is an inconvenience. Cancer or another life-threatening disease is a problem; a cold is an inconvenience. Critical thinking helps you put events in perspective and allows you to focus on creative problem solving, which gives you a positive self-regard. You will focus on your strengths, rather than dwelling on your weaknesses. In a sense, you "wake up" and consciously use your creative mind. Instead of postponing, ignoring, or complaining, you actively engage in exploring solutions. Develop the habit of creative problem solving by practicing critical thinking, using your imagination, and exploring fresh approaches to problems.

9. **Be disciplined.** Peak performers are disciplined and self-managed. They do first things first and do what needs to be done, not what they'd like to do.

PEAK TIP

You can change your habits. Begin to imagine yourself with a new habit or attitude. Notice the sense of confidence you gain. Practice the new habit until it becomes natural.

They keep up on assignments, set goals and priorities, and carve out time throughout the day to focus their attention on the task at hand. Discipline demands mental and physical conditioning, planning, and effort. Using discipline and self-control, you know how to manage your time, stress, money, and emotions—especially anger. As Benjamin Franklin said, "Anger always has its reasons, but seldom good ones." Getting angry rarely solves problems, but it can create big ones. Use the ABCDE Method of Self-Management to dispute negative thoughts and take positive action instead of blaming others or yourself. Learn to master your emotions with such simple tips as counting to 10 or taking a walk. Through discipline and awareness, you can overcome impulsive reactions and learn to use critical thinking before reacting in haste. Develop the habit of discipline by being patient and by investing time, practice, and effort in your goals.

10. **Be grateful.** Peak performers are grateful and have learned to find happiness in simple pleasures. Appreciation prompts them to take care of what they value. They know how to balance their lives so that they are healthy physically, emotionally, mentally, and spiritually. They take time to exercise, rest, be with friends, read, reflect, and laugh. They have not only a sense of humor but also a deep sense of joy and awe at the gift of life. You can practice the habit of being grateful and feel the abundance for all that you have in life—your health, friends, family, and opportunities. Life often seems like a comparison game, with competition for grades, jobs, relationships, and money. Sometimes others seem to have more, and you may feel that your own life is lacking. Reflect on your blessings, strengths, and talents, not on comparing your life with others'. Focus on what you have, not on what you don't have. A sense of humor is vital for keeping things in perspective and developing a grateful heart. Learn to listen to, appreciate, and renew your body, mind, and spirit. Appreciating your body means you take time to rest, invest in exercise, and eat good foods. Appreciating your mind means you spend time reading, visualizing, creatively solving problems, writing, and challenging yourself to learn and be open to new ideas. Appreciating your spirit means you find time for quiet reflection and renewal and you make an effort to listen, develop patience, and love others. The goal is to stay balanced and renewed. Develop the habit of gratitude by appreciating what you have in life and by approaching each day as an opportunity to serve and grow.

Key Teaching Concept
Change is difficult. Most people resist positive changes and rationalize their negative choices.

Teaching Tip
Indicate that billions of dollars are spent by people trying to change destructive habits and quit addictions.

Class Discussion
Ask students how they can use critical thinking when confronted with quick-fix ads.

Hands-On Application
Ask students to think of a habit they want to change. Have them pair up with another person in class and write about their desired change and the barriers. Discuss in groups.

Making a Commitment to Change Your Habits

Most people resist change. Even when you are aware of a bad habit, it is difficult to change it. Consequently, you may find it hard to integrate into your life some of the skills and strategies that you have encountered in this book.

Hands-On Application
Have students write a script
of an action plan, for
example:
- Write your intention.
- List steps.
- Create a schedule.
- Set a date for completion.
- Practice.
- List rewards.
Discuss in small groups.

Teaching Tip
Emphasize the importance of
using the Adult Learning
Cycle for creating interest
and improving skills.

Applying the Adult Learning Cycle to Develop Positive Habits

The Adult Learning Cycle can help you increase your ability to change your behavior and adapt long-lasting positive habits.

1.   **RELATE. Why do I want to learn this?** I know that practicing positive habits and creating long-lasting changes will help me succeed in school, work, and life. What are some of my positive habits, and which ones do I need to change or improve? Do I portray the 10 habits of a peak performer?

2.   **OBSERVE. How does this work?** I can learn a lot about positive habits by watching others and trying new things. I'll observe people who are positive, are motivated, and know how to manage their lives. What do they do? Are their positive habits obvious? I'll also observe people who display negative habits and learn from their mistakes.

3.   **THINK. What does this mean?** I will gather information by going to workshops and taking special classes. I will focus on the 10 habits of a peak performer and create strategies for incorporating them into my everyday routine. I will think about and test new ways of breaking out of old patterns, negative self-talk, and behaviors that are self-defeating. I will look for connections and associations with time management, stress and health issues, and different types of addictive behaviors.

4.   **DO. What can I do with this?** I will focus on and practice one habit for one month. I will reward myself when I make progress. I will focus on my successes, and I'll find simple and practical applications to use my new skills in everyday life. Each day, I'll take small steps. For example, I'll spend more of my social time with my friends who like to hike and do other positive things that I enjoy, instead of hanging out with friends who like to drink.

5.   **TEACH. Whom can I share this with?** I'll share my progress with family and friends and ask if they've noticed a difference.

Something becomes a habit only when it's repeated again and again, just as the learning cycle is more effective the more times you go through it.

Words to Succeed

*"We first make our
habits, and then our
habits make us."*

—JOHN DRYDEN
poet and playwright

Old habits become comfortable, familiar parts of your life. Giving them up leaves you feeling insecure. For example, you want to get better grades, and you know it's a good idea to study only in a quiet study area rather than while watching television or listening to the radio. However, you have always read your assignments while watching television. You might even try studying at your desk for a few days, but then you lapse into your old habit. Many people give up at this point, rather than acknowledge their resistance. Some find it useful to take stock of what common resistors, or barriers, keep them from meeting their goals. However, as a potential peak performer, you will begin to adopt positive techniques to help change your old habits. (See **Peak Progress 13.1** on applying the Adult Learning Cycle to learning new habits.)

Strategies for Creating Positive Change

If you have trouble making changes, realize that habits are learned and can be un-learned. Adopting new habits requires a desire to change, consistent effort, time, and a commitment. Try the following 10 strategies for eliminating old habits and acquiring new ones.

1. **You must want to change.** To change, you must have a real desire and see the value of the change. It helps to identify important goals: "I really want to get better grades. I have a real desire to graduate from business college and start my own small retail business. I see the benefit and value in continuing my education." Your motivation has to be channeled into constructive action.

2. **Develop specific goals.** Setting specific goals is a beginning for change. Statements such as "I wish I could get better grades" or "I hope I can study more" are too general and only help you continue your bad habits. Stating goals such as "I will study for 40 minutes, two times a day, in my study area" are specific and can be assessed and measured for achievement. When completing **Personal Performance Notebook 13.1** on page 13–10, assess your habits and put a star by the areas you most want to work on.

3. **Change only one habit at a time.** You will become discouraged if you try to change too many things about yourself at the same time. If you have decided to study for 40 minutes, two times a day, in your study area, then do this for a month, then two months, then three, and so on and it will become a habit. After you have made one change, move on to the next. Perhaps you want to exercise more, give better speeches, or get up earlier.

4. **Be patient.** It takes at least 30 days to change a habit. Lasting change requires a pattern of consistent behavior. With time and patience, the change will eventually begin to feel comfortable and normal. Don't become discouraged and give up if you haven't seen a complete change in your behavior in a few weeks. Give yourself at least a month of progressing toward your goal. If you fall short one day, get back on tract the next. Don't expect to get all *As* the first few weeks of studying longer hours. Don't become discouraged if you don't feel comfortable instantly studying at your desk instead of lying on the couch.

5. **Use visualization to imagine success.** Imagine yourself progressing through all the steps toward your desired goal. For example, see yourself sitting at your desk in your quiet study area. You are calm and find it easy to concentrate. You enjoy studying and feel good about completing projects. Think back to a time in your life when you had the same positive feelings. Think of a time when you felt warm, confident, safe, and relaxed. Imagine enjoying these feelings and create the same state of mind. Remember, the mind and body produce your state of mind, and this state determines your behaviors.

6. **Observe and model others.** How do successful people think, act, and relate to others? Do students who get good grades have certain habits that contribute

Make a Commitment to Learn and Apply Positive Habits

Committing yourself to good habits is the foundation for reinforcing the cycle of success. Read the following statements concerning habits for success. Check either Yes or No as each statement applies to you.

Success Habit	Yes	No
1. Have you created a study area that helps you concentrate?	_____	_____
2. Do you make learning physical?	_____	_____
3. Do you preview each chapter before you read it?	_____	_____
4. Do you preview other chapters?	_____	_____
5. Do you rewrite your notes before class?	_____	_____
6. Do you outline your papers?	_____	_____
7. Do you proofread your papers several times?	_____	_____
8. Do you rehearse your speeches until you are confident and well prepared?	_____	_____
9. Do you attend every class?	_____	_____
10. Do you sit in the front of the class?	_____	_____
11. Do you actively listen and take good notes?	_____	_____
12. Do you review your notes within 24 hours?	_____	_____
13. Do you monitor your work?	_____	_____
14. Do you get help early, if necessary?	_____	_____
15. Do you participate in class and ask questions?	_____	_____
16. Have you developed rapport with each of your instructors?	_____	_____
17. Have you joined a study team?	_____	_____

Make a Commitment to Learn and Apply Positive Habits –continued

Success Habit	Yes	No
18. Do you study and review regularly each day?	_____	_____
19. Do you complete tasks and assignments first and then socialize?	_____	_____
20. Do you recite and restate to enhance your memory skills?	_____	_____
21. Do you take advantage of campus and community activities?	_____	_____
22. Can you create a motivated and resourceful state of mind?	_____	_____
23. Do you know how to solve problems creatively?	_____	_____
24. Do you use critical thinking in making decisions?	_____	_____
25. Do you exercise daily?	_____	_____
26. Do you maintain your ideal weight?	_____	_____
27. Do you keep your body free of harmful substances and addictions?	_____	_____
28. Do you support your body by eating healthy foods?	_____	_____
29. Do you practice techniques for managing your stress?	_____	_____
30. Have you developed an effective budget?	_____	_____
31. Do you take the time for career planning?	_____	_____

If you find you've answered no to many of these questions, don't be alarmed. When old habits are ingrained, it's difficult to change them. By observing your thoughts, rethinking your beliefs, and reframing your experiences, you can alter your behavior and make lasting changes.

Hands-On Application
Have students:
- Describe the kind of
  person they want to be at
  85 years old. What will
  they be doing? What will
  be their legacy? How do
  they want their children
  and grandchildren to
  relate to them?
- Imagine themselves
  successful. Pretend they
  are already achieving their
  goals.
- Feel their sense of
  accomplishment.
- Write affirmations and
  visualizations in their
  journals.

to their success? Basic success principles produce successful results. Research indicates that successful students study regularly in a quiet study area. They regularly attend classes, are punctual, and sit in or near the front row. Observe successful students. Are they interested, involved, and well prepared in class? Do they seem confident and focused? Now, model this behavior until it feels comfortable and natural. Form study groups with people who are good students, are motivated, and have effective study habits.

7. **Be aware of your behaviors.** Sometimes paying attention to your own behavior can help you change habits. For example, you may notice that the schoolwork you complete late at night is not as thorough as the work you complete earlier in the day. Becoming aware of this characteristic may prompt you to change your time frame for studying and completing schoolwork.

8. **Reward yourself.** One of the best ways to change a habit is to reward yourself when you've made a positive change. Increase your motivation with specific payoffs. Suppose you want to reward yourself for studying for a certain length of time in your study area or for completing a project. For example, you might say to yourself, "After I outline this chapter, I'll watch television for 20 minutes," or "When I finish reading these two chapters, I'll call a friend and talk for 10 minutes." The reward should always come after the results are achieved and be limited in duration.

9. **Use affirmations.** Talking to yourself means that you are reprogramming your thoughts, a successful technique for making change. When you have negative thoughts, tell yourself, "Stop!" Counter negative thoughts with positive statements. Replace the negative thought with something like "I am centered and focused. I have control over my thoughts. When they wander, I gently bring them back. I can concentrate for the next 40 minutes, and then I'll take a short break."

10. **Write a contract for change.** Write a contract with yourself for overcoming your barriers. State the payoffs for meeting your goals: "I agree to take an honest look at where I am now and at my resistors, my shortcomings, my negative thoughts, the ways I sabotage myself, and the barriers I experience. I agree to learn new skills, choose positive thoughts and attitudes, and try new behaviors. I will reward myself for meeting my goals." You may want to discuss this with a study partner. Take the first step by using critical thinking and creative problem solving to complete **Personal Performance Notebook 13.2.**

Peak Performance Success Formula

There isn't any secret to producing an outstanding athlete, a skilled musician, an accomplished performer, or an experienced mountain climber—or academic excellence and success. The same principles of training required to get into Olympic form apply to getting results in school and in work. **Figure 13.2** on page 13–14 describes four components for achieving success in both your personal and career lives. (See **Personal Performance Notebook 13.3** on page 13–15 to assess how you are progressing.)

Commitment Contract

Complete the following statements in your own words.

1. I most want to change _____

_____

_____

_____

2. My biggest barrier is _____

_____

_____

_____

3. The resources I will use to be successful are _____

_____

_____

_____

4. I will reward myself by _____

_____

_____

_____

5. The consequences for not achieving the results I want will be _____

_____

_____

_____

_____

Date _____

Signature _____

Hands-On Application
Have students complete Personal Performance Notebook 13.2 and write a contract for change. Exchange a copy with a trusted friend and review in one month.

Use
TM 13.2 Commitment to Learn Positive Habits.

Figure 13.2   The Secret to Success

The formula for success can be broken down into four components:

1. Confidence is believing in yourself, knowing your worth, and recognizing that you have what it takes to do well. Self-confidence is one of the most important mental qualities you can develop for producing results. When you build on the accomplishments of small victories and successes, you realize that you can achieve almost any goal you set. Confidence is your resolve to win.

2. Vision is mental rehearsal of your victory. You must know clearly what you want to achieve. Be realistic about seeing this vision become a reality. Use encouraging self-talk and imagery. Vision requires you to focus internally, to listen to your positive voice, and to imagine yourself achieving your goal.

3. Method is the process of achieving your goal and knowing the strategies, techniques, tools, and tactics that produce tangible results. Method involves monitoring your actions and techniques, so that you can modify them to excel consistently.

4. Training is the actual practice and the consistent effort required to improve your skills. Training requires the capacity to stay with a vigorous program and hours of rehearsal. Athletes know that they must practice relentlessly to see what may often be only small improvements. Practice is what separates the peak performer from the average person.

The Secret to Success   To apply the formula for success, it takes time, effort, and the determination to succeed. *Which components of this formula do you need to focus on to accomplish your desired goals?*

Practice The ABCDE Method of Self-Management

Throughout this book, you've had an opportunity to practice the ABCDE Method of Self-Management. You have discovered that your thoughts create your feelings, which in turn can affect how you interpret events. Learn to dispel negative thoughts and replace them with realistic, optimistic, and empowering thoughts and behaviors. Developing this habit of being optimistic will keep you centered, calm, rational, productive, and peaceful, even in the midst of confusion and turmoil. You will be empowered to overcome obstacles, resistors, and fears; to maintain a positive attitude; and to reach your goals. (See **Peak Progress 13.2** on page 13–17 on the various positive attitudes of peak performers.)

Assessment Is Lifelong

Read the following skills. Then, rate yourself on a scale of 1 to 5 (1 being poor and 5 being excellent). Refer back to **Personal Performance Notebook 1.1** in Chapter 1 and compare it with your answers here. Have you improved your skills and competencies?

	Excellent	Satisfactory	Poor
	5	4 3 2	1

Teaching Tip

Have students complete Personal Performance Notebook 13.3. Tell them to place a number from 1 to 5 on the line that best indicates their skill in each area. Discuss how they might improve those areas they rated 3 or below.

Area

1. Reading _____

2. Writing _____

3. Speaking _____

4. Mathematics _____

5. Listening _____

6. Critical thinking and reasoning _____

7. Decision making _____

8. Creative problem solving _____

9. Mental visualization _____

10. Knowing how to learn _____

11. Personal qualities (honesty, character, responsibility) _____

12. Sociability _____

13. Self-management and control _____

14. Self-esteem and confidence _____

15. Management of time, money, space, and people _____

16. Interpersonal, team, and leadership skills _____

17. Working well with cultural diversity _____

18. Organization and evaluation of information _____

19. Understanding systems _____

20. Understanding technology _____

21. Commitment and effort _____

—continued

Assessment Is Lifelong—continued

Assess your results. What are your most excellent skills? What are your poor skills that need improvement?

Do you have a better understanding of how you learned these skills and competencies? Do you know how to document and demonstrate these skills and competencies? Your major or career choice may include other skills. Assess additional skills that can be transferred to many situations or jobs. For example, here are six broad skill areas:

Key Teaching Concept
Learning is lifelong.

- Communication skills
- Human relations skills
- Organization, management, and leadership skills
- Technical and mechanical skills
- Innovation and creativity skills
- Research and planning skills

Teaching Tip
Ask students to think of an experience in their lives that they perceived as a setback but actually turned out in their favor.

Resistors and Fears

The following are some resistors that all types of students may experience or feel. These and other obstacles face most people, including peak performers. (See **Figure 13.3** on page 13–18.) Recognize and confront these resistors to create lasting change:

- *Fear of the unknown.* What will happen if I really can't get good grades? Can I compete? I was not a very good student in high school. What makes me think I can do college work? Everyone else seems so much smarter.

- *Familiarity and comfort.* I have a familiar routine of going to work, coming home, preparing dinner, and taking care of the house. How will I find time to study, work, and take care of my family?

- *Independence.* I don't work well in groups. I'd rather study by myself. Beside, some of the students are so young that I may not have anything in common with them.

- *Security.* I felt secure with my beliefs and views. Some of the new ideas that I'm learning are so different. I had thought through my opinions, but now I see that there are lots of ways of looking at issues. This is exciting, but it also makes me feel insecure.

- *Tradition.* I come from a conservative family. I was always expected to stay home and raise my family and take a job only to help supplement the family income. My desire for a college education and career of my own contradicts family tradition. My sister-in-law says that I'm selfish and foolish to go back to school at this time in my life.

Words to Succeed

"You learn that whatever you are doing in life, obstacles don't matter very much. Pain or circumstances can be there, but if you want to do a job bad enough, you'll get it done."

—JACK YOUNGBLOOD
author

Peak Progress 13.2

Use
TM 13.3 Success Principles

Seven Positive Attitudes of Peak Performers

1. *A flexible attitude* means that you are open to new ideas and situations. You are willing to learn new skills and are interested in continual growth.

2. *A mindful attitude* means that you are focused on lasting values. You are mindful of living in the moment, being a person of integrity and character, and acting with kindness and civility. Being is more important than acquiring or doing.

3. *A responsible attitude* means that you take an active role in school and work. You take responsibility for your life and don't rely on others to motivate you. You are a self-starter who takes the initiative to produce positive results.

4. *A supportive attitude* means that you encourage, listen, show empathy, and work well with others. You look for the best and are more concerned about understanding than persuading others. You look for win/win solutions and communicate clearly, concisely, and directly.

5. *A confident attitude* means that you have a balanced perspective about your strengths and limitations. You commit time and effort to grow and to renew yourself physically, mentally, emotionally, and spiritually. You are confident because you use the whole of your intelligence and you are self-disciplined.

6. *A follow-through attitude* means that you are aware of the big picture but are also attentive to details and follow through on essential steps. You see whole systems while attending to essential parts.

Hands-On Application

Have students discuss in small groups the power of habits. Have them observe successful students and people at work. How do they create success? Are there any secrets? List the best habits.

Class Discussion

Ask students what positive attitudes they most appreciate in others at work.

◆ *Embarrassment.* Will I feel embarrassed being in classes with younger students? Can I hold up my end of the team projects and class discussions? I haven't had a math course in 20 years and my study skills are rusty.

◆ *Responsibility.* I am overwhelmed by the responsibility of working, going to school, and caring for my family. I know I am responsible for my life, but sometimes it would be easier if someone would just tell me what to do.

◆ *Expectations.* I have certain expectations of myself. If I go to college, I want to do well. I will not feel successful unless I get mostly *A*'s.

◆ *Environment.* My physical environment is not supportive for studying. Our home is noisy and there is no place where I can create my own study area. My husband and children say they are proud of me, but they complain about hurried meals and a messy house. They resent the time I spend studying.

◆ *Cost.* I am concerned about the cost of going to school. Tuition, textbooks, a computer, day care, and supplies all add up. Is it worth it? Maybe I should be saving for my children's education instead.

Figure 13.3 Courage to Overcome

Elizabeth Garrett Anderson	Although rejected by medical schools because she was female, she still became the first female member of the British Medical Association.
Abraham Lincoln	Although raised in poverty and teased because of his appearance, he was still elected president of the United States.
Glen Cunningham	Although doctors believed he would never walk again after he was severely burned at age three, in 1934 he set the world's record for running a mile in just over four minutes.

Courage to Overcome   These peak performers demonstrated discipline, dedication, and a positive attitude to reach their goals despite obstacles. *What stands in your way of realizing your goals? What steps could you take to overcome obstacles?*

TECH FOR SUCCESS

- **Inspiration** In this text, you have read about many peak performers who have overcome great obstacles to get where they are today. Who truly represents a peak performer to you? If it's even a relatively well-known person, chances are you will find that person's story on-line. Spend at least a few minutes searching and reading about what makes this person stand out. Do you recognize any of the 10 habits?
- **A Log of Positive Habits** Create a Word or Excel document using the 10 habits of a peak performer. Every time you have a significant personal example in which you demonstrated a habit, log it into your document. Eventually, this will create an ideal list of personal examples that you can relay to a future employer. Keep a copy in your Career Development Portfolio.

◆   *Giving up.* I love my classes, the new ideas I'm learning, and the people I've met. My study group is accepting, and they value my opinions and contributions. It is my dream to earn a college degree, but it's too overwhelming. I might as well quit now because I don't want to invest more time and money and then fail.

Rick Torres

CARPENTER

Related Majors: Mathematics, Bookkeeping,
Computer-Aided Design

Good Habits in the Workplace

Rick Torres is a carpenter who, like one-third of carpenters in the United States, works as an independent contractor. This means that Rick is self-employed and does a variety of carpentry jobs for homeowners, from building decks to completing remodeling jobs.

The first thing Rick does is figure out how to accomplish the task. Then, he provides the customer with a written time and cost estimate, purchases materials, completes the work, and hauls away construction debris. Good basic math skills are necessary to provide an accurate estimate and to calculate the amount of materials needed for the job. Basic bookkeeping skills also help Rick keep track of his earnings and help him prepare to pay quarterly taxes. The work is often strenuous, requiring expertise with large tools, such as power saws and sanders; the handling of heavy materials; and prolonged standing, climbing, bending, and kneeling. Rick often works outdoors and enjoys the flexibility and physical activity that his work provides.

Through the years, Rick has learned that good habits are essential to his future. Rick gains new customers through word of mouth. Customers pass his name on to others because he is reliable and possesses excellent skills. Rick's business has been successful because he cultivates positive attitudes and is committed to providing quality service. He shows up on time for appointments, is courteous, and follows through with his commitments. Occasionally, Rick works for neighborhood low-income projects. He occasionally hires younger carpenters to work with him and enjoys teaching them old tricks and new methods of construction.

CRITICAL THINKING
What might be the result of poor work habits for a carpenter working as an independent contractor?

Peak Performer Profile

Mia Hamm

Soccer champion Mia Hamm writes "Dream big" on the soccer balls she autographs for the kids that flock around her at games. Since age five, when she got her start on a coed peewee soccer team, Hamm has lived by that motto.

Born in 1972 in Selma, Alabama, the fourth of six children, Hamm grew up as a "military brat." She got the soccer "bug" in Italy, where her father was stationed. Hamm's mother, a former ballerina, initially tried to interest her young daughter in dancing. Instead, Hamm chose to follow in the footsteps of her father, a soccer enthusiast, who coached his children's soccer teams. Hamm was a natural and too quick even for her male opponents, who sometimes bullied her. The Olympic development team noticed her agility at age 14, and she was signed on. She was the youngest player ever to play on the U.S. national team. Later, Hamm attended the University of North Carolina–Chapel Hill (UNC), where she continued to wow them on the field while earning a degree in political science. The UNC team held the NCAA soccer championship title for four years while she was a student and retired Hamm's college jersey, number 19, when she graduated.

Not long after, Hamm was attracting attention as a world-class champion, "America's secret weapon." The 1996 Olympics in Atlanta, Georgia, were a dream come true when Hamm's team won the gold, defeating China. Then, in the summer of 1999, the U.S. soccer team again faced the Chinese team for the Women's World Cup. The final game—scoreless until the last minute–came down to a single, penalty-free kick by Hamm. For the first time in sports history, female soccer players became national heroes.

Most recently, the U.S. women's team took gold in the 2004 Olympic games and Hamm announced her retirement soon after. Though hailed as the greatest woman soccer play of all time, Hamm deflects individual praise. She told one journalist, "Everything I am, I owe to this team."

PERFORMANCE THINKING Developing good habits has allowed Mia Hamm to become a champion. Which good habits have contributed to her success? Why?

TAKING CHARGE

In summary, in this chapter, I learned to

- *Strive to become a peak performer.* Peak performers are successful because they develop and practice good habits. They are honest, resilient, engaged, curious, responsible, supportive, disciplined, and grateful. They have positive attitudes and creatively solve problems.

- *Make a commitment.* I have made a commitment to turn the strategies I have learned into lasting habits. I have identified specific, meaningful goals and use affirmations and visualization to help me realize them. I observe, listen, and model successful people and practice positive habits until they are a part of my life.

- *Develop a positive attitude.* I have learned to be my own best friend by being positive and approaching each task with a "can-do" attitude. Enthusiasm and a positive attitude help me focus on my strengths and create the thoughts and behaviors that create the results I want.

- *Practice self-management.* By using visualization and affirmations, I can work through difficult situations, dispute any negative thoughts, and focus on positive outcomes.

- *Avoid and overcome resistors and fears.* Fear of the unknown, insecurities, embarrassment, and overwhelming responsibilities are just some of the stressors that can impede my progress if I don't focus on positive outcomes.

Performance Strategies ················

Following are the top 10 tips for developing good habits:

◆ Commit to changing self-defeating behaviors.

◆ Set realistic goals and specify behaviors you want to change.

◆ Assess and monitor your thoughts that create feelings.

◆ Dispute irrational thoughts and describe events in an objective manner.

◆ Work on one habit at a time and focus on success.

◆ Be resilient and get right back on track after setbacks.

◆ Use affirmations and visualization to stay focused.

◆ Reward yourself for making improvements and create penalties if you do not meet realistic goals.

◆ Observe your progress and modify until you achieve the results you want.

◆ Surround yourself with support and positive influences.

Review Questions ····················

1. What are 10 strategies for creating positive change in your life?

2. What is integrity, and how does it affect your ability to be successful?

3. What does it mean to be a team player?

4. Why is self-confidence so important in being successful?

5. How long does it take to change a habit?

Revisualization ·······················

Revisit the Visualization box at the beginning of this chapter and your entry in **Worksheet 13.1.** Now that you have practiced self-management throughout this text, take another look at your scenario and apply the ABCDE Method of Self-Management. How is the outcome different?

A = Actual event: "I have really enjoyed the social aspect of college—too much, though. Too many late nights have translated into missed classes the next day."

B = Beliefs: "I just can't say no to my friends. They might stop asking me to join them."

C = Consequences: "My friends are happy, but my family isn't. I'm letting them and myself down by missing classes and risking doing poorly in class."

D = Dispute: "I know I can and must take control of my life and make school a top priority. True friends want to support me and my goals and don't want to see me fail."

E = Energized: "I'm energized because I know that I can find a balance that supports my success in school and my friendships. I know I must focus on my priorities and responsibilities first."

SPREADING GOOD HABITS

In The Classroom

Craig Bradley is a welding student. He never liked high school, but his mechanical ability helped him get into a trade school. He wants to be successful and knows that this is an opportunity for him to get a good job. Both of Craig's parents worked, so he and his sister had to get themselves off to school, supervise their own homework, and prepare many of their own meals. Money has always been tight, and he hardly ever received encouragement for positive behavior. He never learned positive study or work habits.

1. What kind of a study plan can you suggest to Craig to build his confidence and help him be successful?

   _____

   _____

2. What strategies in this chapter can help him develop positive, lasting habits?

   _____

   _____

In The Workplace

Craig is now working in a large farm equipment manufacturing plant. He has just been promoted to general supervisor in charge of welding and plumbing. He is a valued employee at the firm and has worked hard for several years for this promotion. Craig wants to ensure his success in his new job by getting training in motivation, team building, quality customer service, and communication skills.

3. What suggestions do you have for Craig to help him establish and train his staff in good habits?

   _____

   _____

4. What strategies in this chapter can help him be more successful?

   _____

   _____

APPLYING THE ABCDE METHOD OF SELF-MANAGEMENT

In the Visualization box on page 13–1, you were asked to think of a time when you knew what to do but you kept repeating negative habits. How would positive visualization have helped you?

_____

_____

_____

Now, apply the ABCDE Method of Self-Management. How is the outcome different?

A = Actual event:

B = Beliefs:

C = Consequences:

D = Dispute:

E = Energized:

OVERCOMING RESISTANCE TO CHANGE

Fill in the following.

1. I resist _____

2. I resist _____

3. I resist _____

4. I resist _____

5. I resist _____

6. I resist _____

7. I resist _____

8. I resist _____

9. I resist _____

10. I resist _____

For each item you listed above, write a strategy to overcome your resistance;

1. _____

2. _____

3. _____

4. _____

5. _____

6. _____

7. _____

8. _____

9. _____

10. _____

DEVELOPING POSITIVE HABITS

On the following lines, list five habits you would like to change into positive behavior. It is important to focus on changing one habit at a time for a successful transition. Then, in the following chart, list the steps you will need to take, the difficulties that stand in your way, and the ways in which you can overcome these barriers to reach your goal.

Positive Habits You Want to Develop

1. _____

2. _____

3. _____

4. _____

5. _____

Steps	Barriers	Methods to Overcome Barriers
1.		
2.		
3.		
4.		
5.		

BUILDING POSITIVE ATTITUDES

In your commitment to learning positive habits, you are also integrating positive attitudes into your daily routine. The seven positive attitudes of peak performers will lead to your success in the classroom and in the workplace. In the lines provided, explain how you can change your attitude to reflect the seven peak performance attitudes listed.

1. A flexible attitude

   _____

   _____

2. A mindful attitude

   _____

   _____

3. A responsible attitude

   _____

   _____

4. A supportive attitude

   _____

   _____

5. A confident attitude

   _____

   _____

6. A follow-through attitude

   _____

   _____

7. An innovative attitude

   _____

   _____

CHANGING HABITS

Fill in the grid. You can list more than one habit under each category.

	Habit				Change Perception				Reinforce				Practice			
	Make a commitment to change.	Set a specific goal.	Work on only one habit at a time.	Give yourself time.	Choose to do things differently.	Change negative self-talk to positive.	Imagine success.	Observe and model others.	Reward yourself.	Set negative consequences for setbacks.	Keep a journal of successes.	Write a contract for change.	Act as if you have succeeded.	Practice, practice, practice.	Be persistent and resilient.	Never give up.
Work habit																
Study habit																
Personal habit																

PLANNING YOUR CAREER

Developing good habits in planning will benefit your career. Use the following form to create a career action plan for yourself. Then, add this page to your Career Development Portfolio.

Career objective: _____

What type of job? _____

When do you plan to apply? _____

Where is this job? _____

- City _____

- State _____

- Company _____

Whom should you contact? _____

How should you contact? _____

- Phone _____

- Letter _____

- Walk-in _____

Why do you want this job? _____

Resources available: _____

Skills applicable to this job: _____

Education: _____

- Internship _____

- Courses taken _____

- Grade point average _____

- References _____

Career Development Portfolio: Connecting School with Career

Chapter Objectives

In this chapter, you will learn

▲ How to create your Career Development Portfolio

▲ How to assemble your portfolio

▲ The contents of your portfolio

▲ How to use your portfolio for writing an effective resume

▲ How to use your portfolio to prepare for interviewing

▲ How to explore careers

VISUALIZATION

"I like the subjects I'm studying, but I don't know how to integrate all I'm learning and apply it to real life. Will I have transferable skills that will help me get and keep the job I want?"

Have you ever taken a class and wondered how it relates to real life and if it will help you be more successful? How do you integrate all that you are learning to make it meaningful and personal? In this chapter, you will learn how to translate the information, experiences, and skills you are acquiring in school into a dynamic Career Development Portfolio.

JOURNAL ENTRY In **Worksheet 14.1** on page 14–30, write down one of the classes you are currently taking and list at least three skills you will acquire in this class that will benefit you in your career.

Assessment and feedback will help you progress through the various aspects of your life: school, work, community, family, and personal. One method of assessment is to keep an up-to-date Career Development Portfolio. This chapter will show you how to take control and plan your career by using this self-assessment tool. This can become a lifelong process. As you change and grow, you will want to change and update your portfolio. You will discover that the strategies that helped you plan your education successfully are the same techniques that can help you plan your career.

Artists have traditionally compiled samples of their work in portfolios. Showing samples of their best work, style, and talent is fundamental to getting a job. You can also gain a competitive edge by showing the best of your work and accomplishments in your Career Development Portfolio.

The Importance of a Career Development Portfolio

A Career Development Portfolio is a tool designed to highlight your strengths, skills, and competencies to other people. It helps you to:

◆ Plan and design your educational program and postgraduate learning

◆ Record significant life experiences

◆ Reflect on these experiences and assess what you have learned

◆ Describe how your experiences have helped you grow professionally

◆ Document skills and accomplishments in and out of the classroom

◆ See the connections among educational, extracurricular, community service, internship, job, and leadership learning experiences

◆ Apply patterns of interests, skills, and competencies to career planning

◆ Identify areas you want to enhance, augment, or improve

◆ Record and organize experiences for your resume and job interviews

A portfolio can be used for many different goals:

◆ Satisfy entry requirements for a job if you do not have a degree

◆ Enter an educational program if you do not have course requirements

◆ Obtain a certain job level and demonstrate that you have transferable skills and experience that are not evident from your present position

◆ Receive college credit for prior learning for work you have completed through other colleges; internships; and learning, work, or life experiences

◆ Prepare for a job change

> ## Words to Succeed
>
> *"Your vision will become clear only when you can look into your own heart. Who looks outside, dreams; who looks inside, awakes."*
>
> —CARL JUNG
> *psychologist*

- Prepare a resume
- Document accomplishments during an interview
- Organize a file for a promotion
- Express talents creatively and artistically

The Career Development Portfolio can also help you connect what you have learned in school to your work, and it serves as an organized and documented system to demonstrate that you have the necessary skills, competencies, and personal qualities to perform a job. Even if you have little work experience, you will have assembled examples of your skills and abilities with samples of your work and evidence of courses taken. This documentation can give you an edge when applying for a job. For example, Janet convinced an employer to hire her based on her portfolio: She showed the manager samples of her work and the certificates she had earned. Jake used his portfolio to receive a promotion: He was able to stress his strengths based on documentation of his skills and experiences in his portfolio.

The Career Development Portfolio is an organized place to file documentation of courses, certificates, degrees, and samples of your work. It helps colleges place you in the right courses, it helps employers make the best use of your skills; and it helps you determine what you need to do to obtain a job, an internship, a leadership position, or a promotion or to reach a career goal.

Teaching Tip
Stress that creating a portfolio is a process that takes time, effort, and reflection. Ask students if they know exactly where their grades, major contract, and other important materials are at this moment. A portfolio can save hours of time by keeping important documents and a record of accomplishments in one place.

Teaching Tip
Stress to students:
1. The portfolio is a useful tool for helping students make the transition into a job and for career advancement.
2. They have already been working on their portfolios when they completed the chapter Application Worksheets at the end of each chapter.

When Should You Start Your Portfolio?

You can start your portfolio at any time. If you are a college student, you can begin your Career Development Portfolio during your first term or year in school. As you go through each semester or quarter of a school year, you can make copies of papers or other coursework to add to your portfolio. Make note of courses that relate to your career interests. If you have a work-study job or an internship that is related to your career goal, you can keep records of your experiences, any written work, and letters of recommendation to include in your Career Development Portfolio. By the time you graduate, you will have a tool that is distinctly personal and persuasive.

A sample planning guide appears in **Figure 14.1.** This guide can be used for students in both two- and four-year schools. Students in a two-year school can use freshman and sophomore years for the first year, junior and senior years for the second year. Modify the planning guide to fit your needs.

How to Organize and Assemble Your Portfolio

The exercises, Personal Performance Notebooks, and worksheets that you have completed throughout this book form the basis of your Career Development Portfolio. You will want to type an edited version of this information on the computer

Use
- TM 14.4 Planning Guide Freshman Year
- TM 14.5 Planning Guide Sophomore Year.
- TM 14.6 Planning Guide Junior year.
- TM 14.7 Planning Guide Senior Year.

Figure 14.1   Career Development Portfolio Planning Guide

Freshman Year

- Begin your Career Development Portfolio.
- Assess your interests, skills, values, goals, and personality.
- Go to the career center in your school and explore majors and careers.
- Set goals for your first year.
- Write a resume.
- Network with professors and students. Get good grades.
- Keep a journal. Label the first section *Self-Assessment*. Begin to write your autobiography. Label another section *Exploring Careers*.

Sophomore Year

- Add to your Career Development Portfolio.
- Start a file about careers and majors.
- Join clubs and take a leadership role.
- Read articles and books about your major area.
- Find a part-time job or volunteer your time.
- Update your resume.
- Explore internships and co-op programs.
- Add a section to your journal called *Job Skills and Qualities*.

Junior Year

- Update and expand your Career Development Portfolio.
- Choose a major and career and gain more job experience.
- Network. Join student organizations and professional organizations.
- Develop relationships with faculty, administrators, and other students.
- Obtain and internship or gain additional job experience.
- Update your journal with job tips and articles about your field.
- Update your resume.
- Visit the career center on campus for help with your resume, internships, and job opportunities.

Senior Year

- Refine your Career Development Portfolio.
- Put your job search into high gear. Go to the career center for advice.
- Read recruitment materials. Schedule interviews with companies.
- Update and polish your resume and print copies. Write cover letters.
- Network. Keep a list of contacts and their telephone numbers.
- Join professional organizations and attend conferences.
- Start sending out resumes and attending job fairs.
- Find a mentor to help you with your job search and career planning.
- Log interviews in your journal or notebook.

Career Development Portfolio Planning Guide   This planning guide will help you review your skills and maintain your Career Development Portfolio as you move toward your career goal. *What are some other strategies you can use to prepare for your career?*

and save it, so you can easily make changes and update it often. You will also need these items:

- Three-ring notebook
- Sheet protectors to hold documents and work samples
- Labels and tabs
- Box to store work samples and information

Figure 14.1 lists the steps to organizing your Career Development Portfolio from your freshman year through your senior year and into the workplace. Planning step-by-step will help you reach your career goals.

The steps for organizing and assembling your portfolio will vary, depending on your purpose and the school you are attending. However, they generally include procedures such as these:

- *Step 1: Determine your purpose.* You may want to keep a portfolio as a general documented system of achievements and professional growth, or you may have a specific reason, such as attempting to receive credit for prior learning experiences.
- *Step 2: Determine criteria.* The U.S. Department of Labor created the Secretary's Commission on Achieving Necessary Skills (SCANS) to identify skills and competencies needed for success in the workplace. These skills apply to all kinds of jobs in every occupation. You may add specific criteria to this list as they apply to your situation. (See page 14–9 for a complete list of SCANS skills.)
- *Step 3: Do your homework.* Make certain that you have completed the Career Development Portfolio exercise at the end of each chapter. Assess and review your worksheets.
- *Step 4: Assemble your portfolio.* Print computer copies using quality paper. It often works best to work with a study partner. The following section is a general guideline for the contents of your portfolio.

Class Discussion
Ask students how a portfolio saves them time. What would they do if an interviewer asked them to bring work samples to an interview the next day? Where would they look for examples of work they have completed? A portfolio will save them time by having important documents and samples in one place.

Elements of Your Portfolio

COVER LETTER

Your cover letter should indicate the purpose of the letter, indicate the documents enclosed, give a brief review, and ask for an interview. See **Figure 14.2** for an example of a cover letter.

COVER PAGE

Your cover page should include a title, your name, the name of the college, and the date. You may want to use heavy card stock and put your own logo on the cover to make it unique. Do not number this page. See **Figure 14.2** for an example.

Figure 14.2   Career Development Portfolio Elements

Sample Cover Letter

737 Grandview Avenue
Euclid, OH 43322

October 2, 2005

Dr. Kathryn Keys
Director of Assessment of Prior Learning
Louis College of Business
333 West Street
Columbus, OH 43082

Dear Dr. Keys:

I am submitting my portfolio for credit for prior learning. I am applying for credit for the following courses:

Marketing 201   Retail Marketing
Management 180   Introduction to Management
Business Writing 100   Introduction to Business Writing

I completed my portfolio while taking the course Special Topics 350. My experiences are detailed in the portfolio and I believe they qualify me for six units of college credit. I look forward to meeting you to discuss this further. I will call your office next week to arrange an interview. If you have questions, please call me at 202-555-5556.

Sincerely,
Kim Anderson
Kim Anderson

Sample Cover Page

Kim Anderson
Louis College of Business

CAREER DEVELOPMENT PORTFOLIO

September 20, 2005

Sample Title Page

CAREER DEVELOPMENT PORTFOLIO

Kim Anderson
Louis College of Business

September 20, 2005

Sample Contents Page

CONTENTS

Introduction   1
List of Significant Life Experiences   2
Analysis of Accomplishments   3
Inventory of Interests, Aptitudes, and Values   5
Inventory of Skills and Competencies   6
Inventory of Personal Qualities   7
Documentation   8
Work Philosophy and Goals   10
Resume   12
Interview Planning   14
Samples of Work   15
Summary of Transcripts   16
Credentials, Certificates, Workshops   17
Bibliography   29
Appendix   31

Career Development Portfolio Elements   The presentation of your Career Development Portfolio reflects your personality and makes a valuable first impression. *What are the different ways you can personalize the cover page?*

Figure 14.3 Career Development Portfolio Introduction

INTRODUCTION

The Career Development Portfolio I am submitting reflects many hours of introspection and documentation. The purpose of this portfolio is to gain college credit for similar courses that I completed at Wake View Community College. I am submitting this portfolio to Dr. Kathryn Keys in the Office of Prior Learning at Louis College of Business.

I recently made a career change and want to enter the marketing field. The reason for the change is personal growth and development. I had an internship in marketing, and I know I will excel in this area. I plan to complete my degree in business administration at Louis College of Business. Eventually I want to work my way up to store manager or director of marketing at a large store.

This portfolio contains

- A List of significant life experiences
- Analysis of accomplishments
- Inventory of interests, aptitudes, and values
- Inventory of skills and competencies
- Inventory of personal qualities
- Documentation
- Work philosophy and goals
- Resume
- Interview planning
- Samples of work
- Summary of transcripts
- Credentials, certificates, workshops
- Bibliography
- Appendix

Career Development Portfolio Introduction   A Career Development Portfolio is a record of your goals, progress, skills, and experience. *What are some other elements you should include in your portfolio?*

Teaching Tip
SCANS is a convenient guide to use, but tell students they can add specific criteria that applies to their job or the job they want. Stress:

1. The importance of completing all worksheets from each chapter.
2. The main skills, competencies, and personal qualities that they want to document and demonstrate.
3. The importance of being creative. Their portfolio should be unique and express who they are.
4. The cover letter introduces the portfolio and should be well planned.
5. The importance of being organized.

Have the students use a three-ring binder for their formal portfolio. The information in the portfolio should be stored on a backup disk.

TITLE PAGE

Your title page should include the title of your document, where you are submitting the portfolio, your name, and the date. See **Figure 14.2** on page 14–6 for an example.

CONTENTS PAGE(S)

The contents page lists the contents of the portfolio. You can make a draft when you start your portfolio, but it will be the last item you finish, so that the page numbers and titles are correct. See **Figure 14.2** on page 14–6 for an example of a contents page.

INTRODUCTION

The introduction should discuss why you are submitting the document, your plan of development, and the contents. See **Figure 14.3** for an example of an introduction page.

LIST OF SIGNIFICANT LIFE EXPERIENCES

This section of your portfolio includes a year-by-year account of all your significant life experiences (turning points). You are preparing a chronological record, or time line. Resources that can help you are family members, friends, photo albums, and journals. Don't be concerned about what you learned but concentrate on experiences that are important because you

- Found the experience enjoyable
- Found the experience painful
- Learned something new about yourself

- Achieved something that you value
- Received recognition
- Expended considerable time, energy, or money

This section can also be written as an autobiography. It can include

- Graduation and formal education
- Jobs/promotions
- Marriage/divorce
- Special projects
- Volunteer work
- Training and workshops

- Self-study or reentry into college
- Extensive travel
- Hobbies and crafts
- Relocation
- Military service
- Events in your family

ANALYSIS OF ACCOMPLISHMENTS

Once you have completed your list of significant life experiences, you are now ready to identify and describe what you have learned and how you learned it. Specifically, identify what you learned in terms of knowledge, skills, competencies, and values and how you can demonstrate the learning. Whenever possible, include evidence or a measurement of the learning. Review your list of significant experiences and look for patterns, themes, or trends. Assess your accomplishments. Did these experiences

- Help you make decisions?
- Help you clarify and set goals?
- Help you learn something new?
- Broaden your view of life?
- Accept diversity in people?

- Help you take responsibility?
- Increase confidence and self-esteem?
- Result in self-understanding?
- Change your attitude?
- Change your values?

INVENTORY OFF SKILLS AND COMPETENCIES

Use your completed Career Development Portfolio worksheets to record skills and competencies. Your college may also provide you with a list of specific courses, competencies, or categories. The Department of Labor report from the Secretary's Commission on Achieving Necessary Skills (SCANS) can be a guide. (See **Figure 14.4** on page 14–9.) Complete **Personal Performance Notebook 14.1** on page 14–10 to determine your transferable skills.

Figure 14.4   SCANS Skills

Basic Skills: reading, writing, listening, speaking, and math

Thinking Skills: critical thinking, creative problem solving, knowing how to learn, reasoning, and mental visualization

Personal Qualities: responsibility, positive attitude, dependability, self-esteem, sociability, integrity, and self-management

Interpersonal Skills: teaches others, team member, leadership, works well with diverse groups, and serves clients and customers

Information: acquires, evaluates, organizes, maintains, and uses computers

Systems: understands, monitors, corrects, designs, and improves systems

Resources: allocates time, money, material, people, and space

Technology: selects, applies, maintains, and troubleshoots

SCANS Skills Acquiring these skills and competencies will help you succeed throughout your career. *Which of these skills do you need to develop?*

Use
TM 14.8 SCANS Skills and Competencies.

Teaching Tip
Stress the importance of assessing a work philosophy. Encourage students to think about their work philosophy. It should represent key beliefs and values. You may want to share with students how your philosophy of teaching or work has changed over the years.

SCANS lists several important personal qualities for success in the workplace: responsibility, a positive attitude, dependability, self-esteem, sociability, integrity, and self-management. Cultivate these qualities and apply them to your daily routine. Your personal qualities will set you apart from others in the workplace. In **Personal Performance Notebook 14.2** on page 14–11, use critical thinking to explore ways you've learned and demonstrated your personal qualities.

DOCUMENTATION

For your Career Development Portfolio, document each of the SCANS skills and competencies and personal qualities. Indicate how and when you learned each. Write the names of people who can vouch that you have these skills, competencies, and personal qualities. Include letters of support and recommendation. These letters could be from your employer verifying your skills, from coworkers and community members, and from clients or customers expressing thanks and appreciation. Your skills and competencies may have been learned at college, in vocational training programs, in community work, through on-the-job training, or through travel.

WORK PHILOSOPHY AND GOALS

Your work philosophy is a statement about how you approach work. It can also include changes that you believe are important in your career field. For example, define your educational goals. The following is a sample statement defining your educational goals:

PEAKTIP

Valued employee qualities include
- Honesty and integrity
- A positive, motivated attitude
- Self-management and self-control
- Good communication skills
- A team-player attitude
- Dependability

Transferable Skills

Read the following and comment on the lines provided.

1. What transferable skills do you have?

_____

_____

2. What specific content skills do you have that indicate a specialized knowledge or ability, such as plumbing, computer programming, or cooking?

_____

3. List your daily activities and determine the skills involved in each. Then, consider what you like about this activity. These factors may include the environment, interactions with others, or a certain emotional reaction—for example, "I like bike riding because I am outdoors with friends, and the exercise feels great."

Activity	Skills Involved	Factors
Bike riding	Balance, stamina, discipline	Being outdoors
_____	_____	_____
_____	_____	_____
_____	_____	_____
_____	_____	_____

My immediate educational goal is to graduate with a certificate in fashion design. In five years, I plan to earn a college degree in business with an emphasis in marketing.

Define your career goals—for example,

◆ To hold a leadership role in fashion design
◆ To upgrade my skills
◆ To belong to at least one professional organization

Expand on your short-term, medium-range, and long-term goals. Include a mission statement and career objectives. You may also write your goals according to the roles you perform. What is it you hope to accomplish in each area of your life? **Figure 14.5** on page 14–12 is an example of a mission statement. Ask yourself the following questions:

◆ Do I want to improve my skills?
◆ Do I want to change careers or jobs?

Inventory of Personal Qualities

Indicate how you have learned and demonstrated each of the SCANS qualities. Next, indicate how you would demonstrate them to an employer. Add personal qualities that you think are important. Use additional pages if needed.

1. Responsibility: _____

_____

_____

2. Positive attitude: _____

_____

_____

3. Dependability: _____

_____

_____

4. Self-esteem: _____

_____

_____

5. Sociability: _____

_____

_____

6. Integrity: _____

_____

_____

7. Self-management: _____

_____

_____

Teaching Tip

Stress the importance of learning professional behavior while in college.

Use

- TM 14.9 Most Valued Employee Qualities.
- TM 14.10 Most Desirable Classroom Attitudes.

Hands-On Application

In small groups, ask students to come up with at least three or four habits that are important for professional behavior. Discuss where students can learn how to act professionally. What classes, clubs, organizations, books, and so on, may be helpful?

Figure 14.5   Sample Mission Statement

Name _____

My mission is to use my talent in fashion design to create beauty and art. I want to influence the future development of fashion. I seek to be a lifelong learner because learning keeps me creative and alive. In my family, I want to build strong, healthy, and loving relationships. At work, I want to build creative and open teams. In life, I want to be kind, helpful, and supportive to others. I will live each day with integrity and be an example of outstanding character.

Long-Term Goals
Career goals: I want to own my own fashion design company.
Educational goals: I want to teach and lead workshops.
Family goals: I want to be a supportive parent.
Community goals: I want to belong to different community organizations.
Financial goals: I want to earn enough money to live comfortably and provide my family with the basic needs and more.

Medium-Range Goals
Career goals: I want to be a manager of a fashion company.
Educational goals: I want to earn a college degree in business and marketing.

Short-Term Goals
Career goals: I want to obtain an entry-level job in fashion design.
Educational goals: I want to earn a certificate in fashion design.

Sample Mission Statement   A mission statement reveals your aspirations and your philosophy on work and life. *What other types of personal information can your mission statement reveal?*

◆ Do I want to become more competent in my present job or earn a promotion?
◆ Do I want to obtain a college degree?
◆ Do I want to spend more time in one or more areas of my life?
◆ Do I want to learn a new hobby or explore areas of interest?
◆ Do I want to become more involved in community service?
◆ Do I want to improve my personal qualities?
◆ Do I want to improve my human relations skills?
◆ Do I want to spend more time with my family?
◆ Do I want to assess my interests, aptitudes, and values? (See **Personal Performance Notebook 4.3.**)

Inventory of Interests, Aptitudes, and Values

Aptitudes are abilities or natural inclinations that you have in certain areas. Some people learn certain skills easily and are described by these aptitudes; for example, Joe is a natural salesman or Mary is a born speaker.

Check the following areas in which you have an aptitude. You may add to the list.

_____	Mechanical	_____	Gardening
_____	Clerical	_____	Investigative
_____	Musical	_____	Artistic
_____	Drama/acting	_____	Working with numbers
_____	Writing	_____	Working with people
_____	Persuasive speaking	_____	Working with animals
_____	Sales	_____	Working with things

Use **Personal Performance Notebook 14.4** to list your career, personal, and lifetime goals.

Return to Chapter 3 and review **Personal Performance Notebook 3.3: Looking Ahead.** Reflect on what you wrote and update it. How has it changed in just a few weeks? Make it a habit to reflect and make connections between what you are learning in class and how it relates to work and life. Integrate your experiences between your coursework and your outside learning experiences. How do all of these experiences relate? How are they changing the way you see yourself, others, and the world? How are they changing your values, interests, and goals? How are they changing how you view and work with diverse people? At the end of your college experience, it is very valuable to record these questions in your portfolio and update it often.

RESUME

The purpose of the resume is to show the connections between your strengths, accomplishments, and skills and the needs of a company or employer. The resume is a critical tool because it is a first impression, and first impressions count. Your resume is almost always the first contact an employer will have with you. You want it to look professional, to stand out, and to highlight your skills and competencies. Computer programs can help you format your resume, and resume classes may be offered in the career center. See **Figure 14.6** on page 14–15 for a sample resume.

You may want to include the following components in your resume:

1. **Personal information.** Write your name, address, and telephone number. If you have a temporary or school address, you will also want to include a

> ### PEAKTIP
>
> Your resume should
> - Be honest
> - Be error-free
> - Be clear and concise
> - Use action words
> - Be printed on high-quality paper
> - Focus on skills, achievements, and accomplishments

Assessing Your Goals

Fill in your goals.

Career Goals

1. _____
2. _____
3. _____
_____

Personal Goals

1. _____
2. _____
3. _____
_____

Lifetime Goals

1. _____
2. _____
3. _____
_____

PEAKTIP

Follow up with a phone call in a week or two to make certain that your resume was received. This is also the time to ask if additional information is needed and when a decision will be made. Call or write in a month if you have not heard back.

permanent address and phone number. Don't include marital status, height, weight, health, interests, picture, or hobbies unless you think they are relevant to the job. Keep your resume simple. Adding nonessential information only clutters it and detracts from the essential information.

2. **Job objective.** It is not essential that you include a job objective on your resume. The rule is to include a job objective if you will accept only a specific job. You may be willing to accept various jobs in a company, especially if you're a new graduate with little experience. If you decide not to list a job objective, you can use your cover letter to relate your resume to the specific job for which you are applying.

3. **Work experience.** List the title of your last job first, dates worked, and a brief description of your duties. Don't clutter your resume with needless detail or irrelevant jobs. You can elaborate on specific duties in your cover letter and in the interview.

4. **Educational background.** List your highest degree first, school attended, dates, and major field of study. Include educational experience that may be relevant

Figure 14.6   Sample Resume

KATIE J. JENSEN

Present address:
1423 10th Street
Arlin, Minnesota 52561
(320) 555-2896

Permanent address:
812 La Jolla Avenue
Burlingate, Wisconsin 53791
(414) 555-1928

JOB OBJECTIVE: To obtain and entry-level job as a travel agent

WORK EXPERIENCE

University Travel Agency, Arlin, Minnesota
Tour Guide, August 2000–present
- Arrange tours to historic sites in a four-state area. Responsibilities include contacting rail and bus carriers, arranging for local guides at each site, making hotel and restaurant reservations, and providing historical information about points of interest.

- Develop tours for holidays and special events. Responsibilities include pre-event planning, ticketing, and coordination of travel and event schedules.

- Specialized tour planning resulted in 24 percent increase in tour revenues over the preceding year.

Burlingate Area Convention Center, Burlingate, Wisconsin
Intern Tourist Coordinator, December 1999–June 2000
- Established initial contact with prospective speakers, coordinated schedules, and finalized all arrangements. Set up computerized database of tours using dBase IV.

- Organized receptions for groups up to 250, including reserving meeting rooms, contacting caterers, finalizing menus, preparing seating charts.

EDUCATION
Arlin Community College, Arlin, Minnesota
   Associate of Arts in Business, June 2001
   Magna Cum Laude graduate

Cross Pointe Career School, Arlin Minnesota
   Certificate in Tourism, June 1999

HONORS AND AWARDS
Academic Dean's List
Recipient of Burlingate Rotary Scholarship, 1999

CAMPUS AND COMMUNITY ACTIVITIES
Vice President Tourist Club, 2000–2001
Co-chaired 1999 home-tour fundraising event for Big Sisters

PROFESSIONAL MEMBERSHIP
Burlingate Area Convention and Visitors Bureau

Sample Resume   An effective resume should be clear, concise, and eye-catching to create the best possible first impression. *What is the most important element of your resume?*

to the job, such as certification, licensing, advanced training, intensive seminars, and summer study programs. Don't list individual classes on your resume. If you have special classes that relate directly to the job you are applying for, list them in your cover letter.

5. **Awards and honors.** List awards and honors that are related to the job or indicate excellence. In addition, you may want to list special qualifications that relate to the job, such as fluency in a foreign language. Highlight this information prominently rather than write it as an afterthought. Pack a persuasive punch by displaying your best qualifications at the beginning.

6. **Campus and community activities.** List activities that show leadership abilities and a willingness to contribute.

7. **Professional memberships and activities.** List professional memberships, speeches, or research projects connected with your profession.

8. **References.** You will want three to five references, including employment, academic, and character references. Ask instructors for a general letter before you leave their last class or soon after. Fellow members of professional associations, club advisors, a coach, or students who have worked with you on projects can also provide good character references. See **Figure 14.7** for a sample request for a recommendation letter. Ask your supervisor for a letter before you leave the job. Make certain you ask your references for permission to use their names and phone numbers. Update a list of possible references and their addresses and phone numbers. Don't print your references on the bottom of your resume. List them on a separate sheet of paper, so you can update the list when it is appropriate. Also, you may not want your references to be called until you have an interview. Include recommendations in your Career Development Portfolio. See **Figure 14.7** for an example of a letter of recommendation.

PUTTING YOUR RESUME ON-LINE

Many people put their resume on-line and create their own home page on a web site or job-listing web site. In addition, you can highlight essential aspects of your Career Development Portfolio. Many services are available to scan your resume and help you place it in an electronic database. Some services will help you design your resume and identify trends in your field. Check with your campus career center or a job search agency.

COVER LETTERS

A cover letter is a written introduction and should state the job you are applying for and what you can contribute to the company. If possible, find out to whom you should address your cover letter. Often, a call to the personnel office will yield the correct name and title. Express enthusiasm and highlight how your education, skills, and experience relate to the job and will benefit the company.

Include sample cover letters and other letters that you may find useful in your Career Development Portfolio. See **Figure 14.7** for a sample of a block-style cover letter.

PEAK TIP

Soon after you complete a class or leave a job, ask your instructor, advisor, or supervisor for a letter of recommendation. Supply a list of projects, accomplishments, and skills. Keep these letters in your Career Development Portfolio.

Figure 14.7   Sample Letters

May 2, 2005

Professor Eva Atkins
Chair of the Fashion Department
Green Briar Business Institute
100 North Bank Street
Glenwood, New Hampshire 03827

Dear Professor Atkins:

I was a student of yours last term in Fashion Design and earned and A in your class. I am currently assembling my career development portfolio so I can apply for summer positions in the fashion business. Would you please write a letter of recommendation addressing the following skills and competencies?

* My positive attitude and enthusiasm
* My ability to work with diverse people in teams
* My computer and technical skills
* My skills in design and art

I have also included my resume, which highlights my experience, GPA, and selected classes. If it is convenient, I would like to stop by your office next week and pick up this letter of recommendation. Your advice and counsel have meant so much to me over the last three years. You have served as an instructor, an advisor, and a mentor. Thank you again for all your help and support. Please call or e-mail me if you have questions.

Sincerely,
Susan Sanchos
Susan Sanchos
242 Cherry Lane
Glenwood, New Hampshire 03827
Home phone: (304) 555-8293
e-mail: susans@edu.glow.com

August 12, 2005

Mr. Jason Bently
University Travel Agency
902 Sunnybrae Lane
Pinehill, New Mexico 88503

Dear Mr. Bently:

It is a pleasure to write a letter of support for Ms. Mary Anne Myers. I have worked with Mary Anne for five years at Computer Divisions Corporation. We were part of the same project team for two years and worked well together. For the last year, I have been her supervisor at Computer Divisions. Mary Anne is a team player and works well with a variety of people. She is also well-prepared, knowledgeable, and hard-working. Recently, a major report was due and Mary Anne worked several weekends and nights to meet the deadline.

Mary Anne has a positive attitude and is willing to tackle any assignment. She is self-motivated and creative. In 2001 she won our Creative Employee Award for her new marketing design. Mary Anne is also an excellent listener. She takes the time to build rapport and listen to customers and, as a result, many repeat customers ask for her by name.

Mary Anne is a lifelong learner. She is attending classes for her college degree in the evenings, and she regularly takes additional training in computers.

I highly recommend Mary Anne Myers. She is an excellent employee. Call or e-mail me if you have questions.

Sincerely,
Joyce Morocco, MBA
Joyce Morocco, MBA
Computer Divisions Manager
388 Maple Street
Midland, New Mexico 85802
Office Phone: (606) 555-3948
e-mail: joycem@CDCorp.com

July 1, 2005

Dr. Sonia Murphy
North Clinic Health Care
2331 Terrace Street
Chicago, Illinois 69691

Dear Dr. Murphy:

Mr. David Leeland, Director of Internship at Bakers College, gave me a copy of your advertisement for a medical assistant. I am interested in being considered for the position.

Your medical office has an excellent reputation, especially regarding health care for women. I have taken several courses in women's health and volunteer at the hospital in a women's health support group. I believe I can make a significant contribution to your office.

My work experiences and internships have provided valuable hands-on experience. I set up a new computer-designed program for payroll in my internship position. In addition to excellent office skills, I also have clinical experience and people skills. I speak Spanish and have used it often in my volunteer work in hospitals.

I have paid for most of my college education. My grades are excellent, and I have been on the dean's list in my medical and health classes. I have also completed advanced computer and advanced office procedures classes.

I will call you on Tuesday, July 22, to make sure you received this letter and to find out when you might be able to arrange an interview.

Sincerely,
Julia Andrews
Julia Andrews
Green Briar Business Institute
242 Cherry Lane
Chicago, Illinois 69692
Home phone: (304) 555-5593
e-mail: jullaa@edu.BakersC.com

Sample Letters   Letters of recommendation and cover letters are other important elements in the job search process. Letters can provide a prospective employer with more insight into who you are. *Who might you ask to write a letter of recommendation?*

Interview Planning

Hands-On Application
Role-playing: In pairs, have students choose a job description and write responses for the question "How can you add value to the company?" and practice interviewing with their partners. Have them concentrate on eye contact, poise, and clear communication. Discuss in small groups.

Teaching Tip
Stress the importance of sending a thank-you note. Students may also want to follow up with a phone call if they have not heard from the interviewer in two weeks.

Key Teaching Concept
Research prospective employers and find out about the company. This research shows interest and initiative.

Teaching Tip
Encourage students to assess their interests and skills often. Stress the importance of relating their skills to the company's needs. Remind students to focus also on their personal qualities, such as honesty, responsibility, loyalty, and the ability to work with diverse people.

Just as the resume is important for opening the door, the job interview is critical for putting your best foot forward and clearly articulating why you are the best person for the job. Many of the tips discussed in this text about getting hired and being successful in a career center around both verbal and nonverbal communication skills. These communication skills will be assets during your job interview. Here are some interview strategies that will help you make full use of these skills and others:

1. **Be punctual.** A good first impression is important and can be lasting. If you arrive late, you have already said a great deal about yourself. Make certain you know the location and the time of the interview. Allow time for parking and other preliminaries.

2. **Be professional.** Being too familiar can be a barrier to a professional interview. Never call anyone by his or her first name unless you are asked to. Know the interviewer's name and title, as well as the pronunciation of the interviewer's name, and don't sit down until the interviewer does.

3. **Dress appropriately.** Since much of our communication is nonverbal, dressing appropriately for the interview is important. In most situations, you will be safe if you wear clean, pressed, conservative business clothes in a neutral color. Pay special attention to grooming. Keep makeup light and wear little jewelry. Make certain your nails and hair are clean, trimmed, and neat. Don't carry a large purse, a backpack, books, a coat, or a hat. Leave extra clothing in an outside office, and simply carry a pen, a pad of paper, and a small folder with extra copies of your resume and references.

4. **Learn about the company.** Be prepared; show that you have researched the company. What product(s) does it make? How is it doing? What is the competition? Always refer to the company when you give examples.

5. **Learn about the position.** Before you interview, request a job description from the personnel office. What kind of employee, with what skills, is the company looking for to fill the position? You will likely be asked the common question "Why are you interested in this job?" Be prepared to answer with a reference to the company.

6. **Relate your experience to the job.** Use every question as an opportunity to show how your skills relate to the job. Use examples taken from school, previous jobs, internships, volunteer work, leadership in clubs, and experiences growing up to indicate that you have the personal qualities, aptitudes, and skills needed at this new job.

7. **Be honest.** Although it is important to be confident and stress your strengths, it is equally important to your sense of integrity to be honest. Dishonesty always catches up with you sooner or later. Someone will verify your background, so do not exaggerate your accomplishments, grade point average, or experience.

8. **Focus on how you can benefit the company.** Don't ask about benefits, salary, or vacations until you are offered the job. During a first interview, try to show how you can contribute to the organization. Don't appear to be too eager to move up through the company or suggest that you are more interested in gaining experience than in contributing to the company.

9. **Be poised and relaxed.** Avoid nervous habits, such as tapping your pencil, playing with your hair, or covering your mouth with your hand. Watch language such as *you know, ah, stuff like that.* Don't smoke, chew gum, fidget, or bite your nails.

10. **Maintain comfortable eye contact.** Look people in the eye and speak with confidence. Your eyes reveal much about you; use them to show interest, confidence, poise, and sincerity. Use other nonverbal techniques, such as a firm handshake, to reinforce your confidence.

11. **Practice interviewing.** Consider videotaping a mock interview. Most college campuses have this service available through the career center or media department. Rehearse questions and be prepared to answer directly.

12. **Anticipate question types.** Expect open-ended questions, such as "What are your strengths?" "What are your weaknesses?" "Tell me about your best work experience," and "What are your career goals?" Decide in advance what information and skills are pertinent to the position and reveal your strengths. For example, you could say, "I learned to get along with a diverse group of people when I worked for the park service."

13. **Ending the interview.** Close the interview on a positive note. Thank the interviewer for his or her time, shake hands, and say that you are looking forward to hearing from him or her.

14. **Follow up with a letter.** A follow-up letter is especially important. It serves as a reminder for the interviewer. For you, it is an opportunity to thank the interviewer and a chance to make a positive comment about the position and the company. See **Figure 14.8** on page 14–20 for a sample follow-up letter.

Hands-On Application
Tell students that it is best to work with a study partner when reviewing work samples. Have them bring to class copies of projects, papers, reports, drawings, job descriptions, and anything that demonstrates their abilities, achievements, skills, or competencies.

SAMPLES OF WORK

When appropriate, include samples of your work in your portfolio. Think of how you can demonstrate visually your expertise in your particular area or field. These samples can include articles, portions of a book, artwork, fashion sketches, drawings, photos of work, poetry, pictures, food demonstrations, brochures, a typical day at your job, job descriptions, and performance reviews. If you are in the music field, you can include visual samples of flyers and an audiotape.

SUMMARY OF TRANSCRIPTS

Include a copy of all transcripts of college work.

CREDENTIALS, CERTIFICATES, WORKSHOPS

Include a copy of credentials, certificates, workshops, seminars, training sessions, conferences, continuing education courses, and other examples of lifelong learning.

BIBLIOGRAPHY

Include a bibliography of books you have read that pertain to your major, career goals, or occupation.

It is generally much easier to complete the Career Development Portfolio if students work with a study partner. Have students report progress to their team and use their small group to answer questions, brainstorm ideas, and review one last time. Ask them to use the first meeting with their study partner to discuss the purpose and criteria of the portfolio.

Figure 14.8   Sample Follow-Up Letter

May 29, 2005

Mr. Henry Sanders
The Mountain View Store
10 Rock Lane
Alpine, Montana 79442

Dear Mr. Sanders:

Thank you for taking the time yesterday to meet with me concerning the position of sales representative. I enjoyed meeting you and your employees, learning more about your growing company, and touring your facilities. I was especially impressed with your new line of outdoor wear. It is easy to see why you lead the industry in sales.

I am even more excited about joining your sales team now that I have visited with you. I have the education, training, enthusiasm, and personal qualities necessary to succeed in business. I am confident that I would fit in with your staff and make a real contribution to the sales team.

Thank you again for the interview and an enjoyable morning.

Sincerely,

John A. Bennett

John A. Bennett
124 East Buttermilk Lane
LaCrosse, Wisconsin 54601
Home phone: (608) 555-4958
e-mail: johnb@shast.edu

Sample Follow-Up Letter   A follow-up letter is another opportunity to set yourself apart from other job candidates. *What should you include in your follow-up letter?*

APPENDIX

Include internships, leadership experiences in clubs and sports, volunteer work, service to the community, and travel experiences that relate to your goals. You can also include awards, honors, and certificates of recognition.

Overcoming the Barriers to Portfolio Development

The biggest barrier to career success is procrastination. Maybe you're telling yourself that the idea of a portfolio sounds good, but you also think of these excuses:

- I don't have the time.
- It's a lot of work.
- I don't have enough work samples.
- I wouldn't know where to start.
- I'll do it when I'm ready for a job.

TECH FOR SUCCESS

- **Your Resume On-Line** Many potential employers are willing to receive your resume and supporting documents via a web site or CD. A number of programs and services, such as FolioLive (www.foliolive.com), are available to help you develop your resume on-line. Features include a set amount of space for storing digital files, such as graphic images, video, and PowerPoint presentations. Your school may use a preferred source for developing a portfolio, so consult your advisor as you get started.
- **Job Search Web Sites** There are a number of job search sites, such as monster.com and hotjobs.com. These sites require you to type your resume into their format, which then feeds into their search engine. When you are ready to start your job hunt, it's worth investigating these and more specialized sites that cater to the field you are pursuing. Also, check out any professional organizations in the field, as they may also provide job listings on-line.

A Career Development Portfolio is an ongoing process. It will take time to develop your work philosophy, goals, documentation of your skills and competencies, and work samples. If you are resisting or procrastinating, work with a partner. Together, you can organize supplies, brainstorm ideas, review each other's philosophies and goals, and help assemble the contents.

Another major barrier to career planning is the notion that, once you choose a major and a career, you are on a straight and settled path. Change is part of life. The average student changes majors three times, and the average worker will have four or five career changes. Career planning is a lifelong process, and your Career Development Portfolio should be started during your freshman year and updated throughout your life.

As middle management jobs are eliminated, workers are expected to take more responsibility for managing themselves and their work progress. The job security of lifelong employment will be replaced by a reliance on employees' own portfolios of skills and competencies. Salary increases and advancement will tend to be based on performance and production, rather than seniority or entitlement. You will be responsible for managing your own career and marketing yourself. Career planning gives you the information for making sound decisions, helps you learn how to assess your skills and competencies, and creates a dynamic system that encourages you to adapt to changing jobs and careers. The Internet, computer technology, and telecommunications have fueled major changes. Being prepared, resilient, flexible, and willing to be a lifelong learner will help you overcome many barriers to career success.

Choosing Your Career

A career choice takes time, planning, and effort. You will need time to determine your interests, values, strengths, abilities, skills, and personality. Your Career Development Portfolio will be invaluable for compiling samples of your work, skills, and abilities,

Class Discussion
Ask students if their values are in alignment with their career goals. Why is this important?

Use
TM 14.11 Job Search Steps.

Class Discussion
Discuss the steps that students need to follow for a job search.

Peak Progress 14.1

Tips for Exploring Your Career

The following are some guidelines to help you as you prepare for choosing your career:

- **Talk with professionals.** Try to obtain a realistic view of their various occupations. Find out what they like and dislike about their work.
- **Get work experience.** This is a great way to learn about working conditions in the fields you want to pursue. A part-time job, volunteer work, or an internship can provide valuable experience and help you determine if a specific career path is right for you.
- **Explore careers in depth.** Many careers do not have traditional titles. Focus on your interests and skills and incorporate them into possible careers.
- **Network.** Personal contacts are excellent ways to explore careers and to find a job. Networking provides access to several people who can serve as mentors and help connect you to jobs and opportunities. Personal and professional contacts must be created, cultivated, and expanded. Here are a few tips that can help you:
  - Brainstorm a list of contacts.
  - Talk with instructors, advisors, and counselors.
  - Talk with other students.
  - Collect business cards.
  - Join professional organizations.

PEAKTIP

In the workplace, a positive manager will do these things:

- Communicate with others.
- Motivate others.
- Convey a positive attitude.
- Accept people from all cultures.
- Adapt to new situations.
- Understand a systems approach to motivation.
- Listen and respect others' views.
- Encourage others' self-esteem.
- Bounce back after disappointment or failure.

so that you can highlight your strengths and competencies to others when you begin your job search. This process may take time and effort, but you will be gratified when you decide on an interesting and appropriate career. See **Peak Progress 14.1** for tips on exploring your career. **Peak Progress 14.2** shows how to apply the Adult Learning Cycle to relating your school experience to job success.

Workplace Trends

Keep a section in the appendix of your Career Development Portfolio for workplace trends that relate directly to your occupation. One of the important trends will be education on the job. Some of this education will be informal and consist of acquiring on-the-job training, acquiring new job skills, learning to complete challenging projects, and shifting your work style so that you can work more effectively with others. Other education will be formal, such as seminars, courses, and workshops designed to improve or add to your job skills. These formal courses may include training in these areas:

- Computers
- World Wide Web
- Grant writing

- Financial planning
- Technical skills
- Report writing

Peak Progress 14.2

Applying the Adult Learning Cycle to Connect School with Job Success

1. **RELATE. Why do I want to learn this?** It's motivating for me to see the connection between my coursework and my career opportunities. I know that creating a strong Career Development Portfolio will help highlight my accomplishments, experiences, and skills to a future employer. It will also help me pinpoint the areas where I need more experience or coursework.

2. **OBSERVE. How does this work?** I can learn about job success by observing people who are positive, motivated, and successful in their careers. I can find out what they did to prepare for their first job. I'll assess my skills and personal qualities and list them in my Career Development Portfolio. I'll determine new habits that will help me succeed in any job and observe how I'm improving.

3. **THINK. What does this mean?** What are my strengths? What areas do I need to improve to make me more marketable when looking for a job? I will record the skills and positive habits and qualities necessary for both school and job success and set goals to acquire those skills and change behaviors. I will look for connections between school and work.

4. **DO. What can I do with this?** I'll explore options in the career center and at career days. I will begin and update the Career Development Portfolio. I will focus on my successes and reward myself when I make progress. Each month, I'll determine, demonstrate, and practice a new personal quality and an essential skill.

5. **TEACH. Whom can I share this with?** I'll share my Career Development Portfolio with others and ask for feedback. I'll explain how it is an effective tool for me to assess and demonstrate my skills and personal qualities.

The more you go through the cycle, the more effective you will be at relating your coursework to your future career.

Hands-On Application
Ask students to assess their skills periodically. They should also assess their attitudes and their willingness to change and grow. After answering the questions, have them discuss their answers with study partners. Add to this list.

Teaching Tip
Emphasize the importance of using the Adult Learning Cycle to create interest and improve skills.

Other formal seminars, courses, or workshops may develop better human relations skills, covering these topics:

- Alcohol and other drug abuse
- Sexual harassment
- Cultural and gender diversity
- Team building
- Time and stress management

- Communication
- Motivation
- Negotiation
- Conflict resolution
- Basic supervision

You may decide that you need to earn an advanced degree or certificate by going to lengthy training sessions or attending college in the evenings. However you go about it, lifelong education is a new and significant job trend. The employee who learns new skills, cross-trains in various positions, and has excellent human relations skills will be sought after and promoted.

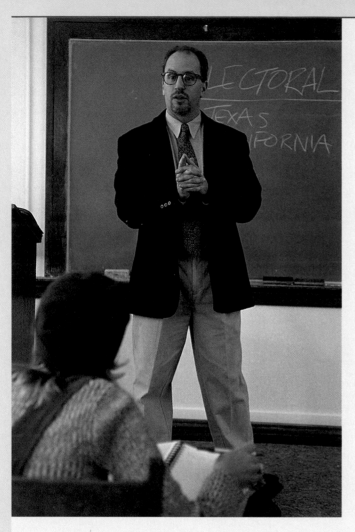

Steven Price

SOCIAL STUDIES TEACHER/LEGISLATOR

Related Majors: Education, Social Studies, Political Science

Career Planning Is Lifelong

Steven Price taught social studies classes at a high school. With an avid interest in politics, Steven soon developed a strong curriculum for teaching government and current affairs. He was well known in the district for his innovative classes in which students researched and debated local issues and then voted on them.

Throughout the years, Steven had remained active in a local political party. Each year, he could be counted on to help hand out flyers and canvass neighborhoods before the September primaries and November elections. One year, a party member suggested that Steven run for state legislator.

Steven took the offer seriously. After 21 years of teaching, he felt ready for a change. He had enjoyed being in the classroom, especially when his students had shared his passion for politics. However, he felt that being a state legislator would allow him to work more directly in bringing about changes in his community. He took a leave of absence from his teaching job. He filed the appropriate papers and worked hard with a campaign manager to get his name out to the voters in his district. Because Steven had already prepared a career portfolio over the years, the manager was able to use the collected information to promote Steven.

Using his years of experience teaching government and current affairs, Steven felt rejuvenated and excited as he worked on his political campaign. His lifelong commitment to politics paid off when he won the election! He was glad that he had taken the risk. A career change was a positive move for both Steven and his community.

CRITICAL THINKING

What might have happened to Steven if he had not taken the risks of moving to a different career?

Business Ethics

Business ethics have become an important issue in today's business world. The go-for-it-at-any-cost attitude of corporate raiders and unethical businesspeople has tarnished the image of big business and has made us all more aware of ethical business practices. Each employee must make decisions based on moral values and conscience and must follow the code of ethics provided by his or her industry. Sometimes this is an unwritten code, and sometimes it is an industrywide set of rules. Whether they are written or unwritten, ethical business standards must be upheld. Sometimes a seemingly small indiscretion or decision can cost a job or result in a tarnished reputation.

Top managers also have a responsibility for setting an ethical code and acting as role models for all employees. They should act with integrity and model ethical behavior. Corporations must set clear guidelines for ethical behavior and insist on accountability. Many corporations have improved their images by being socially responsible and encouraging their employees to become involved in the community and contribute their time and talents to worthwhile community agencies and causes. Make certain you review your campus and workplace codes of ethics. Use **Personal Performance Notebook 14.5** to reflect on your values. Indicate how you have demonstrated them and add any additional values to the list.

Personal Performance Notebook 14.5

Values

Values are qualities that are important to you and enhance your life. Your values are ideals that make you unique, and they act as motivators. When your life's goals, behavior, and major career choices match your values, you are more centered and productive. Following is a partial list of values. You may wish to add to this list and make it more personal. Describe in a few words the values you believe are important to you and how you demonstrate them.

Values	How Values Are Demonstrated
Kindness	_____
Generosity	_____
Citizenship	_____
Integrity	_____
Friendship	_____
Honesty	_____
Work ethic	_____
Spirituality	_____

Peak Performer Profile

David Filo and Jerry Yang

It's a sure thing that anyone seeking information on the World Wide Web knows about Yahoo!—short for Yet Another Hierarchical Officious Oracle. Log on to Yahoo.com and you'll be able to track down the number of times your heart beats per year (40 million beats), search the ancient tombs of Egypt, or even check out your astrological profile. What started as a spare-time activity between friends, David Filo and Jerry Yang has emerged as a successful business and one of the Internet's most popular search engines.

Although Filo and Yang crossed paths as Stanford doctoral candidates, they took a roundabout route. Their lives began, literally, on opposite ends of the earth. At the age of 10, Jerry Yang, born Chih-Yuan Yang, immigrated to America from Taiwan with his grandmother, widowed mother, and little brother in 1968. An only child, David Filo grew up in an alternative community in Louisiana. His family lived with six other families, sharing a garden and a single kitchen. When Filo and Yang both went to Stanford to study electrical engineering in the early 1990s, they discovered common interests—and a great idea.

In 1994, they put together one of the first directories to help net surfers navigate the Internet. Previously, web sites had used only a domain name, such as a personal or company name, making it almost impossible to locate material by topic. Filo and Yang found a novel way to break down and organize the web sites into categories, a system not unlike a library's catalog. They also included such useful features as news and weather, shopping guides, a handy reference section, and even a personalized page, "My Yahoo," for users who wanted to keep favorite links close at hand. Today, Yahoo! receives over 200 million hits each month and has transformed the Internet.

PERFORMANCE THINKING   If you were preparing Filo's and Yang's resumes, what would you write in the job objective section for these "Chief Yahoos"? What are some of their personal experiences that may have contributed to their career success?

In summary, in this chapter, I learned to

- *See the value of portfolios.* My portfolio helps me assess, highlight, and demonstrate my strengths, skills, and competencies. Classes in assessment of prior learning, independent study, and capstone courses often give extra credit for portfolios.

- *Start early and update.* Starting my portfolio early helps me get organized and gives me a chance to add, update, and edit throughout my college experience and into my first career.

- *Organize essential elements.* Assembling my portfolio in a three-ring notebook and box helps me collect and organize work samples, information, lists, examples, transcripts, credentials, certificates, workshops, and documentation of personal qualities.

- *List significant life experiences and accomplishments.* I include such experiences as formal education, special classes and projects, volunteer work and service learning, jobs, self-study, travel, hobbies, military service, special recognition, and accomplishments and events that helped me learn new skills or something about myself or others. I list books that I have read that pertain to my major or career or that have helped me develop a certain philosophy.

- *Document skills and competencies.* I connect essential skills to school and work, and I look for transferable skills. I document critical thinking, interpersonal, computer, financial, and basic skills that are important for school and job success. When appropriate, I include samples of my work.

- *Reflect and write out goals.* I know the importance of having a written mission statement and goals and a philosophy about work, values, interests, and lifelong education.

- *Explore careers and workplace trends.* I take the time to learn more about career opportunities, and I observe workplace trends, especially additional education and training needed. I create a code of ethics and document how I demonstrate character, integrity, and civility.

- *Create a resume and cover letter.* My resume is an essential document that helps me highlight my education, work experience, awards, professional memberships, and campus and community activities. Creating a sample cover letter and updating my resume will make it easy for me to apply for a variety of jobs at a moment's notice.

- *Prepare for an interview.* I save articles and tips on interviewing and practice whenever possible. I assess my performance and strive to improve.

Performance Strategies ••••••••••••••

Following are the top 10 tips for connecting school to job success:

- ◆ See value and meaning in creating a Career Development Portfolio.
- ◆ Know how to connect essential work skills and competencies to school and life and how to transfer skills.
- ◆ Assemble your portfolio in an organized planning guide and review, assess, update, and make additions to your portfolio often.
- ◆ Document skills, competencies, and personal qualities in your portfolio.
- ◆ Include essential elements in your portfolio, such as a resume, transcripts, and accomplishments.
- ◆ Use your portfolio to reflect on your work philosophy and life mission, as well as to set goals and priorities.
- ◆ Observe and reflect upon workplace trends and create a code of ethics.
- ◆ Use affirmations and visualization to stay focused and overcome procrastination.
- ◆ Observe, assess, and make an inventory of personal qualities and document and demonstrate them.
- ◆ Value, document, and demonstrate service learning and volunteer work on campus and in the community.

Review Questions ••••••••••••••••••••

1. What is the purpose of your Career Development Portfolio?
2. What are the four steps for organizing and assembling your portfolio?
3. How can you document your skills, competencies, and personal qualities for your portfolio?
4. What information should be included in a resume?
5. How long should career planning take?

REVISUALIZATION ••

Revisit the Visualization box on the first page of this chapter and your journal entry in **Worksheet 14.1.** It may be easy to see the connections between school and work in a number of your classes, but some may be more difficult. Continue in **Worksheet 14.1** by indicating a class you are taking that doesn't seem to relate directly to your career plans. Use the ABCDE method to analyze what you are learning in that class and how it benefits you either today or later on—for example,

A = Actual event: "I have to take a science class, which doesn't make sense, since I'm an advertising major. What does dissecting a frog in general biology have to do with creating an effective sales campaign?"

B = Beliefs: "This course is a waste of my time that I could be spending learning related skills or getting actual on-the-job experience."

C = Consequences: "I might not do well in this course, since I'm not all that interested in the subject."

D = Dispute: "When I think about it, biology is a lot like connecting the dots—using my critical thinking skills to observe and assess a situation. The scientific method is all about accumulating data, determining an answer or a rationale, and supporting my answer. A good ad campaign does the same—I look at demographics, trends, and what my competitors are doing; I develop a sales strategy or campaign; and I pitch it to clients and to potential customers. Taking biology helps me practice my critical thinking and creativity—two important skills I will need in advertising."

E = Energized: "Now that I see the relevance of this course and its connection to my future career, I'm more motivated to participate and get the most out of this class. I now see this learning experience in a more positive light, and I understand how it will benefit me."

EXPLORING CAREERS

In the Classroom

Maria Lewis likes to make presentations, enjoys working with children, and is a crusader for equality and the environment. She also values family, home, and community. Making a lot of money is not important to her. Her motivation comes from the feeling that she is making a difference and enjoys what she is doing. Now that her own family is grown, she wants to complete a college degree. However, she is hesitant because she has been out of school for many years.

1. How would you help Maria with her decision?

_____

_____

2. What careers would you have Maria explore?

_____

_____

In the Workplace

Maria completed a degree in childhood development. She has been a caregiver at a children's day-care center for two years. She has enjoyed her job, but she feels that it is time for a change. If she wants to stay in her field and advance, she has to travel and go into management. She wants more time off to spend with her family, write, and become more involved in community action groups. Maria would like to stay in a related field. She still likes working with children, but she also enjoys giving presentations and workshops and writing. She has thought about consulting, writing, or starting her own small business.

3. What strategies in this chapter would help Maria with her career change?

_____

_____

4. What one habit would you recommend to Maria to help her with her career planning?

_____

_____

APPLYING THE ABCDE METHOD OF SELF-MANAGEMENT

In the Visualization box on page 14–1, you were asked to write down one of the classes you are currently taking and list at least three skills you will acquire in this class that will benefit you in your career:

_____

_____

_____

Now, think about a class you are taking that doesn't seem to relate directly to your career plans. Use the ABCDE method to analyze what you are learning in that class and how it benefits you either today or later on.

A = Actual event:

B = Beliefs:

C = Consequences:

D = Dispute:

E = Energized:

Use positive visualization to help you achieve the results you want. See yourself creating a portfolio that helps you organize all the information you're learning and relate it to job success. Think of the confidence you'll have when you've developed a cover letter and resume and practiced for job interviews. See yourself focused with a vision and purpose and working in a job you love.

CAREER PLANNING GRID

Use this checklist of strategies to help you with your career planning.

	Assess				Plan				Action Network				Follow-Up			
	Assess your skills.	Assess your abilities.	Assess your interests.	Assess your values and dreams.	Set goals and priorities.	Translate skills into career.	Plan network system.	Plan resume and cover letter.	Volunteer, intern, get job experience.	Network.	Send out resume.	Interview.	Write thank-you notes.	Follow up with phone calls.	Follow up on job leads.	Follow up on network building.
Freshman Year																
Summer																
Sophomore Year																
Summer																
Junior Year																
Summer																
Senior Year																
Summer																

PREPARING YOUR RESUME

In anticipation of preparing your resume, start thinking about the information that will appear on it. On the following lines, summarize your skills and qualifications and match them to the requirements of the job you are seeking. Use proactive words and verbs when writing information for your resume. Here are some examples:

- *Organized* a group of after-school tutors for math and accounting courses
- *Wrote* and *published* articles for the school newspaper
- *Participated* in a student academic advisory board
- *Developed* a new accounting system
- *Managed* the petty cash accounts for the PTA
- Can *keyboard* 60 wpm

You should not be discouraged if you have only a few action phrases to write at this time. You can add to your list as you continue your studies and become an active participant on your campus and with your courses of study.

Skills and Qualifications

1. _____

2. _____

3. _____

4. _____

5. _____

6. _____

7. _____

8. _____

9. _____

10. _____

INTERVIEWING THE EMPLOYED

Make a list of the types of jobs you think you would like. Then, make a list of contacts in those types of jobs. Ask those contacts if you can interview them about their jobs. The purpose of each interview is to find out about the person's career and what the job is really like. Following is a list of questions to ask. (Remember to send a thank-you note after each interview.)

Person interviewed _____

Job title _____ Date _____

1. Why did you choose your career?

   _____

2. What do you do on a typical day?

   _____

3. What do you like best about your job?

   _____

4. What do you like least?

   _____

5. Would you mind telling me the salary range for your job?

   _____

6. If you had to do it again, would you choose the same job? If not, what would you do differently in planning your career?

   _____

7. What advice can you give me for planning my career?

   _____

EXPLORING CAREERS

Go to the library or career center and find 10 careers you've never heard of or are interested in exploring. Do the following exercises. Then, add this page to your Career Development Portfolio.

1. Use the Internet to explore at least one career.

   _____

   _____

   _____

2. Can these careers be grouped into one field?

   _____

   _____

   _____

3. List your skills and interests. Then, list the careers that match these skills and interests. Create names for careers if they are unusual.

Skills/Interests	Possible Careers
_____	_____
_____	_____
_____	_____

4. Review your list of skills and interests. What stands out? Do you like working with people or accomplishing tasks? Think of as many jobs as you can that relate to your skills and interests. Your skills and interests are valuable clues about your future career.

   _____

   _____

   _____

5. Describe an ideal career that involves the skills you enjoy using the most. Include the location of this ideal career and the kinds of coworkers, customers, and employees you would encounter.

   _____

   _____

   _____

Photo Credits

Chapter 1: p. 1–1, Photolink/Getty Images; p. 1–11, Verve Commissioned Series/Getty Images; p. 1–13, Getty Images; p. 1–14, Royalty-Free/Corbis; p. 1–27, Royalty-Free/Corbis; p. 1–31, © James Leynse/Corbis; p. 1–33, Verve Commissioned Series/Getty Images

Chapter 2: p. 2–1, Duncan Smith/Getty Images; p. 2–17, Courtesy Carson Scholars Fund; p. 2–22, PhotoDisc/Getty Images; p. 2–28, Jack Hollingsworth/Getty Images

Chapter 3: p. 3–1, Joaquin Palting/Getty Images; p. 3–21, E. Dygas/Getty Images; p. 3–23, Ryan McVay/Getty Images; p. 3–24, © Bassouls Sophie/Corbis Sygma; p. 3–28, Keith Brofsky/Getty Images

Chapter 4: p. 4–1, Royalty-Free/Corbis; p. 4–21, Ryan McVay/Getty Images; p. 4–22, © Steve Azzara/Corbis; p. 4–23, Ryan McVay/Getty Images

Chapter 5: p. 5–1, PhotoDisc/Getty Images; p. 5–8, D. Berry/PhotoLink/Getty Images; p. 5–13, Doug Menuez/Getty Images; p. 5–17, PhotoDisc/Getty Images; p. 5–19, © Vaughn Youtz/Zuma/Corbis; p. 5–23, Andrew Ward/Life File/Getty Images

Chapter 6: p. 6–1, Eyewire/PhotoDisc/Getty Images; p. 6–7, Adam Crowley/Getty Images; p. 6–11, PhotoDisc/Getty Images; p. 6–20, Ryan McVay/Getty Images; p. 6–21, © Reuters/Corbis; p. 6–23, Antonio Mo/Getty Images; p. 6–30TL, PhotoLink/Getty Images; p. 6–30TM, Steve Cole/Getty Images; p. 6–30TR, PhotoLink/Getty Images; p. 6–30BL, Amanda Clement/Getty Images; p. 6–30BR, Kent Knudson/PhotoLink/Getty Images

Chapter 7: p. 7–1, PhotoDisc/Getty Images; p. 7–15, Royalty-Free/Corbis; p. 7–18, Keith Brofsky/Getty Images; p. 7–22, Courtesy Jamba Juice; p. 7–24, EyeWire/PhotoDisc/Getty Images

Chapter 8: p. 8–1, PhotoDisc/Getty Images; p. 8–16, Jeff Maloney/Getty Images; p. 8–18, Keith Brofsky/Getty Images; p. 8–23, Ryan McVay/Getty Images; p. 8–25, © Marc Brasz/Corbis; p. 8–27, Keith Brofsky/Getty Images

Chapter 9: p. 9–1, Ryan McVay/Getty Images; p. 9–23, © Chuck Savage/Corbis; p. 9–24, © AP/Wide World Photos; p. 9–27, Keith Brofsky/Getty Images

Chapter 10: p. 10–1, Karl Weatherly/Getty Images; p. 10–8, Jeff Maloney/Getty Images; p. 10–10, Jack Star/PhotoLink/Getty Images; p. 10–12, Doug Menuez/Getty Images; p. 10–21, Royalty-Free/Corbis; p. 10–26, © Alex Grimm/Reuters/Corbis; p. 10–29, C. Borland/PhotoLink/Getty Images

Chapter 11: p. 11–1, Ryan McVay/Getty Images; p. 11–5, Keith Brofsky/Getty Images; p. 11–21, PhotoDisc/Getty Images; p. 11–26, © Tony Freeman/PhotoEdit; p. 11–27, © Corbis; p. 11–29, Royalty-Free/Corbis

Chapter 12: p. 12–1, Patrick Clark/Getty Images; p. 12–19, Ryan McVay/Getty Images; p. 12–21, Royalty-Free/Corbis; p. 12–22, © Joe Skipper/Reuters/Corbis; p. 12–25, Ryan McVay/Getty Images

Chapter 13: p. 13–1, EyeWire/PhotoDisc/Getty Images; p. 13–19, Skip Nall/Getty Images; p. 13–20, © Duomo/Corbis; p. 13–23, Adam Crowley/Getty Images

Chapter 14: p. 14–1, Keith Brofsky/Getty Images; p. 14–24, Doug Menuez/Getty Images; p. 14–26, © Ed Kashi/Corbis; p. 14–29, Royalty-Free/Corbis

Subject Index

A

ABCDE method of self-management, 13-14
   active listening-lectures, 4-26
   basic math and science skills, 9-28
   being read to, 5-24
   college classes-skills for careers, 14-30
   confrontational situation, 11-30
   difficult situation, 9-28
   feeling of health, 10-30
   financial goal, 12-24
   goals, 1-34
   losing control of emotions, 2-29
   overwhelmed-too much to do, 3-29
   performance, sporting event, test, 7-23, 8-28
   remembering names/information, 6-24
   repeating negative habits, 13-24
ABCDE visualization method, 1-5
Accepting criticism, 11-14–11-16
Accountant/financial planner, 1-27
Acronym, 6-13
Active listening, 4-1–4-7
   adult learning cycle, 4-6
   building rapport, 11-2
   case study, 4-25
   follow-up activity, 4-7
   recording the message. *See* Note taking
   self-assessment, 4-34
   signal words/phrases, 4-4–4-5
   strategies, 4-2–4-3
   worksheet, 4-33
Active listening strategies, 4-2–4-3
Active reading, 5-1–5-34
   adult learning cycle, 5-4
   analyzing chapters, 5-31
   attitude, 5-13, 5-25
   barriers to, 5-13, 5-32
   case study, 5-23
   five-part reading system, 5-3–5-5
   importance, 5-2
   preparation for reading, 5-5–5-8
   previewing, 5-8
   reading forms, 5-16–5-18
   reading matrix, 5-33
   reading outline, 5-29–5-30
   reading strategies, 5-9–5-10
   reviewing, 5-10–5-11
   SQ3R reading system, 5-5, 5-6–5-7
   technical reading, 5-15–5-16
   worksheets, 5-26–5-28
Adams, Scott, 9-24
Addictions, 10-13–10-15
Adjective, 8-13

Adult learning cycle, 1-23–1-26
   communicator, 11-6
   developing positive habits, 13-8
   exploring majors, 1-29
   financial resource management, 12-18
   healthier lifestyle, 10-25
   listening, 4-6
   math and science anxiety, 9-13
   memory skills, 6-3
   public speaking, 8-21
   reading, 5-4
   school-job success, 14-23
   self-management and control, 4-9
   take control of time and life, 3-12
   test anxiety, 7-17
   test-taking skills, 7-17
Adverb, 8-13
Advising center, 12-6
Aerobic exercise, 10-7
Affirmations, 4-14–4-15, 13-12
Ah-ha exercise, 9-14
AIDS/HIV, 10-17, 10-18
Alcohol abuse, 10-10–10-12
ALEKS, 9-13
Allen, Woody, 4-15
Alumni association, 12-8
American Psychological Association (APA) style of citation, 8-11–8-12
Analyzer, 1-18, 1-24
Anger management, 4-8
Anonymous, 4-8
APA style of citation, 8-11–8-12
Apologize, 11-9, 11-16
Aristotle, 13-2
Armstrong, Lance, 10-26
Armstrong, Thomas, 1-11
Assertive communication, 11-12
Assertive communication role-playing, 11-13
Association, 6-13
Attitude
   math and science anxiety, 9-10
   needs/motives, 2-12–2-13
   negative, 2-11–2-12
   positive, 2-10–2-11, 13-17, 13-27
   problem solving, 9-2
   procrastination, 3-16
   reading, 5-13, 5-25
Audit classes, 3-14
Auditory learners, 1-8, 1-11
Autobiography, 1-40

B

Back-up plans, 6-18
Balance your life, 3-20–3-22
Barriers to
    communication, 11-17–11-18
    memory, 6-17–6-18
    motivation, 2-23–2-25
    note taking, 4-20
    portfolio development, 14-20–14-21
    reading, 5-13, 5-32
    self-assessment, 1-26
Bates, Marilyn, 1-14, 1-15
Beloved (Morrison), 8-25
Benson, Lori, 8-23
Bergstrom, Marla, 6-20
Biased language, 8-14
Bibliography, 8-4, 8-11–8-12
Bibliography card, 8-6
Bill paying on-line, 12-20
Binder, 3-14
Birth control, 10-18
Bluest Eye, The (Morrison), 8-25
Books, 8-15–8-16
Books on-line, 5-14
Brain hemispheres. *See* Left-brain dominant people;
    Right-brain dominant people
Brainstorming, 8-5, 9-12, 9-14
Brainstorming notes, 9-15
Break projects down into smaller tasks, 3-8–3-9
Breathing, 10-24
Briggs, Katherine, 1-14
Brown, Kathy, 11-26
Browser software, 8-17
Budgeting, 12-15–12-16, 12-17, 12-28
Building community, 12-2, 12-3, 12-25, 12-30
Burke, Edmund, 5-9
Burnout, 10-22
Business ethics, 4-25

C

Caffeine, 10-4, 10-10
Calorie counting, 10-9
Campus facilities, 12-8
Campus resources, 12-2–12-9
    campus facilities, 12-8
    financial resources, 12-9
    paper and material resources, 12-4, 12-6
    people resources, 12-4
    program resources, 12-6, 12-8
Cancer warning signs, 10-3
Capitalization, 5-12
Capra, Frank, 9-12
Career development. *See* Job hunting
Career development center, 12-6
Career development portfolio, 14-1–14-34

analysis of accomplishments, 14-8
appendix, 4-20
barriers to portfolio development, 4-20–4-21
bibliography, 4-19
career planning grid, 14-31
choosing a career, 4-21–4-22
college transcripts, 4-19
content page, 14-6–14-7
cover letter, 14-5, 14-6
cover page, 14-5, 14-6
credentials, certificates, workshops, 4-19
documentation, 14-9
elements, 14-5
end-of-chapter exercises. *See* Career development
    portfolio—end-of-chapter exercises
importance, 14-2–14-3
interviewing the employed, 14-33
introduction, 14-7
inventory of skills and goals, 14-8–14-10
job interview, 14-18–14-19
life experiences, 14-8
organizing/assembling the portfolio, 14-3–14-5
planning guide, 14-4
resume, 14-13–14-16, 14-32
samples of work, 14-19
title page, 14-6, 14-7
when to start it, 14-3
work philosophy and goals, 14-9–14-14
workplace trends, 14-22–14-23
Career development portfolio—end-of-chapter exercises
    assessment of personal qualities, 2-33
    assessment of skills/competencies, 7-31
    autobiography, 1-40
    community service, 12-34
    competencies, 5-34
    critical thinking skills, 9-36
    exploring careers, 14-34
    inventory of interests, 10-34
    listening self-assessment, 4-34
    memory skills, 6-32
    planning your career, 13-29
    relationship skills, 11-34
    time management skills, 3-35
    writing and speaking skills, 8-33
Career development portfolio planning guide, 14-4
Career in focus
    accountant/financial planner, 1-27
    carpenter, 13-19
    firefighter, 10-21
    food scientist, 3-23
    human resources director, 8-23
    information technology specialist, 5-17
    journalist, 6-20
    marine biologist, 11-26
    physical therapist, 7-18
    psychologist, 4-21
    restaurant owners, 9-23

Career in focus—*cont.*
   sales representative, 2-22
   school social worker, 12-21
   social studies teacher/legislator, 14-24
Career planning grid, 14-31
Carpenter, 13-19
Carson, Ben, 2-17
Carter, Stephen L., 2-3
Case studies
   active listening, 14-25
   building community, 12-25
   commitment, 1-33
   communication skills, 8-27
   coping with anxiety, 7-24
   energy level, 10-29
   exploring careers, 14-29
   fear of failure, 9-27
   good habits, 13-23
   juggling family and school, 3-28
   memory skills, 6-23
   motivation, 2-28
   reading habits, 5-23
   team work, 11-29
Chamber of commerce, 12-15
Chamberlain, Joshua L., 2-5
Changing your habits, 13-9–13-12, 13-16, 13-18,
   13-25, 13-28
Character, 2-3–2-6
Chatrooms, 11-23
Child care, 12-13
Child-care center, 12-8
Chinese proverb, 5-14, 9-17
Chlamydia, 10-17
Choosing a major, 1-26, 1-28, 1-37–1-38
Cigarette smoking, 10-12, 10-13
Citations, 8-11–8-12
Civility, 2-3
Clarification, 11-15
Classroom behavior, 4-15
Cliché, 8-13
Clubs and organizations, 12-15
Co-op programs, 12-14
Code of ethics, 2-5, 14-25
Codependency, 10-12
Coffee, 10-10
College dropouts, 2-23
College graduates, 2-18–2-19
College/high school, contrasted, 2-16
College transcripts, 14-19
College/university web site, 12-20
Combination note-taking system, 4-11, 4-14
Comfort zone, 2-24
Comma, 8-31
Commitment, 13-7–13-8, 13-10, 13-11
Commitment contract, 13-13
Committed time, 3-3
Communication

adult learning cycle, 11-6
assertive, 11-12, 11-13
barriers to, 11-17–11-18
importance, 11-2
instructors/advisors, with, 11-12–11-14
strategies, 11-5–11-10
Communication strategies, 11-5–11-10
Community involvement, 12-31–12-32
Community resources, 12-13–12-15
Community scholarships and grants, 12-14
Community service, 12-34
Community telephone directories, 12-14
Commuter students, 12-10
Compulsive gambling, 10-14
Computer time savers, 3-21
Confidence, 2-10
Conflict, 4-8
Conflict resolution, 11-15–11-17
Confucius, 6-5
Connecting school with career. *See* Career development
   portfolio
Consolidate similar tasks, 3-9
Contact information, 12-7
Contraceptives, 10-18
Convergent thinkers, 3-11
Cornell method of note taking, 4-10, 4-13
Corporate scandals, 2-3
Counseling service, 12-8
Cover letter, 14-5, 14-6
Cover page, 14-5, 14-6
Creative ideas checklist, 9-22
Creative outline, 4-9–4-10
Creative problem solving, 2-24, 9-12–9-22
Creator, 1-20–1-21, 1-24
Credit card debt, 12-16
Crisis centers, 12-13
Critical reading, 5-5
Critical thinking, 1-3–1-4
   alcohol, 10-11
   attributes of critical thinker, 9-3
   career development portfolio, 9-36
   drugs, 10-12–10-13
   errors in judgment, 9-6
   matrix, 9-35
   problem solving, 9-2, 9-4
   worksheet, 9-30
Criticism, accepting, 11-14–11-16
Cultural awareness pyramid, 11-5
Curiosity, 13-5
Cycle of responsibility, 2-7

D

Daily energy levels, 3-34
Daily planner, 3-8
Dante, 4-5
Date rape, 10-19

Day care, 3-19
De Morgan, Augustus, 9-12
Debold, Elizabeth, 4-3
Debt counseling, 12-18
Deep breathing, 10-24
Delegate and develop, 3-20
Depression, 10-15–10-16
Dewar, Sir James, 11-3
Dewey, John, 9-6
Dictionary, 5-12
Diet, 10-2–10-6
Dilbert, 9-24
Director, 1-19–1-20, 1-24
Disabilities, students with, 12-10–12-11
Discipline, 13-6–13-7
Discouragement, 2-23
Discretionary time, 3-3
Discrimination, 11-7
Dishonesty, 2-3
Distraction, 4-3
Distractions, 6-5
Divergent thinkers, 3-11
Diversity, 11-4–11-10, 11-32
Dole, Elizabeth, 1-6
Douching, 10-18
Drucker, Peter, 1-8, 8-2
Drug addiction, 10-12–10-15
Drunkenness, 10-10–10-20
Dryden, John, 13-8
Duell, Charles H., 2-24

E

E-mail, 11-23
Eating habits, 10-2–10-5
Edison, Thomas, 2-10
Editing, 8-9–8-12
Educational achievement, 2-18–2-20
80/20 rule of time management, 3-15
Eliot, George, 2-13
Emerson, Ralph Waldo, 2-10, 12-16
Emotional health, 10-15–10-16
Emotional intelligence, 2-2–2-3
Empathy, 2-3, 4-3
Encyclopaedia Britannica, 8-17
Encyclopedia Americana, 8-12
Endnotes, 8-12
Endorphins, 10-8, 10-24
Energy level, 3-10, 10-29
Enneagram, 1-21–1-22
Enneagram Made Easy, The (Baron/Wagele), 1-22
Enthusiasm, 2-10
Environmental intelligence, 1-12
Essay test, 7-9–7-13
Essay writing tips, 8-30–8-31
Ethical decision making, 2-6
Ethics, 2-3–2-6, 14-25

Etymology, 5-12
Exam schedule, 7-26
Examples. See Samples
Exams. See Test taking
Exchange program, 12-6
Exercise, 4-16, 10-7–10-8, 10-9
Expectations
    comfort zone, 2-24
    communication, 11-12
    motivational strategies, 2-15
    relationships, 11-20, 11-21
    test taking, 7-2
    time management, 3-19
Experience, 1-28
Extroverts, 1-15
Eye contact, 8-18, 11-19

F

Facts on File, 1941+, 8-17
Failure to graduate college, 2-23
Family ties, 11-21–11-23
Famous sayings. See Words to succeed
Fear of failure, 9-27
Feedback, 1-26, 11-16
Feelers, 1-15
Ferraro, Tony, 4-21
File, 8-5
File Transfer Protocol (FTP), 8-17
Fill-in-the-blank test, 7-9
Filling out forms, 5-18
Filo, David, 14-26
Final draft, 8-12
Financial counseling services, 12-18
Financial problems, 12-16–12-20
Financial resources, 12-9, 12-14
Firefighter, 10-21
First draft, 8-8
First things first, 3-17
First weeks of college, 3-5–3-6
Five-part reading system, 5-2–5-5
Flexibility, 3-11, 3-19
Focus on. See Success principles
Follett, Mary Parker, 11-4
Follow-up letter, 14-20
Food pyramid, 10-4
Food scientist, 3-23
Footnotes, 8-11–8-12
Ford, Henry, 12-2
Formal outline, 4-8
Forms
    filling out, 5-18
    reading, 5-16–5-18
Four-temperament profile, 1-14–1-21
    analyzers, 1-18
    creators, 1-19–1-20
    directors, 1-20–1-21

Four-temperament profile—*cont.*
  follow-up activity, 1-16–1-17
  supporters, 1-18–1-19
  worksheet, 1-39
Free writing, 8-10
FTP, 8-17
Fuentes, Carlos, 7-18

G

Galileo, 9-6
Gambling addiction, 10-14
Games, 9-12
Gardner, Howard, 1-11
General education, 1-26
Genital herpes, 10-17
Genital warts, 10-17
Gide, Andrew, 5-2
Go from general to specific,
Goals, 2-14–2-15
Goethe, J. W. von, 10-2
Goldberg, Natalie, 8-8
Golden Rule, 2-3
Goleman, Daniel, 2-2
Gonzales, Alberto, 6-21
Good character, 2-3–2-6
Government officials, 12-13
Grammar, 8-30–8-31
Grants, 12-9, 12-14
Great speeches, 5-15
Grouping, 6-13
Gymnasium, 12-8, 12-15

H

Habits, 13-1–13-29
  adult learning cycle, 13-8
  changing your, 13-9, 13-12, 13-16, 13-18, 13-25, 13-28
  commitment, 13-7–13-8, 13-10–13-11
  peak performers, of, 13-2–13-7
  resistors and fears, 13-6–13-18
Halo effect, 9-6
Hamm, Mia, 13-20
Hands-on experience, 1-28
Haubegger, Christy, 1-31
Health and wellness, 10-1–10-34
  addictions, 10-13–10-15
  alcohol abuse, 10-10–10-12
  awareness, 10-2
  birth control, 10-18
  caffeine, 10-4, 10-10
  cancer warning signs, 10-3
  cigarette smoking, 10-12, 10-13
  date rape, 10-19
  depression, 10-15–10-16
  eating habits, 10-2–10-5
  emotional health, 10-15–10-16
  exercise, 10-7–10-8, 10-9
  gambling addiction, 10-14
  illegal drug use, 10-12–10-13
  rape, 10-18–10-20
  relationships, 10-8
  sleep, 10-7
  STDs, 10-17–10-18
  strategies, 10-2
  stress, 10-20–10-25, 10-31–10-32
  suicidal person, 10-16
  web sites, 10-9
  weight control, 10-5–10-6
Health center, 12-8
Helping organizations, 12-13
Herstein, I. N., 9-3
Hierarchy of writing, 8-8
High-energy time, 3-9–3-10, 3-16
Higher education, 2-18–2-21
Higher-level needs, 2-12, 2-13
Highway Patrol checkpoints, 10-12
Hippocrates, 1-13
Historical speeches, 8-17
HIV/AIDS, 10-17, 10-18
Hobbies, 10-23
Holt, John, 9-2
Homograph, 5-12
Honesty, 2-3, 2-4, 11-20, 13-2
House Made of Dawn (Momaday), 3-24
Houses of worship, 12-13
Human resources director, 8-23
Humor
  building rapport, 11-4
  idea generation, 9-14
  shyness, 11-19
  stress reduction, 10-24
Hunt, H. L., 3-3
Huxley, T. H., 3-14
Hyperlinks, 8-17

I

"I" statements, 2-8
Iacocca, Lee, 4-2
Idea generation, 8-5
Illegal drug use, 10-12–10-13
Illustrations. *See* Samples
Indefinite pronouns, 8-31
Index cards, 6-5
Index to American Women Speakers, 8-17
iNF temperament, 1-24
Information overload, 6-5
Information technology specialist, 5-17
iNT temperament, 1-24
Integrated brain power, 1-24
Integrating styles, 1-22–1-23
Integrity, 2-3
Intelligence, 1-11–1-12

Internet, 8-17. *See also* Tech for success
Internships, 12-14
Interpersonal intelligence, 1-12
Interruptions, 3-16–3-19
Interviewing the employed, 14-33
Intoxication (drunkenness), 10-10–10-12
Intrapersonal and inner intelligence, 1-12
Introverts, 1-15
Intuitives, 1-15
Inventory
    aptitudes, 14-13
    interests, 10-34, 14-13
    LASSI, 1-21
    learning style, 1-9–1-10
    personal qualities, 14-11
    self-assessment, 1-12–1-13
    self-esteem, 2-31
    skills/competencies, 14-8–14-9

J

Jamba Juice, 7-22
James, Henry, 1-22
James, William, 5-11
Jargon, 8-13
Job hunting portfolio. *See* Career development portfolio
Job interview, 14-18–14-19
Job placement office, 12-6
Job placement services, 12-14
Job search web sites, 14-21
Journal, 8-10, 9-17, 10-25
Journalist, 6-20
Judgers, 1-15
Jung, Carl, 1-13, 14-2

K

Keirsy, David, 1-14, 1-15
Key words
    language courses, 5-14
    note taking, 4-16
    reading, 5-4, 5-10
Kinesthetic learners, 1-11
Kolb, David, 1-23
Koshetz, Marina and Josef, 9-23

L

Language courses, 5-13–5-14
LASSI, 1-21
Latina, 1-31
Laughing, 10-24
Learning and Study Strategies Inventory (LASSI), 1-21
Learning disabilities, 12-11
Learning pyramid, 1-22
Learning style
    auditory learners, 1-8, 1-11

building rapport, 11-4
    kinesthetic learners, 1-11
    memory, 6-10, 6-25
    multiple intelligences, 1-11–1-12
    time management, 3-11
    visual learners, 1-8
    worksheet, 2-32
Learning style inventory, 1-9–1-10
Lecture notes, 4-7. *See also* Note taking
Left-brain dominant people, 1-23
    convergent thinkers, 3-11
    mind mapping, 4-9
    notes, 4-8
    studying, 1-24
Legal aid, 12-14
Letter, 14-17
Letter of recommendation, 14-16
Letter of reference, 11-14
Lewis, C. S., 7-17
Liberal arts education, 2-19–2-20
Library, 8-15–8-17, 12-4
Life area goals, 3-22
Life assessment, 4-31
Lifelong assessment, 13-15–13-16
Lincoln, Abraham, 2-24
Listening. *See* Active listening
Listening self-assessment, 4-34
Local newspapers, 12-14
Log, 10-25
Logical/mathematical intelligence, 1-12
Looking ahead, 3-7
Lower-level needs, 2-12, 2-13
Lying, 2-3

M

Macy, R. H., 1-26
Magazines, 12-14
Maintenance time, 3-3
Major, 1-26, 1-28, 1-37–1-38
Making time for commitments, 12-5
Management process, 3-11–3-13
    delegating, 3-13
    directing and motivating, 3-13
    evaluating, 3-13
    organizing, 3-13
    planning, 3-12
    staffing, 3-13
Manager, 14-22
Managing your resources. *See* Resource management
Managing your time. *See* Time management
Mancuso, Joseph R., 10-8
Marine biologist, 11-26
Maslow, Abraham, 2-12
Maslow's hierarchy of needs, 2-12
Matching test, 7-8
Math and science anxiety, 9-10–9-12, 9-13

Math and science applications, 9-6–9-12
    anxiety, 9-10–9-12, 9-13
    keep up-to-date, 9-12
    problem-solving strategies, 9-7–9-10
    study partner, 9-12
    test taking, 7-6–7-7
Math and science tests, 7-6–7-7
Matrix
    critical thinking, 9-35
    reading, 5-33
    test taking, 7-30
MBTI, 1-14
Mediterranean diet food pyramid, 10-4
Memorandum (memo), 8-24
Memory affirmations, 6-17
Memory assessment, 6-8
Memory map, 6-14–6-16
Memory process, 6-2–6-5
Memory skills, 6-1–6-32
    adult learning cycle, 6-3
    barriers, 6-17–6-18
    learning style, 6-10, 6-25
    memory affirmations, 6-17
    memory assessment, 6-8
    memory map, 6-14–6-16
    memory process, 6-2–6-5
    memory strategies, 6-5–6-13
    memory systems, 6-29
    mental picture, 6-30–6-31
    mnemonic devices, 6-12–6-13
    remembering names, 6-12
    review and reflection, 6-13, 6-17
    stages of memory, 6-11
    worksheets, 6-26–6-28
Memory strategies, 6-5–6-13
Memory systems, 6-29
Mental picture, 6-30–6-31
Mentor, 3-21
Method-of-place technique, 6-13
Mild depression, 10-15
Mind map, 4-9
    follow-up activity, 4-12
    organizing information, 6-6
    sample, 4-10
    sorting information, 4-27
    template, 4-10, 4-11
Mind map template, 4-10, 4-11
Mind-set, 9-14, 9-16
Mind shift, 2-24
Mindfulness, 6-11
Mini-vacations, 10-24
Mission statement, 14-12
MLA style of citation, 8-11
Mnemonic devices, 6-12–6-13
Modern Language Association's (MLA) style of citation, 8-11
Momaday, N. Scott, 3-24
Money management, 12-15–12-20, 12-29

Morrison, Toni, 8-25
Motivation cycle, 2-18
Motivational strategies, 2-13–2-16
Multiple-choice test, 7-8
Multiple intelligences, 1-11–1-12
Multivitamin supplement, 10-5
Myers, Isabel Briggs, 1-14
Myers-Briggs Type indicator (MBTI), 1-14

N

Negative attitude, 2-6–2-7, 2-11–2-12
Networking, 12-33
New York Times index, 8-17
News on-line, 5-14
Newsletters, 12-14
Newspaper, 12-4, 12-14
Nine-dot exercise, 9-14
Nontraditional students, 12-11
Nonverbal cues, 11-15
Note cards, 5-13,
Note taking, 4-5–4-18
    assessment and review, 4-17–4-18
    barriers to, 4-20
    checklist, 4-29
    combination system, 4-11, 4-14
    Cornell method, 4-10, 4-13
    creative outline, 4-9–4-10
    follow-up activity, 4-28
    formal outline, 4-8
    mind mapping, 4-9–4-12
    PDA, 4-18
    revisions/additions, 4-16
    shortcuts, 4-17
    strategies, 4-15–4-16
    structure/format of notes, 4-6–4-18
    writing papers, 8-4
Note-taking checklist, 4-29
Note-taking shortcuts, 4-17
Note-taking strategies, 4-15–4-16
Nutrition, 10-2–10-5

O

Objective test, 7-7–7-9
Observation skills, 4-3, 6-3, 6-4, 8-5
Observing conflict, 11-16
Ochoa, Ellen, 11-27
O'Connor, Flannery, 1-3
Off-campus housing, 12-8
On-line discussion groups, 2-25
On-line journal, 1-29
On-line self-assessment, 1-29
On-line tutors, 7-20
Ongoing assessment and action plan, 4-32
Online research, 8-17
Open-book test, 7-9

Oprah Winfrey Show, 5-19
Oral presentations. *See* Public speaking
Organization
    memory process, 6-3
    planning your education, 3-14
    test taking, 7-5
    time management, 3-10–3-11
    writing plan, 8-6–8-8
Orientation guide, 12-6
Orientation program, 12-6
Outline
    creative, 4-9–4-10
    formal, 4-8
    reading, 5-29–5-30

P

Page, Deborah, 3-23
Paper and material resources, 12-4–12-6, 12-14
Papers. *See* Writing papers
Paraphrase, 5-4
Parker, Louis, 1-27
Parts of speech, 5-12
Passive-aggressive people, 11-12
Paternak, Boris, 10-2
Patience, 3-11
Payne, Calvin, 2-14
PDA, 4-18
Peak performance competency wheel, 1-6
Peak performance self-assessment test, 1-7
Peak performance success formula, 13-12, 13-14
Peak performer, 1-2–1-3
    being engaged, 13-4
    being supportive, 13-5–13-6
    creative problem solving, 13-6
    curiosity, 13-5
    discipline, 13-6–13-7
    honesty, 13-2
    living grateful, 13-7
    positive attitudes, 13-17
    positive thinking, 13-3
    resilience, 13-4
    responsibility, 13-5
    success, formula for, 13-12, 13-13
Peak performer profile
    Adams, Scott, 9-24
    Armstrong, Lance, 10-26
    Carson, Ben, 2-17
    Filo, David, 14-26
    Gonzales, Alberto, 6-21
    Hamm, Mia, 10-20
    Haubegger, Christy, 1-31
    Momaday, N. Scott, 3-24
    Morrison, Toni, 8-25
    Ochoa, Ellen, 11-27
    Perron, Kirk, 7-22
    Rice, Condoleezza, 12-22

Sui, Anna, 4-22
Winfrey, Oprah, 5-19
Yang, Gerry, 14-26
Peak progress
    barriers to note taking, 4-20
    burnout, 10-22
    campus facilities, 12-8
    choosing a career, 14-22
    communicator, 11-6
    creative ideas checklist, 9-22
    dictionary, 5-12
    diversity, 11-7
    eating habits, 10-4
    80/20 rule of time management, 3-15
    essay test, 7-11–7-12, 7-13
    exploring majors, 1-29
    failure to graduate college, 2-23
    financial resource management, 12-18
    healthier lifestyle, 10-25
    high school/college, compared, 2-16
    listening, 4-6
    math and science anxiety, 9-13
    math and science tests, 7-6–7-7
    memory affirmations, 6-17
    memory skills, 6-3
    mindfulness, 6-11
    positive attitude, 13-17
    positive habits, 13-8
    problem-solving checklist, 9-5
    public speaking, 8-21
    reading, 5-4
    remembering names, 6-12
    school-job success, 14-23
    self-esteem and confidence, 2-11
    self-management and control, 2-9
    skills for school and work, 2-20
    student/worker, what kind are you, 2-21
    symbols, 5-11
    take control of time and life, 3-12
    team effectiveness, 11-11
    test taking, 7-3, 7-17
    topic ideas, 8-5
    visualization, 1-4–1-5
    writer's block, 8-10
    writing do's, 8-13–8-14
    writing papers, checklist, 8-16
    writing speeches, checklist, 8-16
Peak tips
    addiction to computers, 10-13
    binder, 3-14
    bouncing back from failure, 1-26, 2-10
    changing your habits, 13-6
    classroom behavior, 4-15
    computer use, 3-17
    effort, 6-17
    employee qualities, 14-9
    filling out forms, 5-16

Peak tips—*cont.*
    follow-up call—after resume, 14-14
    goals/expectations, 2-24
    graphics, 5-15
    learning style, 1-8
    letter of recommendation, 14-16
    math and science anxiety, 9-10, 9-12
    mild depression, 10-15
    newspapers, 12-4
    note taking, 4-6
    performance review, 7-20
    positive attitude, 6-17
    problem solving—keep an open mind, 9-16
    reading, 5-5, 5-15
    resume, 14-13
    saving money, 12-19, 12-20
    stereotyping, 11-10
    studying, how much, 6-9
    successful manager, 14-22
    teaching your study partner, 5-10
    test taking, 7-14
    writing assignments, 8-12
Pell grants, 12-9
People resources, 12-4, 12-13–12-14
Perceivers, 1-15
Perceptual distortion, 9-14
Performance appraisal, 7-17–7-20, 7-29
Periodicals, 8-16
Perkins loans, 12-9
Perron, Kirk, 7-22
Persistence, 3-11, 9-2, 9-22
Personal digital assistant (PDA), 4-18
Personal performance notebook
    assertive communication role-playing, 11-13
    assessing your goals, 14-14
    brainstorming notes, 9-15
    budgeting, 12-17
    building community, 12-3
    character nad ethics, 12-4
    commitment contract, 13-10
    commitment to exercise, 10-9
    conflict resolution, 11-17
    contact information, 12-7
    critical thinking-problem solving, 9-4
    daily energy levels, 3-10
    decision-making application, 9-18–9-19
    diversity, 11-8
    essay test preparation, 7-10
    four-temperament profile, 1-16–1-17
    healthy relationships, 11-22
    interruptions, 3-18
    inventory of interests, aptitudes, and values, 14-13
    inventory of personal qualities, 14-11
    learning style inventory, 1-9–1-10
    learning styles and memory, 6-10
    life area goals, 3-22
    lifelong assessment, 13-15–13-16

listen to your body, 10-3
listening, 4-7
looking ahead, 3-7
making time for commitments, 12-5
math and science anxiety, 9-11
memory assessment, 6-8
memory map, 6-14–6-16
mind map, 4-12
mind map-organizing information, 6-6
mind-set, 9-16
needs, motivation, and commitment, 2-13
nine-dot exercise, 9-14
observation skills, 6-4
observing conflict, 11-16
patterns in relationships, 11-18
peak performance self-assessment tool, 1-7
performance review, 7-19
positive habits, 13-10–13-11
preparing research papers, 8-7
procrastination, 3-16
reflection, 4-19
reviewing your health, 10-6
self-talk and affirmations, 2-15
skills and personal qualities, 2-5
sleep patterns, 10-7
solving problems-making choices, 9-20–9-21
SQ3R system, 5-6–5-7
stage fright, 8-19
stereotypical thinking, 11-9
test anxiety, 7-16
test taking, 7-4
time log, 3-5
time spent on typical activities, 3-6
transferable skills, 14-10
values, 14-25
writer's block, 8-19
Personal qualities
    barriers, 2-23–2-25
    good character, 2-3–2-6
    positive attitude and personal motivation, 2-10–2-18
    responsibility, 2-6–2-7
    self-assessment, 2-33
    self-esteem and confidence, 2-9–2-10, 2-11
    self-management and control, 2-8–2-9
    understanding value of education, 2-18–2-21
Personal reinforcement contract, 2-30
Personality types, 1-13–1-14, 1-15
Physical activity, 4-16, 6-5
Physical activity (exercise), 10-7–10-8, 10-9
Physical and kinesthetic intelligence, 1-12
Physical therapist, 7-18
Pipher, Mary, 11-16
Planning grid, 8-31
Planning your education, 3-13–3-14
Plato, 8-9
PLUS loans, 12-9
Political parties, 12-13

Portfolio. *See* Career development portfolio
Positive attitude, 2-10–2-11, 3-16
Positive attitude and personal motivation, 2-10–2-18
Positive habits, 1-26, 2-14
Positive mind shift, 2-24
Positive self-talk, 11-19
Positive thinking, 13-3
Positive time, 3-19
PowerPoint, 8-21
Praise, 2-8
Prejudice, 11-7
Preliminary reading, 8-4
Presentations. *See* Public speaking
Price, Steven, 14-24
Priorities, 3-4–3-11
Probation, students on, 12-12
Problem gambling, 10-14
Problem solving
    checklist, 9-5
    creative, 9-12–9-22
    math and science, 9-7–9-10
    preparing for, 9-2
    steps in process, 9-3, 9-5
Problem-solving checklist, 9-5
Procrastination, 3-15–3-16
Program resources, 12-6–12-8, 12-15
Project board, 3-8–3-9
Projection, 9-6
Prompters, 8-18
Pronoun, 8-30, 8-31
Pronoun-verb agreement, 8-31
Pronunciation, 5-12
Proofreading, 8-14
Psychologist, 4-21
Public Papers of the Presidents of the United States, 8-17
Public speaking, 8-1–8-33
    adult learning cycle, 8-21
    checklists, 8-16
    conciseness, 8-20
    eye contact, 8-18
    historical speeches, 8-17
    importance, 8-2
    planning grid, 8-32
    prompters, 8-18
    rehearsing, 8-29
    research, 8-15–8-17
    review and assessment, 8-12
    speech evaluation form, 8-20
    stage fright, 8-19
    strategies, 8-17–8-20
    visual aids, 8-18, 8-21
Public transportation, 12-19
Puzzles, 9-12

Q

Questions

    listening, 4-3
    shyness, 11-19
    test taking, 7-2
Quiet time, 3-17
Quotable quotes. *See* Words to succeed

R

RAND Corporation, 8-17
Rape, 10-18–10-20
Reader's Guide to Periodical Literature, 8-5, 8-16
Reading. *See* Active reading
Reading forms, 5-16–5-18
Reading matrix, 5-33
Reading outline, 5-29–5-30
Reading strategies, 5-9–5-10
Reciting, 6-11–6-12
Record keeping, 3-21
Recreation centers, 12-8–12-15
Redmoon, Ambrose, 7-14
Reentry students, 3-20–3-21, 12-11–12-12
Reference materials, 8-16
Reframing, 2-16
Reinforcement, 2-8
Reinforcement contract, 2-30
Relationships, 11-1–11-34
    accepting criticism, 11-14–11-16
    building rapport, 11-2–11-4
    communication. *See* Communication
    conflict resolution, 11-15–11-17
    diversity, 11-9–11-10, 11-32
    energy, 10-8
    family ties, 11-21–11-23
    patterns, 11-18
    roommates, 11-21–11-23
    sexual harassment, 11-10–11-12
    shyness, 11-19
    strategies, 11-19–11-23
Remembering names, 6-12
Representative American Speeches, 1937+, 8-17
Reprogram your mind, 2-24–2-25
Research
    Internet, 8-17
    library, 8-15–8-17
Research papers. *See* Writing papers
Resilience, 13-4
Resistors and fears, 13-6–13-18
Resource management, 12-1–12-34
    budgeting, 12-15–12-16, 12-17, 12-28
    building community, 12-2, 12-3, 12-25, 12-30
    campus resources, 12-2–12-9. *See also* Campus resources
    community resources, 12-13–12-15
    commuter students, 12-10
    financial problems, 12-16–12-20
    money management, 12-15–12-20, 12-29
    networking, 12-33
    reentry students, 12-11–12-12

Resource management—*cont.*
   savings account, 12-20
   students on probation, 12-12
   students with disabilities, 12-10–12-11
   transfer students, 12-12
   yourself as a resource, 12-15
Respect, 4-3
Responsibility, 4-6–4-7
Restaurant owners, 9-23
Restrictive labels, 5-12
Resume, 14-13–14-16, 14-32
Resume on-line, 14-21
Reward yourself, 2-16, 7-6, 13-12
Rhythm and melody intelligence, 1-12
Rhythm and rhymes, 6-13
Rice, Condoleezza, 12-22
Ride and carpooling boards, 12-8
Right-brain dominant people, 1-23
   divergent thinkers, 3-11
   studying, 1-24
   visualization/imagery, 2-14
Robinson, Francis, 5-5
Rohypnol, 10-19
Roofie, 10-19
Roommates, 11-21–11-23
Root words, 5-15
Ruth, Babe, 1-26

S

Sales representative, 2-22
Samples
   career development portfolio elements, 14-6
   creative outline, 4-9
   essay test, 7-11–7-12
   follow-up letter, 14-20
   formal outline, 4-8
   letters, 14-17
   memo, 8-24
   mind map, 4-10
   mission statement, 4-12
   outline, 8-6
   project board, 3-9
   resume, 14-15
   schedule for preparing term paper, 8-3
   time log, 3-4
   title page, 8-15
Saving money, 12-15–12-20
Savings account, 12-20
SCANS, 1-6, 14-8, 14-9
SCANS skills, 14-9
Scheele, Adele, 8-2
Scholarships, 12-9, 12-14
School catalog, 12-4
School-life balance, 3-19–3-22
School newspaper, 12-4
School scholarships and grants, 12-9

School social worker, 12-21
School telephone directory, 12-4, 12-14
School-work connection, 2-20-2-21
Schopenhauer, Arthur, 3-8
Secretary's Commission on Achieving Necessary Skills
   (SCANS), 1-6, 14-8, 14-9
Self-assessment
   assertiveness, 11-33
   barriers to, 1-26
   benefits, 1-3, 1-26
   inventories. *See* Inventory
   lifelong assessment, 13-15–13-16
   listening, 4-34
   peak performance test, 1-7
   personal qualities, 2-33
Self-confidence, 2-10
Self-esteem and confidence, 2-9–2-10, 2-11
Self-esteem inventory, 2-31
Self-management and control, 2-8–2-9
Self-talk, 2-14, 2-15, 11-19
Self-worth, 2-10
Semester calendar, 1-29
Seneca, 1-26
Sensors, 1-15
Service learning, 2-14
Sexual harassment, 11-10–11-12
Sexually transmitted diseases (STDs), 10-17–10-18
Shorthand, 4-16
Shyness, 11-19
sic, 8-4
Sievert, Danielle, 4-21
Signal words/phrases, 4-4–4-5
Singer, Brian, 5-17
SJ temperament, 1-24
Skills for school and job success, 1-5–1-6
Slang, 8-13
Sleep, 10-7
Slouching, 4-16
SLS, 12-9
Smith, Red, 8-2
Smoking, 10-12, 10-13
Snap judgments, 9-6
Social studies teacher/legislator, 14-24
SP temperament, 1-24
Spatial intelligence, 1-11–1-12
Speech evaluation form, 8-20
Speech Index, 8-17
Speeches. *See* Public speaking
Spell-check, 8-21
Sperry, Roger, 1-23
Sports complex, 12-8–12-15
SQ3R reading system, 5-5, 5-6–5-7
Stafford loans, 12-9
Stage fright, 8-19
STDs, 10-17–10-18
Stein, Gertrude, 5-13
Stereotype, 9-6

Stereotypical thinking, 11-9
Stereotyping, 11-8, 11-10
Stress, 10-20–10-25, 10-31–10-32
Stress performance test, 10-31–10-32
Student employment, 12-9
Student loans, 12-9
Student union, 12-8
Students on probation, 12-12
Students with disabilities, 12-10–12-11
Study team, 2-15, 5-13, 7-4
Study-team relationships, 11-31
Studying
    cramming, 7-13, 7-15
    groups, 9-5
    high-energy time, 3-9
    how much, 6-9
    left-brain, 1-24
    mindfulness, 6-11
    right-brain, 1-24
    short segments/sessions, 3-10, 6-9
    team, 2-15, 5-13, 7-4
    when to study, 3-10, 3-17
    where to study, 3-10, 3-17
Subject-verb agreement, 8-30
Success principles
    accomplishments, not entitlement, 14-2
    character, not personality, 13-2
    cooperation, 11-2
    critical thinking, 9-2
    excellence, not perfection, 8-2
    giving, not receiving, 12-2
    meaning, not words, 5-2
    message, not presentation, 4-2
    personal qualities, 2-2
    priorities, 3-2
    quality, not quantity, 10-2
    reality, 1-2
    strengths, not weaknesses, 7-2
    sum, not parts, 6-2
Sugar, 10-5
Sui, Anna, 4-22
Suicidal person, 10-16
Summer school, 3-14
Supplemental loans for students
    (SLS), 12-9
Support groups, 12-13
Support system, 2-24, 3-20, 10-24
Supporter, 1-18–1-19, 1-24
Sweeping generalizations, 9-6
Syllabication, 5-12
Symbols, 5-11

T

T note-taking system, 4-10, 4-13
Taking notes. See Note taking
Team effectiveness, 11-11

Tech for success
    ALEKS, 9-13
    back-up plans, 6-18
    bill paying on-line, 12-20
    books on-line, 5-14
    calorie counting, 10-9
    college/university web site, 12-20
    computer timesavers, 3-21
    ethics information on the Web, 2-25
    health on the Web, 10-9
    inspiration, 13-18
    instructor's visual presentation, 4-18
    job search web sites, 14-21
    log of positive habits, 13-18
    mathematics, 9-13
    news on-line, 5-14
    on-line discussion groups, 2-25
    on-line journal, 1-29
    on-line self-assessment, 1-29
    on-line tutors, 7-20
    PDA, 4-14
    PowerPoint, 8-21
    relationships and computers, 11-23
    resume on-line, 14-21
    semester calendar, 1-29
    spell-check, 8-22
    stored memory, 6-18
    textbooks-ancillary resources, 7-20
    visual aids, 8-21
Technical reading, 5-15–5-16
Telephone directory, 12-4, 12-14
Telnet, 8-17
Temperament. See Four-temperament profile
Term papers. See Writing papers
Test anxiety, 7-14–7-17
Test taking, 7-1–7-31
    adult learning cycle, 7-17
    after the test, 7-6–7-7
    essay test, 7-9–7-13
    exam schedule, 7-26
    fill-in-the-blank test, 7-9
    follow-up activity, 7-4
    how to succeed, 7-3
    last-minute study tips, 7-13–7-14
    matching test, 7-8
    math and science tests, 7-6–7-7
    matrix for test taking, 7-30
    multiple-choice test, 7-8
    open-book test, 7-9
    preparing for a test, 7-2–7-4, 7-27–7-28
    strategies, 7-5, 7-6
    test anxiety, 7-14–7-15
    true/false test, 7-7–7-8
Test-taking strategies, 7-5
Thesis statement, 8-4
Thinkers, 1-15
Time log, 3-4, 3-5

Time management, 3-1–3-35
   adult learning cycle, 3-12
   assessment and reflection, 3-14–3-15
   computer time savers, 3-21
   80/20 rule, 3-15
   first weeks of college, 3-5–3-6
   interruptions, 3-16–3-19
   juggling family, school, job, 3-19–3-22, 3-28
   learning style, 3-11
   priorities, 3-4–3-11
   procrastination, 3-15–3-16
   self-assessment, 3-2–3-4
   strategies, 3-8–3-11
   time, types of, 3-3
   time log, 3-4, 3-5
   time wasters, 3-18, 3-32–3-33
   to-do list, 3-30
   worksheet, 3-32
Time-management strategies, 3-8–3-11
Time wasters, 3-18, 3-32–3-33
Title page,
To-do list, 3-8, 3-30
Tobacco use (smoking), 10-12, 10-13
Togo, Yuki, 6-2
Topic ideas, 8-5
Torres, Rick, 13-19
Transfer students, 12-12
Transferable skills, 14-10
True/false test, 7-7–7-8
Trust, 11-20
Tutoring and special services, 12-6
Twain, Mark, 10-25

U

Understanding the Enneagram: The Practical Guide to Personality Types (Riso/Hudson), 1-22
Unwarranted assumptions, 9-6
U.S.D.A food pyramid, 10-4

V

Value system, 2-3
Values, 14-25
Verbal/linguistic intelligence, 1-11
Veterans programs, 12-9
Visual aids, 8-18, 8-21
Visual learners, 1-8
Visualization, 1-4–1-5, 2-14, 13-9
Vital Speeches of the Day, 1941+, 8-17
Vitamins, 10-5
Vocabulary building, 5-14–5-15

W

Wall Street Journal index, 8-17
Washington, Donna, 12-21

Weight control, 10-5–10-6
Weil, Andrew, 10-23
Wellness. *See* Health and wellness
Whole person, 2-3
Williams, Jacqui, 2-22
WIN, 12-9
Win-win solutions, 2-8
Winfrey, Oprah, 5-19
Winthrop, John, 12-4
Word parts, 5-15
Words to succeed
   Allen, Woody, 4-15
   anonymous, 2-8
   Aristotle, 13-2
   Burke, Edmund, 5-9
   Capra, Frank, 9-12
   Chamberlain, Joshua L., 2-5
   Chinese proverb, 5-14, 9-17
   Confucius, 6-5
   Debold, Elizabeth, 4-3
   Dewar, Sir James, 11-3
   Dewey, John, 9-6
   Drucker, Peter, 1-8
   Dryden, John, 13-8
   Duell, Charles H., 2-24
   Eliot, George, 2-13
   Emerson, Ralph Waldo, 2-10, 12-16
   Follett, Mary Parker, 11-4
   Ford, Henry, 12-2
   Galileo, 9-6
   Gide, Andrew, 5-2
   Goethe, J. W. von, 10-2
   Goldberg, Natalie, 8-8
   Herbert, George, 14-14
   Herstein, I. N., 9-3
   Holt, John, 9-2
   Hunt, H. L., 3-3
   Huxley, T. H., 3-13
   Iacocca, Lee, 4-2
   James, William, 3-11
   Jung, Carl, 14-2
   Lewis, C. S., 7-17
   Lincoln, Abraham, 2-24
   Mancuso, Joseph R., 10-8
   O'Connor, Flannery, 1-3
   Paternak, Boris, 10-2
   Pipher, Mary, 11-16
   Plato, 8-9
   Redmoon, Ambrose, 7-14
   Scheele, Adele, 8-2
   Schopenhauer, Arthur, 3-8
   Seneca, 1-26
   Stein, Gertrude, 5-13
   Togo, Yuki, 6-2
   Twain, Mark, 10-25
   Weil, Andrew, 10-23
   Winthrop, John, 12-4

Wright, Stephen, 8-15
Yarrow, Peter, 11-9
Youngblood, Jack, 13-16
Work-school connection, 2-20–2-21
Work-study, 12-9
Workplace trends, 14-22–14-23
Works Cited, 8-12
Worksheets
    ABCDE method. *See* ABCDE method of
        self-management
    analyzing chapters, 5-31
    attitudes and reading, 5-25
    barriers to reading, 5-32
    budgeting, 12-28
    building community, 12-30
    career planning grid, 14-31
    changing habits, 13-28
    choosing a major, 1-37–1-38
    community involvement, 12-31–12-32
    daily energy levels, 3-34
    different types of reading, 5-26
    diversity, 11-32
    exam schedule, 7-26
    four-temperament profile, 1-39
    grammar, 8-30–8-31
    health, 10-30–10-33
    interviewing the employed, 14-33
    key lecture ideas, 4-28
    learning style and memory, 6-25
    learning styles, 1-35, 2-32
    life assessment, 4-31
    listening habits, 4-33
    listening/note taking in workplace, 4-30
    matrix for critical thinking, 9-35
    matrix for test taking, 7-30
    memory skills, 6-25
    memory systems, 6-29
    mental picture, 6-30–6-31
    mind map, 4-27
    money management, 12-29
    networking, 12-33
    note-taking checklist, 4-29
    ongoing assessment and action plan, 4-32
    performance review, 7-29
    personal reinforcement contract, 2-30
    personality types, 1-35
    planning grid, 8-32
    positive attitudes, 13-27
    positive habits, 13-26
    preparing for tests/exams, 7-27–7-28
    problem solving, 9-28–9-35
    project team, 1-35–1-36
    reading, 5-24–5-33
    reading matrix, 5-33
    reading outline, 5-29–5-30
    resistance to change, 13-25
    resources, 12-27
    resume, 14-32
    self-esteem inventory, 2-31
    stress performance test, 10-31–10-32
    study-team relationships, 11-31
    summarize and teach, 5-27–5-28
    temperaments, 1-35
    test taking, 7-28–7-30
    time management, 3-31
    time wasters, 3-32–3-33
    to-do list, 3-30, 6-28
    writing papers/public speaking, 8-28–8-32
World Wide Web, 8-17
Wright, Stephen, 8-15
Writer's block, 8-10, 8-19
Writing papers, 8-1–8-33
    biased language, 8-14
    bibliography, 8-11–8-12
    checklists, 8-16
    citations, 8-11–8-12
    conclusion, 8-9
    editing, 8-9–8-12
    essay writing tips, 8-30–8-31
    final draft, 8-12
    first draft, 8-8
    follow-up activities, 8-7
    footnotes, 8-11–8-12
    grammar, 8-30–8-31
    hierarchy of writing, 8-8
    idea generation, 8-5
    importance, 8-2
    introduction, 8-8
    main body, 8-8–8-9
    neatness, 8-14
    organizing writing plan, 8-6–8-8
    planning grid, 8-32
    preparing for writing, 8-3
    proofreading, 8-14
    research, 8-15–8-17
    review and assessment, 8-12
    sample schedule, 8-3
    spell-check, 8-21
    title page, 8-12, 8-15
    topic ideas, 8-5
    writer's block, 8-10, 8-19
    writing do's, 8-13–8-14

Y

Yang, Gerry, 14-26
Yarrow, Peter, 11-9
Youngblood, Jack, 10-16

Features Index

Peak performer profile

Adams, Scott, 9-24
Armstrong, Lance, 10-26
Carson, Ben, 2-17
Filo, David, 14-26
Gonzales, Alberto, 6-21
Hamm, Mia, 10-20
Haubegger, Christy, 1-31
Momaday, N. Scott, 3-24
Morrison, Toni, 8-25
Ochoa, Ellen, 11-27
Perron, Kirk, 7-22
Rice, Condoleezza, 12-22
Sui, Anna, 4-22
Winfrey, Oprah, 5-19
Yang, Gerry, 14-26

Peak progress

barriers to note taking, 4-20
burnout, 10-22
campus facilities, 12-8
choosing a career, 14-22
communicator, 11-6
creative ideas checklist, 9-22
dictionary, 5-12
diversity, 11-7
eating habits, 10-4
80/20 rule of time management, 3-15
essay test, 7-11–7-12, 7-13
exploring majors, 1-29
failure to graduate college, 2-23
financial resource management, 12-18
healthier lifestyle, 10-25
high school/college, compared, 2-16
listening, 4-6
math and science anxiety, 9-13
math and science tests, 7-6–7-7
memory affirmations, 6-17
memory skills, 6-3
mindfulness, 6-11
positive attitude, 13-17
positive habits, 13-8
problem-solving checklist, 9-5
public speaking, 8-21
reading, 5-4
remembering names, 6-12
school-job success, 14-23
self-esteem and confidence, 2-11
self-management and control, 2-9
skills for school and work, 2-20

student/worker, what kind are you, 2-21
symbols, 5-11
take control of time and life, 3-12
team effectiveness, 11-11
test taking, 7-3, 7-17
topic ideas, 8-5
visualization, 1-4–1-5
writer's block, 8-10
writing do's, 8-13–8-14
writing papers, checklist, 8-16
writing speeches, checklist, 8-16

Peak tips

addiction to computers, 10-13
binder, 3-4
bouncing back from failure, 1-26, 2-10
changing your habits, 13-6
classroom behavior, 4-15
computer use, 3-17
effort, 6-17
employee qualities, 14-9
filling out forms, 5-16
follow-up call–after resume, 14-14
goals/expectations, 2-24
graphics, 5-5
learning style, 1-8
letter of recommendation, 14-16
math and science anxiety, 9-10, 9-12
mild depression, 10-15
newspapers, 12-4
note taking, 4-6
performance review, 7-20
positive attitude, 6-17
problem solving–keep an open mind, 9-16
reading, 5-5, 5-15
resume, 14-13
saving money, 12-19, 12-20
stereotyping, 11-10
studying, how much, 6-9
successful manager, 14-22
teaching your study partner, 5-10
test taking, 7-14
writing assignments, 8-12

Personal performance notebook

assertive communication role-playing, 11-13
assessing your goals, 14-14
brainstorming notes, 9-15
budgeting, 12-17
building community, 12-3

character nad ethics, 2-4
commitment contract, 13-10
commitment to exercise, 10-9
conflict resolution, 11-17
contact information, 12-7
critical thinking–problem solving, 9-4
daily energy levels, 3-10
decision-making application, 9-18–9-19
diversity, 11-8
essay test preparation, 7-10
four-temperament profile, 1-16–1-17
healthy relationships, 11-22
interruptions, 3-18
inventory of interests, aptitudes, and values, 14-13
inventory of personal qualities, 14-11
learning style inventory, 1-9–1-10
learning styles and memory, 6-10
life area goals, 3-22
lifelong assessment, 13-15–13-16
listen to your body, 10-3
listening, 4-7
looking ahead, 3-7
making time for commitments, 12-5
math and science anxiety, 9-11
memory assessment, 6-8
memory map, 6-14–6-16
mind map, 4-12
mind map–organizing information, 6-6
mind-set, 9-16
needs, motivation, and commitment, 2-13
nine-dot exercise, 9-14
observation skills, 6-4
observing conflict, 11-16
patterns in relationships, 11-18
peak performance self-assessment tool, 1-7
performance review, 7-19
positive habits, 13-10–13-11
preparing research papers, 8-7
procrastination, 3-16
reflection, 4-19
reviewing your health, 10-6
self-talk and affirmations, 2-15
skills and personal qualities, 2-5
sleep patterns, 10-7
solving problems–making choices, 9-20–9-21
SQ3R system, 5-6–5-7
stage fright, 8-19
stereotypical thinking, 11-9
test anxiety, 7-16
test taking, 7-4
time log, 3-5
time spent on typical activities, 3-6
transferable skills, 14-10
values, 14-25
writer's 8-19

Success principles

accomplishments, not entitlement, 14-2
character, not personality, 13-2
cooperation, 11-2
critical thinking, 9-2
excellence, not perfection, 8-2
giving, not receiving, 12-2
meaning, not words, 5-2
message, not presentation, 4-2
personal qualities, 2-2
priorities, 3-2
quality, not quantity, 10-2
reality, 1-2
strengths, not weaknesses, 7-2
sum, not parts, 6-2

Tech for success

ALEKS, 9-13
back-up plans, 6-18
bill paying on-line, 12-20
books on-line, 5-14
calorie counting, 10-9
college/university web site, 12-20
computer timesavers, 3-21
ethics information on the Web, 2-25
health on the Web, 10-9
inspiration, 13-18
instructor's visual presentation, 4-18
job search web sites, 14-21
log of positive habits, 13-28
mathematics, 9-13
news on-line, 5-14
on-line discussion groups, 2-25
on-line journal, 1-29
on-line self-assessment, 1-29
on-line tutors, 7-20
PDA, 4-14
PowerPoint, 8-21
relationships and computers, 11-23
resume on-line, 14-21
semester calendar, 1-29
spell-check, 8-21
stored memory, 6-18
textbooks–ancillary resources, 7-20
visual aids, 8-21

Words to succeed

Allen, Woody, 4-15
anonymous, 2-8
Aristotle, 13-2
Burke, Edmund, 5-9
Capra, Frank, 9-12
Chamberlain, Joshua L., 2-5
Chinese proverb, 5-14, 9-17

Confucius, 6-5
Debold, Elizabeth, 4-3
Dewar, Sir James, 11-3
Dewey, John, 9-6
Drucker, Peter, 1-8
Dryden, John, 13-8
Duell, Charles H., 2-24
Eliot, George, 2-13
Emerson, Ralph Waldo, 2-10, 12-16
Follett, Mary Parker, 11-4
Ford, Henry, 12-2
Galileo, 9-6
Gide, Andrew, 5-2
Goethe, J. W. von, 10-2
Goldberg, Natalie, 8-8
Herbert, George, 14-18
Herstein, I. N., 9-3
Holt, John, 9-2
Hunt, H. L., 3-3
Huxley, T. H., 3-13
Iacocca, Lee, 4-2
James, William, 3-11
Jung, Carl, 14-2
Lewis, C. S., 7-17
Lincoln, Abraham, 2-24
Mancuso, Joseph R., 10-8
O'Connor, Flannery, 1-3
Paternak, Boris, 10-2
Pipher, Mary, 11-16
Plato, 8-9
Redmoon, Ambrose, 7-14
Scheele, Adele, 8-2
Schopenhauer, Arthur, 3-8
Seneca, 1-26
Stein, Gertrude, 5-13
Togo, Yuki, 6-2
Twain, Mark, 10-25
Weil, Andrew, 10-23
Winthrop, John, 12-4
Wright, Stephen, 8-15
Yarrow, Peter, 11-9
Youngblood, Jack, 13-16

Worksheets

analyzing chapters, 5-31
attitudes and reading, 5-25
barriers to reading, 5-32
budgeting, 12-28
building community, 12-30
career planning grid, 14-31
changing habits, 13-28
choosing a major, 1-37–1-38
community involvement, 12-31–12-32

daily energy levels, 3-34
different types of reading, 5-26
diversity, 11-32
exam schedule, 7-26
four-temperament profile, 1-39
grammar, 8-30–8-31
health, 10-30–10-33
interviewing the employed, 14-33
key lecture ideas, 14-28
learning style and memory, 6-25
learning styles, 1-35, 2-32
life assessment, 4-31
listening habits, 4-33
listening/note taking in workplace, 4-30
matrix for critical thinking, 9-35
matrix for test taking, 7-30
memory skills, 6-25
memory systems, 6-29
mental picture, 6-30–6-31
mind map, 4-27
money management, 12-29
networking, 12-33
note-taking checklist, 4-29
ongoing assessment and action plan, 4-32
performance review, 7-29
personal reinforcement contract, 2-30
personality types, 1-35
planning grid, 8-32
positive attitudes, 13-27
positive habits, 13-26
preparing for tests/exams, 7-27–7-28
problem solving, 9-28–9-35
project team, 1-35–1-36
reading, 5-24–5-33
reading matrix, 5-33
reading outline, 5-29–5-30
resistance to change, 13-25
resources, 12-27
resume, 14-32
self-esteem inventory, 2-31
stress performance test, 10-31–10-32
study-team relationships, 11-31
summarize and teach, 5-27–5-28
temperaments, 1-35
test taking, 7-28–7-30
time management, 3-31
time wasters, 3-32–3-33
to-do list, 3-30, 6-28
writing papers/public speaking, 8-28–8-32

PEAK PERFORMANCE: SUCCESS IN COLLEGE AND BEYOND (Annotated Instructors Edition)

Published by McGraw-Hill, a business unit of The McGraw-Hill Companies, Inc., 1221 Avenue of the Americas, New York, NY, 10020. Copyright © 2006, 2002 by The McGraw-Hill Companies, Inc. All rights reserved. No part of this publication may be reproduced or distributed in any form or by any means, or stored in a database or retrieval system, without the prior written consent of The McGraw-Hill Companies, Inc., including, but not limited to, in any network or other electronic storage or transmission, or broadcast for distance learning.

Some ancillaries, including electronic and print components, may not be available to customers outside the United States.

This book is printed on acid-free paper.

1 2 3 4 5 6 7 8 9 0 VNH/VNH 0 9 8 7 6 5

ISBN 0-07-298696-4

Editor in Chief: *Emily Barrosse*
Publisher: *Beth A. Mejia*
Executive Editor: *David S. Patterson*
Senior Marketing Manager: *Leslie Oberhuber*
Freelance Developmental Editor: *Vicki Malinee, VanBrien & Associates*
Managing Editor: *Jean Dal Porto*
Project Manager: *Catherine R. Iammartino*
Manuscript Editor: *Debra DeBord*
Art Director: *Jeanne Schreiber*
Design Manager and Cover Designer: *Violeta Diaz*
Text Designer: *Amy Evans McClure*
Art Editor: *Katherine McNab*
Illustrator(s): *Lotus Art*
Photo Research Manager: *Brian Pecko*
Cover Credit: *© Mike Powell/Getty Images/Allsport*
Print Supplements Producer: *Louis Swaim*
Senior Production Supervisor: *Carol A. Bielski*
Senior Media Producer: *Todd Vaccaro*
Composition: *11/14 Minion by Cenveo*
Printing: *45 # Pub Matte, Von Hoffmann Corporation*

Credits: The credits section for this book begins on page P–1 and is considered an extension of the copyright page.

Library of Congress Cataloging-in-Publication Data

Ferrett, Sharon K.
    Peak performance : success in college and beyond / Sharon K. Ferrett.—5th ed.
      p. cm.
    Includes index.
    ISBN 0-07-298696-4
    1. Academic achievement. 2. Performance. 3. Career development. 4. Success. I. Title.
LB1062.6.F47 2006
378.1'0281—dc22   2004063101

The Internet addresses listed in the text were accurate at the time of publication. The inclusion of a website does not indicate an endorsement by the authors of McGraw-Hill, and McGraw-Hill does not guarantee the accuracy of the information presented at these sites.

www.mhhe.com

FIFTH EDITION

Peak Performance

SUCCESS IN COLLEGE AND BEYOND

Sharon K. Ferrett, Ph.D.
HUMBOLDT STATE UNIVERSITY

Boston   Burr Ridge, IL   Dubuque, IA   Madison, WI   New York   San Francisco   St. Louis
Bangkok   Bogotá   Caracas   Kuala Lumpur   Lisbon   London   Madrid   Mexico City
Milan   Montreal   New Delhi   Santiago   Seoul   Singapore   Sydney   Taipei   Toronto